Studies in the Archaeology and History of
Caesarea Maritima

Ancient Judaism and Early Christianity

Arbeiten zur Geschichte des antiken Judentums und des Urchristentums

VOLUME 77

Studies in the Archaeology and History of Caesarea Maritima

Caput Judaeae, Metropolis Palaestinae

By

Joseph Patrich

BRILL

LEIDEN • BOSTON
2011

This book is printed on acid-free paper.

Library of Congress Cataloging-in-Publication Data

Patrich, J. (Joseph)
  Studies in the archaeology and history of Caesarea Maritima : caput judaeae, metropolis palaestinae / by Joseph Patrich.
    p. cm. — (Ancient Judaism and early Christianity ISSN 1871-6636 ; v. 77)
  Includes bibliographical references and index.
  ISBN 978-90-04-17511-2 (hardback : alk. paper)
  1. Caesarea (Israel)—Antiquities. 2. Excavations (Archaeology)—Israel—Caesarea.
3. Archaeology and history—Israel—Caesarea. I. Title.

  DS110.C13P384 2011
  933.4'9—dc23

2011021399

DS
110
.C13
P384
2011

ISSN 1871-6636
ISBN 978 90 04 17511 2

MIX
Paper from
responsible sources
FSC
www.fsc.org   FSC® C008919

PRINTED BY AD DRUK BV - ZEIST, THE NETHERLANDS

To the blessed memory of my mother Feiga
(January 1, 1919–May 31, 2011).
May she rest in peace.

CONTENTS

ABBREVIATIONS

AASOR	*Annual of the American Schools of Oriental Research*
AB	*Analecta Bollandia*
Ac	*Acts of the Apostles*
ADAJ	*Annual of the Department of Antiquities of Jordan*
AJA	*American Journal of Archaeology*
AJSR	*Association of Jewish Studies Review*
ANRW	*Aufstieg und Niedergang des Römischen Welt*
Ant.	Flavius Josephus, *Antiquities*
AW	*Ancient World*
BA	*Biblical Archaeologist*
BAR	*Biblical Archaeology Review*
BAR Int. Ser.	*British Archaeology Reports. International Series*
BASOR	*Bulletin of the American Schools of Oriental Research*
BCH	*Bulletin de Correspondance Hellénique*
BIA	*Bar-Ilan: Annual of Bar-Ilan University*
CCSL	Corpus Christianorum, Series Latina
CIC	*Corpus Iuris Civilis*
CIG	*Corpus Inscriptionum Graecarum*, A. Boeck ed. Berlin 1828–1877
CIL	*Corpus Inscriptionum Latinarum*, Berlin 1863–.
CIS	*Corpus Inscriptiones Semiticaarum*
CMS	*Center for Maritime Studies*
CNI	*Christian News from Israel*
CPJ	*Corpus Papyrorum Judaicorum*
CSEL	Corpus Scriptorum Ecclesiasticorum Latinorum
CSCO	Corpus Scriptorum Christianorum Orientalium
DOP	*Dumbarton Oaks Papers*
EAEHL	*Encyclopedia of Archaeological Excavations in the Holy Land*
EH	*Ecclesiastical History*
EI	*Eretz Israel*
ESI	*Excavations and Surveys in Israel*
GCS	Die griechischen christlichen Schriftsteller der ersten Jahrhunderte
HA	*Hadshot Arkheologiot* (Hebrew)

HE	*Histoire Ecclésiastique*
HTR	*Harvard Theological Review*
HUCA	*Hebrew Union College Annual*
IEJ	*Israel Exploration Journal*
IJNA	*International Journal of Nautical Archaeology*
ILN	*The Illustrated London News*
ILP	*Israel—Land and People. Eretz Israel Museum Year-book*
IMN	*Israel Museum News*
IMSA	*Israel Museum Studies in Archaeology*
INR	*Israel Numismatic Research*
JGS	*Journal of Glass Studies*
JJS	*Journal of Jewish Studies*
JQR	*Jewish Quarterly Review*
JRA	*Journal of Roman Archaeology*
JRA, Suppl. Ser.	*Journal of Roman Archaeology, Supplementary Series*
JRS	*Journal of Roman Studies*
JSAI	*Jerusalem Studies in Arabic and Islam*
JSP	*Judea and Samaria Publications*
JTS	*Journal of Theological Studies*
LA	*Liber Annuus*
LCL	Loeb Classical Library
M	*Mishnah*
MP	*Eusebius, The Martyrs of Palestine*
NSJ	*New Studies on Jerusalem. Conference Proceedings. Ingeborg Rennert Center for Jerusalem Studies, Bar Ilan University*
NEAEHL	*The New Encyclopedia of Archaeological Excavations in the Holy*
ODB	*The Oxford Dictionary of Byzantium*
ODCC	*The Oxford Dictionary of the Christian Church*
PCPS	*Proceedings of the Cambridge Philological Society*
PEQ	*Palestine Exploration Quarterly*
PG	*Patrologiae cursus completus. Series Graeca* (ed. J.P. Migne)
PL	*Patrologiae cursus completus. Series Latina* (ed. J.P. Migne)
PPTS	Palestine Pilgrims Texts Society

PSI	*Papiri Greci e Latini—Publicazioni della Societa Italiana*
RA	*Révue archéologique*
RB	*Révue Biblique*
RE	*Realencyklopädie der classichen Altertumswissenschaft* (ed. Pauly–Wissowa)
REG	*Révue des Études Grecques*
SC	*Sources Chrétiennes*
SCI	*Scripta Classica Israelica*
SHAJ	*Studies in the History and Archaeology of Jordan*
SJS	*Judaea and Samaria Research Studies*
TB	Talmud Babli
TIR	*Tabula Imperii Romani. Iudaea / Palaestina. Maps and Gazetteer* (ed. Tsafrir Di Segni and Green 1994)
TPR	*Town Planning Review*
TY	Talmud Yerushalmi
War	Flavius Josephus, *War of the Jews*
ZDPV	*Zeitschrift des deutschen Palästina Vereins*
ZPE	*Zeitschrift für Papyrologie und Epigraphik*

INTRODUCTION

Caesarea, on the site of Hellenistic Straton's Tower, is located in a central position on the eastern Mediterranean coast, between Ioppe and Dora—much older maritime cities. Its natural conditions were not favorable as those of the other two for an organic evolution of a prospering settlement in antiquity; its foundation and development were the result of rulers' initiatives. Straton's Tower—the earliest settlement at the site—was founded as a trade post by the Ptolemies. It had a landing-place (*prosormos*), and by the end of the second century BCE, before falling under Hasmonaean control, it became a town subordinate to the tyrant of the much older, larger, and important city of Dora.

The foundation and prosperity of Caesarea were a direct result of Herod's decision to build a large deep-water port, applying the most elaborate Roman harbor-technology, and to found a new city that became the administrative capital of his expanding kingdom (Josephus, *War* 1.408–415; *Ant.* 15.331–341). Its prosperity continued as long as it served as a provincial capital and its harbor functioned, serving the international trade. A network of five radiating routes connected the maritime city with its countryside and with inland cities farther away (Fig. 1).

Following the Arab conquest in 640 or 641 Caesarea underwent a sharp decline, shrinking in size about ten times relative to its former extension (see *infra*, Chapter Six); following the final defeat of the Crusaders it was altogether deserted. In 1884 twenty families of Muslim Bosnians were settled by the Turkish authorities among the ruins, within the confines of the Arab and Crusader walls, staying there until 1948. The scattered houses, each with an extensive garden, appear in the aerial photographs taken in 1918 (Fig. 2), and in 1944 (Fig. 3). In 1940 Kibbutz Sdot Yam (visible in Fig. 3), was founded to the south of the Byzantine city wall. The extra-mural area, within the confines of the Herodian and Byzantine city walls, was already divided into agricultural plots, including the oblong arena of the Roman circus on the south-east. With a somewhat different parceling, such is more or less the condition of this extra-mural area to the present (Fig. 4). When archaeological excavations were begun by A. Negev to the south of the Crusader town in 1960–61, this ground (to be labeled later Areas

CC, KK and NN), served as pasture land (Figs. 5 and 6). The studies presented in this volume are the result of my excavations in these areas during the years 1993–1998 and 2000–2001.[1] On the west, all that is left above sea level of the submerged gigantic Herodian harbor is a tiny touristic haven used for swimming and diving, protected by a simple narrow fishing wharf (Fig. 7).

Nine of the twelve studies presented here (see the list below), were previously published elsewhere, the earliest in 1996 and the latest in 2010; one more (no. **VI**) is forthcoming in 2011, originally having been written for publication elsewhere. Chapter Three has so far been published only in Hebrew, in Joseph Geiger, Hannah M. Cotton, and Guy D. Stiebel (eds.), *Israel's Land. Papers Presented to Israel Shatzman on His Jubilee* (Jerusalem: The Open University of Israel and Israel Exploration Society): 135–56. Articles nos. **I, II, VI, VII**, and **XII** were previously published in Hebrew as well. Chapter Five was written for the present book.

The original articles were slightly modified and updated. An author-date system of references was adopted throughout, and a unified bibliography follows the articles. The illustrations—some of which originally appeared in several articles—are numbered consecutively throughout, with no repetitions. They are brought together at the end of the book.

The idea to collect my dispersed essays and publish them together came to my mind at the end of my term of stay as a Research Fellow at NIAS—the Netherlands Institute for Advanced Studies at Wassenaar (February–July 2008). Work on the volume was concluded in April 2010, while I was a Research Fellow at the Jerusalem Institute for Advanced Studies. Thanks are due to my partners in the Flavius Josephus research group at NIAS—Prof. Jan Willem van Henten of the University of Amsterdam and Prof. Daniel R. Schwartz of the Hebrew University of Jerusalem—for their encouragement. I am also deeply indebted to Prof. Pieter W. van der Horst of the University of Utrecht for his good advice, and to Prof. Martin Goodman of Oxford, chief editor of the Brill series Ancient Judaism and Early Christianity, and

---

[1] For the story of the excavations and preliminary reports on the architectural complexes uncovered in these areas, see Patrich *et al.* 1999; Patrich 2008. Though these articles are not reproduced in the present volume, much of the archaeological information is dispersed in the various articles presented here. For the final report on the objects retrieved from these excavations see Patrich (ed.) 2008.

to the other members of the editorial board of this series for their decision to include this book therein. For the sake of unification of style,
all the articles were style edited anew by Yohai Goell with the exception of Chapter Five, which was style edited by Rachel Wiesen (both of
Jerusalem). The bibliography was unified by my daughter, Aviya and
the index was compiled by Fern Seckbach. Thanks are due to all.

Original Place of Publication

I   Nikos Kokkinos (ed.), *The World of the Herods. Volume 1
of the International Conference The World of the Herods and
the Nabataeans held at the British Museum 17–19 April 2001*
(Oriens et Occidens 14; Stuttgart: Franz Steiner Verlag 2007):
93–130 (with an update on the map of Straton's Tower).

II   Leah Di-Segni, Yizhar Hirschfeld, Rina Talgam, and Joseph
Patrich (eds.), *Man Near a Roman Arch. Studies Presented
to Prof. Yoram Tsafrir* (Jerusalem: Israel Exploration Society
2009): 142*–68*.

IV   Thomas S. Burns and John W. Eadie (eds.), *Urban Centers and
Rural Contexts in Late Antiquity* (East Lansing, MI: Michigan
State University Press 2001): 77–110 (with an update on the
Pagan and Christian communities).

VI   Forthcoming in: Kenneth G. Holum and Haim Lapin (eds.),
The Near East under Transition (Bethesda: University Press of
Maryland): 33–64.

VII   L.V. Rutgers (ed.), *What Has Athens to Do with Jerusalem.
Essays in Honor of Gideon Foerster* (Leuven: P. Peeters 2002):
29–68 (with an update on phase 0 *carceres*).

VIII   Forthcoming in: T. Capelle *et al.* (eds.), *Imperium—Varus und
seine Zeit. Internationales Kolloquium des LWL-Römermuseums am 28. und 29. April 2008 in Münster* (Veröffentlichungen der Altertumskommission für Westfalen, vol. 18; Münster:
Aschendorff-Verlag).

IX   Avner Raban and Kenneth G. Holum (eds.), *Caesrea Maritima.
A Retrospective after two Millennia* (Leiden: Brill 1996): 146–76.

X   *LA* 50 (2000): 363–82, pls. 27–30.

XI   *IMSA* 1 (2002): 21–32.

XII   *LA* 52 (2002): 321–346.

Jerusalem, April 2010

CHAPTER ONE

HERODIAN CAESAREA: THE URBAN SPACE

INTRODUCTION

Caesarea, a newly founded city with large public structures, including a vast and elaborate harbor, was the largest building project of Herod. Caesarea was founded as a maritime city, to serve the economic needs of Herod's kingdom, and as an administrative capital, to serve Herod's political needs. The city and its harbor—Sebastos—were named after Caesar Augustus, Herod's patron in Rome, and a temple dedicated to his cult was built overlooking the harbor and the entire city. This was the showcase of Herod's kingdom, and a lever to its economic prosperity.

Following the wealth of new archaeological data gathered since the 'classical' archaeological summaries by Levine, Ringel, Foerster, and Negev, a much more detailed synthesis of the archaeological finds and the literary sources is now possible.[1] Most of these new finds came to light in the large-scale excavations conducted at the site during the last decade.[2] Although much of this new data is still under study, being so

---

[1] Interestingly, all were published in 1975 (Levine 1975a; 1975b; Ringel 1975: 27–53, 59–65, 75–77; Foerster 1975; Negev 1975). The entry on Caesarea in Stern 1993: 270–91 includes additional information by Raban, Holum, Levine, and Netzer on excavations from the 70s to the early 90s. However, even this revised and updated entry was written before the large-scale excavations began in 1992 (see below, note).

[2] Two expeditions, working all year round from 1992 to 1998, uncovered the south-western zone of the city in a c. 80 m. broad strip parallel to the sea shore, extending from the theater in the south to the harbor in the north. These are the Israel Antiquities Authority (IAA) expedition, headed by Porath, and the University of Haifa expedition, headed by Raban (working within the Crusader city wall) and the present writer (working to the south of that wall), in the framework of the Combined Caesarea Expeditions (CCE), co-directed by Holum. An expedition headed by Holum has been excavating Herod's temple in summer seasons, each several weeks long, since 1989. An expedition of the University of Pennsylvania, headed by Gleason and Burrell, explored the site of Herod's palace in the course of several summer seasons (1990, 1992–94)—a site already explored in 1976, by Netzer and Levine on behalf of the Hebrew University of Jerusalem. In the years 1971–87 the Joint Expedition of Caesarea Maritima (JECM), headed by Bull, Storvick, and Krentz, excavated several areas outside the Crusader city wall, in summer seasons. For the history of

far available only in preliminary reports, a better comprehension of Herodian Caesarea as an urban space is now possible.

Herod's building projects are described in some detail in two passages in the writings of Flavius Josephus:

> And when he <Herod> observed that there was a place near the sea, formerly called Strato's Tower, which was very well suited to be the site of a city (*polin*), he set about making a magnificent plan (*diagraphêi*) and put buildings all over the city, not of ordinary material but of white stone (*leukês petras*). He also adorned it with a very costly palace/palaces (*basileiois*), with civic halls (*diaitais politikais*) and—what was greatest of all and required the most labour—with a well protected harbor (*aklystôi limeni*), of the size of Piraeus, with landing-places and secondary anchorages inside... now this city is located in Phoenicia, on the sea-route to Egypt, between Joppa and Dora... In a circle round the harbor there was a continuous line of dwellings (*oikêseis*) constructed of the most polished stone (*leiotatou lithou*), and in their midst was a mound (*kolônos*) on which there stood a temple of Caesar (*neôs Kaisaros*), visible a great way off to those sailing into the harbor, which had a statue of Rome, and also one of a Caesar. The city itself is called Caesarea and is most beautiful both in material and in construction. But below the city the underground passages and sewers (*hyponomoi te kai laurai*) cost no less effort than the structures built above them. Of these some led at equal distances (*kata symmetra diastêmata*) from one another to the harbor and the sea, while one diagonal (*egkarsia*) passage connected all of them, so that the rainwater and the refuse of the inhabitants were easily carried off together. And whenever the sea was driven in from offshore, it would flow through the whole city and flush it from below. Herod also built a theater of stone (*theatron ek petras*) in the city, and on the south side of the harbor, farther back, an amphitheater (*amphitheatron*) large enough to hold a great crowd of people and conveniently situated for a view of the sea. Now the city was completed in the space of twelve years, for the king did not slacken in the undertaking and he had sufficient means for the expenses (*Ant.* 15.331–341; trans. R. Marcus).[3]

---

exploration of the harbor, and the work of the Caesarea Ancient Harbour Excavation Project (CAHEP), see Raban 1992a. The most detailed survey on the history of the archaeological exploration of Caesarea is in Holum & Raban 1996; for a site map, by Iamim, of all the excavated areas, indicating expedition names and exploration dates, see xxi–xxii. Folded map in that volume (reproduced here with certain modifications as Fig. 8) presents the most updated city plan of Herodian Caesarea, incorporating most of the new archaeological data. See also Roller 1998: 133–44; Lichtenberger 1999: 116–30; Japp 2000: 101–9.

[3] The description of the harbor has been omitted from the quotation.

More details are provided by the second passage:

> His <Herod's> notice was attracted by a town (*polin*) on the coast, called strato's Tower, which, though then dilapidated, was, from its advantageous situation, suited for exercise of his liberality. This he entirely rebuilt with white stone (*leukôi lithôi*), and adorned with the most magnificent palaces (*basileiois*), displaying here, as nowhere else, the innate grandeur of his character. For the whole seaboard from Dora to Joppa, midway between which the city lies, was without a harbor (*alimenon*), so that vessels bound for Egypt along the coast of Phoenicia had to ride at anchor in the open when menaced by the south-west wind...However, by dint of expenditure and enterprise, the king triumphed over nature and constructed a harbor larger than the Piraeus, including other deep roadsteads within its recesses. <Harbor description> Abutting on the harbor were houses (*oikiai*), also of white stone (*leukou lithou*), and upon it converged the streets of the town (*oi stenôpoi tou asteos*), laid at equal distances apart (*hen diastêma memetrêmenoi*). On an eminence (*gêlophou*) facing the harbor-mouth stood Caesar's temple, remarkable for its beauty and grand proportions; it contained a colossal statue of the emperor, not inferior to the Olympian Zeus, which served for its model, and another of Rome, rivalling that of Hera at Argos. The city (*polin*) Herod dedicated to the province (*eparchiai*), the harbor (*limena*) to navigators in these waters, to Caesar the glory of this new foundation, to which he accordingly gave the name of Caesarea. The rest of the buildings—amphitheater (*amphitheatron*), theater (*theatron*), public places (*agoras*)—were constructed in a style worthy of the name which the city bore (*War* 1.408–415; trans. H. St. J. Thackeray).[4]

From these two passages the following information emerges: Caesarea, named after Caesar Augustus, was built between Dor and Joppa on the site of the declining town of Straton's Tower. The city had a large, in-sea, deep-water harbor—a different type from the Hellenistic *limên kleistos* type, built or quarried in-land. It was protected by a breakwater and provided with a wide mole, anchorages, and other harbor facilities. The dwellings and the other structures encircled the harbor, with a temple on top of a mound in their midst. The streets, leading to the harbor or the sea, followed an orthogonal grid plan. An elaborate underground sewage system consisted of conduits under the streets connected by a main diagonal channel (presumably under a diagonal

---

[4] Details pertaining to the construction of the harbor have been omitted here too—see Raban 1992a. Lichtenberger (1999: 197) has suggested that *War* 1.401–31 was derived from a panegyric on Herod's building projects, delivered by Nicolaus of Damascus. But Josephus must have also known Caesarea personally.

street). This system was constructed in such a manner that the tide was prevented from overflowing into the streets themselves.

In addition to the temple dedicated to Augustus and Rome, housing two eminent statues, the public structures included marketplaces (*agorai*), two entertainment structures: a stone theater (*Ant.* 15.341)[5] and an amphitheater (actually a hippodrome/stadium; see below), which was located south of the harbor, overlooking the sea. For his own dwelling Herod built a palatial complex (*basileia*). The work was completed within twelve years (22–10/9 BCE).[6] As will be shown below, the archaeological finds (Fig. 8) correspond remarkably with the literary description. Nonetheless, there are also certain discrepancies.

THE ARCHAEOLOGY OF STRATON'S TOWER: THE STATE OF RESEARCH[7]

After many decades of systematic archaeological exploration and the publication of the 'Caesarea Cup' (see below), several prevalent opinions about Straton's Tower should be revised.

The paucity of Persian finds[8] casts serious doubt on the assumption held by many scholars that the foundation of Straton's Tower should be dated to that period. According to this theory,[9] a king of Sidon named Straton—the Greek form of the Phoenician ʿAbd-Astart ("a servant of the goddess Astarte")—founded a marine and commercial post there. The identification of this founder as Straton I (375/4–361 BCE) has been preferred by some scholars over his identification as

---

[5] The Latin Josephus and one Greek MS (Codex Parisinus Gr. 1419) omit "of stone." For the significance of a stone theater in the period under discussion, see Patrich 2002e.

[6] According to Josephus (*Ant.* 16.136) the work took 10 years, having been prolonged beyond the allotted time. However, the number 12, mentioned in *Ant.* 15.341, should be preferred; see Marcus' notes *ad loc* (LCL 410: 55).

[7] I am indebted to my late colleague, Prof. Avner Raban, for intriguing and fruitful discussions on this topic. For an earlier assessment of the issue and a rejection of pre-Alexandrine foundation on archaeological and historical grounds, see Stieglitz 1993; 1996. Raban (1992a: 17), maintained that "a foundation date in the mid-4th c. BC was possible, but far from probable," while Holum & Raban 1996, xxvii, tended to accept Stieglitz's assertion.

[8] Finds from this period were reported by Avi-Yonah (1956: 260), but the actual finds have not been published so far.

[9] First proposed by Th. Reinach in 1896 (see Ringel 1975: 19, n. 26) and by Schürer (1901, Vol. 2: 134–35).

Straton II (343/2–332 BCE).[10] The earliest mention of Straton's Tower is in the Zenon papyri of 159 BCE (*P. Cairo Zen.* 59004),[11] where it is referred to as the place of his landing on the coast of Syria-Phoenicia, suggesting that the site held a certain maritime and economic significance by that time. The proposal that it was refounded under the Seleucids and renamed Demetrias, in honor of Demetrius I, and issued semiautonomous bronze coins under this name, has met with several strong reservations.[12] In c. 100 BCE it was mentioned by the geographer Artemidorus of Ephesus (9.18) as a town near Dora[13] and later by Strabo (16.8.27), who merely noted a landing-place (*prosormos*) at the site.[14] Later in the second century, with the disintegration of the Seleucid kingdom, it became—together with Dora—a stronghold of a local tyrant named Zoilus, until falling into the hands of Alexander Jannaeus.[15]

Hellenistic pottery, mainly of the second century, was found in significant quantities (Figs. 9–11),[16] but contemporary architecture is still scant and is restricted primarily to the northern zone.[17] These remains suggest, according to Raban, two harbors, one in the north and the other at the site of the later Herodian inner harbor. Both were of the

---

[10] Levine 1973: 75–81; 1975b: 6 and n. 20, with further bibliography. Ringel 1975: 18–21, favors a foundation by the later Straton; see also Schürer 1979: 115; Roller 1982a; 1983: 61. The chronology of these kings is a matter of dispute; see Hauben 1987: 426, n. 71. Straton I was a Phoenician philhellenic king of high reputation, a friend of the Athenian people. The fact that Straton's Pyrgos is not mentioned in *Pseudo-Skylax*, dated 361–357 BCE, does not necessarily exclude a foundation by Straton I, since earlier materials were incorporated in this navigator's manual. Galling is in favor of a Hellenistic foundation. For the date this composition was put into its present form, see Levine 1973: 76, n. 9; 1975: 144, n. 8, referring to Fabre 1965.

[11] Also in *CPJ*, no. 2; Cf. Abel 1923.

[12] Kushnir-Stein 1995. Dated issues are from years 1, 3 and 22, presumably of a Pompeian era starting in 64 or 63 BCE. Depicted deities are Tyche (turreted and veiled head), Nike (walking, holding a wreath and a palm) and Zeus (laureate head). The full name "Demetrias which is on the sea" was inscribed in Greek on a lead weight found near Tyre; cf. Lampinen 1999a; Stieglitz 1999.

[13] See Müller 1855, vol. 1: 576, *apud* Stephanus Byzantinus, *Ethnika* (ed. Meineke, Berlin 1849, reprinted Graz 1958): 255, *s.v. Dôros*.

[14] This reference may reflect the humble condition of the city prior to the foundation of Caesarea by Herod, but does not suggest a deserted town, as stated by Josephus.

[15] Levine 1974a; 1975b: 9.

[16] Roller 1980. Raban 1992a: 7–15, 18–21, and see below on the city walls.

[17] Hellenistic walls were encountered in Avi-Yonah's and Negev's areas A, C and D (dwellings?), in CAHEP areas J3 (harbor facilities) and T1 (harbor round tower), and in JECM area G (wall and dwellings?, see below). For a review of these finds, see Raban 1992a; for areas J3 and T1 see also Raban 1989: 143–49, 177–81.

limên kleistos type. A Hellenistic well was explored in the 1996 IAA excavations at the bottom of the moat near the N Crusader gate (see below). On the temple platform, although rich Hellenistic fills were found in the foundation trenches of the Herodian temple, only a single fragmentary wall was uncovered and stones with drafted margins and a projecting boss reused in the foundations of the Herodian temple.[18] The Herodian city wall in the north might have been a restoration of a second-century Hellenistic wall (see below). Elsewhere, the extension of Straton's Tower might be deduced from the distribution of the Hellenistic burials, which most probably were extra-mural. Burials in amphorae were encountered on the east and south. Further away, on the promontory, rock-cut cists were uncovered under the upper terrace of Herod's palace.[19] The necropolis suggests that Straton's Tower was much smaller than Herodian Caesarea.[20]

In sum, in light of the historical data and archaeological finds, a Ptolemaic foundation, first suggested by Stark,[21] should be preferred. The Louvre Caesarea Cup—a fourth-century CE commemorative bronze cup (8.2 cm high, 20.2 cm upper diameter), decorated with incised drawings inlaid with niello and sheeted with brass and silver—corroborates this conclusion.[22] Since it was published only in 1983, after the 'classical' historical summaries by Ringel, Levine, Foerster,

---

[18] Holum 1999: 15, 17; Berlin 1992: 112–22.

[19] On the southeast and south, see Roller (1983); Hellenistic amphora burials in areas CC, KK and NN (Fig. 12) are reported here for the first time; for the rock-cut cists, see Gleason *et al.* 1998: 28, 34, and fig. 4a.

[20] The map suggested for Straton's Tower by Raban (1987: 85, fig. 21) is also published (although with different graphics) in Holum *et al.* 1988: 46, fig. 24. The positioning of the 'temple mound' outside the walled city has turned out to be erroneous (see below). Later, two different maps were suggested: one in Raban 1993: 287, the southern part of which was reconstructed in a drawing published in Raban 1996: 633, fig. 4, and in Raban 1998a: 60, fig. 3; the other appeared in Raban 1996: 631, fig. 2, where he extends the town wall of Zoilus' era to include the future theater, and not only the harbor, within its southern boundary. The 1993 map seems to me to be the most plausible. Roller's attribution (1983: 61–66; 1992) of the remains uncovered in the northern zone of Herodian Caesarea to a separate village, on the outskirts of Straton's Tower (which he locates within the Crusader city wall), seems, in my opinion, to be untenable. For detailed reservations, see Raban (1992a).

[21] Stark 1852: 450–2, but he also considered the possibility that the founder was Straton of Sidon. A Ptolemaic foundation is also favored by Stieglitz (1993; 1996) and Arav (1989). There was a Straton Island off the Abyssinian coast in the Red Sea (Strabo, 16.4.8). Dura Europos was called Dura Nikanoris in some inscriptions, after Nikanor—an officer of Seleucus I who founded it in c. 300 BCE. This is another example of a site called after a Hellenistic officer, rather than a member of a Royal family.

[22] Will 1983: 1–24; 1987: 245–51.

Negev, and the revised Schürer,[23] its significance to the question under discussion has been overlooked.

Four scenes are depicted on the cup (Fig. 13). Scene I presents a rite of libation before the local Tyche, identified by a Latin inscription as *genio colonia(e)*. This scene is associated with the post-Herodian city—the status of Roman colony having been bestowed upon Caesarea by Vespasian. The three other scenes narrate the foundation myth of Straton's Tower (to be read from left to right, counter-clockwise). As pointed out by Will, it is a typical Greek foundation myth.[24] Scene II presents a consultation in an oracle of Apollo (presumably that of Daphne near Antioch) by three persons whose names are written above: Strato(n), Lysimachos and Ctesipon. Scene III presents in three episodes their sea voyage and landing on a hostile shore haunted by lions; Scene IV depicts a hand-shaking treaty (*dextrarum iunctio*) between Straton and Asclepius, accompanied by his daughter Hygieia. Here too, the names of the three figures appear above the scene.[25] Another point suggesting a Greek, rather than Phoenician, origin is the fact that Isis worshippers in Caesarea adorned her in two aspects—as *Agathê* (the Good) and as *Hellas* (the personification of Greece)—and not as Astarte, with whom she was assimilated at Sidon.[26] All these factors combine to support a Greek foundation for Straton's Tower in the Hellenistic period, certainly prior to Zenon's visit.[27]

---

[23] Above note 1. Levine (1975b: 146, n. 21) refers to a short preliminary note on the cup by Will, published in the *Bulletin de la société nationale des antiquaires de France* 1965: 80–81. No details about the scenes are provided.

[24] Will (1983: 19 and n. 24) draws parallels with the foundation myth of Cyrene by Battos of Thera, and refers to Schmid 1947, and others; see also Malkin 1987.

[25] Will (1983: 22) favors identifying the founder with a Sidonian king, although he is aware of the difficulties of such a person being adulated as a Greek hero (23). A suggestion worthy of further consideration was proposed by Rodan (1999: 146–53), according to which the founder Straton was Philocles, son of Apollodoros, of Sidon (d. 278 BCE), a prestigious general of Ptolemy I and II and King of the Sidonians (according to several inscriptions from Athens and the Aegean islands). After Philocles' death Ptolemy II had abolished the kingship at Sidon, making it a Greek *polis*; see Polyaenus, *Strat.* 3.6; Seibert 1970: 337–51; Hauben 1987.

[26] *P. Oxy.* 1380 (ed. Grenfell & Hunt, Part 11: 190); see also Witt 1966: 53–54.

[27] We may also note that the opponents of the Jews of Caesarea in the conflict about *isopoliteia*, in Jos., *War* 2.266–70, 284, are generally defined as Greeks, not as Phoenicians; in *Ant.* 20.173–78, 182–74 they are called Syrians for literary reasons, see Levine 1974b and 1975b: 167, n. 186; but see Kokkinos 1998: 347–48 and cross-references there. See also *War* 3.442 regarding the Greek nature of the town. A Greek foundation is also echoed in Justinian (*Novella* 103 *praefatio*), according to which the first founder of Caesarea (rather than of Straton's Tower) was Straton, a Greek, and

Stieglitz and others had suggested that a Hellenistic temple of Tyche/ Isis preceded the temple of Augustus and Rome on that same site. I would suggest that this temple was located elsewhere, to the E (see below), and that this prominence near the southern end of the city was rather the location of the citadel of the local tyrant. A citadel located on an eminence at the city edge, rather than at its center, was common in the Seleucid cities in Syria and Phoenicia. In Samaria as well the Hellenistic temple of Kore/Isis was located below the acropolis.[28]

Post Script—Proposed map for Straton's Tower in the time of Zoilus (Fig. 14)

As was mentioned above, according to Flavius Josephus (*War* 1.408; *Ant.* 15.331) Caesarea was founded by Herod on the site of a deserted and dilapidated town called Straton's Tower, which was very well suited to be the site of a city (*polin*).

Can we envision the layout of the town on the basis of the archaeological remains? From the literary sources it can be deduced that Straton's Tower was a fortified town. Two circular towers with Hellenistic foundations built of headers, mark the northern fortification wall (see discussion below). The town had two harbors of the *limen kleistos* type. One to the west of the circular towers; the second on the south, to the west of a hillock that dominated the entire area, on top of which Herod's temple to Rome and Augustus was later built. The distribution of Hellenistic potsherds, mainly of the second century BCE, and few architectural remains indicate the extension of the town. Pottery finds were retrieved in all the areas excavated to the south of the circular towers, as far as the southern harbor and the 'acropolis'—the hillock on which the Herodian temple platform was later located. Farther south they were associated with burials, as was indicated above.

Roller (above, note 20) suggested to locate Straton's Tower within the confines of the Crusaders' city wall. The Hellenistic remains uncovered in the northern zone of Herodian Caesarea were attributed by him to a separate village, on the outskirts of Straton's Tower. Raban had proposed three different maps for the location and extension of Straton's Tower under Zoilus (above, note 20). The first—depicting

---

not Herod; but for the worthlessness of this late statement, see Schürer 1979: 115, n. 156.

[28] Stieglitz 1996: 593–94; see also below notes 56 & 72 (text related to the Tycheon), and Lauffrey 1958. For Samaria, see Crowfoot *et al.* 1942: 62–66.

a town of reduced size, enclosed by a wall that extended from the two circular towers in the north, to the southern harbor, leaving the 'temple mound' outside the walled town. But this has turned out to be erroneous (see below, the discussion on the city wall), and hence was corrected in a later map, in which the 'acropolis,' overlooking the harbor, was included within the confines of the town (above, note 20). In a third version, a maximalist one, Raban had extended the town wall of Zoilus' era to include the future theater within its southern boundary. But there are no archaeological grounds to sustain such a southern extension. As a matter of fact, the Hellenistic burials encountered in areas CC and KK, and in Roller's excavations not far from the SE corner of the Crusaders wall, must have been extra-mural. Hence, the southern wall of Straton's Tower, though not found yet, must have been about in line with the present southern Crusaders Wall, delineating the harbor on the south. Like the second map of Raban, it is suggested here that the eastern wall was in line with the later Herodian wall, as far as the Hellenistic southern wall.

The map presented here gives expression to the proposal that the top of the 'acropolis' was occupied by the palace of Zoilus, the local tyrant, rather than a temple for Tyche/Isis. The map also gives expression to the proposal that this temple was located outside the walled area, to the southeast, below the 'acropolis' (see the argumentation below). The extra-mural location is suggested by the fact that a Hellenistic burial was reported by Roller nearby, and such burials are extra-mural as a rule. In the city of Dor/Dora as well, the large temple of Apollo/Asclepius was located outside the city wall (Dauphin 1999).

BUILDING MATERIALS, METHODS AND DECORATION

The major discrepancy between Josephus' descriptions and the actual finds pertains to the "polished stone" and "white stone," interpreted by some commentators as marble.[29] In fact, all the structures built by Herod were of the local, rough *kurkar* calcareous sandstone, whose "white" hue and "polished" face were attained by the application of a thick layer of high-quality white lime plaster. Stucco of the

---

[29] See Marcus' note on Jos. *Ant.* 15.331; Thackeray renders *War* 1.408 and 414 as "white stone," without comment. On this being marble, see Roller 1998: 136, but this is erroneous. For a survey of building materials and methods and decorations in the Herodian building projects in general, see Japp 2000: 81–89.

masonry style, imitating ashlar masonry with wide flat margins, gave the impression of white polished masonry. Colorful frescoes of the Hellenistic Masonry style and of the second Pompeian style, common to Herodian wall decoration at other sites, adorned inner and outer walls.[30] Column shafts, bases, and capitals of the three orders—Doric, Ionic and Corinthian—were also plastered,[31] and shafts were provided with plaster flutings.[32] The *kurkar* capitals were first stone cut to their draft shape, over which a white layer of plaster was applied.[33] Entablature members were similarly treated.[34] The earliest floors are of *opus signinum*, with mosaic floors of a simple design appearing later.[35] In the theater, the orchestra had a thick plaster floor of many layers, depicting feather and geometric patterns (see below).

Walls were built of *kurkar* ashlars set on foundations of smaller stones in a matrix of brown *hamra* clay cast into the foundation trench.[36] There were also ashlar foundations with stones bonded by gray cement made of lime, into which ashes were added.[37] The N city wall was dry built, with no cement between the blocks; in narrower walls of other structures the stones were cemented with gray mortar. The use of *pozzolana* was restricted mainly to the harbor, its moles and flushing channels, and to the palace pool. Walls were generally isodomic with alternating stretchers and one or two headers in each course. The blocks had either flat margins and a rough boss, or an entirely flat surface, with no margins.[38]

---

[30] Rosenberg 1996; Foerster 1995: 1–44. The final report on the fresco finds from areas CC, KK and NN is in preparation.

[31] For Corinthian Herodian capitals in general, see Fischer 1990: 12–20, capitals nos. 10–34.

[32] Holum *et al.* 1999: 19. A large (2 × 2 m.) curved segment of thick stucco with molded flutings was found in the 1999 season just north of the temple foundation. See Raban & Holum's 1999: 11 (brief report), and Holum 2004a: 41, 45, 57 (although it may be post-Herodian).

[33] Cat. nos. 74 (Ionic), and 75 (Corinthian); Doric capitals similarly treated came from Herod's palace. The catalogue numbers pertain to the catalogue of architectural fragments from areas CC, KK and NN, yet to be published.

[34] Holum *et al.* 1999.

[35] Porath 2000a: 37*–39*.

[36] Such are the foundations of the city wall in area G8 (see below), as well as those of the structures flanking cardo W1 in area KK.

[37] Such were the foundations of the earliest 'phase 0' starting gates (*carceres*) of the Herodian hippo-stadium and of the temple (see below).

[38] Both techniques are present in the northern city wall; the retaining wall of the temple platform also has ashlars of flat margins and a boss. But these might be reused Hellenistic blocks.

THE CITY WALL

Josephus stated explicitly that Caesarea was a fortified city.[39] A wall first surveyed by the Palestine Exploration Fund in the nineteenth century and attributed to Herod[40] was later recognized by the Italian Expedition, headed by Frova, to be Byzantine.[41] This expedition was also the first to uncover the remains of an "inner line"—the Herodian line located between the Byzantine, semi-elliptical outer line and the rectangular and much shorter Crusader wall. The remains of the Herodian line were exposed by the Italian Expedition (Fig. 15), which dug between 1959 and 1964, and by the JECM in the north[42] and, more recently, by the IAA in the south.[43] All three expeditions determined the segments excavated by them to be Herodian, rather than Hellenistic.[44] The line between the northern and the southern segments is recognizable along most of its course in aerial photographs and on the ground by the slight rising of the surface. Soundings and a survey were also conducted along its course.

[39] Contra Negev, see below note 44.

[40] Conder & Kitchener 1882: 13–29; Vann 1992b: 283–86.

[41] Finocchi 1965; Lehmann 1994 (pertaining to CCE area V). The Italian Expedition's dating was based on the small finds and on a comparative architectural study of Hellenistic and Herodian fortifications; the pottery, however, was not published in a manner permitting a critical review of the stratigraphy and chronology.

[42] Blakely 1984; 1989: 79–82; 1992. The JECM G3 sounding was carefully excavated and was published in a clear, detailed, and precise stratigraphical report. Blakely (1984: 3–7) also gives a detailed history of the research up to the JECM 1978 excavations and on archaeological grounds sets the construction date between 128 and the end of the first century BCE, probably within the first century BCE (Blakely 1992: 40), stating that regardless of whether they were originally built by Herod, these were the northern fortification walls of Herod's city.

[43] Porath 2000a: 36*–37* and 41–42, figs. 52 and 53.

[44] It seems that these accumulative results should close the debate concerning the date of the northern segment. Negev (1966a: 343–44; 1966b: 142–43; 1975: 273; 1993: 272) suggested that the segment exposed by the Italians is Hellenistic, and that the Herodian city extended much further to the north and was not fortified. But his "Herodian" streets and sewers in the north are in fact Late Roman or Byzantine. Levine (1975a: 9–13), and Ringel (1975: 74–77), while acknowledging the Herodian date, suggested that this was a reconstruction of the Hellenistic walls of Straton's Tower. Raban (1987: 71–88; 1992) also interpreted the northern wall as Hellenistic, opposing the Herodian date assigned to the Italian and the JECM G8 segments, and contributing several new finds to the discussion. His arguments were rejected in detail by Blakely (1989; 1992). In particular, Raban's interpretation of a corner wall in the southernmost vault below the temple platform as Hellenistic has been categorically refuted by the IAA excavations in two other vaults, which indicate that Raban's "Hellenistic" corner is in fact a corner of the retaining wall of the Herodian temenos.

The new segment exposed in the south suggests that, contrary to earlier conjectures, the theater was encompassed within the walled city.[45] The semi-elliptical wall contour[46] and the location of the temple mound in the centre, overlooking the harbor and the entire city, are in concordance with Josephus' description.[47] The segment uncovered by the Italian Expedition, c. 250 m to the north of the Crusader wall and c. 230 m to the south of the Byzantine wall, is approximately 120 m long, incorporating two circular towers and a polygonal (pentagonal) tower in the northeastern corner of the wall. Here the line takes a southeasterly direction, forming a 40° angle. The JECM dug between 1978 and 1980 one square sounding (10 × 10 m) in this southeastern section of the wall (area G8), exposing (on the outside) the foundations of a c. 12 m long section of the wall.[48]

The circular towers (c. 12 m in diameter; 1.70 m thick) lie 14 m apart. The eastern tower, six courses high (3.5 m), is in a much better state of preservation than the western one (inner diameter: 9.60 m), which is only two courses high on its eastern side. The wall (of the towers as well as the straight segments) is built of courses of alternating headers and stretchers (blocks averaging 1.30 × 0.60 × 0.45 m in size). The protrusion of the central boss is uneven: some blocks have a high boss, while others are almost flat.[49] The lowest course of the eastern tower is exceptional, having been built solely of headers. The straight segments are not bonded with the circular towers; at least technically they are later than the towers. The wall is c. 2.30 m thick, with the exception of

[45] These conjectures were based on extrapolation from the aerial photographs. Thus the Italian *Missione* (Frova *et al.* 1965: 50, fig. 10a), and subsequently Levine (1975a: 11–12 and map facing table of contents), Ringel (1975: 41), Holum *et al.* (1988: 83), and others. The heavy deterioration of the southern segment in antiquity was a factor in the erroneous interpretation.

[46] It is semi-elliptical, rather than semi-circular (the north–south axis being c. 1,300 m and the west–east axis being c. 500 m). Roller (1998: 143, and 1982a: 92–96) refers to a polygonal symmetrical circuit, with five gates set at each of the sides. This approach seems to be too schematic.

[47] Hillard (1992) attributed the wall to Gabinius' reconstructions, but Straton's Tower is not named in the list of cities refounded by him (Jos., *War* 1.165–66). Negev (1975: 271) and Foerster (1975: 10) also maintained that Caesarea was rebuilt by Gabinius; Ringel and Levine are more cautious. The paucity of first-century finds reported for several excavated areas suggests a state of decline after the Hasmonaean occupation.

[48] See Blakely (above note 42).

[49] Such is the external face to the east of the round towers; see Raban 1987: fig. 19. On the masonry of the north wall, see also Blakely (1984: 7), with further references.

the segment (3 m thick) between the circular towers which seems to be a later addition blocking a Herodian gate.

The c. 12 m-long section (2.3 m thick), excavated by the JECM, exposed four foundation courses and six to seven upper courses of the external face, extending 3.9 m above the foundation courses. The latter were laid in a matrix of brown *ḥamra* mud that was poured into the foundation trench, filling it completely from side to side. The six upper courses were laid dry, in courses of alternating headers and stretchers, without any bonding material. The uppermost course, shorter than those underneath but also laid dry, is mainly of headers. The wall section exposed by the Italian Expedition was built in a similar technique.

The south section, c. 60 m long, exposed by IAA in 1998, is 1.75–1.80 m thick. A single round tower (9 m in diameter), of courses built of headers and stretchers, some with carved margins, is incorporated in the wall. Unlike the northern towers, there is no ring wall; it consists of a solid circle. The inner core is built of irregularly laid long blocks.[50] The ring wall must have started at a higher elevation, not preserved. No gate is associated with this tower. The south gate of the city should have been located further to the east. A surface of beaten crushed *kurkar* exposed on the inside is interpreted as a street, or another open space, separating the wall and the theater, which are located in immediate proximity. Later in the first century, the circular tower was replaced by a rectangular one, of smaller dimensions (9.4 × 6.7 m), which encased the western part of the circle, leaving a southern portion of it outside. The eastern end bent northward, thus reducing the fortified area. Porath has suggested that these modifications might have been related to the eruption of the Jewish revolt in 66 CE.[51]

THE STREETS

It is clear from Josephus' writing that the streets were laid on an orthogonal grid, and that there was one diagonal street. This one is recognized in some aerial photographs, leading north of the temple platform from the southeast. An elaborate drainage system ran under the streets. The

---

[50] Porath 2000a: 36*–37*.
[51] Porath 2000a.

excavations indicated that the street plan was indeed orthogonal, consisting of north–south *cardines* and east–west *decumani*. The streets uncovered in the southwestern zone—one cardo and four *decumani*—were marked cardo W1 and *decumani* S2–S5. Their courses were maintained throughout the different levels of occupation; thus streets that have been exposed only to the Roman or Byzantine levels may nevertheless indicate the course of the Herodian level.[52] The surface of the Herodian streets exposed in this zone was of yellow beaten *kurkar* soil; it was not paved by flagstones. These were encountered only in the later phases—pavers of limestone for the Roman streets and of *kurkar* for the Byzantine ones. The streets were c. 5 m wide and each edge was marked by a row of stones, but there were neither pedestrian walks, nor colonnades.[53] The streets were delineated on either side by the buildings. A sewer ran underneath; a water-supply system of lead or terracotta pipes was added next to the sewage system only in the later Roman and Byzantine phases.[54]

The dimensions of the urban blocks (*insulae*) in the southwestern zone were c. 65 × 95 m. If a Roman foot of 31 cm was applied, implying that a land survey was carried out by Roman surveyors,[55] this would result in *insulae* of c. 200 × 300 feet in the southwestern zone, which befit the Roman standard for *insulae* in the ratio of 2:3. The *insulae* in the Seleucid cities were narrow and long, with a ratio of 1:2.[56] An

---

[52] Vann 1983; Porath 1996a; 1998: 41–42.

[53] The stoas by which Herod adorned the broad street of Antioch (Jos., *Ant.* 16.148; *War* 1.425), converting it to a colonnaded street, was an innovation—exceptional in the urban space in the east in the period under discussion (see Lassus 1972; Will 1997: 99–113). New architectural studies of the ancient city have been published in *Syria* 76 (1999). Only later in the Roman period did colonnades become an integral part of a Roman *polis* in the east, including Caesarea, where *the cardo maximus* and *decumanus maximus* were colonnaded streets. The street columns of Caesarea are also mentioned in early fourth-century CE rabbinic and Christian written sources.

[54] Patrich 1998b: 51; 1999: 73–75; Porath 1996a: 111. A north–south sewer (1.8 m deep; c. 1 m wide) uncovered by Negev near the eastern Crusader city gate was attributed by him to the Herodian period (1993: 273). But the street above, being paved in limestone, suggests a later date within the Roman period.

[55] This unit was not applied throughout in the Herodian building projects in Caesarea. In the hippo-stadium and elsewhere, the use of a cubit 50.5 cm long is implied (see Patrich 2001b: esp. 270, n. 10). In the north the *insulae* were 80 m wide east-west, giving c. 270 Roman feet; the original north–south length is uncertain (Holum & Raban, in Stern 1993: 283). In the map given there, traces of north–south alleys dividing each *insula* into two are indicated in areas O and G. This seems to be a later sub-division.

[56] See, for example, Castagnoli 1971: 90–92; Ward-Perkins 1974: 19–21 and figs. 20–25; Barghouti 1982: 209–18; Owens 1991: 80–84.

area 155 m (500 ft) long was left for the temenos. Its axis of symmetry, off the city grid, was determined by the harbor. The diagonal street might have followed the course (determined by local topography) of a pre-existing dirt road, leading N of the hillock of Straton's Tower, on which the Herodian temple was later built.[57]

A "wall street," parallel to the wall and to the inside, is suggested by two Rabbinic sources referring to the graves of Caesarea and their defilement (see below, The Necropolis). This conjectural street—a new feature in the urban plan of Herodian Caesarea—is shown here for the first time in the city plan (Fig. 8).[57a]

Religious Structures

(1) *Herod's Temple of Augustus and Rome* (Fig. 16). The CCE excavations on the temple platform (area TP), directed by Holum since 1989,[58] have contributed significant new information to the previous data on this complex, gleaned in the 1960s excavations by Negev on behalf of the Israeli National Park Service.[59] Below the temple platform larger parts of the western retaining wall and of the piazza extending between this wall and the Herodian quay of the inner harbor have been exposed since 1992 by the IAA expedition headed by Porath (Area II) and by the University of Haifa and CCE expedition headed by Raban (Area I [the letter; not the Roman numeral]).[60] These recent excavations have provided for the first time secure information about the structure, shape, and elevation of the Herodian temenos, and about the location and the shape of the temple.

---

[57] Diagonal or radiating streets are shown outside Herodian Caesarea in the maps of Roman and Byzantine Caesarea (Holum *et al.* 1988: 130 and 163, figs. 86 and 112, respectively). They are not reproduced in the corresponding maps in Raban & Holum 1996. I would suggest that at least one street in a SE–NW orientation is Herodian. For a diagonal street see, for example, the case of Julio-Claudian Verulamium (St. Albans, England), in Ward-Perkins 1974: 71, fig. 69. At its end there is just an intersection.

[57a] See Patrich 2006a; 2009a, reprinted here as Chapter Two.

[58] The most updated and detailed summary to date is Holum 1999 (see also Holum 2004a and b). The foundations of the temple itself were encountered only in the 1995 summer season. For a proposed 3D reconstruction based on the ground plan, and on scattered, fragmentary architectural members, see Kahn 1996. For earlier reports, see Holum *et al.* 1992; Holum 1993: 53–60.

[59] Negev 1963b: 728; 1961: 81–83.

[60] For preliminary reports, see Porath 1996a: 107–9, 115; 1998: 45–48. Toueg 1998: 16.

The temenos, preserved to an elevation of c. 12 m above sea level, faced the harbor and was off-axis relative to the street grid. The platform was extended and leveled on top of the natural hillock by means of longitudinal vaults and a network of walls forming compartments filled with sand. Crushed *kurkar* on top of Herodian fill marks the maximal elevation at certain spots. The temple foundations were preserved to a maximal elevation of 11.37 m. It is assumed that its podium and pavement was actually 1–2 m higher, having been removed after the abandonment of the temple in the Christian regime. None of it survived—neither at the site of the temple, nor on the surrounding temenos.

The temenos had two wings projecting westward, bounding a lower rectangular piazza on the south and north. This piazza (80 × 23 m) was c. 1 m higher than the quay.[61] A massive (20 × 10 m) pier, axially located at the edge of the quay,[62] housed a staircase leading up. The entrance to the staircase was on the eastern side of the pier. The pier also retained a bridge leading to the temple platform. The existence of a second pier, as yet unexposed, is conjectured in the interval between the existing pier and the western temenos wall. Another, regular staircase (c. 6 m wide), was exposed on the south.[63]

The south and north retaining walls of the temenos were perpendicular to the western wall, while the eastern retaining wall was polygonal, or curvilinear—an unusual shape, encompassing an area c. 110 m from north to south and c. 90 m from east to west. It is logical to assume that the temenos was surrounded by colonnades and stoas. Such a structure would need stylobates, bases, or pedestals parallel to the retaining walls. Such supports indeed exist on the south and in the western wings. On the north there was an extension, perhaps of lower elevation. Its western façade served as a *nymphaeum*, built in the first

---

[61] See artistic reconstruction in Porath 1998: 46, fig. 10. In c. 300 CE a series of 10–12 barrel vaults was constructed on this piazza, filling the entire space between the projecting wings and adding space to the upper platform. These vaults have been considered Herodian since first being exposed by Negev. Influenced, no doubt, by this prevalent opinion, Raban (1987) reached the conclusion that the walls on the south and east sides of the southernmost vault, which predate the vault, were Hellenistic, components of Straton's Tower's fortification wall. It is now clear that these are Herodian retaining walls of the temenos, bounding a piazza on the south and on the east.

[62] Holum 1999: 16, fig. 4, reproduced here as Fig. 16.

[63] Stanley 1999.

or second century CE, whose precise relation to the main platform is not yet clear.

The rectangular temple (external dimensions: 28.6 × 46.4 m)[64] was located on an east–west axis, and parts of its foundations were exposed in all wings. It was founded on bedrock, built of *kurkar* ashlars with draft margins with a rough or low boss; gray mortar with flecks of charcoal served as bonding material to bedrock and between the stones. The north, east, and south foundations are 8 m wide, while the western foundations are only 3 m wide, and those on the western side of the *cella* 5 m wide. A *pronaos*, recognized in the foundations to the west of the *cella*, indicates that the temple was facing the harbor. Approximately 50 recorded architectural pieces permit a reconstruction of a Corinthian hexastyle temple with attic bases of c. 2.2 m in diameter; this gives a restored elevation of c. 21 m from base to the top of the entablature. Whether it was peripteral or pseudo-peripteral still remains to be determined. The shafts were coated with a thick layer of white stucco, with flutings.[65] Other members were plastered as well.

The emperor's cult was celebrated annually in the temple and in a street procession. The feast included *munera* and *venationes*, held in the stadium.[66] According to Philo, the emperor Tiberius ordered the golden shields inscribed in his honor, introduced by Pontius Pilatus to his *praetorium* in Jerusalem, thus inciting the wrath of the Jews, to be removed and transported to Caesarea, there to be placed in the temple of Augustus: the Sebasteion. The dynastic character of the cult therein is thus evident.[67]

(2) *Other Temples.* Whether or not the *Tiberieum* mentioned in the famous 'Pontius Pilatus' inscription found in the theater was a shrine or altar for his cult is a matter of debate (see below). The existence of other pagan temples is suggested by the city coins, gems, and statuary, prominent among them Tyche,[68] who could have been venerated

---

[64] The corresponding dimensions of the Herodian temple at Samaria/Sebaste are 23.95 × 34.9 m. The dimensions of the *opus quadratum* temple at Pan's cave, Paneas, attributed to Herod, are c. 22 × 15 m (Maoz 1998: 20). But note E. Netzer's reservation about this identification in *Qadmoniot* 116 (1998): 134 (in Hebrew), who opts for an adjacent *opus reticulatum* structure, c. 28 × 12 m in dimensions.

[65] See above note 32.

[66] For evidence for contests associated with the imperial cult festival at Aphrodisias, see Welch 1998: 558–61.

[67] Philo, *Leg.* 299–305; Maier 1969; Holum 1999: 17.

[68] Kadman 1957: 5–6; Hamburger 1968; 1950; 1955: 118–19, 127–31, pls. X–XI; Ringel 1975: 151–60; Gersht 1996. About one-third of the city coins are of Tyche

already at the Hellenistic Straton's Tower. Her figure as Tyche-Amazon in a marble statue of the early second century CE[69] first occurs on coins of year 68, under Nero, indicating that she was revered in this form already in the period under discussion. She was later conceived in the same form as the genius of the Colony, as stated on the Caesarea Cup. Her annual festival on March 5–7,[70] coinciding with *Navigium Isidis*, adds further weight to *P.Oxy.* 1380, suggesting that Isis was worshipped in Caesarea as Hellas and Agathe—names for the local Tyche.

The marble statue was found in 1971 in JECM Area B, to the south of the 'Byzantine esplanade,' in the debris of a Byzantine complex interpreted as having a commercial or industrial function.[71] It consists of a 'lower market,' surrounded by a colonnade, and an 'upper market,' reached by a stone ramp. A series of stone bases was arranged against the ramp, looking out over the 'lower market.' The Tyche statue was set on one of them. One would assume that the statue had not been carried far from its original location. Could this architectural complex with a basilical hall, extending over two terraces, have been the Tycheon/Isideon of Caesarea in its Hellenistic and Roman phases?[72]

As for other shrines suggested by the coins and Roman statuary, there are no clues about their location. Asclepius is not represented on the city coins, but his daughter Hygieia is (on a coin of Decius). Both are represented in the Roman statuary and gems.

---

type (Kadman 1957: 49–53). She is less prominent on the gems (nos. 71–77, 79–80 out of the 65 gems presented by Hamburger). According to Kadman (1957: 53–56), Tyche/Astarte, Dionysos, and Demeter formed the Caesarean triad. Other deities represented in the city coins (until Trajan Decius) are Serapis (11% by types), Poseidon, and Apollo. Some might have a local cult already in the Herodian period.

[69] Simon & Smith 1971; Gersht 1984: 110–14; Wenning 1986: 113–29; see the "Catalogue of the exhibition" appended at the end of Holum et al. 1988 (without page numbering), description of item 1 (Tyche statue).

[70] Euseb., *De Mart. Pal.* 11.30 (ed. Bardy 1967: 168).

[71] Holum & Raban, in Stern 1993: 283. Earlier, in Holum 1988: 176, and fig. 112 on p. 163, it is described in conjunction with the Byzantine city, as an open square paved with stone slabs, "with what might have been a civil basilica, a public hall for the lawcourts, opening into it."

[72] If this was indeed the location of the Hellenistic *Tychaeon*, one would expect that it should have been located within the wall of Straton's Tower, thus determining its southeastern corner. While only future excavations may establish the veracity of this hypothesis, it is more appealing than to look for the Hellenistic temple on the site of the Herodian temple, which would imply confiscation of sacred property. I would rather suggest that this 'acropolis' was the citadel of the local tyrant (see also above note 28).

(3) *The Jewish Synagogue*.[73] The site, excavated in 1956 and 1962 by Avi-Yonah, with the assistance of Negev, is located in the north-western zone of Herodian Caesarea, overlooking the sea. Of the five defined strata, stratum IV and V can be securely identified as fourth- and fifth-century synagogues respectively on the basis of inscriptions and Jewish symbols on marble capitals. It is assumed that this was also the function of the stratum II structure of the Herodian period, and it has been suggested that this was the synagogue mentioned in Josephus and in Rabbinic sources (*Maradatha* synagogue), in relation to the events that incited the Jewish revolt.[74] (Hellenistic houses were found in stratum I.) The stratum II structure was a square building. The entire east and south walls were uncovered; these were massive walls, up to 1.2 m thick, built of ashlars in alternating headers and stretchers above deep foundations, suggesting a public building. Five such courses were preserved in the southeastern corner of the build-ing, each 28 cm high. Portions of the walls of this building were incor-porated in the later stratum IV synagogue. (In stratum III part was used as a cistern.)

According to Malalas, Vespasian converted a Jewish synagogue located at a great distance from the theater into an odeum.[75] No remains of an odeum were uncovered above the structure under dis-cussion, although it is remote from the theater, so this note of Malalas (if of valid historicity) may refer to another synagogue. Whether or not the Herodian structure under discussion was indeed a synagogue, the Jewish community of Herodian Caesarea did not reside in restricted quarters—the Jewish population was dispersed throughout the city, a source of much friction and hostilities.[76]

As for the Christian community,[77] it used to convene at the pri-vate houses of its members: Peter, for example, has been described as preaching to a crowd assembled at Cornelius' house.[78] A centurion,

---

[73] Avi-Yonah 1956: 260–61; 1960: 44–48; Avi-Yonah & Negev 1963b: 146–47; Negev 1975: 277–79, 281; 1993: 278–80; Levine 1975b: 40–45; Ringel 1975: 117–20; Govaars *et al.* 2009.

[74] *War* 2.285–92; TY *Ber.* 3:6a; *Naz.* 7:6a; *San.* 1: 18a; Levine 1975b: 43, n. 320; 1975a: 30.

[75] Malalas, *Chronographia* X, 338 (ed. Dindorf 1831: 261); X.46 (ed. Thurn 2000: 197); Levine 1975b: 25–26, n. 176.

[76] See Levine's comment (1975a: 41) on *anamemigmenôn* in *War* 2.266. This situa-tion of mixed populations is also evident from the disorders concerning the approach to the synagogue referred to above (*War* 2.285–91).

[77] Downey 1975; Krenz 1992.

[78] Ac 10:27, 34–43.

he and his household were baptized by Peter, thus becoming the first Gentile converts. Similarly, the house of Philip the Evangelist and his four virgin daughters served as a meeting place when Paul and his associates resided there, on their way to Jerusalem.[79] The location of these houses is unknown.

HEROD'S PALACE AND THE *PRAETORIUM* OF THE ROMAN GOVERNORS OF JUDAEA

Herod built a palace (*basileia*) at Caesarea, and in 6 CE, when Judaea came under direct Roman rule, the governor established his seat there. Herod's *praetorium* was the residence of Governor Felix, whence the apostle Paul was brought for a hearing and placed in custody.[80] The Roman governor at Caesarea was first an official of an equestrian rank (with the title 'prefect') and later, after Agrippa I's short reign in the years 4–44 CE, the rank of the equestrian governor became 'procurator.' The Roman governor at Caesarea was subordinate to the governor of the Roman province of Syria—an official of a senatorial rank, who commanded four legions.[81]

Called "Sea Villa" by the Italian Expedition, it was later identified by Netzer and Levine as Herod's palace. The complex was excavated intermittently by several expeditions between 1976 and the late 1990s. An expedition of the Hebrew University of Jerusalem, headed by Netzer and Levine, investigated the lower terrace,[82] and later collaborated with a team of the University of Pennsylvania, headed by

---

[79] Ac 21:8; Philip was preaching in Caesarea years before (Ac 8:40).

[80] Ac 23:35; Patrich 2000b, reprinted here as Chapter Ten.

[81] After the destruction of Jerusalem in 70 CE, Caesarea became a Roman colony under Vespasian, and while Judaea was promoted to a public province ruled by a governor of a senatorial rank (*legatus Augusti pro praetore*), the former palace of Herod, enlarged and elaborated, continued to serve as the *praetorium*. The governor now commanded an army of one—and after 108 CE, two—legions, and the financial affairs of the province was entrusted to an official of an equestrian rank (*procurator provinciae*), for whom another *praetorium* was constructed to serve as his residence and *officium* at Caesarea. The complex was erected immediately after the Herodian period and hence beyond the scope of this paper. For details see Patrich 2000a: 35*–44*; 1999: 84–94, 99–107 and Chapter Eight below. Whether the building that preceded the *praetorium procuratoris*, of fine masonry and frescoes and with a long corridor, was a private or public structure, associated perhaps with harbor taxation, still needs to be examined. The complex was located in the immediate vicinity of the harbor, almost tangential with the southern end of the Herodian inner basin.

[82] Levine & Netzer 1986; Netzer 1996.

Gleason and Burrell, extending its work to the upper terrace as well.[83] The third was an IAA expedition, headed by Porath, which had exposed the larger part of the upper terrace.[84] A synthesis of the various, still preliminary, publications of these contributions is necessary in order to obtain a coherent picture.

Herod's palace (Fig. 17) extended over two terraces with a difference of elevation of c. 3.6 m. The two-storied lower terrace (110 × 55 m),[85] built in the first phase of the building operations at Caesarea (22–15 BCE), served as the private wing. It occupied a natural promontory, extending 100 m into the Mediterranean. The eastern side and the southeastern corner were rock cut. The various wings, founded almost at sea level, surrounded a large, rectangular, rock-cut pool (35 × 8 m; 2 m deep), lined with hydraulic plaster,[86] with a rectangular base—presumably for a statue—at its center. It was a swimming pool, fed by sweet water, typical of Herodian palaces.[87] The pool was surrounded by open walks (2.6 m wide) and on three sides (south, west, and north) by a colonnade (4.2 m wide), with an intercolumniation of 2.3 m, holding rock-cut and masonry-built rectangular pits (0.6 × 1.4 m; 0.7 m apart; more than 0.7 m deep), that served as planters for flowers and shrubs. The south, west, and north wings were severely affected by stone looting and by sea erosion. Nonetheless, the foundation trenches and the first course of some of the walls provide some concept of their plan. The better preserved eastern wing served as a dining suite (looking west), consisting of a central hall (93.5 sq. m), interpreted as a

---

[83] Burrell, Gleason & Netzer 1993; Gleason et al. 1998. In the latter article three Herodian phases are suggested for the complex (see also Gleason 1996; Burrell 1996).

[84] Porath 2000a: 36*–37* and fig. 51 on p. 40. According to Porath, the entire complex, on both terraces, antedates Herod's reign and should be attributed to the Roman procurators of Judaea. However, this interpretation disregards the fact (pointed out by Netzer, in Gleason et al. 1998: 38) that the north wall of the upper terrace is bonded into the west cavea wall of the stadium; nor does it take into consideration the fact that the praetorium where Paul the Apostle was detained at Caesarea under governor Felix is referred to as the praitôrion of Herod (Ac 3:35).

[85] Gleason et al. 1998: 29. According to Burrell (1996: 240) the dimensions of the rectangular structure (without the semi-circular western projection) is 44 × 80 m, while according to Netzer (1996: 198–201) 83 × 51 m—giving a total area of c. 4,400 sq. m for the lower story (including the projections) and 8,000 sq. m for the two stories.

[86] Italian pozzolana cement, imported to Caesarea only in Herod's time, was used in the pool (Gleason et al. 1998: 29; Oleson 1989: 162).

[87] Its identification as a fish pond by Flinder (1976; 1985) should be rejected; it is now clear that it was a part of a palatial complex, not of an industrial plant.

Herodian triclinium, flanked on either side by two small rooms. At least four phases of modifications and mosaic re-flooring were traced.[88] Remains of wall plaster imitating marble incrustation were uncovered *in situ* and glass tesserae point to the existence of wall mosaics. Natural scallop shells were also set into red painted stucco. The thick lateral walls brought to Netzer's mind a vaulted ceiling, but a second story open eastward to the upper palace should not be excluded. The lateral rooms attained heated floors (*hypocaustum*) and furnace in the later periods, serving as a bath. An earlier small bathhouse, including a *miqveh*, was found in the north-western corner of the upper palace (see below).

Access to the second story and to the upper terrace was via a spiral staircase located in the northeastern corner. The western side, which might have served as the living quarters, is poorly preserved. Two projections extended from the main rectangular building. one, semi-circular (26 m in diameter), reconstructed as an elevated exedra, extended westward, while the other, much smaller one, extending southward, might have served as a jetty for small boats.

The upper terrace, on the upper part of the promontory and of a slightly different orientation, served as the public wing. It was built between 15 and 10 BCE around a vast courtyard (42 × 65 m = 2,730 sq. m), paved with compacted crushed stone, and surrounded by porticoes with a 3–m intercolumniation.[89] The *kurkar* columns, with attic bases and Doric capitals, all had a fine plaster coat. A raised square platform, for some monument or a *bêma*, stood in its center, and to its east a vast underground water cistern was constructed, with two compartments, T-shaped in its ground plan.

The north wing held two suites separated by a service corridor. The western suite (in the University of Pennsylvania excavation area) faced south, while the eastern one (in the IAA excavation area) faced north. The symmetrical western suite had a basilical audience hall in its

---

[88] At first the rock-trimmed rear wall of the triclinium was plain and the façade had one or three doorways. Later, an apse was cut in the rear wall, and the entire hall, including the apse, received a new mosaic floor. To the front the wall was replaced by a portico, extending westward, at the expense of the pool. In a yet later phase a fountain was installed in the apse, with a semi-circular pond built over the mosaic floor.

[89] The western half of the upper terrace was excavated by the University of Pennsylvania expedition, directed by Gleason and Burrell, while the eastern half and areas further to the east, belonging to the Roman *praetorium*, as well as the entire south wing, were excavated by the Israel Antiquities Authority expedition headed by Porath.

center (192 sq. m), flanked by smaller rooms and service corridors. The northern part of the hall, which apparently accommodated a dais or a *bêma*,[90] had a heated floor set on stone *suspensurae/hypocaustum*. Later in the Roman period the *suspensurae* were extended to a room on the east, but this extension was built of brick alone. It seems that here the Roman governor and his *concilium* held their assizes. In this case it would have been here that Paul the Apostle, and later the Christian martyrs of Caesarea or members of the Jewish community mentioned in the rabbinic sources, underwent trial.[91] A small bath unit, including a Jewish *miqveh*, was located to the west of this suite. The eastern suite had on its south four rooms facing north, to a stone-paved courtyard with a circular fountain in its center. The southern wing was the latest addition to the upper terrace. In the second and third centuries CE it held a large Roman bathhouse, with an intact furnace that heated a circular hall and with a semi-circular basin. It might have served the staff and guests of the *praetorium*.

The entrance to the palace was from the east, via a square *propylon* of four corner turrets. Only their foundations were preserved. A more massive tower attached to the external side of the northwest corner of the *propylon* could have served as a stronghold, controlling the *sphendone* of the stadium and supervising its entire length.

Under Roman regime Herod's palace was extended further to the east, adding c. 50 m along the southern end of the hippo-stadium, thus encompassing a total area of more than 12,000 sq. m. Latin inscriptions on mosaic floors and architectural members mention various functionaries and identify the function of various rooms of the *officium*.[92]

DWELLINGS

The dwellings in the southwestern zone, of the Roman *domus* type, including a peristyle, were constructed under the first procurators, in the first half of the first century CE, and are thus later than Herod's reign.[93] The development of the city within the insular urban space was gradual. These were wealthy mansions, decorated with mosaic and

---

[90] See plan and reconstruction in Gleason *et al.*, 1998: figs. 4c and 7.
[91] See Patrich 2000a; 2002f, reprinted here as Chapter Twelve.
[92] Cotton & Eck 2001.
[93] Porath 1996a: 110–13; 1998: 37–38.

opus sectile floors and frescoed walls. The Roman *domus* in area KK (extending into the area excavated by the IAA) contained a bathhouse and a *miqveh*.

ENTERTAINMENT STRUCTURES

(1) The Theater (Fig. 18).[94] The theater was one of the venues for the dedication of Caesarea, established as a quinquennial festival in honor of Augustus.[95] King Agrippa I, vested in golden garb, together with a royal retinue and other dignitaries were present at a great festival there, where he fell sick and died after five days in the Caesarea palace.[96] Noticed by travelers and explored more attentively by the SWP team in the nineteenth century, the Herodian theater was exposed in its entirety in the years 1959–63 by the Italian Expedition. Roman rather than Greek in its semi-circular layout, it was exceptional in its construction out of stone (Jos., *Ant.* 15.341) in a period when most

---

[94] Conder & Kitchener 1882: 15–17; Frova *et al.*, 1965: 57–234; Levine 1975b: 23–26; Ringel 1975: 47–51; Segal 1995: 64–69. The latter, however, should be used with reservation, since it contains many discrepancies in measurements and details (see below notes 99–100). Segal (1995: 66, 69) seems to confuse between radius and diameter, and one cannot envisage from his work the Herodian phase—the earliest Roman theater in Judaea/Palaestina; also Josephus' assertion that this was a stone theater is left uncommented by Segal. The Herodian phase was described in detail by Frova *et al.* (1965: 167–74); for a good summary, though with neither plans, nor sections, see Frova 1975: 274–77, and Frova in Stern 1993: 273–74.

[95] Lämmer 1974; Schwartz 1992; Patrich 2002d, reprinted here as Chapter Seven.

[96] Jos., *Ant.* 19.343–50. Following Schwartz (1992: 175–76), who assumes that Caesarea was inaugurated on September 10 BCE (see 175, n. 37), the festival under Agrippa I would have been the 14th 'Herodian' Actiada (running at least one year later than the actual Augustan Actiades—see 175, n. 37), and thus falling in September 43 CE; cf. Lämmer 1981 (who counts from March 11 BCE). Kokkinos (1998: 378–80), who believes that on chronological grounds Herod's Caesarean Games (beginning in March 13 BCE—see 370, point 3) could not have had anything to do with the Actian Games, proposed the interesting suggestion that the festival of Agrippa I was actually a *hyper sôtêrias* festival, held at the beginning of August 44, celebrating the victorious return of Claudius from his campaign in Britain. On one point of Kokkinos' arguments I would comment that the festival referred to by Eusebius, held in Caesarea on March 5–7, 306 CE, was the annual festival of the local Tyche (above note 70), and as I shall suggest elsewhere (see Chapter Three below), it coincided with the *Navigium Isidis* commemorating the foundation of Caesarea as a Roman colony by Vespasian. Does Kokkinos assume that because Eusebius refers to the *genethlia* of Tyche, and as Tyche had to be cognate to the *genius* of Augustus (to whom the city was dedicated), the *genethlia* must equal the *dies natalis* of the city?

theaters in Rome were still made of wood, as was the theater built by Herod earlier (c. 28 BCE) in Jerusalem.[97]

The lower seats were rock-cut; the upper, stone-built and artificially retained. The external diameter of the theater, which faced west to the sea, was 90–100 m;[98] the structure accommodated c. 3,500–4,000 spectators. The Herodian orchestra floor (c. 35 m in diameter)[99] lies 0.70 m below the later, second- to third-century marble floor, with an axial vaulted passage running underneath. This was a multi-colored stucco floor that was frequently refurbished, with a total of 14 successive layers of painted plaster counted over the thick stucco floor. The uppermost layer depicted a polychrome geometric pattern of rectangles and of discs and lozenges in squares, arranged in parallel rows, imitating marble incrustation. A similar band ran around the circumference, with blue, red, and white as the dominant colors. The layer immediately underneath depicted an imitation of multi-colored feathers (*opus pavonaceum*).[100] The sole parallel of a painted, plastered orchestra floor is the Augustan theater at Leptis Magna, where the floor is Flavian in date, approximately a century later than that of Caesarea.

Remains of the Herodian *proscaenium* and *pulpitum* were uncovered under the ones now extant (1 m high; 7 m deep) in the theater. The primitive *proscaenium* had alternating rectilinear and concave niches, 3.5 m wide to the front and c. 0.6 m deep. It was decorated by frescoes resembling the orchestra floor, but depicting lozenges, imitating marble incrustation.[101] The *hyposcaenium* (35.90 m long;

---

[97] Patrich 2002e.

[98] These are the 'official' numbers given for the external diameter by the Italian Expedition (Frova *et al.* 1965: 176, "imperial" phase; Frova 1963: 23, pls. 1–4; Ringel 1975: 48; Levine 1975b: 23, n. 59). Segal (1995: 65 and table on 99), gives a diameter of 62 m, far from the 'official' numbers of the Italians. Lichtenberger (1999: 124–25), relying on Segal, repeats this erroneous data.

[99] Frova 1963, and Frova *et al.* 1965, give a diameter of 30 m for the imperial phase. The Herodian orchestra was more than 5 m larger, as can be gleaned from Frova *et al.* 1965: 86, fig. 64 (reproduced here as Fig. 18a). Segal (1995: 66) gives a figure of 17 m (!) but it is not clear on what grounds. The 0.7 m difference in elevation between the Herodian orchestra floor and the later (marble) floor are not indicated by him at all.

[100] Albricci 1962; 1965. A fragment of this stucco floor was uncovered by the IAA in a rescue excavation in the underground channel, into which it had collapsed due to a winter flood in 1999. The feather pattern (Frova *et al.* 1965: fig. 72 and pl. II, fig. 93) was encountered in a mosaic floor of the Roman urban villa excavated by the IAA— see Porath 2000a: 44, fig. 55 (in Hebrew) and 37* (in English).

[101] Frova *et al.* 1965: 87, fig. 72, and 95, figs. 82–84, marked A and B; pl. I, figs. 86–89, 125–26.

5.5 m wide) was divided by ten pillars, supporting arches, into two unequal naves. It was accessed from both ends. The Herodian *scaenefrons*, of local *kurkar* which had been plastered and stuccoed, rather than the later granite and marble structure, was of a Hellenistic type. It had a central rectangular niche flanked by curvilinear niches and colonnaded wings. The later *scaenefrons*, of marble and red and gray granite, was Roman in type, consisting of a grand semi-circular exedra, flanked by rectangular ones.[102]

The Herodian lower rows of seats (*ima cavea*), buried under the later seats, were partially rock-cut in a moderate hillock. The later *ima cavea* is divided into six sectors of seats (*cunei*), and the upper tribunes (*summa cavea*) into seven. They are separated by a horizontal *praecinctio* to which six radiating vaulted *vomitoria* lead from an external, encircling vaulted corridor. Several architectural features suggest that the *summa cavea* was surmounted by a roofed gallery. It is not known whether the Herodian division of the seats was similar. Only three lowermost rows of these early seats and a single stairway were partially exposed at a depth of c. 2.30 m under a fill of the later *cavea* (Fig. 18b). The seats were of conglomerate. A drainage channel (*euripus*), 0.85 m deep at the circumference of the Herodian orchestra, was uncovered at the foot of these seats.[103] While the later *cavea* was set on top of a c. 1 m-high podium wall, such a wall was not a feature of the Herodian structure.

A *kurkar* slab with a Latin dedication by Pontius Pilatus to Tiberius was found in secondary use in a fourth-century reconstruction of the theater. The *Tiberieum* to which the inscription refers is a matter under debate.[104]

(2) The amphitheater: a Hippodrome-Stadium (hippo-stadium).[105] The 'amphitheater' was a major venue of the games held by Herod

---

[102] Frova *et al.* 1965: 129, figs. 146 and 147 respectively. This *scaenefrons* is also seen here in Fig. 18a. For a proposed reconstruction see Netzer 2006: 112–115, Fig. 26.

[103] Frova *et al.* 1965: 86, fig. 64.

[104] For discussion and full references, see Lehmann and Holum 2000: 67–70, inscription 43. Recently Alföldi (1999 and 2002, with a comprehensive survey of earlier opinions) has suggested that the inscription refers to a tower, perhaps a light tower, in Caesarea's harbor. In any case, the theater was adjacent to the compound of the Roman authority; many other Latin inscriptions were found there, and it seems reasonable that the *Tiberieum* was also located nearby.

[105] The structure was uncovered only in the large-scale excavations which began in 1992. Its larger part was excavated by the IAA expedition headed by Porath. The northern end, including the starting gates of the hippo-stadium, was uncovered by the

in Caesarea in the inauguration festival (dated here to September 9 BCE),[106] described in detail by Josephus (*Ant.* 16.137–41):

> And so, there was, to begin with, a very great festival of dedication and most lavish arrangements. For he had announced a contest in music and athletic exercises, and had prepared a great number of gladiators and wild beasts and also horse races (*hippôn te dromon*) at the very lavish shows that are to be seen at Rome and in various other places. And this contest too he dedicated to Caesar, having arranged to celebrate it every fifth year. And Caesar, adding luster to his (Herod's) munificence, from his own revenues sent all the equipment needed for such games. On her own account Caesar's wife Julia sent many of her greatest treasures from Rome, so that the entire sum was reckoned as no less than five hundred talents. When to see the sights there came to the city a great multitude as well as the envoys sent by communities because of the benefits that they had received. Herod welcomed them all and entertained them with the lodging and meals and continuous feasts. During the day the festivals offered the diversion of spectacles, while at night they provided amusements costing great sums of money, and so they made his generosity famous, for in all the things that he undertook he was ambitious to surpass what had been done before. And they say that Caesar himself and Agrippa often remarked that the extent of Herod's realm was not equal to his magnanimity, for he deserved to be king of all Syria and of Egypt.[107]

The U-shaped structure (Fig. 19) was built on a north–south axis, parallel to the coastline, a location that corresponds to Josephus' description.[108] The local *kurkar* stone served exclusively as the building

---

University of Haifa expedition, headed by the present writer (see Porath 1994; 1995a; 1996b; Patrich 1997a; 2001; 2002c).

[106] A year later than Schwartz (1992: 175, n. 37), two-and-a-half years later than Lämmer (1974: 130–5), and four-and-a-half years later than Kokkinos (1998: 370, point 3). According to the Latin version (prepared at the suggestion of Cassiodorus in the sixth century CE, but preserved in a much older manuscript than the Greek version with which we are familiar) of *Ant.* 16.140, they lasted 15 days: "...*et per dies quindecim spectacula vel delicias ministravit.*" On the occasionally superior tradition of the Latin text, see Niese 1887: xxvii–xxix; Blatt 1985: 17–26. See also Lämmer 1974: 136–37, quoting the full text of the Latin version.

[107] See also *War* 1.415 which agrees with *Ant.* in referring to the 192nd Olympiad, held in July 12 BCE but the cycle of which ended in June 9 BCE. For a more detailed description of the games held by Herod c. 20 years earlier in Jerusalem in honor of Augustus, see *Ant.* 15.268–74.

[108] Earlier, following Reifenberg (1950), the prevalent opinion was that Josephus confused the theater with the amphitheater, which Reifenberg located at the site of an oval depression he had identified in aerial photographs in the north-eastern zone of Caesarea. This now seems to be a later, Roman oval amphitheater. Large scale excavations (non published yet), were carried out in the amphitheater in 2010 on behalf of IAA, headed by Dr. Peter Gendelman.

material. The arena (c. 300 m long; 50.5 m wide; 2.20 m above sea-level) was enclosed on the east, south, and west by the seats (*cavea*), in rows with a seating capacity of c. 10,000.[109] The rounded gallery (*sphendone*) was in the south. The seats were retained on two parallel walls with a fill of earth in between. The straight wings of the *cavea* (entirely preserved on the eastern side, while mostly eroded on the west) did not run along the full length of the arena, but ended c. 65 m from the starting gates (*carceres*). These wings of the *cavea* were c. 175 m long—sufficient to encompass, together with the *sphendone*, a typical stadium long racetrack. The seats were arranged in 18 segments (12 of which are still preserved) and were set on top of a podium wall, 1.1 m above the arena level. An arched entranceway, 3 m wide, ran under the center of the *sphendone*. The *carceres* enclosed the arena on the north. The dimensions and the existence of the starting gates at the northern end indicate that the structure served as a hippodrome.[110] Locally, however, it was known as the "great stadium" (Jos., *War* 2.172) or just the "stadium" (*Ant.* 18.57)[111] of Caesarea.

A trench separated the stadium from the higher *kurkar* ridge and its continuation northward. Access to the top of the gallery was thus prevented from the east until the trench was filled with earth, in the days of Nero, and a double colonnaded portico was built. A passage-way (*vomitorium*), located c. 115 m from the southern gate, ran across the entire width of the eastern gallery, split into two inclined vaults, leading after two successive 90° turns to a platform for the dignitaries (*pulvinar*). This loggia was usually located opposite the finish line of the chariot races, which was marked in lime across the right side of

---

[109] The population of Caesarea by the First Jewish revolt is estimated to be c. 50.000 (Schalit 1964: 172). In 66 CE, when the revolt erupted, over 20,000 Jews were murdered by the Gentiles of Caesarea according to Josephus (*War* 2.457).

[110] On Josephus' terminology, referring to the structure as an amphitheater, see Humphrey 1996.

[111] The context suggests that the event took place near the Roman *praetorium* on the site of Herod's palace, namely, in the Herodian entertainment structure under discussion. Eusebius (*History of the Martyrs in Palestine*, ed. and tr. Cureton, Paris 1861: 21–23 and 51; 6.3–7 in the Greek text), a resident of Caesarea, refers to events witnessed by himself and other citizens: Christian martyrs being thrown into the stadium as prey for the wild beast. His testimony regarding the structure's identification as a stadium by the locals is therefore of utmost significance. The reality of hunt scenes (*venationes*), conducted in a stadium, is also familiar in the Rabbinic sources (see m *Baba Kamma* 4.4; cf. m *Abodah Zarah* 1.7).

the arena. The face of the podium wall was coated with plaster and frescoes that were renewed from time to time.[112]

At the southern end of the arena, about 25 m north of the southern entrance, remains were preserved of the turning post—the *meta prima* (see below). Several architectural phases were discerned here. The starting gates, like all other parts of the hippodrome, were built of *kurkar* stone and coated with white plaster. More than half of the stalls were exposed in a section c. 30 m wide on the eastern part. The stalls further to the west were eroded by the sea. It is logical to assume that they were similar, symmetrically arranged structures. Three phases were discerned in the arrangement of the starting gates. Phase I, with three sub-phases, is of the Herodian period, of interest to our discussion.[113] The Phase I *carceres* had five stalls on either side of the central gate. The ceilings in all three sub-phases were flat and light, apparently made of wooden beams. The stalls were 3.3–3.6 m wide, and their interior depth was 3.75–4 m. They were set parallel to each other and to the long axis of the arena. Each stall was set somewhat further north relative to the stall to its east, so that the façade appeared slightly curved, but symmetrical, relative to the long axis of the arena. The Phase Ib façade piers suggest that the *carceres* had two stories. An architectural analysis gives an elevation of c. 8.9 m.

The arrangement of the Herodian stalls, in all three sub-phases, indicates that the chariots started their race in parallel lanes, as at Olympia (Patrich 2001b, 2002d). The destination of the chariots was the far turning post—the *meta prima*—and not the nearest post, as in the Roman circus system. It appears that Herod instituted Greek-style races, and such remained their style throughout the Herodian period. Such a race course precludes any possibility for the existence of a continuous physical barrier (*euripus*) along the middle of the arena in this phase, as was common in the Circus Maximus at Rome. The nature of

---

[112] One of the layers, in the section preserved south of the dignitaries' platform, presents a scene of running wild animals, as well as vegetation. Porath (2000b) attributes this layer of frescoes to a late phase, when the hippo-stadium was shortened. In another layer, preserved in the curved section between the eastern and southern sides, geometric patterns were depicted. Additional sections of plaster were also found opposite it, on the western side.

[113] For a detailed description of these and the later phases, see Patrich 2001b; 2003b.

Herod's *hippika* as described by Josephus above—horse riding and not just chariot races—is also indicative of their Greek style.[114]

The starting gates of Sub-phase Ic were dismantled and from their stones a massive c. 1.5 m thick wall (W 100), built of headers, was constructed, covering the lower parts of the stalls. While dismantling the three courses left of this wall under Phase II *carceres*, potsherds, including 'Herodian' oil lamps, were found between the stones, resembling those that are found in many sites in a destruction layer corresponding to the end of the second Temple period. These finds enable us to conclude with some confidence that the wall was built at the same time. Its construction brought an end to the operation of the hippo-stadium as such. The arena was converted into a vast walled enclosure. It is tempting to link this physical change with the 66 CE Jewish revolt against Rome, a conclusion permitted by the archaeological data. It is reasonable to assume that with the end of the revolt, in 70 CE, Titus imprisoned the war captives for an entire winter in this walled compound, and not in the prison at the governor's palace (*praetorium*) (Jos., *War* 7. 20).[115] Here Titus also held, in October 70, celebrations in honor of the eighteenth birthday of his brother Domitian, at which over 2,500 of his Jewish captives were slaughtered by being forced to fight with wild beasts, in man-to-man sword duels, or by being hoisted on a stake—traditional Roman types of entertainment (*War* 7.37–8). It can therefore be deduced that the number of imprisoned captives in Caesarea was very large.

Besides chariot races, *munera* and *venationes*—Roman spectacles—constituted an integral component of the Games instituted by Herod (assumed here to be equivalent to the Actian Games). These, too, took place in the hippo-stadium under discussion. Such spectacles were held there on an annual basis, in conjunction with the imperial cult, and not just every four years, in the framework of the *pentaetêris*. Holes

---

[114] For the differences between Greek *hippika* and Roman chariot races, see Humphrey 1986: 5–12; Patrich 2002d.

[115] The stadium in Tiberias also functioned as a prison compound, where in 67, at the end of the battles in the Galilee, Vespasian gathered all the Jewish captives (36,600 according to Josephus) and determined their fate to die or to become slaves (*War* 3.532–42). In Herod's day, Jewish dignitaries were summoned to be put under garrison in the hippodrome in Jericho (*Ant.* 17.193–4; *War* 1.659–69). Netzer (1999a: 56–59) locates the exact place of the arrest in the *palaestra* above and to the north of the theater, and not in the arena of the hippodrome.

(c. 0.8 m apart), cut on top of the podium wall along its entire length and in the first two rows of seats, to hold a protective net (Figs. 102–103), constitute evidence that these spectacles were held in the arena before it had been shortened.

The Necropolis

The necropolis of Caesarea in the various periods is a topic worthy of a separate study. Most finds came from beyond the Byzantine wall. So far, no burials have been found in the entire area between it and the inner, Herodian wall. Nevertheless, these burial grounds are alluded to in an early rabbinic source, which states that the territory of east Caesarea contains graves and is therefore defiling (m *Oholoth* 8.9).[116]

While the Mishnah reflects an earlier (Herodian) urban situation, stating that there are graves east of Caesarea, the later Tosefta interprets it according to a new urban reality. This was necessary due to the extension of the city eastward, over previous burials. Given the new situation, the Tosefta (that may be dated shortly after 200 CE) interprets "east of Caesarea" as "from directly opposite its *tetrapylon* towards its winepress," namely, a territory in the extended, newly built area. Since the graves alluded to in the Mishnah were outside the Herodian city wall, which seems logical, the conjectural location of its east gate may suggest the location of the later *tetrapylon*, which had replaced it.[117] Moreover, the statement of R. Yehuda the baker, in the Tosefta, that the eastern stoa is pure, suggests that a colonnaded street replaced the line of the earlier Herodian wall. This may suggest the existence of a simpler street, parallel to the city wall, in the Herodian city. Future excavations at its course may confirm or reject this hypothesis. This conjectural street is depicted in Fig. 8.

---

[116] See also *t.Oholoth* 18:13 (ed. Zukermandel: 617), and the discussion in Levine 1975b: 38 and 46–47; cf. Patrich 2006a and *infra*, Chapter Two.

[117] Accordingly, it will be located two blocks to the east of the east Gate of the Crusader wall, where the *tetrapylon* is set on the map of Byzantine Caesarea in Holum *et al.* 1988: 163, fig. 112, and 176. According to the Tosefta, *the tetrapylon* was a monument of the Roman city already under Hadrian (see Patrich 2006a, and the next chapter).

The Water Supply

No aqueduct is named by Josephus within Herod's building projects in Caesarea (or in Jerusalem); nonetheless, aqueducts, known in Israel since Hellenistic times, were an integral part of his (and the Hasmonaeans') desert palace fortresses and of the Jericho palaces.[118] Since aqueducts were a common component in Herod's building projects, one would be expected to have been constructed in Caesarea as well. An argument *ex silentio* is therefore not a decisive argument, but on the other hand, there is no decisive archaeological evidence to support this claim. The earliest aqueduct to Caesarea was channel A of the upper-level aqueduct.[119] Its date is under debate: while some claim it to be Herodian, others attribute it to the procurators, and still others to the Flavians.[120] Porath, in a reassessment, opted for the procurators, no later than Vespasian, on the basis of the post-Herodian composition of its waterproof plaster and an examination of the chronology of the water-supply and storage system in the city.[121] However, while plaster composition may be indicative, it is not a definitive dating tool. Certain regional variations in its composition between Jerusalem and its desert and Caesarea should not be excluded.

The aqueduct, c. 7.5 km long, starts at the Shuni springs (11.80 m above sea level; the top of the temple platform in Caesarea, at c. 12.50 m above sea level, certainly could not been reached), c. 6 km northeast of Caesarea. It can be divided into four sections, built in three different methods. The first section, passing the southern tip of Mt. Carmel, is a masonry channel. The second and fourth sections are arched aqueducts—the second crossing through a swampy depression and the fourth through the sand dunes extending along the shore north of Caesarea. The third section is a rock-cut tunnel, 442 m long, cutting through the *kurkar* range of Jisr ez-Zarqa.

Conservation works carried out by the IAA in 1992/3 in the arches of the aqueduct indicate that they rest on a continuous stretch of foundation wall, c. 3.5 m thick, with a graded top. There was no separate foundation for the piers of each arch. The stability of the entire arcade

---

[118] For an updated survey of these and other systems, see Amit, Patrich & Hirschfeld 2002.

[119] Porath 2002, with references therein to earlier studies.

[120] Levine 1975b: 31–35; Patrich and Amit 2002: 16–18.

[121] Porath 2002: 120.

was thus guaranteed. The Jisr ez-Zarqa tunnel (c. 0.9 m wide; 1.8 m high) was lined on the bottom and sides (up to 1.6 m from the floor) with waterproof lime plaster. It had 15 ventilation shafts (6.6–13.4 m deep; 11.5–37.4 m distant from one another), through which it was originally cut in both directions. Such shafts are known from the Hellenistic aqueduct of Acre-Ptolemais and from the Herodian water-supply system to Jerusalem. At the western end of the tunnel the roof was made of two slanting stones, forming a gabled ceiling.

The course of the aqueduct within the walls is not known. It is assumed that it was carried south on top of the city wall. The destination points—apparently city reservoirs or pools, like in Jerusalem—are not known either. A network of lead and terracotta pipes providing running water to private houses, bathhouses, public fountains, and latrines, are later in date. Porath, who dates the aqueduct to the procurators, maintains that private houses, including Herod's palace, had first (until the first half of the first century) wells and cisterns to rely on; running water came later. Wells were 2–5 m deep (the level of the water table is 0.35 m above sea level).[122]

The Urban Plan: A Comparative Discussion

As indicated above, the temenos and the harbor have a different axiality. Is this sufficient to claim that the city, Caesarea, and its harbor, Sebastos, were two completely separate entities, as was suggested by Raban (and later by Barag) on the grounds of the legend *Kaisareia ê pros Sebastôi limeni* ("Caesarea which is near the port of Sebastos"— but literally "the one which faces the port of Sebastos"), on some city coins of Agrippa I and of Nero?[123] In order to sustain such a claim, the legal and administrative status of Sebastos should be compared to the status of other royal, provincial, or municipal harbors throughout the Roman Mediterranean. An interpretation of the legend in such a sense is not enough.

---

[122] Porath 2002: 124. Wells already existed in Straton's Tower. A Hellenistic well was excavated by the IAA in 1996 at the bottom of the Crusader moat near the northern gate (Porath 2002: 105; figures are given in Gendelman 2007).

[123] Raban 1992b; Barag 1996. Interestingly, Pseudo-Skylax (above note 10) names in many cases a city and its harbor as two separate geographical features. But in the case of the much later Caesarea, the harbor is physically within the city.

The Herodian city had a wall, like Sebaste and Jerusalem. Despite the fact that the streets were laid orthogonally, the wall had a semi-elliptical outline, which differed entirely from the square or rectangular wall course in the contemporary Augustan colonies, such as Turin (founded in 27 BCE), Aosta (founded in 25 BCE), and Verona (founded in 28–15 BCE). The flat topography of Caesarea could permit a rectangular layout without any difficulty. However, its curved course is in accord with the traditional local approach (cf. the walls of Dor, located in a quite similar flat landscape, where the curved course of the wall was determined already in the Persian and earlier times), as well as with the Hellenistic approach to fortifications, letting the course of a wall follow the topography freely, even if the layout of the city inside is strictly orthogonal.[124] A citadel was a common feature of a Seleucid city.[125] Herod's palace was an enclosed structure which opened inward. It was protected on the west by the sea, and on the north by the hippo-stadium. Only the gate in the east was protected by four turrets and by a high tower, which also controlled the hippo-stadium. The palace was not a citadel.[126]

An orthogonal plan seems to be an exception in Herodian cities. This feature is entirely absent from Herodian Jerusalem and Samaria (and note that hilly topography did not prevent the application of an orthogonal city plan, as exemplified in Roman Aelia Capitolina). The dominant urban features in both cities were: a temple built on top of a vast, elevated, artificial temenos, isolating the temple from the city; a principal road leading to the temenos from one of the city gates; and a monumental staircase leading up from the street level.[127] In both cities the principal street attained, in addition, the role of a Via Sacra, func-

---

[124] Above note 56.

[125] Above note 56.

[126] One can easily compare it with the adjacent *kastron*, erected around the theater in the Byzantine period to serve as an inner citadel.

[127] Hesberg 1996. In Sebaste the Sebasteion replaced an orthogonal Gabinian neighborhood built on the deserted Hellenistic acropolis. The monumental staircase was on the north, and the course of the main street from the West Gate to the monumental staircase is suggested by both ends and by the orientation of the West Gate with its two round towers, and that of the adjacent buildings exposed not far from the gate. When the colonnaded street was constructed, under Septimius Severus, following an entire different course, cutting through the acropolis slope on the south, the actual opening in the gate was shifted by building two short walls between the circular towers to meet the new orientation (see Crowfoot *et al.* 1942: 35–37, 50–70, 123–39; Reisner, Fisher & Lyon 1924: 167–220; and Netzer 1987). For Jerusalem, see Maoz 1985; Geva 1993: 680, with additional references.

tionally, if not ritually. The diagonal street in Caesarea, the existence of which is alluded to by Josephus and recognized in aerial photographs, might have had a similar role, leading from a southeast gate to the temenos. The hierarchy of the underground sewers—the diagonal being the principal one—may reflect a similar hierarchy in the streets, the diagonal one being perhaps more monumental.

A principal artery serving as a Via Sacra is also to be found at Petra and at Palmyra, leading to Qasr al-Bint and to the Temple of Bel, respectively.[128] This approach to city planning in the east, first encountered in Herodian city planning, can also be recognized in first-century Gerasa, where the 'proto-cardo,' as yet without any columns, led from the north straight to the temple of Zeus. This approach to the streets' hierarchy was maintained into the second and third centuries in the city plans of Philadelphia, Gadara, Sebaste of Septimius Severus, Neapolis, etc.—a colonnaded decumanus being their principal artery (their "armature", to use a term of Macdonald).[129] Its origin might be sought in the principal avenues of the Seleucid cities[130] or in the main avenue of Alexandria, 100 feet wide according to Diodore of Sicily (Diod., 17.52; Strabo, 17.1.6–10).[131] The extra monumentality that the principal street of Antioch attained due to Herod reflects the same approach, to be imitated many decades later in other cities by the introduction of colonnaded streets.

In the urban plan of Caesarea certain affinities to Alexandria should be pointed out:

1. An artificial harbor projecting into the sea; not a *limên kleistos*.
2. A temple overlooking the sea, like Pan temple in Alexandria, built on top of a prominent hill, overlooking the sea and the entire city. Other temples, in less prominent locations but nearer to the sea shore, were that of Poseidon, Isis at Lochias, and the Arseneion.
3. A promontory palace built into the sea, like the much larger Ptolemaic palace compound on Cape Lochias. Another palace was located on the island of Antirhodos, adjacent to Cape Lochias. Above all,

---

[128] Hesberg 1996; for the main street of Petra and its development, see, most recently, *BASOR* 324; for Palmyra, see Schlumberger 1935; Berchem 1976; Barański 1995; Delplace & Dentzer-Feydy 2005: 349–54.

[129] Macdonald 1986: 5–31. For the urban development of Gerasa, see Seigne 1992.

[130] Above note 56.

[131] On the urban development of Alexandria, see MacKenzie 2003.

the resemblance to the Timonion, built by Marcus Antonius on a island connected to the shore by a mole, is noteworthy.

4. The theater of Alexandria also overlooked the sea, like that of Caesarea, and it was located near the Timonion palace.[132]

In the period under discussion Alexandria was a beacon for architectural and artistic influences, spreading its light to Rome itself, and affecting the building project initiated there by Augustus and by Marcus Agrippa. These influences diffused, either directly from Alexandria, or via Rome and Italy, to other regions, including Judaea and Nabataea.[133] Herod passed through Alexandria in his flight from Judaea to Rome in 40 BCE. He received a respectful reception by Cleopatra (Jos., *War* 1.279; *Ant.* 14.375). The second visit of Herod to Alexandria took place ten years later. This time he went to see the victorious Octavian, who had annexed to his kingdom more territories, and granted him a bodyguard of four hundred Gauls, who had formerly served Cleopatra (*War* 1.396–97; *Ant.* 14.216–17). Among the territories added by Octavian to Herod were the land properties of Cleopatra in Judaea. The entire encounter might have taken place in the Timonion, the palace of Marcus Antonius and Cleopatra. In my opinion, the comparison with Alexandria is more pertinent than the comparison with the structures of the Campus Martius in Rome,[134] where Alexandrian influence is in any case evident.[135]

As for the proximity of Caesarea's hippo-stadium to the palace, rather than comparing it to Augustus' house on the palatine and the Circus Maximus, I would suggest a comparison with Antioch, where the hippodrome (donated to the city in 56 BCE by Q. Marcius Rex) was adjacent to the Seleucid palaces on the island in the Orontes. After all, one of the prestigious building projects of Herod was in Antioch.[136]

---

[132] The Lageion—the Ptolemaic hippodrome of Alexandria—is remote from the sea shore. In Caesarea the hippodrome/stadium was constructed over a newly formed piece of land, accumulated and built up as a result of the harbor's construction, forming an obstacle to the sea waves and the sand they carry. The hippodrome/stadium, in its present location, could not have been part of the original building project.

[133] McKenzie 1990: 61–104.

[134] Gleason 1996: 208–27; Gleason *et al.* 1998: 52.

[135] Castagnoli 1984.

[136] Above note 53.

CHAPTER TWO

THE WALL STREET, THE EASTERN STOA, THE LOCATION OF THE *TETRAPYLON*, AND THE HALAKHIC STATUS OF CAESAREA MARITIMA (INTERPRETING *TOSEFTA, AHILOT*, 18:13)*

A thorough examination of *Mishnah Ohalot* 18:10 (9), and *Tosefta Ahilot* 18:13, which derives from it, allows for an interpretation of some topographical demarcations in the urban space of Herodian, Roman, and Byzantine Caesarea. Clarifying these topographical features further makes possible a better understanding of the background for the *halakhic* status of Caesarea with regard to the laws of purity reflected in the aforementioned *Mishnah* and *Tosefta*.

The Tosefta states:

> What is east of Qisri? From directly opposite its *tetrapylon* (טטרפלין) towards its winepress (בית הגת). Testified Judah the baker concerning the eastern *stoa* (סטיו המזרחי) that it is clean [of graves]. And the whole remainder is unclean because of the land of gentiles.[1]

All previous scholars who studied Caesarea examined this *Tosefta* and concluded from it that Caesarea had a *tetrapylon*. I argue that a more attentive analysis can retrieve more information both regarding the urban layout and the development of its cemeteries, as well as about the *halakhic* status of Caesarea with respect to the commandments related to the Land of Israel. But before beginning our discussion of the rabbinic sources, let us briefly present the archaeological remains that are relevant to the subject.

---

* This is an adapted English translation of a Hebrew article published in *Cathedra* 122 (2006): 7–30. A first draft of the text translation was prepared by Sarit Kattan. I am grateful to her. Much of the final work was done while spending a term of my Sabbatical in The Netherlands Institute for Advanced Studies (NIAS), at Wassenaar (Feb.–June 2008). I am indebted to the librarians and to other staff members of the Institute for their kind assistance.

[1] *Tosephta*, ed. Zuckermandel, p. 617. Eng. trans. Neusner 1977: 132 (*Ahilot*). Neusner renders "Mansion-house" for (טטרפלין), "winepress" for (בית הגת), and "eastern side" for (סטיו המזרחי). Therefore his translation cannot be given here *verbatim*.

The Herodian City Wall

In the aerial photograph of Caesarea (Fig. 5), it is easily possible to identify three wall lines: the innermost is an Early Arab/Crusader line; the outer is Byzantine, and in between are the remains of the Herodian wall (Fig. 8). The remains of this wall were exposed in the north by an Italian expedition and by the American Joint Expedition to Caesarea Maritima (JECM);[2] more recently, its remains were uncovered also in the south by the Israel Antiquities Authority (IAA) expedition to Caesarera.[3] The contour of the wall between these two ends is identifiable in aerial photographs along most of its course. It is also recognizable on the ground by a slight elevation of the terrain. All three expeditions dated the segments they had exposed as Herodian. A survey was also conducted along this course and several soundings were dug. The semi-elliptical shape of the wall (the length of the north-south axis is approximately 1,300 m, and that of the east-west axis is approximately 500 m), and the central location of the temple hill within the walled area, dominating the harbor and the entire city, fully match the description of the city by Flavius Josephus.[4]

Cemeteries

Hellenistic cremation burials in amphorae were exposed in various areas east and south of the extant Crusader wall, underlying the Herodian level.[5] A non-Jewish cemetery of Hellenistic cist graves, rock-cut in the kurkar (a local maritime sandstone), was uncovered

---

[2] Finocchi 1965; Blakely 1984; idem 1989; idem 1992. For a detailed exposition on this topic see more recently Patrich 2007: 101–104 and Chapter One, pp. 15–17 above.

[3] Porath 2000a. The new wall section uncovered in the south indicates that the Herodian theater was located within the city wall, unlike the hypothesis of the Italian expedition, Frova 1965: 50, fig. 10A, and following them Levine 1975b: 11–12, and the map opposite the table of contents; Ringel 1975: 41; Holum et al. 1988: 83. This proposal was derived from an extrapolation of lines recognized in aerial photographs. The severe destruction of the southern section of the city wall in antiquity was one of the causes of this mistake.

[4] Flavius Josephus, Ant. 15.332–41 (trans. Marcus 1963: 414–421); War 1.408–415 (trans. Thackeray 1927: 192–197).

[5] For burials to the east and to the south of the Crusaders wall see Roller 1983. Hellenistic internment in amphorae were also found in the excavations I was in charge of in areas CC, KK, and NN, to the south of this wall. See also Chapter One, p. 10 above.

beneath the western section of the upper terrace of Herod's palace.[6] These graves were found completely empty, even without any bones, indicating that they were vacated in an orderly manner. Thus, the Hellenistic city of Straton's Tower was surrounded by gentile graves, the rules pertaining to which were different from those pertaining to Jewish tombs. So far burials from the Roman period have only been discovered in the south. They were built against the Herodian city wall, and include cremation tombs. Thus, in this case as well, we are dealing with non-Jewish graves. They date to after the destruction of the Second Temple, from the end of the first century CE to the third century.[7] We do not know whether there were graves next to the eastern side of the Herodian wall as well. Jewish law prescribes distancing Jewish graves at least 50 cubits (ca. 25 m) from a city wall.[8] A more remote strip of graves, dated to the Late Roman and Byzantine periods, was found beyond the Byzantine city wall, up to several hundred meters away from it. They were uncovered while building the new residential neighborhoods of Caesarea, as well as in the industrial zone of Or Aqiva and even farther.[9] Most of the Jewish graves from the Roman-Byzantine period discovered so far in Caesarea were found in this strip of land, beyond the Byzantine city wall.[10]

THE EXPANSION OF THE CITY BEYOND THE HERODIAN CITY WALL

The two most prominent structures beyond the Herodian wall, still recognizable in the aerial photographs, are the Roman circus/hippodrome in the south-east, and the oval amphitheater in the north-east. The Roman circus was built during Hadrian's rule (Fig. 20). Beneath it were found remains of dwellings dated to the first and second

---

[6] See Gleason *et al.* 1998: 28, 34 and fig. 4a.

[7] Porath 2000a.

[8] *Mishnah, Baba Batra* 2:9: "They put carrion, graves, and tanneries at least fifty cubits away from a town" (tr. Neusner 1988: 561). And see also *The Tractate 'Mourning' (Semahot)* 14: 9 (ed. Zlotnick 1966: 39 and 196; ed. Heiger 1931: 207); *Avot de Rabbi Nathan*, ver. A:35 (ed. Schechter 1887: 104), ibidem, ver. B:39, (ed. Schechter 1887: 107).

[9] Edelstein 1998; Lipkunsky 2000; Peilstöcker 1999; Nagorsky 2003.

[10] Levine 1975b: 46–47. Many burial inscriptions on stone or marble plates were found dispersed throughout the city, and it is evident that they were carried in from their original location in the Byzantine, or in the Muslim period. For a list of burial inscriptions and details about their finding spots see Lehmann and Holum 2000: 24.

centuries CE; the latest finds date to the beginning of the second century. The construction date of the oval amphitheater is unknown; it is
reasonable to date it to the second or third century CE.[11] In the south
were uncovered the remains of another Roman theater (too large to
be a regular *Odeum*), apparently built in the second century CE.[12]
Nearby was found a section of a Byzantine street, with earlier remains
underneath. The location of the public bathhouse (*demosion loutron*)
built by Antoninus Pius in Caesarea[13] is not known; this seems to have
been a large public *therma*, built in the imperial style; it would be
reasonable to look for it outside the Herodian wall. A temple (?) for
Hadrian (*Hadrianeum*) is mentioned in an inscription from the Byzantine period that was found within the confines of the Herodian city.
The red porphyry statue, seemingly of him, seated on a throne, probably served as the cult statue in this temple.[14] The *tetrapylon* was also
erected under Hadrian, as will be discussed below. Three large building projects in Caesarea were constructed under Hadrian: one within
the Herodian city, one outside, and one—the *tetrapylon*—in between.
In addition, under this emperor an aqueduct was added to the city
("Channel B"), built against the earlier aqueduct ("Channel A")[15]
by military units, and the city was expanding. But by that time the

---

[11] Humphrey 1974; idem 1975; idem 1986: 477–491; Porath 2003. Large scale excavations (non published yet), were carried out in the amphitheater in 2010 on behalf
of IAA, headed by Dr. Peter Gendelman.

[12] Porath 2003; Peleg and Reich 1992. According to Malalas, *Chronographia* X, 338
(ed. Dindorf 1831: 261); X.46 (ed. Thurn 2000: 197), an *odeion* holding a large sitting
area (*theatron*) was built by Vespasian over a Jewish synagogue. (I consulted with
Prof. J.W. van Henten and Leah Di Segni about the correct reading of this passage; the
prevailing rendering of this passage so far was that the synagogue was located at a far
distance from the *theatron*, rather than that it held a vast sitting area—*theatron*). As
for the identification, it is impossible to determine whether the second theater should
be identified with this *odeion*, since no remains that can be attributed to an earlier
synagogue were found at the site. Besides, it is located outside the Herodian city wall,
and near the Herodian theater. Would a large Jewish synagogue be constructed in this
place? Besides, it seems that the second theater was constructed only in the 2nd c.

[13] Malalas, *Chronographia* XI, 367 (ed. Dindorf 1831: 281); XI. 25 (ed. Thurn 2000:
212).

[14] For the inscription see Lehmann and Holum 2000: 80–82, inscr. no. 58; as for
the statue see Avi-Yonah 1970. Another statue of Hadrian, larger than life size, was
erected under governor Tineius Rufus by his provincial *beneficiarii*. This is attested by
a Latin inscription found to the north of the main southern entrance to the stadium.
See Cotton and Eck 2001: 235–238; Eck and Cotton 2009. The statue might have been
erected above the arch of the stadium entrance, rather than in the *praetorium* of the
Roman governor—the location suggested by the authors.

[15] Porath 2002.

Herodian city wall had not yet disappeared. Excavations indicate that the wall in the south was not dismantled, nor was the Roman cemetery covered over until the beginning of the fourth century, as a result of the expansion of the city in that area. In the north, too, the Herodian wall stood until the fourth century.[16] It seems that in the east the wall was replaced by new urban structures, both on the inside and outside, much earlier (as will be discussed below). The Byzantine city wall, at a considerable distance from the earlier wall, was not built until the fifth century.[17]

THE WALL STREET

It is known that the Herodian city had an orthogonal layout from both the descriptions of Flavius Josephus and the archaeological remains.[18] Such a layout is consistent with Roman urban planning, a regular feature of which is a street adjacent to the wall, known in scholarly literature as a pomerial road.[19] This feature is to be found in the contemporaneous Augustan colonies, such as Turin (founded in 27 BCE), Aosta (founded in 25 BCE), and Verona (founded in 25–18 BCE).[20] This was already a characteristic feature of Roman town planning in earlier times, as is reflected in the fifth century BCE expansion of Pompei, and in the city of Cosa, founded in the first quarter of the third century BCE. (Greek town planning was completely different: here, the most convenient topographical line for defense was chosen for the city wall, regardless of the layout of the streets inside). Moreover, there was a local tradition: in Dor/Dora, which is adjacent to Caesarea, as early as Hellenistic times a street ran parallel to the wall, within it, on the other side of buildings that were built against the wall.[21]

---

[16] Porath 2000a, Blakely 1984, 1989, 1992; Finocchi 1965: 264; Levine 1975b: 13.

[17] On the Byzantine city wall see Frova 1959; idem 1961–1962; Humphrey 1975; Lehmann 1989; Patrich 2001: 86–88, 103–104 and Chapter Four, pp. 100-101 below.

[18] See Patrich 2007: 94, 104–105 and Chapter One, pp. 17-19 above.

[19] Ward-Perkins 1955; Owens 1991: 108, 111, 115, 150–151.

[20] On these cities and their urban plans see briefly: Castagnoli 1971: 110–111, fig. 48 (Turin); 112–113, fig. 49 (Aosta); Grimal 1983: 115–119 (Aosta), 273–276 (Turin), 280–282 (Verona); Owens 1991: 113–114, fig. 40 (Verona).

[21] Stern 2000: 213–221 and figs. 143–144.

Is there evidence for the existence of a wall street in Caesarea? Not surprisingly, the answer is positive; evidence is found in the two areas that have been thus far excavated within the Herodian wall, the one on the north and the other on the south.

Along the northern section of the wall the Italian Expedition uncovered a street with a drainage channel underneath (Fig. 21). Three levels were identified, the oldest being almost contemporary with the date of construction of the wall. In accordance with the principles of Roman town planning, the street was labeled *via di circonvallazione* by the excavators, namely—a circumvallation street, built along the wall. In short—a Wall Street.[22] On the south, adjacent to the wall on the inside, the IAA exposed a tight surface of crushed *kurkar*; the excavator suggested that this must have been a street or an open square that separated the wall from the adjacent theater.[23]

So far no excavations have been carried out along the eastern wall. However, the two passages from the rabbinic literature mentioned above, pertaining to the location and extension of the burial grounds of Caesarea and their defilement, suggest that a wall street did indeed exist on the eastern side of the city, parallel to the Herodian wall and within it, in accordance with the contemporaneous principles of Roman urban planning.[24]

In *Mishnah Ohalot* 18: 9 it is said:

> East of Qisrin and west of Qisarion are graveyards
> (trans. Neusner 1988: 980).[25]

---

[22] Finocchi 1965. Its date: 'un periodo abbastanza vicino a quello della costruzione della cinta': I sec. dell' Impero (*ibid.*: 258–259).

[23] Thus Porath 2000a.

[24] This interpretation given below was first presented by me in the framework of a seminar of Prof. Ya'acov Sussman, and Prof. David Rosenthal in the Department of Talmud of the Hebrew University, dedicated to the topic of rabbinic sources and archaeological finds. The matter was farther elaborated in the framework of the colloquium News Studies on Caesarea, held in Yad Yizhak Ben Zvi, Jerusalem, on March 11, 2004. I am grateful to Prof. David Rosenthal, Dr. Yuval Shahar and Prof. Zeev Safrai for their valuable comments. Responsibility on what is presented here of course lies with me.

[25] For the Hebrew text Goldberg's edition p. 135 should be consulted. The printed texts, and Albeck's edition read: "East of Qisrin and west of Qisrin are graveyards", but in the commentary Albeck brings the MSS reading "west of Qisarion" (and see also in the additions and complementary to the Division of Purities in his edition, Jerusalem and Tel Aviv 1959: 549). Albeck maintains that the passage deals with cemeteries of Gentiles, and that they are impure, but see *infra*, note 27.

Qisrin here is Caesarea Maritima, to the west of which is the sea. Qisarion, as noted by Neusner and many other commentators, is Caesarea of Philip (Paneas), founded by Herod's son, which is not our concern here. Coastal Caesarea was not known to be a city built on graves (unlike Tiberias).[26] The archaeological evidence described above indicates that graves of Hellenistic gentiles that surrounded Straton's Tower on the east or on the south were vacated or covered under a thick layer of Herodian sand fill. However, the *Mishnah* is certainly not talking about the Hellenistic gentile graves that once existed to the east of the Herodian city, but rather about Jewish graves[27] outside the Herodian city, on the east. It is reasonable to assume that the words of the *Mishnah* "East of Qisrin" refer to the city wall, indicating that a cemetery occupied a certain strip of land that extended to its east.[28]

If this conclusion is accepted, we may better understand *Tosefta Ahilot* 18:13, a text providing more specific topographical indications of the urban landscape on the confines of the strip of Jewish graves. Let us cite it again:

> What is east of Qisri? From directly opposite its *tetrapylon* (טטרפלין)[29] towards its winepress (בית הגת). Testified Judah the baker concerning the eastern *stoa* (סטיו המזרחי) that it is clean [of graves]. And the whole remainder is unclean because of the land of gentiles.[30]

---

[26] *Ant.* XVIII.38; the sources speaking about the purification of Tiberias from its graves are various. See Levine 1978.

[27] According to the *Babylonian Talmud, Baba Meṣia* 114b, the tombs of Gentiles, do not defile; this is also reiterated by Maimonides. R. Shimon Ben Yohai mentioned there is the one who purified Tiberias (see previous note).

[28] According to a late midrash, the cave in which Rabbi Aqiva was buried was located to the east of Caesarea (but see *infra*).

[29] A similar demarcation occurs in the Rehov Synagogue inscription pertaining to the permitted settlements in the district of Beth Shean: the author names a gate and a site adjacent to it outside the city. As will be suggested below, in the section under discussion the *tetrapylon* marks the location of an ancient gate. For a discussion on this *Tosefta* see also Kraus 1902.

[30] For reference to the Hebrew text see *supra*, note 1. See also the supplementary commentry of Lieberman there, p. 40, and in his book, *Tosefeth Rishonim,* III, pp. 157–158, paragraphs 10–11 (in Hebrew); *Tosefta with Hasdei David commentary, VIII: Purities A,* Jerusalem 1994 (first printed in 1970): 312–313 (in Hebrew).

This passage should be divided into four parts:

[1] What is east of Qisri?
[2] From directly opposite its *tetrapylon* (טטרפלין) towards its wine-press (בית הגת).
[3] Testified Judah the baker concerning the eastern *stoa* (סטיו המזרחי) that it is clean [of graves].
[4] And the whole remainder is unclean because of the land of gentiles.

Part 2 gives the words of *tanna qamma* (the technical Aramaic term for an earlier Sage), demarcating "east of Qisrin" in the Mishnah (which is cited in part 1). As explained above, the text addresses the extension of the Jewish cemetery beyond the Herodian city wall, to the east. Part 3 brings the testimony of Judah the baker, the purpose of which is to trace precisely the western border of the cemetery (see below), the nearest one to the city. Finally, part 4 is not the continuation of Judah the baker's testimony but rather continues the words of *tanna qamma* in part 2, as Saul Lieberman stated.[31]

The chronology is essential here for proper understanding. The *Tosefta* under discussion definitely post-dates the *Mishnah*, and the words of the *tanna qamma* there are not later than the time of Judah the baker. Judah the baker was a contemporary of Rabbi Aqiva, and according to some traditions he was one of the ten martyrs under Hadrian.[32] It is clear, therefore, that this *Tosefta* reflects the situation prior to the suppression of the Bar Kokhba revolt, perhaps the state of the city under Hadrian, a time of ambitious building projects in the city. The *Mishnah* is earlier, perhaps from the Second Temple period, when the Jews of the city were thriving. Most probably they had a separate cemetery from that of the gentiles. The *Tosefta* comments on the *Mishnah* in a post-Herodian urban reality, when the outline of the wall seems to have been blurred because buildings were leaning against it both on the inside and the outside (although, as noted above, on the north and on the south the wall stood until the fourth century).[33] The *Tosefta* names more familiar topographical features, apparently along

---

[31] *Op. cit.*
[32] *Midrash Shoher Tov* to Psalms 9:13 (ed. Buber, p. 88); *Lamentations Rabba* 2:2 (ed. Buber, p. 100; the commentated Midrash Rabba, Jerusalem 1989: 285); *TY, Hagigah* 2:1, 77b; Kraus 1925: 112–114 (republished in Oppenheimer 1980: 258–260); Büchler 1956: 183, n. 1. Büchler suggested that Judah the baker was a native of Caesarea.
[33] *Supra*, notes 2, 3.

the road leading east from Caesarea, to indicate the width of the strip of graves: from the *tetrapylon* to the winepress of Caesarea, which seems to have been a large central winepress[34] on the fringes of the agricultural countryside that surrounded the city, beyond the cemetery. Jews were not buried farther to the east. It is reasonable to assume that the *tetrapylon*, like the winepress, was not included within the confines of the cemetery. The two landmarks were external ones.

THE EASTERN *STOA*

A *stoa* is a long structure lined by a row of columns on one side (Fig. 22).[35] According to the present interpretation, the *Tosefta* refers to the eastern roofed side of a colonnaded street. The *stoa* might also have had shops,[36] including Jewish bakeries and ritual baths, enabling

---

[34] *Tosefta, Terumot* 3:7 (ed. Zuckermandel, p. 29); Sion 1998; Qidiocean, Ayalon, and Yosef 1990; Roll and Ayalon 1981. For a reconstruction proposal of such an installation see Drei 2003 (in Hebrew). One should note that a winepress (*gath*) is also mentioned in the Rabbinic sources parallel to the tomb courtyard: "And what is the courtyard of the tomb? That is the floor (גת) to the midst of which the caves open" (*Tosefta, Ahilot* 15:7, [ed. Zuckermandel, p. 612; trans. Neusner 1977: 121]). This comparison derives from the resemblance between the tomb courtyard, surrounded by burial chambers, and the winepress, surrounded by storage compartments for bunches of grapes. Accordingly, two separate entries are given for *gath* as a tomb yard and *gath* as a winepress in Jastrow 1985: 274. One should not conclude from this that the winepress in the *Tosefta* under discussion was a vast burial ground with a central courtyard resembling a winepress.

[35] Stoa—from Gr. στοὰ; Lat. *porticus*. Zuckermandel translated it as Säulengang (*supra* note 1, p. LXXVII); Jastrow 1985: 972 renders 'colonnade'. For a comprehensive survey on the use of this term in the Rabbinic sources see Gordon 1931. On the application of this term in the Greek literary sources see Downey 1937. See also Coulton 1976: 168–183. On the portico built by Herod in Antioch, considered to be the first phase of the main colonnaded street of the city, see Josephus, *War* 1.425; *Ant.* 16.148. On the colonnaded streets of Caesarea in the Roman and Byzantine periods see Patrich 2001 (republished here as Chapter Four), and more generally see Bejor 1999. One of the famous porticos of Caesarea was known as *the portico of Iunia Ba( )ae* and is mentioned in a Greek papyrus from Egypt (*Papiri greci e latini* 9 [Florence 1928]: 1026); it was used for displaying petitions and statutes concerning the Roman soldiers serving in the province. It is reasonable to assume that it was located near the *praetorium* of the Roman governor, who was also the commander in chief of the army. This *praetorium* was located between the stadium and the theater, and not in the eastern part of the city—the location of the stoa under consideration. On this portico and the city streets see also Levine 1975b: 38–40; Ringel 1975: 58.

[36] On a shop which was open to a portico see *Tosefta, Moed Qatan* 2:13 (ed. Zuckermandel, p. 231; trans. Neusner, p. 305). For a portico that was crossed while passing from a shop to wide avenue (*platea*), see *Tosefta Shabbat* 10 (11):1 (ed. Zuckermandel, p. 123; trans. Neusner 1981: 37).

them to maintain the laws pertaining to dough offering in purity. Hence, perhaps, a baker was needed to testify about the purity of the stoa.[37] Thus, it seems that in the new urban situation a portico open to the west marked the western border of the strip of the graves.

Where should this portico be located? As was noted above, the graves about which the *Mishnah* speaks were outside the Herodian city wall. Therefore, the portico was not within the city, for if it were within the wall there would be nothing remarkable about its pure status. Moreover, if it was located within the wall, it would imply that an urban area east of it was impure due to the existence of graves while according to the *Mishnah* there were no graves within the city; moreover, if it was indeed located within the city, remote from the graves, it would not have been appropriate to use it as a marker for the cemetery. The portico under discussion should not thus be sought within the confines of the Herodian city. Was it on the outside? The findings in the south indicate that gentile graves were placed immediately against the city wall there. But for our purpose Jewish graves and the eastern side are most important. So far, no remains of any north-south colonnaded street or a *tetrapylon* have been uncovered in the area east of the Herodian wall. Therefore I would suggest looking for the portico (and the *tetrapylon*), along the line of the Herodian city wall. The *Tosefta* in question does not reduce the area of graves east of Caesarea by moving its western border further east relative to its former border—the Herodian city wall. Rather it provides a clearer and more recognizable marking in the urban landscape of the time, when the city had already expanded beyond its wall. From the testimony of Judah the baker that the eastern portico is pure, one may deduce that

---

[37] On the preparation of dough in ritual purity see below. It is evident that the purpose of Judah the baker's testimony was to be more precise in locating the burial grounds, and that he was not speaking about the Land of Gentiles, since at the beginning of that same *Mishnah* (*Ohalot* 18:9) it is specifically stated that: "Colonnades (האצטווניות) are not subject to the laws applying to the dwellings of gentiles" (trans. Neusner 1988: 980; ed. Goldberg, p. 135). And the *Tosefta* (*ibid.*, 18:11–12) is more specific: "A colonnade (אסטוונות) is not subject to the law of the dwelling of gentiles unless one lives therein…and [the laws of] the dwelling of gentiles and [of] the grave area (בית הפרס) do not apply abroad [where the rabbis' authority does not extend]…The summer-houses (איסטוונות), even though they are joined with the dwelling of the gentiles, are not subject to the law governing the dwelling of the gentiles" (trans. Neusner 1977: 131–132; ed. Zuckermandel, p. 617). I am grateful to Dr. Yuval Shahar for his suggestion to emphasize this point.

it was bounded on its eastern side by the Herodian wall. That is, it was built against the wall or replaced it. In other words, the portico was built on the eastern side of the Wall Street that ran within the eastern wall, parallel to it. It seems that during the Herodian period, this was simply a street, like the segment uncovered in the north, and a portico was built along its eastern side (and perhaps also along its western side) later on, converting it to a colonnaded street.[38] The chronological framework reflected in the *Tosefta* permits to ascribe this building project to the days of Hadrian.

Accordingly, a wall street should be marked on the urban map of Herodian Caesarea, within and parallel to the city wall (see Fig. 8).

THE *TETRAPYLON* OF CAESAREA

The *tetrapylon* was also, so it seems, a component of the Hadrianic building project. A *tetrapylon* is an urban monument ordinarily located at the intersection of two thoroughfares. In Roman urban architecture two types of *tetrapyla* are known: a *tetrakionion* is made of four large pedestals on which columns were set, like the southern *tetrapylon* of Gerasa (dated to the mid-second century CE). The second, known as *quadrifrons*, is a domed structure with four facades that face the intersecting streets, like the northern *tetrapylon* of Gerasa (dated to ca. 200 CE) (Fig. 23).[39]

Caesarea had a most impressive *tetrapylon*, praised in a fourth-century Latin source:

---

[38] Similar urban transformations are known from other cities. In Timgad (Algeria) a Severan colonnaded street replaced the western city wall of the square colony of army veterans (*castrum*) founded by Trajan; this street is known as the Wall Street. An ornamental arch of three openings was built on the inside of the original gate in the wall, which was also dismantled, and the area in between became a rectangular square. In Djemila (a town in western Numidia), founded under Nerva, a long *nymphaeum* with a colonnaded façade was built in about that same time (ca. 200 CE), when the city expanded, against the southern wall. See Grimal 1983: 261–62 (Timgad); Stambaugh 1989: 281–86 (Timgad); MacDonald 1986: 7–13 (Djemila); 26–28 (Timgad). Many years earlier, a colonnaded street was built in Antioch (it originated in the portico donated by Herod, as noted above) along the eastern wall of the Hellenistic city, which was founded by Seleucus I. See Will 1997.

[39] For the *tetrapylon* of Caesarea and other *tetrapyla* in our region see Levine 1975b: 38–39; MacDonald 1986: 87–92; Ball 2000: 273–281; Segal 1997: 140–149; Mühlenbrock 2003. For *tetrapyla* in the Rabbinic sources see Kraus 1898, II: 262.

So Caesarea too, like them (Antioch and Tyre), is quite a pleasant city, and rich in everything, and remarkable in many ways in terms of its urban plan. Indeed, its *tetrapylon* is famous everywhere because it presents a special and extraordinary look (trans. Leah Di Segni).[40]

The *tetrapylon* of Caesarea is also mentioned in a Christian source from the early seventh century CE—the *Acts of Anastasius the Persian*. It is said there that it stood in the center of the Byzantine city (which extended far beyond the Herodian city). The residents of the city erected a chapel adjacent to the *tetrapylon* in memory of the martyr, who was arrested by the Persians in Caesarea and later executed in 628 in Persia; some monks brought back his corpse to Caesarea for burial.[41] According to *Midrash Proverbs*, a ninth or tenth century source,[42] Rabbi Aqiva was interred in a cavern near the *tetrapylon* of Caesarea.[43] This concurs with the words of the *Tosefta*, that Caesarea's *tetrapylon* was adjacent to the cemetery.[44]

---

[40] *Expositio totius mundi et gentium* xxvi (ed. Rougé 1966: 160): *Iam etiam et Caesarea ciuitas est similiter deliciosior et abundans omnibus et dispositione ciuitatis in multa eminens. Tetrapylon enim eius nominator ubique, quod unum et nouum aliquod spectaculum.* In *Hekhalot Rabbati*, where the troughs and horses of the celestial chariot are described, the 'opening of Caesarea' is mentioned as impressive in its dimensions. See *Pirkei Hekhalot Rabbati* 18, 1 (ed. Wertheimer, *Batei Midrashot* I, Jerusalem 1950: 94 [in Hebrew]); Schäfer, *Synopse zur Hekhalot Literature*, §214: 92–93. The context suggests that this was a central gate in the circus/hippodrome of the city, but another urban monument with an impressive opening might also be referred to, perhaps one of the city gates. A *tetrapylon* has four openings, hence it is doubtful that the reference is to this monument.

[41] Kaegi 1978; *Saint Anastase le Perse, Miracles* 8 (ed. Flusin 1992: 130–139; 231–43). I am indebted to Dr. Leah Di Segni, who drew my attention to this important reference.

[42] *Midrash Mishle* 9:18 (ed. Buber, p. 316; ed. Visotzky, pp. 67–69). It is a late Palestinian composition, dated between 860 and 1020 CE. See Visotzky, *ibid.*, p. 45. See also *Yalqut Shimoni to Proverbs*, article 944 (in Hebrew).

[43] The toponym is very corrupted in many MSS of *Midrash Mishle* and *Yalqut Shimoni* (including Tripolin, and Antipatris of Qisrin). According to Visotzky the correct version for *Midrash Mishle* should read '*tetrapylon* of Qisrin' following Cambridge MS, University Library 329.815 TS-NS. See also Sperber 1977: 37–38. For this reason many locations were proposed in the scholarly literature for the burial place of R. Aqiva (among them Appelbaum 1977 [Qaqun]). For a full list of references see the Hebrew article, Patrich 2006, footnote 43.

[44] However, Dr. Hillel Newman (in a lecture delivered in the 14th World Congress for Jewish Studies, July 31st—August 4th 2005, the Hebrew University of Jerusalem, Mt. Scopus), suggested that this late *Midrash* was influenced by the seventh century Christian martyrology, including the *Acts of Anastasius the Persian*, and for this reason the *Midrash* may not reflect the authentic urban reality. The subject merits further study.

It is quite possible that the *tetrapylon* under discussion was built to commemorate the visit of emperor Hadrian to the Roman province of Judaea in 130 CE, or even beforehand.[45] In any case, it was older than the southern *tetrapylon* of Gerasa, a city of secondary administrative significance relatively to Caesarea. From the *Tosefta* it is possible to conclude that this was a prominent monument at the eastern confines of the area that was considered by Jews to be clear of graves, which was located along the line of the Eastern *Stoa*. Namely, it was located on the line of a colonnaded street, the Eastern *Stoa* of which was pure, while the area behind it was a burial ground. It seems reasonable to assume that the *tetrapylon* replaced the eastern gate in the Herodian city wall, on the road that went from Caesarea eastward.

What was the shape of this *tetrapylon* of Caesarea? Was it of the *tetrakionion* type or of the *quadrifrons* type, with a dome? In the *Palestinian Talmud* (*TY*), *Nazir*, "the dome of Caesarea" is mentioned—perhaps a *tetrapylon* of the *quadrifrons* type, which was built over a colonnaded street (פלטיא דקיסרין). R. Hiyya bar Abba, an Amora of the third generation, who was a priest, refrained from passing underneath this dome, for fear of becoming defiled. Therefore he bypassed it, while his comrades, who were engaged in the words of Torah while strolling along the street, passed underneath it without the fear of becoming impure.[46] A possible but not necessarily certain interpretation of this passage is to assume that the avenue and the dome mentioned here are the colonnaded street with the *stoa* and the *tetrapylon* of the *Tosefta* under discussion. The Rabbis were walking in the open avenue (perhaps they refrained from walking in the eastern *stoa*, which was roofed, since they held the opinion that it was suspected to be impure, contrary to the opinion of Judah the baker several generations earlier, that this *stoa* was pure). Farther along the street stood the domed *tetrapylon*, and R. Hiyya bar Abba, being a priest, bypassed it, perhaps since he was afraid that he might be contaminated by tent defilement

---

[45] Holum 1992b: 58.

[46] *TY, Nazir* 7:1, 56a. See discussion in Levine 1975b: 39. Some hold the opinion that the reason of bypassing the dome was fear of idolatry, rather than a tent defilement (*infra*). In the *TY, Berakhot* 3:1, 6a there is a similar anecdote, with the same people, but the place name in the printed text is the street of Sepphoris (פלטיותא דציפורי). However, MS R Vatikan says Caesarea.

of the dome if he passed under it. Up to this point he had been walking in the street with the others, under the open sky.[47]

Is the *tetrapylon* of the Latin and Greek sources mentioned above identical with that of the *Tosefta* and of *Midrash Proverbs*? Again, this is possible but not certain. For there might have been two *tetrapyla* in Caesarea, as in Gerasa, perhaps even three.

So far it has been suggested to locate the *tetrapylon* two urban *insulae* farther west, on the site of the Crusaders eastern gate.[48] As a matter of fact, the remains of two massive piers are preserved within this gate, perhaps remains of a *tetrapylon* (Fig. 24).[49] However, with respect to the *Tetrapylon* mentioned in the *Tosefta*, the location proposed here—at the intersection of the Wall Street and the *decumanus maximus*—should be preferred, for the reasons presented above. When it was constructed it stood on the margins of a densely built urban area, but the future extension of the city was taken into consideration.[50] Indeed, it occupies a central position in the expanded Byzantine city, as is mentioned in the *Acts of Anastasius the Persian*.

Under Hadrian large-scale building projects were certainly carried out in Caesarea, including a *tetrapylon* and a *stoa*, and the city was expanded greatly, a process that continued in the subsequent Roman

---

[47] However, it is quite possible that we are dealing here with two distinct monuments, since in the *Tosefta* under consideration it is not said that the *tetrapylon* defiles, on the contrary, it is located outside the impure area. It is possible that the avenue under discussion was located in the eastern part of the city, where there were tombs in the past, that were most probably vacated when being surrounded by the expanding city (in accord with *Tractate Mourning* 14:9 [ed. Zlotnick, pp. 39 and 196]; *TY, Nazir* 9:3, 57d; *Avot de Rabbi Nathan*, ver. A, 35 [ed. Schechter, p. 104]; *ibid.*, ver. B, 39 [ed. Schechter, p. 107]; *Ramban, Torath HaAdam*, Venice 1555: 39b). The street was most probably paved (and a pavement annuls the impurity of a grave area [בית הפרס]; see "He who paves a grave area with stones which one cannot move—it is clean" (*Mishnah, Ohalot* 18:5, trans. Neusner 1988: 980; ed. Goldberg 18:6, p. 132), and there is no fear of tent defilement; the matter deserves farther study. On vacating of tombs at Caesarea, like the one that took place in Tiberias, there is no reference in the Rabbinic sources. This seems to have been a common matter, and as was indicated above, it was also applied in case of the Hellenistic tombs in the upper terrace of Herod's palace.

[48] Thus in the map of the Byzantine city in Holum *et al.* 1988: 163, fig. 112 and p. 176; and accordingly it was also graphically reconstructed. See Holum 1999: 28, fig. 13.

[49] See Patrich 2001: 86.

[50] Similarly, in Leptis/Lepcis Magna Trajan's *tetrapylon* (of the *quadrifrons* type), was located on the fringes of a planned new quarter, and so, too, the *tetrapylon* of Septimius Severus there, located farther south, seems to have marked an intention to develop a new quarter. See Tomlinson 1992: 193–94; MacDonald 1986: 87–92, and p. 40, fig. 36.

and Byzantine periods. Future excavations will provide more information about these developments, confirming or refuting our conjectures
regarding the location of the *tetrapylon* and the transformation of the
Herodian Wall Street into a *stoa* on the eastern side.

The Halakhic Status of Caesarea and its Borders —
of the Land of Israel or of the Land of Gentiles?

How should part 4 of the *Tosefta* be interpreted, bringing the end
words of *tanna qamma*: "And the whole remainder is unclean because
of the land of gentiles"? A study of this part entails a broader topic:
what was the *halakhic* status of Caesarea and of Straton's Tower and
of their borders with regard to regulations of purity and impurity and
laws related to the Land of Israel, such as religious obligations pertaining to the seventh year (*shebi'it*), and tithes (*ma'aserot*)? Were they
considered a part of the Land of Israel or of the Land of Gentiles?[51]
This is a difficult topic, fraught with debate; a detailed study of all its
aspects would go far beyond interpreting the *Tosefta* under consideration. Even experts in the history of Jewish law have difficulties in
understanding this matter fully, and hence the task is so challenging.[52]

Lee Levine, Zeev Safrai, and Efrat Habas have concluded from
the *Tosefta* that the city of Caesarea was considered to be impure.
Levine took the end of this passage to be evidence that between the
two revolts, with the decrease in the Jewish population in the city, the

---

[51] The Land of Gentiles is outside of the Land of Israel and held to be impure
according to an ancient tradition given in the *Babylonian Talmud* (*TB*), *Shabbat* 15a,
and in the *TY, ibid.*, 1:4, 3d, and: *TY, Pesahim* 27d; *Ketubot* 32c. According to what is
said there, Yose ben Yoezer of Seridah, and Yose ben Yohanan of Jerusalem, the first
pair of sages in the generation that preceded the Hasmonaean revolt, declared that the
territory of gentiles was unclean. According to the *TY ibid.* 32c, the impurity of the
Land of Gentiles was one of the Eighteen Decrees, issued when the great revolt had
erupted, but these were rather much older decrees, reiterated. Some traditions attribute this sanction to Hillel and Shamai. See *Talmudic Encyclopedia*, II, pp. 196–199
(in Hebrew). About the transformations in understanding the causes for the impurity
of the Land of Gentiles see Alon 1957: 121–147. According to Alon the conception
underlying the impurity of the Land of Gentiles was in effect already since the First
Temple period. See also Safrai 1996: 632–639; Ben Shalom 1994: 252–272. More recent
studies claim that the impurity of Gentiles land and houses is a rabbinic principle that
derives from the corpse impurity generated by Gentile corpses, refuting Alon's statement that it is derived from an ancient principle of intrisic Gentile ritual impurity. See
Klawans 1995; 2000: 134–135, 207; Hayes 2002: 199–204.

[52] See Safrai 1967: 29 (reprinted in idem 1996: 449–450); Sussman 1974 and 1975.

rabbis declared much of Caesarea as impure and equated it with areas not considered part of Jewish Palestine, namely—as a Land of Gentiles, in contrast with its status earlier and later, after the Bar Kokhba revolt. Then Caesarea was again declared part of Jewish Palestine with respect to religious obligations (as is said in *Tosefta, Ahilot* 18:16), and therefore regulations related to the Land of Israel apply in it, and Rabbi Yehuda HaNasi exempted Caesarea from these observances.[53] Safrai also maintained that the *Tosefta*, including the testimony of Judah the baker, indicates that the city was impure and considered to be outside of the Land of Israel all the way to the portico in the east of the city. Thus the city and a small area around it were considered to be a Land of Gentiles.[54] Habas suggested that up to and including the days of Usha, Caesarea in the wider sense, the whole city territory, was considered mostly as the Land of Israel, though the city itself was not in this status. In the days of Rabbi Yehuda HaNasi, through local initiative, Caesarea was released (by vote) from the status of the Land of Gentiles, and he sanctioned it.[55] Relying on the topographical considerations given above, which will be elaborated later, and on the analysis of the *Tosefta*, I maintain that one cannot conclude from the *baraita* under consideration that the city was considered impure on the eve of the Bar Kokhba revolt, but rather, on the contrary, that it was considered pure, as it was before the destruction of the Second Temple.

Part 4 of the *Tosefta* aims to clarify the *halakhic* status of the area farther east of Caesarea, not of Caesarea itself. Lieberman already commented about this point: "This is the continuation of the words of *tanna qamma* that defines as impure the east of Caesarea because of the graves, and he adds that the rest is not impure because of graves, but rather due to being Land of Gentiles, and the testimony of Judah the baker is a parenthetical clause" (trans. Patrich).[56] The purpose of the words of *tanna qamma* is, therefore, to define the status of the strip east of Caesarea, not of Caesarea itself, and he determined that the area beyond the cemetery is impure because it is Land of Gentiles; he did not rule at all on the urban area of Caesarea.

---

[53] Levine 1975a: 67–68; *Tosefta Ahilot* 18:16 is cited *infra*, next to note 62.
[54] Z. Safrai 1985: 318. And see also idem 1980: 155–159.
[55] Habas 1996: 464; Fredkin (Habas) 1980: 70–97.
[56] Thus Lieberman, *Tosefeth Rishonim*, III, p. 157.

We may add a topographical consideration to Lieberman's statement: it is impossible to define a roofed portico[57] (generally not more
than 5 meters wide) as pure, when there is an impure cemetery to its
east, and to its west a city which is impure since it is Land of Gentiles. On what grounds could this narrow and roofed strip of land be
considered pure while it is flanked on either side by impure land and
inaccessible without crossing that impure land? Following the same
reasoning, it is impossible to assume that the *baraita* reflects a situation in which both the city and its territory were considered as Land
of Gentiles, while in between there was a cemetery and a pure *stoa*.
Thus, we must inevitably conclude that according to the *Tosefta* the
city was pure, and that the end passage of *tanna qamma*, "And the
whole remainder is unclean because of the land of gentiles," refers not
to the rest of the city of Caesarea but rather to the rest of "east of Qisrin," mentioned at the beginning of the *Tosefta*, as Lieberman asserted.
In the period under discussion Jews refrained from burying their dead
east of the winepress of Caesarea. This area, farther east of the Jewish
cemetery, was considered impure because it was Land of Gentiles, and
not because of Jewish graves.[58]

The conclusion that Caesarea was considered, at that time, to be
Land of Israel, can also be gathered from what follows in the *Tosefta*,
Ahilot 18:16–17, according to some commentators and scholars. There,
it states:

> Testified Judah b. Jacob of Bet Guvrin and Jacob b. Isaac of Bet Gufnin[59]
> concerning Qisri that they possessed it from ancient times and declared
> it free without a vote.[60] Said R. Hanin (חנן), "That year was the seventh

---

[57] On the abstention from walking under a roofed portico in Caesarea, and the
preference for walking in the colonnaded street (פלטיאה) under the open sky (unlike
the sanction of Judah the baker), see *supra*, the text next to notes 46 and 47.

[58] Cf. Lieberman, *Tosefeth Rishonim*, III, p. 158, on the graves to the west of Qisarion (according to a specific version in the *Tosefta*). I cannot understand why Z. Safrai
(1980: 157) concluded from the *Mishnah* under consideration that the east of Caesarea
is impure as Land of Gentiles, though it speaks about the impurity of graves; in his
article (1985: 218–219) as well there is a confusion between the impurity of graves and
that of Land of Gentiles.

[59] These Sages are considered to be among the last *Tannaim*, but their words reflect
an ancient conception. Their words pertain to a permit that preceded that of Rabbi
Yehudah HaNasi.

[60] According to the commentary of R. Samson of Sens (ר"ש; ca. 1150–1230) Caesarea was always considered as Land of Israel, liable to tithe and *shebi'it*, and it was
exempted without a quorum, namely the people there used to behave as if they were
exempt from tithe and *shebi'it*, although no quorum of Sages permitted the people

year, and gentiles went to their circuses and left the market full of fruits, and Israelites came and swiped them, and when they came back, they said, 'Come let us go to sages, lest they permit them pigs also'."[61] Said R. Zeriqa, "On the fifth of Second Adar twenty-four elders voted concerning it and declared it free, for all were entering it [and it was clean, not regarded as gentile land].[62]

According to Samson of Sens (and similarly more recently Abraham-Adolf Büchler and Jacob Neusner in his translation), Caesarea was always considered to be Land of Israel and had no impurity of the Land of Gentiles.[63] On the other hand, Gaon Rabbi Elijah ben Solomon Zalman of Vilna (1720–1797, הגר"א) took the opposite opinion: "they held it [Caesarea] from the beginning to be impure and they exempted it; thus it should be understood" (trans. Patrich).[64] Here we have two opposing conceptions about the status of Caesarea before it was permitted. According to the first, that of Rabbi Samson, Caesarea was always a part of the Land of Israel, and the permission exempted it from the liability of ma'aser (tithes) and shebi'it (seventh year). According to the other opinion, that of Gaon Rabbi Elijah (הגר"א), and the

---

to do this (אף על פי שלא נמנו חכמים להתירם) (Lieberman, *Tosefeth Rishonim*, III, p. 159, renders here להתירה במנין—a permit given to the city).

According to the Halakhah, regulations related to the Land apply especially within the confines of Eretz Israel settled by those who had returned from Babylon; but in this territory some areas were exempt from *shebi'it* and tithes, since they were considered to be settled exclusively by gentiles; these areas were known as "permitted." However, even in these "permitted areas" (as well as beyond the main boundaries of Eretz Israel), some specific towns were not exempt, since they were considered to be settled by Jews, and even in the "permitted areas" some fruits were forbidden, having the status of being imported from the reduced Land of Israel, which was liable to tithes and *shebi'it*. And see Sussman 1974: 97–98.

[61] Levine 1975a: 30, had suggested that the seventh year referred to here is that of 61/2 CE, but it rather seems that the events took place in the days of the named sages.

[62] Ed. Zuckermandel, p. 617; trans. Neusner 1977: 132–133.

[63] Samson of Sens brings the words of R. Zeriqa as: "and it was permitted for all to enter it" (והתירוה שיהו הכל נכנסים לתוכה), (instead of "for all were entering it"—והתירוה שהיו הכל נכנסים לתוכה, as it stands in Zuckermandel's printed edition and in Lieberman's book, *ibid.*), and the commentary of Samson of Sens is: "and it has no impurity due to the Land of Gentiles". In this spirit is also Neusner's translation cited above. See also Büchler 1956: 181–182 (but he had a corrupt version of the sources, and his conclusions should be taken with precaution).

[64] The author of *Yehusei Tannaim VeAmoraim* as well, under the entry R. Hanan, held the opinion that the correct commentary should be "that it was permitted not to render impurity due to Land of Gentiles" (according to Lieberman, *op. cit., ibid.*). Similarly Klein 1965: 150, note 127 (in Hebrew), but he, like Büchler 1956 had a corrupted version of the *Mishnah*: "East of Qisrin and west of Qisrin are graves."

author of *Yehusei Tannaim VeAmoraim*, it was impure as Land of Gentiles, and the permission freed it from its impurity. Lieberman suggested that the quorum referred to by Rabbi Zeriqa in the continuation of the *baraita* occurred "after they saw that the habit prevailing there was as if it was exempt from *shebiit* and *ma'aserot*," and in this quorum "it was exempted from being considered as Land of Gentiles, and it was considered to be in the category of Enclaved Towns (עיירות המובלעות), that are exempt from *shebi'it* and *ma'aserot*, but are not considered to be Land of Gentiles (trans. Patrich)."[65] This seems to be the right interpretation. His words imply that before the first exemption, Caesarea was considered as the Land of Israel, and was liable to *ma'aser* and *shebiit*. The later permission of Rabbi Yehuda HaNasi,[66] therefore, ratified earlier exemptions.

In summary, according to *tanna qamma* in the last part of the *Tosefta*, the area beyond the strip of graves, farther east, was impure as Land of Gentiles (and he did not determine the width of that strip). We have thus learned that even before the Bar Kokhba revolt there was a strip east of Caesarea that was considered to be Land of Gentiles, while the city itself was regarded as Land of Israel, which is liable to regulations related to the Land. Or, in Lieberman's words: Caesarea was like the Enclaved Towns (עיירות המובלעות), which were exempt from *shebi'it* and *ma'aserot*, but were not considered Land of Gentiles.[67] The implications of this conclusion regarding the changes in the settlement pattern in the territory of Caesarea immediately following the

---

[65] See Lieberman, *Tosefeth Rishonim,* III, pp. 159–160.

[66] *TY Demai* 2:1, 22c: "[It has been taught (in a baraita)]: Rabbi permitted [produce sold in] Beth Shean [to be eaten without separating tithes], Rabbi permitted Caesaria, Rabbi permitted Bet Guvrin, Rabbi permitted Kfar Semah" (trans. Sarason 1993: 69).

[67] Caesarea was later accorded a different status, that of Towns of the Samaritans (Kutim), rather than that of Enclaved Towns (end of third-beginning of fourth century), as emerges from what is written in the *TY Shebiit* 6:1, 36c: Said R. Abbahu, "There are Samaritan cities that have been treated with leniency since the days of Joshua, son of Nun, and these [cities] are permitted" (trans. Avery-Peck 1991: 209). According to Lieberman these words do not refer to the towns of the Kutim in Samaria, but rather to Rabbi Abbahu's own city—Caesarea and its surroundings, which had a large population of Samaritans at that time. See Lieberman 1931: 107. A differentiation between the Land of the Kutim and the Land of the Gentiles also emerges from what is said in *Tosefta Miqvaot* 6:1 (ed. Zuckermandel p. 657): "Samaritan territory [in the Land of Israel] is clean [and] its immersion-pools and its dwellings and its paths are clean. The Land of the Gentiles [in the Land of Israel] is unclean, [and] its immersion-pools and its dwellings and its paths are unclean" (trans. Neusner 1977: 253). According to Reish Laqish in the *TB Hagiga* 25a, a strip of land inhabited by Kutim (Samaritans) separated between Judaea and Galilee.

Jewish war of 66–70 CE, during which many of Caesarea's Jews died
and others fled to the region of Narbata is noteworthy. The transformation of Caesarea into a Roman colony and the reestablishment
of the provincial administration increased the proportion of Latin
speakers in the city. The non-Jewish component of the population also
increased in the rural region along the coastal strip—in particular the
expansion of the Samaritans, which is generally dated to the period
following the Bar Kokhba revolt.[68]

Further evidence that Caesarea (within its ancient wall) was pure,
and that to its east lay a strip considered as Land of Gentiles, more
than four miles wide, can be gleaned from the *TY Hallah*; this testimony pertains to a later period, the time of Rabbi Abbahu (second half
of the third century and beginning of the fourth century CE). After the
statement: "For dough-offering and for washing of hands, a man goes
four *mils* [to find water]," the Talmud Yerushalmi asks:

> What is the law as to requiring one to go less than four *mils* in order
> to prepare the dough-offering in a state of cleanness, [or if water is no
> nearer than] four *mils*, then letting one prepare it in *qab*-sized portions?
> [Is that distinction viable?]. Let us derive the answer from the following:
> For R. Hiyya bar Va said, "For example, Caesarea [would be a distance
> to go to find water for attaining cleanness]." Now was Caesarea not four
> *mils* [from where Hiyya lived]? That then proves that, in the case of
> one's being four *mils* from water, let him prepare the dough in a state of
> cleanness [by going for the needed water], but for a greater distance than
> this, let him prepare the dough in *qab*-sized portions.[69] R. Ammi gave
> instructions in Kepar Shimi to prepare a large piece of dough in state of
> uncleanness. Now was not that location not four *mils* from water? Since
> a river ran between his locale and the source of usable water, it was as if
> distance was [more than] four *mils*.[70]

---

[68] See for example, Alon 1971: 242–251; Neeman 1997; Mor 1983: 183; Eck 2007:
224.

[69] See *Pnei Moshe* commentary *ad loc.* R. Hiyya bar Va (=Abba), and R. Ammi were
Amoraim of the third generation, contemporary of Rabbi Abbahu who renewed the
assertion that Caesarea is as the Land of Israel. But the region of Caesarea was Land of
Gentiles, and it was permissible to come to Caesarea from a distance of up to 4 miles
and prepare dough there in a state of purity.

[70] *TY Hallah* 2:3, 58c, trans. Neusner 1991: 65. See also *TY, Berakhot* 8:2, 12a, and
Lieberman 1931: 108. Lieberman noted that the commentaries are not satisfactory and
it seems that in Caesarea the sages were afraid of a possible impurity of the Land of
Gentiles. Therefore they went to places which were certainly Land of Israel to prepare
their Hallah in purity, and the distance from Caesarea to what was certainly the Land
of Israel was less than 4 miles. However, Caesarea was always considered to be Land of
Israel, as was indicated above. Guggenheimer in his translation was of the opinion that

What emerges from this text (and such is *Pnei Moshe* commentary) is that according to R. Hiyya bar Abba, it was customary to come to Caesarea from a distance of four miles for the sake of preparing a dough in purity, and whoever lived farther away was allowed to make his dough in smaller, *qab*-sized portions (which were not susceptible to ritual impurity). In the strip of Gentiles' Land that surrounded Caesarea, Jews also settled places that were more than four miles distant from the city; these Jews were exempt from going to Caesarea in order to prepare dough in purity. As for Kepar Shimi (Shumi/Shuni, adjacent to Binyamina), it was located within the Land of Gentiles, but its distance from Caesarea was less than four miles; therefore it would have been appropriate to go to Caesarea from there and prepare the dough in purity. However, since a river (Nahal Tanninim) separates between them, Kepar Shimi was considered as being located more than four miles from the Land of Israel. Therefore Rabbi Ami ruled that they should prepare the dough there in impurity. (It is evident that Kepar Shimi was distant more than four miles from the Land of Israel in any other direction).[71]

Sources that mark a piece of land to the east of Caesarea as a Land of Gentiles, as small as it might be, disagree with the *Baraita* of the borders of the Land of Israel (*Baraita deThumin*),[72] which sets the wall of Straton's Tower as one of the western demarcation points of the Land of Israel settled by those who returned from Babylon. According to this *Baraita*, all the area to the east of this border is Land of Israel. This topographical demarcation of the *Baraita*, according to which Straton's Tower was outside the area inhabited by those who returned from Babylon (that is, outside the Land of Israel), is also, of course, inconsistent with the conclusion that all of Caesarea was considered

---

the passage speaks about Caesarea of Phillipus, and had difficulties in understanding the issue. He also maintained that we have to do here with Kepar Shimi or Kephar Shami which is located between Sepphoris and Acre (*TY Gittin* 1:2, 43c), rather than with Shumi/Shuni in the borders of Caesarea, but he is wrong. See his translation to *TY Hallah*, 2003: 302, n. 57. On Kephar Shami, or Kephar Sasi adjacent to Acre see Di Segni and Frankel 2000, with farther references; the authors rightly refrain from addressing *TY Hallah* in this context. These were two different sites.

[71] Z. Safrai (*supra*, note 54) held however the opinion that the text does not speak about the distance from Caesarea, but about the distance from the Land of Israel to the east of the Land of Gentiles strip. If such were indeed the case, the exact site in the Land of Israel, which is less than 4 miles distance from Kfar Shami, with a river separating them, should have been mentioned.

[72] See Klein 1965; Sussman 1976.

as Land of Israel for the purpose of laws of purity and regulations related to the Land of Israel, since Straton's Tower was entirely within the urban confines of Herodian Caesarea.[73] The inevitable conclusion appears to be that this passage of the *Baraita*, concerning Straton's Tower, must have originated prior to the foundation of Caesarea by Herod, although the final text of the extant *Baraita* is much later.[74]

The conclusion that a strip of Gentiles' Land had existed east of Caesarea bears implications on understanding Jewish burial customs there during the Talmudic period.

THE LATER CEMETERY

The urban expansion beyond the limits of the old cemetery, into the Land of Gentiles, and the development of a new cemetery farther away, within the Land of Gentiles, may explain the later custom of transferring Caesarea's dead for burial in various places that were without any doubt Land of Israel, for fear of burying them abroad. This custom is mentioned in the *TY Mo'ed Qatan*, according to the version of The Early [Sages] (נוסח ראשונים):

> ...they used to bring the deceased from one place to another, for instance, those [of Qisrin] whom they bury in Beth Sharii....[75]

---

[73] The version given by Sussman 1976, following the MS tradition of *Sifre* is: 'and the wall of Migdal Sharoshan'. In Erfurt MS of the *Tosefta*, *Shebiit* 4:11 (ed. Zuckermandel, p. 66) there is a gloss: 'the wall of Migdal Sarshan of Qisri'. According to Sussman it seems that this refers to the ancient part of Caesarea, the Hellenic town. See Sussman, *ibid*.: 228, 256–257; and Lieberman, *Tosefta KiPshuta, Zeraim B: Shebiit*, p. 534.

[74] Scholars had difficulties in dating the *Baraita*. The Rehov inscription solved many problems pertaining to the text, but it is not determinative about the dating. Hildesheimer was of the opinion that the list reflects the territorial expansion in the days of John Hyrcanus and Alexander Jannaeus, although edited in a later period; see Hildesheimer 1965: 19–20. Klein dated the *Baraita* to the time of Herod, but prior to the inauguration of Caesarea in 10 BCE; see Klein 1965: 162–164. Others dated it to the generation of Usha, after the Bar Kokhba revolt, namely, the second half of the second century, or even somewhat later. According to Sussman the list had crystallized at the end of the Tannaitic period, the end of the second century, prior to the issue of the permit of Caesarea by Rabbi Yehuda HaNasi; see Sussman 1976: 254–255. Safrai 1996: 636–639.

[75] *TY Mo'ed Qatan* 3:5, 82c. Sites mentioned in the variant readings include Beth Shean, Beth Kira, Beth Biri, Beth Sara; see Ratner 1967: 114; Lieberman 1931: 108; Safrai 1959: 211, note 74; Rosental 1993: 496, note 41.

One need not go so far as to say that Caesarea had no cemetery at all,[76] contrary to what it says explicitly in the *Mishnah* mentioned above, and implicitly in the *Tosefta* under discussion.[77] The development of the new burial custom is understandable only in relation to a new cemetery, located farther away from the city, which came into existence during the third and fourth centuries, and not in relation to the old cemetery, with which the aforementioned *Mishnah* and *Tosefta* deal. The custom of transferring the Jews of Caesarea to be buried in Beth Sharaii (בית-שריי), which is Beth She'arim, and in other places, reflects a reality in which it was no longer possible to bury Jews in the old Jewish cemetery, which the city already encompassed. In this reality, Jews who feared burial outside of the Land of Israel farther east, preferred to be buried in what was considered undoubtedly Land of Israel, rather than in the strip of Gentiles Land that extended beyond the old Jewish cemetery. One should not conclude from this that Caesarea itself was not considered as the Land of Israel.[78]

In the same time, it should be emphasized that Jewish graves and burial inscriptions uncovered beyond the Byzantine wall, seemingly within the confines of the Land of Gentiles, beyond the old cemetery, indicate that Jews were buried in the Gentiles' strip as well. The transfer of the dead for interment in Beth She'arim, or in other locations within the confines of the Land of Israel proper, was thus, seemingly, a custom of the more conservative and wealthy.

In summary, from the aforementioned *Mishnah* and *Tosefta*, it is possible not only to learn about the existence and location of several topographical elements in the urban landscape of Caesarea—the wall street, the eastern *stoa*, and the *tetrapylon*; the two sources also make it possible to comprehend properly several questions in the rabbinic literature that pertain to the *halakhic* status of Caesarea and its borders with regard to regulations related to the Land of Israel, as well as the status of the Land of Gentiles adjacent to the city and the expansion of a second cemetery into this land. The following chronological development is suggested:

---

[76] Lieberman, *Yerushalmi KiPshuto*[2], I.1, p. 426.
[77] And contrary to what is said in the *TY Pesahim* 3:7, 30b, about a message Rabbi Abbahu had sent to his son: "Have I sent you to Tiberias because 'there are no graves' in Caesarea?..." (trans. Bokser and Shiffman 1994: 141). See Lieberman, *ibid*.
[78] As is rendered by Safrai 1959: 211.

- Caesarea in its Herodian confines was always considered to be pure.
- Beyond the city to the east, was a strip of Jewish graves, and the area farther east was a strip of Gentiles Land, the width of which exceeded four miles from the Herodian city wall.
- When the city grew beyond the Herodian walls, and it was no longer possible to continue to bury Jews in the old cemetery, some people preferred to be buried in Beth She'arim and in other locations that were within the confines of the Land of Israel proper, rather than be buried in the strip of Gentiles' Land to the east of Caesarea.
- The Byzantine city wall, built in the fifth century, seemingly encompassed the old cemetery (whose remains have not yet been found) and additional area, which was previously within the Gentiles' strip.

The Jews of Caesarea, as far as they adhered to the *Halakhah*, were meticulous in confining themselves within the borders of the Herodian city. The implications of this conclusion for the daily life of the Jewish congregation of Caesarea in the Mishnaic and Talmudic period deserve further consideration.

THE BOUNDARIES OF THE GENTILES' STRIP

As mentioned above, *tanna qamma*, prior to the Bar Kokhba revolt, did not indicate the width of the Gentiles' strip east of Caesarea.[79] Kepar Shimi was within this strip, as was indicated above. Topographical features that may determine the width of the Gentiles' strip east of Caesarea can be found, perhaps, in the *Mishnah* dealing with the boundaries of exemption from tithes on pressed figs (תחום היתר דבלה), and other fruits (although there is not necessarily an overlap between the area of exemption from regulations related to the Land of Israel—תחום ההיתר—and the Gentiles' strip). In *Mishnah, Demai* 2:1 it is stated:

---

[79] For an attempt to define precisely the width of Land of Gentiles in the boundaries of Caesarea and to trace changes in the definition of this area throughout the period see Safrai 1980: 217–228. His point of departure, that Caesarea was impure, is in disaccord with what was concluded above.

These items are tithed as *demai* produce in every place [viz., both in and outside the Land of Israel]: pressed figs, and dates, and carobs, and rice, and cumin.[80]

According to H. Albeck, in his commentary on the *Mishnah*, these are fruits with *demai* status[81] which were taken from *Am HaAretz* everywhere, regardless of where they were living, i.e., even in those places that were not conquered by those who returned from Babylon, since it is assumed that they were grown in a territory conquered by those who returned from Babylon and brought from there. In the ensuing discussion on this passage in the *TY Demai* 2:1, 22c, which can be dated to the first half of the fourth century, it is said that in Caesarea the exemption of pressed fig was in effect:

> Said R. Mana: "I went to Caesarea and saw them treating figcakes as permitted. I asked R. Isaac bar Eleazar [about this], and he said, 'Thus did Zugga treated them, as permitted'."[82]

And further down are given the boundaries of this permission:

> R. Isaac bar Eleazar in the name of Zugga of Caesaria [said], "[In] every place from which the [Mediterranean] Sea can be seen, they [fig-cakes] are permitted."[83] Some hold [that this permission obtains] as far as Migdal Malha,[84] and others hold [that it obtains] as far as Ma'arat Telimon.[85]

---

[80] Trans. Sarason, in Neusner, p. 37.

[81] All agricultural products of *Am HaAretz* are suspect as to whether tithes were appropriately levied from it, and therefore it is called *demai*. It was ruled that the buyer should set aside a tithe and *trumah* on their behalf. See Albeck's introduction to tractate *Demai*: H. Albeck, *Seder Zeraim*, p. 69.

[82] Trans. Sarason 1993: 66. R. Yizhak bar Elazar mentioned there is R. Yizhak bar Elazar the second, an Amora of the fourth generation, and so is Zugga, and both were active in Caesarea. See Frankel 1967: 77a, 107a; Margalioth 1976: 584–585.

[83] The translation follows here Rome—Vatican Apostolic Library, Cod. Ebr. 133 MS that renders *yma* (sea), which is a preferred reading. Leiden MS renders here *mya* (water). Z. Safrai (1980: 159; 1985: 221–222) suggested that the reference is to a western strip of the Sharon area, which stretches to the east up to the second line of hills, and is delineated by the higher lowland area. He apparently means the *hamra* hills to the west of the *Marzeva*; see Yizhaki 1979: 3–5 (in Hebrew). The width of this strip from the sea is 5–6km; the width of the entire Sharon, including the *Marzeva*, up to the feet of the Samaria Hills is ca. 15km.

[84] Hildesheimer suggested identifying it with Kh. Malha, at the feet of Mt. Carmel, to the N-W of Geva Carmel. See Hildesheimer 1965: 31. And similarly Klein, who wrote Kh. Mliha, see Klein 1965: 152–153. This identification is also shared by Avi Yonah 1976: 80, as well as by Tsafrir, Di Segni and Green 1994: 187.

[85] Trans. Sarason, p. 66. According to Hildesheimer 1965: 32, one should read the Cave of Salimon, and it refers to a cave near Kh. es Suleimaniye, to the NW of el Fureidis, about 3km to the SE of Dor. This is also shared by Avi Yonah 1963: 126;

Later on, after a list of items that are permitted during the seventh year (but during the other years of the sabbatical cycle these items are deemed to be *demai*), the boundaries are given:

> How far [south does the market area of Caesaria extend, in which the above rules pertain]? [From] the way station of Amuda (פונדקא דעמודא),[86] the way station of Tibta (פונדקא דטיבתא),[87] as far as Kfar Saba[88] and Zoran[89] and Dora is deemed to be like Caesaria.[90]

In the halakhic inscription of the Rehov synagogue there is a similar list of sites, presented after a list of fruits that were permitted in the seventh year in Caesarea, and in other years of the sabbatical cycle they were considered *demai*:

---

idem 1976: 79, and by Z. Safrai (1980: 159), who wrote Kh. a Talamania, to the NW of el Fureidis. The cave is marked on trails map (מפת סימון שבילים).

[86] Safrai, *ibid.*, suggested an identification with Kh. Hamdan, to the south of Tul Karem. Tsafrir, Di Segni and Green 1994: 201 suggested Fandaqumiyya, a village in Samaria, to the NE of Sebastia. This location is not reasonable, being too far from Caesarea.

[87] Hildesheimer (1965: 32) held the opinion that the Arab village of Funduq, on the Jaffa-Shechem road, to the west of Shechem, is a descendent of the two Inns referred to here. Avi Yonah (1963: 128, and 1976: 101—Tibetah), as well as Safrai (1980: 159) suggested Taiyibe, in the "Triangle", which is 27km distant from Caesarea to SSE, ca. 5km to the south of Tul Karem, and ca. 16 km from the sea.

[88] Hildesheimer (1965: 32) identified it with modern Kfar Saba, and similarly Safrai (1980: 160). Tsafrir, Di Segni and Green 1994: 99—Caphar Saba, bring a more precise location—Kh. Sabiye, near Antipatris. Kfar Saba is located to the east of Apollonia, ca. 7km from the sea. It is 35km distant from Caesarea to the south. One should consider identifying it with Kh. Kafr Sibb, only 20km distant from Caesarea to the SE, and about 15 km from the sea. Avi Yonah (1976: 70), identified it as the site of Yeshuv—a Samaritan village. Accordingly, under the entry Caphar Saba (*ibid.*: 46), he did not referred to *TY Demai*.

[89] Zoran (Zowarna of the Rehov inscriptrion) was identified by Klein (1965: 159) with Tell Tsur to the south of Dor. Avi Yonah (1963: 126, and 1976: 97—Soran), identified it with Umm Sur, 7.5km distant from the sea. This was also adopted by Tsafrir, Di Segni and Green 1994: 263—Zoran. Safrai (1985: 226) identified it with Tira, to the north of Atlit (namely, in the district of Dora), or with Tell Tsur/ H. Tsorim on the south of Mt. Carmel. At this site, adjacent to Ain Tsur, in the confines of Ramat HaNadiv park, a farmhouse was excavated, around which a village came into being in the Second Temple period. The site was thereafter destroyed, without being renewed.

[90] *TY Demai* 2:1, 22c, trans. Sarason 1993: 68. The version "and Dora is deemed to be like Caesaria" is in Vatican, Apostolic Library, Cod. Ebr. 133 MS. The final passage addresses various items of agricultural products which were forbidden in Caesarea (namely, which were liable to tithe), but were permitted in the sabbatical year, and in other years they were considered *demai*: wheat, bread, wine, oil, dates, rice and cumin.

...And until where is the region of Caesarea? Till Soran, and the Inn of Tibetah, and Amuda, and Dor, and Kefar Saba.[91]

The permitted halakhic district of Caesarea was a narrow north-south strip, from which the sea could be seen (Fig. 25). On the north it stretched beyond Dora and on the south up to the boundaries of Apollonia. Two of the demarcating points (Migdal [= Tower of] Malha and Ma'arat [= Cave of] Telimon) are located to the north and northeast of Caesarea, on the western slopes of Mt. Carmel, and actually within the district of Dora. In this context the final clause, "and Dora is deemed to be like Caesaria," is understandable. We have to do here with the narrow agricultural strip between Mt. Carmel and the sea, north of Caesarea, from which the sea can indeed be seen. This strip extended beyond the lake that was created by damming Nahal Tanninim in the fourth or third centuries. The two demarcating points are located along roads, and are recorded from the farther to the nearer. The Tower of Malha is a marker on the road along the seashore, and the Cave of Telimon is next to an eastern route, along the foot of Mt. Carmel, on the eastern side of the aforementioned lake.[92]

The four other points are located more to the south, demarcating the agricultural zone of the northern coastal plain, comprising the

---

[91] The translation follows Levine 1981: 152–153, lines 25–26. Sussman (1974: 132–135, 159–160, with references to the studies of Neubauer, Klein, Luntz, and Avi Yonah, given in footnote 322). According to Avi Yonah (1963: 126–128), the passage of the *Yerushalmi* defines the district of Caesarea, which included also the toparchy of Nabrata. Its northern limit was Nahal Daliyah (Nahr ed-Difle)—Chorseos, and Telimon Cave is located nearby (near Kh. es Suleimaniye), in the south—Nahal Poleg (Nahr Faliq)—Bdellopotamos, Soran (Umm Sur). According to Z. Safrai the text defines the Gentiles' strip, and one should differentiate between this matter and the administrative boundaries of Caesarea. The administrative district of Narbata extended to the east of that of Caesarea; it was considered as the Land of Israel. Later on, in the beginning of the fourth century CE, the district of Narbata was included within the district of Caesarea. Z. Safrai (1980: 155–159) proposed various identifications, given above. If we accept that the demarcating points were Umm Sur, Taiyibe and Kh. Hamdan, then they are located too close together, rather than being scattered, and they are quite distant from Caesarea to the south, being nearer to Apollonia. Sussman too emphasized that one should not confuse between the borders given in the Rehov inscription and in the *Yerushalmi*, which deal with regulations related to the Land of Israel, and the administrative district of Caesarea. He also suggested that the demarcating points should be sought nearer to the city, so they did not cut too large a territory from the Land of Israel. He therefore rejected the identification of the way-station Tibta with Fandaqumiyya/Pentakomia, located in the heart of Samaria, and that of Kfar Saba with the present day city, both being too remote from Caesarea.

[92] See the roads mapped in Tsafrir, Di Segni and Green 1994.

kurkar ridges and the valleys in between, up to the "gutter" (*Marzeva*). All four markers were probably located in the agricultural zone of the Sharon plain, beyond the oak forest. It is reasonable to assume that these marking points as well, especially the two way-stations, actually inns, were located on local roads. The Inn of Tibta seems to have been located next to a main road adjacent to Tibta, and not in Tibta itself (today the Israeli Arab city of Taiyibe). The sites marked on the map (Fig. 25) were thus identified: the way-station of *Amuda* was an inn adjacent to Umm Hamdan, south of Tul Karem; the way-station of Tibta was an inn adjacent to Taiyibe; Kfar Saba is Kh. Kafr Sibb, which is adjacent to a main road; and Soran is Umm Sur (Fig. 25).

Post Script

What was the layout of the expanded city beyond the Herodian wall? Was it orthogonal, following the inner grid,[93] as was suggested by Holum 2009: Fig. 1, or was it a network of curving streets (reflecting the outline of the presumed Wall Street), intersected by a series of radiating streets, like the map of Byzantine Caesarea (Fig. 26) published by him more than twenty years ago?[94] None of the extra-mural entertainment structures followed the internal orthogonal grid. The axis of the eastern hippodrome, a Roman circus built under Hadrian in an early stage of the extra-mural expansion, is markedly offset to the internal grid. The *scaenae frons* of the *odeum* and the axes of the oval amphitheatre, are slightly offset, with no apparent reason if the Herodian grid was indeed applied outside the wall. One also wonders why was the Byzantine wall (erected in the fifth century) semi-oval, rather than rectilinear, if it was to encompass an orthogonal city? All these data suggest a *curved and radiating* disposition for the area outside the Herodian wall, like in Holum *et. al.*'s 1988 map.

Are there other archaeological remains to sustain this conclusion? So far not much was exposed in this area other than parts of the entertainment structures mentioned above. The Italian Mission uncovered,

---

[93] It should be noted that even inside the Herodian city there was a diagonal "radiating" street, and that the Temple Platform was curvilinear, not rectilinear, on its rear side, facing the city wall. A network of five roads radiated from Caesarea in all directions (Fig. 25).

[94] Holum *et al.* 1988: 163.

immediately to the south of the pentagonal tower on the north-eastern corner of the Herodian wall, a draining channel that runs across the wall due east (Fig. 27), while the internal grid follows an eastern south-eastern orientation.[95] Hence, this channel and the presumed street of the expanded city built above, deviate from the Herodian grid.[96]

The uncovered remains along the inside of the eastern wall are only briefly described, and the short description is not clear enough. The graded *crepizoma* built against the eastern wall (seemingly in order to retain it) suggests in my opinion that the north Wall Street attained here a south easterly direction, running parallel to the city wall on the inside.[97] Farther north, near the Byzantine city wall, the main sewage channel (*cloaca*) is also offset to the Herodian grid. The street above it ran somewhat parallel to the later Byzantine wall that encompassed it. In the south-eastern zone of the city the 1949 aerial photo[98] suggests that a large compound or quarter was laid out, aligned on the axes of the Roman circus. A 80m long tessellated pavement uncovered in 1932 and 1942, and mentioned by Holum, was associated with a street connecting the hippodrome with the Herodian city. In this zone Holum set four "radiating" streets. But there is no apparent reason not to start them from the Wall Street (the exact location of which is conjectural in this section of the wall run).

Holum *et al.*'s 1988 map can be modified in a few details: a curved longitudinal Wall Street in line with the Herodian city wall; a due east street to the south and off the north-eastern Herodian tower; a segment of street above the *cloaca* in the north; and another street parallel and to the north of the *scaenae frons* of the *odeum*. Hopefully future excavations will further clarify the picture.

Hence, it is easier to understand why such an extraordinary city plan, which could have been seen at glance from the top of the temple

---

[95] Wall 8024 in Area G8 of the Joint Expedition to Caesarea Maritima, exposed farther south along the Herodian wall, and discussed by Holum, is just 3.20m long; it should be interpreted as a fortification tower, rather than as the starting point of a new city wall of an expanding city, as is suggested by Holum, adding a new northern gate based on this speculation.

[96] A section of a paved street was uncovered nearby, but its location on fig. 375 is not clear.

[97] Finocchi, in Frova 1965: 248, 280, 286–87, Fig. 375. Anna Iamim drew my attention to the fact that the north arrow on fig. 375 is actually 23 degrees east of north, and not as drawn. Hence the channel runs almost due east, deviating from the Herodian grid given by Holum.

[98] Frova 1965: Fig. 1 and p. 287; Levine 1975b: Pl. 1 = Fig. 3 here.

platform, would have ignited the enthusiasm of the anonymous author of the *Expositio totius mundi et gentium*, Ch. 26: *et dispositione civitatis in multa eminens*[99]—a passage that is at the core of Holum's 2009 article. The orthogonal layout suggested by Holum is so common in Roman urbanism (like in the case of Alexandria, Antioch, Laodicea, to name just a few), that one wonders why in the case of Caesarea such a conventional disposition would have merited the praises of the ancient author. A curved and radiating disposition, which could be observed in a single glance from the top of the temple platform, is an extraordinary layout. One should also notice that such a layout resembles that of the adjacent city of Dora,[100] where since Persian times and throughout the Hellenistic and Roman periods two parallel streets followed the curvilinear line of the city wall. It seems that this was an ancient tradition of urban planning, known in the region since ancient times.[101]

There are no archaeological finds that can sustain Holum's claim that the orthogonal grid was applied outside the Herodian city wall. There is nothing in the archaeological data or in the aerial photographs to sustain the very existence of Cardo E3 on his map. This hypothetical street should not have served him as a point of departure for the rendition of *Tosefta, Ahilot*, 18: 13, for locating the eastern *stoa* mentioned there, and for the bearing of this text on the evolution of the urban space. As was indicated above, the "eastern *stoa*" could not have run outside the Herodian city wall. It must have been on the eastern walk of the Wall Street.

---

[99] Ed. Rougé 1966: 160.
[100] *Supra*, note 21.
[101] See many city maps in Kempinski and Reich 1992.

CHAPTER THREE

ON THE PROCLAMATION OF CAESAREA AS A ROMAN COLONY*

Caesarea as a Colony

Caesarea, the city founded by King Herod, was transformed into *Colonia Prima Flavia Augusta Caesarea or Caesarensis* by Vespasian (69–79 CE)[1] after the suppression of the Great Jewish Revolt. This was a change of status, not a foundation of a new city as a colony of military veterans. The question, whether such Latin-speaking colonists were added at all to the city in significant numbers, joining the old Greek- and Aramaic-speaking citizens, is a matter of dispute.[2] Benjamin Isaac put forward several convincing arguments against colonization by veterans. He claimed that since, on the basis of the literary and epigraphical sources, and from the fact that whereas veteran-colonies invariably issued coinage marking the military origins of the settlers and the units from which they were discharged, there is no such military insignia on the city coins of Caesarea, the inevitable conclusion is that Caesarea was an honorary colony. It was granted a new status as an act of gratitude for the assistance provided by its citizens to Vespasian in suppressing the Jewish revolt in the province of Judaea. According to Isaac, the promotion in status was not accompanied by

---

* I began writing this chapter while I was staying in the Netherlands Institute for Advanced Studies (NIAS). I am grateful to the librarians and the entire staff and administration for the excellent working conditions which they placed at my disposal.

[1] Plinius, *Historia Naturalis* 5.14.69: "*Stratonis Turris, eadem Caesarea, ab Herode rege condita, nunc colonia prima Flavia a Vespasianus imperatore deducta....*" Its official name on the city coins: *Colonia Prima Flavia Augusta Caesarea/Caesarensis.* See, for example, Kadman 1957. Such was its official name in inscriptions as well; see Lehmann and Holum 2000: inscr. nos. 3, 24, 44.

The principal discussions on Caesarea as a Roman colony are: Levine 1975a: 34–45; Ringel 1975: 144–46; Schürer 1973–87, 2:117–18; Isaac 1980–81: 38–43, 48, 50–52 (repr. in *idem* 1998: 87–111); Millar 1990: 26–28 (repr. in *idem* 2006: 164–222); Cotton and Eck 2002; Eck 2007: 216–26; Alon 1967: 84–85.

[2] Already under the procurators, there were also Latin-speakers in the city, such as Cornelius, the centurion of the Italian cohort (Gr. σπεῖρα; Ac 10:1), as well as the governor and his council (*ibid.* 25:12).

the settlement of veterans. Fergus Millar shares this opinion.[3] On the other hand, Leo Haefle, and later also Lee Israel Levine, opined that the granting of the new status was accompanied by settling of soldiers, veterans of the war against the Jews.[4] More recently, with much more epigraphical data at hand, Werner Eck had reached a similar conclusion.[5] He argues that this is indicated by the vast and almost exclusive use of Latin from the time of Vespasian (the earliest monumental Latin buildings inscription—Fig. 28—is dated to 77/78 CE) and throughout the second and third centuries. And we are dealing not only with administrative inscriptions, but also with commemoration of individual euergetism and burial inscriptions. Latin is also the sole script on the city coins of the colony (coinage started under Domitian). All these lead to the inevitable conclusion, he claims, that the proclamation was accompanied by the settlement of a large group of Latin-speaking veterans familiar with Roman law and administration. The subject of the present chapter does not call for a decision on this issue.[6]

---

[3] Isaac 1980–81; 1998, and more recently 2009; Millar, 1990 and 2006. Prior to Isaac, such was also the position of Kadman 1957: 64, and of Ringel 1975: 145. Their conclusion was based mainly on the numismatic argument. Already Jones 1971: 277 was bothered by the question whether Vespasian had settled veterans in Caesarea.

[4] Haefeli 1923: 31, 74; Levine 1975a: 35 and 171, n. 14.

[5] Eck 2007; see also Cotton and Eck 2002, and more recently 2009.

[6] However, it should be noted that the image of Tyche adopted for the Tyche of the colony (see below), is the one already adopted by the local citizens before the city had acquired a colonial status, and that it is related to the an ancient myth of the older citizens of the city, which was not associated with the colonial status and which had no relations with the new military settlers. These are additional arguments to sustain Isaac's approach.

Cremation tombs—a burial practice common to the Latin west—in the Roman cemetery located to the south of the theater (four out of the eleven that were excavated), indicate that a new Roman population was indeed added to the city. But this was a quite small cemetery, which can be interpreted in relation to the *officium* of the Roman governor, whose compound was located nearby, rather than as a municipal cemetery. In itself it does not bear enough evidence that a sizeable colony of veterans was added to the city. Few pottery sherds were found, dated to the second and third centuries. Some of the tombs were lined with stamped tiles of the Tenth Legion. In one of them a coin of Hadrian was found. The burial inscriptions are in Latin or in Greek. See Porath 2008: 1660.

The weights, mostly bearing Greek—but two with Latin—inscriptions, reflect a variegated market life. Those bearing Latin inscriptions—the only ones of this kind found so far in Israel—were published recently; see Kushnir-Stein 2007. One weighs 40.2 gr., the second 36.6 gr. Despite the Latin script, the weight is according to the local standard, rather than following the Roman *libra/litra* standard. On the other hand, a weight of Caesarea of 1 litra—the Roman standard—published by Lifshitz, bears a

The citizens of a colony were granted Roman citizenship[7] and hence the preparation of a new list of citizens[8] (*coloni*/κολωνὸι)—both new and old—of the colony Caesarea was required, and the *territorium*— its administrative territory—had to be defined.[9] In a colony, like in any other city, there were also inhabitants who were not citizens; they had a different legal status. If any Jews remained in the city after the revolt ended,[10] their number must have been very small after the severe massacre carried out by the Greek/Syrian population during the events that led to the revolt, while other fled to the adjacent toparchy of Narbata.[11] The lands of the Jews were seized and reserved by Vespasian as his private property.[12] In Caesarea and its territory there was enough land and property to be distributed to veterans (if we accept the conclusion of Cotton and Eck which is not beyond doubt, as was

Greek inscription; see Lifshitz 1961: 121. Its correct reading is given by Kushnir-Stein 2007. Its suggested date is the beginning of the 4th c.

[7] Aulus Gellius, *Attic Nights* XVI 13.8–9, ed. Rolfe 1952: 180–81. Aulus Gellius was a second-century CE author.

[8] A list of citezens (ἀναγραφαί τῶν πολιτῶν) of Caesarea is mentioned by Eusebius in his early fourth-century CE *Martyrs of Palestine* (*De Mart. Pal.* IV.8, ed. Bardy 1967: 131 in the shorter recension). A list of citizens was also common in Greek cities.

[9] Eck 2007: 217.

[10] A military *diploma* of April 5, 71 (*CIL* XVI, 15.29 = CIL III, Suppl. 3, IX.30) mentions a Jewish soldier of Caesarea named L. Cornelius Simon as one of the witnesses. He served in the Roman army during the First Revolt; (see Isaac 1980–81: 50). This *diploma*, found in Pompeii in 1874, was also published in ed., *CIL* III, Suppl. 3, IX.30, edited by Herbert Nesselhauf (Berlin: Walter de Gruyter, 1936), 14. See also note 72 below. A topic deserving of a separate study is the civil status of the Jews in the city immediately after the revolt, and in the second and third centuries. They had already lost their *isopoliteia* under Nero (see below).

[11] According to Josephus (*War* II.457; VII.361–62), more than 20,000 Jews were massacred in Caesarea in one hour on a Sabbath at the beginning of the revolt, and since then Caesarea lost its Jewish population. Those who survived were put in chains and led to the harbor by the procurator Florus (whence they were apparently deported abroad as slaves). Later on the governor of Syria, Cestius Gallus, proceeding from Ptolemais to Caesarea, dispatched a cavalry detachment to the toparchy of Narbata, bordering on the territory of Caesarea, where the Jews had found refuge in May 66, following the struggle over free passage to a synagogue, carrying with them their holy scriptures. The death toll caused by this cavalry unit in the toparchy was enormous, as it looted property and setting villages on fire (*War* II.509).

[12] *War* VII.216–17: κελεύων πᾶσαν γῆν ἀποδόσται τῶν Ἰουδαίων,.. ἰδίαν αὐτῶι τὴν χώραν φυλάττων. He issued his order to the governor of Judaea, Bassus, and to the financial procurator—L. Laberius Maximus (known also from inscriptions), after the fortress of Mechaerus was captured at the end of 71 or early in 72. See also Josephus, *Vita* 422. On the significance of this statement of Josephus, the meaning of ἀποδόσται here, and the judicial status of the seized lands, see Applebaum 1977; Smallwood 1976: 340–42; Isaac 1984 (repr. in *idem* 1998: 112–19, with a new postscript: 120–21).

mentioned above).[13] The provincial governor—from now on of the senatorial class, holding the rank of *legatus Augusti pro-praetore*—and the financial procurator (*procurator provinciae*), of the cavalry class, who was appointed alongside him already during the revolt, also resided in Caesarea during their term in office. Both had a staff of clerks familiar with Roman law and administration,[14] and each had a separate government compound.[15] The elite of the pagan Greco-Syrian population of the city might also have integrated into the new provincial, as well as the municipal, administration. The administrative language throughout the colony was Latin, which was also the language of the social elite of the city.[16]

Vespasian exempted the Caesareans from poll-tax (*tributum capitis*) and Titus extended the exemption to land tax (*tributum soli*).[17] But

---

[13] Cotton and Eck 2002; Eck 2007: 224–25. Jones 1971: 277, suggested that the lands of the Jewish toparchy of Narbata were also distributed to the colonists, if Vespasian had indeed settled veterans there.

[14] On some of the personnel of the provincial governor of Judaea-Palaestina residing in Caesarea, mentioned in the epigraphical material, see Cotton and Eck 2001. On the *officium* of the provincial Roman governors, in general, see Rankov 1999; Palm 1999; Eck 2000. On the financial procurators in Caesarea and their staff, see Eck and Cotton 2009.

[15] Patrich 1999; *idem* 2000a; *idem*, 2010, reproduced here as Chapter Eight). See also Eck 2007: 79–103. A fragment of a building inscription dated to 77–78 CE is apparently to be attributed to the inauguration in that year of the *praetorium* of the financial procurator, which was financed by the imperial treasury. This was already suggested by Eck 2002: 538–39; Cotton and Eck 2003: 30–35; Eck 2007: 219 (reading emendation of Lehmann and Holum 2000, inscr. no. 27). The inscription (Fig. 28), was incised on a local sand stone (*kurkar*)—the common building material in Caesarea, of which the *praetorium* was built. It was found nearby, on the sea shore. Avraham Negev, in whose excavations it was found, uncovered the northern part of this compound.

Vespasian also converted a large Jewish synagogue into an *odeion* with a large seating area (θέατρον); see John Malalas, *Chronographia* X.338, ed. Dindorf 1831: 261; *idem*, *Chronographia* X.46, ed. Thurn 2000: 197; English trans. Jeffreys *et al.* 1986: 138. The year is not given. Seemingly, this θέατρον served as the assembly place of the senate/curia of the colony. It was suggested that this was the theater-like structure excavated by the Israel Antiquities Authority in Area VII, ca. 200m to the south-east of the Herodian theater, located within the compound of the floor-tiles plant of Kibbutz Sdot Yam. Its diameter is ca. 85m (Porath 2008: 1657 [map], and 1660). But this is far from being certain. In any case, the inscription under consideration was found far away from these remains, and it is clear that it does not refer to this architectural complex.

[16] Cotton and Eck 2002; Eck 2007: 223–26; Levine 1975a: 40; Lehmann and Holum 2000: 6, 26.

[17] *Digest.* L 15, 8, 7, ed. Mommsen 1902, I: 857: "*Divus Vespasianus Caesarienses colonos fecit non adiecto, ut et iuris Italici essent, sed tributum his remisit capitis; sed divus Titus etiam solum immune factum interpretatus est*" (according to the jurist Paulus): "The Divine Vespasian made the Caesarienses *coloni* without adding *the ius*

they did not acquire *ius Italicum*—the right to enjoy the judicial and fiscal privileges of Italy, including the privilege of a colonus to posses his land, in addition to immunity (*immunitas*) from the above mentioned taxes.[18]

Before becoming a Roman colony, the affairs of the polis Caesarea were administered by a city council, the *boule*.[19] Apollonius of Tyana, who apparently had visited the city some time during the first century CE, before it became a Roman colony, praises the size, rules and Greek customs (ἤθη Ἑλληνικά) of the polis Caesarea.[20] Upon its establishment as a Roman colony, it received a foundation constitution, and municipal institutions were set, resembling those of Rome.[21] Instead of the former *boule* of the polis Caesarea, the city's affairs and its budget were managed by a new city council, the senate/*curia*/*ordo*, whose members—the *decuriones*/*curiales*—were registered in a list—*album ordinis*,[22] in an hierarchical order. Their number in Caesarea is not known. The decisions of the council were published in Latin, and it was in charge of the public treasury (*pecunia publica*). Its members,

---

Italicum, but remitted the poll-tax; but the Divine Titus decided that the soil had been made immune also" (translated by Isaac 1980–81: 41–42).

[18] *Digest.* L 15, 1, 6, ed. Mommsen 1902, I: 856): "*In Palaestina duae fuerunt coloniae, Caesariensis et Aelia Capitolina, sed neutra ius Italicum habet*" (according to the jurist Ulpianus). See also previous note. On *ius Italicum*, see Sherwin-White 1973: 276–77, 316–22; Schürer, above note 1: 96, note 43, with farther bibliography.

[19] A city council (*boule*) was a feature of any Hellenistic polis; see Jones 1940: 162–69. According to Otto 1913: 120ff, and Schalit 1964: 158–159, Herod granted a constitution (πολιτεία) to Caesarea and to the other cities he had founded, in accordance with the "Civil Laws" (πολιτίκοι νόμοι) of the Hellenistic cities, Athens serving as their paragon. See also Schalit 1969: 219–223; Kasher1978; Schürer, above note 1: 93–95; Levine 1975a: 17; Lehmann and Holum 2000: 6, and 233, n. 16.

[20] *Philostratus, The life of Apollonius of Tyana*, Ep. XI, ed. Jones 2005–2006: 16–19; ed. Penella 1979: 38–41, 97–98. Letter 11, in praise of Caesarea, was sent to the chief magistrates (πρόβουλοι) of the city in gratitude for a honor he had received from them—perhaps in a letter granting him citizenship (thus Penella 1979: 98). Its title there as the greatest of Palaestina (μεγίστη τῆς Παλαιστίνης) is an anachronistic term, reflecting the administrative conditions at the time of Philostratus—end of the second century, not that of Apollonius, when the province was called Judaea. Apollonius praises there the heroism of its ancestors in times of war, and their ethics in days of peace. The precise date of the letter is not known. Ringel (1975: 141) is of the opinion that it reflects a pre-colonial reality; Levine 1975a: 35 and 170, n. 6 attributes it to the early colony.

[21] Aulus Gellius, *Attic Nights* XVI xiii. On Roman citizenship, see Sherwin-White 1973: 176–81; *idem* 1970a. On the civil administration of colonies see: Kornemann 1900: 578–88; Sandys 1963: 371–79, 388; Sherwin-White 1970b: 266; Schürer, above note 1: 96–97. On Roman municipal administration, see Abbott and Johnson 1926; Reynolds 1988; Sartre 1991: 121–65; *idem* 2001: 649–63.

[22] Jones 1964 (repr. 1973): 730–31; Chastagnol 1978.

or a smaller committee from among them, were personally responsible
for collecting the imperial taxes in the amount imposed on the city,
and they were obliged to add from their own burse any missing sum.
In addition to imperial taxes, they had to guarantee the collection of
the municipal taxes. The city also had regular incomes from the leasing
of property, credit on loans, etc.[23] In Caesarea there were also various
incomes from the harbor.[24] The municipal leadership was entrusted to
magistrates that were elected by the assembly of the people for a term
in office of one year. They were headed by two members of the council,
who formerly held lower-ranking magistracies (such as *quaestor* and
aedilis). These were the duovirs (*duoviri iure dicundo*),[25] who together
with the two *aediles* and the other magistrates administered all the
municipal affairs: finances, civil order, municipal legislation and law,
civil building and maintenance, games, attribution of honors, dispatching of delegations to the emperor or to the provincial governor,
and so forth. They were also in charge of the municipal mint. Roman
law was in effect in the Roman colonies, and they enjoyed autonomy
from any interference by the governor in their affairs. The duovirs
and the *aediles* had official garb (*toga praetexta*) and a staff of clerks
and bearers of *fasces* within the territory of the city. Every four years

---

[23] From Trajan's time on, the provincial governors had nominated civil curators for
the cities (*curatores civitatum*/λογίσται), i.e., municipal inspectors, who were charged
with supervising their administration, especially the financial affairs. See Reynolds
1988: 41–42. City curators (λογίσται) are mentioned by Eusebius, *The Martyrs of Palestine* (see note 8), IX.2, p. 148 in the Greek recension; 34, p. 31 in the Syriac.

[24] A Greek inscription dating from the second or third century CE, found in the
praetorium of the Roman governor, mentions Varios Seleukos, a curator of ships
(κυράτορ πλοίων sic!) (Lehmann and Holum 2000, inscr. no. 12). Seemingly, we are
dealing here with a high municipal official—the harbormaster, who was in charge of
the docking facilities for ships. He might have also been in charge of the taxes to be
paid on maritime commerce and as docking fees. On this inscription, see also Burrell
1993. Harbor taxes on imports and exports, or on goods in transit, and anchorage
fees are mentioned in the "*hippotrophoi* inscription" so called after those in charge
of the stables of the race horses in Caesarea. The inscription (Lehmann and Holum
2000: 112–14, inscr. no. 109), in Greek, is dated to the fourth to the seventh centuries.
Raban and Barag held the opinion that the Herodian harbor was a separate entity than
the city, issuing its own coins. According to Barag, this state of affairs had continued
up to 81–83 CE, when the harbor was given over to the municipal authorities by the
imperial authorities. See Raban 1992b; Barag 1996.

[25] *Duovir* and decisions of the senate (*decuriones*) in Caesarea are mentioned in
inscriptions nos. 3, 8, 10, 11, and 15 in Lehmann and Holum 2000. The public treasury (*pecunia publica*) is mentioned there in inscriptions nos. 3, 8, and 10. *Questores*,
or *aediles* are not mentioned in the Caesarea inscriptions. See also Schalit 1937: 126,
n. 78.

a census was conducted, supervised by the "duovirs of the fifth year" (*duoviri quinquennales*).[26] This included an updating of the list of citizens and their family members, and a property assessment. On that occasion new *decuriones* were elected to the senate from among those who had already served as magistrates, or from among the wealthy citizens. A decurion had to be a free-born citizen of the colony and a resident of the city; there were restrictions of age (25, but this was not always strictly kept) and of property size; the absence of any ethical or judicial dint was also required. When elected, the decurion served for life. All the magistrates, from among the city's wealthy and dignitaries, were not paid (indeed, in many cases, in the second century, they were even required to pay the city council a sizeable amount of money— *summa honoraria*—in order to be elected to the honorary office). A five-year break was required between two successive terms in office, as well as active military service. In order to be appointed to a more senior position, a pause of three years was enough. The magistrates were assisted by a staff of paid clerks (the tasks and number of which were determined by the municipal regulations), who were inhabitants of a lower social rank, including slaves. The handling of religious affairs was entrusted to priests—*pontifices*, who were elected for life, but the priesthood was not hereditary, and there was also a collegium of *augures*.[27] The cult of the ruling emperor, and the games associated with it, were administered and partially financed by six *augustales* (*severi Augustales*), a group of free men from among the wealthiest citizens of the city.[28]

There is a consensus of opinion that Caesarea was established as a colony at the beginning of Vespasian's reign, but no definite date is given by Schürer (in the revised updated version), by Levine in his book on Caesarea, by Isaac and Millar in their articles on the Roman colonies, or by other historians who deal with Vespasian.[29] Vespasian

---

[26] They were nominated at the beginning of a new four-years circle. A similar four-years circle was in affect in city or crown games, like the Olympian games that were held each four years, but were known as the games of the fifth year.

[27] A *pontifex* of Caesarea is mentioned in Lehmann and Holum 2000, inscr. no. 3; for a collegium of *augures*, see *ibid.*, inscr. no. 123.

[28] Lehmann and Holum 2000: 120–21, inscr. no. 122 and 253, n. 122, with bibliographical references.

[29] See note 1, and also Homo 1949: 342–43; Bengtson 1979: 101; Levick 1999: 149–50 and 251, n. 39 ; 255, nn. 74–75; Amit 2002: 391. Stein 1990: 137–38, 145, notes specifically that the date of the establishment of Caesarea as a Roman colony is unknown. Caesarea coins lack a colonial city era; (neither is there a Herodian city era).

was proclaimed Emperor by his troops, first in Alexandria on July 1, 69 CE and then, in July 3, in Caesarea.[30] The Roman Senate conferred on him full powers only after Vitellius was killed on December 20, 69 CE. In the military *diploma* of April 5, 71 CE found in Pompeii, mentioned above,[31] Caesarea is not defined as a colony, and hence Ringel suggested, and similarly Eck and Cotton, that its promotion to the status of colony took place only later.[32] While there is no precise information about the year, it seems that we do have precise information about the month and day, and from it we may deduce the year.

THE LOUVRE CUP AND ITS SIGNIFICANCE

The key to a solution of this problem lies in two sources of information dated to the beginning of the fourth century. On a ceremonial bronze cup from the first half of the that century, seemingly produced in Caesarea, now in the Louvre—a commemorative liturgical cup (8.2 cm high, 20.2 cm upper diameter) decorated with incised drawings inlaid in niello overlaid by leafs of silver and copper—[33] is depicted a libation scene in front of the local Tyche by a Roman official, probably the governor, clad in a mantle that covers his head (*velato capite*) (Fig. 13a). He is holding a scroll (*volumen*) in his left hand, and a libation bowl (*patera*) above a libation altar, in his right; behind him is a young cult attendant (*camillus*) holding an incense box (*acerra*). The goddess, larger in her dimensions than the officiating figure, wears a turreted crown. She is depicted as an Amazon, clad in a short toga held tight to her body by a girdle on which a sword is hanging; her raised

---

Kindler 1968 attributed to Caesarea a "foundation coin" of the year 81/82 which, he maintained, bears the Greek letter Γ, and suggested that this mark on this provincial coin refers to a city era starting in 78/79—the beginning of Titus' reign. However, Pliny states clearly that the colony was established by Vespasian, not by Titus, and such a city era is unknown from any other coin. On this point Stein (1990: 145, n. 2) adds that the letter is not the Greek Γ, but rather the Latin P, an abbreviation for PATER, and the complete inscription on the coin should be read: DIVUS VESPA-SIANUS PATER.

[30] Tacitus, *Hist.* II.74–76; *War* IV.488–506.
[31] See note 10.
[32] Ringel 1975: 144, n. 207; Eck and Cotton 2009. Wenning (1986: 116), however, is of the opinion that this took place already in 69 CE. He is mistaken.
[33] Will 1983; *idem* 1987. On the identity of Straton and the historical context for the foundation of Straton's Tower according to the archaeological finds, see Patrich 2007: 95–100, reproduced here in pp. 8–13.

right hand is holding a spear, and her right leg is standing on a ship's prow. A small figure is leaning against the left leg of Tyche, the genius (guardian spirit) of the harbor, with a ship's rudder on his shoulder. The goddess is identified by an inscription as GENIO COΛONIA (in a corrupted script and language, a mixture of Greek and Latin letters, and wrong cause). Another inscription: AGONES IEROI, namely, sacred games, is incised above the libation scene and five busts, seemingly of deities. The turreted crown indicates that the scene depicts a religious rite on the occasion of an official feast in honor of the city Tyche, associated with her identification as the genius of the colony; a feast in which the governor took part. It seems that we are dealing here with a rite commemorating the proclamation of Caesarea as a Roman colony, taking place in the framework of a feast in which sacred games were held.

The Tyche on the cup was depicted in that same shape much earlier, on coins of the Roman administration minted in Caesarea, at first on a coin from 67/68 struck there by Vespasian as legate, under the authorization (AUCTORITAS AUGUSTI) of emperor Nero. (Caesarea was granted the right to strike city coins only later, under Domitian.)[34] A similar representation is also known on Roman gems, and thus is the goddess also depicted on bronze statuettes and large marble statues.[35] A tyche of this type is known as Tyche-Amazone. It derived its inspiration from the depiction of Roma Victrix or Virtus—the deification of the virtues of vigor and military power embodied in Rome. Such a depiction of *Dea Romae* is also found on imperial coins of Nero beginning in 60/61, on coins of Galba, and later also on coins of Vespasian in Rome.[36] It was suggested that this type of Tyche was introduced to Caesarea by Vespasian and his troops.[37] The new type of Tyche, emphasizing loyalty to Rome, replaced an earlier type in which she is depicted turreted, clad in a long robe, holding a palm branch in her left hand and a rudder of a ship in her right. Thus is she represented on coins of Agrippa I from his seventh and eighth regnal years (42/43

---

[34] Hamburger 1970: 81–91; Will 1983: 6; Ringel 1975: 154, Pl. XX:11; Barag 1996; Wenning 1986; Burnett *et al.* 1992: coins nos. 4862–65.

[35] Seyrig 1972; Simon and Smith 1971; Gersht 1984: 111.

[36] Vermeule 1959; Wenning 1986: 118–19. In Rome there was a temple to this goddess, erected in the third century BCE. It was restored by Vespasian.

[37] Wenning 1986: 118–19. Gersht 1984 is of the opinion that in this shape of Tyche-Amazon holding the emperor's bust she represents a cult common to Rome and to Augustus.

and 43/44 CE respectively).[38] The inscription and the scene on the cup indicate that when Caesarea was established as a Roman Colony by Vespasian, a few years after the new type of Tyche first appeared on a coin of Nero, the new iconographic type was adopted as the genius of the colony. Thus the city goddess was given an image expressing fidelity to victorious Rome.

The other three scenes on the cup depict the foundation myth of Straton's Tower, unknown from any other source (Figs. 13b–d). Scene II presents three figures consulting an oracle of Apollo. They are identified by inscriptions set above as Strato(n), Lysimachos, and Ctesipon. Scene III presents the maritime voyage of the three and their landing on a hostile shore, haunted by lions. Scene IV depicts an alliance concluded by shaking of hands (*dextrarum iunctio*) between Straton and the god Aesclapios, accompanied by his daughter Hygieia. Here, as well, the three names are incised above. Will recognized that the foundation myth depicted is Greek, not Phoenician.[39] The foundation took place before the visit of Zenon at the site in 259/8 BCE—the earliest source to mention Straton's Tower. The commemoration of the foundation myth of Straton's Tower was thus an integral part of the feast commemorating the proclamation of Caesarea as a Roman colony. Thus was the myth preserved as a living memory, coming down to us in its artistic rendition on a cup from the first half of the fourth century. The foundation of Caesarea (not of Straton's Tower) by a Greek founder named Straton (not by Herod) is also mentioned

---

[38] See Will 1983: 6 and n. 12; Barag 1996: 611, figs. 1, 2, 4, 5. The Greek inscription surrounding the figure reads: "Caesarea which is near the port of Sebastos." The genius of the harbor, depicted on the cup at the left foot of Tyche, appears on the city coins from the time of Trajan onwards, in 117–19 CE; it was not yet represented on Nero's coins. Wenning 1986: 117–22, 127, had already observed this. See also Ringel 1972–75: Pl. II.

[39] On Straton's identity see Patrich 2007 and in Chapter One above. The archaeological data given there indicates that Straton's Tower was founded in the Hellenistic, and not in the Persian, period. Gersht had put forward the proposal—strange, one must admit—that scenes II–IV do not depict the foundation myth of Straton's Tower, but rather episodes related to the birthday of Tyche and the *Navigium Isidis*—the sailing feast of Isis. According to her, Straton, whose name is incised above the three scenes, is the name of the official who was in charge at that time of the supply of the wild animals to the arena! scene III, presenting these beasts, the arrival of a ship, and the discharge of these animals from its dock; in scene IV Asclepius is blessing the people who had reached the shore, and scenes I and II depict scenes of benedictions given by Tyche and by Apollo. See Gersht 1996: 316–17.

in the *praefatio* to Novella 103 of Justinian.[40] The official chronicle adopted a version that left Herod in oblivion, attributing to Straton the foundation of Caesarea.

The foundation myth of Straton's Tower as narrated on the cup adds a new dimension to the dispute about the *isopoliteia* between the Greeks and the Syrians of Caesarea and the Jews that had erupted in 59/60 CE.[41] According to Josephus, the Jews were wealthier and stronger, being dispersed throughout the city, intermingled (ἀναμεμιγμένων) with the Gentiles rather than living in a separate quarter. Their claim was that they deserve precedence, since King Herod, the founder of Caesarea, was of Jewish origin. Their opponents, while acknowledging this, responded that the earlier Caesarea was called Straton's Tower, and at that time no Jews were living there.[42] This claim is presented more forcefully on the Louvre Cup. The cup, and the information provided by Eusebius (see below), indicate that the Greeks/Syrians perceived themselves as descendants of the earlier settlement—Straton's Tower, and this was a living tradition, maintained throughout the ages, up to the time of Justinian.

The controversy between the Jews and the Greeks/Syrians evolved into a violent struggle in the streets of the city and in the agora, leading to bloodshed. An appeal of the Jews to Governor Felix only worsened matters, and finally delegations of the two parties reached Rome, for judgment before Nero's tribunal. There, with the intervention of Pallas—Felix's brother—and a large bribe transferred by the Syrians of Caesarea to Beryllus—the tutor (παιδαγωγός) of Nero, who was also appointed secretary of Nero's Greek correspondence (τάξιν τὴν ἐπὶ τῶν Ἑλληνικῶν ἐπιστολῶν)—the *isopoliteia* (ἰσοπολιτεία) of the Jews

---

[40] *CIC Nov.* 103, *praefatio*, eds. Schöll and Kroll 1899: 496–497; Eng. Tr. Scott, Vol. XV, 1932 (rprt. New York 1973): 12–13.

[41] *Ant.* XX.173–78, 182–84; *War* II.266–70, XIV.284–92. On this conflict, see Levine 1974b: 381–97; Kasher 1978. The opponents of the Jews are generally called Greeks in *War*; while in *Antiquities* they are called Syrians. According to Levine's opinion (*ibid.* and 1975: 167 n. 186), this was for literary reasons, since each composition was addressed to a different audience. Levine also pointed out in detail the differences between the two accounts, sometimes arousing difficulties in understanding the issues at stake. On the Greek character of the city, see also *War* III.409.

[42] Thus in *Ant.* XX.173; another argument of the Greeks/Syrians was that Herod, as a second founder, intended to give it to the Greeks, otherwise he would not have erected temples and statues there (*War* II.266).

was annulled.[43] Nero issued a letter (ἐπιστολή) to this effect.[44] The Greeks/Syrians won the case and received from the emperor the government of the city (τῆς πόλεως ἄρχειν), bringing back with them the text of the decision (τὰ τῆς κρίσεως γράμματα).[45] It is reasonable to assume that the foundation myth of Straton's Tower was mentioned in this document.

This myth was a living tradition, reiterated year after year in the celebration commemorating the establishment of the colony, attributing its original foundation to Straton, no longer to Herod. And indeed, whereas Pliny, while mentioning the establishment of the colony by Vespasian, also mentions its first foundation by Herod,[46] already in the military diploma of April 5, 71 mentioned above, one of the witnesses (a Jewish legionary!) names his *patria* as Caesarea Stratonis,[47] indicating that this was a current name already before the proclamation of the colony. It is thus also named in yet later sources.[48] Its association with Herod was obliterated. An anonymous novel dated to ca. 225 CE mentions the arrival of Clemens the Roman in Caesarea Stratonis.[49] Such, too, is its name in the *praefatio* of Novelle 103 of Justinian of 532 CE, as was mentioned above. Thus, Nero's anti-Jewish decision resulted in the obliteration of Herod as the founder of Caesarea and in the adoption of the foundation myth of Straton's Tower prevalent

---

[43] Opinions vary about the meaning of this term. Some opine that it designates equal rights given the Jews by the civic authorities, like those of all other citizens of the city. According to others, it designates recognition by the central authorities, that the Jewish community constitutes a separate *politeuma* within the city, with autonomy to lead their life in accord with their religion and tradition, and also recognition of its leadership, separate from that of the polis. See the discussion in Kasher 1978.

[44] *Ant.* XX.183.

[45] *War* II.284.

[46] See note 1.

[47] See note 10.

[48] See references in Schürer, above note 1, 2:115.

[49] Pseudo Clemens Romanus, *Recognitiones* I 12,1 (ed. Rehm 1965: 13); *Homiliae* XX, I, xv; I, xx; XIII, vii (*PG* 2: 69–70; 73–74; 333–334 respectively). This is a Christian novel of a didactic purpose, narrating the meeting of Clemens—a Roman nobleman—with St. Peter in Caesarea Stratonis. About the date of this novel, see Quasten 1950: 59–62; Krentz, 1992: 262; Tsafrir, Di Segni and Green 1994: 94. But Caesarea was also known as Caesarea of Palestine, without any attribute. See, for example, Malalas' reference to building projects in the city under Vespasian and Antoninus Pius: Malalas, *Chronographia*, X.46 (ed. Dindorf, 261; ed. Thurn, 197; Eng. trans., 138); XI.25 (ed. Dindorf, 281; ed. Thurn, 212; Eng. trans., 149).

among the Graeco-Syrian component in the population of the city, as described on the bronze cup.[50]

The Cult of Isis-Tyche and the "Navigation Feast" at Caesarea

An unknown aspect in the pagan life of Caesarea associated with the celebration of its establishment as a Roman colony, in the framework of which "sacred games" were held, as depicted on the cup, is illuminated by a short passage in Eusebius—the bishop of Caesarea in the early fourth century CE. Eusebius records it in the story of the two brother martyrs—Hadrian and Euboulus of Batanaea—who were made prey for beasts in Caesarea in 310 CE. Hadrian was thrown to a lion on March 5, "The birthday of the one called Tyche by the people of Caesarea" (Τύχης ημέραι γενεθλιῶν τῆς κατά Καισάρειαν νομιζομένης). This seems to be the feast of Tyche depicted on the Caesarea Cup. His brother, Euboulus (the last martyr of Caesarea) was thrown to the beasts on March 7.[51] Such was not a daily affair. We have to deal here with a birthday feast (*dies natalis*) that extended for three days, from March 5 to March 7, which included sacred games (the AGONES IEROI mentioned on the cup). These were apparently held in the city stadium, located between the two compounds of Roman rule in city— the *praetorium* of the governor and that of the financial procurator, as well as in the other entertainment structures of the city. Interestingly, March 5 is the date of the Isis Navigation Feast (*Isidis Navigium*), or the feast of launching a bark (τὰ πλοιαφέσια), accompanied by processions, which marked the renewal of the sailing season in the Mediterranean.[52] This was a pan-Roman festival, recorded already in the first century BCE, which might have begun even earlier. It is mentioned

---

[50] This is a point emphasized by Will 1983: 23.

[51] Eusebius, *De Mart. Pal.* XI.30 (ed. Bardy 1967: 168).

[52] Merkelbach 1963 suggested that this festival originated in Ptolemaic Egypt. Griffiths (1975: 40–46) has reservations about Merkelbach's proposal concerning the origin of the Isis Navigation Feast. According to Dunand (2000: 96–97), the Navigation Feast was originally a Greek festival, not an Egyptian one; later it was brought under the patronage of Isis. It began in the first century BCE in Eretria, whence it was propagated to maritime cities and Greek island cities throughout the Mediterranean. Its most detailed description is given by Apuleius (see below).

in Latin calendars since the first century CE[53] and up to the calendar
of Filocalus of 354 CE.[54] Claudius Claudianus (d. 404 CE), the court
poet of emperor Honorius and the apparent official spokesman of his
chief aid Stilichus, a pagan who had reached Rome from Alexandria,
composed a poem on this feast in honor of Isis Pelagia as the goddess
of the sea, grain, and fertility.[55] John Lydus, in the sixth century CE,
calls this feast ὁ πλοῦς τῆς Ἰσίδος.[56] In Rome, too, it is mentioned in
the sixth century.[57]

The coincidence of the birthday of Tyche in Caesarea with the *Isidis
Navigium* raises another aspect of the yearly feast of Tyche, in addition
to the commemoration of the establishment of Caesarea as a Roman
colony, since according to Isis aretalogy, her worshipers in Straton's
Tower adored her as Hellas (Ἕλλας) and Agathe (Ἀγαθή) (the good
one)—her epithets as the city Goddess.[58] The birthday of Tyche was
accompanied in Caesarea by sacred games.[59]

---

[53] These are two agricultural calendars (*Menologia Rustica*), dated between 36/39 to
the end of the first century CE; CIL I².1, ed. Mommsen 1893: 280–281.

[54] The Filocalus Calendar, named after Furius Dionysius Filocalus, a famous Christian caligrapher, is an illuminated calendar of the city of Rome for the year 354, part of
a codex prepared for Valentianus—one of its wealthy Christian citizens—in which the
public festivals and holydays of Rome are listed. *Chronographus Anni CCCLIIII*, ed.
Mommsen 1892 (repr. Munich 1981): 13–148; CIL I².1, ed. Mommsen 1893: 254–279
(text); 305–339 (commentar). On the composition and its illustrations, see Stern 1953;
Salzman 1991.

[55] Claudianus, *De Isidis navigio*. The original text with an English translation are
given in Salzman 1991: 173. Stern 1953: 101, 103 mentions more fourth-century
sources, up to the end of the century, in which the festival is mentioned. As a fertility goddess, Isis was also identified with Kore. Thus in neighboring Samaria, where
Isis-Kore was the principal goddess of the city since Hellenistic times, as well as in
Caesarea. For the cult of Isis-Kore in Samaria, see Flusser 1975; Magness 2001. For a
proposal to identify Kore with Isis also in Caesarea see Gersht 1996a.

[56] *Liber de mensibus* [*On the Months*] 4.45, ed. Wünsch 1898.

[57] Salzman 1991: 239–40.

[58] *Pap. Oxyrhynchus* 1380: 94–95, ed. Grenfell and Hunt XI, 1915: 197. The papy-
rus, bringing acclamations of Isis by the worshipers, was written in the second century
CE (*ibid.*, 190). Ἀγαθή is a regular epithet of Tyche; see Matheson 1994; Rodan 1999;
Witt, 1966.

[59] According to the Latin calendars mentioned above, the *Isidis Navigium* was not
associated with *agones*, gladiatorial combats (*ludi*), or with chariot races in the circus
(*circenses*); see Salzman 1991: 124–25, Tables 3–4. Hence, it seems that the sacred
games in Colonia Caesarea, mentioned on the Louvre Cup, which seemingly lasted
for 3 days, are associated with the festival of proclamation of the colony, whereas the
Isidis Navigium, generally a non-*ludi* festival, constituted just a part of this Caesarean celebration. The *Iunonalia* was celebrated in Rome on March 7. This festival was
added to the official calendar of Roman festivals after the mid-first century CE. This,

Details about the Sailing Feast of Isis are preserved in Book XI of the *Metamophoses* of Apuleius of Madaurus, North Africa (the "Isis Book"), written in Latin in ca. 170 CE, seemingly in Carthage. The pages that concern us describe a parade and a ship-launching ceremony during the Sailing Feast at Kenchreai—the harbor of Corinth.[60] The launching ceremony of a real new ship, named after the goddess, included a purification rite. The ship was dedicated to her and launched into the open sea. Later, back in the temple, a concluding ceremony was conducted.

Leading the parade down to the sea marched young girls, in white robes with garlands of flowers on their heads, who scattered flowers along the route. They were followed by women with mirrors hanging on their backs, while others held ivory combs, and still others sprinkled perfumes and drops of balsam. A crowd of men and women, bearing lanterns, torches of wax tapers, and other kinds of artificial lighting accompanied the procession. They were followed by a band of musicians with various instruments, including a pipe and a flute, and a choir of youth in white festal tunics, singing a song in praise of Serapis and Isis. The parade proceeded with acclamations: "Make way for the holy parade." A group of initiates, men and women of every rank and age, clad in white linen grab, followed them. The men's heads were shaven while those of the women were veiled by a linen scarf. They held chiming sistra of bronze, silver, or gold. After them came six priests in long, white linen robes, holding various golden vessels sacred to the goddess: a golden boat-shaped lantern (*aureum cymbium*) giving off bright light, a high altar marking the help of the goddess, a palm branch, a winged staff of Mercury, an outstreched palm of a left hand—an emblem of justice, and a woman's breast-shaped rounded vessel used for pouring milk libation, a winnowing-

---

too, was not accompanied by games. See Salzman 1991: 125, Table 5. The testimony of Eusebius brings to mind that in Caesarea the *Iunonalia* was celebrated together with the *Isidis Navigium*, jointly forming a prolonged festival, three days long, and accompanied by games (which elsewhere were not held in these two festivals, commemorating the establishment of the colony).

[60] The Latin text with a French translation on opposite pages, are given in Apulée, *Les Metamorphoses*, 3 ed. Robertson, tr. Vallette 1965: 138–68. For an English translation, see Apuleius, *The Isis-Book*, tr. Griffiths 1975: 70–109 (text), 111–354 (commentry). The text that concerns us is given in chapters 8–17 of Book XI (145–54 in the French edition; 78–91 in the English). It is also discussed in the introduction to Griffith's edition, 1975: 31–47.

basket made of laurel twigs, and an amphora. Another priest carried
a covered box (*cista mistica*, perhaps holding the sacred serpent of
Horos/Harpocrates). Others were carrying effigies of the deities. The
high priest (*summus sacerdos/sacerdos maximus*) held in his hands a
systrum, and a crown of roses (that was given to Lucius—the hero of
this tale—to eat, thus bringing about his metamorphosis from an ass
back to human form).

When the procession reached the beach, the images and vessels were
put aside in an orderly manner, and all turned their attention to a new
ship that had been decorated in advance. It had a tall mast made of a
pine trunk, and a linen sail on which were written prayers, in hiero-
glyphic script, for a fortunate sailing. Milk and honey were poured on
the waves, and the ship was loaded with baskets of spices and similar
offerings. After a rite of purification with a bright torch, an egg, and
sulphur, the high priest publicly named the ship and dedicated it to
Isis. The anchor was lifted, the ropes were released, and a wind drove
the ship toward the horizon.

When the ship had disappeared from sight, all returned in a procession to the temple, in the same order and each bearing the images
and the vessel he had carried before. The high priest, the bearers of the
divine images, and the initiates were received into the chamber of the
goddess (*cubiculum deae*), and there they set down in orderly fashion
the breathing effigies (*simulacra spirantia*). The Lector (*grammatea*,
from Gr. γραμματεύς), standing near the entrance, summoned a gathering of the *pastophoroi*—thus was called the sacred collegium (*sacro-
sancti collegii*). From a high pedestal he recited from a book prayers
for the prosperity and welfare of the emperor, the senate, the equestrian class, the whole Roman people, as well as for the peaceful voyage
of all the ships and the sailors navigating the seas under Roman rule.
This was a public declaration of loyalty (*votum publicum*), read from
a written text. The ceremony was concluded by a proclamation, in
Greek, of the Launching of the Ships (Πλοιαφεσία) with the applause
of the people. Then, carrying branches, greenery, and garlands, they
kissed the feet of the silver-wrought statue of the goddess that stood
at top of the staircase, and departed to their homes.

Was a similar ceremony conducted in Caesarea? In the procession
going down to the sea one of the priests was carrying a symbol of the
goddess—a boat-shaped oil lamp, known as *cymbium*, representing
the boat of Isis and Osiris. Such oil lamps are quite common archaeo-

logical finds.[61] Two fragments of such a lamp were also found in our excavations in Caesarea.[62] Its elongated base bears the Greek inscription ΕΥΠ(Λ)ΟΙΑ—the epithet of Isis as a guarantor of a good and safe sea-voyage.[63] This seems to indicate that a sailing feast was indeed celebrated in Caesarea—a maritime city. A safe voyage was crucial for its economic prosperity.

In Caesarea, too, there was a temple of Tyche-Isis. This is attested not only by the city coins; the marble statue of the Tyche of Caesarea seemingly stood in that temple. The architectural complex where the statue was found, extending over two terraces—a lower antecourt surrounded by columns, and an upper compound, where the temple proper was presumably standing—seems to have been this temple. A slanting ramp connected between the two levels.[64]

Isis the Lady of the Seas (*Pelagia*), or the guarantor of a safe sailing (*Euploia*), is sometimes depicted as holding a ship's rudder (like in a Pompeian fresco), resembling the rendition of the Tyche on the coins of Agrippa I. Seemingly, such was the early image of Tyche Agathe/Isis in Straton's Tower since its foundation under the Ptolemies. The iconographic reform in the image of the city-goddess under Nero by Vespasian as *legatus Augusti* (in 68 CE) described above, was in accord

---

[61] On boat-shaped oil lamps associated with this festival of Isis, see Merkelbach 1963: 40; Apuleius, *The Isis-Book*, ed. Griffiths 1975: 195–96. A boat-shaped oil lamp from the British Museum is mentioned there, found in the sea opposite Poteoli bearing a Greek inscription εὔπλοια. Isis and Serapis are also depicted on this lamp. Boat-shaped lamps of bronze and clay were also found in Pompeii and elsewhere. See the following note.

[62] Sussman 2008: 255 (oil lamp no. 229). The Caesarea lamp was found with pot sherds dated to the third and fourth centuries CE, and various coins—the earliest of them Herodian, the latest dating from 222–35 CE. Fragments of elongated votive terra-cotta altars, perhaps representing the altar carried in the procession, were also found. See Patrich 2008: 315, 321, 329–30, objects nos. 316–20.

Such lamps were also found in Athens; see Böttger 2002: 209–10, nos. 2683–2712, Pl. 50–51. Lamp no. 2711 there has the beginning of an inscription: EYPL. It is dated to 337–50 CE, almost contemporary with the Caesarea Louvre Cup, the Filocalus Calendar, and not much later than Eusebius' testimony. See also Picard 1962: 228–30; Bruneau, 1965: nos. 4535–50 (type XV.4: lampes en forme de navires).

[63] Such was the epithet of Isis in Gaza (*Pap. Oxyrhynch.* Part XI, line 98). It is also attested in an inscription from Delos of 106/5 BCE. Such was also the epithet of Aphrodite in the Greek colonies of Ischia and Neapolis, and of Aphrodite of Knidos. These facts facilitated the distribution of the Isis cult as the Lady of the Sea in the Mediterranean basin; see Bruneau 1961; 1963; Miranda 1989. See also Flusser 1975.

[64] See Patrich 2007: 109. On the archaeological context of this finding, see Simon and Smith 1971.

with the spirit and events of the time—the Jewish revolt and its suppression—and also was an expression of loyalty to the Romans. Since
then, Tyche was depicted as a warring Amazon and *Dea Romae*. But
it seems that the substance and date of the yearly rite did not change.
A declaration of loyalty to the emperor and to the Roman Empire
was an integral part of the navigation feast conducted in the temple
of Isis/Tyche. Such was the case in the days of Marcus Aurelius, as
described by Apuleius, and it is reasonable to assume that such was
also the character of the ceremony in the time of Vespasian. The new
iconographic type adopted for the goddess in Caesarea expressed fidelity to the militant and victorious Rome. It was a clever measure on
the part of the Roman government and of the municipal authorities
to enlist a declaration of loyalty to the emperor, the members of the
Senate, the equestrian class, and the Roman people in the framework
of this religious feast, and to proclaim Caesarea a Roman colony on
that occasion. Thus, the ancient patroness of the ancient maritime
city was also acknowledged as the guardian spirit of the colony. In
this manner, continuity and a connection were established with an
ancient civic rite of paramount significance in the life of a maritime
city. By linking the date of proclamation to the great feast of naval
Isis—the feast of the sailing renewal—it was assured that each year it
would remain an impressive ceremony, that at the same time would
express loyalty to Rome due to the participation of the governor, who
played a prominent role in the celebration, as is depicted in the libation scene on the Cup.[65] The scene depicts a rite of libation during the
yearly celebration associated with the colony, not with the sailing feast,
such as the launching of a new ship in a calm sea, or a mass procession. When it became an official municipal ceremony, Actian games
resembling those established by Herod in the inauguration celebration
of Caesarea were added. But whereas the games instituted by Herod
had lasted for fifteen days[66] and were held every four years, the sacred

---

[65] In Apuleius, *Metamorphosis* XI.8–17, the high priest of Isis, carrying a wreath
of roses and a tanburine in his right, led the procession down to the sea, and the one
who delivered the discourse of blessing in the temple is the *grammatea*/γραμματεύς.
On the festival of Isis as an expression of loyalty to the emperor also under Christian
emperors, see Alföldi 1937.

[66] According to the Latin version of *Ant.* XVI.140, preserved in a much older manuscript than the Greek version with which we are familiar, they lasted for fifteen days:
"...et per dies quindecim spectacula vel delicias ministravit." For a detailed discussion
of these games, and their connection to the emperor's cult and to Herod's policy, see

games in honor of Tyche/Isis on the occasion of the proclamation of the Roman colony lasted for only three days, but were held every year between March 5 and 7.[67]

The Date of Caesarea's Proclamation as a Roman Colony

Let us now return to the date Caesarea was proclaimed a Roman colony. As was mentioned above, the scene on the Cup indicates that Tyche, the city goddess, was also acknowledged as the guardian spirit of the new colony. This association began when the city was first proclaimed a colony, and it is reasonable to assume that this took place when the celebrations had begun, on March 5. But in which year did this event take place? As noted earlier, the consensus of opinion held by many scholars is that it occurred early during Vespasian's reign, but they do not specify the year. Vespasian was proclaimed emperor by his Alexandrian troops on July 1 69 CE, and on July 3 in Caesarea.[68] The continuation of the siege on Jerusalem was entrusted to his son Titus, after which Vespasian went to Egypt. In Rome he was acknowledged as emperor by the Senate only at the end of December 69, after Vitellius was killed. On January 1, 70 Vespasian and Titus began their consulship, but both were not at Rome at that time, Vespasian still being in Egypt. Since in March 69 Vespasian was not yet an emperor, the earliest possible date would be March 5, 70.[69] But at that time the battle in Judaea was not yet resolved, and the Roman army was still preoccupied with it. The Temple was set on fire on August 29 or 30, 70 CE,[70] and the upper city was conquered about one month later. On October 24, 70, Titus celebrated the eighteenth birthday of his brother Domitian

---

Lämmer 1974: 136–37, where he brings the Latin translation in full. The festival began on September 23, Augustus' birthday; see Schwartz 1992: 175.

[67] Will 1983: 7 was of the opinion that the sacred games mentioned on the Cup were the periodical games instituted by Herod in honor of Augustus, and that such were also the games in the annual festival of Tyche of March 7–9, mentioned by Eusebius. The Actian games commemorate Augustus' victory at Actium, and hence were held in September, not in March. Will did not pay attention to the fact that the date in March coincides with the *Isidis Navigium*. Wenning 1986: 128 also conceived the annual games mentioned by Eusebius as the Actian games instituted by Herod, and so did Kokkinos 1998: 379. But this is a mistake.

[68] See also note 30 above.

[69] Therefore Wenning's 1986 proposal, that Caesarea became a Roman colony in 69 should be rejected. At that time Jerusalem was not yet conquered.

[70] *War* VI.249–53.

in the stadium at Caesarea. More than 2,500 captives were thrown as prey to wild beasts, forced to fight each other, or were burnt alive.[71] Hence, March 5, 71, about five months after the conquest of Jerusalem and the conclusion of large-scale military action, seems to be the earliest plausible date for the proclamation of Caesarea as a Roman colony. But in the military diploma from Pompeii, noted above, dated April 5, 71, Caesarea Stratonis is mentioned as the native land (*patria*) of one of the witnesses, without the addition "Colonia."[72] Hence, Ringel, as well as Eck and Cotton, concluded that at that time Caesarea had not yet been proclaimed a colony.[73] If such is indeed the case, then the event took place only on March 5, 72 CE. In that year Flavia Neapolis was founded as a new city, on the site of Ma'abrata.[74] A further delay in the proclamation of Caesarea as a Roman colony would be doubtful,[75] since it constituted a central stronghold for Roman rule in the reviving province. But can the military diploma be taken as decisive evidence against March 5, 71 CE? The soldier, being remote from his home city, could have hardly received news about an event that had occurred a month earlier. In addition, we should note that even later the title "colony" was not always mentioned in the literary and epigraphical sources.[76] Therefore, in my opinion, March 5, 71 CE, not too long after the suppression of the Jewish revolt and the beginning of the recovery of the inflicted province, seems to be a more plausible date for the proclamation of Caesarea as a Roman colony.

---

[71] *War* VII.37–38.

[72] *CIL* XVI, 15.29, and see note 10 above. The witness was a Jewish soldier who apparently had been dispatched to the West in 69 CE, after previously taking part in the suppression of the revolt in Judaea (thus Isaac 1980–81: 50).

[73] See note 32 above.

[74] *War* IV.449; Plinius, *Historia Naturalis*; 5.14.69; Schalit 1937: 25, 129, note 125; Stein 1990.

[75] Pliny's *Historia Naturalis*, where Caesarea is mentioned as a colony, was published in 77; clearly the proclamation took place earlier.

[76] Thus, in a list of triumphs of a pankratist from Aphrodisias, dated 165 CE (Moretti 1953: no. 72), Caesarea Stratonis is mentioned without its title as a colony. There are more examples, later ones, including Origen, and Eusebius—in the early 4th century, where that status is not mentioned. See Millar 1990: 8, 27.

CHAPTER FOUR

URBAN SPACE IN CAESAREA MARITIMA IN THE LATE ANTIQUITY

Caesarea Maritima was founded by Herod, king of Judaea, in 22–10/9 BCE on the site of a deserted Hellenistic coastal town called Straton's Tower. According to Josephus Flavius (*War* 1.408–15; *Ant.* 15.331–41), Herod founded there an elaborate harbor called Sebastos, and a city with streets laid in a grid pattern. The city, like the harbor, was named after emperor Caesar Augustus, Herod's patron in Rome. Herod erected in the city a temple which he dedicated to Rome and Augustus, a theater and an amphitheater, a royal palace, market places, dwellings, and an underground sewer system.

Caesarea served as the main harbor and capital city of Herod's kingdom, and of the later Roman province of *Iudaea/Syria Palaestina*, the seat of the Roman governors and of the financial procurators of the province. Vespasian made Caesarea a Roman colony, and Alexander Severus raised it to the rank of metropolis. In the Byzantine period[1] it was the capital of *Palaestina Prima*, and a Metropolitan See. During this period urban space expanded about three times relative to the Herodian period, reflecting a large increase in population (Fig. 29). It was a prosperous maritime city, of a heterogeneous ethnicity and a cosmopolitan flavor, as is reflected by the archaeological record: the city coins, statuary, and inscriptions, attesting to its pantheon, and the imported ware and numismatic finds, attesting to its international commerce. During the third and fourth centuries it was the seat of a Jewish academy, led by Rabbi Oshayah and Rabbi Abbahu, and of a Christian academy, founded by Origen. (On Caesarea as an intellectual center in Late Antiquity, see Post Script below). The Christian

---

[1] The term *Byzantine* denotes here the period from Constantine's conquest of the East in 324, to the Arab conquest of Palestine in c. 640, as is common in Israeli archaeology. For the rationale behind this terminology pertaining to the Holy Land, see, for example, Tsafrir and Foerster, *DOP* 50: 85, note 1. However, being aware that the period from Diocletian to the mid-sixth or early seventh century is considered by many historians as *Late Antiquity*, the terms *Byzantine period* or *Late Antiquity* will be used here indifferently.

community suffered martyrdom in the persecutions under Decius, Valerian, and Diocletian. The Samaritans were another vital component in the Caesarean society, representing the lucrative peasantry of the fertile agricultural hinterland of the city—the Sharon plain and the hilly country of Samaria.

The division of the province of *Syria Palaestina* into smaller provinces during the fourth or early fifth centuries (*T.A.Q.* 409 CE), and the emergence of Scythopolis as a capital of *Palaestina Secunda*, resulted in a decline in the administrative status of the city within the Empire, and in the economic prosperity associated with it. Similarly, in the mid-fifth century the ecclesiastical status of the city decreased, when the Metropolitan of Caesarea became subordinate to the Patriarch of Jerusalem. The demise of the harbor, and three Samaritan revolts in the years 484, 529–30, and 555, were other reasons of gradual deterioration, yet it was a thriving city throughout Late Antiquity.

The Arab conquest in 640 or 641 brought a sharp decline of urban life, a process that had already started following the Persian conquest of 614. Islamic and Crusader Qaisariye was a small town of marginal importance, located around its decaying harbor.[2]

LATE ANTIQUE/BYZANTINE CAESAREA[3]

The excavations, since the 1950s to the present, shed light mainly on the SW Zone, the temple platform, and the harbor. But good information, though segmented, was accumulated in other sectors as well. In most of the excavated areas the Late Antique/Byzantine stratum was exposed in its entirety. Our information on this period in the history of the city is therefore by far better than on any of the earlier periods.

The local *kurkar* stone continued to be the major building material, yet, public *kurkar* structures of the Herodian age were gradually replaced in the Roman period by marble structures. This is evident in the *skenefrons* of the theater, as well as in the main temple. Marble was applied for column shafts, capitals (Fig. 30) and bases, entablature,

---

[2] For historical studies see Abel 1952, Vol. l: 369–70, 470, 478; Vol. II: 182–84, 250–53, 404–405; Ringel 1975; Levine 1975a; Fritch 1975; Lifshitz 1977: 490–518; Schürer 1979, Vol. II: 34–35, 115–18; Holum *et al.* 1988. For a comprehensive references to the literary sources and scholarly studies see Tsafrir, Di Segni and Green 1994: 94–96.

[3] Since so far only preliminary reports on the large scale 1992–98 excavations have appeared, and the huge amount of new data is still being processed, this synthesis should be considered as preliminary.

statuary, pavement, and wall revetment. Isotope analysis of Corinthian marble capitals had indicated that major locations of marble import were Proconnesos and Afyon/Aphrodisias.[4] Marble, reused as well as imported, continued to be applied in Late Antiquity as well, as is evident in the octagonal church, but in some cases marble floor-plates were replaced by mosaic floors, and in some rare cases marble columns were whitewashed. The intensive burning, later, under the Islamic regime, of marble architectural members in lime kilns, in order to produce slake lime, encountered in Caesarea as well as in so many ancient Roman cities, had masked the extent to which the Roman and Late Antique city was clad in marble, yet there is enough evidence for this. *Opus sectile* floors of a rich pallet of colorful stones, and of intricate patterns—mostly geometric and floral, but depicting dolphins and crosses as well, became popular in the sixth century, but mosaic floors were the most prevalent, both in the private as well as in the public domain.[5] Frescos depicting Christian saints (Fig. 31) and crosses were applied even in structures of mundane function.[6]

The Herodian, orthogonal city-plan (Fig. 8) was maintained through-out antiquity with only minor modifications, expressed in narrowing the Roman streets, elevating the street level in accordance with the raised sills of the adjoining buildings, and replacing thick limestone pavers by thinner pavers of the local *kurkar*. The latest repavement of cardo W1 took place in the mid-sixth century, and on the same occa-sion a comprehensive renovation of the sewer system and a replacement of lead water pipes by terracotta pipes took place.[7] Roman trabeated colonnades gave way to arcades supported by square pilasters.

The Late Antique/Byzantine city (Fig. 29) extended beyond the Herodian wall, reflecting a great increase of population, but it seems that the settlement of this zone had started already in the second and third centuries, following the construction of the eastern hippodrome and the amphitheater. But since no excavations were carried out in this zone, other than those of the hippodrome, we have no informa-tion about the exact process of inhabitation of this zone during the second to the fourth century. However, the addition of the lower level aqueduct in c. 385 CE may indicate that a significant increase of popu-lation was reached already before the end of the fourth century, and it

---

[4] Fisher *et al.* 1992.
[5] Spiro 1992.
[6] Avner 1999; Patrich 1996: 169–71, figs. 22–24; Horton 1996: 180, fig. 2.
[7] Patrich *et al.* 1999: 75.

seems that the settlement of this zone was dense enough, by the time the wall was erected in the fifth century, to dictate its line. This wall confronted the three Samaritan revolts mentioned above, and the Arab siege that lasted seven years (633/34–640/41 CE). In this siege some of the urban statuary was piled up in the southern city gate to block it against the penetration of the Arab troops.[8] And indeed, monumental Roman statuary was reused in the urban sphere of the Byzantine city to decorate its streets, plazas, and *nymphaea*.[9]

The estimated population at its apogee, when it occupied an area of c. 111.5 hectares, varies between c. 35,000 and 100,000.[10] As for the ethnic composition, like everywhere throughout the east, after the crisis of the third century and the reforms of Diocletian and Constantine, the Latinate element in the provincial and municipal administration gave way to Greek-speaking *officiales*. The Late Antique inscriptions are all in Greek or in the local Semitic scripts and languages (Aramaic, Hebrew, and Samaritan).[11] The Greek, that returned to be the language of administration in the entire east, was spoken by all three religious groups: Christians, Jews, and Samaritans.

The Jewish quarter is considered to be in the northern part of the city, at the site of ancient Straton Tower, around the third-century synagogue. The synagogue, which yielded Jewish inscriptions in Hebrew

---

[8] Peleg Reich 1992. Later excavations had indicated that this was a gate in the *scaenefrons* of a theater, not of a city wall!

[9] Yevin 1955; 1957; Avi Yonah 1970; Porath 1998: 47, fig. 11; Gersht 1999. The view that ancient temple statuary has artistic value, deprived of its previous pagan connotation, was expressed by the early-fifth-century Christian poet Prudentius (*Contra Symmachum*, 1.499–505). On this, and in general on Late Antique legislative attitude toward urban buildings of the past, see Alchermes 1994: 167–178; Saradi-Mendelovici 1990.

[10] The lower figure can be gleaned from Broshi 1980: 5, if we correct the figure of the city area to 124.5 hectares instead of 95 hectares given by Broshi. A population of 100,000 is given by Avi Yonah 1964: 121 (Hebrew) and Levine 1975b: 9 and note 37, who brings references to even higher, purely speculative estimates of 200,000 inhabitants. Holum *et al.* 1988: 174, adhere also to the 100,000 figure, but more recently (1998a: 163–4, and note 20), he speaks of a population of only 25,000 people within the Byzantine fortification wall. Broshi discusses various methods for calculating population density and size. According to al-Balādhuri (*Futuh al-buldān* 141–42, ed. Hitti 1916: 217–18), in his account of the Arab conquest of the city, the entire number of soldiers was 700,000 [sic!, clearly a mistake], the Jews numbered 20,000, the Samaritans 30,000, and the city was guarded every night by 100,000 men stationed on its wall.

[11] Hamburger 1959; Ben Zvi 1961: 139–42. On the use of the old Hebrew script by the Samaritans, see *TB, Sanhedrin* 21b; Jerome, *Comm. In Ezech.* 3.9.4., *CCSL* 75, 106. Crown 1989: 59, the Samaritans at Caesarea comprised about one third of the population.

and Greek, and Corinthian capitals with the menorah symbol, was destroyed in the mid-fourth century, and rebuilt in the mid-fifth. It was destroyed in a fire. After the death of R. Abbahu—the head of the local Jewish academy—in 309, there was no Jewish leader of his magnitude. Beryllos, archisynagogue and *phrontistes* (treasurer or administrator), who made a mosaic floor from his own funds, is mentioned in a Greek inscription from the synagogue.[12] The predominance of Greek inscriptions, their content, as well as references in the rabbinic sources, attest to the high degree of Hellenization and acculturation of the local community, like in other urban Jewish congregations, both in Palestine and in the Jewish diaspora.[13] In spite of the fact that in the literary sources there is almost no reference to the Jews of Caesarea in the Byzantine period, the Jewish community continued to form a significant component of the local population, though its status declined relative to that held in the third and early fourth century.[14] The general Jewish revolt against Gallus in 351–52, might have been a decisive factor in this decline. A second riot of the Jews of Palestine, especially those of Caesarea, in which some Christians were killed, took place in c. 439, during the reign of Theodosius II and Pulcheria. The Jews of Caesarea joined ranks with the Samaritans in the revolt of 555, burning Christian churches and slaughtering the provincial governor in his *praetorium*; one of them assisted the Arab troops to sneak into the besieged city through a secret water tunnel in 640/41.[15]

As for the Samaritans, a large quantity of "Samaritan" oil lamps retrieved from the excavated area in the SW zone bears evidence of their presence and activity in this part of the city. According to a rabbinic source, the staff (*taxis*) of the Byzantine governor of the province in the city (as opposed to that of the *dux*) was composed mainly of Samaritans. There were also separate Samaritan units in the Roman

---

[12] Roth-Gerson 1987: nos. 25–29 (Hebrew), 115, inscr. 27. Capitals and architectural fragments with Jewish symbols are presented there in pp. 122–24. A marble column with the Hebrew inscription "*shalom*" (peace) was found by Levine and Netzer (1986: 45, Ill. 64) in their principal area of excavation, to the NW of the inner harbor. A fragment of a stone slab decorated with a menorah was found to the S of the temple platform (Area Z). See Raban 1998b: 32, fig. 4. On the synagogue see also note 62 below.

[13] Levine 1996.

[14] On the population size at the end of the period, see above, note 10.

[15] John Malalas, *Chronographia*, XV, ed. Dindorf 1831: 487–88; Theophanes, *Chronographia*, A. M. 6048, ed. de Boor 1883, 1: 230; Al-Balādhuri, above, note 10. See also below, Chapter Six.

army.[16] Their involvement in the provincial administration might be alluded to by two Greek mosaic inscriptions found in Area NN in the SW zone. One (Fig. 136), of the fifth century, reads: "May the one and only God (*heis theos monos*), help Eusebius the accountant (*noumerarios*)." On the one hand, there is no cross at the beginning of the inscription, as was common in Christian epigraphy, and on the other hand, the opening formula was very common among the Samaritans.[17] The second inscription, of the sixth century, reads: "May the peace of the Christians persist,"[18] a declaration that may allude that its author was a non-Christian, perhaps a Samaritan, or a nominal Christian.[19] In this case the inscription may be conceived as a declaration of loyalty related perhaps to one of the Samaritan revolts of the sixth century. A notable Samaritan of Palestine who accepted nominal Christianity was Faustinus, of an old Samaritan family. Under Justinian he assumed a senator rank of *clarissimus* and became governor (*consularis*) of his province. Later he became *epitropos* of the imperial domains in Palestine and Phoenicia.[20] Inscriptions from Scythopolis and literary sources bring some interesting details about another prominent Samaritan family of that city. Silvanus and his brother, Sallustius, lawyers (*scholastici*), acted as patrons of the city and obtained grants from emperor Anastasius for the erection of public buildings in Scythopolis (year 515/16). Silvanus held consular rank, and maintained close connections with the emperor. His son, Arsenius, accepted the Christian faith, and had

---

[16] *TY, Avodah Zarah* 1.2–39c; Lieberman 1939–44: 405–406. The period alluded to in this text is the time of the Diocletianic persecutions. Samaritan troops suppressed the uprising of the Monophysite monks against Juvenal at the wake of the Council of Chalcedon (Ps. Zacharia Rhetor, *Historia Ecclesiastica*, 3.5, trans. Brooks, *CSCO*, series 3, vol. 5, 109). According to Malalas (*Chron.* XV.8, ed. Dindorf 1831: 382–83), following the Samaritan revolt of 484, Zeno issued an edict that no Samaritans be admitted into the army. But the exclusion of the Samaritans from the army (and the civil service), was first issued by Honorius in 404 (*Cod. Theod.* 16.8.12), and repeated by Theodosius II in his *Novella* 3 of 438 or 439. A re-enactment by Zeno is not mentioned neither in *Cod. Just.* 1.5.18, issued between 527 and 531, where Justinian repeated it, nor in his *Novellae.* See Di Segni 1998: 65.

[17] Three *heis theos* inscriptions were found at Caesarea (Lehmann and Holum 2000, inscriptions nos. 138–40), suggesting the existence of Samaritan synagogues in the city. As was noted by Di Segni 1990: 346; *eadem.* 1994: 94–115, although this formula is known in Jewish and Christian circles, in Palestine most inscriptions of this kind come from a Samaritan milieu.

[18] For a drawing and a photo of the inscriptions, see Patrich *et al.* 1999: 96–97, figs. 31, 32.

[19] As a result of the anti-Samaritan legislation many of them assumed nominal Christianity. See Procopius, *Anecdota* XI, 15. 24–30.

[20] Procopius, *Anecdota* XXVII. 8–10.

a successful career at the imperial court of Justinian and Theodora, yet he maintained close relations with his family in Scythopolis. He had procured an imperial donation for rebuilding the walls of Scythopolis.[21] Similar Samaritan families, involved in the municipal and provincial affairs, might have existed also in Caesarea. A basilical structure to the south of the deserted Herodian hippodrome might have been a Samaritan synagogue, rather than a Christian church.

The Christians constituted the majority of the population. Their major church in the sixth century was the octagonal church on the site of the former Roman temple—the most prominent position in Caesarea's landscape, overlooking the entire city and the harbor. The bishop, assisted by the clergy, was most influential in municipal affairs, second only to the governor. Being renowned since the days of Origen in the third century and Eusebius, in the fourth, as a center of learning and Christian theology (see Post Script below), Caesarea preserved its prestige down to the sixth century as a school of theology, rhetoric, and law.[22] Procopius of Caesarea, the famous historian at the courts of Belisarius and Justinian, was its most renowned author (although his writing was done remote from his city of origin). Another prominent author was John the Grammarian, an important Neochalcedonian theologian in the late fifth and early sixth century, against whom the Monophysite leader Severus of Antioch composed in 520 a polemical treatise.[23] An echo of the Christological controversy of the sixth century can be heard in a Greek mosaic inscription found at the site of the inner harbor (Area I1), reading: "May the Lord sustain the Orthodoxy forever."[24]

THE ARCHAEOLOGICAL RESEARCH

Archaeological excavations started in the early fifties,[25] and included many expeditions, both Israeli and foreign, working in many locations:

---

[21] Tsafrir and Foerster 1997: 124–26. For the Samaritans at Caesarea see Holum 1983.

[22] Schemmel 1925; Downey 1958: 301–302.

[23] John of Caesarea, *Opera quae supersunt*, ed. Richard 1977; *idem, Capitula XVII contra Monophysita, ibid.*, 1977: 59–66. Severus of Antioch, *Liber contra impium grammaticum* (ed. J. Lebon), *Corpus Scriptorum Cristianorum Orientalium, Scriptores Syri IV, 4, 5, 6*, Paris—Louvain 1928, 1929, 1933.

[24] Raban 1998a: 63–4, fig. 35.

[25] For the history of research, and summary of archaeological finds, excluding the 1992–98 large-scale excavations, see Levine 1975b; Holum and Raban 1993; Holum

Yeivin, Avi Yonah and Negev,[26] and the Italian Mission headed by
Frova excavated there during the fifties and early sixties.[27] The Joint
Expedition to Caesarea Maritima (JECM)—a consortium of American colleges and universities headed by Bull,[28] working at the site in
the seventies and early eighties, was followed since the late eighties to
the present by the Combined Caesarea Excavations (CCE) headed by
Holum, in cooperation with Raban from the University of Haifa.[29] The
Hebrew University excavations in the seventies, headed by Netzer and
Levine,[30] were followed by the University of Pennsylvania excavations,
led by Burrell and Gleason.[31] The large-scale excavations in the SW
zone of the city during 1992–98, working year round in the framework of the Caesarea Tourist Development Project by two expeditions:
that of the Israel Antiquities Authority (IAA), directed by Porath, and
that of the University of Haifa, directed by Raban and myself, had
augmented tremendously the previous archaeological record.[32] This
SW zone, c. 80m wide and 800m long, extending along the sea from
the harbor and the temple platform, in the North, to the Roman theater in the South (inclusively), is today almost entirely exposed to its
Byzantine and Roman layers. Our information about the northern and
eastern sectors of the city is segmented and fragmentary, yet informa-
tive and significant.

Underwater work, which started in 1960 by Link,[33] was followed
in the eighties by the Caesarea Ancient Harbors Excavation Project
(CAHEP),[34] moderated by Raban of the Center for Maritime Studies of
the University of Haifa, and since the late eighties by the underwater

---

1997; Patrich 1997c; Holum and Raban 1996: xxvii–xliv. For the results of the more
recent excavations, see Holum 2008; Patrich 2008b; Porath 2008; Raban 2008; with
more bibliographical references.

[26] Yevin 1955; 1957; Avi Yonah 1956; *idem* and Negev 1963. Negev 1963a; 1963b;
1967; 1975.

[27] Frova, *et al.* 1965, and Frova 1959; 1961–62.

[28] Bull *et al.* 1985.

[29] Holum *et al.* 1992: 79–193; Raban *et al.* 1993; 1999; Raban 1996, and the Field
Reports in Holum, Raban and Patrich 1999.

[30] Levine and Netzer 1986.

[31] Burrell, Gleason, and Netzer 1993; Burrell and Gleason 1995; Netzer 1996; Gleason 1996; Burrell 1996; Gleason *et al.*, 1998.

[32] Porath, Patrich and Raban 1998; Porath 1994; 1995; 1996a; 1996b; 1998; Patrich
1996; 2000a; 2001b. See also Patrich *et al.* 1999, and Raban *et al.* 1999.

[33] Fritsch and Ben-Dor 1961. See also: Hohlfelder 1989; 1992.

[34] Raban *et al.* 1989; Oleson 1994.

team of the CCE.[35] This research supplied a wealth of information on the construction of the harbor, its later history, and its gradual demise.

THE HARBOR

The harbor was a huge enterprise, compared by Josephus (*War* 1.410; *Ant.* 15.332) to Piraeus, with many quays, landing places, and secondary anchorage. It was constructed of huge stones, including *pozzolana*—volcanic ashes imported from Italy, used by Romans for making hydraulic cement applied in harbor architecture, and other advanced Roman harbor technology.[36] The outer mole and breakwater, on the S and W, penetrated c. 400m into the sea, enclosing the outer and intermediate basins; the inner basin was rock-cut in land, incorporating the closed harbor (*limen kleistos*) of Hellenistic Straton's Tower. Work of recent years indicated that the inner harbor extended over a much vaster area than previously assumed. Its E pier extended to the S beyond the Crusader wall, and it encompassed an area 250m long (NS) by 150m broad (EW). The entrance to the outer harbor, flanked by three colossal statues on either side, was from N, at the W end of the N mole. Several inscribed lead ingots found in 1993 over the NW end of the mole[37] suggest that this section of the pier was submerged already at the end of the first century CE due to tectonic slumping, causing a rapid silting of parts of the inner harbor, that became a lagoon.[38] The intermediate and outer harbors underwent a large scale reconstruction by Anastasius in the late fifth–early sixth century.[39] By that time the inner harbor was already silted, giving new ground for the construction of new buildings, and later, under Arab dominion, of a new neighborhood of dwellings.

Though no lighthouse is mentioned in Josephus' narrative, we may assume its existence. However, its exact location is a matter of dispute.[40]

---

[35] Raban 1996; Raban *et al.* 1992; 1993; 1999.
[36] Raban 1992c; Oleson and Branton 1992; Brandon 1996; Vann 1983b.
[37] Raban 1999.
[38] Raban 1996; Yule *et al.* 1999; Toueg 1998.
[39] Procopius of Gaza, *Panagyr. Anast.* 19, *PG* 87: 2817.
[40] Vann 1991; Hohlfelder 1996: 85; Alföldi 1999.

WALLS AND GATES

Two semi-circular city walls are still recognizable in aerial photographs (Fig. 5), beyond the rectilinear shorter line of the Arab-Crusader wall. The inner line is Herodian and the outer—Byzantine. The Herodian wall (Fig. 8) had a N gate flanked by two circular towers. A third, rectilinear tower, was exposed nearby.[41] At the S part of the Herodian city wall, to the S of the Roman theater, another circular tower was exposed in the excavation of recent years, attached to the external face of the wall. Later during the Roman period the round tower got a rectilinear encasement. The fortification line was abandoned in the mid-fourth century.

Like other Roman cities, such as Jerusalem, Gerasa, Scythopolis, or Neapolis, the Roman and Early Byzantine city, that expanded beyond the Herodian wall, had no outer wall for more than three centuries. These extra-mural quarters comprised also an amphitheater and a hippodrome. So far there is not enough data to reconstruct in detail the history of this extra-mural settlement. It is also not clear to what extent the Herodian wall retained its defensive features during this period. But while Roman Jerusalem and Gerasa were encircled by walls already in c. 300 CE, Caesarea got its wall more than a century later—only in the fifth century. The southern quarter of Jerusalem likewise got a wall, by Eudocia, in the first half of the fifth century. The date of construction of the wall of Scythopolis is as yet unknown; what is known is that it was renovated in the first quarter of the sixth century.[42]

Segments of the Byzantine wall of Caesarea, in the N, E, and S, were exposed and explored by three different expeditions.[43] It encompassed an area of 111.5 hectares (1500 x 830m maximal dimensions)—two to

---

[41] Finocchi 1965; A construction date within the first century BCE was concluded by Blakely 1984, who excavated near its NE tower. See also *idem* 1992. The Herodian date suggested by the Italians was questioned by Levine (1975b: 10–12), Negev, and disputed by Raban 1987. Excavating in the northernmost vault of the Temple Platform, and noticing that the stones of its lower courses have similar margin drafts, he claimed that the remains of the towers and wall in the north belong to the Hellenistic town of Straton's Tower. See also Raban 1992a. Hillard 1992 favors a Gabinian date. The more recent excavations in the vaults of the Temple Platform had refuted Raban's claim. The present prevalent opinion is that the fortification remains at the north are Herodian. On the abandonment of this fortification line, see Blakely, *op. cit.* The city gates are mentioned in the early fourth century by Eusebius. See Chapter Twelve below.

[42] Tsafrir and Foerster 1997: 102.

[43] Frova 1959; 1961–62; Humphrey 1975; Lehmann 1994.

three times larger than before (Fig. 29). The road system emerging from the city[44] suggests the existence of four gates. The north Byzantine gate was eroded by the sea, the southern was a triple entrance monumental gate.[45] A Greek inscription mentioning a *bourgos* was uncovered near the conjectural location of the E gate.[46] A Roman monumental arch with a Greek inscription referring to the city as metropolis, a rank granted to the city by Alexander Severus, was located nearby,[47] indicating that like in the case of Gerasa, Jerusalem, Scythopolis, Gadara, (and Athens), the outskirts of the city were indicated by a monumental arch long before a city wall was actually constructed.

In the sixth century an inner fortress or citadel (*kastron*) with semicircular towers was constructed around the theater that went out of use already by the fourth century.[48] Byzantine cities from the sixth century onwards were usually equipped with citadels. Zenobia with its *citadel*, on the Euphrates, fortified by Justinian, is a good example.[49]

THE STREET SYSTEM AND URBAN PLAN

Archaeology confirmed Josephus' account (*Ant.* 15.340; *War* 1.408, 413) that Herod laid a magnificent city plan, with equal distance between its streets (Fig. 8), and a sophisticated sewage system underneath. The JECM, as well as the recent excavations in the SW zone, uncovered at least three successive street levels, adhering to the same urban plan.[50] In this regard Caesarea is the exception among the cities built by Herod. Jerusalem and Samaria followed an entirely different city plan, with a main thoroughfare leading from the city gate to the main temple. So far there is not enough data to indicate whether the extra-mural quarters, developed in the Roman and Byzantine periods beyond the Herodian city wall, followed throughout the same grid pattern recognized within the inner perimeter wall (Fig. 29).[51]

---

[44] Roll 1996.
[45] Peleg and Reich 1992, but see *supra*, note 8.
[46] Schwabe 1950a; Lifshitz 1961: 115–26, inscr. no. 16.
[47] Abel and Barrois 1931.
[48] Frova *et al.* 1965: 57–159, 165–86.
[49] Foss and Winfield 1986: 7–14.
[50] Vann 1983a; Patrich *et al.* 1999: 74–75; Porath 1996a; 1998: 41–42.
[51] Therefore Holum was right in refraining from depicting the grid beyond the Herodian wall in the city plan of year 500 CE. See Raban and Holum 1996, Map 3 (The Byzantine/Late Antique Period), reproduced here as Fig. 29, but see his more recent proposal for the city layout in Holum 2009: 170*, Fig. 1.

Cardo W1, exposed in the SW zone for a length of c. 400m (Fig. 32), was not a colonnaded street. Its width—c. 5m, was slightly reduced during the centuries of its existence due to retaining the walls of the buildings along its course. The line of the *cardo maximus* is marked by the line of the eastern Crusader wall. Several columns are still preserved on the inside of the northern section of this wall, suggesting that it was a colonnaded street. As for the *decumanus maximus*, its western end was exposed in the recent excavations by the IAA team at the northeastern corner of the Temple Platform, its line being parallel to *decumani* S2 and S3 (see map—Fig. 29 and Fig. 33). Its course eastward is suggested by the remains of a *tetrapylon* in the eastern gate of the Crusader wall (Fig. 24). So far, no remains indicate that it was a colonnaded street. But colonnaded streets (*platea* and stoa) in Caesarea are mentioned in rabbinic and Christian sources (*TY, Nazir* VII, 1, 56a; *Tosefta Oholot* XVIII, 13; Eusebius, *Mart. Pal.* IX.12).

The N–S street exposed by the JECM in the NW zone of the city, indicates that the size of the urban *insulae* in this zone—a neighborhood of dwellings (see map—Fig. 29), was different than their size in the SW zone. In Gerasa as well, the dimensions of the dwelling *insulae* in the eastern part of the city were different than those of the *insulae* in the western part of the city, comprising mainly of public structures.

Religious Buildings

Temples

Of the many temples suggested by the deities depicted on the city coins (Tyche, Isis, Serapis, Demeter, Apollo),[52] and inscriptions (Jupiter Dolichenus),[53] only three temples yielded architectural remains. As for the evidence of the statuary of deities (Tyche, Isis and Serapis, Apollo, Aphrodite, Athena, Asklepius and Hygieia, the Ephesian Artemis, Cybele or Nemesis, and the Dioscuri),[54] one should be precautionary not to interpret each statue as an indication for the existence of a temple for that particular deity. Statues were commonly used for decoration alone, though expressing religious piety.

On top of the temple platform, dominating both city and harbor, the foundations and scattered architectural members of Herod's

---

[52] Kadman 1957; Ringel 1975: 151–162.
[53] Lifshitz 1966: 255–56.
[54] Gerst 1984; 1987; 1995; 1996; Frova 1962; Wenning 1986.

temple to Rome and Augustus (*War* 1.415; *Ant.* 15.339) were found.[55]
The podium, 28.6 x 46.4m in dimensions, was constructed on top of
a U-shaped elevated platform, leaving an open esplanade below, to
the W, in a lower terrace, along the E mole of the inner harbor.[56] In
c. 300 twelve vaults were erected on the esplanade, between the arms
of the elevated platform. Their roof established an additional square in
front of the Roman temple. Certain modifications in the facade of the
temple might have occurred on this occasion.

The Imperial cult is also attested by two inscriptions, one, in Latin,
mentioning a *Tiberieum*,[57] and the second, in Greek, a *Hadrianeion*.
The porphyry statue of this emperor, found reused, decorating a Byzantine esplanade, originated perhaps from his temple.[58] A marble head
of Hadrian, of almost life size, was found during the recent excavations in a late seventh-century layer of debris (Fig. 20). Its original
location is unknown.

In the SW zone a Mithraeum was installed in the second or third
century in one of the vaults underneath the audience hall of the *praetorium* of the Roman financial procurator (see below).[59] A *naos* (presumably of this *praetorium*), is mentioned in a Greek papyrus from
Egypt.[60] The shrine (*sacellum*) of the Western hippodrome (Herod's
amphitheatron, see below) was, seemingly, dedicated to Kore, since
a dedicatory inscription to her on a marble foot—one of seven—was
found therein. Snakes—a common attribute of Isis—entwining four
of the ex-voto feet, suggest an assimilation between Kore and Isis.
Kore was the principal deity of the adjacent city of Samaria in Roman
times. A Greek inscription found in the stadium there reads: "One

---

[55] Holum *et al.* 1992: 100–109; Raban *et al.* 1993: 53–60; Raban 1998a: 68–69; For
summery of recent excavations, see Holum 1999. For the reconstruction of the temple
on the evidence of scattered architectural fragments, see Kahn 1996.

[56] See drawing in Porath 1998: 46, fig. 10. The dimensions of the podium are given
in Holum 1999: 21.

[57] The common opinion is that in spite of Tiberius' refraining from encouraging
his veneration as a god, the inscription attests to this cult. Recently G. Alföldi (1999;
2002) had suggested that the reference is to a light tower, a twin of the "Druseion"
tower mentioned by Josephus (*War* 1.413; *Ant.* 15.336), named after Drusus—Tiberius' brother.

[58] The *Hadrianeion* is mentioned in a sixth-century Greek inscription at the site:
Moulton 1919–20; Avi Yonah 1970. On the presumed visit of Hadrian to Caesarea,
and his endowments to the city, see Holum, 1992a.

[59] Bull 1974a; 1978. (At the time when these articles of Bull were written the relation
of this sanctuary to the *praetorium* of the Roman procurators was not yet perceived).

[60] Rea 1977; Eck 1998.

god, the ruler of all, great Kore, the invincible." In Samaria Kore was also assimilated with Isis.[61]

Synagogues

Of the various synagogues that existed in Caesarea, only one was exposed in the N part of the city,[62] the site of Straton's Tower. Another Jewish synagogue was converted by Vespasian to an odeum (Malalas, *Chronographia*, X, 338, ed. Dindorf, 1831, 261; X.46, ed. Thurn 2000, 197). A Jewish house of learning (*bêt midrāšâ*) open onto the agora of Caesarea is mentioned in the Babylonian Talmud, *Hulin* 86d.

Christian Buildings

Several Christian Buildings associated with New Testament events and with the persecutions of martyrs, are mentioned in the Byzantine itineraria: the houses of Philip (Ac 8:40; 21:8) and of Cornelius (Ac 10:1–48), the chamber of the four virgin prophetesses—Philip's daughters, the burial place of Pamphilus and Procopius, and the latter's chapel.[63] More chapels and churches are known from literary sources. In the Acts and Miracles of Saint Anastasius (martyred 627 CE), are mentioned the following churches: St. Euphemia, St. Mary the Younger (perhaps not distinct from the unspecified St. Mary), a chapel of Saint Anastasius the Persian, the "most holy church of Christ," and a building associated with the martyr Cornelius.[64] The church of St. Procopius was set on fire in the Samaritan revolt of year 484.

Of these only two churches (one being dubious) were so far exposed. In c. 525–50 CE, an octagonal church, decorated and revetted in marble, had replaced Herod's temple to Rome and Augustus. Access from the W was by means of a monumental staircase that rose over a broad

---

[61] Flusser 1975. For the ex-voto feet and the dedicatory inscription for Kore, see Gersht 1996: 310–11; Porath 1995a: 23, fig. 10; a photograph of the *Sacellum* is given there on p. 21, fig. 9a, and p. 272, color fig. 9. For a picture of the feet, see also *idem* 1998: 41, fig. 3.

[62] Avi Yonah 1956; 1960 and recently Govaars, Spiro and White 2009. For the Synagogue inscriptions, see Schwabe 1950b; Lifshitz 1967b; Roth-Gerson 1987. See also Levine 1975b: 40–45.

[63] Downey 1975; Krenz 1992; Levine 1975b: 45–46. *Ac* 21:13; Jerome, *Epistulae* 108.8; *PPTS* VI: 32 (a 13th c. anonymous travelogue referring to the chamber of the four virgin prophetesses). Antoninus of Placentia, *Itinerarium* 45, ed. Geyer 1965: 174 (reference to the burial place of Pamphilus and Procopius); Malalas, *Chronographia*, XIV, ed. Dindorf 1831: 93–94; *Chronicon Paschale*, 327, *PG* 92: 840–41 (reference to the chapel of Procopius).

[64] Kaegi 1992.

arch.[65] The W end of this staircase was founded on a platform of huge stones laid inside the partially silted inner harbor, adjoining the edge of the Herodian mole.[66] The E end of the staircase was leaning against the vaults. A second, simpler staircase let access from the south.[67]

The process of Christianization of urban space at Caesarea was slower than assumed.[68] The temple, although ruinous, was replaced by a Christian monument many decades after such a process occurred in Jerusalem (under Constantine), or in Gaza (under Theodosius I and Eudoxia).[69]

A second structure identified as a church was exposed during the recent excavation to the south of the deserted Herodian hippodrome, overlying the NE part of the Roman *praetorium*. It is a basilica, 32 x 17.5m in dimensions, with a 16m-long atrium to its west, with a small cistern in its center.[70] It seems that the *sacellum* of Kore mentioned above was converted in the fourth century into a martyrs chapel (Fig. 34).

PALACES AND *PRAETORIA*

Herod's palace, constructed on a promontory to the south of the harbor, was enlarged and elaborated, becoming the *praetorium* of the

---

[65] Holum *et al.*, 1992: 100–107; Raban *et al.*, 1993: 37–42, 50–51; 53–55. For the date of construction of the octagonal church, see most recently Holum 1999: 26.

[66] Raban 1996: 657–58, and fig. 23, refers to this platform as a "reflecting pool." In my opinion this is an erroneous interpretation. The massive platform was needed to retain the staircase, and leave reasonable open space to its front. A later looting of some of the *kurkar* blocks of this platform gave the wrong impression that the extant remains are those of a basin.

[67] Stanley 1999.

[68] For the intentional preservation of pagan or Jewish precincts as void spaces in Christian town-planning, see Wharton 1995.

[69] See Eusebius, *Life of Constantine* III. cc. xxvi–xl on the erection of the Church of the Holy Sepulcher in Jerusalem, on the order of Constantine, on the site of the temple of Aphrodite; Mark the Deacon, *Vita Porphyrii* (ed. Gregoire and Kugener 1930), about the erection of the Eudoxia church at Gaza on the site of the local temple of Marnas. On the conversion of temples to churches and the Christianization of the urban space in Palestine, see Holum 1996a; Tsafrir 1998.

[70] However, since the Greek inscriptions of this basilical building, with its apse-oriented east, do not commence with a cross, as is common with Christian inscriptions, the interpretation of the architectural remains as a Christian church (Porath 1998: 44, fig. 8) is dubious. The eastern orientation of the apse can also befit a Samaritan synagogue, since Mt. Garizim, to which Samaritan synagogues were oriented, is located to the east of Caesarea.

Roman governors.[71] Late in the first century, a second *praetorium* was constructed in the first urban insula to the south of the harbor, for the use of the financial procurators of the province. This palace became later the residence and *officium* of the Byzantine governor (Fig. 35).[72] Both *praetoria* had vast courtyards, gardens, and elaborate bathhouses. Two other palatial mansions were constructed in Late Antiquity in the SW zone (Fig. 36), between the two *praetoria* mentioned above. The northern one, exposed in its entirety, had an elaborate bathhouse in a good state of preservation.[73] It was constructed in the fourth century over a first-century Roman "villa" that extended over a vaster area. The second, constructed in the sixth century, had a two-story peristyle courtyard with a tri-conch triclinium. In a lower terrace, on the west, a garden and a fountain were installed, leading to a private beach (see Chapter Five below).[74] A unique *opus sectile* workshop with magnificent designs was uncovered in one of the side rooms of this Byzantine palace. Urban dwelling quarters of palatial mansions are known in many Late Antique cities, like Apamea in Syria, Ephesus and Aphrodisias in Asia Minor, Paphos in Cyprus, Volubilis in Morocco, and elsewhere.[75]

Dwellings of a more regular type, yet quite spacious, were uncovered in several locations in Caesarea, mainly in the NW zone.[76]

Sports Arenas

Herod's theater is located at the southern end of the city. In its Severan Roman imperial phase (Figs. 37–38), it comprised two blocks of seats, accommodating c. 4,000 spectators.[77] Herod's *amphitheatron*

---

[71] See above, note 31, and Netzer and Bar Nathan, "The Promontory Palace," in: Levine and Netzer 1986: 149–77.

[72] Patrich 2000a; *idem et al.* 1999, and Chapter Eight below.

[73] Porath 1998: 42–43, fig. 4. During the IAA excavations this complex was identified as a bathhouse. However, now, after being entirely exposed, it is clear that the bathhouse, being the first part to be exposed, formed just a wing of this palatial mansion.

[74] See plan in Porath 1998: 43–44, fig. 6; and garden reconstruction in *idem* 1996a: 118–19, figs. 2, 3.

[75] For bibliographical references, see Sodini 1995; 1997.

[76] See, for example, Bull and Storvick 1993.

[77] Albricci 1965; Levine 1975b. The diameter of the theater was 90m, and that of the orchestra 30m. It is not clear wherefrom Segal (1995: 99) had derived his dimensions of 62m and 16m respectively. Just a glance at the plans reproduced as figs. 70 and 71 in that book indicate that these dimensions are wrong.

(*Ant.* 15.341; *War* 1.415),[78] uncovered in the recent excavation along the sea, between the palace and the harbor, turned out to be a hippodrome (Figs. 8 and 19).[79] The estimated number of spectators is 13,000. The arrangement of the starting gates—five on either side of a central wide gate—and their layout parallel to each other, rather than radial, indicate that the races established by Herod followed the Olympian tradition of chariot racing, rather than that of the Roman circus, with its four factions. Later transformations in the arrangement of the starting gates with a radial layout, reflect a process of Romanization (see Chapter Seven below).[80] Chronologically, this architectural and cultural transformation is contemporary with the refoundation of Caesarea as a Roman colony by Vespasian. The Latin factor associated with the Roman army and administration became dominant since that time and until the Diocletianic reforms in the late-third–early fourth century, as is reflected by the language of the local inscriptions.[81]

At the final phase of the hippodrome—perhaps in the early, or mid third century, the arena was truncated, and the hippodrome was converted to an amphitheater, being deserted later in the fourth century due to erosion by the sea waves (Figs. 39–40). Similar conversion of a hippodrome into an oval amphitheater was encountered in Gerasa, Neapolis, and Scythopolis. But while the converted amphitheaters at Scythopolis and Neapolis were monumental in their truncated end, that at Gerasa is a thin wall, and at Caesarea there are four distinct lines of thin walls, just one stone thick, suggesting a casual or temporary construction, perhaps on occasion for special events.[82]

A "canonical," oval, Roman amphitheater (recognized only by aerial photographs—Fig. 5),[83] and a second hippodrome were installed in the NE and SE zones respectively, presumably in the early second century. The eastern hippodrome (Fig. 41), with obelisks and *metae* decorating

[78] On the ambiguity in applying technical terms to spectacle structures that existed in the Late Hellenistic/Late Republican and Early Imperial periods, see Humphrey 1996 and Porath 1995a: 23–27.

[79] Porath 1994; 1995a; 1996b; 1998: 40–41.

[80] Patrich 2001b. For a thorough survey of Roman circuses, and the two major styles of chariot races, see Humphrey 1986: 1–24.

[81] Lifshitz 1961; 1963b: 256; 1965; 1966; 1967a; 1962; 1963a; Negev 1971; Eck 1996; Lehmann and Holum 2000.

[82] Müller 1938; Ostrasz 1989; Magen 1993; Tsafrir and Foerster 1997: 99 and fig. E on p. 91.

[83] Reifenberg 1950; 1951. Large scale excavations (non published yet), were carried out in the amphitheater in 2010 on behalf of IAA, headed by Dr. Peter Gendelman.

its *spina*, continued to function during the Byzantine period, until it went out of use, and was systematically demolished well before the end of that era, perhaps already early in the sixth century.[84]

According to Malalas (*Chronographia*, X, 338, ed. Niebuhr, 1831, 261), Vespasian converted a Jewish synagogue into an odeum. Its location is as yet unknown.

OTHER MONUMENTS AND BUILDINGS

More monuments and buildings are mentioned in the literary sources—both Greco-Roman and rabbinic,[85] and in the inscriptions: a *tetrapylon*,[86] remains of which are still recognized inside the East Gate of the Crusader wall (Fig. 24), porticos (one of which, the portico of Iunia Ba( )ae, was used for displaying petitions and statutes concerning the Roman soldiers serving in the province),[87] stoas and colonnaded streets (*platea*), a dome-like structure overlaying a public thoroughfare, and market places.[88] A sigma-shaped market building of Roman and Byzantine date was exposed in recent excavations on the S side of the temple platform.[89]

WAREHOUSES AND HORREA

As a maritime city and provincial capital, the city was provided with plenty of warehouses and *horrea* for both import-export trade, and for stocking foodstuffs in adequate quantities to prevent inflation of prices. Warehouses of several types were uncovered in the SW zone (Figs. 42–43), and around the harbor, mostly dated to the late Roman and early Byzantine periods: long vaulted *horrea*, and warehouses of

---

[84] Humphrey 1975: 6; Toombs 1978: 229. On this hippodrome of Caesarea in the wider context of Eastern hippodromes, see also Humphrey 1974; 1986: 438–540 (Caesarea—pp. 477–91). See also Jeremias 1931.

[85] Habas 1996; Weiss 1996; Levine 1975b.

[86] Holum 1992a. See also Chapter Two above.

[87] This portico is mentioned in a Greek papyrus from Egypt: *PSI* IX, 36f, no. 1026. See also Degrassi 1926.

[88] Levine 1975b: 38–40.

[89] Raban and Stieglitz 1988. A much larger *sigma* complex, dated to the early sixth century was exposed in Beth Shean. See Bar-Nathan and Mazor 1992: 43–44; Mazor and Bar-Nathan 1998: 15; Tsafrir and Foerster 1997: 120–21.

the "courtyard" and of the "corridor" types.[90] Particular features of these warehouses are vast halls with crude mosaic floors that held vast *dolia* for the storage of oil (*dolium olearium*), and underground granaries with thick walls revetted by well-drafted blocks imbedded in a thick layer of oily lime mortar. Granaries of similar structure were found in Shuni—a site of an Askelapeion and water celebration near Caesarea—and in Apollonia—the adjacent city to Caesarea on the south. Warehouses with *dolia* were uncovered in Iamnia—another maritime city of *Palaestina*, and in Sepphoris.

THE WATER SUPPLY SYSTEM[91]

The Roman city got its water supply from the north by means of two aqueducts (Fig. 44). The high level aqueduct reached the city as a double arcade supporting two channels. The western, later one, is dated by inscriptions to the reign of Hadrian. The earlier channel is attributed, alternatively, to Herod, the Roman procurators, or Vespasian. The lower level aqueduct is a masonry tunnel, c. 1.20m wide and 2.00m high, that got its water from an artificial lake (Fig. 45), constructed in the late fourth century (c. 385 CE).[92] A Byzantine terra cotta pipeline reached the city from the north.[93] A network of lead and terra cotta pipes running under the paved streets led the water to various public amenities: fountains, *nymphaea*, bathhouses, latrines, and gardens. The palaces and rich mansions benefited from this network of pipes, enjoying a private water supply. In the late Byzantine period the water system deteriorated, and wells replaced the pipelines in some parts of the city. Stephanus, the governor of *Palaestina Prima* in the early thirties of the sixth century, is praised in his encomium, written by Choricius of Gaza in 534/36, for improving the water supply system of Caesarea by maintenance work, clearing the high-level aqueduct's channels of obstructions.[94]

---

[90] Patrich 1996. For a comprehensive survey, see Rickman 1971: 148–55. See also Chapter Nine above.

[91] Negev 1964; Barag 1964; Olami and Ringel 1975: 148–50; Peleg 1986; Everman 1992; Porath 2002.

[92] Negev 1972; Di Segni 2002b. Recent excavations at the Tanninim Dam had indicated that it was constructed in the early 3rd c. CE.

[93] Porath 1990.

[94] Mayerson 1986.

Bathhouses, *Nymphaea*, and Latrines

All the bathhouses uncovered so far in Caesarea, are associated with the palaces and villas mentioned above. A possible exception is a small bathhouse, in an impressive state of preservation, exposed in the 1997–98 excavations below the temple platform, to the east. This one might have been an urban *balaneum*, unless it formed part of another palace, perhaps that of the metropolites, that might have existed adjacent to the octagonal church. But until the excavated area will be expanded, this suggestion is a mere speculation. None of the Caesarean bathhouses uncovered so far was a huge *therma* of the Roman imperial type, like those known at Scythopolis, Eleutheropolis, Gerasa, Gadara, or Bostra.[95] Yet, according to Malalas, Antoninus Pius erected a public bath at Caesarea.[96] The "baths of Cornelius" are mentioned in the fourth-century *Itinerarium Burdigalense*.[97]

Nymphaea, fountains,[98] and latrines,[99] both public (Fig. 46) and private, were abundant throughout the city. A network of lead and terra-cotta pipes lead water to street and private fountains, and to the latrines. An elaborate *nymphaeum*, with three niches holding statues, adorned the NW projections of the temple platform (Fig. 47),[100] yet it

---

[95] Yegul 1992; Nielsen 1990. See also Berger 1982: 90–93. The bathhouse below the temple platform, occupied in this period by the octagonal church, can be compared with the Baths of Bishop Placcus at Gerasa, erected in 454/55, and renovated in 584. The baths are located to the north of St. Theodore Church, in the ecclesiastical complex that comprised also of the "Cathedral" and the clergy house. See Kraeling 1938: 265–81, Plans XLIV–XLV, and Pls. LIII–LVI.

[96] *Chronographia*, XI, 367, ed. Dindorf 1831: 281; XI.25, ed. Thurn 2000: 212.

[97] *Itinerarium Burdigalense* 4, ed. Geyer 1965: 13.

[98] The following is a list of *nymphaea* and fountains found so far in the city: two small niche fountains on E facade of the "western stoa," Area KK; a fountain to the W of vault 4 in Area CV; the central, garden fountain in the *praetorium* of the financial procurator, phases 1 and 2, and a second, "mundane" fountain in CC 59; a niche fountain in the "library" of that *praetorium*, phases 1 and 2; two fountains and an octagonal basin in the bathhouse of that *praetorium*; an elaborate latrine fountain in IAA "bathhouse" (Porath 1998: 43, fig. 5), and several "basin fountains" in the "palaestra" and "frigidarium" of that "bathhouse"; A central, portico fountain in the upper terrace of the IAA "Byzantine palace," and a second, garden fountain, in its lower terrace (Porath 1998: 43, fig. 6). An apse fountain in the triclinium of Herod's lower palace, and a courtyard fountain in the N wing of the upper palace. A *nymphaeum* in the facade of the NW projection of the temple platform (see note 100 below).

[99] The following is a list of latrines: Public: at the cardo-decumanus junction in Area CC; in the S passage to the Hippodrome; Private: adjacent to the "Ibex Mosaics" hall in Area NN; in vault 54 of area CC; in IAA "bathhouse"; in CCE Area I, over the Herodian mole (Byzantine in date; first exposed by Negev).

[100] Levine 1975b: Pl. 3:2; Porath 1998: 47, fig. 11.

is not as elaborate as the *nymphaea* of Philadelphia, Gerasa, or Bostra.[101] Smaller fountains were located in street corners, and in the private domain, fountains and reflecting pools were incorporated into the gardens and courtyards. Being located on the seashore, Caesarea also enjoyed the pleasant and refreshing panorama of the sea.

The southern part of the SW zone was occupied in the sixth century by the citadel (*kastron*) erected around the theater; it was a military zone.[102] The adjacent, former *praetorium* of the Roman governor on the site of Herod's Palace, was partially dismantled during the construction of the *kastron*. In its reduced size it might have served the *dux* while in the city. In the northern part of this zone extended the *praetorium* of the Byzantine governor, the public part of which comprised a revenue office flanked by waiting rooms with benches, an audience hall that served as a law court, offices for the clerks, and an archive or library.[103] The *officiales* mentioned in the inscriptions from the *praetorium* of Caesarea included *ypoboethoi, chartularioi, noumerarioi*, a *magister* or *magistrianos*, and various staff of the law court.[104] Another Late Antique *praetorium* with a law court was found in Gortyn (Crete), the capital of the Roman province of Crete and Cyrene. Inscriptions of the fourth and fifth century specify that they originally stood beside, or before, the doors of Justice.[105]

The rest of the SW zone was occupied by two or three palatial mansions of the local landowners (*ktetores*), each having its own complex of warehouses. In Late Antique Apamea, we encounter along its *cardo maximus* the same phenomenon of a neighborhood of palatial mansions, one of which—the house called "*au triclinos*"—is believed to be the palace of the governor of Syria II.[106] Neither in Apamea, nor in Caesarea, was the governor's palace the most elaborate residence.

[101] Segal 1997: 161–180.

[102] A police chief or sheriff (*lestodioktes*) and a garrison of Arcadiani is mentioned in Caesarea in conjunction with the suppression of the Samaritan revolt of 484 (Ps. Zacharias Rhetor, note 16 above; Jo. Malalas, *Chron.* XV.8 ed. Dindorf 1831: 382–83).

[103] Patrich 2000a; Patrich *et al.* 1999; Holum 1995. See also Chapter Eight below.

[104] The final epigraphical report on the new Greek inscriptions from the Byzantine *praetorium* is being prepared for publication by Leah Di Segni. For previous publications of some of them see Patrich *et al.* 1999 and Holum 1995. See also Di Segni *et al.* 2003.

[105] See Burrell 1996, where she discusses also the Roman palace of the *Dux Ripae* at Dura Europos, the *praetorium* at Cologne, and the governor's palace at Aquincum.

[106] Balty 1969. For the other mansions in that quarter of Apamea, see Balty 1984. For other palatial mansions that belong to this group, see Ellis 1985; Erim 1969—the so called 'Governor's Palace' with a private bath suite. Another quarter of wealthy mansions in a late antique city is the NE quadrant in Ptolemais (Cyrene). See Little 1985.

The provincial governors who resided in the *praetorium* were replaced quite frequently, after a relatively short period of office, while the other mansions served as the permanent residences of the aristocracy of the city. The more simple dwellings, in the NW zone, were quite spacious as well, reflecting the wealth of the population. In one of them, comprising a peristyle courtyard and three shops in the street front, an under-floor hoard of 99 gold coins, dated to the second half of the fourth century, was found (Fig. 48).[107]

The wealth of the city and its function as a commercial center is also reflected in its warehouses. The imported ware—both amphorae and tableware—reflect commercial contacts with large parts of the Mediterranean basin: North Africa, Egypt, Cyprus, Asia Minor, and the Aegeans.[108] The harbor, undergoing a gradual demise, was renovated by Emperor Anastasius, but its inner basin was already silted by sand, and it never reassumed its grandeur of the Herodian and early imperial times.[109]

The eastern hippodrome was the sole sport arena that survived into Late Antiquity. Chariot races and circus factions were popular in Caesarea as they were in other cities of the eastern Mediterranean.[110] The "*hippotrophoi* inscription," found not far from the eastern hippodrome, specifies sums of money that went from various municipal taxes and levies to pay for the maintenance of the stables and the races.[111] In the Samaritan revolt of 484, Justasas, their leader, presided over victory celebration games in this circus.[112] Like in other cities of the east, other spectacles lost their popularity.[113] The theater went out of use already by the fourth century and later, in the sixth century, its site was surrounded by a *kastron*. The amphitheater, unexcavated as yet, might have gone out of use much earlier. The hippodrome went out of use and was systematically demolished already in the first half of the sixth century. So far no public *therma* was uncovered, but bathing in the private sphere—in the palatial mansions mentioned above—was a popular entertainment among the local élite.

---

[107] Lampinen 1999b; Bull and Storvick 1993.

[108] For the final report on the imported amphorae and the table ware from Areas KK, CC and NN see Johnson 2008.

[109] Raban 1996; Raban *et al.* 1992; 1993; 1999; Raban 2009.

[110] Humphrey 1974; Cameron 1976; Liebeschuetz 1991; Dan 1981.

[111] Lifshitz 1977: 510–12; Lehmann and Holum 2000: inscr. 110.

[112] Jo. Malalas, *Chron.* XV.8, ed. Dindorf 1831: 382–83; Crown 1989: 72. According to Di Segni 1998: 60, Justasas just attended the chariot races, and did not preside over them.

[113] Kennedy 1985: 3–27; Liebeschuetz 1992.

The **necropolis** extended on all three sides around the city wall, but mainly to the east, as is attested by burial caves, burial inscriptions, and sarcophagi.[114] A first–second-century Roman cemetery with cremation burials was uncovered in IAA excavations to the south of the theater, adjacent to the Herodian city wall, on the outside. This alien burial practice should be attributed to the Latinate element in the population, associated with the governor's *praetorium*, located nearby.

The **extra-mural** territory was densely settled and cultivated. Dwellings and suburban villas with mosaic floors were encountered in several locations,[115] and Roman and Byzantine farmsteads were exposed farther away, in the agricultural countryside.[116]

Conclusion

It seems that the city reached its apogee by the end of the fourth century, after serving for more than four centuries as the capital of a large province. As was already mentioned above, the division of the Roman province of *Iudaea Palaestina* into two, and later three, smaller provinces in the mid-fourth to early-fifth centuries, decreased its administrative and ecclesiastical status. A further decline in the ecclesiastical status was caused by the proclamation of Jerusalem as the fifth Patriarchate of the Christian world, recognizing the superiority of its *episcopos* over the *metropolites* of Caesarea. The anti-Jewish and anti-Samaritan imperial legislation affected the security and prosperity of these important ethnic groups in the local society. All parties suffered due to the Samaritan revolts. Especially severe were the damages and casualties caused in the 529/30 revolt, that inflicted a severe blow on the Samaritan peasantry and on the agricultural estates. All these were causes of a gradual process of decline in urban life and economy.[117] A certain improvement was caused by the partial

---

[114] *Mishnah, Oholoth* 17:49; Lifshitz 1964. It seems that the Tell Mevorakh (3km distant from the city) sarcophagi were found in the confines of a private estate; they should not be conceived as an indicator for the continuous extension of the urban necropolis of Caesarea. See Stern 1978; Gersht 1996b.

[115] Struffolino in Frova 1965: 294–304; Reich 1985; Horton 1996.

[116] Hirschfeld and Birger-Calderon 1991; Hirschfeld 1995; 2000.

[117] In this I share the opinion expressed by Levine (1975a: 135–39), about Byzantine Caesarea.

restoration of the harbor by Emperor Anastasius, and the erection of the octagonal church, perhaps under this emperor as well.

The demise of Caesarea following its capture by the Muslim troops, after a prolonged siege, was quite abrupt (see Chapter Six below). Deserted by its élite during the siege, it underwent a rapid transformation, although there is no evidence for a large-scale hostile destruction. The Islamic town occupied only a small area, centered in the immediate vicinity of the harbor, reflecting a severe decrease In the population. The buildings of the Roman and Byzantine city were stripped of their masonry and marble elements were burned for lime. The SW zone, the administrative and aristocratic center, underwent a process of ruralization by being converted, already in the second half of the seventh century, into terraced gardens fed by wells.[118] The fate of Caesarea—the capital of *Palaestina Prima*, located on the sea shore, within easy reach for the Byzantine fleet—was different than that of Scythopolis—the provincial capital of *Palaestina Secunda*—and of Jerusalem—the religious capital of *Palaestina*, both located inland. All of them survived, though more humbly, under the new regime.*

Post Script—Caesarea as an intellectual center in Late Antiquity

The period that followed the Diocletianic persecutions and the "Peace of the Church" marks the beginning of a new age for the Roman Empire, but the end of paganism and the takeover of Christianization in the urban space were gradual; their pace in Caesarea is not reported by any ancient source. Seemingly, like in other cities, such as Gaza (see above), or Alexandria, it took about a century until the pagan temples were abandoned.

Although the epigraphic habit had changed (see above), Latin was still a living language among the more educated people of Caesarea.[119] Under Roman rule Caesarea became a center of Greek wisdom—

---

[118] Patrich 1998a; Holum 1998b.

* The original article was written while I was on Sabbatical in 1998–99 at the University of Miami, Coral Gables, FL. I am grateful for the facilities and services offered me there. The Post Script are excerpts from: Caesarea in the Time of Eusebius, forthcoming in: *Reconsidering Eusebius:A Fresh Look at His Life, Work and Thought*, edited by Sabrina Inowlocki and Claudio Zamagni.

[119] Geiger 1994; 1996.

philosophy, grammar and rhetoric—and a school of Roman law.[120] Its Hellenistic culture was praised already in the 1st c. CE by the famous philosopher Apollonius of Tyana in his letter to the city council.[121] Shortly after it became a Roman colony a Latin rhetor of the city, named Flavius Agrippa was honored by the city council.[122] In the first half of the 3rd c. Theodore of Neocaesarea in Pontus, the future bishop of the city better known as Gregorius *Thaumatourgos* came and studied Latin in the city, planning to move and study law in Berytus. His encounter in Caesarea with Origen brought a change in the course of his life. In his youth, Eusebius attended classes in the Holy Scripture with the priest Dorotheus of Antioch, who was well acquainted with the Hebrew Bible, and Greek learning.[123] Apphianus of Lycia, the future martyr of the city, and his brother Aedesius went to study law in Berytus and then reached Caesarea, joining the company of Pamphilus. Similarly in the early 4th c. Gregorius of Nazianzus, the future Cappadocian father, first acquired his learning in Caesarea. His teacher there was Thespasius, who was active in the city in the 340's.[124] According to Libanius due to its wealth Caesarea could compete with Antioch in attracting the best teachers. In ca. 361–365 active there was the rhetor Acacius (a contemporaneous of the bishop of that name, who had succeeded Eusebius on the See of Caesarea). He was an epical poet, and an author of drama,[125] as well as a correspondent of Libanius, friend and adversary. His sons and son-in-law were sent by him to study with Libanius in Antioch. His nephew was the Latin historian Eutropius, the author of *Breviarium ab urbe condita*—an abridged history of Rome, in ten books. It was dedicated to Emperor Valens in 369. Paenius, another Caesarean, translated shortly thereafter (in ca. 380) this composition into Greek, and Hieronymus used it. This translation is still extant almost in its entirety. Another Palestinian

---

[120] Geiger 2001. See also Levine 1975a: 57–60.

[121] *Philostratus, The life of Apollonius of Tyana, Ep.* 11, ed. Jones 2005–2006: 16–19; ed. Penella 1979: 38–41, 97–98. The authenticity of the letter is discussed there on pp. 23–29.

[122] Lehmann and Holum 2000: 36–37, inscr. no. 3.

[123] Eusebius, *HE* VII, 32, 2–4.

[124] He is also mentioned as a *rhetor* by Hieronymus. For references about him and about other persons and notices mentioned in the short survey on Greek wisdom in Caesarea given below see Geiger 2001.

[125] According to Geiger, *ibid.*, the *Okypous* (the "fast feet"—an adjective of horses in Homer)—a drama full of humor, generally attributed to Lucianus, should be attributed to Acacius.

rhetor mentioned by Libanius, seemingly a Caesarean as well, was Helpidius, who was teaching later in Athens and finally settled in Constantinople. Two other Palestinian sophists, seemingly Caesareans, were the late 4th c. sophists Pangyrius and Priskion.[126]

As was mentioned above, during the third and fourth centuries Caesarea was the seat of a Jewish academy, led by Rabbi Oshayah (first half of the 3rd c.) and Rabbi Abbahu (d. 309 CE),[127] and of a Christian academy, founded by Origen (d. ca. 254), and headed by Pamphilus and then by Eusebius. Pamphilus (martyred in 309 CE in Caesarea) collected and copied the writings of Origen. He established a school in Caesarea, which was open to pagans and Christian alike, and provided elementary education for both. The library he established comprised 30,000 scrolls.[128] It included many secular books on Greek science, philosophy, history, drama, poetry, rhetoric etc., and compositions of Jewish Greek authors, residues of which were preserved in the writings of Eusebius.[129] Pamphilus and Eusebius took upon themselves to catalogue this collection.[130] He and his successors in the See of Caesarea—Acacius and Euzoius took care to copy the papyri scrolls to codices of parchment.[131] Scribal work at Caesarea started already in the time of Origen, with the financial assistance of his wealthy companion Ambrose.[132] Later its *scriptorium* was famous by its attentive work in producing copies of scriptures for the free use of scholars, disciples and pious women. In ca. 325 CE, at the request of Constantine, fifty copies of scripture, in codices of parchment, were dispatched by Eusebius to Constantinople.[133]

John the Grammarian, the important Neochalcedonian theologian in the late fifth and early sixth century, and the sixth century historian Procopius of Caesarea, mentioned above, were late offsprings of an old, well established center of learning.

---

[126] For a Greek dedication of a statue of a local philosopher named Titus Flavius Maximus in the palace of the Roman governor see Lehmann and Holum 2000: 47–48, inscr. no. 12. In the 5th c. we hear of two pro-Hermogenean Caesarean rhetors—Paul, and his disciple John. The Hermogenean school of rhetorics stood at odds with the Antiochean school. See Geiger 2001: 33.

[127] Levine 1975c; 1975a: 61–106; 1992; Lieberman 1963. See also Zuri 1926.

[128] *HE* VII, 32, 25. On his activity in Caesarea see: Kofsky 2006, with farther references; Geiger 2001: 30–31.

[129] Runia 1996.

[130] *HE* VI, 32. On the library, see Carriker 2003.

[131] Hieron. *Ep.* 34.

[132] *HE* VI, 23, 1–2.

[133] Eusebius, *Vit. Const.* IV, 36; Robins 1987; Kofsky 2006: 55.

CHAPTER FIVE

SEVERAL ASPECTS OF COMMERCE AND ECONOMY
IN LATE ANTIQUE CAESAREA

According to a 3rd c. Jewish sage, speaking about Caesarea and its
dependent cities, "there prices are low; there abundance obtains".[1]
Similarly, according to a 4th c. geographical treatise, Caesarea (like
Antioch and Tyre) was "a pleasant city and rich in everything",[2] being
distinguished in exporting purple dye, and celebrated for its produc-
tivity in corn, wine and oil.[3] The immediate hinterland of Caesarea
comprises of the southern end of Mt. Carmel, and of the northern
part of the Sharon plain and of the Samaria Hills. The Sharon was
renown already from earlier periods as a land of wheat,[4] and good pasture.[5] Five trade roads radiating in all directions[6] established the infrastructure for the inland commerce (Fig. 1): north to Dora; northeast
to Gabae and Ptolemais; east to Legio/Maximianopolis and Scythopolis, Sepphoris and Tiberias; southeast—with two branches, one leading to Samaria and Neapolis, the other to Antipatris, Lydda/Diospolis,
and hence to Aelia Capitolona/Hierosolyma, or to Eleutheropolis; and
south, to Apollonia/Sozousa, Ioppe, and hence to Ascalon and Gaza.
The harbor served the maritime trade. Since Herodian times the city had
a steady water supply by several aqueducts.[7] These aqueducts had provided abundance of drinking water to meet the needs of the increasing
population, and of the public and private amenities such as bathhouses,
nymphaea and fountains. Several branches extended from the aqueducts

---

[1] TY *Kelaim* 9.4: 32c; TY *Ketubot* 12.3: 35b. These qualifications, attributed to Caesarea and its dependent cities—namely, the towns and villages included in its administrative territory (*territorium*), are also attributed to Tyre and its dependent cities. The
Sage is Rabbi Simeon ben Lakish (Reish Laqish; fl. 250–290 CE). (In *Genesis Rabba* 74.1,
only Tyre and its dependent cities are mentioned). Hence, it seems that Caesarea was
not affected by the 3rd c. crisis. See also Levine 1975a: 49 and note 29 on p. 181; 68.

[2] *Expositio totius mundi et gentium* XXVI: 160–61.

[3] *Ibid.* XXXI and XXXII: 162–167. The city was also renowned for its pantomime
artists.

[4] Galling 1938: 90.

[5] I *Chronicles* 27: 29–31; M *Bava Qama* 10: 9; T *Menahot* 9: 13.

[6] Roll 1996.

[7] Porath 2002.

to provide water to some villas[8] but they did not fed a network of irrigation channels for agriculture in the countryside. For this springs, wells
and rain water where available. In the *territorium* of Caesarea there was
also a lot of pasture land both in rocky hills and along the river brooks,
unsuitable for tilling. Bone analysis[9] indicates that meat were provided
mainly from sheep, goat, cattle (and pig, raised in enclosed pens, not in
open pasture). The first three provided also milk; cattle provided also
hides and material for the bone industry (see below).

An ample amount of information on daily life and material culture
that pertains to Late Antique Caesarea is imbedded in the Rabbinic
sources. Certain aspects of the local economy and commerce alluded
to in these sources reflect the general conditions in the city, applicable
also for non-Jewish Caesareans.[10]

A rich variety of agricultural products was available in the city markets: wheat, bread, wine, oil, dates, rice, cumin and bulbous onions; it
was famous by the size of its citrons, by the quality of its wheat, grapes
and figs. Corn and fruits were brought there not only from the Samaria
Hills but also from farther away: from the Northern Judaea Hills (Har
HaMelech), and even from Sepphoris and Tiberias. Caesarea markets
attracted merchants from all over the province. Its industry included
glass,[11] purple dye, flax growing and linen weaving, washing, bleaching
and dying; textiles (or shoes) manufactured following the Babylonian
style;[12] trade and manufacture of fine veils[13] and of silk textiles from

---

[8] See sites nos. 32, 33 and 59 in Olami *et al.* 2005. The hewn outlet 3m wide near
Nahal Ada, barred by a wooden barrier, that let water irrigate adjacent farming plots,
might have been cut in the Islamic period; an Arabic inscription was carved on the
rock surface nearby.

[9] Cope 1999.

[10] A good survey based mainly on the Rabbinic literature is to be found in Levine
1975a: 48–54, 68–70; its main points are given in the introduction that follows.
Levine's survey was much reiterated by McGuckin 1992: 11–15. See also Ringel 1975:
147–150; Harel 1988. On the economy of Palestine in general in the periods under
consideration see Safrai 1994. For the Herodian period see Pastor 1997; for luxury
provisions—fish sauces, Italian wines (*Philonianum* from Brundisium, *Massicum*,
Tarentinum and apples from Cumae (*mala Cumana*) imported for Herod, see Cotton
and Geiger 1996.

[11] TY *Qidushin* 1: 60b; TY *Shabbat* 7.4: 10d; Levine 1975a: 52, note 59. On Palestinian glass industry see Y. Brand, *Glass Vessels in Talmud Literature*, Jerusalem 1978
(Hebrew); Safrai 1994: 202–204. See also *infra*, notes 62–65.

[12] Lehmann and Holum 2002: 152–153, inscr. no. 184.

[13] R. Zeʻira was dealing with linen (כיתנא, כתנא דרומא); R. Yose b. Hanina and
R. Abbahu seem to have been merchants in linen, handling with לסוטיא—fine veils
(TY *Bava Mezia* 4.9: 9d). See Zori 1926: 174–176.

raw silk.[14] Some Palestinian Rabbinic sages of the third century were silk merchants who had business in Tyre.[15] Contacts with Babylonian Jewry made easier the import of raw silk from the Far East through the territories of Sassanian Persia under the protection of which the Babylonian Jewry lived. R. Abba, a 4th c. Babylonian sage who immigrated to Palestine was a producer, or an importer of raw silk. He addressed the sages of Caesarea a question pertaining to silk commerce, indicating that silk commerce was a local reality.[16]

There was also a type of Caesarean couches or beds (פלטירה/ערסתא קיסרייתא/קלטירא), famous throughout Palestine. The necessary wood could be obtained from the adjacent oaks woodland (*drymus*) of the Sharon.[17] Pottery vessels were produced there as well,[18] and there was also a market of leather products.[19] The products of the local workshops, and goods imported from overseas were transported to the inland markets of its rural territory and farther away to other cities. The variety of coins—city, provincial and imperial—bear evidence for this network of commercial connections. The literary sources attest to an inland international trade with Babylon (mainly silk, jewels, gold and incense; local wine was exported) and Bostra (figs), and Emesa.[20] These sources bear evidence for maritime trade, mainly with Rome (export of olive oil, dates and leeks) and Egypt (jewelry, import of dry fish, and brinefish—מורייס).[21] Wheat was imported from Cyprus. Five hundred recipes of baking required five years of apprenticeship.[22] One of the Jewish sages in the early 2nd c. was Judah the Baker. The

---

[14] On the silk trade and textile industry in Roman and Byzantine Palestine as reflected mainly in the Rabbinic sources, see Safrai 1994: 161–162, 192–202.

[15] *Midrash Rabbah. Genesis*, Ch. LXXVII, ed. Mirkin: 188, Eng. tr. H. Freedman, Vol. II 1951: 711 and the comment *ad loc.* on the Sages names.

[16] TY *Bava Mezia* ch. 4: 2, 9c; TY *Bava Mezia* 4.2: 9c; BT *Bava Qama* 117b. The three sages named were Caesareans. On silk commerce in Caesarea in the 3rd–4th c., according to the Rabbinic sources, especially those mentioned in the Talmud of Qisrin ("תלמודה של קיסרין"), see Levine 1975: 53, 55.

[17] *TIR*: 114.

[18] On this industry in Roman and Byzantine Palestine see Safrai 1994: 205–211.

[19] Zori 1926: 74–75.

[20] Zori 1926: 74. Incidentally, one of the 6th–7th c. lead seals found at the site are of the Church of Emesa, indicating ecclesiastical contacts between these two cities (Nesbitt 1999: 131—no. 10).

[21] Zori 1926: 30–48. Muria was a salty liquid similar to garum but of lower quality; it was used for conserving vegetables, fruits, olives or fish, rather than as a spice for its own sake. See Cotton *et al.* 1996: 231.

[22] *Ecclesiastes Rabba* I, 23.

prosperity of the city had attracted investment in wine, farming, maritime trade, local businesses, and financial transactions.

This picture, derived mainly from the Rabbinic literature, can now be augmented and modified by some new architectural structures and by the evidence of the various objects retrieved in the recent excavations.[23] Pottery, oil lamps, clay objects, stone objects and vessels, jewelry, glass vessels, metal artifacts and bone objects,[24] bear evidence on the various aspects of the economic life in the city.[25] There were workshops (not yet uncovered), where these objects were manufactured; shops where they were sold; some goods were imported, bearing evidence for overseas trade; other objects had arrived over land, from the rural countryside of Caesarea and from farther away.

I. The evidence of the objects/Small Finds retrieved in the Excavations

A. *Import*

The maritime commerce was one of the main resources of wealth of the Herodian kingdom, and later of Caesarea itself. Throughout the Roman and Byzantine periods it was the best harbor of Judaea/Palaestina.[26] In the 1st c. CE, on the eve of the Great Revolt against Rome, one of the Jewish leaders was a tax-collector (*telones*), seemingly in the harbor.[27] A Greek inscription of the 2nd or 3rd c. mentions Varios Seleukos, curator of ships.[28] He was a municipal official of high rank—the manager of the harbor, or the one in charge of anchoring services. It is possible that such an official was in charge of collect-

---

[23] Patrich 2008. The survey below is based mainly on this publication, being the largest catalogue of finds retrieved from the archaeological excavations carried out at the site. Since these excavations do not include dwelling quarters, they may not be wholly representative. Yet, it seems that much of the dump fills transported from other areas do represent dwelling contexts, even if not *in situ*. More finds were retrieved in previous excavations in the city, and in other excavation areas, some of them not published yet. In the present framework it would be impossible to address them all; many of them were taken into consideration in the various chapters of Patrich 2008.

[24] Ayalon 2005.

[25] Construction works and related professions and expertise, such as masonry, stone and marble cut, fresco, stucco, mosaics and opus *sectile* artisans, and water works are not included in the following survey.

[26] Raban 2009.

[27] Josephus, *War* II.287.

[28] Lehmann and Holum 2000: 47–48, inscr. no. 12.

ing the taxes on maritime commerce and for anchoring in the harbor detailed in the "*hippotrophoi* inscription"—a Greek inscription dated to the 4th to 7th c. named after those in charge of the imperial circus stables.[29]

1. *Goods imported in amphorae*[30]

The international character of the city, expressed in its maritime commerce, is best attested by its imported clay ware, coming from the entire Mediterranean basin. Amphorae were the regular containers for various goods, mainly liquids, such as oil and wine, but *garum* sauce, fish[31] and dry fruits as well. Pottery kilns excavated throughout the Mediterranean, and the study of the ware and shape of amphorae, and of residues left therein, enable locating the original place of manufacture of many containers, and even identifying the products transported therein. Yet, there are still numerous types of amphorae that could be identified as imported, yet no specific production center could be assigned to them other than generally "Eastern Mediterranean," "Aegean" etc.

---

[29] Lifshitz 1957; Lehmann and Holum 2000: 112–114, inscr. no. 109. Tolls on the taxes on maritime transit commerce and on various anchoring services (*stolos, dikeration, tetrakeration*). There were also tolls on the directors of the games and on income from city games (*synarchiai*); capital taxes (*epikephalion*), and levies on buildings (*hypopyrgion*); import and export taxes in the amount of 12.5% (one eighth/*octava*); a levy on weights and measures was laid on the merchants, and there were also tolls on the perfumes and lentils merchants, the corn customs magistrate (*mesites*) and the money changers (*nomismatapuloi*). See Lehmann and Holum, *ibid*.

[30] Johnson 2008. In this study Johnson addresses all previous finds in the city. Not included are Hellenistic and Early Roman assemblages of pottery from the IAA excavations, studied by Gendelman 2007, and an assemblage from area LL warehouse near the harbor, that represents the final phase of urban life in the city prior to its Arab conquest, published by M. Oren Paskal in Holum *et al.* 2008: 49–58. This last assemblage is similar to assemblages studied by Johnson. On inland and maritime trade as reflected in the Caesarea pottery finds see also Adan Bayevitz in Levine and Netzer 1986: 120–121; Blakely 1988; Oleson *et al.* 1994: 149–160. Much of the imported goods to Judaea/Palaestina seem to have passed through the harbor of Caesarea. Such goods and their containers/amphorae, even if found elsewhere, remote from Caesarea, like in Herodian Masada (see, for example, Cotton and Geiger 1996; Cotton *et al.* 1996), are relevant to the assessment of import through the city (though much of these goods were shipped to Herod, in person). Hence a total assessment deserves a much more thorough study of imported amphorae in Judaea/Palaestina. This is beyond the scope of the present study.

[31] On fish-hash imported from Pelusium see B *Avoda Zara* 34b; on fish merchants: TY *Shvi'it* 7.3: 37c; TY *Terumot* 10.3: 47a. See Levine 1975a: 54; Safrai 1994: 163–165.

A rich variety of amphora types, from all over the Mediterranean, is present in the catalogue (Fig. 49–50): Spain and Western Mediterranean; North Africa (Tripolitania, Central Tunisia and Mauritania), producing Early Roman, Mid Roman and Late Roman types; Italy; Rhodes and other Aegean sites; Asia Minor; Antioch and its area; the Phoenician litoral; and Egypt. One amphora type even seems to origin in Miremeki area, in the eastern corner of the Crimea.[32] Being a maritime city, the variety of amphora-types (and of goods delivered therein) that had reached Caesarea, exceeded those found in inland sites.

Unfortunately, the contents itself cannot always be identified, yet, certain types were associated with specific products, their sherds thus indicate goods that were imported to Caesarea, being available in the local markets. These include: Spanish fish sauce (*garum*),[33] olive oil from North Africa and from Spain,[34] fruit conserves from Italy,[35] wine and olive oil from Antioch area,[36] and Egyptian wine.[37]

2. *Import of pottery vessels*

The imported merchandise included also clay vessels, such as table (Fig. 51) and cooking ware, tiny pots for medicine and ointments, oil lamps, figurines, and other non-pottery ceramics. But one should bear

---

[32] Johnson 2008: 103. Other rare types of amphorae, almost not to be found elsewhere in Israel, yet present in Caesarea, include: Peacock and Williams amphorae classes 7 and 8, dated to the 1st c. CE; class 25, with a date range from the 1st to the 3rd c. CE; Richborough Amphora 527 of a western Mediterranean origin; Benghazi Middle Roman amphora no. 3 of the 1st to early 4th c. CE; Benghazi Middle Roman amphora no. 1a, of the 2nd to 4th c. CE, and no. 13; Benghazi Late Roman amphora no. 10 of Eastern Mediterranean origin, that was in use until around mid 6th c.; and a long and narrow Spatheion (North African?), produced from late 4th to the 5th c. CE.

[33] Johnson 2008: 99 and 101. On various fish sauces—*garum*, and *allec*—imported for Herod, see Cotton *et al.* 1996. See also *supra*, note 31.

[34] Olive oil was transported in Peacock and Williams amphorae class 8, of the 1st c. CE; North African olive oil was transported in Tripolitanian Benghazi Early Roman amphorae 11a of the 1st c. and later, and in Peacock and Williams amphorae class 37 (= Tripolitania III Amphora) of the 2nd half of 3rd c. CE into the 4th c. CE, and class 34 (= *Africana Grande* IIB), of the 3rd to 4th c. CE; Spanish olive oil was transported in Peacock and Williams amphorae class 25, dated to the 1st to 3rd c. CE. Johnson 2008: 99–100, 102–104.

[35] These were shipped in wide-mouth Peacock and Williams amphorae class 7, of the 1st c. CE. Johnson 2008: 100.

[36] These were shipped in Late Roman 1 amphorae, dated to the 4th to 7th c. CE. Johnson 2008: 105–106.

[37] It was transported in Peacock and Williams amphorae class 53 of the 4th to 6th c. CE, and class 52 of the 4th to 7th c. CE. Johnson 2008: 107.

in mind that the imported table ware (plates, bowls, jugs and juglets), was encountered in much smaller quantities than the local table ware. Table ware came from all over the Mediterranean:

Italy and Gaul (Western Sigillata, Pompeian Red Ware and other Italian fine wares); Greece (Corinthian Relief Bowl), and the Aegean Islands; Cyprus (Eastern Sigillata D = Cypriot Sigillata, popular in the Early Roman period, it was replaced by Cypriot Red Slip Ware in the Late Roman/Byzantine period); Asia Minor (Gray Ware—produced mainly in the 1st c. BCE to the 1st c. CE; Lead Glaze Ware; Eastern Sigillata B; Knidian Ware, Sagalassos Ware, Çandarli Ware; Phocaean Red Slip = Late Roman C Ware, prominent from around the mid 4th to early 7th c. CE); Syria (Eastern Sigillata A—the most common Late Hellenistic Early Roman Fine Ware in use in Palestine, seemingly produced in Southern Syria; North Syrian Mortarium); Egypt (Egyptian Red Slip Ware A and Variant with Cream/Yellow slip—dated to the 2nd half of the 5th to 7th c.; B—6th to 7th c.; C—of 7th c.; Coptic Painted Ware); North Africa (African Red Slip Ware—the most renown table ware throughout the Mediterranean from the 1st to the 7th c. CE).

In the Early Roman period the most popular fine table ware were Eastern Sigillata A and Eastern Sigillata D (Cypriot Sigillata). Italian Sigillata, Gaulish Sigillata, and other imported early fine wares are present only in small quantities and limited shapes. African Red Slip Ware was imported to Palestine only from the 4th c. CE and on—the Late Roman/Byzantine periods, being the most popular table ware at that period,[38] along with Late Roman C (Phocaean Red Slip Ware), and Cypriot Red Slip Ware. Other imported fine wares are represented by a single example, or slightly more, each. Such are the Knidian Gray Ware Carinated Bowl, and the Corinthian Relief Bowl depicting a chasing scene (dated to the 2nd half of the 2nd c. through the 1st half of the 3rd c. CE) (Fig. 52).[39]

---

[38] Mainly forms 50, 59, 61, 67, 91, 104, 105 and 106; more rare forms are 23, 49, 171/174–75 and 181. Johnson 2008: 20, 58–62.

[39] Other table ware types, rare or not to be found elsewhere in Palestine, include Italian Fine Wares with sanded or barbotine decoration, dated to the 1st c. CE; Pompeian Red Ware (1st c. BCE to 1st c. CE); Aegean Basin (Blakely Basin Class 1, dated to the 2nd–4th c. CE); a pinched-mouth jug (of the 2nd and 3rd c. CE); Lead Glazed Ware from Tarsus in Asia Minor (dated to the 2nd half of the 1st c. BCE to the early 1st c. CE); Sagalassos Fine Ware (ca. 1st to 2nd c. CE); Çandarli Ware of the 1st to 3rd c. CE. Nabataean pottery, common in the Negev, but rare elsewhere in Palestine, was

Cooking pots and pans were mostly local, but there are also a few imported cooking vessels that came from Italy, North Africa, the Aegean, Asia Minor and Egypt. However, for the most part, the imported cooking pots could not be assigned to a specific place of manufacture.

3. Imported oil lamps[40]

Mold-made lamps are easy to copy; yet, an attentive examination of ware and technique makes it possible to differentiate between local and imported lamps. Imported lamps were found indeed, and their variety in Caesarea is larger than elsewhere in Israel.[41] They might have been brought from abroad by officials or soldiers, but also as imported goods. In the Roman period wheel-made lamps came from Italy and Asia Minor, but mold-made lamps predominated by large. In the early Roman period these were imported from the West—mainly from Italian factories, but also from North Africa, Corinth and Athens, and from the Levant—Syria and Phoenicia. One type came from the Decapolis. But since discus and other mold-made types were easily copied or imitated in many workshops in Asia Minor, Cyprus and Egypt, it is not always easy to determine the actual source of import. In the Byzantine period (4th to 7th c.) there was a sharp decline in import of lamps. Almost all the lamps came from regional and local-Caesarean workshops. The few mold-made imports came from North Africa, Asia Minor, and Cyprus.

4. Glass Import [42]

From the Augustan era and on, everywhere, the blowing technology had gradually over-shadowed the earlier casting technology. This enabled mass production, and the introduction of a large variety of new shapes of vessels—beakers, jugs, bottles, flasks, etc. There were also mold-blown vessels—bowls and bottles.[43] Some Early Roman vessels were imported from Asia Minor.

---

found in very low quantities. Other rare wares are Egyptian Red Slip C of the 7th c., the least common among the three Egyptian Red Slip Wares, and Coptic painted ware, of the late 6th to 7th c.

[40] Sussman 2008.

[41] R12, R16 and R17 are rare in Israel. Sussman 2008: 223, 227–228.

[42] Israeli 2008.

[43] Such are bowl no. 20, and bottles nos. 217–220. Israeli 2008: 372 and 387, respectively.

Luxury glass vessels of the Caesarea elite were found as well.[44] Extraordinary finds, rare, or not found so far elsewhere in Israel, include a fragment of a mold-blown cup of the 1st c. CE (no. 243), resembling one with the name of Aristeas the Cypriote—a famous glassmaker—marked on the mold. According to Yael Israeli, only two cups made and signed by Aristeas are known to date.[45] Few Sidonian vessels of the same type bear the names of five glassmakers, one of them Ennion—a great glass artist, who had influenced Aristeas.[46] A "cage cup" (*Vasa Diatreta*)—an extraordinary vessel made of two glass layers of different colours, in which the upper layer is carved in various designs and the lower one serves as the background (Fig. 53). Such cups are dated to the end of the 3rd c. and 4th c. CE. Their place of manufacture is not known.[47]

B. *Local Industries*

1. *Pottery*

A potter of Caesarea is mentioned in TY *Bava Mezia* 4.8, 11a. Unfortunately, no petrographical analysis was done so far to any of our finds, and no potter kiln was so far excavated.[48] Thus, the attribution of a certain jar type to a Caesarean workshop is based on more general considerations and on examination of the clay in bare eye. Similar is the case regarding many other Palestinian types, which it is still impossible to attribute to a specific workshop or production center, other than in general. The Kfar Hananya ware, studied thoroughly by David Adan Bayevitz, is a case apart.[49] Nevertheless, there are types

---

[44] Such is the cast of plate no. 19 (from the end of the 1st c. to the first half of the 2nd c. CE), produced in Egypt. Just a tiny rim fragment was actually found. Israeli 2008: 372.

[45] Israeli 2008: 389.

[46] Other extraordinary finds include the cylindrical bowl no. 245, decorated with facet-cutting. Such decoration is rare; the nearest parallel, dated to the 2nd to mid 3rd c. CE, comes from Dura Europos. No. 246 is a rare blown fish flask, considered to be of the 3rd c. CE, that seems to originate from an Eastern Mediterranean workshop. No. 247 possibly depicted a dolphin. Israeli 2008: 389–390.

[47] Israeli 2008: 390. It is represented by a tiny fragment (no. 249).

[48] Site no. 99 in Olami *et al.* (2005: 58 and 42*), yielded wastes from a potter's workshop and pottery fragments warped by the heat of a kiln. The site was not excavated yet. Byzantine, Crusader and Mamluk pottery was collected in the archaeological survey.

[49] D. Adan Bayevitz, *Common Pottery in Roman Galilee. A Study of Local Trade*, Ramat Gan 1993. For 9 petrographic samples of pottery imported to Caesarea see Goldberg in Levine and Netzer 1986: 130–131.

that can be attributed on good grounds to various localities or production centers: the Phoenician coast, Galilee, Beth Shean region, Jerusalem, the Negev, Gaza and Ashkelon.

Local Jars (Fig. 54). Most popular was the local Palestinian Baggy Jar, especially that in a gritty orange fabric,[50] believed to be manufactured in the litoral region adjacent to Caesarea. The Black Baggy Jar, hard fired, manufactured in Galilee, especially in the region of Beth Shean,[51] was less popular in Caesarea. There were also Gaza Jars of various types. Gaza Jars were found in larger quantities than the Beth Shean type, reflecting the fact that over sea transportation costs were much cheaper than over land costs. Other local types, rarer, include a Lebanese Amphora, Jalame Amphora Form 1, and more.

The Palestinian fine and utilitarian ware—table and cooking ware— came mainly from the northern part of the country, including Kefar Hananya. Smaller quantities came from the region of Jerusalem and the south. The Fine Byzantine Ware of the Late Roman/Byzantine period seems to be locally made, and an earlier date is now assigned to the beginning of its production.[52]

The utilitarian ware includes also antals—vessels that were attached to a water-wheel of the *saqiya* type for hauling water,[53] like the one installed in the bathhouse of the villa to be described below. They were assigned to the 4th to 6th centuries CE. *Pithoi* (Gr.) or *Dolia* (Lat.), dated to the 5th to 7th c. CE, were very huge, un-transportable containers that stood in warehouses for the storage of oil, wine, or lentils.[54] There were also miniature pots, seemingly used as containers for medicinal salves, unguents, or ointments. (Perfumes and cosmetics might have been held in more fancy and delicate containers, made of glass, or of a more expensive material, such as bronze, silver or gold).

The non-pottery ceramic industry included terracotta pipes and roof tiles, found in abundance in the excavations. Bricks were used

---

[50] Riley Caesarea Types 1A, 1B and 1C shapes. Johnson 2008: 87–88.
[51] Riley Caesarea Type 3. Johnson 2008: 91–93.
[52] J. Magness, "The Roman Legionary Pottery", in: B. Arubas and H. Goldfus (eds.), *Excavations on the site of the Jerusalem International Convention Center (Binyanei Ha'uma): a settlement of the late First to Second Temple period, the tenth legion's kilnworks, and a Byzantine monastic complex. The pottery and other small finds* [*JRA Suppl. Ser.* 60], Portsmouth RI 2006: 105–106. However, just a single example of Jerusalem Fine Ware (Magness Rouletted Bowl Form 1), is represented in the corpus.
[53] Ayalon 2000.
[54] Patrich 1996: 156–164. See below, Chapter Nine.

mainly in the under-floor heating system (*hypocaust*) of the various bathhouses.[55]

2. Clay objects[56]

The sort of clay indicates that most of these objects were locally manufactured. Lids of various shapes and sizes were fitted for particular vessels, like jars or *pixides* (that might have been used to store spices, powders, ointments etc.). A decorated lid, 8.3 cm. in diameter, depicting a male face with a open mouth shaped as a slot (Fig. 55), suggests that it covered a safe-box, the slot serving for the insertion of coins.[57] Figurines—anthropomorphic and zoomorphic, and miniature altars were manufactured to respond to the domestic religious needs of the gentile population. Spindle whorls of both clay and stone, bear farther evidence on the weaving industry.

3. Local oil lamps (Fig. 56)

In the Late Hellenistic—Early Roman period (end of the 1st c. BCE– to Herod's days), like in later periods, two local workshops could be differentiated, reflecting the immediate inland commercial contacts of the city: the one "Samarian", the second "Judaean". In the Roman period Judaean volute lamps, made in Jerusalem, and "Darom" Samaria type, were encountered in the city side by side. Recently it was found out that knife pared "Herodian" lamps, were transported from Jerusalem to the towns of Galilee and to Gamla in the Golan, while in mixed Jewish-Pagan cities such as Beth Shean/Scythopolis and Dor/ Dora such lamps were produced from a local ware.[58] Since Caesarea was also a city of mixed population, it seems that such was also the case of the local knife pared lamps (one of the largest group in our finds), though they were not included in that study. One wheel-made type seems to originate from the Christian communities near Nazareth, and another one might have come from Judaea, but at the lack of petrographical analyses these proposals cannot be conclusive. The

---

[55] These finds were studied by Uri Davidovitch, and will be published in a next volume of the Final Reports.

[56] Patrich and Abu Shaneb 2008.

[57] *Op. cit.*, lid no. 209: 301, 310 and 323.

[58] D. Adan-Bayewitz, F. Asaro, M. Wieder, and R.D. Giauque, Preferential distribution of lamps from the Jerusalem area in the late Second Temple period (late first c. BCE–70 CE), *BASOR* 350 (2008): 37–85.

most prevalent lamp in the country from the last third of the 1st c. to the 3rd c. CE was the round local "Provincial" Syria-Palaestina type.

In the Byzantine period Samaritan types predominated in the local industry.[59] Two types are identified as Caesarea types, being found in abundance at the site (and similarly the Samaritan types B4 and B5). The case of one of them (B10) is clear, since limestone molds for lamps of this type were found there (Fig. 57).[60] A subtype of the other (B11B) is seldom found outside Caesarea. Since the distribution of workshops in the hinterland of Caesarea is not known, some of the "Samaritan" types, like B4, very common in Caesarea, might have been manufactured in the immediate vicinity of the city. Such is also the case of another type (B9, dated to the 4th and 5th c.). Three types came from Scythopolis/Beth Shean.[61]

In the late Byzantine period–5th to 7th c. and beyond, there is a revival in Palestine of local wheel-made lamps of two types: high (B14) and low (B15) boot-shaped (Fig. 58), different than the previous wheel-made lamps. Luchnaria (candlestick/slipper lamps = B13), prevalent throughout the Byzantine period (4th to 7th c.), were found in the entire Levant; In Caesarea this type was not very common.

4. Glass industry[62]

Glass was produced out of sand and lime. Phoenicia, extending to the north of Caesarea, was always a prominent center of glass industry; other workshops were dispersed in the Eastern Mediterranean. But glass workshops were found also in the countryside not too far from Caesarea. And indeed, most vessels in the corpus seem to come from local or adjacent workshops. Late Roman/Early Byzantine (4th to 5th c.) workshops or furnaces were found in Jalame,[63] Sebastia, Apollonia and

---

    [59] These are B2–B6, B8–B9. B2–B5 are of the 3rd to 5th c.; B8 and B9 are of the 4th and 5th c.; B6—of the 5th to 6th c.—Sussman 2008: 239, 243–245. R21 (3rd/4th to 5th c. CE), also manufactured in the region of Samaria, was a latter offspring of R20—the round local "Provincial" Syria-Palaestina type.
    [60] Patrih and Pinkas 2008: 296–300.
    [61] These are R22, dated to the 4th and 5th c., B7 (4th and 5th c.), and B12 (mid 4th to 5th c.). Some of the "Samaritan" types found in Beth Shean differ in their ware from the same types found in Caesarea. Sussman 2008: 233, 244, 249–250.
    [62] Israeli 2008.
    [63] G.D. Weinberg and S.S. Goldstein, "The Glass Vessels," in G.D. Weinberg (ed.), *Excavations at Jalame, Site of a Glass Factory in Late Roman Palestine*, Columbia, MO 1988: 38–102.

in the Valley of Acco.[64] Hence, there was a local glass industry. This is corroborated also by several types of glass oil lamps unknown from any other place that seem to be local products, like the small bowls (nos. 155–168 in the catalogue—Fig. 59), found in large quantities at the site. The existence of local glass manufacture is also suggested by glass slags found in dump fills,[65] and from the Rabbinic passages mentioned above.

Among the finds are also perfume bottles and flasks, ointment and kohl (single and double) vessels, and fine table vessels. Late Roman/ Early Byzantine vessels (4th to 5th c.) include also storage vessels.

5. *Textile, purple dye and silk*

As was noted above, Caesarea was renowned for its purple dye, and linen fabrics. The manufacture of textiles is also indicated by the clay and stone spindle whorls and loom weights uncovered at the site.[66] The variety of shapes and sizes, and the distribution pattern may suggest that these ones were used in domestic spindles and looms, rather than in a central weaving plant, where more uniform objects should have been expected.

Purple dye was an ancient industry throughout the Mediterranean litoral, known already in the Bronze Age. Muricid snails (*Murex brandaris*) from which purple dye was extracted were found scattered in the excavated areas (CC, KK and NN—administrative center and a complex of warehouses), but not in high numbers. Hence, the purple dye workshops were located elsewhere in the city.[67]

---

[64] D. Barag, Glass Vessels of the Roman and Byzantine Periods in Palestine, Ph.D. dissertation, Jerusalem 1970, Vol. II: 1–5; Roll and Ayalon 1989: 217–221, who mention in addition to Apollonia glass workshops also in Kh. Jius, and Kh. Sabiya (Caphar Saba), and in a dozen other smaller sites in the southern Sharon, as well as in the northern Sharon, Ramat Menashe and the Carmel; Yael Gorin-Rosen, 'The Ancient Glass Industry in Eretz-Israel: a brief summary,' *Michmanim* 16 (2002): 7*–18*. See also *supra*, note 11. It was suggested that the finds from Beth She'arim are from the Early Islamic Period. See: I.C. Freestone, 'The great glass slab at Bet She'arim, Israel: An Early Islamic glassmaking experiment,' *JGS* 41 (1999): 105–116. The one excavated at Beth Eliezer, near Hadera, some 12 km away from Caesarea, is Umayyad as well. See: Yael Gorin-Rosen, 'Hadera, Bet Eli'ezer,' *ESI* 13 (1993): 42–43; Neemam *et al.* 2000, site no. 88, and remains of another glass workshop at site no. 78, Hadera. The wood needed for the melting process determined the location of workshops in woodlands.

[65] Evidence for the existence of a major glass industry in Caesarea during the Abbasid period was indicated by Toombs 1978: 230.

[66] Patrich and Abu Shaneb 2008: 303–306; Patrich 2008: 335–336.

[67] On this industry in antiquity along the Phoenician coast and in Apollonia-Arsuf, to the south of Caesarea see: N. Karmon, 'Remains of Purple Dye Industry found at

Justinian made the silk trade a state monopoly.[68] But as was indicated above, already before the 6th c the Phoenician cities, especially Berytus and Tyre were renown as centers for the manufacture and dying of silk textiles. The recent archaeological finds provide more evidence on the silk trade through Caesarea: A lead seal found at the site (Fig. 60) bears the monogram "Georgios *kommerki[a]rios*" on both sides.[69] In the Byzantine imperial administration the *kommerkiarios* was a high official who collected transit taxes on merchandise. Such a title is known also in later Byzantine seals as the official in charge of warehouses and on the silk commerce. A literary source from the end of the Byzantine period describing events during the Persian occupation of the city (614–627 CE), refers to the *kommerkiarios* as the most prominent Christian citizen, having direct access to the Persian governor who had resided in the city. Presumably he held a high position in the Persian administration. This literary source renders this title in Caesarea as the "archon of silk".[70] The high position he held suggests that commerce in silk through the harbor of the city was maintained also under the Persian regime.

6. Jewelry

Jewelry found in the excavations, mainly of bronze, but also of silver and gold, included rings, some of them inlaid with engraved gem stones (Fig. 61),[71] bracelets, earrings, pendants (crosses and of other shapes), and necklaces. A member of the guild of goldsmiths of Caesarea named Leontios was brought to burial in Beth She'arim.[72]

Tel Shiqmona,' *IEJ* 38 (1988): 184–186; *eadem*, 'The Purple Dye Industry in Antiquity,' *The Maritime Holy Land*, Haifa 1992: 53–60; *eadem*, 'Muricid Shells of the Persian and Hellenistic Periods,' in: *Apollonia-Arsuf: final report of the excavations* 1, Tel Aviv 1999: 269–280; I. Ziderman, 'Seashells and ancient purple dyeing,' *BA* 53 (1990): 98–101. On its imperial importance, see: W.T. Avery, 'The *adoratio purpurae* and the importance of the Imperial purple in the fourth century of the Christian era,' *Memoirs of the American Academy in Rome* 17 (1940): 66–80. Speaking about the production process, Pliny (*HN* IX 60, 126; 62, 133–134) tells that lead vats were used in the production process.

[68] Procopius, *Anecdota* 25.

[69] Nesbitt 1999: 130, no. 5.

[70] Flusin 1992, 1: 242, 2: 235. See discussion in Chapter Six below.

[71] Patrich and Refael 2008: 419–431. On gem stones see also Hamburger 1968.

[72] Levine 1975a: 70 and notes 101–104 on p. 197, had suggested that Leontios and his sons (one of them, Julianos, buried nearby, was a *palatinos*—a tax official serving in the governor's administration), were Caesareans. On the inscription see also Schwabe and Lifshitz 1967: 21 (inscr. no. 61).

7. *Metal industry*

Though no metal workshop was so far uncovered, metal slags found in the dump fills suggest that such workshops in iron, bronze and lead indeed existed. One of the Jewish Caesarean sages was a blacksmith— R. Isaac Napaha (*napah* being a blacksmith).

The metal objects found in the excavations,[73] include a large variety of bronze and iron nails, four iron tools: a heavy square axe, two agricultural implements that could have served a gardener, and a punch that might have been used by a smith, a carpenter, or in a leather workshop. Other iron finds include door and yard fittings: rings, keys and hinges. One key, of bronze, 2.5 cm long, might have locked a box of jewelry or documents. There is good reason to assume that most of these and other objects were manufactured by local blacksmiths and bronze-smiths. Other metal objects include hinges and bands of trunks, bronze revetment pegs, and a few weapons. Also were found several surgical and cosmetical instruments—*ligulae, spatula*, tweezers, probes, kohl sticks and scalpel. There were also buckles,[74] needles, a silver set of shears (Fig. 62), bells (used as charms, or as musical instruments in daily life, or in religious ceremonies), kitchen and tableware: a knife and a silver spoon (elaborately decorated, with a handle shaped like a swan head) (Fig. 63),[75] pots, candelabra hooks and chains. Sounding lead weight served navigators maneuvering while fishing in shallow waters, or while getting in or out the harbor.[76]

Lead was imported to Caesarea as ingots;[77] it was used for the sheeting of ships, for construction works, fishing, water pipes, and for magical amulets.

8. *Stone vessels industry*

This was a local industry of all kinds of stones: local *kurkar*, limestone, basalt and recycled marble and porphyry. The stone objects found in the excavations (Patrich 2008, 333–343) include spindle whorls and loom

---

[73] Refael 2008.

[74] Gold belt ornaments and a buckle that decorated the belt of one of the Caesarea elite named Stephanos, dated to the late 6th–early 7th c., was recently published by M.K. Risser in Holum *et al.* 2008: 59–65. It was suggested that the belt originated in Constantinople, and that Stephanos was an imperial magistrate.

[75] Below, Chapter Eleven; Patrich and Refael 2008: 449 (no. 250).

[76] Refael 2008: 450—nos. 269–271. See also Oleson 2000.

[77] Raban 1999.

weights associated with the local weaving industry addressed above. Grinding and filing stones as well as stone pestles, plates, bowls and mortars of various shapes and sizes,[78] could have served for the preparation of cosmetics or color powders. The stone weights found in the excavations discussed here, are of various shapes and standards; not official ones.

9. Bone and ivory (Fig. 64)

The existence of this industry in the city throughout the Roman and Byzantine periods is attested by the finds of blanks, unfinished objects and production waste.[79] The artifacts produced include handles, decorative pins, needles, dice, rings, beads, whorls or buttons, carved pieces, inlays, disks, some weapon parts and pegs for musical instruments. Knife, chisel, saw and lathe were used in the manufacture process. This industry is associated with the eating customs of the local population: the consumption of cattle (and horse) meat,[80] left abundance of bones required for this industry. Ivory objects were manufactured on a much smaller scale, and the manufacture had started only in the Byzantine period, although finished ivory artifacts were available at Caesarea already at the earlier Roman period.

10. Cosmetics and medicine

Miniature clay pots, and various glass vessels, among them single or double kohl bottles could be used as containers for medicinal salves, unguents, ointments and perfumes. Bronze kohl sticks were found as well (Fig. 65). As was indicated above small grinding plats, mortars and pestles could be used for the preparation of powders, and some metal objects served medical purposes. Perfumes merchants are listed in the "hippotrophoi inscription" mentioned above, as one of the groups (or actually guilds, like that of the goldsmiths), who had to pay a certain levy for the maintenance of the circus stables.[81]

---

[78] Patrich 2008: 337–338—nos. 69–77, 83–91; Patrich and Shadmi 2008: 345–365. The unfinished marble basins nos. 118–122, made of a recycled marble plate, indicate that these were manufactured locally.

[79] Ayalon 2005.

[80] Cope 1999.

[81] See supra, note 29. On guilds see Safrai 1994: 197–202, 296–297.

11. Food production

i. Fishery

The fishing tackle (Fig. 66) include: bronze fishing-net needles, lead fishing-net weights or sinkers, and bronze fishing hooks.[82] The study of the fish bones retrieved from two excavated areas[83] indicated that in terms of both variety and quantity, most fish consumed in the city were local marine or fresh water fish; imported fish was less evident. Those imported date to the Byzantine period, and are Egyptian Nile fish. Ponds for fish breeding in fresh water were uncovered in the South-Western zone of Caesarea, in a suburban villa, and in Tel Tanninim, located not far away to the north of the city.[84] All are dated to the Byzantine period. But it seems that each pond provided fish for the consumption of the proprietor's family (and perhaps also for his clientele); this was not a real industry. Evangelius, a rhetor of Caesarea, a noble and rich landlord, had increased his property by purchasing for 300 gold coins (*solidi*) a village on the sea shore named Porphyreon (shortly thereafter being seized from his possession by emperor Justinian).[85] Its exact location is disputed; perhaps near Haifa or Castra, to the north of Caesarea, beyond its official *territorium*. Being located on the sea shore it must have been a village of fishermen and much of its fishery yield could have been directed by its owner to Caesarea—his city.

Salt (*malha* in Aramaic) as a spice, and for the food industry, could have been easily obtained from sea water in evaporation pools. One of the 3rd c. Caesarea sages—R. Abdimi Malha,[86] was a salt merchant; Migdal Malha[87] (namely—*Malha* Tower), located on the seashore to the north of Dor, seems to be called after salt industry that had prevailed there. Nearer to Caesarea El Mallaha attests for the same industry, though no installations were so far traced at both sites.[88]

---

[82] Refael 2008: 443–444. See also Oleson *et al.* 1994: 67–73; Galili *et al.* 2010.
[83] Fradkin and Lernau 2008.
[84] Porath 1996; Holum *et al.* 1988: 184; Horton 1996: 189; Stieglitz 1998.
[85] Procopius, *Anecdota* 30.
[86] TY *Bava Mezia* 4, 9d.
[87] TY *Demai* 2, 22c. See Safrai 1994: 186.
[88] Olami *et al.* 2005, site no. 78.

ii. Wheat, oil and wine

An artificial outlet cut through the coastal *kurkar* ridge to the north and to the south of Caesarea in the Roman and Byzantine periods, had drained swamps, increasing the agricultural land, and improving health.[89] It also seems that the size of the oaks woodland (*drymus*) was decreased to let more land for agriculture.[90] In the proper *territorium* of Caesarea, a dam was built across Nahal Tanninim, before its outlet into the Mediterranean, and another one to its North-East, in the late 3rd early 4th c. These two dams created an artificial lake, whence the low-level aqueduct to Caesarea had started. On the other side of the Tanninim dam numerous watermills were constructed, thereby affording an industry of corn flour for Caesarea.[91] Basalt mill stones were also found in the city.[92]

The warehouses uncovered in the excavations inside and to the south of the Crusader town, for the storage of grain in underground granaries, and of oil and wine in *dolia* and jars, dispersed throughout the excavated area mainly next to urban villas, had occupied altogether ca. 25% of that area (Fig. 67). These goods were stored for local consumption, not for export. It was the interest of the municipal and imperial administration to guarantee adequate supply of food at reasonable prices. The Roman and Byzantine emperors also issued statutes and edicts to regulate the price of grain and other food products and to control their orderly supply. Many of them are preserved in the *Codex Theodosianus*. The "grain buyer" (*sitonos*)—a prominent municipal magistrate in each city—was in charge of supplying grain for the city.[93] Interestingly, an amulet against lumbago uncovered near one of the underground granaries depicts on its obverse a reaper with a broken back holding a sickle, harvesting corn ears. On the reverse a Greek inscription reads CXIWN, which stands for (ὑπὲρ) ἰσχίων, "for the hips" (Fig. 68).

---

[89] Nir 1959.

[90] Roll and Ayalon 1989: 216.

[91] Oleson 1984; 'Ad 2005.

[92] Patrich and Shadmi 2008: 348, 359 (in a fill); Bull and Storvick 1993 (in domestic context).

[93] On all these see discussion and references in Patrich 1996 (Chapter Nine below). On the wheat trade in Palestine see Safrai 1994: 316–320, 417–419.

Numerous wine and oil presses, as well as farmhouses,[94] were found dispersed in the countryside of Caesarea, and in the Samaria Hills.[95] These provided the necessary food supply to the city. A prominent wine press was a land mark to the east of the city.[96]

R. Yohanan interpreted thus the phrase *blessed shalt thou be in the field* (Deut. 28:3)—"that thy estate shall be divided in three [equal] portions of cereals, olives and vines".[97]

The warehouses and granaries found next to the urban palatial mansions to be described below, in which the three basic agricultural products—grain, oil and wine—were stored,[98] indicate that property division into three portion recommended by this Jewish *midrash* was a common practice.

---

[94] Hirschfeld 2000.

[95] For the immediate vicinity of Caesarea see the archaeological survey of Binyamina map (Olami *et al.* 2005), sites nos. 9, 10, 14, 28, 45, 99, 107 and 114. (Site no. 22—Kh. Zeituna—suggests olive horticulture, but no remains of an oil press was traced there in the survey). To the north-east, in Daliya survey map (Olami 1981), remains of wine or oil presses were encountered in sites nos. 16, 19, 24, 25, 28, 30?, 43?, 44, 46, 47, 52, 59, 63, 75, 77, 79, 91, 151. Within the areas of these maps, and farther away from Caesarea, wine and oil presses were excavated in Ramat HaNadiv and Kh. Jalame, an oil press in H. Sumaqa on the Carmel, an oil press at Nahal Hagit and in Shuni, and a wine press in Tel Hefer. Not all of them can be considered as located in the *territorium* of Caesarea (see Ayalon *et al.* 2009, with farther references). Farther south, in Hadera survey map (Neemam *et al.* 2000), remains of an olive press were traced in site no. 43, and of a wine press in site no. 70. But no comprehensive study of the agricultural installations in the *territorium* of Caesarea (on this territory see discussion and references in Patrich 2009a: 159*–161* = Chapter Two above), was so far undertaken. The survey map of Regavim (Gadot and Tepper 2008), is an exception—a case apart. Ca. 30 wine presses and 15 oil presses were recorded there, and there is a detailed discussion on typology, distribution and more. Such thematic study was carried out by Roll and Ayalon 1989 for the southern Sharon—the *territorium* of Apollonia. Most recent studies on wine and oil presses are Frankel 1999 and Magen 2008 (on oil presses in Southern Samaria and Southern Judaea), who in pp. 294–95 addresses installations found in the Sharon. Magen (2008: 258–59, 309–329) claims that two new types of pressing technology were introduced in the Umayyad period: a lever-screw-and-cylindrical weight and pier-shaped weights and a screw, and that this period, until the 9th c., had witnessed a peak in oil industry in the areas he examined. These conclusions stand in contrast with previous studies, according to which this peak had occurred earlier, in the Byzantine period. They deserve a careful re-examination. (In any case, for our sake, Early Arab Caesarea was a much smaller city than the Roman-Byzantine city). Magen also maintains that this oil industry was an initiative of the central government and that the olive oil was exported eastward, to the Umayyad territories. On the oil industry in Late Roman Palestine see also Safrai 1994: 118–127; on the grape and wine industry—*ibid.*: 126–136.

[96] T *Oholot* XVII:13.

[97] TB *Bava Mezia* 107a.

[98] Patrich 1996. See below, Chapter Nine.

A wine merchant named Isidoros is mentioned in one of the burial inscriptions of a family tomb.[99] In the 3rd and 4th c there were also wealthy Jewish wine merchants in Caesarea. One of them was R. Isaac son of Joseph, a Babylonian wine merchant who was active also in Caesarea and its region. The Rabbis of Caesarea were discussing how to calculate the number of jars to be given as priestly tithe by a merchant who has in his cellar one hundred wine jars arranged in rows.[100] It is reasonable to assume that this issue was discussed by the city sages under the background of a concrete reality, according to which there were in the city rich people who possessed in their cellars large quantities of wine jars. Jews used to purchase wine from the Samaritans until this was prohibited by Rabbi Abbahu and by other Sages.[101]

Weights (Fig. 69). These were essential, of course, for commerce. The standards for weight and measures were controlled on behalf of the municipal and provincial authorities by the local *agoranomos*, latter *episkopos*—the inspector in charge of the markets.[102] Three of the five (or six) stone weights mentioned above (of limestone, basalt and porphyry), weight 40, 116 and 424 grams; the 13 metal weights (10 of bronze, 3 of lead) are of a few grams, and hence seemingly were used by merchants of spices, perfumes and ointments, by jewelers or in financial transactions. Most of the metal weights fit (though not with absolute precision), the Roman and Byzantine system of pounds, ounces and *nomismata*. One of them may be of the Phoenician standard.[103] A fragment of a scale pan of the *bilanx* type, might have also served one of the above mentioned merchants.[104] Another find seems to have been part of an axle of a coin scale.[105] Money changers (*nomismatapuloi*) are listed in the "*hippotrophoi* inscription" mentioned above as one of

---

[99] Lehmann and Holum 2000: 162—no. 205.

[100] M *Demai* 7: 8.

[101] TY *Abodah Zarah* 5.4: 44d; TB *Hulin* 6a.

[102] For inscribed lead weights from Caesarea see Lifshitz 1961: 121; Kushnir-Stein 2007 and 2008; Holum 1986b: 231–232, 239 mentions two bronze weights from Caesarea of the type used by jewelers and in financial transactions, bearing the name of Flavius Stephanus—proconsul of Byzantine Palestine later than 536 as the issuing authority. On the weights systems that had prevailed in Palestine from the Bronze Age to the Early Arab period, see: L. Di Segni, The Weights System in Palestine," in: B.Z. Kedar, T. Dothan Sh. Safrai (eds.), *Commerce in Palestine Throughout the Ages*, Jerusalem 1990: 202–220 (Hebrew).

[103] Refael 2008: 444–445—nos. 170–182.

[104] Refael 2008, no. 183.

[105] Refael 2008, no. 184.

the guilds, who had to pay a certain toll for the maintenance of the circus stables.[106]

Lead seals (bullae) (Fig. 70). These were used to seal a folded letter, or to authenticate a signature on a sealed package or merchandise. Altogether, 46 lead seals were found, 36 of them readable; all of them from the 6th-7th c. In addition to the seal of Georgios *kommrerkiarios* mentioned above, there is another seal indicative of the commercial life in the city. It is a seal of an un-named customs imperial official who had the right to levy and collect customs on goods in transit. It is dated to 638–641 CE. Imprints of burlap on its reverse indicate that it was attached to a sack of merchandise by that official.[107]

II. DWELLINGS OF THE WEALTHY

Our Rabbis taught: Who is wealthy? He who has pleasure in his wealth: this is R. Meir's view. R. Tarfon said: He who possesses a hundred vineyards, a hundred fields and a hundred slaves working in them.... R. Jose said: He who has a privy near his table.[108]

While it is self evident that much land and many servants are indicators of wealth, why is a privy mentioned here? Dwelling conditions in ancient times, as at present, are among the proper criteria for defining a wealthy person. In antiquity, most people had their privy in the courtyard, rather than within the house. Only the rich could afford such amenities. A nice example of a private privy was found at the northern end of area NN, next to a spacious reception hall decorated with the "Ibexes Mosaic" (Fig. 71). The privy is located at the western end of a corridor that delineated this hall on the north. A Greek inscription located nearby says "Good Luck Dionysius" (Fig. 72)—presumably the owner's name. Another reception hall,

---

[106] See *supra*, note 29.
[107] Nesbitt 1999: 129—no. 2. It is recognized as a seal of a customs official by its iconography: the figures of Heraclius, Heraclius Constantine and Heraklonas (638–641), standing, are depicted on its obverse. Two other seals were classified as of the civil administration: One, monogramatic, reads Leon *chartoulariou* or *magistrou*, in which civil department it is not known; the other—Bardas *notarios* (Nesbitt 1999: 130—nos. 4 and 6), was involved in the administration of law. Other seals bear honorific titles, and there are also ecclesiastical and private seals. One was imperial, depicting the bust of Justinian on its obverse, and victory standing to front, holding a wreath on each hand on the reverse.
[108] TB *Shabbath* 25b, tr. I. Epstein, London: Soncino.

apsidal in shape, that was uncovered nearby, had a colorful tiles pavement (*opus sectile*)—the fanciest floor type. This elaborate architectonic complex extended farther east, in an area that has not yet been excavated.

A palatial mansion with a private latrine was uncovered in its entirety by the IAA expedition farther south.[109] The latrine occupied a separate wing of a bathhouse.[110] Access to both was via a small courtyard decorated with fonts. The palatial mansion under discussion (Fig. 73) extended over a vast area between Cardo W1 and the seashore. Besides the bathhouse and the latrine, located in the southern part of the complex, it also comprised dwelling quarters and reception halls arranged around a vast courtyard adorned with fountains and surrounded by columns. The main reception-hall was on the western side. It comprised an apsidal nave flanked by aisles. The two columns of the *di-stylos in-antis* façade, were taller and thicker than the other columns around the courtyard. A wide staircase, occupying the entire western side of the courtyard was leading-up to the façade. The reception hall and the aisles were erected on top of four subterranean chambers, roofed by lateral arches. Another apsidal hall extended on the southern side of the courtyard, while to its east was the dwelling wing. The lavishness of the vast complex is also expressed by the high quality of the building materials applied, and by its decorative mosaics, including wall and ceiling ones. To the north of this palatial mansion, a large complex of six spacious warehouses had extended (Fig. 74). It seems that all of them were owned by the proprietor of the villa.[111] The warehouses were of two types—a courtyard type and a corridor type. Large *pithoi* (Gr.)[112]/*dolia* (Lat.), that held oil, stood along the walls of long halls, paved with crude white *tesserae*. Wine was held in local jars, stored in other rooms of the warehouses, and grain was stored in underground granaries. The warehouses thus served for the storage of agricultural provisions destined for the inhabitants of Caesarea. These provisions seemingly came from the estates of the villa owner—a wealthy landlord like the one mentioned in the proverb of Rabbi Tarfon mentioned above. Another complex of warehouses, near

---

[109] Porath 1996: 105–120; 1998: 42–43, fig. 4.
[110] The excavators had identified the entire complex as a bathhouse, rather than as a vast palatial mansion with a private bathhouse. In the 5th and 6th centuries, and even earlier, a private bathhouse was a regular component of wealthy dwellings.
[111] Patrich 1996: 146–176, and Chapter Nine below.
[112] Cf. M *Bava Batra* 6: 2.

the harbor (in area LL), first erected in the Herodian period, and in continuous use until the end of the Byzantine period, seems to had served the maritime trade.[113]

A similar picture of wealth—a palatial mansion with a complex of warehouses and shops—was uncovered by the IAA expedition in the next urban block (*insula*) to the south. This vast structure extends as well between Cardo W1 and the seashore. Adjacent to the sea it held a pleasure garden with a fountain and irrigation channels. A wide corridor was leading to a broad staircase that descended to a pergola paved by marble slabs and delineated by piers and hence to the beach (Fig. 75). There were two courtyards. The eastern one served a two-storied wing with marble columns. In its northern side was a trilobate dining hall (*stibadium*).[114] One of the rooms held a workshop for colorful tiny sawed *opus sectile* tiles, for the decoration of the floors and walls of the villa. Three parallel warehouses of the corridor type occupied the southern part of this *insula*.[115]

Elaborate villas were also uncovered outside the city walls. The most impressive was the one located at the top of the *kurkar* ridge, to the north-east of the city, several hundred meters from its wall, overlooking the city and the sea. Its central courtyard was adorned by the "Birds Mosaic" (Fig. 76).[116] An extraordinary item found therein is a table plate inlaid with golden glass *tesserae*. In the more remote countryside, in Ramat HaNadiv, on the southern end of the Carmel ridge, two farmhouses were excavated; one—Herodian, the other—Byzantine. Both might have belonged to the affluent people of Caesarea.[117]

The literary sources, together with the small finds and architectural remains uncovered in the archaeological excavations enable to better understand several aspects of commerce and economy in Late Antique Caesarea and get a more detailed and refined picture of the living conditions there at that period.

---

[113] Levine and Netzer 1986; Stabler and Holum 2008.

[114] Porath 1996: 105–120; 1998: 42–43, fig. 4. On the unique plan of this zone of Caesarea—a line of villas along the cardo, with comparisons to other sites, such as Apamea in Syria, see Patrich 2001a, and Chapter Four above.

[115] There were also Jews who owned houses: Zeira son of Hama was the owner of the house where R. Ami, R. Asi, R. Joshua son of Levi and the entire Rabbis of Caesarea were residing (BT *Yoma* 78a).

[116] Porath 2006; Spiro 1992.

[117] Hirschfeld and Birger-Calderon 1991: 81–111; Hirschfeld 2000.

CHAPTER SIX

CAESAREA IN TRANSITION: THE ARCHAEOLOGICAL
EVIDENCE FROM THE SOUTHWEST ZONE
(AREAS CC, KK, NN)

The impact of the Muslim conquest of 641[1] on urban life in the South-west Zone of Caesarea (Figs. 29 and 77) is at the core of our topic. Were urban space and urban life just modified, or did they come to an abrupt end following this historical event? Or perhaps was the process of transformation gradual, beginning earlier in the sixth century, the result of internal, long-term processes, such as the sixth-century Samaritan revolts or the plague, enhanced by the Persian occupation of Palestine (614–627)?[2] K.G. Holum examined the transition period at Caesarea in several places,[3] as L.E. Toombs had earlier.[4] While Toombs was of the opinion that these events, and especially the Arab conquest, were major causes of urban decline,[5] Holum, in his more recent

---

[1] On the conquest of Palestine see Gil 1983, 1: 9–61; 1992: 59–60; Schick 1995: 68–84. On the conquest of Syria in general, see Hill 1971: 59–84; Donner 1981: 91–155, 301–23. For the historical background as reflected in the Syriac sources, see Palmer 1993: xiv–xxviii.

[2] Stratos 1968: 134–65; 248–93; Schick 1995: 20–67; Flusin 1992: 67–365; Baras 1982: 300–349.

[3] Wiemken and Holum 1981: 29, 40–41; Holum *et al.* 1988: 202–6; Holum 1989; 1992b. The transition period was also a topic of Lenzen 1983.

[4] Toombs 1978. Reifenberg 1951 is a general survey derived from analysis of aerial photographs, and written before any excavations took place at the site.

[5] The Toombs article pertains to excavations in 1971–1974 of the American Joint Expedition to Caesarea Maritima (JECM) in its fields A, B (both to the east of the Old City), C (our field CC, now recognized as the site of the *praetorium* of the Byzantine governor), and H (the eastern hippodrome, or Roman circus of Caesarea). In order to establish an overall stratigraphy valid for excavation areas remote from one another, JECM adopted the destruction layers overlying the latest Byzantine occupation as the stratigraphic key to the site, and then adopted a system of "general phases" by working upward and downward in the balk section from this reference layer. The result was checked against the ceramic and coin evidence, and if the results matched the phases were considered contemporary (1978: 223). This method seems to have been most logical. In squares C10 (at the western entrance to vault 1) and C16 (above vaults 5 and 6) "the final Byzantine surfaces rest on leveled destruction debris, and are overlaid by the massive destruction layers which mark the end of the Byzantine period. They are associated with poorly-constructed rebuilds of earlier Byzantine structures" (1978: 228). In the "archive building" (now recognized as the provincial revenue office of the

articles, emphasized that it was not the purposeful, physical plundering and destruction of the city, for which there is little evidence, so he
claimed, that was the cause of decline but the desertion of the elite,
of the bouleutic class.[6] The more we explore and excavate, the more

---

praetorium), the floors of the "Main Byzantine Period" (330–614 CE), were overlaid
by debris attributed tentatively to the Persian conquest, which was leveled off and
became the base for the surfacing of the "Final Byzantine Period" (614–40 CE). This is
overlaid by a heavy destruction layer (attributed to the Arab conquest), characteristic
of the close of the Byzantine era (1978: 228). Toombs' concluding remarks pertaining
to the effects of these two conquests on the urban space of Caesarea at large are these:
"This <the Persian> invasion caused widespread destruction and brought the Main
Byzantine Period to a close, but recovery was rapid and the city was restored, although
its magnificence was greatly reduced. In A.D. 640 Caesarea fell to Arab invaders. This
time the destruction was complete and irretrievable. Battered columns and the empty
shells of buildings stood naked above heaps of tangled debris. Among these ruins a
few survivors attempted to clear enough space among the rubble to make life possible"
(1978: 230).

  [6] Whereas in his early article (Wiemken and Holum 1981), Holum agreed with
Toombs' stratigraphic and historical interpretation, in his later publications, he
expressed reservations on various grounds. On the literary sources on the Arab conquest he claimed in his 1992 article (1992b: 74) that "the relevant literary sources are
brief, late, and mostly unreliable," and that "no literary evidence suggests pillage, burning, and destruction on a scale catastrophic enough to interrupt urban life." As will
be indicated below, the literary sources do suggest an abrupt and violent end, though
not widespread purposeful plundering or destruction caused by the conquering Arabs.
About Toombs' method of stratigraphy he argues (*ibid.*), that "without positive evidence there is no reason to associate so-called 'destruction' layers in various parts of
the site with one another in a single episode of Muslim pillage. These layers might just
as well present discrete cases of conflagration and collapse separated from one another
by decades or even centuries and of completely innocent or even natural etiology."
But, one wonders, would *loci* "separated from one another by decades or even centuries" yield similar small finds? This was an essential point in Toombs' methodology,
and if sustained by a reliable pottery and numismatics reading, it seems to be sound.
As for the finds in area LL, formerly excavated by Netzer and Levine on behalf of the
Hebrew University (Holum 1992b: 75), cf. their present interpretation by Holum in
Holum and Lapin (forthcoming), which corresponds very much with finds in other
areas, indicating a ruined layer of desertion, a result of the Arab conquest, followed
by a new stage of resettlement with floors raised over the earlier ruins, and humbler
architecture. In Field K (our Area KK, located to south of the Joint Expedition's Field
C), no remains that could be associated with the Persian conquest came to light, but
deposits associated with the Muslim sack were reported (namely, by Wiemken and
Holum 1981), but in 1992 he preferred to attribute "much of the alleged Muslim
destruction to accidental or natural causes" (199b: 80). He also suggests that "the long
Muslim siege and subsequent storming of Caesarea may have proven much more
devastating ultimately to the city's society and economy than to its buildings. During
the siege many of the Caesarea's wealthy, Christian, Greek-speaking inhabitants, may
have elected to escape by sea, and other Christian Caesareans, especially the wealthy
and prominent, may have preferred to emigrate to Byzantine lands after the conquest
rather than live in their native city under Muslim rule" (199b: 83). See also Holum
et al. 1988: 204. The present excavations indicate that he was right about the effect of
the conquest on the local society; the result was an abrupt architectural transformation

detailed and refined is our understanding. Different excavated zones of the city reveal somewhat different stories. Therefore, a reassessment of previous theories has become indispensable, after the large-scale excavations of the 1990s, in which vast sectors of the city were uncovered, mainly in its Southwest Zone, on the Temple Platform, and in the area below the Temple Platform to the west, including the harbor. Moreover, we now have a new, local, non-Muslim literary source, published only in 2002,[7] that permits a better evaluation of the other literary sources available.

The focus here is on the Southwest Zone of Caesarea Maritima (Fig. 77), a tract ca. 80 m. wide and 800 m. long extending along the sea between the Harbor and the Temple Platform in the north and the Roman theater in the south. Today it has been exposed almost entirely down to its Byzantine and Roman levels. Until the end of its urban phase it constituted a significant part of Caesarea; here the administrative and military centers were located, with the dwellings of the elite in between.[8] Its fate in the transition period will provide a telling story about the history of Caesarea at large. In this paper will be examined the final urban stage of two large Late Roman/Byzantine architectural

---

of the urban sphere in the zone under consideration. Holum elaborated this theory best in his 1996 article (1996b: 626–27). In his 1989 article, critical about Toombs' stratigraphy and interpretation of destruction layers in various areas in two distinct phases, representing the Persian and the Muslim conquests, he had not yet developed the thesis of desertion of the bouleutic class. Like Kennedy (1985a and 1985b), he favored a decline of *longe durée* (1989: 83). In Caesarea, so he claimed, decline might have started with the Samaritan and Jewish revolts of the late fifth and sixth centuries. Accordingly, he maintained (1989: 95) that "for the historian of classical antiquity, the correct approach is to recognize that in general the Muslim conquest did not bring an end to ancient urbanism in the Middle East but only accelerated the transformation of the ancient *polis* into a Muslim *madina*." Though he admits that during the conquest Caesarea lost population by violent death, captivity, and flight, and that the warfare caused damage, he would recommend that "as they explore the transition from classical urbanism to Muslim *madina* at Caesarea Maritima, archaeologists and historians should keep this or similar model in mind, abandoning the destruction theory" (1989: 96). As we will see below, urban structures in the Southwest Zone of Caesarea indeed turned into ruins as a result of the conquest. The Muslim conquest did result in an abrupt physical decline, though neither due to setting the entire city on fire nor due to a systematic destruction by the storming conquerors, as was argued by Toombs. The process was more complicated. In this regard there is a clear distinction between the fate of Caesarea and that of other cities discussed in Holum and Lapin (forthcoming).

[7] The Continuatio *of the Samaritan Chronicle of Abu al-Fath al-Samiri al-Danafi*, ed. Levy-Rubin 2002. Amikam El'ad of the Hebrew University of Jerusalem is currently accumulating more Arabic sources related to Islamic Caesarea.

[8] For a general description of Late Antique/Byzantine Caesarea see Patrich 2001a (= Chapter Four above).

complexes located in the northern end of this zone, immediately to the south of the Crusader wall: the public wing of the palace of the Byzantine governor, the *praetorium*, and a Late Roman/Byzantine complex of six warehouses extending all over area KK adjacent on the south to the *praetorium*. The *praetorium* occupied the first urban block (*insula*) to the south of the harbor and the octagonal *martyrion*. The complex of warehouses and a palatial mansion associated with it occupied the next *insulae* (Fig. 78).[9]

THE ARCHAEOLOGICAL EVIDENCE

In all, we defined nine strata and sub-strata in the excavations under discussion, representing major phases of construction, settlement, or destruction. Of these, our present concern is with the five strata and sub-strata in the following table:[10]

Stratum	Period	Findings
IVB	Fifth–sixth centuries CE, the Byzantine period	Warehouse complex in Area KK, the Byzantine governor's palace (*praetorium*) in Areas CC and NN
IVA	634–41 CE, the seven-year siege leading to the Arab conquest	End of the urban era: the Byzantine buildings (warehouses in Area KK and the *praetorium* in Areas CC and NN) were abandoned.
IIIB	634–41 CE, end of the Byzantine period	A layer of rubble inside the abandoned Byzantine buildings
IIIA	634–50 CE, transition from the Byzantine to the Early Arab period	The siege and the first few years after the Arab conquest. Wells were dug and terraced, irrigated gardens were installed on top of the ruins of the Byzantine buildings. A layer of garden soil rich in organic waste
II	700–800 CE, the Umayyad-Abbasid period	Sand layer with eroded Byzantine potsherds, perhaps the result of dredging operations in the silted harbor

---

[9] For more details on the finds in these areas, located in the north of the SW Zone, and on their stratigraphy, see below, Chapters Eight, Nine and Ten; Patrich *et al.* 1999. For the finds further south, see Porath 1998; 1996a; 2001.

[10] The reader should note that after further study I modified the date I assigned to stratum IIIA in my preliminary report, Patrich *et al.*, 1999: 72.

The stratigraphy is quite neat. The last urban layer was followed by a layer of terraced gardens installed on top of the abandoned and ruined buildings. Later, in the Abbasid, Fatimid, and Crusader periods the area became a cemetery of cist tombs and simple burials. Assigning a precise date to each stratum, though a more intricate problem, is quite clear and precise as well.

In the *praetorium* (Fig. 35) and its annexes there are indications of decline in municipal and architectural standards and negligence in its physical maintenance already in the final urban phases of the Byzantine period. These are expressed in the following:

Deterioration in the water supply:
1. The water supply system fed by aqueducts, repaired early in the sixth century,[11] ceased serving the Southwest Zone.
2. At the northwest corner of the decumanus S1 and cardo W1 intersection, two tiny street fountains were located facing cardo W1, one on each end of the Western Stoa. At an earlier stage these fountains had apparently been connected by two subfloor pipes to the aqueduct-fed pipeline system, which also had provided water to the adjacent latrine. Later, however, a well located nearby served as the source of water. In the final phase the mosaic floor of the stoa was cut through and the (lead?) pipes were looted.
3. An octagonal fountain in the bathhouse of the *praetorium* and its adjacent reservoir, previously fed by channels and pipes from the east, later took its water from a new circular well (no. 14) located to the south.
4. The bath of the palatial mansion to the south of Area KK, earlier fed by water pipes running beneath cardo W1, took its water in its final stage likewise from a well that employed a wheeled mechanical lifting device for drawing water.[12]
5. New wells were also dug within the warehouses, in buildings I (well no. 13), II (no. 9), III (no. 14), and IV (no. 16), so there was clearly a shortage in running (aqueduct) water available to this zone.
6. The latrine at the intersection of cardo W1 and decumanus S2 was reduced to half of its original size (Fig. 79).

---

[11] On the restoration of the water supply system earlier in the sixth century, under Justinian, see Mayerson 1986. On the water supply system of Caesarea in general see Porath 2002. For the end of water supply from the aqueducts to the Southwest Zone at the end of the Byzantine period, see *ibid.* 125.

[12] *Ibid.* and see also Porath 1996a: 114, and 1998: 42–43.

Deterioration of the praetorium and in its maintenance:

1. In the revenue office a stone floor replaced a mosaic floor in one of the waiting rooms.[13] Similarly, the uppermost mosaic in the central hall of the revenue office was fashioned from very crude tesserae.
2. Various "industrial" installations were installed in the vaults beneath the *praetorium*: tabuns near the open, western ends of vaults 2 and 11, a stable with a drainage channel in vault 12, a basin and a channel in vaults 6 and 7 respectively (Figs. 80a–c).
3. A tavern and a wine cellar were installed in vaults 4, 13, and 5. Two openings were cut through the south wall of vault 13, leading into the tavern from decumanus S2. Benches were installed in the open court in the corner between vaults 13 and 5 (Figs. 81–82).
4. Streets were apparently left uncleaned. A layer of soil ca. 5 cm. thick covered decumanus S1, but this might have been accumulated in the very final years, when Caesarea was under the Muslim siege.

Dating the deterioriation

While the deterioration in the water supply, resulting in a shift from aqueduct-fed, running water to well water, might have occurred already in the second half of the sixth century, the deterioration in the maintenance of the Byzantine *praetorium* occurred later, during its occupation by the Persian administration in Caesarea (614–627 CE) or in the following years. The stone floor laid over mosaics in the revenue office (*skrinion*) of the *praetorium*, covering a Christian inscription, was attributed by Toombs to the Persian period.[14] A fresco depicting Christ and the Twelve Apostles in vault 10 seems similarly to have been concealed then by white-washing.[15] It seems that during this phase the elaborate latrine, comprising three wings of seats around a paved courtyard, was reduced to just the long, southern wing. Elsewhere at Caesarea, in Fields A and B east of the Old City, Toombs suggested that modifications, more minor in scale, likewise resulted from the Persian conquest.[16] It is true that the Persian occupation did not bring urban life to an end, yet it seems to have caused deteriora-

---

[13] JECM excavated this room; see Holum 1995.
[14] Toombs 1978: 226–29.
[15] Avner 1999.
[16] Toombs 1978: 223–26.

tion of the urban space, especially in the *praetorium* and some other public structures.

For certain the Persian conquest affected the population, especially when Caesarea's inhabitants learned of the massacre the Persians perpetrated in Jerusalem and in the Great Laura of Saint Sabas.[17] Though the city capitulated,[18] unlike Jerusalem, it is reasonable to assume that peasants from the countryside had fled to the walled city, and that some of its citizens sought refuge abroad, as was the case with Maximus the Confessor and other communities of monks, fleeing from the Desert of Jerusalem across the Jordan or to Alexandria, North Africa, Rome, Constantinople, and other territories still under the Byzantine regime.[19]

UNDER THE PERSIAN OCCUPATION

After the Persian conquest, the Jerusalem bishop Modestus, assisted by John the Almsgiver, patriarch of Alexandria, restored some life to the Christian communities.[20] Some details about the situation in Caesarea during and after the Persian occupation are provided by the *Acts* of Anastasius the Persian, martyred in 627 CE, formerly a Persian cavalryman named Magundat who had converted to Christianity and in 620 had joined a monastery near Jerusalem.[21] During the occupation,

---

[17] Flusin 1992: 20–21, 151–72, 179–80, with references to earlier studies. On the fate of the Great Laura of Saint Sabas, see Patrich 1995a: 326–28.

[18] Flusin 1992: 153.

[19] On the fate of Maximus Confessor and other Palestinian monks during this period, see Boudignon 2004.

[20] Flusin 1992: 173–77.

[21] Kaegi 1978; Flusin 1992: 231–43. The Greek *Acta martyris Anastasii Persae*, ed. Usener 1894; ed. Flusin 1992, comprises the *Vita, Translatio,* and *Miracula* performed by his relics in several places, including Caesarea (Mirac. 7–10, ed. Usener 1894: 22–24; ed. Flusin 1992: 130–39). The accounts of the Caesarea miracles were originally composed in Syriac by a contemporary (Usener 1894: 20–21). (Another edition of the *Vita*, based on a different manuscript, was published by Papadopoulos-Kerameus in 1897.) An *Encomium*, based on the *Vita*, published by A. Pertusi *AB* 76 1958: 5–63, was attributed in three MSS to a contemporary poet in the court of Heraclius, George of Pisidia. In a fourth MS from Berlin it is attributed instead to Sophronius of Jerusalem. Usener was of the opinion that the actual author of the *Encomium* was indeed Sophronius, and that later, at Constantinople during the Monotheletic period, it was reattributed to Pisides. Pertusi refuted this theory, and Flusin, in his comprehensive, more recent publication of all these Greek texts with French translation and extensive commentary, followed Pertusi (*Saint Anastase le Perse* ed. Flusin 1992: 191–97). However, the *Encomium*'s acquaintance with the urban space of Caesarea (see n. 23

the Persian administration and judicial system had functioned effectively, maintaining regular correspondence with the Persian king at Dastagerd in Persia. The Persian district governor (*marzabanas*),[22] apparently in charge of *Palaestina Secunda* as well, resided in the *debras*, the *praetorium*,[23] that was guarded by a unit of soldiers under the command of a *sellarios*, a Persian officer. The garrison was stationed in the *kastron*, the Byzantine fortress built in the sixth century surrounding the deteriorating Roman theater. In the *kastron* was a military prison where Anastasius was detained. There was also a more public prison under a less stringent regime. The attitude towards the Christian community was lenient, since pious Christians seeking to encourage Anastasius quite easily entered and left his prison. The highest Christian dignitary, who enjoyed open access to the governor, was the *kommerkiarios*, who appears to have been integrated into the Persian administration. His office was perhaps an innovation of this period.[24] At his request Anastasius was permitted to celebrate the feast of the Exaltation of the Cross (September 14, 627) outside of the prison, in one of the churches, after a vigil service during the previous night celebrated inside the prison without any restrictions. In the prison the congregation included other members of the Christian community, among them two monks who had come to Caesarea from their monastery near Jerusalem. Anastasius, the two monks, and another Christian were also invited to dine with the *kommerkiarios* in his house. On January 22, 628, however, Anastasius, having been transported from Caesarea, was executed and became a martyr. After the restoration of

---

below) and its functionaries (see n. 24 below) may lend more credence to Palestinian authorship, as Usener suggested already in 1894.

[22] Gignoux 1984; Flusin 1992: 234.

[23] Pisides renders *debras* as *archeion*, the headquarters of a magistrate. The reference is to the *praetorium* of the Byzantine governor, which seems to have been converted to serve as the residence of the Persian governor in Palestine, the *marzabanas* (Flusin 1992: 233–34).

[24] Kaegi 1978: 179, renders this term as "revenue official," but the *Encomium* is more specific about his actual function, rendering this term as the "silk archon (ed. Flusin 1992: 242; and vol. 2: 235). Flusin points out that such a functionary is not known at Caesarea before this period in any of the Byzantine sources. But a lead seal found in area KK bear on its two faces the monogram *Georgios kommerki[a]rios* (Fig. 60). See Nesbitt 1999: 130 (cat. no. 5, from the "garden soil" layer). The *kommerkiarios* collected imposts on goods in transit. Such an official, known from other Byzantine seals, was in charge of warehouses and associated with the silk trade. See Zacos and Veglery 1972: 135; Oikonomides 1986: 33–53. This may suggest silk trade through the harbor of Caesarea during this period.

Byzantine rule, his remains were translated back to Caesarea, where they were displayed for veneration and performed miracles. A chapel was constructed near the *tetrapylon*, in the center of the city, to commemorate the new martyr, and his icon placed on the *tetrapylon* received veneration. From Caesarea his relics were taken to a final resting place in his monastery near Jerusalem (November 2, 631), although a fragment remained in Caesarea. A small Persian community also existed in Caesarea, which installed a fire-temple discretely in a private house where magi conducted sacred rites.[25]

THE ARAB CONQUEST OF CAESAREA AND ITS CONSEQUENCES

The Arab conquest was a different story. As will be indicated below, the available sources, Muslim, Christian, and Samaritan, agree that Caesarea was conquered in war, after a siege that lasted six or seven years. There was killing, deportation, and desertion on a large scale.

Can the traces of the siege and fight be recognized in the archaeological record in Caesarea and its countryside? A suburban villa with a mosaic pavement depicting birds in its center,[26] excavated and preserved by the Israel Antiquities Authority, was apparently destroyed by fire during the Arab conquest. Northeast of Caesarea, the excavators linked the demise of the Byzantine manor at Ramat ha-Nadiv with the Arab conquest. In the absence of evidence for deliberate damage or conflagration, they suggested that faced with the Arab menace the inhabitants of the estate abandoned it in an orderly manner shortly after the conquest.[27]

The excavations also provided evidence for the fate of Caesarea's Southwest Zone during the Arab siege and thereafter. The end of urban life in the areas that we excavated was abrupt, but it was marked by desertion, not by a large scale conflagration, as was proposed by Toombs. Stratum IVA is a layer of fill some dozens of cm. thick that accumulated over the floors inside the abandoned Byzantine structures. The small finds suggest that the *praetorium* and the adjacent

[25] Flusin 1992: 231.
[26] The mosaic floors was exposed long ago; see Spiro 1992. In conjunction with recent restoration of the mosaic, the excavated area was extended and further wings of the villa were uncovered; see Porath 2006.
[27] Hirschfeld and Birger-Calderon 1991: 109; Hirschfeld 2000: 13–87, esp. 78.

palatial mansion excavated by the Israel Antiquities Authority (Fig. 73) had been abandoned during the Muslim siege (634–41 CE) but that the walls were left standing. Later on, building materials, including roof tiles, ceiling beams, and building blocks, were gradually looted rather than set on fire *in situ*. This occurred mainly along the cardo, on both sides. Next we witness an initiative to convert a large area into terraced, irrigated garden plots. Their traces occurred all over the warehouses in area KK (Figs. 42, 83), including the western, lower level of the adjacent IAA mansion; on the south fringes of the former *praetorium* in area CC, in front and above vaults 6 and 7; and above the latrine and the western stoa delineating cardo W1 (see map, Fig. 84).

Establishing the gardens involved the following operations:

First, the plots were terraced and leveled. This operation is best illustrated in the so-called *dolia* hall of the warehouse designated as building I, where we discovered a difference of ca. 3 m. between its floor and the area to its east and south. Above the accumulated stratum IVA there was a thick, distinctive layer, stratum IIIB, of rubble from a second story, the walls of which were deliberately demolished in order to decrease elevation differences (Fig. 85).[28] Then a network of poor walls, one or two courses deep, was constructed, forming terraces. Another well-stratified plot was set over the stone-paved courtyard of building I, delineated on the north by a barrier wall built of standing kurkar column drums. The irrigated gardens extended over several terraces, descending gradually from east to west. Soil rich in organic waste, comprising stratum IIIA, was poured over the flattened debris.

Second, wells were dug, or the shafts of existing wells were built upward, a total of twelve wells altogether (see the map, Fig. 84). Of these, seven wells were dug anew (Fig. 86), and the tops of five older wells were raised to meet the level of the garden plots. Thus the walls of well 13 (in building I) were elevated, and a stone pavement was laid on its south side to facilitate drawing water. A path leading to it from the shelter installed in building V and from the ruined mansion to the south was marked by stones and by a fallen column. Similarly, the walls of well 16 in building IV and of well 5 in the latrine at the street intersection were extended upward to meet the elevated ground level

---

[28] For a description of the remains, including a suggested reconstruction of the upper storey, see Patrich 2000b; 2001c, and below, Chapters Nine and Ten.

of the terraced gardens. Two new wells, nos. 11 and 12, were dug in building II, and three, nos. 15, 18, 19, in building III; another, no. 6, to the south of vault 6, and a seventh, no. 3, to the west of vault 12. The wells, actually more than twelve altogether, were dispersed throughout the area, in about five north-south lines, each intended to irrigate several plots by gravitational flow.

Third, the irrigation channels were laid (Figs. 86–87). Within the plots, stones were laid lengthwise abutting one another in north-south or east-west lines. Channels 10 cm. wide and ca. 10 cm. deep were cut into the top of the rectangular blocks, creating a single, in-line channel. V-shaped notches at intervals of ca. 0.5–1 m. opened to right or left of the main channel, through which water flowed from the wells to adjacent planting beds. Stone vats were placed near the openings of the wells, at the beginning points of the channels, to receive the water as it was drawn. In two cases, wells 6 and 13, stone sarcophagi served this purpose. The irrigation channels uncovered in the basement of the apsidal hall of the palatial mansion suggest that this building was already in ruins as well.[29]

Fourth, in three places shelters were installed for the gardeners and their equipment. Above decumanus S2, in front of vaults 9 and 10, a path delineated by two rows of stones occupied the position of the earlier street, leading from the west. Above the vaults, in the south wing of the *praetorium*, rooms that formerly had served as offices for clerks were adapted for new functions. Their openings to the north were blocked, and various crude installations for tools and storage shelves were installed. Several rooms of warehouse building V were occupied as well. The courtyard floor was elevated to reach the new ground level of the garden. The columns surrounding the courtyard were shifted. The location of this shelter overlooking the entire area, its structure, and the adjacent large well with a paved floor for drawing water, suggest that this shelter controlled the entire enterprise, at least the Area KK gardens. In spite of the multiplicity of wells, the absence of separate paths to each plot or well precludes the possibility of 12 separate proprietors. Suggested instead is a more centralized administration, perhaps under the former steward of the adjacent palatial mansion, and under another one or two overseers who controlled the southern fringe of the former *praetorium*.

---

[29] Porath 1996a: 127–28, fig. 23.

This garden enterprise and the earlier looting of building materials were not associated yet with the construction of lime kilns and the burning of marble pieces. Several marble columns, still extant, were incorporated into the terrace walls in Area KK, as mentioned above, and others remained exposed above the former latrine (Fig. 88). An Ionic capital of the latrine courtyard, broken to two pieces when it fell, was likewise incorporated into a terrace built there (Fig. 89), rather than going into an adjacent lime-kiln. As the stratification indicates, the lime-kilns were constructed later, apparently in conjunction with the next major building project in the adjacent area, the establishment of the cemetery and building of the city wall in the Abbasid period.

This sequence of events was even clearer in the apsidal basement of the palatial mansion to the south, where a thick layer of burned lime accumulated above the garden plots installed there, indicating that the lime-kiln uncovered in the upper level of the mansion, the source of the burned lime, was established well after the period of the irrigated gardens. By that time many columns had already been buried and thus escaped the fate of marble pieces still on the surface.

Dating the terraced gardens

One wonders who were the initiators of the terraced gardens, whether they were Muslims or Christians. It struck us that on one of the two columns found above the former latrine someone incised a cross when the column was already lying horizontally (Fig. 88), incorporated into the terrace. Clearly the person who inscribed this cross was a Christian.

The dating of the garden stratum is the main question. The leveled garden soil was rich in urban garbage including potsherds and other finds from the Byzantine period, fragments of glass vessels, coins, lead seals, long bronze needles, and pieces of lead. The ceramic evidence, illustrated by the four plates published here (Pls. I–IV),[30] as well as the finds inside the wells, are typical of the Byzantine period. Many types continued indeed into the second half of the seventh century, but post-700 CE types are altogether missing. The numismatic evidence is even more decisive. Out of the 12,426 coins recorded from

---

[30] Julia Idelson prepared the plates, and Barbara Johnson examined them. I am grateful for their contributions.

our excavation, only 584 are dated to the seventh century or later.[31] Most are not later than Heraclius. Of these coins, only 19 came from the garden soil, from five different loci. Of these 16 are attributed to the seventh century in general, but eight of them are of the Alexandria I+B type (*dodecanumiae*) that are probably local imitations rather than minted in Alexandria. Such coins served as the common small change of the early seventh century, and after Heraclius this type was not minted anymore. Of the remaining three coins, one is dated to the years 582–602 (Mauricius) and the other two to 613–18 and 618–28, both from the reign of Heraclius (610–41). Another coin,[32] identified as a "Persian I+B" type, was minted in the years 618–28, during the Persian occupation. Nine of our lead seals (Fig. 70), all of them Byzantine, came from the layer of garden soil.[33]

It seems that the transformation of the urban space in the area under discussion began already during the lengthy Muslim siege when the wealthy proprietor of the warehouses and the palatial mansion, a landlord and member of the local elite, deserted these buildings. The Byzantine governor seems also to have left the besieged city by sea (below), if he was not killed in battle. The deserted structures began to be stripped of their building materials, roof-tiles and ceiling beams, but walls were not yet dismantled. When the Byzantine defeat was final, and the change in regime had become evident—if not already during the siege—walls were torn down and terraced gardens were installed, in order to provide a food supply inside the city walls during a period of insecurity when people were abandoning nearby estates like the one at Ramat ha-Nadiv. It appears that such a drastic transformation in the use of urban space could occur only after it had become clear that the well-to-do citizens, including the great landowners, had deserted the city, never to return. The terraced gardens thus provide archeological evidence for a very dramatic period in the history of the city. The garden enterprise was actually a ruralization of a previously urban zone. This is a clear case of discontinuity, of a *caesura*, rather than of a gradual demise and transformation.

---

[31] Peter Lampinen read all the coins. I am also indebted to Gabriella Bijovski for advice, and to Julia Idelson for assistance in cataloguing the coins and lead seals relevant to this chapter.

[32] Coin registration number 42/93 KK29 B.0008 001, L.000, was found on the surface, not in archaeological context.

[33] On the lead seals see Nesbitt 1999.

Excavations in the city center, in Areas I, Z, and TP, and elsewhere indicated that other zones of the Byzantine city suffered a different fate. Some structures in the city center, like the octagonal church and the bathhouse adjacent to the east (area TPS) survived unscathed,[34] while other Byzantine structures, such as those in Areas LL, A, and B, were reoccupied after a certain period of abandonment, but Islamic Qaisāriyah, encircled by a new wall in the ninth century, occupied just a tenth of the area of its Byzantine predecessor. Accordingly, its population decreased drastically, its role as an administrative center was lost for good, and the harbor also declined seriously.[35]

When were the gardens deserted?

Our excavations also provided some evidence for the abandonment of the garden enterprise. The two sarcophagi incorporated into the irrigation systems, one serving well 13, the other above vault 7 serving well 6, were displaced from their original location, the first into the well, the other thrown down from above the vault. These were acts of vandalism. Perhaps they were associated with the violent Byzantine assault against Muslim Caesarea initiated by Justinian II in ca. 686, during the revolt of ʿAbdallah Ibn al-Zubayr (683–93) against the Umayyads. According to the Islamic sources Caesarea and Ascalon were destroyed in this assault and their citizens exiled.[36] It is difficult to tell whether on this occasion the gardens spoiled, but this seems reasonable. Upon becoming ruler, ʿAbd al-Malik ibn Marwan (685–705) rebuilt Caesarea, restored its mosque, and garrisoned it, policies that marked a

---

[34] See Holum 2004b; Stabler et al. 2008: 8–9, 30–31; also Holum in Holum and Lapin (forthcoming), and Toombs 1978. About Caesarea and its harbor one should note that in 610 CE Bonosus, the comes orientis of Phocas, organized under his command an army and a fleet in Caesarea to be fetched to Alexandria against Niketas and Heraclius. He sailed from Caesarea to Alexandria while the army marched on land. See John of Nikiu, Chronicle 107. 23, ed. Charles 1916: 169; Stratos 1968: 85–86. For another note about the harbor, a person sailing from there to Sykamina in 634, see below, n. 44.

[35] Arnon 2004. (On p. 24, however, about the terraced gardens, Arnon attributes to me words I never wrote.) On Early Islamic structures see also Raban et al. 1999, and Holum in Holum and Lapin (forthcoming). On the harbor see Raban 2004: 21.

[36] al-Balādhuri, futuh 143, 144, ed. Hitti 1916: 220: "In the days of Ibn al-Zubayr the Greeks went out against Kaisārîyah and devastated it and razed its mosque to the ground." See also Elʿad 1982: 149; Sharon 1986: 89–90; Gil 1983: 65–67; 1992: 78–81.

new chapter in the history of the Muslim city.[37] As for the terraced gardens, the ceramic evidence shows that by about 700 they had ceased to be cultivated. In the entire excavated area not a single potsherd was found in the garden stratum that could be dated to only after 700 CE. The types are all Byzantine. After the Byzantine assault, when Caesarea was restored and garrisoned by ʿAbd al-Malik, the entire garden system, including the wells, was abandoned. Then it was covered by a layer of beach sand, as thick as 1 m. or more, especially in the west, that contained many Byzantine sherds, mainly of amphorae or jars. This layer (Figs. 85, 91) constitutes stratum II, dated to 700–800 CE. Many of the sherds in the layer were water-worn and coated with marine fauna, *virmitids* (barnacles) and *ostreae*. A study of this layer suggested that it was deposited by purposeful human activity, not by *tsunami* waves.[38] Moreover, Raban also suggested that a plausible origin of this man-made deposit was dredging of the harbor, apparently in the Abbasid period, though no such dredging is mentioned in written sources.[39]

Nothing of the garden phase was integrated into the next stratum, phase I, that of the Abbasid cemetery.[40] The burials were Muslim and thus indicate a religious and ethnic transformation of the population. The cemetery remained in use until the Ottoman period. In the Crusader period (1101–1265) Christians and not Muslims were buried there, indicating another change of population, and thereafter the cemetery became Muslim again.

Literary evidence for the Muslim conquest

The written sources contain much evidence about the siege and capture of Caesarea and about events in the countryside, complementing the archaeological results from the Southwest Zone and providing a framework in which it can be interpreted. Most of these sources, Muslim, Christian, and Samaritan, seem to be trustworthy, deriving from contemporary chronicles and other accounts, even if they were

---

[37] Al-Balādhuri (previous note); also Whitcomb in Holum and Lapin (forthcoming).

[38] Thomas and Buyce 1992; 1993, part 1: 74–75, part 2: 105, fig. 144. On the stratigraphic context of stratum II, see Patrich *et al.*, 1999: 82, and n. 10 above.

[39] Raban 2004.

[40] A possible exception is well no. 2 in area NN. On the cemetery stratum see Patrich *et al.* 1999: 82–83.

compiled several centuries after the events took place. Although there is
some variation in details, these accounts accord well with one another
on the general outline of events. They reveal that Caesarea did not
capitulate formally to the Muslims. There was a siege and an armed
struggle with associated casualties. Instead of seeking for contradic-
tion in detail between the sources, I suggest a cumulative approach, in
which we allow details in one source to complement those given by
another—without, of course, abandoning caution and critical inspec-
tion of each source. Some sources speak for themselves and are worthy
to be cited *verbatim* below. Examined together, the written sources
permit to suggest the following sequence of events:

634 CE: Defeat of patrikios Sergius, commander of Caesarea, leading a combined force of Romans and Samaritans caught in an ambush in the countryside, away from the city

Our source for this event is the lost Syriac chronicle of Dionysius of
Tel-Mahre, as reconstituted by Andrew Palmer from a chronicle of
1234 CE that preserved Dionysius faithfully, and from Michael the Syrian, Patriarch of Antioch (d. 1199), who tended more to paraphrase:[41]

> §49*. <The Patrikios Sergius[42] was the officer> to whom Heraclius had
> committed Palestinian Caesarea and its region. When he learned of the
> Arab army's approach he assembled his own forces and sent for 5,000
> Samaritan foot-soldiers to strengthen his army in the coming encounter
> with the Arabs. When the Arabs heard about these preparations they
> concentrated their forces and laid an ambush by which to surprise and
> destroy the Romans.
>
> §50. Already the Romans were on the march. They had reached the place
> were the ambush had been laid. Unaware, as yet, of the presence of the
> Arabs, they requested permission from Sergius to rest a little and to lay
> down their burdens—for most of them were foot-soldiers. The Patrikios
> refused. He knew by this time that the enemy were close at hand. He
> ordered the trumpets to be sounded, the drums to be beaten. The
> Romans were just preparing to charge, when the Arabs, mightily armed,
> sprang out of their hiding places and advanced on them with deafening

---

[41] Palmer *et al.* 1993: 83–104; 146–147 (text no. 13).

[42] Interestingly, two of our lead seals from Caesarea are of Sergius, (son of) John,
the *patrikios* (Fig. 90). Both came from the garden soil layer. The name Sergius is
written in Latin on the obverse (Nesbitt 1999: cat. nos. 17a and 17b). But the Sergius
under discussion, *dux Palaestinae*, was known as *ho kata Nikētan*, so he was either a
son of Nicetas, or perhaps had served under a Nicetas. See Martindale 1992: 1134–35,
Sergius 43.

angry shouts. The first ranks to meet their onslaught were those of the Samaritans, for these had marched at the head of the column. Under the attack they collapsed and every one of them perished by the sword. The Patrikios saw this and began to flee headlong to save his skin. The Arabs pursued the Romans, like harvesters scything a ripe field of corn. Sergius fell from his horse, but his attendants came to his aid and set him back on again. He stayed briefly in the saddle, then fell again. Again his companions held ranks and set him back on his mount. A few steps further on he fell to the ground for the third time. They were making as if to put him back in the saddle, when he said: "Leave me! Save yourselves! Otherwise you and I shall drink the cup of death together."

§51*. So they left him behind; and indeed they had not gone far before the pursuers swooped in on him and killed him on the spot. They continued their pursuit and slaughter of the Romans until darkness fell. A few got away by hiding in trees, behind stone walls, and in vineyards. And so the Arabs entered Caesarea.[43]

§52. <The news about> the death of the Patrikios Sergius and of the defeat of the combined forces of the Romans and the Samaritans had reached Heraclius.[44]

In this text the location of the battle is not given. R. Hoyland put forward the appealing suggestion[45] that this ambush is actually the battle of Dāthin, described by al-Balādhuri as a village of Gaza,[46] and it is likewise the battle lost by Sergius, Patrikios of Caesarea, mentioned by the ninth-century chronicler Theophanes.[47] Hoyland suggested

---

[43] We should understand here the urban territory of Caesarea, the countryside, since this was the beginning of a siege that lasted seven years.

[44] In *Doctrina Jacobi* 5.16, ed. Bonwetsch Berlin 1910: 86.9-25—a contemporary source composed in Carthage ca. 640—we hear that a Jew of Caesarea named Abraam had sent in a letter to his brother in Acre news about the killing of the *kandidatos* Sergius by the Saracens (among whom "a false prophet" had appeared). Sailing in a boat to Sykamina/Shiqmona, Abraam brought the news to the Jews there, who rejoiced at hearing it.

[45] See Palmer *et al.* 1993: 19, n. 119, referring to a Syriac chronicle composed A.D. 640 (text no. 2), mentioning on Friday, February 4, AG 945 (= 634 CE) a battle between the Romans and the Arabs 12 miles east of Gaza, in which the Romans, led by another *Patrikios*, the Son of YRDN (Syriac BRYRDN), were defeated and their commander killed. Hoyland therefore suggests that according to this source the battle near Gaza was not the one led by Sergius.

[46] Al-Balādhurī, *Futūh*, 109, ed. Hitti 1916: 167. In this passage the Byzantine commander at the battle of Dāthin is called "the Patrician of Ghazzah," but his name is not given.

[47] Theophanes, *Chronographia*, AM 6124, ed. de Boor, Leipzig 1883: 336; ed. Mango and Scott, Oxford and New York 1997: 467–68. Theophanes reports the event in AM 6124=631/2 CE and presents the following narrative (Mango and Scott, trans.): "In this year Aboubacharos sent four generals who were conducted, as I said earlier, by the Arabs and so came and took Hera and the whole territory of Gaza. At length, Sergius

that Dāthin should be identified with Biblical Dothan and the nearby 'Araba, where, according to al-Balādhuri,[48] the Byzantines regrouped after the initial defeat in Dāthin, with Araboth. These sites lay ca. 20 miles east of Caesarea and three miles apart.[49]

July 634 CE: The siege of Caesarea began, under 'Amr ibn-al-'As, and lasted for seven years, with intermissions

Details about the dates and the six- or seven-year siege come from many authorities, Muslim, Samaritan, and Christian (see below). The ninth century historiographer al-Balādhurī got his information from earlier authorities, mainly from Muhammad ibn-Sa'd, citing al-Wākidi, and from 'Abdallāh ibn-'Āmir.[50] According to al-Wākidi (d. 823), the siege began on 1 Jumada (July) of the 13th year (634) under the command of 'Amr ibn-al-'As, and concluded late in the 19th or early in the 20th year under the command of Mu'āwiyah. He tells that "'Amr would camp around it [Caesarea] as long as he could, and whenever the Muslim forces wanted to combine against their enemy, he would go to them. Thus he witnessed the battles of Ajnadayn[51] (634), Fihl (December 634–January 635), al-Marj,[52] Damascus, and the Yarmūk (August 636). He then returned to Palestine and after taking Jerusalem (638) laid siege to Kaisāriyah. From Kaisāriyah he left for Egypt."[53] Thus the siege conducted by 'Amr ibn-al-'As in the years from 634 to 639/40, when he left for Egypt, was not a continuous one. When Yazid ibn-abi-Sufyan was nominated governor, after al-'As departed, he renewed the siege with a force of 17,000 men. The besieged people resisted. When Yazid fell ill in the last part of year 18, and departed for Damascus, his brother Mu'āwiyah took his place at Kaisāriyah and conquered the city.

---

arrived with some difficulty with a few soldiers from Caesarea in Palestine. He gave battle and was the first to be killed along with his soldiers, who were 300. Taking many captives and much booty, the Arabs returned home after their brilliant victory."

[48] Al-Balādhurī, above, note 46.

[49] Palmer *et al.*, above, note 45.

[50] Al-Balādhurī, *Futūh*, 140–43, ed. Hitti 1916: 216–20. See also Caetani 1911: 31–32, 156–63; Hill 1971: 63, 65, 75–84; Donner 1981: 153, 323, nn. 295–97.

[51] Near Beit Govrin, according to others in Syria, e.g. Sharon 2002: 62–73.

[52] Location unknown, in the region of Damascus.

[53] Al-Balādhurī, *Futūh*, 140, ed. Hitti 1916: 216.

September 634 CE: An earthquake and a portent in the sky

Michael the Syrian adds at this point:[54] "AG 945 [= 634]: There was a violent earthquake in the month of September and afterwards a portent in the sky, resembling a sword stretched out from the south to the north. It stayed there for thirty days and it seemed to many that it stood for the coming of the Arabs."[55]

Romans and Samaritans [apparently members of the upper classes, and the more wealthy], feeling threatened, decided to flee from cities and villages along the coastal plain to Byzantium, the Samaritans leaving their possessions with the Samaritan high priest 'Aqbūn ben El'azar, at Bayt Ṣāma

Our source for this is the Arabic *Continuatio* of the Samaritan chronicle of Abu al-Fath al-Samiri al-Danafi, a resident of Nablus in Samaria, or one of its neighboring villages, deriving from ancient sources:[56]

> The *imām* in those days was 'Aqbūn ben El'azar, who lived in Bayt Ṣāma [a Samaritan village in the province of Nablus]. When the Muslims attacked and the Byzantines fled, all of the Samaritans who lived along the coast fled with the Byzantines from the advancing Muslims, [thinking] that they would return. When the Samaritans began to leave with the Byzantines for Byzantium (Rūmīya), they came to the *ra'īs* 'Aqbūn ben El'azar, to Bayt Ṣāma, because he lived there, and said to him: "You are a trustworthy man, so we will deposit our possessions with you until we return," thinking that they would be returning soon. They collected their possessions and deposited them with him, and there accumulated in his charge an amount of wealth greater than anything either encountered or known. The people who deposited [their wealth] were people of Caesarea (Qaysārīya), Arsūf, Maioumas (Mīmās), Jaffa (Yāffa), Lydda, Ascalon ('Asqalān), Gaza (Ghazza), and all of the interior villages and those along the coast. After this they left for Byzantium and remained there and have not returned to this day.[57]

---

[54] Palmer *et al.* 1993: 147, n. 347.

[55] Theophanes reports this earthquake in AM 6124=631/632 CE (*Chronographia*, ed. de Boor 1883: 336, ed. Mango and Scott 1997: 467). Russell 1985: 37–59, dates the same earthquake to September 633 and suggests that it is attested archaeologically in Scythopolis/Beth Shean. See also Guidoboni *et al.* 1994: 355–356.

[56] *Continuatio*, ed. Levy-Rubin 2002: 28–29, 51–53.

[57] *Continuatio*, ed. Levy-Rubin 2002: 51. For a small hoard of gold objects, including jewelry, crosses, and a silver box, found in the Byzantine fortress (*kastron*) built around the Roman theater of Caesarea, see Frova *et al.* 1965: 235–42. The circumstances

Next in our sequence comes the story of the final conquest of Caesarea.

The capture of Caesarea (October 640, or the early part of year 641)

Detailed and fascinating, reflecting familiarity with the layout of the Byzantine city and the story of its conquest, yet not stereotypical, is the account given in the *Continuatio* of the Samaritan chronicler Abu al-Fath,[58] especially since it does not reflect the uniform *topoi* of the Islamic historiography of city conquest, to which Noth has drawn attention:[59]

> [The Muslims] set camp against it [Caesarea], and besieged it for six years before they conquered it. Now the Byzantines were making use of the sea before the Muslims were acquainted with it. In the fortress of Caesarea, at its north, in the northwest corner, there was a small gate which was hidden from view. The Byzantines used to come and go through it without the Muslims knowing. The Byzantines forgot and left it open, and a dog came out of it. When [the Muslims] saw it, they followed it to the gate without raising the alarm. They rode in, and there was killing in the city. They continued killing for a whole day in the lower market before it was known in the upper [market], because it was built in the form of one city above another. Whoever was able to flee fled by sea, whoever opposed them they killed, and whoever submitted to them was unharmed. The city was captured, and they inhabited it. After they captured it, every place else stood in awe of them.[60]

In line with reports of heavy fighting and of horrors outside and inside the besieged city is the narrative given in the reconstituted chronicle of Dionysius of Tel-Mahre:[61]

> AG 950 [= 638/639 CE]: Mu'awiya besieged Caesarea with vigorous assaults, taking captives from the surrounding country and laying it waste. He sustained the hostilities by night and day for a long time until

---

in which this hoard was hidden could not be determined, but it was never recovered in antiquity.

[58] On the historicity of this source see *Continuatio*, ed. Levy-Rubin 2002: 10–45, esp. 27–29 on the conquest of Caesarea. The archaeological evidence we know today, as presented here, accords much better with the *Continuatio* account than that was available to Levy-Rubin in 29, n. 129.

[59] Noth 1994: 19–20, 167–68; cf. Gil 1983: 49, n. 72, and 1992: 59–60.

[60] *Continuatio*, ed. Levy-Rubin 2002: 52–53. The date of the capture fell in the seventh year of the reign of 'Umar ibn al-Khattāb, in 641 (*ibid.*, 54). A small gate (wicket) was actually found in the northern wall (Fig. 92). But at the moment it is impossible to say that this is the small gate mentioned in the *Continuatio*.

[61] Palmer *et al.* 1993: 165–66, par. 83*.

he conquered it by the sword. All those in the city, including the 7,000 Romans sent there to guard it, were put to death. The city was plundered of vast quantities of gold and silver and then abandoned to its grief. Those who settled there afterwards became tributaries of the Arabs.

Michael the Syrian's description of the final assault accords well with this account, giving the same number for the garrison size: "For three days the fighting continued, before ultimate Arab victory. Of the 7,000–strong Roman garrison some escaped on ships. Muʿawiya took the treasures and obliged the population to pay tribute."[62]

More details are in al-Balādhurī, but most numbers he provides should be divided by 100,[63] and his account of the Arab penetration into the city is at variance with that provided by Abu al-Fath. According to other sources the final conquest occurred in the early part of 20/641, while al-Balādhurī states that it took place in Shauāl, year 19 (October 640):

> When Muʿāwiyah at last took it by storm [namely, by force, and not following a surrender with a peace treaty, which had legal implications pertaining to taxation], he found in it 700,000 [*sic!*] soldiers with fixed stipends [*mortazica*], 30,000 Samaritans and 200,000 [*sic!*] Jews. He found in the city 300 markets (*suq*), all in good shape. It was guarded every night by 100,000 men stationed on its wall. The city was reduced in the following way: A Jew named Yūsuf came to the Moslems at night

---

[62] Palmer *et al.* 1993: 179, n. 445. About the final stage of the siege (placed in ca. AG 953/4=641/6422 CE), some details in Michael's description appear to be fantastic: "At this time…the Arabs destroyed Caesarea in Palestine. […] Muʿawiya surrounded it by sea and by land and kept it under attack by day and by night, from the beginning of December until the month of May. Yet they would not take the word for their lives. Though seventy-two catapults bombarded it continually with rocks, the wall was so solid that it did not crack. Finally the attackers made a breach, through which some entered, while others climbed onto the wall with ladders." But according to bar-Hebraeus (d. 1286), the 72 catapults were located on the walls, in the service of the besieged, not of the attackers. This would better explain the stubborn resistance. And after the walls were breached, 7,000 Byzantine soldiers escaped Caesarea by sea. See Bar Hebraeus, *Chronography* 104b, ed. Wallis Budge 1932: 97; also Gil 1983: 49, n. 72, and 1992: 59–60.

[63] Gil 1983: 49, n. 72, and 1992: 59–60, suggested dividing al-Balādhuri's numbers by 100 in order to get valid ones. According to al-Yaqubi, whose capture date is 18/639, 80,000 soldiers were stationed in Caesarea. According to Yaqut, the siege had lasted seven years less a month, the guide was a certain Lentaq, one of their hostages, whom he does not claim to have been a Jew, and the city was seized on Sunday when all were attending church (Gil, *loc. cit.*). For the typology of the siege stories, repeated for many cities, see Noth 1994, with details provided by Gil, *loc. cit.*, and by Levy-Rubin in *Continuatio*, ed. Levy-Rubin 2002: 27–29, n. 7. On numbers in the Arab narratives of the conquests conveying symbolic significance only, rather than having a statistical validity, see also Conrad 1992: 354–58.

and pointed out to them a road through a tunnel, the water in which would reach a man's waist; in consideration for which information, safety was guaranteed him and his relatives. Mu'āwiyah sanctioned the conditions [made to Yûsuf] and the Moslems entered the city by night, calling 'Allah is great!' The Greeks seeking to flee through the tunnel found it occupied by Moslems. The Moslems opened the city gate and Mu'āwiyah with his men went in.[64]

Al-Balādhurī also reports that many Arabs were already inside the city when it was captured.[65] A special messenger sent by Mu'āwiyah carried the news to 'Umar.[66] The conquest of Caesarea had caused serious difficulties for the Muslim army, and its conquest was a great relief. Al-Balādhurī exaggerated the numbers, adhering to a literary *topos*,[67] in order to glorify the Arab achievement and thus accounting for the prolongation of the siege, but he does make it clear that Caesarea was taken in war, with the regular usual horrors and damage associated with it.

Theophanes also reports briefly that Mu'āwiya was the Arab commander who took Caesarea in the year 641 (AM 6133) after a siege of seven years.[68] Bar-Hebraeus (13th century) tells us that the siege (in its final stage?) lasted five months, from December to May. The besieged had 72 fire engines on the walls. The attacking Muslims, using ladders to climb the walls, could not manage for three days to descend from the walls into the city, until the wall was pierced and the defenders were defeated. 7,000 Byzantine soldiers then escaped Caesarea by sea.[69]

---

[64] Al-Balādhurī, *Futūh*, 141, ed. Hitti 1916: 217–18. It has been suggested that the tunnel mentioned in this narrative was Caesarea's low-level aqueduct (Fig. 93), on which see Porath 2002.

[65] Were these Arabs prisoners, as suggested *ibid.* by Hitti 1916: 218? In oral communication El'ad put forward the possibility that the reference is to local Arab *foederati* of the Byzantine army. On the conquest story see also Gil 1883: 49, paragraph 72; 1992: 59–60.

[66] Al-Balādhurī, *Futūh*, 142, ed. Hitti 1916: 218–19.

[67] Above, n. 63.

[68] Theophanes, *Chronographia*, AM 6133, de Boor 1883: 341; ed. Mango and Scott 1997: 475.

[69] *Chronography*, 104b, ed. Wallis Budge 1932: 97. See also Gil 1983: 51, n. 72; 1992: 60, and Schick 1995: 72, 76. The twelfth-century patriarch of Antioch and chronicler Michael the Syrian confuses the issue by claiming that it was the Arabs who employed 72 siege engines; for his text see Palmer *et al.* 1993: 147 with n. 347.

The death toll

The figure of 7,000 is given by the ninth century Christian Greek chronographer Theophanes. Though not as fantastic as the numbers of the besieged population, this might nevertheless be an exaggeration, intended to glorify the bravery of the besieged and to demonize the Muslims.[70] In any case, a high death toll is surely to be expected following a long siege.

Captives exiled

Captives are also reported. According to al-Balādhurī the captives numbered 4,000, and they were sent to 'Umar ibn-al-Khattab in Medina, who gave the orders to settle them in al-Jurf. The children were distributed to orphanages of the Ansar, the first supporters of Muhammed at Medina, and some of the mature captives were employed as clerks and manual laborers for the Muslims.[71] The exiled captives appear to have comprised the literate intellectuals and artisans of Caesarea, two important components in its society. Others were killed, and some of the population managed to escape by land or sea.[72]

These deaths, flights, and deportations accord with the words of the seventh century chronicler John of Nikiu preserved in Ethiopic, our earliest source on the fate of Caesarea during this period of turmoil, who speaks about "horrors committed in the city of Caesarea in Palestine."[73] Unlike the case of Jerusalem, which was also besieged, and the case of other cities such as Fahl, Beth Shean, and Tiberias, no surrender treaty is reported in the case of Caesarea.[74]

---

[70] Theophanes, above, n. 68. According to Dionysius of Tel Mahre, the entire population found in the city, including the Roman garrison of 7,000 soldiers, was put to death. The details in bar-Hebraeus do not correspond with Theophanes either. Perhaps we can conclude only that the garrison size was 7,000 soldiers.

[71] Al-Balādhurī, Futūh, 142, ed. Hitti 1916: 218.

[72] For further details on the flight and deportation of Christians during the Arab conquest of the Near East see Levy-Rubin 2006 and eadem in Holum and Lapin (forthcoming).

[73] Chronicle 108.10, ed. Charles 1916: 188.

[74] Gil 1983: 49, n. 72; 1992: 59–60, n. 61; Schick 1995. In many cities that were captured or capitulated, deserted houses were repopulated by Arabs after the conquest. This was not the case in Caesarea; after the conquest there were no homes to resettle in the zone under discussion.

CONCLUSIONS

The archaeological record of desertion and abrupt end of urban life in the Southwest Zone and elsewhere in Caesarea is best understood in light of these written sources. The Arabs did not set Caesarea entirely on fire, nor did they demolish the city systematically. Instead, the population evacuated large parts of the city, and those who had the means emigrated overseas. Many more were captives or were killed. Yet many Christians still remained, among them those who tilled the terraced gardens. These were deserted before about 700 CE, perhaps a result of the brief Byzantine re-conquest in the early 680's. The cemetery established subsequently above the garden phase provides evidence for the transformation of the local population from Christian to Muslim, a result of settlement policy, garrisoning with Muslim soldiers, and perhaps also of forced conversions to Islam.

Now back to the beginning. The Joint Expedition's stratigraphic interpretation of archaeological evidence for the Late Byzantine and transition periods corresponds very much with my own.[75] Toombs in 1978, as well as Wiemken and Holum in 1981, were correct in their interpretation of the archaeological record regarding the impact of the Arab conquest on the Southwest Zone, bringing urban life there to an abrupt end. But the deterioration was a result of desertion of the population in the face of the Arab menace, and the ensuing looting of building materials and leveling of the structures, during the long years of siege and afterwards, under the new regime. In the zone under discussion, remote from the city walls where most of the fighting took place, there is no evidence of systematic destruction caused by the conquering force.[76] The fate of the zones nearer to the harbor and the

---

[75] Compare my stratigraphic table (above) with Toombs 1978: 231, fig. 4.

[76] *Pace* Toombs 1978, Holum had stressed this factor in his post-1982 articles. Compare, for example, the fate of the island city of Arwad/Aradus as described by Dionysius of Tel Mahre: "Muʿawiya ordered its walls to be demolished and its buildings to be set on fire. In this way the Arabs razed it to the ground: and they resolved never to let the city be rebuilt or resettled." See Palmer *et al.* 1993: 178, par. 99; Conrad 1992: 317–401. On p. 323 Conrad gives a slightly different translation: "...Muʿawyā gave orders, its walls were razed, and the city was put to the torch and destroyed. They made the city into [a state in which] it could never again be rebuilt and inhabited."

Temple Platform was different.[77] Life continued there, but urban space in Umayyad and Abbasid Qaisāriyah was drastically altered.[78]

Almost ten years ago Holum suggested that the desertion of the bouleutic class was a major factor in urban decline at Caesarea.[79] Now we have a new literary source and new archaeological finds that confirm this point, setting the decline more precisely in time and place: namely, the *continuatio* of Abu al-Fath and the large-scale excavations in the Southwest Zone. The archaeology and the written sources are in perfect accord with each other. The *continuatio* relates that the more wealthy, what Holum calls the "bouleutic class," deserted already before Caesarea was captured, not within a generation following the capture. The Southwest Zone (Fig. 77), comprising the Byzantine *praetorium* (Fig. 35) and two or three palatial mansions (Fig. 73), represent some of the property deserted at that time. The stratigraphy and the small finds retrieved in the excavations seem to indicate, as discussed above, that this occurred indeed in the earlier part of the siege. Due to the administrative and social significance of this zone for urban life, its fate represents clear evidence for a swift decline of urban life in Caesarea at large. But even beyond this limited zone, vital for urban life in the Byzantine city, Early Arab Qaisāriyah was a small Muslim town, with new population, much reduced in size and entirely different in the layout of its lanes and in the architecture of its structures, in comparison with those of Roman and Byzantine Caesarea.[80]

Caesarea was a coastal city and metropolis of *Palaestina Prima*. It was conquered after a long struggle, and before long was positioned on the maritime front between Muslim and Byzantine powers. Thus its fate differed, for instance, from that of Jerusalem/al-Quds, located inland and a Holy City, conquered after a briefer conflict. Caesarea's fate differed also from the fate of Scythopolis/Beisan, an inland city and metropolis of *Palaestina Secunda*, that capitulated to the Arab forces.[81] When one writes on the Near East in the transition period, one should

---

[77] See Holum in Holum and Lapin (forthcoming).

[78] Above, n. 35.

[79] Holum 1996b: 626–27.

[80] For the transformation of the area above the Inner Harbor and the Temple Platform see above, n. 35, and Holum in Holum and Lapin (forthcoming). For comparison with Byzantine Caesarea and its wealth see Patrich 2001a (reproduced here as Chapter Four); Holum, *op. cit.*, Holum 2009 and Magness 2003: 209–13.

[81] On Jerusalem see Avni in Holum and Lapin (forthcoming). On Scythopolis cf. Tsafrir and Foerster 1989; 1997.

look for the nuances that differentiated between regions and sites,[82] and even between distinct zones in the same site. One should focus on variations, not just on points in common. For reconstructing the transition period, one should (so to speak) employ a fine paintbrush allowing representation of exact details with precise brush strokes, rather than a broad brush suitable only for creating a grosser depiction.[83]

---

[82] This point is best made by Magness 2003.

[83] Research for this paper was made possible by grants of the Israel Science Foundation.

APPENDIX

POTTERY RETRIEVED IN THE GARDEN-SOIL LAYER
(PLS. 1–4)

Barbara Johnson and Julia Idelson

Plate I (1–17)

No.	Vessel Type	Description	Date Range
	Table and Fine Ware Locally Produced		
1	Magness Fine Byzantine Ware bowl form 1A	Core gray/red, surface light red/red, overlapped incised wavy lines around upper body just below rim	Mid 6th c. to late 7th/early 8th c. CE
2	Magness Fine Byzantine Ware bowl form 2D	Core reddish yellow, surface reddish yellow	Mid 7th c. to 9th/10th c. CE
3	Magness Fine Byzantine Ware juglet form 2A	Core and surface light reddish yellow, incised nicks around shoulder	Mid 6th c. to early 8th c. CE
4	Local plain ware bowl with incurved rim	Core reddish yellow, surface reddish yellow; some minute white grits	
5	Local plain ware bowl with incurved rim	Core brown, surface reddish yellow, some minute black and white grits	
6	Local ware bowl with carinated side	Core yellowish red, surface reddish yellow, a few minute white grits	
7	Local ware bowl with carinated side	Core red, surface reddish brown slip, many small white grits	
8	Palestinian bowl with thickened rounded-off rim	Core brown, surface pinkish brown, some small white grits	
9	Local ware basin with thickened rim and comb decoration	Core light reddish brown, surface pale brown (slip?)	Byzantine-Umayyad periods
	Imported Table and Fine Ware		
10	Imported bowl with variegated slip	Core pink, surface dark reddish-gray slip on upper, dribbled lower	
11	CRS Form 7	Core red, surface red slip	Mainly 2nd half of 6th c. to early 7th c. CE
12	CRS Form 8	Core red, surface red slip	Perhaps 6th c. CE
13	CRS Form 9, Type B	Core red, surface red slip	Ca. 580/600 to end of 7th c. CE
14	CRS Form 10	Core red, surface red slip	Ca. mid–7th c. CE
15	CRS unclassified bowl	Core red, surface red slip	
16	CRS unclassified bowl	Core red, surface red slip	
17	CRS unclassified bowl	Core red, surface red slip	

Plate I

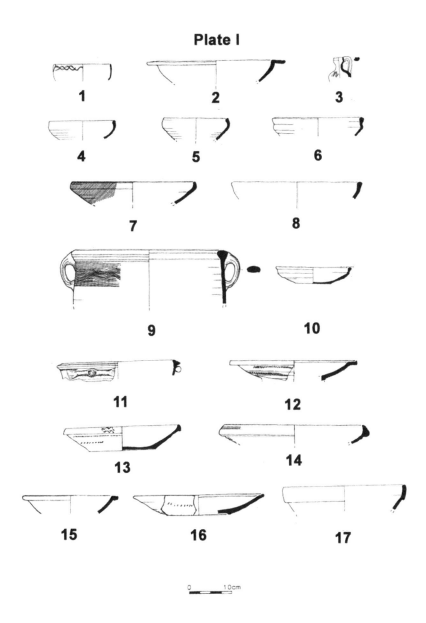

PLATE II (18–32)

No.	Vessel Type	Description	Date Range
18	CRS Form 11	Core red, surface red slip	Ca. 550–650 CE and later
19	LRC (PRS) Form 3, Type F	Core red, surface red slip	6th c. CE
20	LRC (PRS) Form 3, Type H	Core red, surface red slip	6th c. CE
21	LRC (PRS) Form 10, Type B	Core red, surface red slip	Late 6th c. to early 7th c. CE
22	LRC (PRS) Form 10, Type C	Core red, surface red slip	Early to mid 7th c. CE
23	ERS A Bowl Form J, Type 2	Core light red, surface mainly light red slip, reddish brown on outside of rim	Late 6th c. to 7th c. CE
24	ERS B bowl	Core gray, surface red slip on the interior, many small white grits, many minute sparkling inclusions	Late 4th c. to early 5th c. CE and later
25	ERS B bowl base with ring foot	Core gray, surface red slip, one groove on the bottom inside the vessel, many small and large white grits	6th c. to 7th c. CE
26	ERS B bowl with knob rim	Core weak red, surface red slip	6th c. to 7th c. CE
27	ERS B krater with painted decoration	Core gray, surface reddish brown (slip on the exterior?), some small and large white grits, minute sparkling inclusions	6th c to 7th c. CE
28	ERS C bowl Form b	Core brownish red, surface red slip, many large white inclusions, many small sparkling inclusions (mica)	7th c. CE
29	ARS Form 99, Type C	Core dark red, surface dark red slip	Ca. 560/580–620 CE
30	ARS Form 104, Type C	Core red, surface red slip, many minute white and some minute dark grits	Ca. 550–625 CE
31	ARS unclassified bowl	Core red, surface red slip	
32	ARS stamped fragment with Type 234d saint surrounded by Type 166–172 lambs	Core red, surface red slip	2nd half of 6th c. CE

Plate II

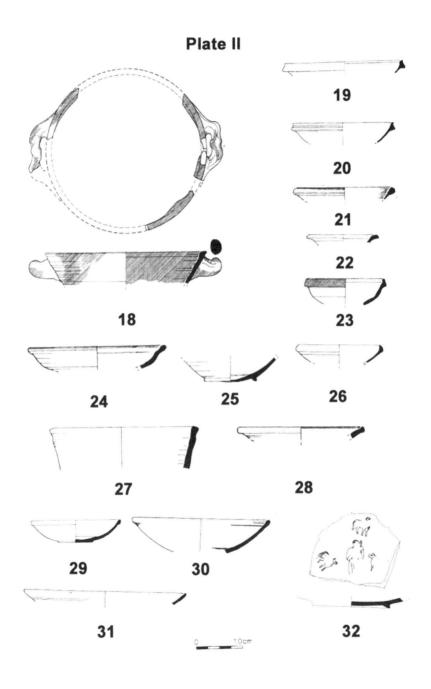

PLATE III (33–49)

No.	Vessel Type	Description	Date Range
	Coarse Ware Locally Produced		
33	Adan-Bayewitz Caesarea cooking pot Type 3	Core and surface reddish brown	6th c. to 7th c. CE
34	Magness casserole Form 1	Core and surface grayish brown, many small white grits, sandy ware	1st/2nd c. to 8th/9th c. CE
35	Local ware open cooking pot with carinated thin wall	Core and surface reddish brown, many small white grits	
36	Magness cooking pot lid, Variant 1	Core variegated reddish brown and brown, surface reddish brown, many small to medium white grits	1st/2nd c. to 8th/9th c. CE
	Imported Coarse Ware		
37	Egyptian pot with grooved rim in cooking pot fabric	Core reddish brown, surface white slip, some small white and many miniature sparkling inclusions	6th c. to 7th c. CE
	Coarse Ware Locally Produced		
39	Riley Caesarea Type 3 (black baggy jar)	Core reddish brown, surface grayish brown, many large and small white and dark inclusions	
40	Bottle	Core pale pinkish brown, surface very pale brown, hard fired, many small white and large dark inclusions	
41	Jug with flanged neck	Core reddish yellow, surface variegated light reddish brown and reddish yellow, some minute to small white grits	
42	2–handled local ware jug with grooved neck	Core light reddish brown, surface pale brown, some miniature and large white grits	
43	Local ware pot in cooking pot fabric	Core reddish brown, surface gray, some miniature white and dark inclusions	
44	Local ware jug with grooved lower neck	Core red, surface reddish brown, many small white grits	Ca. 6th c. to 7th c. CE and later
45	Jalame Form 1 strainer jug	Core and surface reddish brown, many small white and dark grits	4th c. to 7th c. CE
46	Jalame orm 1 strainer jug	Core and surface reddish brown	4th c. to 7th c. CE
47	1–Handled local ware strainer jug	Core red, surface weak red, some minute to small white grits	4th c. to 7th c. CE
48	2–Handled imported (?) jug with inward-beveled rim	Core reddish yellow, surface partial red, a few minute white and dark grits	
49	Local ware (?) wide mouth jug with spherical body	Core reddish yellow, surface partial red slip	

Plate III

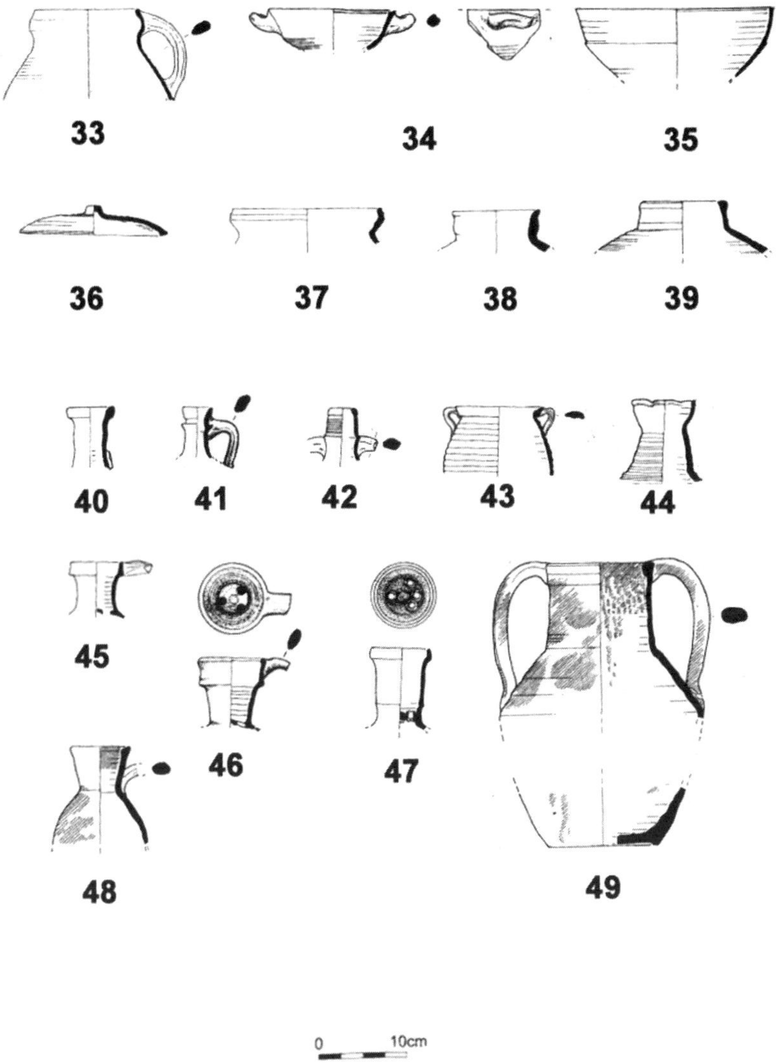

33

34

35

36

37

38

39

40

41

42

43

44

45

46

47

48

49

0   10cm

PLATE IV (50–67)

No.	Vessel Type	Description	Date Range
50	Palestinian ware pilgrim flask	Core yellowish red, surface reddish yellow, some minute to small white and dark grits, some small voids, surfaces feel gritty to the touch	Ca. 4th c. to 7th c. CE
51	Palestinian ware pilgrim flask	Core red, surface reddish brown, some minute to small white grits, a few minute to small dark grits	Ca. 4th c. to 6th c. CE, perhaps a little later
	Various Imported Vessels		
52	Egyptian Coptic jug	Core reddish brown, surface white/cream slip, many small white and sparkling inclusions	5th c. to 7th c. CE
53	Egyptian Coptic jug	Core reddish brown, surface white/cream slip, many small and large white grits and some miniature sparkling inclusions	5th c. to 7th c. CE
54	Egyptian Coptic jug	Core red, surface pale brown slip, many minute black and some minute white grits	5th c. to 7th c. CE
55	Hayes Early Christian ampulla	Core yellowish red, surface partial dark red slip, many minute sparkling inclusions	5th c. to 6th c. CE and later
56	ERS A variant, cream/mellow slip melon-shaped jug	Core red, surface cream slip	5th c. to 6th c. CE and later
	Jars and Amphorae		
57	Tall Gaza jar	Core and surface grayish brown, some small and large white inclusions	4th c. to 7th c. CE and later
58	Tall Gaza jar	Core and surface light reddish brown; some small and large white inclusions	4th c. to 7th c. CE and later
59	Tall Gaza jar	Core reddish brown, surface light reddish brown, some small and large white inclusions	4th c. to 7th c. CE and later
60	Tall Gaza jar	Core and surface light reddish brown, some small and large white inclusions	4th c. to 7th c. CE and later
61	Tall Gaza jar	Core and surface light brown	4th c. to 7th c. CE and later
62	Tall Gaza jar	Core and surface light reddish brown, some small and large white inclusions	4th c. to 7th c. CE and later

Plate IV

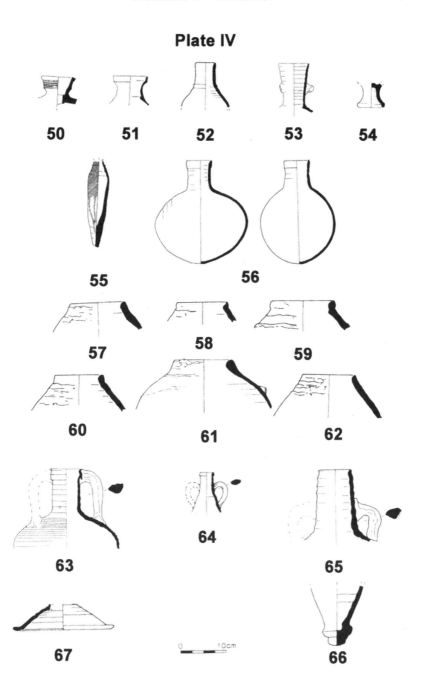

Plate IV (*cont.*)

No.	Vessel Type	Description	Date Range
63	Adan-Bayewitz Caesarea amphora Type 10	Core and surface red, gritty fabric, some minute white grits. There is a hole (ca. 0.5 cm. in diameter) in the lower neck.	6th c. to 7th c. CE
64	Benghazi Late Roman amphora 10 or related	Core light reddish brown micaceous, surface light brown	4th c. to mid 6th c. CE
65	Peacock and Williams amphora Class 52, Type B	Core and surface brown, many small white and sparkling inclusions	6th c. to 7th c. CE
66	Peacock and Williams amphora Class 53	Core and surface brown, many minute sparkling inclusions	Late 4th c. to mid 6th c. CE
67	Adan-Bayewitz Caesarea amphora lid Type 1A	Core light red, surface pale brown	

CHAPTER SEVEN

HEROD'S HIPPODROME/STADIUM AT CAESAREA AND THE GAMES CONDUCTED THEREIN

An arena for chariot races and other games uncovered in the archaeological excavations conducted at Caesarea in the years 1982–88 (Fig. 94)[1] is identified with the "amphitheater" mentioned by Josephus Flavius:

> Herod also built a theater of stone in the city, and on the south side of the harbor, farther back, an amphitheater large enough to hold a great crowd of people and conveniently situated for a view of the sea.[2]

And indeed, the location on the seashore, and the architecture of the structure exposed, befit this description. The structure, U-shaped, was built on a north–south axis, parallel to the coastline (Fig. 95). The local *kurkar* stone served as the exclusive building material. The arena was about 300 m long and 50.5 m wide. The seats (*cavea*), holding 12 rows with a seating capacity for c. 10,000 spectators,[3] enclosed it on the east, south, and west. They were arranged in 18 segments (12 of which are still preserved), and were set on top of a podium wall 1.1m high above the arena level (Fig. 96). The southern gallery (*sphendone*), semicircular in shape, had an arched entranceway, 3 m wide, in its center. The starting gates (*carceres*) enclosed the arena on the north.

---

[1] The structure was excavated by two expeditions. One, on behalf of the Israel Antiquities Authority, directed by Y. Porath, had exposed most of the *cavea* and the arena. The second, on behalf of the University of Haifa directed by the present author, had exposed the starting gates and the adjacent arena. For preliminary reports, see Porath 1994; 1995a; 1996b—an update to the 1995 excavations; Patrich 2001b.

[2] *Ant.* 15.9, 6, 341; *War* 1.21, 8, 415 mentions only the amphitheater. In the period under discussion, the term amphitheater was use indifferently to designate a stadium, or a hippodrome, rather then an oval Roman *amphitheatrum*, known in the first century BCE as *spectaculum*. See Etienne 1966. Such is also the case in the writing of Josephus Flavius, when he is speaking about the hippodrome/amphitheater at Jerusalem, and Jericho. See Jeremias 1931; Humphrey 1996.

[3] Porath 1996b: 96, estimated it to be 7,000–8,000 spectators (assuming that the western side did not have seats). A careful analysis by the conservation works architect, Daniel Abu Hatzeira (interim publication), presents the following estimations for the maximum number of spectators, assuming that there were 12 rows of seats in the west as well: 10,250 (according to a 55 cm seat width), 9,410 (according to a 60 cm seat width), and 8,684 (according to a 65 cm seat width).

The dimensions, and the existence of starting gates, indicate that the structure served as a hippodrome. But locally it was known as the "great stadium,"[4] or just the "stadium"[5] of Caesarea. Hence the name of the structure in the title of this chapter.

A trench separated the hippodrome from the higher *kurkar* ridge and its continuation northward. Access to the top of the gallery was thus prevented from the east, and in a later period (in the days of Nero) the trench was filled with earth, on top of which a double colonnaded portico was built.

A passageway—*vomitorium*—located about 115 m from the southern gate, ran across the entire width of the eastern gallery, split farther away to two inclined vaults, leading after two successive 90° turns to a platform for the dignitaries (*pulvinar*). This loggia was usually located opposite the finish line of the chariot races that was marked in lime across the right side of the arena. The face of the podium wall was coated with plaster and frescoes that were renewed from time to time.[6]

At the southern end of the arena, about 25 m north of the southern entrance, remains were preserved of the turning post—the *meta prima* (see below). Several architectural phases were discerned here. Two parallel subterranean walls, standing 1.7 m apart, ran from near the *meta prima* northward, forming an underground drainage channel. In a later stage, when the arena was shortened and the hippodrome/stadium was converted to an amphitheater, underground amphitheatrical tunnels were installed (Fig. 39). The southernmost transversal tunnel was connected by a narrower underground passage with a rock-cut

---

[4] *War* 2.9, 3, 172; in *Ant.* 18.3, 1, 57, simply a stadium is mentioned. The context suggests that the event took place near the Roman *praetorium* on the site of Herod's palace, namely, in the Herodian entertainment structure under discussion.

[5] Eusebius, *History of The martyrs in Palestine*, ed. Cureton 1861: 21–23 (Syr.), 19–21 (Eng.); 51 (Syr.), 47 (Eng.); *de Mart. Pal.* VI.3–7, ed. Bardy 1967: 139–40 (Gr.). Eusebius, a resident of Caesarea, speaks about events to which he and other citizens were eye witnesses, therefore his testimony as for the identification of the structure as a stadium by the locals is of utmost significance. Christian martyrs were thrown into the stadium as prey for the wild beast. The reality of hunt scenes (*venationes*), conducted in a stadium, is also familiar in the rabbinic sources. See: *M Bava Qamma* 4: 4; cf. M 'Avodah Zarah 1, 7.

[6] One of the layers, in the section preserved south of the dignitaries' platform, presents a scene of wild animals running, as well as vegetation. Porath attributes this layer of frescos to a late phase, when the hippodrome was shortened (see below). In another layer that was preserved in the curved section between the eastern and southern sides, geometric patterns were preserved. Additional sections of plaster were also found opposite it, on the western side. Porath 2000b.

cell that was attached to a *sacellum* located under the eastern *cavea*. These subterranean tunnels should be interpreted in conjunction with the gladiatorial combats and hunting shows that were also held in this structure (see below).[7]

In his description of the games held in Caesarea in honor of Augustus, which were part of the celebrations for the inauguration of the new city, details are given about the various contests and shows:

> And so, there was, to begin with, a very great festival of dedication and most lavish arrangements. For he had announced a contest in music and athletic exercises, and had prepared a great number of gladiators and wild beasts and also horse races ("ἵππων δρόμος) at the very lavish shows that are to be seen at Rome and in various other places. And this contest too he dedicated to Caesar, having arranged to celebrate it every fifth year. And Caesar, adding luster to his (Herod's) munificence, from his own revenues sent all the equipment needed for such games. On her own account Caesar's wife Julia sent many of her greatest treasures from Rome, so that the entire sum was reckoned as no less than five hundred talents. When to see the sights there came to the city a great multitude as well as the envoys sent by communities because of the benefits that they had received. Herod welcomed them all and entertained them with the lodging and meals and continuous feasts. During the day the festivals offered the diversion of spectacles, while at night they provided amusements costing great sums of money, and so they made his generosity famous, for in all the things that he undertook he was ambitious to surpass what had been done before. And they say that Caesar himself and Agrippa often remarked that the extent of Herod's realm was not equal to his magnanimity, for he deserved to be king of all Syria and of Egypt.[8]

---

[7] Porath 1994: 17; 1996b: 95–96) interprets the north–south tunnel as remains of a *spina*—the barrier along the circus arena. He believes that these walls carried a vault that protruded above the surface level of the arena and served as partitions. A similar subterranean structure, 30 m long, discovered in the hippodrome of Gerasa, was also interpreted in this—erroneous, in my opinion—manner. There as well no evidence was found for the existence of a vault. See Ostrasz 1991 and a re-evaluation of this structure in Patrich (forthcoming-b). A circus *spina* had the shape of elongated narrow pools set above the arena level, or of a series of monuments, like obelisks, columns, pavilions, fountains, and other decorative installations, all set above the ground (see also below).

[8] *Ant.* 16.5, 1, 137–41; and see *War* 1.21, 8, 415, where a date corresponding to September 9 BCE is mentioned. (This date will not fall in the Actian calendar, if it indeed occurred for the first time in Nicopolis, Greece, and Jerusalem in 28 BCE—as claimed by many scholars; see Schalit 1964: 193. Some scholars date the celebrations in Jerusalem to 29 BCE and the celebrations dedicating Caesarea together with the Sixth Actiad at year 9 BCE. See Marcus' remark in the LCL translation of *Ant.*, p. 263; other scholars adhering to the 28 BCE date fix the Caesarea celebration in the year

The celebrations and spectacles were held in September.[9] According to the Latin version of *Ant.* 16.5, 1, 140, preserved in a much older manuscript than the Greek one with which we are familiar, they lasted 15 days.[10] The event was established as a quinquennial festival, celebrated every four years. King Agrippa I together with a royal retinue, and other dignitaries were present at the fourteenth festival (September 43 CE).[11] Here we hear that on the second day of the festivities, events in the theater started early in the morning.

Even more detailed is the description of the games instituted by Herod 20 years earlier in Jerusalem, in honor of the Caesar—an expression of the ruler worship, soon to become the emperor cult, as were the later games at Caesarea:

> For in the first place he established athletic contests every fifth year in honor of Caesar (Augustus), and he built a theater in Jerusalem, and after that a very large amphitheater in the plain,[12] both being spectacularly lavish but foreign to Jewish custom, for the use of such buildings and the exhibition of such spectacles have not been traditional (with the Jews). Herod, however, celebrated the quinquennial festival in the most splendid way, sending notices of it to the neighboring peoples and inviting participants from the whole nation. Athletes and other classes of contestants were invited from every land, being attracted by the hope of winning the prizes offered and by the glory of the victory. And the leading men in various fields were assembled, for Herod offered very great

---

12 BCE, i.e., the Fifth Actiad. Clarification of the chronological issue here deviates from the subject at hand. On the Actian calendar used by Josephus, see: *War* 1.20, 4, 398).

[9] Schwartz 1992: 175.

[10] "...*et per dies quindecim spectacula vel delicias ministravit.*" On the superior textual tradition of the Latin, preserved in a ninth-century MS, see Niese 1887: xxvii–xxix; Blatt 1985: 17–26. See also Lämmer 1974: 136–37 a quotation of the full text of the Latin version. Given the involvement of the imperial family in supplying utensils and equipment, we may assume that the scope and grandeur of the events, that so impressed even Augustus and Agrippa, were inspired by the "Centennial Games"— *ludi saeculares* (the Secular Games) of 17 BCE in Rome, held on the tenth anniversary of the Principate.

[11] *Ant.* 19.8, 2, 343–50; and see Schwartz 1992: 175–76. Five days later Agrippa died in the palace in Caesarea. See also Lämmer 1981.

[12] The Latin text renders here "*in campo maximo*" ("in the Great Plain"). Therefore, Milik, like others previously, had suggested that the reference is to the Jordan Valley, or more specifically to the amphitheater of Jericho. However, the toponym μέγα πεδίον, or *campo maximo*, as used by Josephus, and other ancient sources (The Book of Judith; Eusebius; the "Bordeau Pilgrime"), generally refer to the Jezreel Valley, not to the Jordan Valley. See Tsafrir, Di Segni, and Green 1994: 182. No Herodian amphitheater is known in that valley, so it seems that the Greek version should be preferred in this case.

prizes not only to the winners in gymnastic games but also to those who engaged in music and those who are called *thymelikoi*.[13] And an effort was made to have all the most famous persons come to the contest. He also offered considerable gifts to drivers of four-horse and two-horse chariots and to those mounted on race-horses. And whatever costly or magnificent efforts had been made by others, all these did Herod imitate in his ambition to see his spectacle become famous. All round the theater were inscriptions concerning Caesar and trophies of the nations which he had won in war, all of them made for Herod of pure gold and silver. As for serviceable objects, there were no valuable garment or vessel of precious stones which was not also on exhibition along with the contests. There was also a supply of wild beasts, a great many lions and other animals having been brought together for him, such as were of extraordinary strength or of very rare kinds. When the practice began of involving them in combat with one another or setting condemned men to fight against them, foreigners were astonished at the expense and at the same time entertained by the dangerous spectacle, but to the natives it meant an open break with the customs held in honor by them. For it seemed glaring impiety to throw men to wild beasts for the pleasure of other men as spectators, and it seemed a further impiety to change their established ways for foreign practices.[14]

The celebrations at both Caesarea and Jerusalem thus included music (*mousika*) and gymnastic (*gymnika*) competitions, as well as horse and chariot races (*hippika*). These were three regular elements of the Greek-style games, but in addition, Roman spectacles were included: inciting various types of wild beasts one against the other, combats between gladiators (*munera gladiatorum*), leaving men condemned to death to be devoured by beasts, and hunting spectacles (*venationes*). Such a combination of Greek-style games and Roman spectacles constituted the common program in games associated with the emperor's imperial cult.[15] The *mousika* could be held in the theater, but the Greek contests of *gymnika* and *hippika*, and the Roman spectacles—*munera*

---

[13] A guild of professional actors and musicians. An artists' guild by this name is also mentioned by Plutarch (*Sulla* 36) alongside mime artists and kithara musicians. Such guilds were known in the Hellenistic world, primarily with regard to the Dionysos cult and the Hellenistic royal cults. See the remark of Marcus in the LCL translation of Josephus' works, who refers to Rostovtzeff 1941: 1048–50. See also Le-Guen 2001.

[14] *Ant.* 15.8, 1, 268–74. For a detailed discussion of these celebrations and their political significance, see Lämmer 1973.

[15] Competitions and games following this program were an integral part of the emperor cult. See Schürer 1973: 304–5; 1979: 45–47. On the proliferation of the Augustan cult in the eastern Empire, see Zanker 1990: 297–306. Zanker (*ibid.*, 299) stresses that the annual emperor cult celebrations involved processions, public feasts, impressive games, and fairs. See also Suetonius, *Lives, Augustus* 52; Fears 1988, with extended bibliography.

gladiatorum and *venationes*, were held in the "amphitheater"—the hippodrome/stadium under discussion. Let us examine to what extent the exposed structure was equipped to meet the operational needs of the various activities conducted therein. An acquaintance with the various types of contests, and with Greco-Roman entertainment structures uncovered in Judaea and beyond, will afford a correct interpretation of the remains at Caesarea.[16]

ATHLETICS (GYMNIKA)

Gymnika normally included all branches of athletics: the *pentathalon* (comprising five events:the long-distance jump, discus throwing, the javelin lunge, three-round wrestling, and the short, one-stadium run); the "double run" (*diaulos*), which was a full, two-stadia long, course; the "long run" (*dolichos*) of an unset length that could range between three quarters of a mile and three miles; and the foot race of hoplites with helmet and shield. There were also boxing, and the *pankration*— a wrestling competition that included kicking and choking, as well as separate events for children (*paides*), young men (*ageneioi*), and adults (*andres*).[17]

The structure used for the athletic competitions in the Greek and Hellenistic world was the stadium (Fig. 97).[18] That of Olympia is an example of a simple Greek stadium. The minimal length required for a racetrack was one *stadium* (600 ft, 177–92 m, depending on the standard length of the foot that was used). The average width of the rectangular racetrack (*dromos*) in known stadiums is about 30m (100 ft). The spectators were standing, or sitting on raised mounds of earth, flanking the racetrack. Stone seats, first restricted only to the judges' box, appear gradually during the Hellenistic period. In the second century CE, apparently influenced by the Domitian stadium in Rome, building began in the East of stadium seats on inclined vaults that could be

---

[16] For a good survey of the entertainment structures in Roman Palestine, and the games conducted therein, including an examination of the rabbinic literature in this regard, see Weiss 1995; 1999. For a specific discussion of the games in Caesarea, see *idem* 1996. On the games in the Hellenistic and Roman East, see also the next note.

[17] For a succinct survey, see Swaddling 1980. More detailed are Finley and Pleket 1976; Harris 1964: 64–109; 1972: 13–74; Young 1988: 1131–42; Matz 1991, and the references in the next note.

[18] Gardiner 1930: 128–43; Harris 1964: 136–47; Miller 1980; Aupert 1994.

built on a flat surface. Such was the case, for example, at Perge, Aspendos, Ephesus, and Sardis. The seats were also set above a podium wall c. 1 m or more high above the level of the arena (e.g., Delphi, Aphrodisias, Miletus, Perge, and elsewhere). The most impressive stadium was the Panathenaean, built by Herodes Atticus in Athens in 143 CE, that could hold 50,000 spectators—like the Colosseum in Rome.[19]

The structure in Caesarea was a much earlier stone-built stadium, with the seats retained on two parallel walls with a fill of earth in between. The straight wings of the *cavea* (entirely preserved on the east side, while mostly eroded on the west), did not run along the full length of the arena, but ended at c. 65 m from the *carceres*. These wings of the *cavea* were c. 175 m long—enough to encompass, together with the *sphendone*, a typical 1 stadium long racetrack. But any permanent installation along the racetrack, such as a barrier of a hippodrome, or pavilions and cages associated with Roman spectacles, would have prevented the running contests, which were major events of athletics. They could have been obstacles to other contests—like the discus and the javelin—as well.

In regular stadiums, with permanent rather then shift installations, the starting and finish lines were marked by a row of hewn stones, just slightly projecting above the ground. Two grooves cut along the stones gave a good grip for one's toes. The width of each lane was about 1.5 m. A mechanical starting device that simultaneously opened a simple rod at the beginning of each lane, known as a *hysplex* (ὕσπληξ), was widespread since the Hellenistic period.[20] It was anchored to a large triangular stone surface, with incised lines radiating from the center of the mechanism toward the starting posts. No remains of such devices, or of the starting stones, were found at Caesarea. It seems that here these were shift devices, set in place before each running contest, and thus causing no obstacle for the operation of the *hippika* (see below).

The athletic events continued to comprise a component of the periodic games held in Caesarea also years after Herod's day. In a second-century CE inscription (the time of Marcus Aurelius) found at Aphrodisias in Caria, mention is made of a glorified winner of the

---

[19] Welch 1998a; 1998b.

[20] Humphrey 1986: 132–33. Remains of "starting stones" were found in Delphi, Epidaurus, Miletus, Olympia, and Priene. The start mechanism can be reconstructed at Cos, Priene, and Miletus.

pankration held in Caesarea,[21] thus confirming that athletic events held in Caesarea had still attracted athletes of the highest degree.

An inscription from Laodicea dated 221 CE, listing the victories of a glorified boxer, refer to the games in Caesarea as the "Isactium," namely—"Actian Games," instituted to commemorate Augustus' victory in the war at Actium in September 31 BCE. These were still the same games first established by Herod. The same inscription also mentions that Caesarea held the "World Pythian Games" instituted by Septimius Severus (Σεουήρειος Οίκουμενικος πυθικός).[22] The "Pythian Games" were one of the Greek "Crown Games,"[23] and the inscription indicates that Greek-style games, renewed by Septimius Severus throughout the Roman Empire, were also held in Caesarea. Namely, the stadium still was active at that time.[24] In 304–5 CE, Caesarea, as elsewhere throughout the Empire, held celebrations for the twentieth anniversary of Diocletian's rule. Gymnastics, boxing, and wrestling, regularly held in a stadium, still took place in Caesarea in this period.[25]

CHARIOT AND HORSE RACES (*HIPPIKA*)

Horse and chariot races (*hippika*), were part of the program in Greek-style games throughout the Greek and Hellenistic world. This was not a Roman innovation. *Hippika* included four-horse chariots (*tetrahip-*

---

[21] Moretti 1953: no. 72 (= Les Bas-Waddington III, no. 1620).

[22] *Ibid.*, no. 85 (= Les Bas-Waddington III, no. 1839); *CIG* 4472. On the identification of Caesarea in which the Isactium Games were held as Caesarea Maritima, and not Caesarea Philippi (Paneas), see Schwartz 1992: 167–81. On the two abovementioned inscriptions from Aphrodisias and Laodicea, see also Schürer 1979: 45–47, notes 90, 91, and 109; Harris 1976: 37.

[23] These were the games held in Olympia in honor of Zeus, Delphi (the "Pythian Games"), in honor of Apollo, Nemea in honor of Zeus, Isthmia, near Corinth in honor of Poseidon. The games in the latter two cities were held every two years, and not every four years. The "Pythian Games" were the only ones that also included music contests. They were known as the "Crown Games", since the winners were presented with only wreaths (of olive leaves at Olympia, of laurel plus a handful of apples at Delphi, of pine, or in some eras of celeriac at the Isthmus, and of celeriac at Nemea), and had to wait until they returned to their city-states to receive valuables or monetary rewards. These games gained a special reputation in the Greek world, thus determining the format of the games throughout the Greek and Hellenistic East. See Gardiner 1910; 1930; Garland 1988. Herod's games in Caesarea and Jerusalem included *mousika*, resembling in this aspect the "Pythian Games".

[24] The archaeological finds retrieved in the excavations near the *carceres* (see below), indicate that the structure was still functioning also as a hippodrome under Septimius Severus.

[25] Eusebius (*supra* n. 5), p. 11 (Syr.), pp. 10–11 (Eng.); III.2 p. 126 (Gr.).

pon/quadriga), two-horse chariots (*synoris/biga*), colt and horseback riding, and *desultores/kalpe* in which the riders finish the race running on foot aside their horses. The various riding races comprised an important part of these games, no less than the chariot races. On the organizational end, the competitors in the horse or chariot races were wealthy individuals (men or women), owners of horse and rider (although the owners could ride for themselves), and not "clubs" such as the four "circus factions" that organized the races in the Roman-style competitions (see below). The number of competitors was therefore not restricted to multiples of four; any number was possible.

The hippodrome was the racetrack of the Greek world. The archaeological finds indicate that even as late as the Hellenistic period the hippodrome could have been a temporary installation, which did not require much of a permanent architecture. The racetracks were arranged so that the spectators could sit or stand on a naturally sloped surface or raised mounds flanking the track. The starting stalls, as well as the turning posts, could have been shift structures, built expressly for the competitions. Special emphasis was placed on the start and a device was developed for opening the gates, similar to the one used in the stadium, that would ensure each competitor an equal chance at reaching the first turning post without endangering himself and without giving anyone of them a distinct advantage over the others.[26] The convergence of all the tracks was at the far turning post, located at the far end of the arena, and therefore the competitors began their run in lines parallel to the long axis of the arena. Races in this format, held since early times in Greece, were adopted in the Hellenistic cities in the East and continued there for a long time even under Roman rule.[27] Hippodromes as permanent structures were rare there. The most famous of them was the Lageion in Alexandria that apparently was built by Ptolemy Lagos (after whom it was named).[28] A permanent hippodrome was built in Antioch only in 56 BCE, few years after the establishment of Provincia Syria, and in Cyrene, the hippodrome—that also functioned as a stadium—was even older; it is possible that it

---

[26] In Olympia, the stalls were arranged in the shape of an inverted V (see Humphrey 1986: 7–9, figs. 2a, 2b; Harris 1968, and every pair of stalls was opened with a time delay relative to the opening of the pair of stalls behind. In this manner, all the chariots would reach the starting line at the same time. This early method was later replaced by a mechanism ensuring the simultaneous opening of all the stalls. The location of the stalls was also changed accordingly.

[27] Humphrey 1986: 535; Harris 1972: 151–83.

[28] Humphrey 1986: 505–12; Maricq 1951.

was built already in the sixth century BCE, and certainly was used in the Hellenistic period.[29]

Unlike the temporary structures of the Greek and Hellenistic world, the Romans developed a sophisticated architectural complex for horse and chariot races—the Circus (Fig. 97). This complex met the needs of all parties involved in the races, both spectators and contestants. The Circus Maximus of Rome set the standard. Its occupancy under Augustus reached 250,000 spectators. It was the source of architectural inspiration for all other circuses in the entire Roman world. Though only partially preserved and excavated, a meticulous study of all the sources pertaining to the Circus Maximus—historical and epigraphical, as well as the archaeological finds and artistic depictions on mosaic floors, gems, reliefs, etc.—furnish information about the race procedures, the decorations along its barrier, the starting gates, and the various decorative installations that stood in the arena. Especially detailed are the mosaic floor scenes from Lyon, Carthage, Silin, Piazza Armerina, Dougga, Gerona, Italica, Ravenna, Barcelona, and Gafsa. The best-preserved circus is the one at Lepcis Magna in Libya.[30]

The seats (*cavea*) in a typical circus were built of stone, and a network of built passageways and steps enabled orderly, easy, and quick movement of spectators to their seats. The starting gates were built on a curved line, whose axis was slightly inclined in relation to the long axis of the arena, so that each chariot would pass an equal distance up to the "starting line." This line, marked in white lime, cut across the right side of the arena, from the nearer turning post to the right battery of seats. All lanes had converged from the starting stalls to this line. The games commenced with a ceremonial procession (*pompa*) around the arena, after which the chariots would set themselves up at the starting gates (*carceres*),[31] each in a stall of his choice. This was determined by lots in a special lottery machine (κυλίστρα) comprised of an amphora turned on a horizontal axis. The starting gates had a mechanical device for opening all the gates simultaneously.[32] The signal for opening the

---

[29] Humphrey 1986: 520–23.

[30] On all of these, see in detail in Humphrey 1986: 86, 142–51; 1988: 1153–65; Harris 1972: 184–243; as well as: Olivová 1989; Vogel 1969; Hönle and Henze 1981 and more recently Nelis-Clément and Roddaz 2008: 17–46, 235–258.

[31] Latin; literally, prison cells. In the Roman amphitheater, this term denotes cells or cages for the wild beast; the two should not be confused.

[32] See a reconstruction by Humphrey (1986: 157–70 and figs. 74–76) for the circus at Lepcis Magna.

gates and commencing the race was marked by a piece of white cloth (*mappa*) that was thrown from the hands of the presiding magistrate, whose box was located high up, above the stalls. The turning posts were denoted *meta*. The one farther from the starting gates was the *meta prima*, and the other, nearer to the starting gates, the *meta secunda*. It is here that the starting line—"the white line"—was marked. The lanes as well were marked with white lime, and during the start of the race—until "the white line"—each chariot was confined to its lane. The layout of the lanes at the first section of the arena was a kind of a radial layout; they were not set parallel to the arena axis, as in the Greek-style hippodrome. From this point on, until the *meta prima*, the chariots could deviate and pass each other. The race comprised seven counter-clockwise laps around a central barrier, comprised of a series of elongated pools (*euripi*)[33] protruding above the arena. The basins were decorated with statues and other monuments. Such a continuous barrier was built in the Circus Maximus only in Trajan's time.[34] Earlier, a temporary, wooden barrier was set when races were held. The turning posts (*metae*) acquired a monumental character in the shape of three vertical cones standing on a high platform already many years earlier—probably in the Etruscan period; eggs and dolphins were added at the *metae* by Agrippa, under Augustus, as a counting device for the laps. The "finish line"—about halfway between the two *metae* and on the right hand side of the arena—was also marked with white lime. The judges' box (*tribunal*) was also located on this side, with the

---

[33] The term *spina*, mentioned for the first time only by Cassiodorus—a sixth-century author—is widespread in modern research. However, Humphrey (1986: 175) has shown that in the Roman period the term *euripus* was actually widespread for describing the continuous barrier in the Circus Maximus. This term denotes its shape—a series of narrow, elongated basins (*euripi*), while *spina* (spine), is just a general term for the barrier which does not denote its shape. The term *euripus* reflects faithfully the shape of the barrier in the Roman circuses, as it emerges from sites like Lepcis Magna, Carthage, and the eastern circus at Caesarea (recent excavations by Y. Porath on behalf of the Israel Antiquities Authority), in which clear remains of the barrier have been preserved. Nothing similar ever existed in the Herodian hippodrome (see also *supra*, n. 7).

[34] A roofed drainage channel ran along the center of the arena of the Circus Maximus for hundreds of years. Permanent monuments began to be erected on this line only in the early Empire. Augustus was the first to erect an Egyptian obelisk in the middle of the barrier line, and in the course of the first century CE more altars and pavilions were added. The monumental shape of the barrier comprising of *euripi* was rendered only under Trajan, as one can glean from depictions on his coins. The *euripus* is mentioned explicitly for the first time only by Tertullian at the end of the second century (Humphrey 1986: 11, 292–93).

"finish line" to its front. On the opposite side of the *cavea* (on the left side of the arena), were the dignitaries' seats in the *pulvinar*.[35]

The emphasis in the Roman circus was placed on the chariot race, especially the *quadriga*, rather than on horse riding. The race engaged teams, or "clubs," not individuals. The teams were known by their representative colors and had large followings of partisans. During the Republic, there were only two colors—the Whites and the Reds. In the first century BCE or CE, the Blues and the Greens joined them. Domitian added the Purple and Gold factions, but these were cancelled after his death. The competitions were therefore restricted to a number of chariots in multiples of four (twelve in the Circus Maximus since the time of Julius Caesar). This organization also enabled the existence of double and triple races, in which each faction was represented by two or three chariots that cooperated with each other in order to ensure that the winner would be a representative of the faction. In the Early Empire, the "president" of the races (*editor ludorum/agonothetes*), who also funded them, was aided by businessmen (*domini factionum*), who rented them the horses, chariots, and other required equipment (to a certain extent the way Augustus had assisted Herod), and they also supplied the charioteers and their assistants. These businessmen, and not the chariot drivers, thus managed the factions.

In the fourth century CE, and perhaps even earlier, management was taken from private hands. The stables of the "circus factions" were transferred to the emperor, who financed their upkeep, the food supply for the horses, and the entire staff. The manager of each league was a professional, sometimes the head driver; he was an official in the imperial administration and was known as the *factionarius*. Later on, the faction became a professional guild of sorts and was headed by a wealthy patron who represented the faction's teams and fans, however complete funding continued to come from the imperial treasury. The patron became the head of the faction, which was no longer headed by a professional. In the East, private race managers continued to fund

---

[35] It is thus clear that in Caesarea the dignitaries' box was the one located above the vaulted passageway mentioned above, and not in the place set by Porath (*supra* n. 1), which belongs to a phase when the arena was shortened and converted into a Roman amphitheater.

races for a longer period than in the West. We have no information about "circus factions" prior to 315 CE.[36]

The Starting Gates (CARCERES) at Caesarea[37]

The starting gates of the Herodian hippodrome at Caesarea are most instructive concerning the type of chariot races conducted therein, and the transformation they underwent during a period of c. 250 years of its operation.

Located at the northern end of the hippodrome, the stalls, like all other parts of the hippodrome, were built of *kurkar* stone and coated with white plaster. Only the stalls on the eastern side were exposed in the excavations, in a section c. 30 m wide from east to west. The western stalls were eroded long ago by the sea, but it is reasonable to assume that they were similar, symmetrically arranged, structures.

Three phases were discerned in the arrangement of the starting gates (Fig. 98). Phase I has three sub-phases, while the two later phases (II and III) have no sub-phases. A thick wall was built on top of Phase Ic stalls, that were almost completely dismantled, rendering the complex inoperable as a hippodrome for a while. Phase II was built on top of the lower courses of this wall, raising the level of the arena by 0.7 m. The Phase III stalls were moved about 3 m south of Phase II stalls. The Phase I *carceres* had 12 stalls without a central gate, Phase II had 5 stalls on either side of the central gate, and Phase III had 4 stalls on either side of the central gate.

Architecturally, the stalls of the Roman circus can be divided into two categories: (1) four-pier stalls; and (2) double-pilaster stalls. The stalls of the first type are the earlier ones. The table below presents the essential features and data concerning each phase and sub-phase.

---

[36] Cameron 1976; Humphrey 1986: 11–24; Matz 1991: 58. See also: Roueché 1993: 143–156.

[37] The excavation of this complex, and a c. 40 m broad section of the area to its front was undertaken by the University of Haifa expedition under the direction of the author. Shalom Rotgaizer and Alon Moscu were area supervisors; measurements were taken by Illya and Nadia Levitt, and the photographs were taken by Zaraza Friedman and Jonathan Gottlieb. Anna Iamim entered the field measurements into the computer and produced the computerized plans. Registration of the finds was done by Michal Oren-Pascal and Yael Arnon. Moshe Tzadik and Zeev Ginat served as the expedition supervisors. My gratitude is extended to everyone.

Phase	Type and Façade Ornamentation	No. of Stalls	Date	Elevation of Arena (above sea level)
1a	4–pier stalls on trapezoidal platform. Ornamentation: depressed horizontal band	12*	Herod; dedicated in the year 9 BCE celebrations	2.20
1b	4–pier stalls; front piers take the shape of two half-columns attached to each other; rear piers diamond-shaped in cross section; wooden partitions between stalls	12*		2.20
1c	4–pier stalls; front piers more massive; vertical band protruding to the front; stone partitions between stalls	12*	Coin of Agrippa I, 42–43 CE in arena fill	2.50
W100	Built on top of Phase Ic's piers that were largely dismantled; preserved to an elevation of 3.00		66–70 CE; pottery typical to end of Second Temple period, including "Destruction lamps"	Built on 2.50
II	Double-pilaster stalls; attached half-column to the front	5+5**	Coin of Trajan (98–117 CE), from arena fill	3.20
III	Double-pilaster stalls; attached pilaster to the front	4+4**	Coin of Septimius Severus, from arena fill	3.40

   * The dimensions also allow for an alternative reconstruction of 5 stalls on either side of the main gate; however comparative architectural research prefers the proposed reconstruction of 12 stalls without a main gate, and not 10 stalls with a main gate.
   ** Central gate conjectural.

PHASE I

The three sub-phases can be distinguished from each other by the structure and the ornamentation of the piers, preserved up to 1–2 courses. The first sub-phase (Ia), corresponding to 2.20 m arena level, was built by Herod. The subsequent sub-phases exhibit a growing monumentalization. A coin of Agrippa I, dating to 42–43 CE, was found in a fill beneath the Phase Ic arena. This sub-phase, therefore, should be attributed to his day. The ceilings in all three sub-phases were flat and light, seemingly made of wooden beams. The stalls were 3.3–3.6 m wide, and their interior depth was 3.75–4 m. They were set parallel to each other and to the long axis of the arena. Each stall was set a bit further north relative to the stall to its east, so that the façade appeared slightly curved, but symmetrical, relative to the long axis of the arena. The Phase Ib facade is especially noteworthy (Fig. 99): a half-column 0.5 m in diameter to the front is attached to a 1 m diameter half-column, indicating that the *carceres* had two stories. An architectural analysis suggests an elevation of c. 8.9 m.

The arrangement of the stalls in Phase I, in all its three sub-phases, indicates that the chariots started their run in parallel lanes, as at Olympia (Fig. 100). The destination of the chariots was the far turn-ing post—the *meta prima*. Herod instituted Greek-style races, and such was their style throughout phase I. Such a racecourse precludes any possibility for the existence of a continuous physical barrier along the middle of the arena in this phase. The nature of Herod's *hippika* as described by Josephus above—horse riding and chariot races—also indicates their Greek style.

The starting gates of sub-phase Ic were dismantled and from their stones a massive c. 1.5 m-thick wall (W100), built of headers, was constructed, covering the lower parts of the stalls. While dismantling the three courses left of this wall under Phase II *carceres*, potsherds, including "Herodian" oil lamps were found between the stones, resembling those that are found in many sites in a destruction layer that corresponds to the end of the Second Temple period. These finds enable us to conclude with some certainty that the wall was built at the same time. Its construction brought an end to the operation of the hippodrome as such. The arena was converted into a vast walled enclosure. It is tempting to link this physical change with the Jewish revolt against Rome that broke out in Caesarea in 66 CE. The archae-ological data permit this conclusion. It is reasonable to assume that with the end of the revolt, in 70 CE, it was in this walled compound, and not in the prison at the governor's palace (*praetorium*), that Titus imprisoned for an entire winter the war captives.[38] Here Titus also

---

[38] *War* 7.1, 3, 20. Also the stadium in Tiberias functioned as an imprisonment compound, when in 67, at the end of the battles in the Galilee, Vespasian gathered there all the Jewish captives—36,600 in number, and there determined their fate—to

held, in October 70—early in that winter—celebrations in honor of
the eighteenth birthday of his brother Domitian, at which over 2,500
of his Jewish captives were slaughtered by being forced to fight with
wild beasts, by man-to-man sword duels, or by being hoisted on a
stake—accepted types of entertainment for Romans.[39] The number of
imprisoned captives in Caesarea was thus very large.

PHASES II AND III

Phase II involved raising the elevation of the arena by c. 0.7 m (from
2.50 m to 3.20 m a.s.l.). The stalls of the new *carceres*, built on top of
W100, took a radial rather than a parallel orientation and had a different structure than those of Phase I. The width of each pilaster was
1.2 m and its length (without the engaged half-column) was c. 3 m.
The width of each stall in this phase was 3m. The structure, arrangement, and dimensions are similar to the stalls of Gerasa (second half
of the second century CE),[40] and therefore the ceiling of each stall can
be reconstructed as a vault 4.5m high (Fig. 101).[41] A coin of Trajan
(98–117 CE) found in the fill of arena 3.20 m a.s.l., dates Phase II *carceres* to the reign of Trajan (or to the beginning of Hadrian's reign).

Phase III pilasters were more massive 1.4–1.5 m wide and 3m long.
The width of each stall was 3.5 m. The pilasters supported vaults, as
in Phase II. Since the stalls were now wider, they probably stood to a
higher elevation than the stalls of Phase II. The arched central entrance
stood to an even greater height. Incorporated into the easternmost,
first, pilaster of Phase III was a massive pedestal stretching eastward—
perhaps of a stair tower. A coin of Septimius Severus (198–211 CE),
found beneath arena 3.40 m a.s.l. dates the construction of Phase III
carceres, associated with this arena level, to the reign of this emperor.

When the competitions recommenced after the Jewish Revolt, in
Phase II, there was a change in the direction of the starting lanes. Now

---

die or become slaves (*War* 3.10, 10, 532–42). In Herod's day, Jewish dignitaries were
summoned to be put under garrison in the hippodrome in Jericho (*Ant.* 17.6, 5, 175;
8, 2, 193–94; *War* 1.33, 6–8, 659–69). Netzer 1999a: 56–59, suggests viewing the exact
place of the arrest in the *palaestra* above and to the north of the theater, and not in
the arena of the hippodrome.

[39] *War* 7.3, 1, 37–38.
[40] Ostrasz 1989: 71.
[41] In the reconstruction proposed here, the same 2:3 ratio exists between the width
and the height of each stall. For a reconstruction of the circus at Gerasa on the basis
of its remains, see: Ostrasz 1989: 51–77, 67–70, figs. 4–6.

the chariots began their run in radial tracks, their destination being the "white line" extending to the right of the *meta secunda*. The number of stalls in this phase—5 on either side of the central arch—indicates that also in this phase the circus factions were not yet a determining factor in the organization of the races. But even in Phase III, with 4 stalls on either side of the central passage, it seems that one can hardly speak of the introduction of full-fledged circus factions in the operation of the games, but rather of imitation of the four teams of Rome. The circus factions are first attested in the literary sources pertaining to the Greek East not earlier than 315 CE. Phase III date seems by far too early.

The "Isactian Games" were still conducted, one would assume, in their regular structure—the city stadium—as late as year 221 CE, as is attested by the inscription from Laodicea mentioned above, rather than in the eastern hippodrome—a typical Roman circus, that was already standing at that time.[42] It had a continuous barrier that would have presented an obstacle for proper conduct of the athletics. The continued periodic celebration of the Isactian Games, in the stadium, would have precluded the construction of a continuous barrier there even in phase III. And indeed, as we have noted above, there is no archaeological evidence to indicate that an *euripus* had ever existed in this arena.

Munera Gladiatorum and *Venationes*—Roman-Style Games

All the games mentioned so far—the athletics (*gymnika*) and the equestrian games (*hippika*)—were already widespread in the Hellenistic world, before the Roman period. The classic Roman games were

---

[42] Humphrey 1974; 1975; Bull 1973: 262. This circus, whose continuous barrier was decorated with an obelisk and pink granite cones, was built in the first half of the second century on the eastern side of the city, while—on the basis of information at our disposal—the Herodian hippodrome was still operative and functioned as the stadium of the city. Excavations were recently renewed at the site and work had commenced for erecting the obelisk anew. In the course of these excavations, under the direction of Y. Porath on behalf of the Israel Antiquities Authority, long sections of the *euripus* were exposed, as well as the *meta prima*, columns, and statues. See Porath 2003; 2008: 1659. As for the oval amphitheater, owing to the lack of excavations we cannot know when it was built on the eastern side of the city. On this amphitheater, see Reifenberg 1951; Roller 1982a. In a survey and in a sounding of a limited scale excavated by Negev, few architectural fragments were found. See Negev 1966b: 144. The estimated size of the arena are: 62 × 95 m. Large scale excavations (non published yet), were carried out in the amphitheater in 2010 on behalf of IAA, headed by Dr. Peter Gendelman.

the ravaging spectacles—the gladiatorial combats, the hunting shows, and the executions in the arena. Despite Josephus' complaint against Herod regarding the introduction of such despicable games into Jerusalem, there were Jews who were curious to watch them already many years earlier.[43] In the imperial era, these spectacles were associated with the annual emperor cult, and such were the games instituted by Herod in Caesarea. In Rome, under Julius Caesar and Augustus, these shows were also held in the Circus Maximus.

The combats commenced with a procession (*pompa*/πομπή) that included a brief ceremony in the chapel (*sacellum*). The games ran for a number of days and included three daily events: hunting (*venatio*) in the morning, gladiator combats (*munus/munera*) in the afternoon, and in between various afternoon games (*meridiani*), such as an exhibition of exotic animals, acrobatic and athletic performances, as well as executions of convicts by leaving them prey for wild beasts, or by crucifixion and hoisting on a stake.[44] All three elements are referred to in the detailed description given by Josephus of the celebrations organized by Herod in both Jerusalem and Caesarea.

A special structure was invented in the Roman world for these games—the oval amphitheater (Fig. 97), the Colosseum being one of the best examples. Many of them had a complex network of corridors and staircases leading to the seats (*cavea*) and an intricate system of underground passageways and subterranean cells that served as cells (*carceres*) for the wild beasts, for lifts and lifting devices for scenery, and as a place for the combatants to stay until the time of their performance. A structure with external dimensions of 100 × 80 or 70 m

---

[43] Among the rights granted by the Senate to Hyrcanus II, his children, and the envoys sent by him, in the time of Julius Caesar, in a Senate decree (*senatus consultum*) quoted *verbatim* by Josephus, was the right to sit in Rome among the senatorial order when watching the contests of gladiators and wild beasts (*Ant.* 14.10, 6, 210). A very similar right was granted by the Senate in 39 BCE to the ambassadors of Aphrodisias and Plarasa in Rome. See Reynolds 1982: 60, 63, 88, inscr. No. 8, lines 76–77; Welch 1998a: 563. These sources also inform us that the seating order at the various entertainment structures of performances was determined by social hierarchy.

[44] For a description of the daily routine in these shows in the imperial era, see Golvin and Landes, 1990: 189–92. Among the arena combats were also exhibitions that included fighting on horseback or even from chariots. The fighting rider was called an "*eques*" (horserider) and was armed with body armor, a shield, a helmet, and a javelin. The fighter on the chariot was called "*essedarius*." The battle was held between two chariots holding two people, one the charioteer and the other the gladiator. The combatants alighted the chariot and fought one another while the chariots waited on the side. See Matz 1991.

was considered a large structure.[45] First called in Latin *spectaculum*, it later—since the beginning of the first century CE— received the term *amphitheatrum*, borrowed from the Greek ἀμφιθέατρον.[46] This term is composed of two words: ἀμφί, meaning "around," and θέατρον, meaning "place for seeing." In the Greek world, during the Late Hellenistic and Early Roman period, this term was commonly used to denote a hippodrome or a stadium—a structure with a seating arrangement encompassing an arena, no matter what the context of the performances conducted therein. Thus it is used by Josephus, Strabo, and other Hellenistic authors.[47] Only in a later period, when the Roman games replaced the Greek-style games, was a separate structure designated for each type of entertainment—horse and chariot races in the hippodrome/circus, *munera* and *venationes* in the amphitheater. However, even following the process of monumentalization and differentiation that characterized Roman entertainment architecture, when a separate structure was designated for each show, *munera* and *venationes* in the hippodrome/circus, or horse races in the stadium, were still the norm in the East. Actually, Roman style amphitheaters (as well as circuses), were relatively rare in the East, although *munera* and *venationes* were widespread there as they were in the west.[48]

In the eastern provinces of the Empire the various hunting and gladiatorial spectacles were held primarily in stadia,[49] and since the first

---

[45] Tables summarizing the dimensions are presented by Golvin 1988: 283–88.

[46] The term "amphitheater" appears for the first time before year 2 BCE in the *Res gestae Augustii* of Ankara. See Etiénne 1966. The famous Colosseum in Rome—a name originating only in the Middle Ages—was known as "the Flavian Amphitheater" in the Roman period. The Latin term *spectaculum* appears in a dedicatory inscription of the gladiators' arena in Pompeii, the earliest stone structure of its type, dedicated in 70 or 65 BCE. See: CIL X, 852.

[47] Humphrey 1996.

[48] The evidence from various sources for the existence of gladiatorial combats in the eastern provinces were compiled by Robert 1940 (reprinted Amsterdam 1971); *idem* 1960.

[49] Humphrey 1996; Welch 1998a; 1998b. This reality was known to the rabbis as well. See, for example, "an ox from the stadium" mentioned in *M Bava Qamma* 4, 4; cf. *M 'Abodah Zarah* 1, 7. The acts of the martyrs—let prey to the wild beast, as narrated by Eusebius (above, note 5), occurred in the "stadium" of Caesarea.
The term "amphitheater" is not mentioned in rabbinic literature. R. Abbahu, a resident of Caesarea, speaks of theaters and circuses in the city (*Lamentations Rabbah*, Prolegomenon 17), but he does not mention an amphitheater. This conjunction of only theaters and circuses, also appears in the sayings of other *amoraim* (*TB 'Abodah Zarah* 18b; *Pesiqta de Rav Kahana* 15, 2; *Genesis Rabbah* 67, 4). Yet, the reality of the gladiatorial and hunting spectacles was known to the rabbis (*Pesiqta de Rav Kahana* 28, 3; *TY Gittin* 4, 9, 46b; *TB Gittin* 47a), and see also: Brettler and Poliakoff 1990. It

century CE such spectacles were also held in many places throughout the Empire in theaters that were adapted for this purpose: the orchestra was surrounded by a high partition wall, or its level was lowered in such a way that the *cavea* would be high above it, on top of a podium wall measuring more than 2 m.[50] In the stadiums and theaters that served this purpose, a special net fence propped on a series of poles was built on top of the podium wall, to protect the spectators.[51]

We shall now return to Caesarea. It is clear that the *munera* and *venationes*—the "Roman spectacles" component of the "Actian Games" instituted by Herod—took place in the hippodrome/stadium under discussion.[52] Such spectacles were held there on a yearly basis, in conjunction with the imperial cult, not just every four years in the framework of the "Actian Games." Similar is the case with the shows given by Titus in Caesarea in October 70 CE on the occasion of Domitian's eighteenth birthday.[53] The city stadium was the natural candidate to hold these shows. The stadium is mentioned explicitly by

---

seems that the word קניגין (Greek: κυνήγιον; see Jastrow 1985: 1392), meaning "hunt," denotes not only the spectacle but, at the same time, the setting in which it occurred (e.g. *TB 'Abodah Zarah* 18b). At Constantinople, for instance, the amphitheater of Septimius Severus was known by the name *Kynegion*. This may have also been the name used by rabbis for the amphitheater in Caesarea that could have already been built in the time of R. Abbahu.

Also in the *Martyrs of Palestine* of Eusebius—a contemporary of R. Abbahu—the term "amphitheater" is not mentioned; just circus, stadium, and theater.

[50] This was the situation in the following theaters (partial list): Miletus, Ephesus, Priene, Magnesia, Sagalassus, Sidé, Hierapolis, Termessus (all in Asia Minor), Athens (Dionysos theater), Corinth, Thassos, and Philippi (Greece), Stobi (Macedonia), and Cyrene (Libya), which are essentially mixed structures ('édifices mixtes', 'théâtres transformés', according to Golvin). See: Golvin 1988: 237–49, 317; Golvin and Landes 1990: 8–10, 204–6; Welch 1999. This phenomenon of transformation of theaters is, according to Golvin, not to be found in the provinces of Syria and Palaestina, where oval amphitheaters were built from the outset in Antioch, Bostra, Caesarea, and Eleutheropolis, and perhaps also Berytus.

[51] Gebhard 1975; Golvin 1988: 237–46; Stillwell 1952: 84–98; Welch 1998a: 560, fig. 12; 1998b 125, fig. 9 and n. 8.

[52] The *cavea* of the Herodian theater at Caesarea had no podium wall. *Munera* and *venationes* could not be held there. Golvin (1988: 246–47) excludes this option also for the later phase of the theater, attributed by Frova *et al.*, 1965: 57–159, 165–86, to Septimius Severus. Yet, according to Eusebius (*supra* n. 25, Syriac version), Christian martyrs were let prey to wild beasts in the theater, not only in the stadium. A protective net could be installed on top of the "*naumachea*" wall exposed by Frova. In any case, even in theaters that were certainly equipped with a protective net, the show had to be reduced to a small number of beasts or combatants—no more than a few couples—unlike the much larger arena of the stadium, even in its shortened phase.

[53] Above, note 39.

Eusebius as the site of the martyrdom of Agapius in the presence of Emperor Maximinus, and of an earlier confession of Silvanus—two famous martyrs of Palaestina.[54] But in this late period the stadium was already shortened (see below).

Holes cut on top of the podium wall throughout its length, and in the first two rows of seats (Fig. 102), to hold the protective net (Fig. 103), provide archaeological evidence that these spectacles were already held in the arena before it was shortened. The holes, c. 0.8 m apart, were cut through the molded projected profile, decorating the upper course of the podium wall. They are seen along the entire length of the podium wall, everywhere the molding is still preserved, and they are large enough to permit a rope to go through, not more than that. They are also found along the margins of the first two rows of seats. Larger square or round depressions were also cut into the upper face of the podium wall, c. 1.5 m apart. These depressions could have been related to the awning (*vellum*).[55]

THE SHORTENING OF THE STADIUM

We know of cases in which stadiums having a podium wall and a U-shaped hippodrome were shortened, so that part of the arena bordered by the curved end (*sphendone*) and the nearby galleries of seats were cut off from the rest of the arena by a concave wall and converted into oval amphitheaters.[56] The phenomenon of shortening stadiums and hippodromes began only in the late Roman period, reflecting (in addition to the disappearance of chariot races and athletics from these structures) a distinct decline in amphitheater spectacles relative to the earlier period, when the various gladiatorial spectacles were held for hundreds of years (with a protective net installed), in the unshortened structures, accommodating a much larger audience. Welch has suggested that the shortening attests to the disappearance of the *munera*

---

[54] See note 64 below.

[55] The significance of these intrusive holes along the margins of the podium and of the depressions on its top is obvious. They were not mentioned in the preliminary reports published so far by Porath, but they can be seen by any visitor to the site.

[56] This was the situation in the following stadia: Aphrodisias, Ephesus, Perge, Aspendos, Laodicea, and the Panathenaean stadium in Athens. See Welch 1998a: 565–60. See also Patrich forthcoming-b.

component of the shows during the fourth century (*inter alia*, under the pressure of the church), with the *venationes* still remaining.[57]

In Caesarea, four thin and curved walls, 91.5–136.5 m distant from the southern gate, indicate the reduction of the arena and its conversion into an oval amphitheater on four different occasions. Each of these northern walls were just one stone (c. 50 cm thick) laid as a stretcher, rendering it impossible for the wall to stand very high—the higher the wall, the poorer its stability. The wall delimiting the shortened arena on the north never attained a monumental character, as was the case at Beth Shean (where the second-century hippodrome was converted into an amphitheater in the fourth century), and at Neapolis/Nablus (where the shortening dates to the third century).[58] Therefore, it seems that one should conceive each of these walls as a one-time event held in the arena, rather than a permanent construction. Such a shortening, by a thin wall, is known also in the hippodrome at Gerasa (second half of the fourth century and perhaps even later), and in several stadia of Asia Minor and Greece, as was mentioned above, where the modification was dated to the Late Roman period (mid-fourth and fifth century), when the athletics declined.[59]

Porath dated the shortening to the second century and related it to the construction of the eastern circus at that time.[60] According to him, the shortened complex went out of use in the early third century.[61] But the data from my excavations near the *carceres* indicated that the Phase III *carceres* was constructed under Septimius Severus, indicating that the hippodrome was still in operation in the early third century. The construction of the eastern circus—much larger than the Herodian stadium—featuring thus chariot races in the style of the Circus Maximus, was not caused by the deterioration of the stadium, and

---

[57] Welch 1998a: 568. The games at Olympia were cancelled by an edict of 392 CE. On the disappearance of gladiatorial combats from the Roman world, see also Golvin and Landes 1990: 221–25.

[58] For Beth Shean, see Tsafrir and Foerster 1994: 113–15; 1997: 99, figs. E, 17. For Neapolis/Nablus, see Magen 1993: 1357–58, and n. 62 below.

[59] For Gerasa, see Ostrasz 1989: 74; for the stadia in Asia Minor and Greece, see *supra* n. 56.

[60] Porath 1996b: 98. In *TB Megillah* 6a and *Midrash Tanhuma, Exodus*, 6 (ed. S. Buber; reprint Jerusalem 1964) 4, mention is made of the circuses (in plural) of Caesarea. See Levine 1975a: 188, n. 135.

Joshua Drei, who is well acquainted with the stratigraphy of the Herodian hippodrome, reached the conclusion (in a private communication, dated June 11, 1998) that the first shortening occurred between two periods of use as a hippodrome.

[61] Porath 1996b: 99; 1995a: 23.

its construction did not bring an end to the activities in the Herodian hippodrome. Moreover, parallels from most of the sites mentioned above indicate that the shortening of stadia and hippodromes, and their conversion into amphitheaters, is a phenomenon of the fourth–fifth centuries.[62] The shortening at Caesarea should be placed, at the earliest, in the third century, later than Septimius Severus, or even at the very beginning of the fourth century, and the abandonment of the shortened structure should be accordingly postponed to a later time in that century, later than Maximinus.

The frescos on the podium wall, depicting hunting scenes, are attributed by Porath to this phase.[63] Identifiable here are the deer, fox, wild boar, and tiger. A subterranean system of tunnels was also installed in the reduced amphitheater of Caesarea, and the loggia for dignitaries was moved northward, to be located more or less opposite the center of the shortened arena. A great deal of work was invested in these new features that did not constitute a part of the original stadium, in its full length.

In the shortened arena—still called a stadium—took place (in year 306–7 CE) the martyrdom of Agapius, who was left prey to a bear by order of Emperor Maximinus, who sat in the dignitaries' platform. A year later the confession of Silvanus took place there.[64]

THE *SACELLUM* (Fig. 34)

Beneath the new platform was a chapel, *sacellum*, roofed by two arches supporting the floor of the platform above it. A central niche is cut in the eastern rock wall, and smaller niches, some elongated and horizontal, are distributed on this wall. The finds tell us about the cult

---

[62] The case of Neapolis is an enigma, since according to Malalas (*Chronographia*, ed. Dindorf 1831: 446) the Samaritan rebel Julian attended a chariot race in the local hippodrome in year 529, in which Samaritan, Jewish, and Christian charioteers competed. How could this be if the hippodrome was already converted into an amphitheater in the third century? We'll have to wait for the final report to check whether there are sufficient grounds for this claim of the excavator.

[63] Above, note 6.

[64] Eusebius (*supra* n. 5) relates the detailed stories. These events occurred according to Eusebius in the stadium—Herod's hippodrome, even if in its reduced form. This structure was situated next to the Roman governor's palace wherein the persecuted Christians were incarcerated, and it was there that they were brought to trial before the governor.

that took place there.[65] According to Porath, many clay lamps were found in the fill that was accumulated there, as well as 5 marble votive feet, as it were, for receiving a blessing and strength for the legs of the contestants. One of them bears a dedicatory inscription to the goddess Kore, apparently the patroness of the *sacellum*. This goddess was also worshiped in the stadium at Samaria.[66] Furthermore, three stone altars incorporated into a wall from the Byzantine period were discovered, as well as a small marble plaque with the Greek inscription: Μερισμος ἡνίοχος (Merismos the charioteer), and a decoration of ivy leaves with a date palm in between. These finds indicate that the religious ceremonies conducted therein were connected expressly with athletics and chariot races, and not only gladiatorial combats or wild beast spectacles. Thus, it is not inconceivable that this *sacellum* existed as a cult place in the arena already before the shortening.

It seems that at the beginning of the Byzantine period the *sacellum* was converted into a Christian martyrs' chapel.[67] Three foundation stones for altar legs were found *in situ*—a common find in chapels and churches. It seems that at least some of the niches carved in the rock wall are from this phase. In any event, the large niche in the middle room, the aedicule of the pagan *sacellum*, certainly functioned in this phase as an apsidal niche, and the elongated niches in the side room were perhaps burial or hiding *loculi* for the remains of martyrs, as was the case in the Christian catacombs in Rome.[68]

ARCHITECTURAL DISCUSSION

An examination of the preserved remains of Herod's sports facilities reveals a development from the simpler to the more complex (Fig. 104). The oldest of these edifices—the amphitheater/hippodrome in

---

[65] On chapels in amphitheaters, see Golvin 1988: 337–40. Many of them were dedicated to Nemesis. Several were dedicated to Hercules, Mars, or Diana. In many cases, the *sacellum* was located at the end of the short axis, beneath the dignitaries' box—the *loggia*, to which there was access from the arena. Such was the case at Mérida, Lyon, Casino, Perge, Pozzuoli, and Italica, as well as Caesarea.

[66] Flusser 1975. Regarding the votive feet, see Gersht 1996a: 310–11; Porath 1995a: 23, fig. 10; a photograph of the *Sacellum* is given there on p. 21, fig. 9a, and p. 272, color fig. 9. For a picture of the feet, see also *idem*. 1998: 41, fig. 3.

[67] Also the *sacellum* in the amphitheater of Salonae was converted into a Christian chapel in the fourth century. See Dyggve 1933: 102–7.

[68] See, for example: Fiocchi-Nicolai, *et al.* 1999; Rutgers 2000.

Jerusalem built in 29 BCE—left no standing remains. The stadium in Samaria, whose construction began in 27 BCE, was a rectangular field (194.5 × 58.5) surrounded by porticos. The hippodrome in Jericho was a more complex stadium: a rectangular race track (315 × 83 m), apparently surrounded by porticos on three sides, the northern side was occupied by the *sphendone*, and behind it, on higher ground than the arena, extended the *palaestra*.[69] The amphitheater/hippodrome in Caesarea, known as the stadium of the city, already had built seats not only in the *sphendone* but also along the two long sides. The dimensions of its arena (301 × 50.5), somewhat smaller than those given for Jericho.

Most instructive is the resemblance of the Herodian hippodrome in Caesarea to the Caesarean and Augustan circus in Bovillea (Fig. 105), not far from Rome,[70] that had the following features: the circus was also built on a north–south axis, and the measurements of the arena—60 × 328.5 m—closely resemble those at Caesarea. A passageway cuts through the center of the *cavea* from one side to the other, above which stood the dignitaries' platform, as in Caesarea. The eastern seats rest on a natural slope, while the western ones have a gallery resting on two parallel walls, as at Caesarea. It is not clear whether there was a passageway or a fill of earth between these walls. Since the western gallery in Caesarea was practically not preserved, it is difficult to ascertain if this side inclined slightly in the direction of the stalls, as at Bovillea. However, the fact that the arena at Caesarea was narrower detracts from such a possibility. In every gallery at Bovillea there were six rows of seats, and the overall capacity is estimated to have been c. 8,000 spectators. Here there was an early cult place to *gens Juliae*—the forefathers of Julius Caesar and Augustus. At the end of 16 CE a temple was dedicated there by Tiberius, with a statue of divine Augustus inside. In other words, the emperor cult was celebrated in this private

---

[69] Crowfoot *et al.* 1942: 41–50. On the hippodrome/stadium in Jericho, see Netzer 1999a: 56–59. The location of the hippodrome of Jerusalem is a matter of debate. See Patrich 2002b. On Herodian entertainment structures see also Netzer 2006: 277–281 and Patrich 2009c.

[70] On the hippodrome of Bovillea, see Humphrey 1986: 561–66. A direct influence of the building projects of Augustus and Agrippa in Rome was also recognized in other building projects of Herod. This is expressed, inter alia, by sending teams of masons familiar with the *opus reticulatum* and *quadratum* building techniques. These techniques are encountered in Israel only in Herod's building projects in Jericho, Jerusalem, and Paneas.

circus as well. There is also a resemblance between the games held in both places; these included athletics, chariot races in the Greek tradition, and entertainment in the Roman-style—gladiatorial combats and wild beast spectacles.[71] Also at Bovillea the stalls, twelve in number, were of the four piers type (however there the piers supported arches) and also a grid of wooden rods served as a partition between the stalls, as in Phases Ia and Ib at Caesarea. Their width was 2.72–3.13 m and the depth 3.9 m, dimensions quite similar to those at Caesarea. Also, in the first phase at Bovillea there was no central arch; it was added only at a later phase at the expense of the two central stalls, being 4.8 m wide[72] (in Phase II *carceres* at Caesarea it was 4.5 m wide).

The foundation of the seats on two parallel walls, having a fill or vaulted passageway between them, corresponds with Hellenistic tradition, since it appears in the earliest hippodromes and circuses. Such was the case in the Hellenistic *lageion* of Alexandria and in the hippodrome of Cyrene. Such was also the seating arrangement in the Circus Maximus during the reigns of Julius Caesar and Augustus.[73] The typical layout in the Roman circuses and stadia in a later period (as well as in the Roman amphitheaters) had a seating arrangement built on a network of parallel vaults perpendicular to the arena's long axis. Such was the layout at Gerasa (second half of the second century CE) and Tyre (early third century CE).

The excavations in Caesarea provide, then, more data for reconstructing ancient civic games. In addition, they also help to document an important stage in the development of Herodian architecture.

Update Addendum

Further elements of the foundations of the starting gates were uncovered in excavations conducted in 2002, including the foundations of two new piers (nos. 7 and 8), to the west of those known so far. The new finds indicate that during Phase I there were 5, and not 12, stalls on either side of a central gate.

---

[71] This, as noted, is the typical program of games associated with the emperor cult. Similar celebrations were also held in a first-century CE stadium at Aphrodisias and in any other place where such games took place. See Welch 1998a: 561–68.

[72] Humphrey 1986: 563–66.

[73] This early Roman practice, under Greek influence, reappears in Rome about 300 years later, in the Circus of Maxentius (306–12), where seats resting on a quadrant vault were supported by two parallel walls. On this feature, see Humphrey 1986: 586–98, fig. 281.

We now have more details about an earlier Herodian phase, the foundations of which were uncovered already in 1997, a phase which was not mentioned in the original article. These foundations are arranged in a radial, rather than in a parallel layout. Only a single course is preserved, sometimes two, with a top elevations of only 1.50–1.71 m a.s.l. The phase I stalls, of a different layout, are only partially set on top of the earlier foundations. It is therefore puzzling that no higher courses of the earlier stalls were preserved, unless they were never completed. However, two square depressions on the top face of the new western foundation 7 (the only one of the earlier phase uncovered in its entirety, though its western face was eroded by the sea), suggest that the stalls on top of these foundations were of wood.[74] Moreover, already in 1997 it was noticed that a tight layer of beaten *kurkar* at an elevation of 1.55–1.62 is reaching these foundations—an intermediary layer in the arena fill (the arena level of Phase I *carceres*, in which the structure was inaugurated, was 2.20 m a.s.l.). It was therefore evident that the earlier stalls were a casual construction, related perhaps to a specific event that preceded the inaugural celebrations of the city.

What was this event? Why were stalls built in relation to an intermediary layer in the arena fill? Why were these earlier stalls laid radially, to be later replaced by permanent parallel stalls with which the hippodrome was inaugurated? We may get reasonable answers to the last two question if we assume that the event in question was the visit of Marcus Agrippa to Herod in Caesarea, in 15 BCE, when the hippodrome was still under construction, five years prior to its inauguration.

This is how Flavius Josephus describes this visit in Judaea:

> And Herod, omitting nothing that might please him, received him in his newly founded cities and, while showing him his buildings, diverted him and his friends with enjoyable food and luxury; this he did both in Sebaste and in Caesarea, at the harbor which had been constructed by him, and in the fortresses which he had built at great expense, Alexandrion, Herodeion and Hyrcania....[75]

---

[74] In the period under discussion—the Early Principate—like in the Late Republic, most public theaters in Rome were still temporary wooden structures, constructed for a specific event and dismantled immediately thereafter. The testimony of the contemporary Roman architect Vitruvius (*De Architectura* 5.5.7, ed. Granger 1970: 280–281), is crystal clear in this respect. For further details about this issue, see Patrich 2002e.

[75] *Ant.* 16.13 (tr. Marcus 1963: 6–7). It seems that Agrippa sailed away from the Caesarea harbor (Philo, *Legatio ad Gaium*, 37, 294–297, ed. M. Smallwood, Leiden 1970). See Schürer 1973: 318 and note 115. Richardson (1996: 263–264), deemed it proper to suggest that the visit included spectacles and entertainment in the theaters,

In light of the archaeological record mentioned above, it would not be a speculation to assume that the entertainment in honor of Agrippa and his entourage at Caesarea included chariot races in the hippodrome, though still under construction. A layer of beaten *kurkar* was compressed on top of the sand fill to serve as an arena, and on its north end starting gates were installed. It was only to be expected that the races in honor of the notable guest would be in the Roman style, with radial stalls.

But in order to ensure the status of Caesarea as a center of games in the east, Herod instructed that in the permanent structure the races would be à la Olympia,[76] and accordingly, for the inaugural games, new stalls were built in a parallel layout and the arena was elevated to the pre-conceived level, following the master plan, to be in accord with the *cavea* and the staircases leading from the arena to the seats. The starting gates of Phase I, in its three sub-phases, served the hippodrome from its inauguration to their end, when wall W100 was built on top of them, as was detailed above.

---

stadia, and hippodromes constructed by Herod throughout his kingdom, for the pleasure of both retinues. The suggestion that the pleasures vested by Herod on Agrippa at Caesarea included chariot races was mentioned to me by my colleague in the Caesarea excavations, Prof. Avner Raban. In spite of the fact that this is not stated plainly in the short description of Josephus, I tend to accept it, especially in light of the archaeological data mentioned above, indicating that the structure was operative with a lower arena level and separate starting gates, anterior to the inauguration feasts.

[76] Herod was well acquainted with the Olympic Games. In the Olympiade of 12 BCE (two year before the inauguration feast of Caesarea), he served as the president (ἀγωνοθέτης) of the Olympic Games. Observing that these games were in decline for lack of funds, he endowed revenues and gave the games greater dignity in respect of sacrifices and other ceremonies. For his munificence his name was recorded by the people of Elis as perpetual president of the games (*Ant.* 16.5.3–149; *War* 1.21.12–426–427). In this capacity he could easily enlist the best athletes for the consecration games of Caesarea. On Herod's involvement in the Olympic Games, see Lämmer 1972.

CHAPTER EIGHT

THE *PRAETORIA* AT CAESAREA MARITIMA

Caesarea Maritima, a prosperous city, was founded by Herod the Great—a client king of Rome—during the years 22–10 BCE to serve as a harbor and an administrative capital of the expanding kingdom of Judaea. Yet, the major city of Herod's kingdom, and its religious and cultural center was Jerusalem—the Jewish holy city. Five routes connected Caesarea to the hinterland—the fertile land of Samaria—and hence to the Judaean Hills. The Herodian city had a royal palace, a deep-water harbor, a temple overlooking the harbor and the entire city, and two entertainment structures—a theater and a hippo-stadium.

In 6 CE, when Judaea came under direct Roman rule, the governor established his seat in Herod's palace, known as Herod's *praetorium* in *Ac* 23:35. Paul was detained there for two years (58–60 CE) before being fetched to Rome to be sentenced at the emperor's court. In this Palace Herod Agrippa I (41–44 CE), king of Judaea, died after a short illness. Earlier, in 26 CE, the Jews of Jerusalem sent a delegation to Pontius Pilate to protest against the introduction into Jerusalem of military standards with the images of Emperor Tiberius, in contrast to earlier custom. They assembled in the Great Stadium, adjacent to the palace.

Under Vespasian, after the destruction of Jerusalem in 70 CE, Caesarea became a Roman colony and the province was promoted to be ruled by a *legatus Augusti* of senatorial rank. Caesarea became the capital of the province—*Iudaeae caput* according to Tacitus (*Hist.* 2.78). At this stage, its financial affairs were entrusted to an official of an equestrian rank—the *procurator provinciae*. The first known procurator was L. Laberius Maximus (*War* 7.6. 6 [216]). He served under the governor Lucilius Bassus, who captured the fortresses of Herodium and Machaerus.[1]

Archaeological excavations carried out in Caesarea since the 1970s uncovered the remains of these two *praetoria*—that of the *legatus*

---

[1] *War* 7.6.1–6 (163–218); 7.8.1 (252); Schürer 1973: 515.

Augsti pro praetore and that of the *procurator provinciae*. These structures yielded also a wealth of inscriptions, which enable us to identify
the function of some of their wings.

HEROD's PALACE AND THE *PRAETORIUM* OF THE ROMAN GOVERNOR
(FIGS. 17, 106, 107)[2]

Herod's palace extended over two terraces with a difference of elevation of ca. 3.6 m. The two-storied lower-terrace palace (110 × 55 m in
size),[3] built in the first phase (22–15 BCE) of the building operations at
Caesarea, served as the private wing. It occupied a natural promontory
extending 100 m into the Mediterranean. The E side and the SE corner
were cut out of the bed-rock. The various wings, whose foundations
were almost at sea level, surrounded a large, rectangular, rock-cut pool
(35 × 18 m), 2 m deep, lined with hydraulic plaster[4] with a rectangular
base, presumably for a statue, at its center. It was a swimming pool, fed
by sweet water, typical of Herodian palaces.[5] The pool was surrounded
by open walks 2.6 m wide, and on three sides (S, W and N) by colonnades 4.2 m wide, with a 2.3 m intercolumniation. Rectangular planters filled with garden soil were rock-cut between the columns. The
E wing, in a better state of preservation, constituted a dinning suite
looking west, comprising of a central hall (93.5 sq m) interpreted as
a Herodian triclinium, flanked on either side by two small rooms. At
least four phases of modifications and mosaic reflooring were traced.[6]

---

[2] On this complex, excavated by several expeditions (Hebrew University of Jerusalem, University of Pennsylvania, and the Israel Antiquities Authority), see Levine
and Netzer 1986; Netzer 1999a: 109–14; Netzer 1996; Gleason 1996; Burrell 1996.
See also Burrell, Gleason, and Netzer 1993. Gleason *et al.* 1998. During the years
1995–97, in the framework of Israel Antiquities Authority excavations directed by
Y. Porath, further parts of the N, S, and E wings of the *praetorium* were exposed. For
a short preliminary note, see Rochman 1998; Porath 2001. See also Cotton and Eck
2001; Porath 2008; Netzer 2006: 106–112.
[3] Gleason *et al.* 1998: 29. According to Burrell 1996: 240, the dimensions of the
rectangular structure (without the semicircular western projection) are 40 × 80 m;
according to Netzer 1996: 198-201, they are 83 × 51 m, giving a total area of c. 4400
sq m for the lower story (including the projections), and 8000 sq m in two stories.
[4] Italian *pozzolana* cement, imported to Caesarea only in Herod's time, was used in
the pool (Gleason *et al.*, 1998: 29.
[5] Swimming pools were also found in Herod's palaces at Jericho, Masada, Herodium
and Hyrcania. See Netzer 1986. For Hyrcania, see Patrich 1992. See also Elitzur 2008.
[6] At first the rock-trimmed back wall of the triclinium was plain, and the facade
had one or three doorways. Later an apse was cut in the back wall, and the entire hall,

Remains of wall plaster imitating marble revetment were uncovered *in situ*, and glass *tesserae* indicate the existence of wall mosaics. In the northernmost room of the unit a furnace and a hypocaust floor were installed later, in the Roman period. A tile used in the furnace bears the stamp of the Legio X Fretensis, indicating a post-67 CE date. In a still later phase this smaller hypocaust was replaced by the southernmost room which was also heated by a hypocaust. These were interpreted as indications of a small bath unit, but in the absence of any tubs or basins one should not exclude the possibility that these were just heated rooms without any bathing activity associated with them. The more so since a small bathhouse, including a *miqveh*, was found in the NW corner of the upper palace (see below).

Access to the second story and to the upper terrace was through a staircase located in the NE corner. The western side of the lower terrace, that might have served as the living quarters, is poorly preserved. Two projections extended from the main rectangular building. One, semicircular, 26 m in diameter and reconstructed as an elevated exedra, extended westward, and the second, much smaller, extending southward, might have served as a jetty for small boats.

The upper terrace, on the upper part of the promontory and of a slightly different orientation, served as the public wing. The entrance to the palace was from the E, via a square propylon of four turrets set at its corners. Only their foundations had been preserved. The upper terrace was built around a vast courtyard (42 × 65 m = 2730 sq m), paved by a compacted crushed stone, and surrounded by porticoes.[7] The columns, made of local sandstone (*kurkar*), had a fine plaster coat. The bases were Attic, and the capitals Doric. A raised square platform, for some monument or for the emplacement of a *bema*, stood in its center, and to its east was constructed a vast underground water cistern of two compartments, T-shaped in its ground plan.

The N wing of the upper terrace held on the west a bathhouse with a *miqveh* built over a spring house, but the larger part of this wing was occupied by two suites separated from each other by a service

---

including the apse, got a new mosaic floor. To the front the wall was replaced by a portico, extending westward, at the expense of the pool. In a still later phase a fountain was installed in the apse, with a semicircular pond built over the mosaic floor.

[7] The W half of the upper terrace was excavated by the University of Pennsylvania expedition, directed by Gleason and Burrell. The E half, and farther areas to its E, which belonged to the Roman *praetorium*, as well as the entire S wing, were excavated by the Israel Antiquities Authority (IAA) expedition, headed by Yosef Porath.

corridor. The W suite (in the Penn excavation area) was facing S, while the E one (on the IAA excavation area) was facing N. The W suite, symmetrical in its layout, held in its center a basilical audience hall (192 sq m) flanked by smaller rooms and service corridors. It seems that the Roman governor and his *concillium* held their assizes in this basilical hall, to be identified with the law court, or audience hall, called *akroaterion* in Ac 25:23. The N part of the hall, accommodated a dais, or a *bema* (Ac 25:6), occupied by the governor and his council (*sumboulion* Ac 25:12) during the assizes. It had a heated floor set on stone *suspensurae/hypocaust*.[8] Later in the Roman period the *suspensurae* was extended to a room on the E, but this extension was built of brick alone. The *bema* can be identified with a high degree of certainty.

It was here where St. Paul was brought for a hearing,[9] and later the Christian martyrs of Caesarea[10] or members of the Jewish community mentioned in the rabbinic sources were brought to trial.[11] In the persecution under Decius, Origen was imprisoned and tortured severely on the rack in Caesarea. The right to inflict a death penalty—the *ius gladii*—belonged to the provincial governor.[12] He presided over the court of justice in such affairs, and therefore the governor (*hegemon*) is regularly referred to as the judge (*dikastes*) in Eusebius' *Martyrs of Palestine*. Christians were brought to his tribunal (*dikasterion*), where he interrogated them about their name, place of origin, family, and faith.

A lively description of the effect of law court assizes on city life and economics is given by Dio Chrysostom. Writing around the turn of the second century, he describes the extent to which Celaenae (Apamaea of Phrygia) profited from hosting biennial assizes:

> And what is more, the courts are in session every other year in Celaenae, and they bring together an unnumbered throng of people—litigants, jurymen, orators, princes, attendants, slaves, pimps, muleteers, hucksters, harlots, and artisans. Consequently not only can those who have goods to sell obtain the highest prices, but also nothing in the city is out of work, neither the teams nor the houses nor the women. And this contributes not a little to prosperity; for wherever the greatest throng

---

[8] See plan and reconstruction in Gleason *et al.*, 1998: figs. 4c and 7.
[9] *Ac* 21:15–27:1.
[10] Patrich 2002f, reprinted here as Chapter Twelve.
[11] See, for example, *TY Megilla*, III, 2, 74a.
[12] Garnsey 1968: 51f. See also Schalit 1937: 91–93, 98–99.

of people comes together, there necessarily we find money in greatest abundance, and it stands to reason that the place should thrive… So it is, you see, that the business of the courts is deemed of highest importance toward a city's strength and all men are interested in that as in nothing else. And the foremost cities share this business each in its turn in alternate years.[13]

Levine, citing this passage, adds: "If infrequent assizes added so much to prosperity of a locale, the benefits accruing to a city where the government was regularly present for such proceedings must have been great indeed."[14]

An elaborate Roman bathhouse with a nicely preserved furnace and a circular basin was added under Roman rule next to the SE corner of the courtyard. At that stage Herod's palace was extended farther to the east, adding ca. 50 m along the S end of the hippo-stadium.[15] Latin inscriptions found in this extension mention military personnel active in the governor's *officium*.[16] In a room west of the bathhouse a Latin inscription reading: *spes bona adiutorib(us) offici custodiar(um)*— "Good hope to the Assistants of the Office in charge of Prisoners (or the Prison"), was incorporated in the mosaic floor (Fig. 108a).[17] Hence, the room was occupied by a guard in charge of the prisoners. The prison must have been located nearby, but so far it has not been identified archaeologically. However, the T-shaped water cistern mentioned above, located under the courtyard, was converted in a later phase into a vast subterranean space with a narrow subterranean corridor leading in. This gloomy space apparently served as a prison, as is attested by Greek Christian inscriptions that were smeared in mud on its walls by a certain Procopia, seeking help from the Lord: *kyrie boethi Prokopia*—a most dramatic find pertaining, perhaps, to a woman confessor.

---

[13] Dio Chrysostom, *Discourse*, 35, 15–17 (ed. Cahoon and Crosby 1940, III: 389, 405–7).

[14] Levine 1975a: 48.

[15] According to Porath (2008: 1658), the entire complex postdates Herod's reign. However, this interpretation disregards the fact (pointed out by Netzer, in Gleason *et al.* 1998: 38 with n. 29), that the N wall of the palace's upper terrace is bonded in the W *cavea* wall of the hippo-stadium, and the fact that the *praetorium* where St. Paul was put to trial at Caesarea under the governor Felix is referred to as Herod's *Praetorium* (*Ac* 23:35).

[16] See Cotton and Eck 2001.

[17] Cotton and Eck 2001: 230–32.

Another mosaic inscription (Fig. 108b), found in a room that flanks an entrance to the extended *praetorium* from the W, reads: *Sanct[o] Genio fru[m]entarioru[m] omnia felicitia*—"To the sacred Genius of the *frumentarii*. Good luck in all things." The *frumentarii* were imperial couriers, and the room served for their social gathering.[18] Nearby was located a clubroom (*schola*) of the centurions.[19] Another inscription, on a marble plate, refers to a statue of Hadrian that was dedicated by the *beneficiarii*—soldiers who received an administrative job from the governor (in this case Tineius Rufus, the governor of Judaea when the Bar Kokhba revolt broke out), numbering as many as 120 in Judaea. The statue seems to have been erected near the place in the *praetorium* that served as their official and social center, perhaps their social club—their *schola*.[20]

More inscriptions, on statue bases or shafts that carried statues, attest that the *praetorium* was adorned with statues of emperors, governors, and other dignitaries (Fig. 109).[21] Seemingly they stood in the porticoes that surrounded the central courtyard, or in the courtyard itself, under the open sky.

---

[18] Cotton and Eck 2001: 232–234. For a *frumentarius* sent by Sabinus, the prefect of Egypt, to pursue Bishop Dionysius in the streets of Alexandria in the persecution under Decius, see Eusebius, *Historia Ecclesiastica* VI.40.2–3 (ed. Oulton and Jugh 1973: 97). Also, a *frumentarius* escorted Cyprian, after his arrest, to face trial in Utica (Cyprian, *Letter* 81.1, tr. G.W. Clarke, Vol. 3 [*Ancient Christian Writers* 47], New York: Newman Press, 1989).

[19] The inscription, engraved on a cylindrical stand of blue-grey marble, found lying in front of a *mensa* in that room, reads: *Cl(audius) Severus cust(os) sc(olae) (centurionum) s(ua) p(ecunia) f(ecit)*—"Claudius Severus, warden of the centurions' clubroom, paid (for it) with his own money." See Cotton and Eck 2001: 234–35.

[20] Cotton and Eck 2001: 235–38. For governor's *officiales*, see Rankov 1999; Palm 1999.

[21] Lehmann and Holum 2000: inscr. no. 12 (Gr.): Varios Seleukos, curator of ships for the colony Caesarea, honors as his patron the philosopher Titos Flavios Maximos, after 71 CE; no. 13 (Lat.): Dedication to Emperor Probus by the governor [P]assenianus, 276–82 CE; no. 14 (Lat.): Governor Aufidius Priscus honors Caesar Galerius, 293–305 CE; no. 15 (Lat.): The Cornelii honor D. Seius Seneca, *legatus Augusti pro praetor*, ca. 157–58 CE; no. 16 (Lat.): Governor Acilius Cleobulus honors emperor Probus, 276–82 CE; no. 17 (Lat.): Governor Aufidius Priscus honors Caesar Constantius, 293–305 CE. More similar honorific inscriptions related to Caesarea are, either of unknown provenance, or where found remote from the *praetorium* under consideration.

THE PALACE OF THE ROMAN FINANCIAL PROCURATOR, AND OF THE BYZANTINE GOVERNOR (FIG. 110)[22]

After the suppression of the Jewish Revolt, when *Provincia Judaea* was promoted in status, to be governed by a governor of a senatorial rank—*legatus Augusti pro praetor*, the financial affairs of the province were entrusted to the provincial procurator (*procurator provinciae*). A new compound was constructed for him to serve as his residence and *officium*, thus adding a second *praetorium* to the one on the site of the former palace of Herod, which had served the Roman governor. This complex was erected by Vespasian and Titus in 77/78 CE according to the evidence of the earliest Latin inscription from Caesarea (Fig. 28).[23] In the early fourth century the palace of the Roman procurator became the *praetorium* of the Byzantine governor. This shift of residence should be attributed to the physical deterioration of "Herod's *praetorium*" by that time, being eroded by the sea, and to the administrative reforms of Diocletian and Constantine. The Byzantine *praetorium* served until the end in urban life at this zone of Caesarea, caused by the Arab conquest of 640 or 641.

The *praetorium* of the Roman financial procurator and the Byzantine governor is located in the first *insula* of the city to the south of the temple platform, adjacent to the harbor, overlooking the sea—a prominent location. Its uncovered remains occupy an area 65 × 55 m, c. two-thirds of the 65 × 90 m grid block (*insula*). The northern third of this *insula* was destroyed by the later Abbasid and Crusader wall and moat of the tiny town of Qaisariye. The complex is delineated on the south and on the east by paved streets—a decumanus and a cardo. Following the westward slant of the terrain, the western and southern parts of the *praetorium* were constructed on top of vaults which served as substructures (Fig. 111). On the west a series of four parallel vaults, c. 30 m long and 5 m wide, are facing the sea. On the south, along the decumanus, there are eight shorter vaults, of various dimensions, some oriented E–W, and others N–S. Large parts of these vaults still stand solid and well preserved; five of them are intact.

---

[22] Patrich 2000a; Patrich *et al.* 1999; Patrich 2008b: 1676–78.

[23] Eck 2002: 538–39; Cotton and Eck 2003: 34; Eck 2007: 219. The inscription was incised on *kurkar*, of which the *praetorium* was built. It was found nearby, on the sea shore.

Certain structures on the second floor, above the vaults or to their E and N, are also quite well preserved.

Three major phases were discerned in the architectural history of the complex (Figs. 112a–c): phases 1 and 2 belong to the Roman period; phase 3 reflects the layout of the complex during the Byzantine period.

Access was from cardo W1 on the east by means of two staircases of similar dimensions that led to a courtyard (the height difference being ca. 2m, requiring just ten stairs to cover). This arrangement and the layout of the phase 3 cardo pavement in front of the staircases— a parallel rather than the regular diagonal arrangement in the other sections of the street—emphasize the axial layout of this architectural complex. In phase 3 a circular, domed water cistern occupied the center of the courtyard.[24] To the north of the upper courtyard, at street level, the NE corner of the compound was occupied by a "revenue office" (attributed to phase 3), comprising a vast hall surrounded on three sides by seven rooms with mosaic floors bearing Greek inscriptions that identify the complex as a provincial office—*skrinion*, where an accountant (*noumerarios*) and clerks (*chartularioi*) were in office (Fig. 113).[25] The inscription in the western room, facing east, reads: "Christ help Ampelios the *chartularios* and Musonios the *numerarios* and the rest of the *chartularioi* of the same *skrinion*" (tr. Holum 1995) (Fig. 114). Another, in the central hall, facing north, reads: "Christ help Marinos the *magistrianos* (or magister) and Ampelios and Musonios." The two rooms on either side of the main entrance from the street served as waiting rooms. Inscriptions therein encourage the people to cooperate with the authorities: In the center of the southern room a Greek inscription in a medallion reads: "Do you wish not to fear the authority? Do good and you will receive praise from it" (tr. Holum 1995)—a citation of Romans 13:3 (Fig. 115a). The inscription in the northern room is a shortened version of the first, reading: "Do you wish not to fear the authority? Then do good!" (tr. Holum 1995) (Figs. 115b–c). In front of the *skrinion* there is a portico that was delin-

---

[24] A small sounding was already conducted in this cistern by the Joint Expedition in 1980. See Bull Krentz and Storvick 1986: 38–40, and fig. 12. This sounding was extended by us.

[25] Holum 1995; Lehmann and Holum 2000: 96–102. The translations given below are from these publications.

eated on its east by an arcade,[26] and paved by three successive, super-
imposed mosaic floors. A Greek inscription found *in situ* in the lowest
of these floors (Fig. 116a–b), reads: "The *hypoboethoi* (subadjutors)
made this in thanksgiving" (tr. Leah Di Segni). The *hypoboethoi* were
assistants of lower rank in the judicial or fiscal administration.[27] This
inscription provides further evidence for the administrative function
of this complex.

To the S, on the other side of the stair rooms, along the *cardo*, was
another mosaic-paved portico with an arcade of square piers on its E
side (Fig. 117). To its west was a public latrine (Fig. 79).

The upper terrace to the west of the courtyard comprised a basilical
structure that served as an audience hall, 13 × 18m in size, which was
surrounded by other offices and installations. The southeastern corner of
the hall is still preserved. It was erected on top of two inner vaults
of the four vaults facing west mentioned above. The roof and ceiling
of the basilical hall were supported by marble columns standing on
an inner rectangular stylobate, partially preserved on the east and on
the south. The phase 1 marble floor was replaced by a mosaic floor in
phase 3. Patches of these two floors were preserved (Fig. 118).

The phase 1 facade of this elevated hall was on the west, overlooking
the sea (Fig. 119). On the other three sides the hall was surrounded by
a reflection-pool. This facade is not preserved, since the western part
of the underlying vaults had collapsed. A square graded fountain was
installed to the east of the reflection-pool (Fig. 120).[28] Access from the

---

[26] The present colonnade of marble columns re-erected there has no archaeological
basis. The northern section of the portico was exposed by Negev. A later lime kiln
mutilated its mosaic floor, including a Greek inscription holding at least 8 lines within
a medallion, 3 m in diameter. Its fragmentary text suggests that it should be dated to
the 6th, or early 7th c. Negev uncovered another Greek inscription holding three lines
within a smaller medallion in that same area, decorating the lowest of three superim-
posed mosaic floors. It says: "Enter rejoicing, with good fortune" (Negev 1971, inscr.
32 and 31; Lehmann and Holum 2000, inscr. 92 and 85, respectively). It seems that
both inscriptions were located at the entrance to the private wing of the *praetorium*
(see below). A marble statue of the "Good Shepherd," now in the Roman Theater
compound, was found in debris above and to the south (Negev 1971: 258).

[27] Such an official, in a latinized form (*subadiuva* written in Greek—*soubadios*) is
mentioned in the *Miracles of St. Artemios* (ed. Crisafulli and Nesbitt 1997: 114–121),
a collection of seventh-century miracle stories by an anonymous Greek author of Byzantium. This *soubadios* or deputy in the office of the eparch assisted a litigant in the
law court. I am indebted to K.G. Holum for bringing this interesting and vivid source
to my attention.

[28] This graded structure was interpreted as a small *bouleterion* by the Joint Expedition. See Bull *et al.* 1986: 37.

western lower level to the rear area and to the square fountain behind the hall was via an alley partially vaulted (vault no. 3), and two other vaults (nos. 19 and 54). In phases 1 and 2 vault 54 served as a latrine of the *praetorium* (Fig. 121). A wide staircase led there down from the rear area, westward. In phase 2 this vault was separated from vault 19 by a wall, preventing access to the latrine from the west.

The major modification of the compound marking phase 2 was the filling up of the reflection-pool with brown soil (*hamra*), which was set over an elevated surface of tiles placed above the floor of the pool.[29] Thus, the reflection-pool was converted into a "hanging garden" of the *horti pensiles* type.[30] The purpose of the elevated surface of tiles was to protect the underlying vaults from humidity. In this phase the rear fountain (Fig. 120) was reduced in size, and an irrigation water-tank was installed in the strip of land separating the fountain from the rear wall of the audience hall.

During phase 2 the audience hall was still facing west. It was only in phase 3 that the facade was moved to the east, and the entire area to its front was converted to an open plaza, paved by a mosaic floor, depicting a geometric lozenges pattern. This pavement was laid over the entire garden, including the water-tank that was dismantled, and over the fountain and vault 54 that were filled in. A large room decorated by a "Seasons Mosaic" was added to the south of the audience hall.[31] In spite of the fact that the western end of the hall had collapsed, it is quite possible that the transition of the facade from the west to the east was accompanied by replacing the western wall by an apse (Figs. 112c and 35). Apsidal halls were popular in Late Antiquity. In any case, the lengthening of the hall westward at this phase is suggested by the addition of two supporting arches near the western end of the underlying vaults.

The audience hall was flanked on the south by a row of rooms constructed on top of the southern vaults, along the decumanus. These

---

[29] This structure was interpreted by the Joint Expedition as a "honorific esplanade," "a U-shaped building" (Bull *et al.* 1986: 34, 36), or "a U-shaped honorific portico" (Spiro 1992: 257).

[30] I am indebted to Lynne Lancaster for bringing to my attention literary references and archaeological parallels for such gardens on the Palatine, Rome, dated from Nero to Hadrian. These are discussed in her dissertation (1995: 213–19). A later possible example is to be found in the Severan Baths there (*eadem.*, personal communication). Thanks are also extended to Kathryn Gleason for her advice.

[31] Spiro 1992.

seem to be the offices of the law court clerks and officials. In phase 3 access to these rooms from the northeast was through an arcaded portico with a mosaic floor depicting a geometric pattern of squares and octagons. A similar portico might have been constructed on the northern side of the esplanade; however, the state of preservation on this side is very poor.

To the north, the audience hall was flanked in phase 3 by an apsidal building.[32] The upper level was approached by a square, spiral staircase, three flights of which are still preserved (Fig. 122). A circular room served as an antechamber for the staircase room. A mid-sixth-century Greek inscription in honor of the Byzantine governor Andreas, reading: "May the years of the most glorious proconsul Andreas, devoted to building, be many!" is inserted in its mosaic floor (Fig. 123).[33]

The apsidal building had replaced a rectangular structure paved with colorful mosaic floors of geometric patterns exposed by the Joint Expedition, that was part of the complex during phases 1 and 2 (Fig. 124). A series of rectangular wall niches, presumably intended to house wooden cupboards (*armaria*), were installed along its S wall (Fig. 125). Such niches are common to ancient libraries. This fact, and the proximity of the rectangular structure to the "law court" and to the "revenue office" (*skrinion*), lend support to the interpretation that it served as an archive (*tabularium*) or a library for law or finances. Legal or financial records or codices could have been stored in *armaria* set in the niches. The later, apsidal building that replaced the rectangular structure might have retained this function.[34] A record-office (*tablarion*), in Caesarea, perhaps that of the *praetorium* of the financial procurator (if not in the *praetorium* of the *legatus Augusti*), is mentioned in a papyrus found in Egypt, but originating from Caesarea, dated to 152 CE.[35]

---

[32] Impressive remains of its substructure were exposed already in 1960 by Avraham Negev, and in the 70s by the Joint Expedition. See Negev 1963a; 1963b; Bull *et al.* 1986: 38–39 and fig. 8.

[33] Holum 1986a; Lehmann and Holum 2000: 65, inscr. 39.

[34] A nice example of an apsidal library, though of an earlier date, was found at Timgad (Callmer 1954: 144–93).

[35] Rea 1977, and for a different reading, see Eck 1998. See also Haensch 1997: 556. Evidence for a procurator's *tabularium* were also found in the Roman governor's palace in London, see Marsden 1980: 79–106; Scullard 1979: 54–55.

Another possible function for the apsidal hall (on the upper level, that disappeared, not in the extant substructure), is an apsidal dining hall, or a *stibadium*, with dinning couches arranged in a semicircle.[36]

The bathhouse that had formed a part of this *praetorium* was partially exposed in the NW corner of the compound. Its layout is diagonal relative to the other components of the *praetorium*, described so far.[37] It had a rectangular hall 6 × 12 m in size, with a marble flooring and wall revetment (Fig. 126). In its center was an octagonal basin c. 3 m wide, that got its water through a lead pipe from a large water tank located to the W of the circular room mentioned above. A one-line Greek inscription (not deciphered yet) was painted in red on its marble floor. On the SW and NW the marble hall was flanked by various rooms with typical under floor brick hypocaust and wall *tubuli* that were part of the heating system. Other parts of the bathhouse are still buried under a dirt road that delineates the excavated area on the north.

The exposed wings of the *praetorium* comprise of courtyards, a garden, offices, and an audience hall where law court assizes could take place—all components of the public wing. Of the private wing, only part of the bathhouse was exposed. Other components of this wing, that might have held the dwelling quarters and presumably more halls, courtyards, and gardens, were almost entirely destroyed by the Islamic/Crusader wall and moat of Qaisariye, located immediately to the north of the area under discussion. The exposed components occupy only two thirds of the urban *insula*. The remaining, northern, third was large enough to accommodate the residence itself.

Out of 22 fragmentary Latin inscriptions of the second and third century retrieved from Areas KK and CC, five (and perhaps four more) are associated with provincial procurators of Syria Palaestinae, being dedications on their behalf or acclamations in their honor (Figs. 127–128).[38] These inscriptions were seemingly attached to bases of statues or busts of procurators serving in this precinct, of the imperial fam-

---

[36] Holum (1995: 345), had put forward this possible interpretation for the ground floor of the apsidal building, actually a basement floor. On the replacement of rectilinear triclinia by semi-circular *stibadia* in late antiquity, see Duval 1984.

[37] For a nice parallel of a bathhouse set diagonally to the main complex in a fourth-century palace, see Wilson 1983.

[38] Eck and Cotton 2009. These finds bring to mind the villa of the financial procurator at Colonia Ulpia Triana Sarmizegetusa in Dacia Superior (later Dacia Apulensis). See Alicu and Paki 1995.

ily, or of gifts to certain divinities. Such and other statues (Fig. 129) were dispersed in the precinct. Subordination to the ruling emperor and loyalty to the empire were expressed in some sort of an imperial cult. Hence, Hadrian's head (smaller than life size) found in a Byzantine debris in area KK (Figs. 20 and 130), might have originated from the *praetorium* under discussion. A 3rd c. Mithraeum was exposed in Vault 1 by the Joint Expedition (Fig. 131).[39] A staircase leading down from the upper floor was later blocked. A private sanctuary was a common component of a *Villa procuratoris*.[40]

The Joint Expedition attributed vault 1 to Herod, but more recent excavations in area CV and in vaults 1, 2, 11, and 12 (Fig. 132) indicated that the vaults were constructed in the late 1st c. In all vaults walls of an earlier period were discovered, founded on bedrock and belonging to buildings with a different layout.

The vaults remained in use until the Late Byzantine period but underwent modifications. Lateral openings were blocked, the vaults were extended *c*.2 m to the west, and vaults 2 and 11 were reinforced by two arches 16.4–16.6 m apart, one near the east end, the other near the west end. Similarly, the east part of vault 12 was buttressed through the installation of an inner vault 7.65 m long that reduced the width to 3.25 m. In each vault several levels of plaster floors or *kurkar* flagstones were uncovered. The Joint Expedition assumed that the vaults served both as substructures for the upper-storey buildings and as *horrea*. It appears, however, that in their original phase the vaults were open at their W end and so could not have been *horrea*. The Mithraeum constructed inside vault 1 was separated by a grille from the space to its west. At a later phase, the vaults had been elongated, and an arcaded portico was constructed in front of the vaults. In the same later phase a wall with doorways was constructed at the west end of the vaults. In a still later phase, the portico was converted into a corridor entered from a stone paved courtyard in front of vault 2.[41] A hall decorated with a colourful mosaic floor depicting vine medallions incorporating birds and figures (Fig. 133) was constructed in the 6th c. to the west of the corridor.[42]

---

[39] Bull 1974; 1978.
[40] Thus, for instance, in Ulpia Traiana Sarmizegetusa, *op. cit.*, and more generally in Lavan 1999 and 2001.
[41] Lehmann 1999, 145.
[42] Lehmann, *op. cit.*

A change of function also occurred over the roughly four centuries of use of the vaults. Of particular interest is a painting of three Christian saints preserved on the south wall of vault 11 (Fig. 134).[43] Since this was an enclosed space, and not just a passage-like vault 9 (above), the painting may indicate a religious or charitable function for vault 11. On the N wall of vault 12 were the faint remains of a figure holding a sceptre, a spear, or a cross. At some later phase it appears that this vault was converted into a stable, with a drain channel running down the vault (Fig. 80). Near the front of vault 11 an oven 1.6 m in diameter was constructed.[44]

The identification of the hall on top of the four western vaults as a law court is indicated by eight (perhaps nine) fragments of a large Greek inscription retrieved from several adjacent locations. The fragments belong to a marble plate, ca. 155 × 47 cm (5 × 1.5 Byzantine feet) in size (Fig. 135). The inscription was arranged in three columns of 20 lines. The top line has larger letters and ran across all three columns. The inscription is a copy of an imperial edict, issued by Flavius Pouseus, the praetorian prefect of the East in the years 465–67,[45] listing fees permitted for specific judicial procedures and services in the civil law court of the provincial governor. It is logical to assume that originally such an edict was placed outside a law court, visible to the public. The audience hall is the best candidate for this law court.[46]

Another *noumerarios*, named Eusebius, is mentioned in a Greek inscription on the eastern side of the cardo (Fig. 136). Two spacious halls that were exposed on this side, one being apsidal, suggest that during the Byzantine period the administrative center had also extended over the *insula* to the east of the cardo. In this case this cardo might have actually been an inner street in a vast government compound, the E–W width of which had extended over two urban *insulae*.

---

[43] Avner 1999.

[44] Additional study will be required to understand the chronology of the various installations in these vaults and how they functioned.

[45] Di Segni, Patrich and Holum 2003.

[46] In the *praetorium* at Gortyn (Crete), capital of the Roman province of Crete and Cyrene, inscriptions of the fourth and fifth century specify that they originally stood beside, or before, the doors of Justice. See Borrell 1996: 236–38.

APPENDIX

THE TARIFF INSCRIPTION
(DECIPHERED AND TRANSLATED BY LEAH DI SEGNI)*

THE TEXT

1 - - ΔΟΘΕΝΤΕ - - - ca. 42 ll. - - - ΚΑΙΕΞΟΧ῾Χ῾ΕΠΑΡΧ῾Χ῾ΦΛ῾ΠΟΥCΕΟ
ΥΤΟΥΜΕΓΑΛΟΠΡ῾ΚΑΙΕΝΔΟΞ῾ΕΠΑΡΧΟΥ
2   ΤWΝΙΕΡ.ΝΠΡΑΙΙ̣

Col. I
3   ...ΗΑΝΑΤΟΛΙΚΗΤΟΝΕΠΑΡΧΙΚΟΝΤΟΝΜΕΘΟΔ - - -
4   .ΟΜΙ̣ΖΕCΘΑΙΛΟΓΩCΠΟΡΤΟΥΛWΝΚΑΤΑΝ°Ρ̄ Ν°Ā
5   ΠΕΡΕΤΕΡWΔΕΝ°Η̄ΜΗΠΑΡΕΧΕCΘΑΙΚ῾ΑΝΥΠΕΡΟΓΚCΕΙΗΗΠ
       ΟCΟ...
6   ΤWΠΑΡΑCΤΑCΙΜΟΝΕΧΟΝΤΙΑΠΟΤΗCΑΝΑΤΟΛΗCΝ°Ī̄Β̄
       vacat
7   ΓΝWCΙCΤWΝΤΥΠWΘΕΝΤ̣ẈΝ̣ΑΝΑΛWΜΑΤWΝΠΑ̣ - -
8   vacat   ΧWΡ̣Α̣Κ̣ΤΑΞΙ
9   ΥΠΕΡΚΛΗΤΙΚΟ̣Υ̣Μ̣Ο̣ΝΟΜΕΡ - -
10   vacat   ΠΡ̣Α̣Γ - - -
11   ΕΙCΕΚΔ̣Ο̣C̣Ι̣Ν̣Τ̣Ο̣Υ̣Υ̣Π̣Ο̣Μ̣Ν̣ΗΜΑ - - -
12   ΥΠΕΡΔΕΚΑΘΑΡΟΥΥΠΟΜΝΗΜ - - -
13   ΥΠΕΡΑΝΑΓΝWCΙΜΟΥΕΙCΤ - - -
14   vacat   ΚΛΗΤΙΚΟΝ vacat
15   ῾Υ῾ΠΕΡΚΟΜΠΛΕΥΤΡWΝ vacat
16   ΠΑΡΑΤΟΥΠΑΡΑΒΑΛΛΟΜΕ̣ - - -
17   ΑΠΟΝΟΜΙCΜΑΤWΝ Ī̄
18   ΑΠΟΔΕ Ν° Ρ̄ΕWCΝ̣° - - -
19   ΑΠΟΔΕ Ν° Ρ̄Ν̄ ΕW - - -

* Originally published in Di Segni, Patrich and Holum 2003, it was commented by
D. Feissel in *Bulletin épigraphique* 2004, no. 394 = *Chroniques d'épigraphie byzantine*
(2006), pp. 224–226, no. 718, summarized in *Supplementum Epigraphicum Graecum*
LIII, no. 1841.

Col. II

2	- - - -	vacat	N° Ā -
3	- - - - ca. 26 ll. - - - - - - -		IOICTETYΠWTAI
4	- - - - ca. 26 ll. - - - - - - -		ẠZHOYΔENHTTON
5	- - - - ca. 29 ll. - - - - - - - - -		KAIEΠITOICCINΓOY
6	- - - -	vacat	
7	- -ΛΛETAITW		
8	- CŸΠEPBEN		
9	- Ạ		
10	- ETWN°ĀΓ'		
11	- ÇN°A<'		

Col. III

2	EΞEΠTOPCINYΠEPXAPTWN		KEP̣ S̄
3	EKΔOCIMOYΔIAΓNWCEWCΠEPEWΘICHC		N°Ā
4	EIΔEEKΛABINBOYΛOITOTICTHNYΠEPΘICANΔIAΓNWCIN		
5	vacat XAPTWNMEN		KEP̣ Δ̄
6	EKΔOCIMOYΔEΠAPEKATEPOYMEPOYCEKΛAMBANONTOC		
	KEP̣S̄		
7	KOMΠΛEYEIMOYΔIAΓNWCEWC		KEP̣ H̄
8	KAIEΠITWNENKΛHMATIKWNΔEYΠOΘECEWNTAAYTAXPHΠ		
	APẸ - -		
9	YΠEPΔHKPHTOYKOYPATOPOCΠPOBOΛHCNEΠITPOΠOYΓEN		
	IKỌ - -		
10	vacat WΔIAΦEPI		K- - -
11	IΔIKOY		
12	EKΠOIHCEWCENEKENBOYΛEYTIKOYΠPAΓMATO - - - -		
13	EΠITPOΠOYΔEHKOYPATOPOCΠPOCTHNAΞIANTỌ - - - -		
14	vacat AXPI N° Φ̄ TIMHMATOC OM°		
15	- - - - - - - - - - - vacat		KEP̣ -
16	- - - - - - - - - - - vacat		KEP̣ IB
17	- - max. 22 ll. - - - - - - - - PETEP - - -		N° A
18	- - max. 15 ll. - - - - - ṆWNCKΔOCIMO.... ΔHKPHTWN		KEP̣ S
19	- - max. 15 ll. - - vacat		KEP̣ Δ
20	- - max. 12 ll. - ỴΠPATTOMENOYWΔIA . EPI		KEP̣ Γ

1   [Τύποι] δοθέντε[ς κατὰ τῶν θείων διαταγμάτων παρὰ τῶν μεγαλοφυεσ(τάτων)] καὶ ἐξοχ(ωτάτων) ἐπάρχ(ων) Φλ(αουίου) Πουσέου τοῦ μεγαλοπρ(επεστάτου) καὶ ἐνδοξ(οτάτου) ἐπάρχου

2   τῶν ἱερ[ῶ]ν πραιτ[ωρίων, - - - κὲ - - -]

Col. I

3   ['Εν τ]ῇ ἀνατολικῇ τὸν ἐπαρχικὸν τὸν μεθοδ[εύοντα]

4   [κ]ομιζέσθαι λόγῳ σπορτουλῶν κατὰ νο(μίσματα) ρ' νό(μισμα)
    α'·

5   περετερω δὲ νο(μισμάτων) η' μὴ παρέσχεσθαι κ' ἂν ὑπερογκ<ο>ς
    εἴη ἡ ποσό[της.]

6   Τῷ παραστάσιμον ἔχοντι ἀπὸ τῆς ἀνατολῆς ν(ομίσματα) ιβ'.

7   Γνῶσις τῶν τυπωθέντων ἀναλωμάτων πά[σῃ]

8   χώρᾳ κ(αὶ) τάξι·

9   Ὑπὲρ κλητικοῦ μονομερ[οῦς]

10   πράγ[ματος   κερ(άτια) -]

11 Εἰς ἔκδοσιν τοῦ ὑπομνήμα[τος   κερ(άτια) -]

12 Ὑπὲρ δὲ καθαροῦ ὑπομνήμ[ατος   κερ(άτια) -]

13 Ὑπὲρ ἀναγνωσίμου εἰς τ[ὸ πράγμα]

14   κλητικόν   [κερ(άτια) -]

15 Ὑπὲρ κομπλευτρῶν

16 παρὰ τοῦ παραβαλλομέ[νου]

17 ἀπὸ νομισμάτων ν' (?) [ἕως νο(μισμάτων) ρ'   κερ(άτια) -]

18 ἀπὸ δὲ νο(μισμάτων) ρ' ἕως νο(μισμάτων) [ρν'   κερ(άτια) -]

19 ἀπὸ δὲ νο(μισμάτων) ρν' ἕω[ς νο(μισμάτων) σ'   νό(μισμα) α' ?]

Col. II

2   [? Οὐδὲν πλέον ἀπαιτείσθω] ν(ομίσματος) α'.

3   - - - - - - - ca. 26 ll. - - - - -]ίοις τετύπωται

4   - - - - - - - ca. 26 ll. - - - - - ΑΖΗ οὐδὲν ἧττον

5   - - - - - - - ca. 29 ll. - - - - - - - καὶ ἐπὶ τοῖς σινγου-

6   [λαρίοις - - - - - - - - - -]

7   [- - - - - - - - - - - - - ? καταβά]λλεται τῷ

8   [- - - - - - - - - - - - - ? ἡ ποσότη]ς ὑπερβ<αί>ν-

9   [ει? - - - - - - - - - - - - - - - - - - -]Α

10 [- - - - - - - - - - - - - - - - - - - παρεχ]έτω νο(μισματα) α' γ̄

11 [-]ς νο(μισματα) α' <̄
    - - - - -

Col. III

2   Ἐξ(κ)έπτορσιν ὑπὲρ χαρτῶν   κερ(άτια) ς'·

3   ἐκδοσίμου διαγνώσεως περεωθίσης   νό(μισμα) α'.

4   Εἰ δὲ ἐκλαβῖν βούλοιτό τις τὴν ὑπερτεθῖσαν διάγνωσιν,

5   χαρτῶν μὲν   κερ(άτια) δ'·

6   ἐκδοσίμου δὲ παρ' ἑκατέρου μέρους ἐκλαμβάνοντος
    κερ(άτια) ς'·

7   κομπλευ<σ>ίμου διαγνώσεως   κερ(άτια) η'.

8   Καὶ ἐπὶ τῶν ἐνκληματικῶν δὲ ὑποθέσεων τὰ αὐτὰ χρὴ
    παρέ[χειν.]

9   Ὑπὲρ δηκρητοῦ κουράτορος προβολῆς ἢ ἐπιτρόπου γενικο[ῦ]

10   ᾧ διαφέρι   κ[ερ(άτια) - ·]

11 ἰδικοῦ

12 ἐκποιήσεως ἕνεκεν βουλευτικοῦ πράγματο[ς   κερ(άτια) - ·]

13 ἐπιτρόπου δὲ ἢ κουράτορος πρὸς τὴν ἀξίαν το[ῦ πράγματος?]

14 ἄχρι νο(μισμάτων) φ' τιμήματος ὁμο(ῦ)·

15 [ἀπὸ δὲ νο(μισμάτων) φ' ἕως νο(μισμάτων) ψ' ?]   κερ(άτια) [-]

16 [ἀπὸ δὲ νο(μισμάτων) ψ' ? ἕως νο(μισμάτων) -] κερ(άτια) ιβ'·

17 [? ἀπὸ—κἂν εἴη μεῖζον (τὸ τίμημα) οὐδὲν πε]ρετέρ[ω]
    νο(μίσματος) α'.

18 [- - max. 15 ll. - -]ṆWN ἐκδοσίμο[υ τῶν] δηκρητῶν   κερ(άτια) ς'

19 [ὑπὲρ χαρτῶν ?]   κερ(άτια) δ'

20 [- - max. 12 ll. - - - το]ῦ πραττομένου ᾧ δια[φ]έρι   κερ(άτια) γ'.

TRANSLATION

(1) Edicts issued [according to the imperial orders by the most noble] and most eminent prefects, Flavius Puseus the most magnificent and most glorious prefect (2) of the sacred praet[oria, so-and-so (prefect of Italy) and so-and-so (prefect of Illyricum)].

(I:3) In the (prefecture of) Orient, the *praefectianus* sent to collect taxes (I:4) shall receive on account of *sportulae* one solidus on each hundred; (I:5) but beyond 8 solidi nothing shall be exacted, even if the amount is in excess. (I:6) For whoever has a post outside the Orient (the maximum permitted amount is) 12 solidi.

(I:7) Schedule of the legal costs fixed by law for each (I:8) province and office.

(I:9–10) For a writ of summons *ex parte*   [x]
(I:11) For delivery of the memorandum   [x]
(I:12) For a clean copy of the memorandum   [x]
(I:13-14) For a reader for the [writ] of summons   [x]
(I:15) For those who write out (the memorandum)
(I:16) from the party that is sued:
(I:17) from 50 (?) solidi [to 100 solidi   x]
(I:18) and from 100 solidi to [150 solidi   x]
(I:19) and from 150 solidi to [200 solidi (?)   1 solidus (?)]

(II:2) [Nothing must be required beyond (?)]   1 solidus.

(II:3) [- - - - - - - - - - - - - - - - -] it is ordered

(II:4) [- - - - - - - - - - - - - - - - -] nothing less

(II:5) [- - - - - - - - - - - - - - - - -] and for the *singu-*

(II:6) [*lares* - - - - - -]

(II:7) [- - - - - - - - - - - - - - - - -] is paid (?) to the

(II:8) [- - - - - - - - the quantity] exceeds (?)

(II:9) [- - - - - - - - - - - - - - - - -]

(II:10) [- - - - - - - - - - - - - - - -] should pay 1 solidus and 1/3

(II:11) [- - - - - - - - - - - - - - - -] 1 solidus 1/2

(II:12-) - - - - - - - - - - - - - - - - -

(III:2) To the *exceptores* for papyri   6 siliquae;

(III:3) for issue of a *definita causa*   1 solidus.

(III:4) And if one wants to receive (the record of) a deferred trial:

(III:5) for papyri   4 siliquae

(III:6) and for the issue from each party who receives (the record)
    6 siliquae.

(III:7) For writing out the record of a trial   8 siliquae.

(III:8) And in criminal trials the same amounts are to be paid.

(III:9) For a decree of appointment of a general curator or guardian,

(III:10) (cost) to the interested party   [- siliquae].

(III:11) For a special (curator or guardian):

(III:12) in a matter of sale of property belonging to a decurion [- siliquae]

(III:13) and for a (special) guardian or curator according to the value
    of the [transaction]

(III:14) up to 500 (solidi) in value, the same,

(III):15) [and from 500 to 700? solidi]   [- siliquae]

(III:16) [and from 700? to ? solidi]   12 siliquae.

(III:17) [Beyond ?, even if (the value) is larger, nothing be]yond 1 solidus.

(III:18) [- - - - - - - - - -] of the issue of the decrees   6 siliquae

(III:19) [for papyri (?)]   4 siliquae

(III:20) [- - - - - - -] of the transacted (business) to the interested party
    3 siliquae

CHAPTER NINE

WAREHOUSES AND GRANARIES IN CAESAREA MARITIMA

Introduction

Caesarea was a maritime city with an elaborate harbor. Later it also became the provincial capital of Judaea/Palaestina. Storage facilities occupied no doubt large areas of the city. The 1990's excavations enable us to distinguish several different types of storage facilities, to locate many of them on the actual city plan, and to evaluate their significance in the economy and administration of Caesarea.[1]

The storage facilities uncovered in the recent excavations of the Combined Caesarea Expeditions (CCE) and the Israel Antiquities Authority (IAA) south of the Crusader town cover c. 25% of the excavated area (Fig. 67), a most significant percentage. In fact, area KK—an entire insula of the Byzantine city (Fig. 83)—consists almost entirely of warehouses. As for the location of the warehouses on the city plan, except for those of the Inner Harbor *horrea*, all are located at some distance from the harbor area. This does not mean, however, that ships docked at the opposite shore. At Ostia, for example, the warehouses (*horrea*) are distributed throughout the city, not necessarily in the immediate vicinity of the Tiber. Besides, warehouses were required not only for import-export trade through the harbor, but for storing the local food supply of the city's residents.

---

[1] The excavations, in the framework of the Project for Promoting Tourism to Caesarea, were carried out by two expeditions: the IAA expedition (areas I, II and III), directed by Dr. Yosef Porath, and the University of Haifa expedition, as part of the CEE, directed by Avner Raban (areas I and Z) and Dr. Joseph Patrich (areas CC, KK, and NN). The excavations began on March 15, 1992, and have continued year round since then. The excavations at area KK began on May 16, 1993, at area CC in November 1993, and at area NN on July 1, 1994. I am indebted to my team members for their collaboration: field supervisors, David Reshef, Dror Ben-Yosef, Shalom Rotgeizer, Ziev Bar-Or, Alon Mosko, Shery Pinkas, Hedva Van-Dam, and Saar Nudel; registrars, Michal Oren-Paskal and Yael Arnon; photographers, Zaraza Friedman and Jonathan Gottlieb; pottery restorers, Rachel Polak and Stanley Richman; administrative manager, Moshe Tsadiq; and surveyors, Ofra Lazar, Anna Iamim, and Yavgeni Preisman. Architectural conservation work in the field was carried out by a team headed by David Tsel and Jacques Neger. Joshua Drei (Yeshu) operated the metal detector.

This study concerns large warehouses and storage facilities, rather than the small storage spaces of retail shops. Large warehouses were used to store every type of merchandise. The containers used—mainly jars and amphoras found at the site—help to suggest the type of goods that were stored within them. It is reasonable to assume that for purposes of the import-export trade, when a warehouse served as a relatively short-term storage area, the merchandise remained in its original containers (perishable sacks and basketry, or longer-lasting jars and amphoras), whereas for long-term storage purposes, the merchandise was transferred from the smaller, space-consuming amphoras to larger containers, such as underground granaries and large *dolia*.

It is useful to examine briefly the architectural and urban aspect of warehouses and granaries in general. According to Rickman,[2] the commercial structure par excellence for the Greeks was the stoa, which could be adapted to a multitude of uses and was so suitable for flanking the sides of an agora or a harbor, as in the case of the harbor stoa at Miletos. The *porticus* was the Roman transformation of the Greek stoa for storage purposes. In Republican Rome, the Porticus Aemilia, constructed in 193 BCE, served as the first emporium; later the Porticus Minucia became the great storage and distribution center. *Horrea*, that is, warehouses for commercial storage, first occurred in Rome by the end of the second century BCE. Their basic ground plan included a row of deep, narrow rooms. The same is true at Ostia and in the provinces. In both Rome and Ostia the rows of rooms are arranged mainly in two ways, defining two types of *horrea*: the corridor type and the courtyard or quadrangle type. The concept of the courtyard *horrea* in Rome derived from an Eastern, Hellenistic influence. At Portus (the harbor of Ostia) and sometimes in Rome, the courtyard design was abandoned and the rows of rooms were arranged back to back. This arrangement fits well mole *horrea*, as in the case of the harbor *horrea* of Portus and of Leptis Magna.[3]

In the provinces of Asia Minor and Africa and in Judaea/Palaestina, the *horrea* consisted of only one row of very deep rooms, all opening onto the same side. According to Rickman,[4] such *horrea* reflect a Middle Eastern tradition, their origin being in the great palaces and temple

² Rickman 1971: 148–55.
³ Rickman 1971: 123–37, 148.
⁴ Rickman 1971: 151–55.

ensembles of that region, although such storage rooms are also well known in Minoan Crete, for example, in the Great Palace at Knossos and in Phaestos.

The roofs of the various types of Roman *horrea* could be either vaulted or gabled, built of beams and tiles,[5] or flat, built of beams and mortar, as in the warehouses of the Northern and Western Palaces at Masada.[6]

Types of *Horrea* at Caesarea Maritima

In Josephus' description of the Herodian harbor (*War* 1.408–14; *Ant.* 15.331–41), there is no reference to any storage buildings along the moles, only to vaulted chambers (ψαλίδες) for lodging sailors. Nor have underwater surveys and excavations along the submerged moles revealed the existence of any mole *horrea*.

On land, four types of *horrea* can be distinguished: (1) Vaulted; (2) Courtyard; (3) Corridor; and (4) Composite *horrea*.

Whereas vaulted *horrea* have been known for some time in the antiquities of Caesarea, the other three types have been uncovered and identified only in more recent excavations. In chronology, the first type is the earliest, appearing already in the Late Roman and Early Byzantine periods; the other three types are Byzantine structures. Their components and features (see below) indicate that they served for a multiplicity of storage purposes.

At present, then, the following *horrea* are known at Caesarea:

(1) Vaulted *horrea*. Two groups of *horrea* belong to this type: the Mithraeum *horrea* and the Inner Harbor *horrea*. The Mithraeum *horrea* consists of a series of four parallel vaults c. 30 m long, 5 m wide and 5 m high, all opening to the west (Figs. 80b, 111, 137).[7] In their

---

[5] Rickman 1971: 83.

[6] Netzer 1991: 37–75, 171–98, 301–7.

[7] Vault 1 was excavated by JECM during two seasons in 1973 and 1974; see Bull in Blakely 1987: 7. During this time the other vaults were surveyed and sounding were dug therein. Since 1989 the excavation of Vault 2 has been the undertaking of the Caesarea Maritima Vault Project (CMVP), directed by J.A. Blakely and W.J. Bennett, Jr. on behalf of Archaeological Assessments, Inc. The western part of the vaults, identified as area CV, has been excavated by CCE since 1993. Excavations of Vaults 1, 11 and 12 were resumed on a large scale on January 1, 1995 on behalf of CCE by the University of Haifa expedition.

ground plan they resemble the Masada and Samaria warehouses, but the roofs of these warehouses were flat. The Masada warehouses were constructed by Herod, while those of Samaria are post-Herodian, being attributed to the third Roman period.[8] The Mithraeum *horrea* reflect a Middle Eastern tradition. They constitute one architectural complex. Arched openings near the front and a second toward the rear end of the lateral walls provide access between adjacent vaults. When first explored in the early 1970s by the Joint Expedition to Caesarea Maritima (JECM), they were considered to be *horrea*; however, in light of more recent excavations, this generally accepted assumption still needs to be confirmed. A serious issue is the means by which these vaults were closed on the west and the date of this closure. The JECM excavations in Vault 1 claimed that it was originally constructed under Herod the Great and served as a *horreum* until the mid-first century CE. At the end of that century or at the beginning of the next, the rear part of Vault 1 was transformed into a Mithraeum and remained a shrine until the mid- to late third century. It later reverted to use as a warehouse until the seventh century.[9] However, CCE excavations at area CV11 in the summer of 1994 indicated that Vault 12 was constructed in the late Roman Period.[10] Similar results were obtained by the University of Haifa excavations at Vault 3 (= CC3), and by Caesarea Maritima Vault Project excavations at Vault 2 in the summer of 1995. The construction of the Mithraeum *horrea* should be dated to the second or third century.[11]

The Inner Harbor *horrea* (Figs. 138–139) had been considered Herodian in date[12] until the IAA excavations indicated that they were constructed c. 300 CE. The complex consists of two series of six parallel vaults flanking a broad staircase. The vaults were erected over the open square below the Herodian temple platform. They are 21 m long, 5–5.2 m wide and 6 m high, and open to the west; the side walls are 1.4 m thick. At each end of the side walls arched openings 2.6 m broad

---

[8] Netzer 1991: 37–75, 171–98, 301–7; Crowfoot *et al.* 1942: 133, Pls. V and LXXI.

[9] Blakely 1987: 38–39, 149–51.

[10] Mills, A. Shaffer, and J. Stabler, Field Report, Area CV, July 23, 1994, unpublished manuscript, Caesarea, 1994: 5.

[11] Later excavations had indicated that the four vaults were laid out by the Flavians at 77/78 CE to serve as a substructure for the *praetorium* of the provincial financial procurator. See above, p. 211ff. At that stage they were open to the west. At a later stage they became lockable, and some of them might have served as warehouses for a while.

[12] Negev 1993: 273; Holum *et al.* 1988: 88–89.

allowed passage from one vault to another. A window in the upper part of the rear wall provided access to light and ventilation through a vertical shaft (Fig. 139). Their plan and location suggest that these vaults served as *horrea*, although it is not yet clear how these *horrea* were closed on the west side.

The other vaults in area CC, on the north side of the decumanus (Fig. 111) were constructed in the same time as the four long vaults. They are smaller than the Mithraeum *horrea* and seem to belong to two separate structures, each of two stories. Some vaults (nos. 4–7) served as warehouses; others (nos. 8–10, 19 and 54)[13] served as passages and support for structures on the upper story. Vault 13 served, in its final stage, as a tavern, and Vault 3 was an alley.

(2) Courtyard *horrea*. The main structure (i.e., building I) uncovered in area KK (Fig. 67), south of the decumanus, is of this type. The building (Figs. 42, 140) consists of several rooms and halls surrounding a courtyard (5.35 × 5.65 m) paved with flagstones and surrounded by porticos 2.05–2.50 m wide, lined by two corner pilasters and a central one. It is entered from the north through an antechamber (3.8 × 5.5 m). The entrance (1.8 m wide), is flanked by two jambs with trapezoidal bases. The south wing is a transverse *dolia* hall (Fig. 141), c. 32 m wide and 5.6 m deep, the roof of which was supported by arches resting on six pairs of pilasters attached to the side walls. The walls are plastered, and the floor is paved in white mosaic. Access was through two doors, one from the south portico, near its southwest corner, and the other from the western extension of this portico. Many fragments of *pithoi* or *dolia*, smashed into tiny pieces, covered the floor. At either end of the hall, two large *dolia* are inserted under the floor up to rims, which are 42 cm in diameter.

Building I also contains a *dolia* room with a single sunken *dolium* west of the antechamber (Fig. 142). A *dolia* hall is a feature that reappears in the corridor *horreum* (building II), and the composite *horreum* (building III), described below, and in building VI along the cardo (dimensions 5 × 6 m). Yet another *dolia* hall was uncovered in the IAA excavations along the Inner Harbor, and a *dolia* room also in CCE area Z.

---

[13] The system of vaults was first explored by the JECM, which also published a general plan; see Bull, Krentz, and Storvick 1986: 41, fig. 13. Excavations of the vault system were resumed in 1993 within the framework of the current project. Vault 19 was discovered in November 1994, and Vault 54 in November 1995.

In building I, underground granaries are located under two of the rooms (Fig. 143). A large room (6.5 × 7.3 m) located at the structure's northwest corner contains a colorful mosaic floor and two benches (Fig. 144), and might have served as the office or archive of the *horrea*. Two niches next to its east wall might have held cupboards for files and documents. Many lead bullae were retrieved throughout the area.

(3) Corridor *horrea*. Building II (Fig. 145), which is the next building along the decumanus, west of building I, is a corridor *horreum*. The corridor is 15.5 m long and 1.8–1.9 m wide. Jambs with trapezoidal bases flank the entrance, which is 1.2 m wide. On the east side of the corridor there is a *dolia* hall 15.9 m long and 4.5 m wide, with one pair of pilasters and a single *dolium* under the mosaic floor. The *dolium* is small, 24 cm in diameter at its rim. A well is located near the west wall on the inside. On the west side of the corridor there are three simple storerooms, 5.8 m long and c. 5 m wide. Another room (6.4 × 2.9 m), on the northeast corner of the building, might have served as an office.

Two other *horrea* of this type were uncovered south of the bathhouse of the palatial mansion by the IAA expedition. They are parallel to each other, each with a corridor c. 33 m long (Figs. 67, 146, 147). The east unit deserves special attention. The entrance to the corridor was through an opening in the north end that was 2 m wide and had a marble sill. The corridor is 3 m wide for its first 9.5 m and 6.75 m wide thereafter. Each wing comprises ten rooms, 2.8–2.9 m wide, and at the inner end there is a portico 1.85 m wide with two columns between a pair of pilasters (*distylos in antis*) forming a facade leading to a lateral room (6.90 × 5.65 m) and an inner space. This spacious part of the complex, paved with colorful mosaic floor, may have served as the office or archive of the *horreum*. The patterns of the mosaic pavement are similar to those found in the office of building I described above.[14]

---

[14] The north-south, stratum 4 building in squares A–E/2–3 of the main excavated area of Levine and Netzer (1986: 17, 44–48, 59–65), overlooking the present harbor from the north (if indeed a single structure), might have been a corridor *horreum* as well. The excavators also considered this identification as a warehouse as a possibility. Stratum 4 is dated to the Late Byzantine period. A cluster of six granaries was uncovered at the south end of the building, but Levine and Netzer (1986: 62) could not determine its date. See also Raban *et al.* 1989: 176, who dates these bins (in CAHEP area S) to the Early Arab period, suggesting that they served for storing oil. Levine and

(4) Composite *horrea*. Building III (Fig. 148), located southwest of building I, is of this type. On the west there is a corridor 17 m long and 3.95 m wide. It is entered from the north and is paved with a crude white mosaic floor. Three openings lead east to the storage rooms and halls. The storage halls consist of a very long ward (19 × 5 m) with an opening 1.85 m wide and a shorter one (9.15 × 4.90 m) with an opening 1.95 m wide, both of the ancient Palestinian tradition; a *dolia* hall (7.25 × 5.30 m) with a single *dolium* under its floor; and three underground granaries (nos. 7, 8, 9 in Table 1).

CHARACTERISTIC FEATURES AND INSTALLATIONS IN THE STORE BUILDINGS

(a) There are simple storerooms 3–6 m long, paved with flagstones, plaster floor, beaten earth or mosaic floors. The barrier walls between adjacent rooms are 20–30 cm thick (in one case just 18 cm thick), being constructed of stretchers.

(b) There are transverse *dolia* halls with flat ceilings and tile roofs supported by arches that spring from pairs of pilasters attached to the longitudinal walls. The walls are of white plaster, and the paving is crude white mosaic. Large *dolia* were standing on the mosaic floor, and one or two *dolia* were inserted under the floor, on the longitudinal axis of the hall, to collect the contents of an entire vessel in case of breakage. There are instances of a single *dolium* inserted under the mosaic floor of a room. (Such rooms are thus referred to as "dolia rooms.") These arrangements indicate that liquids, rather than grains, were stored in the freestanding *dolia*. A somewhat similar arrangement for draining a warehouse where liquids were stored was found in two of the Masada storage halls.[15] This arrangement may be considered equivalent to the *dolia defossa* type of *horrea*, encountered at Ostia and Boscoreale.[16]

A dolium (Greek πίθος), is a large storage jar for wine, oil, grain, and so on (Fig. 149). In the literary sources there are references to *dolium vinarium* and *dolium olearium*. The wine *dolium* was lined

---

Netzer's excavations were extended by CCE, designating the entire area as LL. For a preliminary report with farther references see Stabler and Holum 2008.

[15] Netzer 1991: 40–41, 117–19.

[16] White 1975: 147; Meiggs 1973: Pl. XXVd; Rickman 1971: 73–76.

with pitch, and oil storage containers were steeped in oil-lees (*amurca*) for a week.[17] In our finds, no resins are observed on the sherds, so it is likely that these were oil *dolia*.

At Sepphoris, a hall with eight free-standing *dolia* containing lentils was found; no vessel was inserted under the floor of this room.[18] *Dolia* or *dolia* sherds were found in many coastal sites, from Yavneh Yam in the south to Ramat ha-Nadiv on the Carmel, not far from Caesarea.[19] In Yavneh Yam, a vessel was found sunken under a mosaic floor.[20]

Noteworthy is the transverse arrangement of a *dolia* hall in a store building, whether on a wing of a courtyard *horreum* or as a wing of a corridor *horreum*, which facilitated movement and activities inside the hall between the *dolia*.

(c) Underground granaries, appearing singly or in a group, have been known for many years from various excavations within the Crusader walls of Caesarea. Until now, most were dated to the Umayyad to Fatimid period.[21] Approximately six more clusters were found in the IAA and CCE excavation. Area KK is, for the time being, the only place where the ground floors of the buildings in which the underground granaries were incorporated were preserved to a considerable height. There is good stratigraphic evidence to date them to the Byzantine period. Those in IAA area I should be similarly dated.[22]

Most granaries were partially looted before being covered by debris. Granaries 8 and 9 in KK building III (see Table 1) are exceptional because they are preserved to their entire height (Figs. 150, 151). They were roofed by four lateral wooden beams set into depressions in the inner reveting walls (Figs. 151, 152). The height of the depressions indicates that the beams were c. 25 cm thick and 18 cm wide; they sup-

---

[17] White 1975: 146.

[18] I thank Ze'ev Weiss for this information. See now Weiss and Netzer 1994: 26–27.

[19] Hirschfeld and R. Birger-Calderon 1991: 86, fig. 5.

[20] Ayalon 1991: 80–88.

[21] Holum *et al.* 1988: 208–11; Negev 1967: 67–68; Levine and Netzer 1986: 62, 64–65; Raban *et al.* 1989: 176–77, figs. 164–66; Raban *et al.* 1993: 25, fig. 48; 56–57, figs. 120–22.

[22] Byzantine granaries of similar type were found in Apollonia, under the Muslim wall, which was erected at the end of the seventh century. I thank the excavator, Israel Roll, for this information. However, there seems to be good reason to date the silos in areas TP and I to the Early Fatimid period (Raban *et al.* 1993: 57). It seems that silos that look quite similar were built in Caesarea in two separate periods, Late Byzantine and Early Fatimid. But the quality of the later mortar was inferior to that of the Byzantine (Tsatskin 1994).

ported the mosaic floor of the upper, ground floor rooms. It is likely that all the underground granaries were roofed in this manner. The fill opening of each silo was presumably in the middle of the upper room, that is, in the middle of the silo's ceiling.

Each unit is rectangular in shape, reveted from the inside by ashlars embedded in a thick layer of white lime mortar, and paved by a mosaic floor or by flagstones with a cavity in the middle. Since the walls are not plastered, the containers were not used for the storage of oil, as has been suggested,[23] but rather for grain storage (Fig. 152).[24] In fact, in the process of sifting and flotation of the fill above the floor in the three silos in Areas KK9 and KK29, a significant quantity of carbonized kernels of grain were retrieved.[25]

The region of Caesarea, the Sharon Plain, was known as a land of grain and was praised as such as early as the Eshmunezer inscription, dated to the late Persian or early Ptolemaic period.[26] Many centuries later, the tenth-century author al-Muqaddasī praised the white bread of Caesarea.[27]

Grain must be kept dry when stored. The safe limit for moisture in stored grain is usually between 10% and 15%, depending upon the type of grain, the climate, and the length of storage. Grain also must be kept cool, if possible below 60 degrees F (16 degrees C) and free from vermin, which tend to breed if the grain overheats. If grain is stored loose, or in bins, the walls of a granary must be capable of supporting considerable lateral thrust, as the lateral pressure of grain is about two thirds of the vertical pressure.[28] The mortar recommended by Pliny and others was lime and marble mortar, mixed with oil-lees (*amurca*), which also served as an insect repellent.[29] It seems that the oily white mortar characteristic of the Caesarean granaries is due to its mixture with *amurca*.[30]

---

[23] Raban *et al.* 1989: 176–77; Holum *et al.* 1988: 208–9.

[24] As also Negev 1967: 67–68. Negev (1975: 275) refers to the numerous cellars or underground storage areas within the walls of the Crusader town as Byzantine remains, suggesting that goods brought in by sea were stored therein.

[25] A similar process of examination is being undertaken for all the other bins. The botanical analysis is being done by Prof. M. Kislev of Bar Ilan University.

[26] *CIS, pars prima*, t. I.1, Paris, 1881: 13–15.

[27] Le Strange 1965: 474.

[28] Rickman 1971: 1–2.

[29] White 1970: 189, 196–97; 1984: 62–63.

[30] This is perhaps the reason for the oily character of the under-floor cement encountered in the area S bins (Raban *et al.* 1989: 176–77). A microscopic examination

(d) Offices are distinguished from the simple storage rooms by having colorful mosaic floors, more elaborate architecture, and sometimes even stone benches and alcove niches in the walls.

(e) The water supply of the Byzantine structures under discussion did not depend on the aqueducts of Caesarea or on underground cisterns that collected rainwater, but on wells that access the nearby aquifer (the present elevation of which is c. 1.5 m at NN, and 0.5 m at the western part of KK). The wells were constructed in or near the courtyard or the corridor of the *horreum*.

Discussion

The greatest part of maritime commerce in ancient times involved the transport of food products.[31] In a Roman-Byzantine city, warehouses for long-term storage were constructed primarily to collect the *annona* and to insure a regular supply of grain and of other foodstuffs, at reasonable prices, to the inhabitants. These responsibilities belonged to the authorities—imperial, municipal, or ecclesiastical. Such was the case at Rome already in Republican times, as well as in other cities. The larger the city and its population, the larger the extent of its warehouses and granaries.

Who owned and who operated the storage facilities of Caesarea, especially those that occupied insula KK (which, although divided into six separate buildings, is one architectural unit)? Were they private enterprises or municipal facilities? Were they operated by the imperial government under the governor of Palaestina Prima (a resident of Caesarea)? Were these *annona*-collecting facilities controlled by the *dux Palaestinae* (also a resident of the city) or were they operated by the Church? Perhaps different buildings belonged to different authorities, and the managers were different from the owners?[32]

One of the municipal officials in each city was the "grain buyer" (*sitones*),[33] who was in charge of supplying grain for the city. In the

---

of two mortar specimens, one from a Fatimid bin and the other from a granary in area KK22, indicated the superior quality of the latter (Tsatskin 1994). The partition walls encountered in many cases were intended to decrease the lateral pressure.

[31] Parker 1992: 17–20.

[32] Concerning the organization and operation of Roman civilian *horrea* during both the Early and the Late Empire, see Rickman 1971: 163–212, 307–11.

[33] Dan 1984: 87, 99; Jones 1964: 735; Claude 1969: 114.

Late Roman and Byzantine administrative system, which was bureau-
cratic and centralized, the proper supply of grain and other food for
the citizens was the concern of the imperial government, not only of
the municipal authorities, especially in the case of a provincial capital
such as Caesarea. The *mesites* is known from Greek papyri in Egypt
as the official in charge of the government granaries and of weighing
the grain.[34] A *mesites* is mentioned in one of the Caesarean inscriptions, but it is not certain whether his function was similar to that
in Egypt.[35] Large warehouses should therefore be conceived as public
buildings, constructed and operated by the city or imperial authorities,
rather than private enterprises. The Roman and Byzantine emperors
also issued statutes and edicts to regulate the price of grain and other
food products and to control their orderly supply. Many of them are
preserved in the *Codex Theodosianus*.[36] The proximity of the area KK
storerooms, the Mithraeum *horrea*, and the area NN granaries to area
CC, which seems to be a provincial administrative center, suggest that
these areas were state warehouses. On the other hand, many finds
imply that the Church might have played a significant role in operat-
ing them.

For example, frescoes depicting icons of saints (Fig. 153) were
uncovered in the debris of the antechamber of building I,[37] and in its
dolia hall plaster blocks with depictions of crosses of the *crux gemmata* type were retrieved (Figs. 154–155). These, as well as a eucharistic bread stamp (Fig. 156), two ampules depicting St. Menas (Fig. 157),
indicating connections with Egypt; an ampule depicting a stylite saint
(originating from Syria?) (Figs. 158–159), retrieved from the well of
building II, and a marble screen plate depicting a cross surrounded by
a wreath (Fig. 160) from building VI, may all indicate that the buildings were operated by persons of religious piety, perhaps ecclesiastical
officials. (A chapel might have been located in an upper story of building I).[38] The buildings might have served as welfare facilities operated

---

[34] Dan 1984: 112.
[35] Lifschitz 1957: 124; Lehmann and Holum 2000: no. 110.
[36] *Codex Theodosianus* 2.33, 1; 14.16, 17, 19, 25, 26; 15.1.12, ed. and trans. Pharr
1952.
[37] Depictions of Christ and the twelve apostles are found on the west wall of CC
Vault 9, which served as a passage vault, and drawings of three saints have been
uncovered on the south wall of CC Vault 11. See now Avner 1999.
[38] See below, Chapter Ten, and on the bread stamp and the ampules—Chapter
Eleven.

by the church to distribute food to the poor rather than as *horrea* oper-ated by imperial or municipal authorities. On the other hand, one can-not exclude the possibility that all these finds indicate simply religious piety, not ecclesiastical property or welfare activities.[39] Considering the evidence as a whole, it seems that these *horrea* were for civilian use and were under the supervision of the provincial governor.[40]

Taken together, the storage facilities of Caesarea shed light on the city's economic, administrative, and social life. These topics have not yet received the attention they deserve, and this study should be con-sidered a preliminary one undertaken while the excavations are still in progress.

KK	Bldg.	Cluster	Single	Area (sq m)	Courses	Preserved ht.	Orig. ht.	Capacity (cu m)
1	I	+		1.6 × 2.3	2	0.55	2.1	7.73
2	I	+		1.6 × 2.3	2	0.55	2.1	7.73
3	I	+		1.6 × 2.3	2	0.55	2.1	7.73
4	I	+		1.6 × 2.3	2	0.55	2.1	7.73
5	I		+	2.5 × 3.5	7	2.40	3.15	27.56
6	I		+	2.8 × 3.1	3	1.15	2.40	20.83
7	III		+	4.4 × 2.7	6	2.40	2.40	19.49
8	III	+		2.8 × 2.9	7	2.40	2.40	19.49
9	III	+		2.8 × 3.0	6	2.25	2.25	18.90
NN								
10		+		1.8 × 1.7	2	0.55	1.80	5.51
11		+		1.8 × 1.7	2	0.55	1.80	5.51
12		+		1.8 × 1.7	2	0.55	1.80	5.51
13		+		1.8 × 1.7	2	0.55	1.80	5.51
14		+		1.8 × 1.7	2	0.55	1.80	5.51
15		+		1.8 × 1.7	2	0.55	1.80	5.51
								Total: 177.19

---

[39] For pagan religious dedications in *horrea*, see Rickman 1971: 312–15.

[40] Later considerations had led me to the conclusion that the KK warehouses were the property of the landlord who resided in the palatial mansion, or villa, extending immediately to their south. See above, Chapter Five, pp. 138–139.

CHAPTER TEN

A CHAPEL OF ST. PAUL AT CAESAREA MARITIMA?

St. Paul at Caesarea

St. Paul[1] was in confinement for two years (c. 58–60? CE)[2] in Caesarea. This chapter in his life took place at the end of his third missionary journey to the Gentiles. He was brought to Caesarea in chains, under a heavy military escort of 200 soldiers, 70 horsemen, and 200 spearmen, commanded by two centurions, after being arrested in Jerusalem by the Roman tribune (χιλίαρχος) in the city, Claudius Lysias. The arrest took place in Pentecost 58 CE, after a Jewish mob had attacked him in the Temple, suspecting that he had polluted the holy precinct by letting Gentiles in, among them one—Trophimas the Ephesian— with whom he was seen together in the streets of Jerusalem. The mob was incited by Jewish pilgrims from Asia, who opposed his missionary activity in their synagogues and among the Greeks in their cities, blaming him that he is preaching to the Jews living among the Gentiles not to circumcise their sons and to abandon the Law. Before being brought to Caesarea he was already interrogated by the tribune in the barracks (παρεμβολή) of Jerusalem (i.e., the Antonia fortress) about his identity, origin, and behavior, being exempt from scourges when he told his interrogaters that he is a Roman citizen. The tribune first suspected that he was the Egyptian who a few days earlier led out into

---

[1] For Paul's biography, see *Bibliotheca Sanctorum* X, Roma 1968: 164–94; Cross and Livingstone 1974: 1046–49; Kazhdan 1991: 1604–5; Attwater 1965: 266–68; Farmer 1987: 339–40. See also Baslez 1991; Becker 1995.

The Greek critical edition of *Acts* was published by C. Tischendorf, *Novum Testamentum Graece*, Leipzig 1872 (rprt. Graz 1965). The English translations consulted were Nestle and Marshal, *The Interlinear Greek-English New Testament*[2], London 1959 (rprt. 1969); *The New Revised Version*; *The Inclusive Version*; *The New Testament in Hebrew and English*, published by The Society for Distributing the Holy Scriptures to the Jews, London, and R.B. Rackham, *The Acts of the Apostles*, London 1901 (rprt. Ann Arbor, Michigan 1964).

[2] Paul's arrest in Jerusalem and his confinement and trial in Caesarea are given in *Ac* 21:15–27:1. For the chronology, in the last two years of procurator Felix, see Schürer 1973: 459–66. See also Ogg 1968.

the wilderness 4,000 men of the Assassins (*Sicarii*),[3] thus breaking the civil order, but when realizing that he was accused by the Jews for breaking their Law, Paul was given to the sentence of the Jewish council (Sanhedrin/συνέδριον). Paul aroused discord among the Pharisees and Sadducees of the council, by presenting his stance (pertaining to the resurrection of Christ, and the Holy Spirit), as beliefs in personal resurrection, in the angels, and in the spirits—disputed issues between the two Jewish sects. The dissension aroused in the council was so immense that the tribune had to remove Paul from there by force, for fear that he would be torn to pieces by the two parties. Back in custody in the barracks, a plot of the high priests, the elders, and more than forty people to murder Paul next time he would be on his way to their court was brought to the attention of the tribune by Paul's nephew—the son of his sister—residing in Jerusalem. In order to prevent it the tribune decided to dispatch him, under a military escort, with a letter, to stand trial before the procurator Felix at Caesarea.

Felix (procurator c. 52–60? CE) put Paul in custody in the *praetorium* of Herod—the palace and *officium* of the Roman procurator—until his accusers would come from Jerusalem. Ananias the high priest and the elders arrived after five days, and the prosecutor was a certain rhetor, named Tertullus.[4] After hearing both sides, the verdict was postponed until the arrival of the tribune Claudius Lysias. Paul was given over to a lenient custody (*custodia libera*) under the surveillance of a centurion, being permitted to be visited and served by his acquaintances. Paul was known to the local community. Some of its members had departed with him to Jerusalem for Pentecost. Among the disciples in Caesarea was the evangelist Philip and his four virgin daughters who did prophecy, at whose house Paul and his company had spent several days before getting to Jerusalem.[5] Imprisoned with Paul was Aristarchos, and he was served by St. Luke, a Gentile, the author of *Acts*, his companion for many years in the voyages to the Gentiles and an eye witness to his adventures in Jerusalem and Caesarea. It seems that

---

[3] The event of the "Egyptian" ringleader of a rebellious group is also narrated by Josephus *War* 2.13.5 (261–63); *Ant.* 20.8.6 (169–72). According to *War* they were 30,000 in number, and they gathered on the Mount of Olives. The governor Felix attacked them with his troops, killed and scattered the followers of the Egyptian, or took them prisoners, but the Egyptian himself escaped the massacre and disappeared. The event took place shortly before Paul's arrest. See Schürer 1973: 464.

[4] *Ac* 24. The trial took place 12 days after Paul first arrived in Jerusalem.

[5] *Ac* 21:8–16.

Luke had completed his Gospel during this sojourn of two years in the province, having easy access to the Palestinian apostolic tradition. Some of Paul's *Epistles* (*to the Ephesians, Colossians,* and *Philemon*) might have been written in this period and sent from Caesarea. His messenger to the churches in Asia was Tychicus.[6]

Actually the trial was not resumed for two years, until the end of Felix's governorship,[7] although Paul was summoned to Felix many times, hoping to get from him a bribe for his release. One of these encounters was together with his consort Drusilla—a beautiful Jewish princess, daughter of Agrippa I and sister of Agrippa II, that he had married through the intervention of a magician from Cyprus called Simon, in defiance of the law which strictly forbade the marriage of a Jewess with a pagan.[8] Paul was asked to present before them the essentials of his creed.

Under Porcius Festus (procurator c. 60?–62 CE) the conclusion of the trial was not delayed any longer.[9] About two weeks after assuming the procuratorship he ordered Paul to be brought before him, sitting on the judgment platform (ἐπι τοῦ βήματος).[10] A Jewish delegation that arrived from Jerusalem presented the accusations, and Paul defended himself. But he refused the suggestion of the judge to transfer the issue of sentence to the Sanhedrin in Jerusalem and be judged there in his presence. Being a Roman citizen he appealed unto Caesar to be sentenced in Rome.[11] The appeal was approved by the judge. But before being dispatched from the harbor of Caesarea by boat to Rome, together with other prisoners, under a guard of a centurion named Julius, Paul encountered two other members of the Jewish

---

[6] For St. Paul's and St. Luke's work at Caesarea, see Rackham 1901: 449–51. See also Downey 1975. Krentz 1992, mentions the *Epistle to the Philippians* as the best candidate of "Prison epistles" written in Caesarea, though Christian tradition suggests Rome. Kümmel 1975: 328–29, brings the pros and cons of each place, and favors (*ibid.* 346–47) Caesarea as the place where the *Epistle to the Colossians* was written. According to Kümmel (1975: 347) Mark also was with Paul in Caesarea, and the runaway slave Onesimus met Paul there (*ibid.* 348–49). Paul's biography and chronology are given by Kümmel 1975: 252–55. He places Paul's arrival in Jerusalem in 55/56 CE.

[7] The prolonged delay might have been the result of the dispute aroused at that time in the city between the Jews and the Syrian inhabitants, over the equality of citizenship (ἰσοπολιτεία). See Schürer 1973: 465.

[8] *Ant.* 20.7.2 (141–43).

[9] *Ac* 25.

[10] *Ibid.* 25:6.

[11] *Ibid.* 25:11.

royal family—Agrippa II and his other sister, Berenice,[12] who came to Caesarea to greet Festus on his appointment. Paul was summoned into the audience hall (τὸ ἀκροατήριον),[13] in the presence of Festus, Agrippa, and Berenice, the military tribunes, and the prominent men of the city, to present his case. Festus asked Agrippa's advice in formulating the letter to the emperor concerning Paul's affair. After the hearing the king, accompanied by Festus, Berenice, and the others, withdrew (presumably to a side chamber, or to an adjacent suite), saying to each other that the man had done nothing worthy of death or imprisonment.[14] But since he had appealed to Caesar, he could not be set free. A few days later Paul, together with other prisoners, sailed for Italy.

The *"Praetorium"* of Herod: The Site of St. Paul's Custody and Hearing

The archaeological excavations carried out in Caesarea since the mid-1970s, brought to light the entire complex of the *"praetorium* of Herod" (Fig. 106). Within it the law court, or audience hall (τὸ ἀκροατήριον of *Ac* 25:23), and the *bema* (*ibid.* 6) occupied by the governor and his council (συμβούλιον—*ibid.* 12) during the assizes, can be identified with a high degree of certainty.[15]

Herod's palace extended over two terraces with a difference of elevation of c. 3.6 m. The two-storied lower-terrace palace (110 × 55 m in size),[16] built in the first phase of the building operations at Caesarea,

---

[12] Renowned for her beauty, Berenice later attracted the attention of Vespasian. Later she became the mistress of Titus, his son, until she had to leave Rome after he was proclaimed emperor.

[13] *Ac* 25:23. According to Rackham (1901: 461), this auditorium was a different hall than the regular governor's hall of justice.

[14] *Ibid.* 25:31.

[15] On this complex, excavated by several expeditions (Hebrew University of Jerusalem, University of Pennsylvania, and the Israel Antiquities Authority), see Levine and Netzer 1986; Netzer 1999a: 109–14; Netzer 1996; Gleason 1996; Burrell 1996. See also Burrell, Gleason and E. Netzer 1993; Gleason *et al.* 1998. During the years 1995–97, in the framework of the Israel Antiquities Authority excavations directed by Y. Porath, further parts of the N, S, and E wings of the praetorium were exposed. For a short preliminary note, see Rochman 1998; Porath 2001. See also Cotton and Eck 2001 and Chapter Eight above.

[16] Thus Gleason *et al.* 1998: 29, but according to Burrell 1996: 240, the dimensions of the rectangular structure (without the semicircular W projection) was 40 × 80,

(dated to the years 22–15 BCE), served as the private wing. It occupied a natural promontory, extending 100 m into the Mediterranean. The E side and the SE corner were cut out of the rock. A large, rectangular, rock-cut swimming pool (35 × 18 m), 2 m deep, lined with hydraulic plaster, fed by sweet water, was surrounded by various wings, founded almost at sea level. A rectangular base, presumably for a statue, was located in the center of the pool.[17] The E wing, best preserved, constituted a dining suite looking west, comprised of a central hall flanked on either side by two small rooms. The thick lateral walls of the Herodian triclinium suggest a vaulted ceiling; there was no second story above this hall. The western side, that might have served as the living quarters, is poorly preserved. Access to the second story and to the upper terrace was through a staircase located in the NE corner.

The upper terrace, on an upper part of the promontory and of a slightly different orientation, served as the public wing. It was built around a vast courtyard (42 × 65 m) surrounded by porticoes.[18] A raised square platform, for some monument, or for the emplacement of a *bema*, stood in its center, and to its east was constructed a vast underground water cistern, of two compartments, T-shaped in its ground plan.

The N wing of the upper terrace held two suites separated from each other by a service corridor. The W suite (in the Penn excavation area) was facing S, while the E one (in the IAA excavation area) was facing N. The W suite, of symmetrical layout, contained in its center a basilical audience hall (192 sq m), flanked by smaller rooms and service corridors. The N part of the hall, that accommodated, so it seems, a dais, or a *bema*,[19] had a heated floor set on stone *suspensurae/hypocaust*. It seems that over this *bema* the Roman governor and his

---

while according to Netzer 1996: 198, 200, 201, it was 83 × 51, giving a total area of ca. 4,400 sq m for the lower story, including the projections, and 8,000 in two stories.

[17] Swimming pools were typical in Herodian palaces; they were found in Herod's palaces at Jericho, Masada, Herodium, and Hyrcania. See Netzer 1985; 1988. For Hyrcania, see Patrich 1992.

[18] The W half of the upper terrace was excavated by the University of Pennsylvania expedition, directed by Glieson and Burrell, while the E half, and farther areas to its E, belonging to the Roman *praetorium*, and the entire S wing, all yet unpublished, were excavated by the Israel Antiquities Authority expedition headed by Yosef Porath. See note 15 above.

[19] See plan and reconstruction in Gleason *et al.* 1998: figs. 4c and 7 and 13, and discussion in Burrell 1996: 229.

council (*concillium*/συμβούλιον) held their assizes, including those pertaining to St. Paul mentioned above.[20]

A small bath unit, including a Jewish *miqveh*, was located to the west of this suite. The E suite had on its S four rooms facing N, to a stone paved courtyard, with a circular fountain at its center. It is likely that to this suite, overlooking the sea and the city, Festus, Agrippa, and the other magnates present at St. Paul's hearing withdrew.

The S wing of the upper palace was occupied by a large Roman bathhouse. The entrance to the palace was from the E, via a square propylon of four turrets set at its corners. Another, higher tower, rose above this propylon, overlooking the hippodrome/stadium. Only the foundations of the propylon and the adjacent tower had been preserved. Under Roman rule Herod's palace was extended farther to the east, adding c. 50 m along the southern curved end of the hippodrome/stadium.[21] Latin inscriptions mentioning various functionaries and rooms of the *officium* were found in this extension.[22]

Although still standing in the Byzantine period, according to the excavators,[23] the audience hall of the W suite was never converted into a chapel. A Byzantine apsidal structure located farther to the east, within the bounds of the former Roman *praetorium*, had a Greek inscription calling for the salvation of Silvanus and Nonna. No cross accompanies the inscription—a common feature in Christian Greek epigraphy, to be expected also here if the structure was used by Christians. The apse, oriented to the east, is very shallow, leaving no room for a *synthronon*, and there was neither a *bema*, nor an altar. Thus, it should not be excluded that the structure was actually a Samaritan synagogue, oriented eastward to Mt. Garizim, located to the east of Caesarea.

---

[20] For the audience hall see Gleason *et al.* 1998: 33, 45–48, figs. 4c and 7 and 13. The side chamber whence Agrippa and Berenice, together with Festus and the other magnates withdrew can be identified as R.6 in fig. 7 there, unless it was to the E suite, depicted in fig. 4c.

[21] According to Porath (oral information) the entire complex of the two-terraces palace postdates Herod's reign. However, this interpretation disregards the fact (pointed out by Netzer, in Gleason *et al.* 1998: 38, n. 29), according to which the N wall of the palace's upper terrace is bonded to the W *cavea* wall of the hippodrome/stadium, and ignores the fact that the *praetorium* where St. Paul was put in custody was known as the *Praetorium* of Herod (*Ac* 23:35).

[22] See Cotton and Eck 2001.

[23] Gleason *et al.* 1998; Burrell 1996: 240–47.

A Chapel of St. Paul?

In the extant literary sources there is no record of a church or chapel dedicated to St. Paul in Caesarea.[24] Nevertheless, several finds from area KK, located in the southwestern zone of the city, may suggest that such a chapel did exist there.[25]

St. Paul Eulogia Bread stamp (Fig. 156)[26]

The stamp was found in building I of the complex of warehouses. It is circular in shape (10.4 cm in diameter), like a disk, 1 cm thick, made of pink-reddish clay, well fired. A pyramidal, knob shaped handle, 3.5 cm wide and 3 cm thick is attached to the center of the rear side. More than half of the original disk is preserved. For a detailed description and discussion, see Chapter Eleven below.

Frescos depicting crosses and wall inscriptions

Several plastered building stones found in debris in the *"dolium* hall" (Fig. 141) of Building I, in the Area KK complex of warehouses (Fig. 161), depicted large painted crosses of the *crux gemmata* type, with the abbreviated formula IC XC A W above and below the arms, and Greek inscriptions, in a single line underneath (Fig. 155).[27] At least three such crosses can be restored.[28] Their location in the debris, and the fact that the lower story walls are preserved on either side to a considerable height, indicate that they came from the second story. This upper story hall, located above the central section of the *"dolium* hall" and overlooking the entire compound of warehouses, is our candidate for the suggested chapel (Fig. 162). One of the inscriptions, referring perhaps to the Holy Cross, as suggested by Di Segni, might be associated with the cross depicted on the above mentioned *eulogia* bread stamp.

---

[24] For a brief survey, with references, on the churches and chapels of Caesarea, see Patrich 2001a.

[25] For a preliminary report on the excavation in area KK, see Patrich *et al.* 1999.

[26] Object no. 10/94 KK17 L.012 B.0086 001. For a detailed description, including artistic and liturgical significance, see Patrich 2002c.

[27] For a detailed description of the KK complex of warehouses, see Patrich 1996. figs. 23–24 on pp. 170–71 depict one of the painted crosses reproduced here as Fig. 155. For the Greek inscriptions, see Di Segni 2000.

[28] One cross with an underline inscription, presented by Di Segni 2000 as inscription 1, and already reconstructed graphically in Patrich 1996, was restored by the conservation team of the Israel Antiquities Authority. See Israeli and Mevorah 2000: 34.

Two masonry blocks depict red painted branches (Fig. 163), one with traces of a cross to its left. These branches were perhaps placed at the beginning and end of the inscriptions.

The central section of the "*dolium* hall" of Building I is retained on the inside and on the outside by five pairs of attached pilasters. The retaining pairs of pilasters, and the thick accumulation of *kurkar* plastered blocks retrieved therein, including fragments of white mosaic floor, suggest the existence of a second story above this section, which is preserved up to the springing course of the arches. Blocks plastered on three of their faces originated from the arches.

The presumed upper story chapel (Fig. 162), could have been 10.25 m long and c. 5.65 m wide (internal dimensions). On its west the chapel might had a small 5.65 × 4.40 m courtyard. Access from the lower floor could have been by a wooden staircase installed in the room (3.8 × 4.7 m, internal dimensions) on the southern side of the "*dolium* hall," leading directly to the prayer hall.[29]

The architectural members

Besides the above mentioned frescos and wall inscriptions, found in the upper story debris, the following decorated architectural fragments, mostly of marble, might have originated in the suggested chapel, although found dispersed throughout KK area, in a post-occupational fill, or reused in a later stratum. These are not finds to be expected in a mundane context of warehouses, yet, their attribution to a one and single hall, interpreted as a chapel—although possible—is far from being certain.

All members are made of gray Proconessian marble, unless otherwise specified.

Ciborium (baldachino) columns (Fig. 164)

1. 10/94 KK23 L.018 B0076 001
Marble, complete, but broken into two pieces. 2.04 m high; lower section, 70 cm high, vertically fluted; upper part diagonally fluted upward

---

[29] Aspects of engineering and architectural stability of the possible existence of an upper story chapel in this place were discussed with our conservation architect at the Caesarea excavations, Daniel Abu Hazeira, who had expressed his absolute confidence that an upper story did exist over the central section of the "*dolium* hall." I am indebted to him for his opinion. But the hypothesis presented below is based more on the interpretation of the archaeological data, suggesting an upper story chapel, than on the possible existence of an upper story on purely architectural grounds.

to the right. Lower diameter 28 cm, top diameter 27 cm, 22 cm below the top, and 24 cm at an elevation of 1.40 m.

2. 10/94 KK23 L.008 B0046 001
Marble, complete, but broken into two pieces. 2.12 m high, diagonally fluted upward to the right. Lower diameter 23 cm, top diameter 21 cm.

In spite of the variance in shape and size, the columns might have been used as a kind of ciborium, as suggested in Figs 162a–e.

Table legs (Fig. 165)

3. 10/94 KK27 L.009 B0021 001
Marble, upper part, 21 cm long. Lower diameter 9 cm, upper diameter 11 cm.

4. 42/93 KK18 L000 B0066 001
Leg fragment, 14 cm high, marble, 10 cm in diameter.

5. 10/94 KK15 L.550 B0221 001
Capital of an altar leg (?), marble, 8 cm high, upper surface c. 8.5 × 8.5 cm, has a shallow cavity. The tiny size excludes the possibility that this was a table leg of regular size. It might have served as a decorative piece of a smaller installation, such as a decorative tiny niche.

Table Plates (Fig. 166)

It is hard to tell which (if any) of the plates detailed below, four of which were certainly circular, actually belonged to the presumed chapel, and which, if any, had served as an altar table plate.

6. 42/93 KK20 L.231 B0110 001
Small fragment, 13 cm long, of a circular table plate, of the Theodosian relief type,[30] c. 3 cm deep, and 2 cm thick. White marble, inner diameter c. 52 cm, preserved rim c. 5.5 cm wide, depicting a feline tail to

---

[30] For a catalogue of these table plates, see Dresken-Weiland 1991. I am indebted to David Amit for bringing this publication to my attention. A larger fragment of an altar of this type depicting on the rim a hunting scene was found recently in a monastery in Jerusalem. See Amit, Seligman, and Zilberbod 2000.

the right of an acanthus flower, presumably of an heraldic, antithetic arrangement.

7. 10/94 KK28 L.035 B0059 001
Ten fragments of a circular table plate, 77 cm in diameter, 1.4 cm thick and 2.8 cm deep. Rim width 6.4 cm. White marble.

8. 03/96 KK35 L.079 B0111 001
Four fragments of a circular table plate, marble, 100 cm in diameter, ca. 2 cm thick, very shallow concavity. Rim decorated by a pattern of beads.

9. 42/93 KK21 L.122 B0090 001
Three fragments of a circular table plate, white marble, 109 cm in diameter, 4 cm deep, 3.5 cm thick, 4 cm high rim (on the inside).

10. 42/93 KK20 L.000 B0057 001
White marble, fragment 10 × 11 cm, 1.5–3 cm thick, diameter c. 20 cm.

Screen and other Plates (Fig. 167)

11. 10/94 KK24 L.024 B0103 001
Screen plate upper fragment 22 × 22 cm, 3 cm thick, grey marble, rear face rough. Upper band incised by a 1.2 cm-wide chisel; decoration depicting poppy cob and buds.

12. 10/94 KK24 L.026 B0107 004
Screen plate corner. Grey marble, 26 × 24 cm, 2 cm thick, rear face smooth. Decoration incised with a 1 cm-wide chisel.

13. a. 10/94 KK24 L. 026 B0107; b. 07/95 KK08 L.035 B0130
Decorative plates, grey marble, decorated in *champs levée* technique, depicting vegetal motives. a. Right part, 34 cm long, 15.5–11 cm broad, 3.4 cm thick, drill in upper edge. b. fragment, 10 × 10 cm, 1.75 cm thick.

14. 10/94 KK17 L000 B0070 001
Screen plate? Fragment, 16 cm long, 5 cm thick, grey marble. Depicting a conch and a wreath? in relief. 42/93 KK21 L.127 B0105, 13 cm

long, of similar thickness and motif, might have been another piece of the same screen.

15. 42/93 KK13 L.327 B.0075[31]

Decorative plate. Marble, ca. 30 × 30 cm, 3 cm thick; left lower corner and right upper corner missing. Dimensions too small for a screen plate. Floral? emblem emerging from a vase flanked by two crosses surrounded by a strip connecting two palmettes. Two buds, or fleur de lis, decorate both lower corners, and an awning the uppermost part.

Burial inscriptions and sarcophagi

Several Greek mortuary inscriptions on marble plates retrieved in area KK may indicate that the chapel also served for burial, or that a burial chamber was attached to it.[32] One inscription (Fig. 168a) reads +Μημόριον Κορν(η)λιας (Tomb of Cornelia). Another (Fig. 168b) reads +Θήκη [δ(ια)φ(έρουσα)] Άνα(σ)τασ[ίου] καὶ Άξίας+ ([Private] tomb of Anastasius and Axia) referring perhaps to a communal burial.[33] In this context should be mentioned two sarcophagi found in this area, that were reused as water basins in the irrigation system of a terraced garden constructed over the ruined and abandoned Byzantine structures in Areas KK and CC.[34] One (Fig. 169) was found thrown in Well KK16.171,[35] and the other was found fallen at the entrance to Vault CC07, near another well (Fig. 170).[36] The occurrence of sarcophagi

---

[31] This plate was already presented in Patrich 1996: 175, fig. 29.

[32] For a survey of burial practice in the churches and chapels in Palestine, see Goldfus 1997. Christian burials (unlike veneration of martyrs' relics), were quite rare within urban confines, and when occurring within the wall it was near the outskirts of the city, as in the case of the "Mortuary Church" at Jerash, or "Kyria Maria Monastery" and the "Martyr's Church" in Scythopolis—both within an *intra*-mural cemetery. "Kyria Maria Monastery" served as a burial ground for monks and their relatives, and for persons of high rank. Tombs were also found in the narthex of the tri-apsidal church at Horvat Soger in western Galilee. See Aviam 1999. Although imperial legislation and ecclesiastical stance forbade *intra*-mural burial (see Di Segni 2000), these finds, and the necessity to re-enact these laws time and again, indicate that such a practice did occur. Although one cannot exclude the possibility that both sarcophagi and burial inscriptions to be mentioned below came from the *extra*-mural cemeteries of Caesarea, in my opinion an origin adjacent to the finding spot should be preferred.

[33] The inscriptions were deciphered and translated by Leah Di Segni.

[34] This "irrigated garden" constitutes our stratum IIIa. See Patrich *et al.* 1999: 72. See also Patrich 1998: 56, fig. 26.

[35] Object no. 10/94 KK16 L.171 B0001.

[36] Object no. 10/94 CC07 L.002; Photo no. C94-29-13.

together with the burial inscriptions in area KK, may not be accidental. Taking in consideration their heavy weight, it seems unlikely that
the sarcophagi were brought from the *extra*-mural burial grounds, at
a distance of c. 700 m to the east, just to serve as irrigation basins.
It would have been much simpler to construct such basins near the
wells, using masonry blocks. Therefore, it is much more reasonable to
assume that they originally stood in proximity to the wells where they
were found.

Due to their weight it would be more reasonable to suggest the
room annexed to the chapel on the south, c. 3 × 3.5 m in size (Figs. 161
and 162), with a fill of earth under its floor, as their original location,
rather than to set them in the chapel itself, having a space underneath.
The only possible entrance to this room was from the north, and since
its floor level was 2.75 m lower than the chapel's floor, it was a kind
of a crypt, and we should assume several wooden stairs, or a ladder,
leading down from the chapel.

Eulogia flasks

Four St. Menas flasks (Fig. 157), and one *eulogia* flask of St. Simeon
the Elder (Figs. 158–159), and a silver (eucharistic?) spoon (Fig. 63)
were also retrieved in the post-occupational dirt and "garden soil" that
covered area KK,[37] but again one cannot insist that they came from the
presumed chapel rather than being owned by private individuals.

---

[37] For a detailed description of these objects, see Patrich 2002c.

CHAPTER ELEVEN

FOUR CHRISTIAN OBJECTS FROM
CAESAREA MARITIMA

The four objects described below—a *eulogia* bread stamp, a St. Menas ampulla, an ampulla depicting a stylite saint, and a silver spoon—were found in the course of the University of Haifa archaeological excavations of a complex of warehouses and granaries adjacent to the palace of the Byzantine governor, located to the south of the Crusader wall of Caesarea.[1] The objects were found in a layer of debris that accumulated over the Byzantine structures after their desertion following the Arab siege and conquest of the city in 640 or 641 CE. Various fragments of marble architectural elements retrieved in this area, such as chancel screen plates, a diagonally fluted colonnette, and altar legs, in addition to the items under discussion, suggest the possible existence of a chapel on a second story, above the warehouse complex. This proposal is further supported by the discovery—in the debris of the *dolia* hall of Building I at the complex—of plastered building stones from the second story, which depict large painted crosses of the *crux gemmata* type surmounting Greek inscriptions.[2]

The first three objects described here are *eulogiae* (Christian objects of various kinds believed to impart blessings), while the fourth may be considered Christian only in general terms, having been retrieved in the debris of an architectural complex that belonged to Christians.

1. *Eulogia* bread stamp (Figs. 156). The bread stamp[3] was found in Building I of the warehouse complex.[4] It is made of well-fired clay and is disk-shaped (dia. 10.4 cm; Th. 1 cm). A pyramidal, knob-shaped

---

[1] The excavations took place in the years 1993–98. For a preliminary archaeological report, see Patrich 1999, 70–108. Objects nos. 1–3 appear in Patrich 1996, 146–76, figs. 25–28. The Christian identity of the architectural complex is evident from the frescoes and inscriptions on its walls.

[2] Patrich 1996: 175, fig. 29 (marble plate); 170–71, figs. 23–24 (painted cross). See also Patrich 2000b; Di Segni 2000.

[3] Registration number 10/94 KK17 L.012 B.0086 001.

[4] For a map of the complex, see Patrich 1996: 148, fig. 2, and Patrich 1999: 76, fig. 7.

handle (w. 3.5 cm; th. 3 cm) is attached at the back, in the center. More than half the original disk is preserved.

The decorations were incised on the clay before firing. The circumference of the stamp is decorated by two concentric bands, the outer bearing a zigzag line and the inner a Greek inscription, more than half of which is preserved. The suggested reconstructed reading of the complete inscription is: "Blessing of the Lord upon us, and of Saint Paul."[5] The inner area of the medallion depicts an arched ciborium over a cross.[6] The arch, decorated by a zigzag line, is supported by two columns, also decorated by zigzag lines. A surrounding circle of dots is interrupted at the bottom by a smaller cross in a circle—seemingly one of a pair. Similar dots are depicted between the arms of the larger cross. The arms of both crosses have flaring ends. Another cross with flaring arms is depicted on the back. The other markings on this side, however, are unclear.

This bread stamp is the only one of its kind found to date in Caesarea. On the basis of the clay, which is different from that of the local jars and lamps,[7] it seems that the object was not produced locally.

Eulogia bread stamps differ in their shape and inscriptions from eucharistic bread stamps.[8] While the eucharistic bread was served to the faithful as part of the rite of communion, after it had been consecrated on the altar, the *eulogia* bread was distributed as a *eulogia* to the faithful after the conclusion of the rite and the dismissal of the assembly. It was also acquired by pilgrims at churches, monasteries, and martyrs' shrines, and distributed to the poor at feasts. In addition, *eulogia* bread was given out to the faithful in conjunction with important feasts and saints' days, without any connection to a particular site.[9] It is also possible that a stamp could serve as a *eulogia* in its own

---

[5] See Di Segni 2000.

[6] For a somewhat similar depiction of an arched ciborium over a cross, with a surrounding Greek inscription reading: "Blessing of the Lord on us," see Galavaris 1970: 119, fig. 64 (from the Byzantine Museum, Athens). The provenance of the stamp, dated to c. 600 CE, is unknown.

[7] On the local jars, see Johnson 2008; on the local oil lamps, see Sussman 2008.

[8] Galavaris 1970. The identification of this object as a eucharistic bread stamp in Patrich 1996: 172, fig. 25 was erroneous.

[9] Galavaris 1970: 132–33, 137–61. Of particular relevance for the stamp under discussion is the one from Thessaloniki, of c. the sixth century, depicted there as fig. 77. The blessing of the Lord is followed by the blessings of St. Andrew and (presumably) St. Paul (Galavaris 1970: 128, 141–43). On another stamp, from Vienna, SS. Peter and

right, rather than as a functional object in the baking process. This would explain the dissemination of these objects and the discovery of identical stamps in different parts of the Early Christian world.[10]

How should the depiction on this bread stamp be interpreted? There is no feature beneath the central cross that would identify it as the cross on Golgotha—a Greek-type cross regularly depicted on grades or on a trilobated mound. Similarly, the two smaller crosses appear below the central cross, not beside it—the common position of the crosses of the two thieves crucified with Christ on Golgotha. The two smaller crosses may have represented two of the Apostles, such as Peter and Paul, if there were originally two names in the inscription. According to Di Segni, there is no space in the inscription for another name besides that of St. Paul.[11] Nevertheless, in my opinion, the missing part of the inscription is long enough to have included a second name, consisting of a few extra letters, preceding that of Paul, without making the spacing of the letters in the missing part denser than that in the extant part. The other name could have been that of an apostle or of a local martyr.

If the stamp was not a *eulogia* in its own right, brought to Caesarea from Jerusalem (like nos. 2 and 3 below, from Egypt and Syria respectively), it is reasonable to assume that it was used locally in conjunction with a shrine or a feast. The identity of the shrine or feast depends on the completion of the inscription.

The inscription, as deciphered by Di Segni, associates the stamp with a shrine dedicated to St. Paul, presumably Paul the Apostle. This is the first indication so far for the possible existence of such a shrine

Paul, identified by their names, are shown flanking a cross. The surrounding Greek inscription reads: "The blessing of the Lord on us. The cross is the beginning of life." Galavaris (1970: 146–48, fig. 79) associates this stamp with bread distributed on the feast of SS. Peter and Paul. The shape of the handle of this stamp resembles ours. To the list of bread stamps given by Di Segni 2000 one can add two un-inscribed stamps depicting crosses. The first, made of gypsum and cylindrical in shape (dia. 5 cm), is from Sinai, Wadi Sigaliya (Dahari 2000: 132, fig. 84) and the second, made of clay and round (dia. 15 cm), with a hollow, cylindrical handle (dia. 7.2 cm), is from Tiberias (Feig 1994: 591–94). Feig (1994: n. 7) mentions a similar, as yet unpublished stamp from Kefar Barʿam in the Upper Galilee (a Jewish village during the Byzantine period) and two others from Kh. Kerak and from Susita, with a different ornamentation, all housed in the IAA storerooms.

[10] Galavaris 1970: 127, 142.
[11] See discussion by Di Segni 2000.

in Caesarea.[12] The literary sources pertaining to the city make no mention of such a shrine.[13]

According to Acts 23–25, after being arrested in Jerusalem Paul was imprisoned by the procurator Felix in Herod's *praetorium* at Caesarea (58 CE). Since Felix refrained from making any decision concerning the case, Paul remained in prison for two years. Porcius Festus, Felix's successor, decided to send Paul to Rome after Paul invoked his right to be tried in the court of Caesar (as a Roman citizen, he was outside the jurisdiction of the local procurator). Yet before being sent to Rome, Paul was given a second hearing in the audience hall of the *praetorium* (Acts 25:23), in front of a large assembly that included, besides Festus, his guests Agrippa II and Agrippa's sister Berenice, as well as high-ranking officers and prominent citizens of Caesarea. Sometime later, Paul was sent to Italy (60 CE). Based on this tradition, it would not be surprising to find a shrine of St. Paul in Caesarea. The archaeological evidence at our disposal suggests that the chapel was located on the upper story above the warehouse complex, in the immediate vicinity of the spots where the objects under discussion were found.[14]

The following two objects (nos. 2–3) are clay ampullae. As tiny containers for liquids, ampullae could serve as receptacles for water that was used by a saint to wash his hands; for water that was drawn from a well or cistern near his pillar; or for dust (Syr—*hnana*, Gr—*konis*) from his shrine, mixed with water or oil.[15] Similarly, such flasks might hold oil blessed by a saint, taken from the vigil lamp burning in a

---

[12] St. Paul is also mentioned in a fragmentary Greek inscription on a clay *plate* found in this area (10/94 KK17 L.001 B.0096), to be published by Di Segni together with the other Greek inscriptions from these excavations.

[13] The most detailed list of the churches and chapels of Caesarea is given in the Acts of St. Anastasius the Persian. See Kaegi 1978; Flusin 1992: 231–43. For a brief survey of this topic, presenting all literary and archaeological evidence, see Patrich 2001a, reprinted here as Chapter Four. A church of St. Paul's prison at Caesarea is mentioned by an anonymous pilgrim of the later thirteenth century. See Pringle 1990: 181. See also Patrich 2000b, reprinted here as Chapter Ten.

[14] For a detailed exposition of the archaeological data and the considerations leading to this proposal, see Patrich 2000b; Di Segni 2000b. The location of the proposed chapel near the Byzantine *praetorium* may reflect that, in this period, the Byzantine *praetorium* was regarded by the Christian populace of Caesarea as the site of St. Paul's detention, rather than the Roman *praetorium* in Herod's palace, which by that time was already in ruins.

[15] The Syriac *hnana*—literally "grace"—was martyr's dust mixed with oil or water (Brockelmann 1928: 243; John of Ephesus, *Lives of Eastern Saints*, ed. Brooks 1923: chap. 4, n. 70; Magoulias 1967: 254, n.1; Lafontaine-Dosogne and Orgels 1967: 175–76; Duran 1992: 19). The terracotta tokens were also made of this blessed earth.

martyr's tomb, or sanctified by contact with relics.[16] Hagiographic literature is replete with tales of healing and other apotropaic miracles
performed by means of such *eulogiae*. They were considered instruments by which the grace and supernatural powers of the holy man
were delivered to his supplicants and were attributed with the ability
to cure sickness, to protect the faithful and their relatives and property
from demons and the Evil Eye, to perform all kinds of miracles, and to
safeguard pilgrims against any hazards they might encounter on their
journeys.[17] Shipowners even sprinkled the contents of ampullae over
their ships before they were about to set sail.[18]

2. St. Menas ampulla (Figs. 157a–b). The ampulla[19] was found in
Building I, in Area KK. It is 10.7 cm high, with a round, flat body, a
projecting neck, and a pair of large handles. On both sides St. Menas
is depicted frontally as an orant, his arms raised in prayer. He wears
a short tunic tied by a belt and a *paladamentum* over both shoulders,
and flanking him are two kneeling camels. Two crosses are depicted
above his shoulders. The scene is surrounded by a circle of grains.
Three more Menas ampullae of the same type were also found in Area
KK.[20] Based on its size, the ampulla belongs to the group of small

---

[16] John Chrysostom (*Homelia in Martyres*, PG 50: 664–65) encouraged the Christians of Antioch to take from the sanctified oil while visiting martyrs' shrines and use
it as an ointment for the body and all its members, as a remedy for the soul. Theodoret
of Cyrrhus hung a flask of oil by his bed, for protection against the nocturnal visits of
demons: *Historia Religiosa*, XXI.16, trans. Price 1985: 139–40. On the use of oil from
martyrs' shrines, see Lassus 1947: 163–67. The prophylactic powers of stylites' *eulogiae*
containing sacred dust mixed with water or oil were obviously similar.

[17] The reddish dust from the base of the pillar of seclusion of St. Symeon the
Younger could also calm tempests; see van den Ven 1970: chap. 235. According to
this account, when the captain and the crew were ready to abandon ship, one of the
passengers, a monk, "took the dust (*konis*) of the saintly servant of God that he carried with him as a blessing (*eulogia*), and after having put it into water, he threw it
on the sea and sprinkled all the boat, saying: 'Holy servant of God, Simeon, direct us
and save us.' With these words, all those on the boat were impregnated with perfume,
the sea water surrounded the boat like a wall, and the waves were powerless against
it." See also Magoulias 1967: 256; Vikan 1991a: 75; and Vikan 1997: 56–59. A similar
episode of a "calm tempest" associated with the *hnana* of St. Symeon the Elder is given
in chapter 71 of the Syriac Life. The ship was carrying passengers from Arabia (Sinai?)
back to their homes in Syria. See Duran 1992: 151. These sea episodes bear, of course,
special significance for the people of a maritime city like Caesarea.

[18] Vikan 1991a: 78, following the Piacenza pilgrim, *Itinerarium*, 11.

[19] Registration number 10/94 KK24 L.003 B.0026 001.

[20] These are 10/94 KK24 L.003 B.0026 003 (a second ampulla from the same basket), 42/93 KK22 L607 B.0063 001, and 3/96 KK27 L.055 B.0130 001.

flasks as classified by Kaufmann; according to the typology of Kiss, this type dates to 610–50 CE,[21] which corresponds to the last urban stage at Caesarea.

According to Christian lore, Menas, a Roman soldier of Phrygian origin, suffered martyrdom during the reign of Diocletian. His corpse was transported secretly to Egypt and buried in the western desert, near a spring that acquired miraculous properties due to its proximity to the saint's tomb. Presumably, St. Menas ampullae contained drops of water from this spring. Menas was regarded as a protector of pilgrims and merchants.[22] His burial place at Abu Mina, southwest of Alexandria, beyond Lake Mareotis, became a famous pilgrimage site for Christians from all over the world. It was first monumentalized by Arcadius and Theodosius II and later by Zeno and Justinian.[23] The center for the production of St. Menas ampullae was located at this site, and several pottery kilns have been excavated there. Although the camels appearing on the ampullae suggest that Menas was popular with desert-farers, the fact that such objects have been found throughout the Mediterranean basin and beyond,[24] and not just in Egypt (or Alexandria), points to Menas' role as a guardian of all travelers, whether overland or by sea.[25] A church of St. Menas was erected in Jerusalem in the fifth century by Bassa, a wealthy matron associated with the empress Eudocia.[26] A martyrion of this saint has been known since the early fifth century in Constantinople.[27] This ampulla, together with the others of the same type found at the site, attests to the fact that the Christians of Caesarea made pilgrimages to the famous shrine of St. Menas near Alexandria, unless, of course, the ampullae were acquired at the saint's shrine in Constantinople or Jerusalem.

---

[21] Kaufmann 1910a: 68–78; Kiss 1989: 15, cat. nos. 43–106; Kiss 1990: 195–202.

[22] Kazhdan and Ševchenko 1991: 1339.

[23] For the history of the site and its architecture, see Kaufmann 1910b; Grossmann 1989; Meinardus 1961: 351–52. For a brief summary, see Maraval 1985: 319–22.

[24] For a distribution map, see Lambert and Pedemonte Demeglio 1994: figs. 1–4, 6. See also Lapp 2000. Menas ampullae constitute the largest sub-category among all known pilgrims' flasks throughout the Christian world (Lambert and Pedemonte Demeglio 1994: fig. 5 and Vikan 1991b: 1340).

[25] According to one account, two sea monsters that threatened the ship carrying Menas' corpse to Egypt were appeased by the relics of the saint (Kiss 1989: 9, n. 4). According to the Ethiopian version, the sea monsters had thick long necks and their faces were "like those of camels" (Wallis Budge 1909: 28–29). For the prophylactic property of pilgrims' flasks and tokens on journeys, see Vikan 1991a: 74–92.

[26] Cyril of Scythopolis, V. Euth. 30, ed. Schwartz 1939: 49.22.

[27] Maraval 1985: 407; Delehaye 1910: 117–50.

3. Clay ampulla depicting a stylite saint (Figs. 158–159). The ampulla[28] was found in an unsealed layer that accumulated in the well of Building II. This layer can be broadly dated to the fifth–seventh century. The ampulla is a squat bottle (h 9 cm, w 5 cm, th. 2.5 cm); the rim and top of the neck are missing. Both sides present a schematic depiction, in relief, of a stylite saint wearing a hood, on top of a pillar. The pillar is flanked by two Greek crosses, and the scene is framed by two palm branches.

The scene is derived from the iconography of stylite saints, inspired by the life of St. Symeon the Elder (ca. 389–459), the famous Syrian monk who introduced the ascetic practice of living on top of a pillar into Syria. His pillar of seclusion at Telanissus (present-day Qal'at Sem'an) became a popular pilgrimage site during his lifetime and thereafter.[29] Another famous Syrian stylite was Symeon's sixth-century namesake—St. Symeon the Younger (521–92), who lived on top of a pillar on Mt. Admirabilis (the Wondrous Mountain), to the west of Antioch.[30] This kind of asceticism was most popular in the region of Antiochene in Syria.[31]

Stylite ampullae are very rare. Most stylite *eulogiae* known so far are tokens or medallions, mainly associated with Symeon the Younger; these are usually made of clay, but a few are of lead and fewer still of glass. Several clay objects (an oil lamp, a cup, and an oil lampstand), two glass bottles, a silver reliquary plaque, a sandstone plaque, and

---

[28] Registration number 10/94 KK24 L.030 B.0118 001.

[29] Tchalenko 1953: 229ff; Maraval 1985: 342–44. The monumental structures at the site were constructed only after the saint's death (459), under the emperor Zeno, during the years 476–90. Symeon the Elder's corpse was transferred to Antioch, and some of his relics were conveyed to Constantinople in 468 by Emperor Leo I, who had constructed a martyrion near the pillar of seclusion of Daniel the Stylite, outside the city wall. Nevertheless, St. Symeon's shrine at Qal'at Sem'an continued to be a major pilgrimage center up until the Arab conquest, even after it came under Monophysitic influence in the early sixth century and lost its attraction for the Chalcedonians. Symeon's shrines in Antioch and Constantinople were also centers of pilgrimage (Lafontaine-Dosogne and Orgels 1967: 192–93; Maraval 1985: 342–44, 409). In 560, Evagrius visited the great shrine in Antioch, where St. Symeon's relics were kept (*Historia Ecclesiasticae* I, 13–14, ed. Bidez and Parmentier 1898: 20, 33–25, 2). He had also visited Qal'at Sem'an. The popularity of the saint in north Syria is also attested by the multiplicity of monasteries bearing his name there. See Nasrallah 1972.

[30] Mércérian 1952: 299–302; Lafontaine-Dosogne and Orgels 1967: 67–135; Djobadze 1986: 57–115; Maraval 1985: 344–45. The pilgrimage center around the pillar was constructed between 541 and 551, already during his lifetime. Other components were added after his death.

[31] Delehaye 1923; Peña, Castellana, and Fernandez 1975.

several seals, all bearing images of stylites, are also known.[32] Another stylite ampulla, similar in shape and dimensions to the one presented here but with different representations, is known from Beirut (Fig. 171).[33] Its dimensions are h 9 cm, w 6.3 cm, th. 2.5 cm. On the obverse, the pillar is shaped like a palm-tree trunk; the two crosses flank the hooded bust, rather than the pillar, and are elevated on top of similar tree trunks, which, in turn, rest on top of two P-shaped stands. The cabin on top of the pillar, masking the lower part of the stylite saint, is covered by branches of a similar pattern to that of the trunks. The curving lines flanking the pillar have been variously interpreted as floral motifs or snakes. The reverse side presents a cross and other motifs, framed on both sides by palm-tree trunks. According to Sodini, this ampulla depicts St. Symeon Stylites the Elder, since the scenes on the *eulogiae* of St. Symeon the Younger are different from those depicted here.[34] However, St. Symeon the Younger touched his supplicants with palm branches when granting them a benedicition, rather than by placing his bare hands upon them. Palm trunks and branches are dominant motifs in the two ampullae under discussion. It is thus likely that this ampulla, as well as the one from Beirut, represents St. Symeon Stylites the Younger.

The reputations of both stylites—the Elder and the Younger—reached as far as the boundaries of the provinces of Palestine and Arabia.[35]

---

[32] See the lists and descriptions in Lassus 1932: 140–58, 169–218; Sodini 1989: 29–53.

[33] Formerly in the Sarafyan Collection, Beirut, no. 1262, published by Lassus (1932: 75–76 and pl. xx [no. XI]). At present it is in the Elderkin Collection, Princeton. See also Lafontaine-Dosogne and Orgels 1967: 157; Peña, Castellana, and Fernandez 1975: 178, figs. 29, and 213, fig. 59. For palm trees and branches on stylite *eulogiae*, see Lafontaine-Dosogne and Orgels 1967: 157, 184–85, and fig. 94 (a limestone medallion); Peña, Castellana, and Fernandez 1975: 205–6 and also 196, fig. 47, interpreting the trees as symbols of hope, immortality, and Christ's Cross. Two crosses flanking a stylite are also depicted on a glass medallion published by Lassus (1932: 75, no. XI, pl. xx). According to Sodini (1989: 33), St. Symeon the Elder is depicted on this glass medallion.

[34] Sodini 1989: 33.

[35] Empress Eudocia sent her delegates to consult St. Symeon the Elder during her sojourn in the Holy Land (Cyril of Scythopolis, *Vita Euthymii* 30, ed. Schwartz 1939: 47.22); Theodosius passed through the Saint's precinct of seclusion at the very beginning of his monastic career, on his way from Cappadocia to Jerusalem (Theodore of Petra, *Vita Theodosii* 3, ed. Usener 1890: 9–10). A Georgian monk from Jerusalem, named Sergius, went to St. Symeon the Younger to seek a cure for his infirmity. According to another narrative in *Vita Marthae* (Symeon's mother), a portion of the Holy Cross and pieces of the Holy Rock of Golgotha were sent to Symeon the Younger by Thomas, the *staurophylax* of the Anastasis in Jerusalem (*Vita S. Marthae*, *Acta*

A few stylites were also known in Palestine itself.[36] Like the St. Menas ampullae, this find suggests that the Christians of Caesarea made pilgrimages to the shrine of Symeon the Elder at Qal'at Sem'an or the Younger, at Mt. Admirabilis; alternatively, the ampulla may have been acquired at Symeon's shrine in Antioch or Constantinople.[37]

4. Silver spoon (Fig. 63). The spoon,[38] a fine cast *ligula*, was found in Building III. The oval bowl (l. 3.9 cm) has a molded rim and is decorated by a shell. The handle (l. 11.5 cm) is divided into three segments, and the scroll commonly found at the point of attachment between the bowl and the handle is only alluded to. The first segment has a square cross section and its upper side bears a separate quadrangular pattern; the second, with a round cross section, terminates in a double bulb; the third is shaped like a stylized swan head with a pointed beak. Such elaborate spoons are generally dated to the fourth–fifth century and later.[39]

Though silver spoons are commonly found in church hoards, not all of them were used in the celebration of the Eucharist. Similarly, in the present case, there is nothing to suggest that this particular piece was a communion spoon, though such a function cannot be entirely excluded.[40] It may have simply served as a luxurious table piece. Yet when examined together with the other objects described above, their possible origin in a chapel that might have existed in this area should be considered as well.[41]

Sanctorum, Maii V, 3a éd. Cap. 7, 418 and 422–24 respectively); Magoulias 1967: 248–49, 257.

[36] A Palestinian stylite named Pancratius was among the delegates sent by the Patriarch Eustochius to Constantinople for the Fifth Ecumenical Council of 553 (Cyril of Scythopolis, *Vita Sabae* 90, ed. Schwartz 1939: 198:28); another stylite lived near Petra (John Moschus, *Leimonarion* 129). See also Festugière 1962: 129, n. 303. A Sinaite monk named John later became a stylite in Diospolis; see Nau 1903. A tower of seclusion, exceptional in its state of preservation, is located c. 1 km to the north of Umm al-Rasas in Jordan; see Piccirillo 1992: fig. 330. An incision on a stone from the church of Umm er-Rus, in the Judean hills, interpreted by Bagatti (1971: 286–87, fig. 144.2) as a depiction of the "cosmic ladder," should preferably be conceived as a rendition of a stylite saint, whose name—*amba* (= *abba*) *el.*—written in Greek, flanked the drawing. I owe this last reference and interpretation to Leah Di Segni.

[37] See note 29 above.

[38] Registration number 07/95 KK28 L.117 B.0253 002.

[39] Strong 1966: 204–6.

[40] This point was well emphasized by Taft 1996.

[41] See Patrich 2000b, reprinted here as Chapter Ten; Di Segni 2000.

The four Christian objects described above augment our knowledge on Christian Caesarea, attesting to the piety of the local population, and to maritime connections with centers of pilgrimage in Egypt and Syria. Besides Menas flasks, which is a relatively common object, all other three are unique objects. The *eulogia* bread stamp, conveying the blessings of Christ and St. Paul, may identify the above mentioned chapel. The object bears evidence to the veneration of St. Paul in the city where he was kept in detention for two years. The stylite ampulla add another species to a type of squat rectangular bottles known so far by a single example from Beirut. Due to the prominence of palm branches in the decoration of both, it is suggested here that both relate to St. Symeon the Younger, rather than the Elder.

CHAPTER TWELVE

THE MARTYRS OF CAESAREA: THE URBAN CONTEXT

The archaeological excavations conducted in Caesarea over the last 30 years enable us to conceive better the *Acts of the Martyrs of Caesarea* in the urban context, and to examine several issues pertaining to the urban topography. Much of the new material so far has been published only in preliminary reports;[1] several of the large urban complexes were excavated by more than a single expedition, and the interpretation and chronology of some structures are therefore debated issues. But in spite of these difficulties, pertaining to the availability and interpretation of the archaeological data, there is room for the examination of the topographical details incorporated in these *Acts* in light of the new archaeological finds, even if not all may share my conclusions.

The Acts of the Martyrs of Caesarea are given by Eusebius, the future bishop of the city, in his *Ecclesiastical History* (=*HE*) and in much more detail in the *Martyrs of Palestine* (=*MP*),[2] recording "the persecution in his own days," to which he was an eyewitness.[3] The work has reached us in two recensions, of which only the shorter is extant in Greek. The longer recension is extant only in a Syriac translation, the vernacular of Palestine, dated to 411 CE, and in some Greek

---

[1] For an updated archaeological survey of the Late Roman/Byzantine city, with further references, see Patrich 2001a.

[2] Eusèbe de Césarée, *Histoire Ecclésiastique*, ed. Bardy 1952–1967; Eusebius, *The Ecclesiastical History*, ed. Oulton and Lawlor 1973. The Greek texts of *The Martyrs of Palestine* are given in Vol. III of Bardy's edition, Paris 1967. The Syriac: Eusebius, *History of The Martyrs in Palestine*, ed. Cureton London and Paris 1861. Also consulted was the English translation of Cruse 1850: 349–78: The Book of Martyrs. The references below to the Greek text of *MP* indicate paragraph and page in Bardy's edition. The references to the Syriac text indicate page number of the Syriac text. I am indebted to Ofer Livneh for assistance in reading the Syriac. On Christian martyrdom, see Gregoire 1950; Ste. Croix 1954; Frend 1965; Musurillo 1972; Fox 1986: 419–92; Davies 1989; Bowersock 1995; Shaw 1996; Mendels 1999: 51–109. On the persecutions at Caesarea, see also Barnes 1981: 148–63.

Another contemporary Latin source for the persecutions of Diocletian and his co-rulers is Lactantius' *The Death of the Persecutors* (*De mortibus persecutorum*, ed. Brandt 1897; Eng. tr. Fletcher 1871; Latin text with Fr. tr. Moreau 1954). Lactantius was an eyewitness to the events; living at the court of Diocletian in Nicomedia he had first-hand information.

[3] See explicitly his words in *HE* 8.13.7.

fragments.[4] Both recensions were the work of Eusebius.[5] The long one, a separate treatise, was intended for the instruction of the people of Caesarea, who were eyewitnesses to the events.[6] Therefore, although preserved only in a redaction made about a century after the events, it is of the utmost interest, especially with regard to the urban topography. The shorter recension, intended for wider circulation, was incorporated by Eusebius into his *Ecclesiastical History*. Eusebius must have also published a collection of more ancient Acts, pertaining to the persecutions of earlier days, to which he refers repeatedly in *Ecclesiastical History*.[7] But this composition has perished, and thus there are only brief allusions to these events in *Ecclesiastical History*.

The first martyrs of Caesarea were Ambrose, the patron and associate of Origen, and Protoctetus, a presbyter. Both became martyrs in 235 CE, in the persecutions under Maximin.[8] Origen's treatise *On Martyrdom* was dedicated to their memory. Origen, who made Caesarea his residence after leaving Alexandria, found refuge in Cappadocia during this period. But 15 years later, in the persecution under Decius, he was imprisoned and tortured severely on the rack in Caesarea.[9] A short while later he died. Under Valerian, in the persecution of 258, three martyrs of the countryside, Priscus, Malchus, and Alexander, and a woman of the sect of Marcion, were cast to the wild

---

[4] The Greek fragments of the long recension were published by H. Delehaye, *AB* 16 (1897): 113–38. The fragments are also found in Bardy's edition. On Syriac/Palestinian Aramaic being a vernacular of Palestine, see Égérie, *Journal de Voyage* 47.3–4, ed. Maraval 1982: 314–15; in the Church of the Holy Sepulcher there was a priest whose task was to translate for the neophytes the Mystagogical Cathecheseis of the bishop from Greek to Syriac; Procopius was an interpreter from Greek to Aramaic/Syriac— *MP* Syr.4, p. 4; Cyril of Scythopolis, *Vita Euthymii* 18, 38 (ed. Schwartz 1939: 28, 56). See also *Vita Hilarionis* 22, 23, 25 and the discussion of these passages in Weingarten 2000: 81–82, 104–7.

[5] Bardy 1967: 35–36; Cureton 1861: i–xi: preface; Quasten 1990: 317–19.

[6] Lightfoot 1877–87, 2: 320–21; Lawlor 1973: 179–80; 1912 (rprt. 1973): 279–83.

[7] *HE* 4.15.47; 5. Pref.2; 4.3; 21.5.

[8] *HE* 6.28, ed. Oulton and Lawlor 1973: 81. No martyrs are recorded for the persecutions under Septimius Severus in 203 CE. A few years earlier, c. 190, the Quatrodeciman synod was convened in Caesarea, at which bishop Theophilus was the leading personality. There are only few details about the local Church from year 60, when St. Paul was dispatched in a ship from Caesarea to Rome, to the convening of the Quatrodeciman synod. See I.L. Levine, *Caesarea under Roman Rule*: 127–34. Only nine bishops are recorded up to the episcopate of Eusebius (315/16–39). See Fedalto, *Hierarchia Ecclesiastica Orientalis*, Padova 1988, 1014. To his list should perhaps be added, as Eusebius' immediate predecessor, Agricola, who subscribed to the synod of Ancyra in 314 CE, according to the Latin minutes of that synod (Bardy, *op. cit.*, p. 34; Valesius, in: Cruse, *op. cit.*, p. x).

[9] *HE* 6.39, ed. Oulton and Lawlor 1973: 95.

beasts.[10] Under Gallienus, in the persecution of 260 CE, Marinus was beheaded by the governor Achaeus. His act was not a typical one, but it illustrates the role of the governor as a judge. Marinus, distinguished by birth and wealth, was an officer in the army. He wished to be promoted and become a centurion. During the process, before the tribunal (*bema*) presided over by the judge-governor, who was also the commander-in-chief of the army, he was accused by another officer of being a Christian who did not sacrifice to the emperors. After an interrogation the hearing was postponed, and Marinus was given three hours to reflect. After the appointed time was over he was summoned again by the herald (*kerux*) to the court of justice (*dikesterion*). Refusing to repudiate his faith, he was beheaded straightaway.[11] In the same *dikesterion* the later martyrs were sentenced after being imprisoned in the same compound in which Origen (and earlier St. Paul[12]) had been incarcerated.

Persecutions were resumed in 303–11 CE under Diocletian and his successors—Galerius and Constantius as Augusti and Maximinus Daia and Severus as Caesars—who assumed the government on May 1, 305, upon the abdication of Diocletian and his co-ruler Maximian. Maximinus ruled the prefecture of Oriens, in which the province Syria Palaestina was included. The number of martyrs in Palestine during this period was 83. Far more numerous was the number of confessors. There were also Christians who had renounced their faith and apostatized, unable to bear the hardship and torture. Eusebius was at that time already a presbyter of the church of Caesarea. There are no clear details how he managed to escape the fate of his confrere Pamphilus and his circle, but it is certain that he did not renounce his faith and sacrifice.[13] Sometime after 307 he escaped to Tyre, and later to the Thebaid in Upper Egypt and to Alexandria, becoming an eyewitness to and a reporter of the massacre of Christians there as well.

According to Lawlor, a careful examination of the chronology indicates that at Caesarea the persecution took the form of five intermittent onslaughts on the Church, of which four were initiated by imperial edicts and the fifth by a visit by Maximinus himself to

---

[10] *Ibid.* 7.12: 167–69.
[11] *Ibid.* 7.15: 171–73.
[12] *Ac* 21:15–27:1; see also Patrich 2000b, reprinted here as Chapter Ten.
[13] Lightfoot 1877–87: 311–12; Valesius, in: Cruse 1851: ix–x; ed. Bardy 1967: 30–33; Quasten 1990: 310. His accusation of apostasy occurred only at the Council of Tyre of 335, made by his opponents.

Caesarea for the celebration of his birthday. Each assault was followed by a period of inactivity; in all they lasted no more than three years and a half.[14] Thereafter a similar time elapsed until the end of the persecution. But even in the intervals that were free of martyrdoms there was persecution of a sort: the Christians were not allowed full liberty of worship, and confessors who had been imprisoned were not released (Pamphilus and his companions were kept in prison about two years, as was Agapius).[15]

THE URBAN CONTEXT

Caesarea was the capital of the province of Syria Palaestina, the seat of the provincial governor. Edicts issued by the tetrarchs ordered the leaders (*archontes*) of each city to ensure that all Christians in each city sacrificed and offered libations. In Caesarea, by the order of the governor, public heralds (*kerukes*) called upon men, women, slaves, and even children to assemble in the pagan temples. In addition, the tribunes (*chiliarchoi*) and centurions summoned them by name, according to a list of citizens, going from house to house in all quarters (*amphoda*).[16] Those who violated these orders were brought for interrogation and sentencing before the governor in the law court located in his *praetorium*. During their trial they were also imprisoned and tortured in the *praetorium*. Apart from this seat of power, the gates, streets, porticos, and entertainment structures of Caesarea are all mentioned in the *Acts*.

WALLS AND GATES[17]

Some of the non-local martyrs and confessors were arrested by the guards before the city gates (πρὸ τῶν τῆς πόλεως πυλῶν), prior to

---

[14] Lawlor 1973: 210. The first lasted about six months, from June to November 303. The second and third seem to have been very brief, and may be dated respectively March 305 and March–April 306. The fourth was much the longest, continuing for about a year and eight months, from November 307 to July 309. The last covered some five months, from November 309 to March 310.

[15] *Idem, ibid.*

[16] *MP* Gr. 4.8, ed. Bardy 1967: 131 (the long recension is more detailed); 9.2, ed. Bardy 1967: 148. See also Ste Croix 1954: 99, 112–13.

[17] Patrich 2001a: 84–86, with references. See also pp. 100–101 above.

entering the city. These were Procopius of Scythopolis, Adrianus and Eubulus from Batanea, and five Egyptians.[18]

Two semicircular city walls are still recognizable beyond the rectilinear shorter line of the Arab-Crusader wall (Fig. 172). The inner line is Herodian and the outer Byzantine. The Herodian fortification line was abandoned in the mid-fourth century. The Roman city, extending beyond the Herodian wall, had no outer wall for more than three centuries. Caesarea acquired a new wall only in the fifth century. The road system emerging from the city suggests the existence of four gates. The southern one was a monumental triple-entrance gate.[19] A Greek inscription from a Roman monumental arch referring to the city as metropolis, a rank granted to the city by Alexander Severus, was uncovered near the conjectured location of the east gate,[20] indicating that—as in the case of Gerasa, Jerusalem, Scythopolis, Gadara (and Athens)—the limits of the city were indicated by a monumental arch long before a city wall was actually constructed. Procopius, Adrianus, and Eubulus were apparently arrested at this gate, as it is located on the road from Batanea and Scythopolis to Caesarea. The five Egyptians were presumably arrested at the north gate, since they were on their way back home to Egypt from Cilicia. The north Byzantine gate disappeared, being eroded by the sea. Topographically, it must have laid at a lower elevation above sea level relative to the Herodian/Early Roman north gate, exposed by the Italian Expedition. Here, as well, like in the east, a gate without a wall might have marked the outskirts of the expanded city, although the Herodian/Early Roman north gate might still have been in use.

The corpse of another martyr, Apphianus, cast with stones into the sea, was vomited back by a storm (*tsunami*) following an earthquake,

---

[18] *MP* Syr. 4—ed. Cureton 1861: 4 (Procopius); *MP* Syr. 48—ed. Cureton 1861: 45; Gr. XI.29—ed. Bardy 1967: 168 (Adrianus and Eubulus); *MP* Syr. 43—ed. Cureton 1861: 40; Gr. XI.6—ed. Bardy 1967: 157–58 (Egyptians). Three other Egyptians were similarly arrested at the Gates of Ascalon—*MP* Syr. 38, Gr. X.1—ed. Bardy 1967: 151. The Syriac (4—ed. Cureton 1861: 4) renders: *thr'aya dmdyntha* and (43—ed. Cureton 1861: 40): *bthr'a dqsrya mdyntha*. Arrest and interrogation by the guards (φυλακές) are mentioned in the case of the Egyptians in Caesarea and Ascalon, and of Adrianus and Eubulus.

[19] Thus Peleg and Reich 1992, but recent IAA excavations had indicated that this was the royal entrance of a theatre stage! If so, the southern gate in the Byzantine city wall, running more to the south, has still not been uncovered.

[20] Abel and Barrois 1931.

washed ashore by the waves, and deposited before the gate of the city.[21] This may have been the northern extra-mural gate mentioned above, located near the sea shore. The Herodian/Early Roman north gate is located too high above sea level.

Eusebius defines the earthquake that occurred on April 2, 306 as extraordinary and severe (παράδοξος σεισμός/zw'a qshya). It made the entire city tremble, and people supposed that the whole place, together with its inhabitants, was about to be destroyed on that day. But neither casualties nor damages are recorded. It seems, therefore, that it was not devastating for Caesarea.[22] The effects of this earthquake have not been recognized so far in the archaeological excavations at the site.

Procopius was put to death on June 7, 303, the first martyr of Caesarea under Diocletian. He was a lector, an interpreter from Greek into Aramaic, and exorcist of the church of Scythopolis. His Acts are typical in their outlines. He was first brought to be interrogated before the tribunal of the governor. Refusing to sacrifice to the gods or offer libations to the four emperors, he was beheaded.[23]

The most renowned martyr of Caesarea was Pamphilus, a priest and admired teacher of the local church, head of the Christian academy founded by Origen, and friend of Eusebius, after whom he called himself Eusebius Pamphili. Pamphilus and his household and students were put to death in 309 CE, after a confinement of two years and many tortures of all sorts.[24]

---

[21] *MP* Syr. 18, ed. Cureton 1861: 17 (Epiphanius), Gr. 4.15, ed. Bardy 1967: 135–36 (Apphianus). The πρόπυλα in the long recension may suggest a more articulated and architecturally elaborate city gate, unless it refers to a square or a piazza in front of the gate. Eusebius emphasizes that he was an eyewitness to this prodigy. The burial of some other martyrs was forbidden by the order of Governor Urbanus, their corpses being left outside the city gates as prey for beasts and birds (*MP* Gr. 9.11, ed. Bardy 1967: 151, Syr.34, ed. Cureton 1861: 33: Ennathas/Mannathus and others). For refusal of burial by the Roman authorities cf. *HE* 5.1.59–62, ed. Oulton and Lawlor 1973: 435–37, pertaining to the devoured and charred corpses of the Martyrs of Lyons and Vienne.

[22] Eusebius, *Chronicon* (Migne, PG 27: 664) mentions a terrible earthquake which destroyed many buildings in Tyre and Sidon and crushed innumerable people. In a marginal note in Migne's edition the date 306 CE is given for this event. If correct, one would expect that the earthquake at Caesarea in that same year, recorded by him in *MP*, would also be mentioned. Russell 1985 suggested, on p. 42, that a date c. 303 may be more correct for the earthquake that had struck Tyre and Sidon. The earthquake at Caesarea in 306 is not mentioned neither by Russell, *ibid.*, nor in: Guidoboni, Comastri, and Traina 1994.

[23] *MP* Gr. 1.1–2; Syr. 3–5.

[24] *MP.* Gr. 11.1–3; Syr. 26–28, 38–42. The long recension of the martyrdom of Pamphilus, first published in *Analecta Bollandiana* 16 (1897): 129ff., is reproduced by

The right to inflict a death penalty—the *ius gladii*—belonged to the provincial governor.[25] The law court was a wing of the *praetorium* of the Roman governor at Caesarea. He presided over the court of justice in such affairs, and therefore the governor (*hegemon*) is regularly referred to as the judge (*dikastes*). The Christians were brought to his tribunal (*dikasterion*), where he interrogated them about their name, place of origin, family, and faith. But the governor held assizes in other cities, as in the case of the martyrs and confessors sentenced in Gaza, Lud/Lydda, and Ascalon.[26]

The degree of harshness with which the edicts were imposed on the Christians in each province depended greatly on the provincial governor. Three governors were in office in Caesarea during this period: Flaminius (303–4), Urbanus (304–7), and Firmilianus (308–9).[27] The governors had an escort of military bodyguards (περὶ τὸν ἡγεμόνα στρατιωτικὸν στῖφος)[28] while walking in the city. Soldiers were also on guard outside the law court, where the prisoners sat awaiting their trial.[29]

THE *PRAETORIUM* OF THE GOVERNOR

Herod's palace, constructed on a promontory to the south of the harbor, was enlarged and elaborated, becoming the *praetorium* of the

---

Bardy 1967: 153–56. Eusebius wrote an account of his life, now lost. See *HE* 6.32.3; 7.32.25; *MP, ibid.*

[25] Garnsey 1968: p. 51f. See also Schalit 1937: 91–93, 98–99.

[26] *MP* Gr. 3.1; Syr. 9–10 (Gaza); Syr. 29 (Lud/Lydda; it is said there that the Greek name of the city is Diocaesarea, instead of Diospolis; the Gr. recension omits any city name; only the territory of the Jews is indicated); Syr. 37–38 (Ascalon). The trials in Zauara/Zoora and Phaeno (Syr. 49–50) were by the *dux*. On assizes held by the governors while on an administrative itinerary in the province, see Burton 1975; Di Segni 1996. See also Ronchey 2000.

[27] Urbanus and Firmilianus, each in his turn, were finally put to death at the order of the emperors: *MP* Gr. 7.7, ed. Bardy 1967: 143–44 (Urbanus); 11.31, ed. Bardy 1967: 168 (Firmilianus).

[28] *MP* Gr. 4.8, ed. Bardy 1967: 132. See also 2.4, ed. Bardy 1967: 127; 4.10, ed. Bardy 1967: 133; 7.7, ed. Bardy 1967: 143. Being a military escort, it should be differentiated from the escort of civilian *lictores*, mentioned also in a contemporary rabbinic source (*TY* Megilla, III.2, 74a). The *lictores*, five in number, were the only civilian *apparitores* allocated during the Principate to a *legatus Augusti pro praetore*, see Rankov 1999: 17. Military bodyguards serving in the *officium* of a governor were the legionary *protectores* and the *singulares*, who were auxiliaries (Rankov 1999: 22). The escort under discussion seems to have been composed of such soldiers, presumably the legionary *protectores*.

[29] *MP* Gr. 7.2, ed. Bardy 1967: 141; 11.20, ed. Bardy 1967: 164.

Roman governors. According to the inscriptions, the *praetorium* was still in full activity under the tetrarchy.[30] It housed the hall of justice (*dikasterion*).[31]

The archaeological excavations carried out in Caesarea since the mid-1970s have brought to light the entire complex, including the law court (*dikasterion* of the *Acts of the Martyrs*), with a permanent elevated platform (*bema*) at its inner end.[32] A small altar (βωμός) with a sacrificial fire (ἡ πυρά) burning on it was also located inside.[33] A large prison can also be identified in this huge complex.[34]

The *praetorium* extended over two terraces with a difference of elevation of c. 3.6 m. The lower terrace served as the private wing. It occupied a natural promontory, extending 100 m into the Mediterranean. The upper terrace, on an upper part of the promontory, and of a slightly different orientation, served as the public wing. It was built around a vast courtyard surrounded by porticoes.[35] A raised square

---

[30] Burrell 1993.

[31] For *dikasterion*, see *MP* Gr. 1.1, ed. Bardy 1967: 122; 4.11, ed. Bardy 1967: 133; 7.1, ed. Bardy 1967: 140, including the long Gr. recension, here preserved. The Syriac (16, ed. Cureton 1861: 15) renders *byth dyna*, or *dyqstryn* (31, ed. Cureton 1861: 29).

[32] Roman legal institutions referred to in the *Martyrs of Palestine* (and the contemporary rabbinic literature) were discussed in great detail by Lieberman, and there is no need for a repetition here. See Lieberman 1944. The platform (*bema*) of the judge is mentioned in *MP* Gr. 7.7, ed. Bardy 1967: 143 (the judge hands down his verdict from the elevated platform—ἐφ᾽ ὑψηλοῦ βήματος δικάζοντα—surrounded by a guard of soldiers); 9.8, ed. Bardy 1967: 150. See also *HE* 8.9.5, ed. Oulton and Lawlor 1973: 276–77, refering to the persecutions in the Thebaid.
I am of the opinion that the law court of the *Acts of the Martyrs* is the same hall as the audience hall (τό ἀκροατήριον) of *Ac* 25:23, where the hearing of St. Paul before Festus took place. See Patrich 2000b, reprinted here as Chapter Ten. Archaeologically, only a single hall that could fulfill these functions was uncovered in the excavations of the *praetorium*.

[33] *MP* Gr. 8.7, ed. Bardy 1967: 146; Syr. 31, ed. Cureton 1861: 29.

[34] On this complex, excavated by several expeditions (Hebrew University of Jerusalem, University of Pennsylvania, and the Israel Antiquities Authority) see: Levine and Netzer 1986; Netzer 1999; Netzer 1996; Gleason 1996; Burrell 1996. See also: Burrell, Gleason, and Netzer 1993; Gleason *et al.*, 1998. During 1995–97, in the framework of the Israel Antiquities Authority excavations directed by Y. Porath, more parts of the N, S, and E wings of the *praetorium* were exposed. For a short preliminary note see: Rochman 1998; Porath 2000a: 36*. See also Patrich 2000a; 2001a: 90, and Chapter Eight above.

[35] The W half of the upper terrace was excavated by the University of Pennsylvania expedition, directed by Glieson and Burrell, while the E half, and areas farther to its E, belonging to the Roman *praetorium*, and the entire S wing, all yet unpublished, were excavated by the Israel Antiquities Authority expedition headed by Yosef Porath (*supra*, n. 34).

platform, for some monument, or for the emplacement of an outdoor *bema*, stood in its center.

The northern wing of the upper terrace held two suites separated from each other by a service corridor. The western suite (on the excavation area of the Pennsylvania expedition) faced south, while the eastern one (in the IAA excavation area) faced north. The western suite, of symmetrical layout, had in its center a basilical audience hall. This was the law court of the *praetorium*. The elevated northern part of the hall accommodated, so it seems, the dais, or the *bema*.[36] It had a heated floor set on stone *suspensurae/hypocaust*. Over this *bema* the Roman governor and his *concillium* of friends and relations held their assizes, including trials of martyrs.[37]

The entrance to Herod's palace was from the east, via a square propylon with four turrets set at its corners. Another, higher, tower rose above this propylon overlooking the hippodrome/stadium. Under Roman rule Herod's palace was extended farther to the east, adding about 50 m along the southern curved end of the hippodrome/stadium. Four Latin inscriptions found in this extension mention military personnel active in the governor's *officium*. They mention Assistants of the Office in charge of the Prisoners or the Prison (*adiutores custodiarum*), imperial couriers (*frumentarii*) (Fig. 108), *beneficiarii*—soldiers who received an administrative job from the governor (in this case Tineius Rufus, the governor of Judaea when the Bar Kokhba revolt broke out)—numbering as many as 120 in Judaea, and a Club Room of the Centurions (*schola centurionum*).[38]

There were also women martyrs: Thecla of Gaza, who was cast to the wild beasts; Theodosia of Tyre, who was thrown into the sea,[39] and similarly Valentina of Caesarea together with Hatha, another Gazaean.

---

[36] See plan and reconstruction in Gleason *et al.* 1998: 33, 45–48, figs. 4c and 7 and 13, and discussion in Burrell 1996: 229.

[37] The συμβούλιον, or *concillium*, is mentioned in *Ac* 25:12, pertaining to St. Paul's hearing before Festus in the *praetorium* of Caesarea. Eusebius regularly mentions the judge (*dikastes*) alone. In *MP* Gr. 10.2, ed. Bardy 1967: 152 mention is also made of "those around him" (τῶν ἀφ᾿ αὐτόν).

[38] Cotton and Eck 2001. For governor's *officiales* see: Rankov 1999; Palm 1999. For a *frumentarius* sent by Sabinus, the prefect of Egypt, to pursue bishop Dionysius in the streets of Alexandria in the persecution under Decius see *HE* VI.40.2–3, ed. Oulton and Lawlor 1973: 97. Also, a *frumentarius* escorted Cyprian, after his arrest, to face trial in Utica (Cyprian, *Epistle* 81.1, tr. G.W. Clarke, Vol. 3 [*Ancient Christian Writers* 47], New York: Newman Press, 1989).

[39] *MP* Gr. III.1, VI.3, Syr. 10–11 (Thecla); Gr. VII.1–2, Syr. 23–25 (Theodosia).

All were virgins. Valentina, protesting against the judge for the prolonged tortures inflicted against Hatha—being first scourged, then
raised on high on the rack, lacerated and galled in the sides—was
seized and driven to the midst of the place of judgment. They dragged
her to the altar and tried to force her to sacrifice, but she kicked the
altar and overturned the fire. The judge, infuriated, ordered the two
young women to be bound together and hurled into the sea.[40] An
altar for libation that stood in the law court was not discovered in
the excavations.

The Prison

The prison (τὸ δεσμωτήριον, ἡ εἱρκτή, *beth asyra*) is frequently mentioned. Pamphilus and his circle spent two years in the jail before
being executed.[41] A Latin mosaic inscription mentioning the prison
wardens was found in a room in the southern wing of the upper terrace. It reads: *Spes bona adiutorib(us) offici custodiar(um)*—"Good
hope to the Assistants of the Office in charge of Prisoners (or of the
Prison)."[42] Presumably, the prison was located nearby, but so far it has
not been identified archaeologically. However, an enormous underground water cistern, with two compartments, T-shaped in its ground
plan, constructed under the courtyard, was later converted into a vast
subterranean space and a narrow subterranean corridor led into it.
This gloomy space apparently served as a prison, as Greek Christian
inscriptions were smeared in mud on its walls, by a certain Procopia,
seeking help from the Lord (Κύριε βοήθι Προκοπία)—a most dramatic
find pertaining, perhaps, to another woman confessor.

The need to convert a water cistern into a jail might be reflected
in Eusebius' words that the number of prisoners increased tremendously during this period: "everywhere the prisons, that long ago
had been prepared for murderers and grave-robbers, were then filled
with bishops and presbyters and deacons, readers and exorcists, so

---

[40] *MP* Gr. VIII.5–8, Syr. 30–32 (Valentina and Hatha). See also Clark 1992; Hall
1993.

[41] *Desmoterion*: *MP* Gr. 3.4, ed. Bardy 1967: 127, Syr. 12, ed. Cureton 1861: 11; 4.10,
ed. Bardy 1967: 133; 7.4, ed. Bardy 1967: 142–43; 7.6, ed. Bardy 1967: 143; 11.7, ed.
Bardy 1967: 158. *Eirkte*: Gr. 4.10, ed. Bardy 1967: 133 (Apphianus, long recension);
11.5, ed. Bardy 1967: 157 (Pamphilus and his circle being detained for two years). Gr.
1.1, ed. Bardy 1967: 122: ἡ φυλακή.

[42] Cotton and Eck 2001: 230; Rochman 1998.

that there was no longer any room left there for those condemned for wrongdoing."⁴³ This might have been the dungeon into which Origen was cast, or the "deep dark prison" into which Apphianus was cast⁴⁴ (if this is not a literary expression, of course).

THE CITY STREETS

The confession and martyrdom of Ennathas in the streets of Caesarea, in the sixth year of the persecutions (Nov. 13, 308 CE) was extraordinary in its cruelty:⁴⁵ She had been brought by force from Scythopolis. Maxys, "who was set over the streets of the city,"⁴⁶ stripped her naked down to her groin and carried her about through the whole city, being tortured with leather straps, even without the approval of the superior authority. Then she was taken before the tribunal of the governor. After suffering tortures of every sort she was condemned to be burnt, together with other martyrs. Moreover, the governor Urbanus forbade their burial, ordering that their bodies be guarded day and night before the gates of the city, until they be completely devoured by wild beasts and consumed by birds. After this had gone on for many days, a prodigy occurred in the midst of the city:

> The atmosphere was perfectly calm and clear, when, all of a sudden, the columns supporting the public stoas of the city (τὴν πόλιν κιόνων οἱ τὰς δημοσίας ὑπήρειδον στοάς) emitted spots, as it were of blood, while the market places (ἀγοραί) and the colonnaded streets (πλατεῖαι) became sprinkled and wet as with water, although not a single drop had fallen from the heavens. And it was declared by the mouth of every one that the stones shed tears, and the ground wept.⁴⁷

---

⁴³ HE 8.6.9.

⁴⁴ For Origen's dungeon (μυχός εἰρκτή) see supra, n. 9. For Apphianus/Epiphanius see MP Gr. 4.10 (long recension, ed. Bardy 1967: 133: εἰς τὸν τῆς εἰρκτῆς σκοτεινὸν μυχὸν ἀνελαμβάνετο), Syr. 16, ed. Cureton 1861: 15.

⁴⁵ MP Gr. 9.6–8, Syr. 34 (Mannathus).

⁴⁶ Thus the Syr. 35, ed. Cureton 1861: 32, while the Gr. 9.7, ed. Bardy 1967: 150 refers to him as an army tribune (chiliarch) stationed in the vicinity of the city. The Syr. text, derived from the long Greek recension, written for the Christians of Caesarea, seems preferable in this case; but he might have been an officer in charge of internal security on the city streets, a post which would meet both designations. Cf. the fate of the martyrs of Lyons and Vienne under Marcus Aurelius, being dragged into the market-place by the tribune (chiliarch) and the chief authorities of the city, and at last being shut up in the prison until the coming of the governor (HE 5.1.7–8).

⁴⁷ MP Syr. 35, ed. Curton 1861: 33–34; Gr. 9.12, ed. Bardy 1967: 151. We may have here a literary topos, since a similar prodigy is given in the rabbinic sources: TB Moed Katan 25b: "When R. Abbahu died the pillars of Caesarea shed tears"; TY, Avodah

The Herodian, orthogonal city-plan was maintained throughout antiquity with only minor modifications. Colonnaded streets (*platea* and *stoai*) in Caesarea are also mentioned in other rabbinic sources.[48] The line of the *cardo maximus* seems to be preserved in the line of the Crusader eastern city wall; the *decumanus maximus* was seemingly parallel to the present asphalt road. Many of the street columns were incorporated in the Muslim and Crusader city wall and in the north quay of the Crusader harbor. Other public structures mentioned by Eusebius are the temples and the bathing places (τὰ λουτρά).[49]

TORTURES

Tortures inflicted in the prison, or publicly at or near the law court, by tormentors (βασανισταί, *qstwnra*)[50] on behalf of the judge/governor as a means of coercion to renounce the Christian faith, included hunger, hanging head down, flagellation, scourging and lacerations of the sides, and castration. The instruments of torture included iron combs and the rack. This was a frame on which a person was stretched by having the feet placed in holes set apart at intervals (the fifth hole being at the largest interval), or by wheels. Sharp reeds were also driven through

---

Zarah III.1, 42c, interpreted as an expression of mourning the death of R. Abbahu. See Lieberman 1939–44: 400–2, who comments that Eusebius' dating of the occurrence, between mid-November to mid-December 309, in the sixth year of the persecutions, establishes the *terminus ante quem* for R. Abbahu's death. The city market places (*agorai*) are also mentioned in *MP* Gr. 9.2, ed. Bardy 1967: 148; Syr. 34, ed. Curton 1861: 31 (*shwqa*).

[48] *TY Nazir* VII, 1, 56a; *Tosefta, Ahilot* XVIII, 13.

[49] *MP* Gr. 9.2, ed. Bardy 1967: 148 (baths; bath attendants are also mentioned); Gr. 4.8, ed. Bardy 1967: 131, Syr. 15, ed. Curton 1861: 14, and 34, ed. Curton 1861: 31 (temples). In autumn 308 Maximinus issued edicts ordering the reconstruction of all temples and the revival of cult therein, with specific instructions to the provincial governor and *dux* in each province, and to the city magistrates—the accountants (λογισταί), στρατηγοί (*duumviri* in case of a Roman colony) and *tabularii* (*MP* Gr. 9.2, ed. Bardy 1967: 148, Syr. 34, ed. Curton 1861: 31. On λογισταί or *curatores* appointed by the central government to control cities accounts, see Reynolds 1988: 41–42.

[50] *MP* Gr. 8.6, ed. Bardy 1967: 145, 11,16, ed. Bardy 1967: 162; Syr. 8, ed. Curton 1861: 7, line 27 (in Antioch), 47, ed. Curton 1861: 44, line 19 (Julianus); here the Gr. 9.26, ed. Bardy 1967: 167) has οἱ τῶν φονῶν διάκονοι. Syr. 31, ed. Curton 1861: 29, and 45, ed. Curton 1861: 42 (*hnwn dsrqyn*). *Quaestionarii*, from which the Syriac *qstwnra* is derived, who constituted an integral part of the governor's *officium*, serving as judicial interrogators (Rankov 1999: 23), are not mentioned in the corresponding passages in the Greek recension of *MP*.

the fingers, under the tips of the nails.[51] Torture by slow fire was the
fate of Apphianus (Syr. Epiphanius), after suffering various other tor-
ments: flagellation, scourges, and the rack. His feet were wrapped in
linen (Gr.; the Syr. renders cotton) dipped in oil, which was set alight
at the command of the governor. "The fire, after consuming his flesh,
penetrated to the bones, so that the humours of the body, liquefied
like wax, fell in drops."[52] Final execution was decapitation by sword,
burning, strangling, and casting into the sea.[53] Boats could sail out to
the deep sea directly from a short jetty projecting from the north wing
of the lower terrace of the *praetorium*, rather than from the harbor.
The site of execution and decapitation was open to the public, which
included Jews and Samaritans, not just pagans.[54]

When the death penalty was annulled for a while, "orders were given
that their eyes should be gouged out, and one of their legs maimed....
The right eye was first cut out with a sword and then cauterized with
fire, and the left foot rendered useless by the further application of
branding irons to the joints, and after this they were condemned to
the provincial copper mines (at Phaeno)."[55]

Some were condemned to be left as prey for the wild beasts—lions,
leopards, bears of different kinds, wild boars, and bulls goaded with
hot iron (see below), a common form of execution for criminals under
Roman law.[56] Youth of fine and bold stature were dispatched to the
ludus.

---

[51] *HE* 5.1.27, 8.7.1–8.1, 8.10.8, 8.12.6–7, ed. Oulton and Lawlor 1973: 419 (Vol. I),
271–75, 283, 291 (Vol. II) respectively; *MP* Gr. 7.4, ed. Bardy 1967: 142 (castration).

[52] *MP* Gr. 4.12, ed. Cruse 1851: 356, ed. Bardy 1967: 133–34; Syr. 16, ed. Cureton
1861: 15.

[53] Martyrs thrown into the sea were Apphianus/Epiphanius, Agapius ("of the stadium"), Theodosia of Tyre, Valentina, and Hatha.

[54] *MP* Gr. 8.11–12, ed. Bardy 1967: 147, Syr. 32, ed. Cureton 1861: 30.

[55] *HE* 8.12.10, ed. Oulton and Lawlor 1973: 293. On this penalty, see Millar 1984.

[56] Coleman 1990; Potter 1993; Veyne 1999. For condemnation to the wild beasts see
farther below and compare *HE* 5.1.37–57, ed. Oulton and Lawlor 1973: 425–35, pertaining to Maturus, Sanctus, Blandina, and Alexander the Phrygian, martyrs of Lyons
and Vienne in the amphitheater of Lyons under Marcus Aurelius in 177 CE; *ibid*,
8.12, ed. Oulton and Lawlor 1973: 167–69, concerning the martyrs of 258 in Caesarea
under Valentinian; *ibid*, 8.7.5–7, ed. Oulton and Lawlor 1973: 273—the martyrdom
of five Christians in Tyre during these great persecutions; and that of Perpetua and
Felicitas in Carthage in the persecution of 203 CE under Septimius Severus: *Passion
de Perpétue et de Félicité*, ed. Amat 1996; Shaw 1993.

THE *LUDUS*

In the fifth year of the persecution (307), three young Christians, Timotheus, Theophilus, and Theotimus,[57] were condemned by Urbanus to take part in pugilistic combat (Gr. εἰς μονομαχίαν ἐπὶ πυγμῇ καταδικάζει—to contest in gladiatorial fights; Syr. *lwdwn/ludus*).[58] The next year (308), under governor Firmilianus, they refused to be nourished from the imperial treasury (which attests that this was an imperial *ludus*, see below, not a municipal or private one), or to train and obey the *epitropoi* and *hegoumenoi*. They were summoned to Maximinus himself, but to no avail.[59] Back in the law court of the governor, his verdict was that the right eye and left leg of each of them be mutilated, and that they were to be sent to the mines.

The fact that the final sentence of the three martyrs was before Firmilianus, the provincial governor, indicates that the *ludus* under discussion, and the entire affair, were in Palestine. It is reasonable to assume that this *ludus* was located in Caesarea, no doubt in conjunction with the oval amphitheater.

The *ludus* was a school or caserne for training gladiators. In the Roman world there were three types of *ludus*, imperial, municipal, and private. The references by Eusebius to the imperial treasury and to Maximinus indicate that the *ludus* under discussion was an imperial one, being a component in the framework of the imperial *munera*, not

---

[57] Their names are given only in the Menologia; see Bardy 1967: 142, n. 7.

[58] *MP* Gr. 7.4 and 8.2–3, ed. Bardy 1967: 142, 145; Syr. 26 and 30, ed. Cureton 1861: 24 and 28. In the rabbinic sources there are references also to Jews, including the third-century sage Reish Lakish, who sold themselves to the *ludus* (*TY Gitt.* IV 46b and 47a; Ter. VIII 45d; *Pesikta de Rav Kahana* 12b). See also Brettler and Poliakoff 1990. It is reasonable to assume that this was the same *ludus* at Caesarea.

[59] The phrasing of Eusebius with reference to Maximinus seems to indicate that the latter was in Palestine at that time, though not in Caesarea. Otherwise, if the three had been summoned to him in another province, once outside the jurisdiction of the provincial governor of Palestine, they would have been sentenced abroad rather than being brought back to Palestine. Was Maximinus' stay a continuous one, since celebrating his birthday in Caesarea on Nov. 20, 306 (*MP* 6.1, ed. Bardy 1967: 138)? A *terminus ante quem* for their case being brought before Maximinus is July 15 or 25, 308—*MP* Gr. 8.5 and 12, ed. Bardy 1967: 145 and 147 respectively. Leah di Segni is of the opinion that some details in the martyrdom of the three martyrs under discussion, especially their summons to Maximinus, are void of any historicity, since the narrative is structured according to that of Daniel and his three companions, refusing to eat from the meat and wine allotted to them by Nebuchadnezzar (Dan. 1:5–16). Although I am not sure whether her conclusion in this case is correct, I am indebted to her for many other useful comments on the present Chapter.

a municipal establishment. Each imperial *ludus* was headed by a *procurator ludorum*, while this imperial system as a whole was directed (in the Early Empire) by the procurator of the *Ludus Magnus* in Rome.[60]

Bardy renders both *epitropoi* and *hegoumenoi* as governors, and similarly Cruse (p. 362).[61] But Robert, Ville (and earlier Valesius) are right in noting that the *epitropoi*, the equivalent of the Latin *procuratores*, were those in charge of the *ludus* and their assistants.[62] In Rome, the *Ludus Magnus*, and the *Ludus Matutinus*, or *Bestiarius* (for the practice of the *bestiarii*—the hunters in the *venationes*, held in the mornings), were each headed by a procurator. Outside Rome, a Latin inscription mentions *procur(ator) ludi famil(iae) glad(iatoriae) Caes(aris) Alexandriae ad Aegyptum*.[63] A *proc(urator) Aug(usti) familiae glad(iatoriae)* is mentioned in a Latin inscription from Pergamon.[64] Galen served as a physician at the Pergamon *ludus*. Elsewhere we hear of a *proc(urator) fam(iliarum) glad(iatoriarum)*, or *proc(urator) Aug(ustorum) ad famil(ias) gladiator(ias)* in charge of several provinces in Asia Minor.[65] An *epitropos* of a *ludus* is mentioned in two Greek inscriptions, one

---

[60] Robert 1940 (reprint Amsterdam 1971): 267–68; Pflaum 1950: 51; Ville 1981: 277–87, 295–306; Golvin 1988: 148–56. In the eastern provinces imperial *ludi* are known to have existed at Pergamon, Cyzicus, Ancyra, Thessalonike, and Alexandria. Robert, Pflaum, and Ville are aware of the reference to the *ludus* in the *MP* (but not in the rabbinic sources). See Robert 1960: *Hellenica* III, 120–21; Pflaum 1950: 76; Ville 1981: 287, n. 140.

[61] Eusebius refers regularly to the governor as *hegemon*—ἡγεμών (*MP* Gr. 7.2, ed. Bardy 1967: 141), but at times also as *hegoumenos* (*MP* Gr. 8.1, ed. Bardy 1967: 144). But the event under discussion took place after the abdication of Diocletian on May 1, 305, namely, in a post-reform period, when the province was already governed by a civil governor (*praeses/hegemon*), and a military governor (*dux*), and not in the pre-reform system of double regime of a governor and a financial procurator (Gr.—*epitropos*). This is another indication that Bardy's translation (if meaning provincial governors) is wrong (see below). Pflaum also interprets these *epitropoi* as the regional equestrian procurator and his "adjoint affrachi." See Ville 1981: 287, n. 140.

[62] For Robert, and Ville see *supra*, end of n. 60. These are Valesius' words: "He means, as I judge, the Procurators of the company of gladiators and of the morning exercises...for the gladiators...were committed to their care, and they gave them their allowances out of their treasury (*Ecclesiastical History*, Eng. tr., Cruse 1851: 163, note b, *apud* Cureton 1861: 66). According to Robert, these are "sans doute, le responsible provincial, ses adjoints et le directeur de *ludus*."

[63] CIL, X, 1685; Robert, *supra*, n. 60 (1971), inscr. 70, 124–25 (from Naples).

[64] Robert, *op. cit.*, inscr. 258, p. 215. In cities, like Aphrodisias, *familiae* (= troupes) of gladiators and wild beast fighters were maintained by the high priests of the imperial cult, in order to mount gladiatorial contests which were characteristic elements of the civic festivals of the cult. See Robert, *op. cit.*, 56–64; Roueché 1993: 61–80.

[65] CIL, III, 6753 (from Ancyra), 6994 (from Prousa). See Robert, *op. cit.*, 267, note 1.

from Ancyra, the other from Thessalonike.[66] The *procurator ludorum* (Latin), or *epitropos loudon* (Greek), and their staff were in charge of recruiting gladiators for the imperial *munera*, training and feeding them, providing for all their needs from the imperial treasury, and dispatching them to the imperial spectacles in Rome or elsewhere.[67]

The number of known structures throughout the Roman world that might be identified as *ludi* is relatively small compared with the number of amphitheaters (or amphitheatrical theaters).[68] Some were rectilinear, with a large courtyard that served as a training ground, surrounded by porticoes, dwelling rooms for the gladiators and their trainers, and offices. Any wealthy mansion with a fairly spacious inner courtyard could have served this purpose. In the more elaborate structures, like the *Ludus Magnus* and *Ludus Matutinus* in Rome, an oval or circular arena was inserted into the courtyard.

The location and shape of the *ludus* in Caesarea are not known, but these *Acts* of Eusebius indicate that gladiatorial combats (*munera*) were still a living practice in Caesarea in the early fourth century, and its *ludus* constituted an integral component of the infrastructure established for the imperial *munera*.

Several martyrs were condemned to be devoured by wild beasts: Auxentius, a venerable old man (5th year, 307),[69] and the last two martyrs of Caesarea, Adrianus and Eubulus. Each was thrown to a lion and then put to death by the sword. Their executions took place on March 5 and 7, 310 CE, during the feast of the local Tyche.[70] But the arena in which the events took place is not mentioned. Far more detailed is the case of Agapius (see below).

---

[66] Robert, *op. cit.*: 267–68, note 1. Pflaum (1950: 698–99) had suggested to read in a Greek honorary inscription from Prusias (*IGRom* III, no. 1420; *SEG* XXVIII, no. 1043) *procurator ludorum* (*epitropon epi loudon*) in the provinces of Phoenicia, Arabia, and Syria Palaestina. But I. Piso, *Chiron* 8 (1978), 517 is of the opinion that the reference might have been to the *procurator vicesimae hereditatium* (*epitropon eikostes kleronomon*), in charge of the 5 percent tax on inheritances for these provinces. I owe the references to this inscription to Dr. Leah Di Segni.

[67] Papyrus Leipzig, 57 mentions the provision of clothing for the gladiators (Robert, *op. cit.*, 125).

[68] Golvin 1988: 148–56; Golvin and Landes 1990: 156–59. They are not aware to the existence of an imperial *ludus* in Palestine, located, most probably, in Caesarea.

[69] *MP* Gr. 7.4, ed. Bardy 1967: 142; Syr. 26, ed. Cureton 1861: 24. The name of the old man is given only in the Gr. recension; Eusebius does not give the date in the year. The name is not mentioned in the *menologia*.

[70] *MP* Gr. 11.30, ed. Bardy 1967: 168; Syr. 48, ed. Cureton 1861: 45. The wild beasts, namely lions, and the local feast of Tyche are mentioned only in the Gr. recension.

The reference to the feast of the local Tyche is of interest. Tyche is depicted on many of the city coins as an Amazon-like figure holding a spear or a standard in her left hand, and the emperor's bust in the right.[71] Similarly she is depicted in a marble statue, where her right leg is set on the prow of a ship and near her right leg a smaller half figure, depicting a sea creature holding a harness, is shown.[72] She is shown in this posture also on a bronze cup with silver and enamel decorations, now at the Louvre, in a scene of sacrifice before her, accompanied by the Latin inscription *genio colonia(e)*. Three other scenes on the cup portray the mythical foundation of Straton's Tower—the Hellenistic city that preceded Caesarea.[73] This depiction of Tyche indicates her close association with the foundation of the colony. The commemoration of this event might have been the actual celebration in the feast mentioned by Eusebius. If so, a date c. March 5–7 would be the date of the refoundation of Caesarea as a Roman colony by Vespasian in about 70 CE.[74] This date has remained unnoticed so far.

It would be reasonable to assume that the feast of the local Tyche was celebrated in Caesarea annually. Did this feast regularly include fatal spectacles in the arena? One would assume that gladiatorial combats (*munera*) and hunting spectacles (*venationes*), including execution of criminals (see below), were indeed an integral part of this yearly feast, although it is only for the year 310 that we are told that Christians underwent martyrdom in the arena on that occasion. The *dies imperii*, celebrated annually on Nov. 20 (see below), was another occasion when such spectacles took place.

---

[71] Kadman 1957.

[72] Gerst 1984; Wenning 1986; Holum *et al.*, 1988: 10–16, and Ann Guida's description of item 1 (Tyche statue), in the Catalogue of the Exhibition appended (without page numbering) at the end of this book.

[73] Will 1983. The inscription *agones ieroi* in Latin characters on the rim of the cup above the Tyche scene indicates that her feast included games, as is also indicated by Eusebius. These games must have been different than the "Isactian Games" established by Herod (see next note).

[74] The inauguration of the Herodian city was in September—a different date, with a festival in honor of Augustus, after whom the city and its harbor were named. The games, established as "Isactian Games" celebrated every four years, were related to the victory of Augustus in the battle of Actium. For the date, see Schwartz 1992: 167–81. On the association of the feast under discussion with the proclamation of Caesarea as a Roman colony by Vespasian, see Chapter Three above.

Agapius in the Stadium

Agapius[75] and Thecla, citizens of Gaza, were condemned there by governor Urbanus in the second year of the persecution (304) to be devoured by wild beasts. They were dispatched to Caesarea and imprisoned there, waiting for their future execution. On the occasion of a pagan public feast celebrated in all the cities,[76] there were horse races in the circus, a show was performed in the theater, and it was also customary to give a barbarous spectacle in the stadium (Syriac recension). According to the Greek recension, governor Urbanus staged a hunting spectacle (κυνηγέσιον).[77] The rumor was that Agapius and Thecla, together with a group of Phrygians, where to be sent to the combat so that they might be devoured by the wild beasts, as a gift of governor Urbanus to the spectators. Six young Christians had voluntarily addressed the governor on his way to the theater, asking to be thrown to the wild beasts in the theater[78] together with Agapius and the others. They were put in prison for many days, until being beheaded on March 24, 305.[79]

Kynegion is known in the rabbinic sources as the place for hunting performances (*venationes*).[80] This was the name of the great amphitheater of Byzantium/Constantinople, erected by Septimius Severus.

---

[75] The Agapius under discussion should not be confused with another Agapius, a Gazaean as well, brother of one of the six youngsters who was beheaded with them in the second year of the persecutions (see below).

[76] *MP* Gr. 3.2, ed. Bardy 1967: 126; Syr. 11, ed. 1861: 10. The feast seems to be the *dies imperii* of year 304, celebrated on Nov. 20. See also *HE* 8.13.9, ed. Oulton and Lawlor 1973: 298–99. The *Vicennalia* of Diocletian's reign was celebrated already on Nov. 20, 303, marking the beginning of the twentieth regnal year, rather than its end. It is mentioned in a Latin inscription from the *limes* fortress of Yotvata in southern Palestine. See Roll 1989 (I owe this reference to Dr. Leah Di Segni). Agapius was martyred only on Nov. 20, 306 (see below), without Thecla. Her feast is on August 19, as is that of Timotheus, a martyr of Gaza. See Bardy 1967: 126, n.6.

[77] *MP* Gr. 3.3, ed. Bardy 1967: 127; Syr. 11, ed. Cureton 1861: 10. The term κυνηγέσιον may cover every kind of show involving wild animals: combats of animals with one another, armed men (*venatores*) fighting and killing animals, men performing feints and tricks with the animals, and animals attacking and killing convicts. See Roueché 1993: 64. From the context it is clear that the last category was included in the show under discussion.

[78] The text says that the show of persecution was to be staged in the theater, but it is clear from the context that the arena of the κυνηγέσιον—presumably the amphitheater—is meant, since the theater of Caesarea was never equipped with installations required to hold *munera* or *venationes*. See Golvin 1988: 246–47.

[79] *MP* Gr. 3.1–3, ed. Bardy 1967: 126–27; Syr. 11, ed. Cureton 1861: 10–11.

[80] See, for example, *TB Abodah Zarah* 18b; *Yalkut Shimoni, Psalms*, 613, and Jastrow 1971: 1392.

Such might have been also the name of the Roman amphitheatre of Caesarea, though there is no explicit indication of this. It is logical to assume that the hunting spectacle given by Urbanus in 304, in which Agapius, in the end, did not take part, was staged in the oval amphitheater of Caesarea,[81] the usual arena for such a show.

The martyrdom of Agapius finally occurred only in the fourth year of the persecution, on the occasion of Maximinus' birthday (Nov. 20, 306), celebrated by him personally in Caesarea.[82] The event took place in the stadium of Caesarea,[83] not in the amphitheatere! Was the amphitheatere one of the structures damaged seven months earlier, during the earthquake of April 2, 306, its vaults having disintegrated? Only when this monument will be entirely excavated and published, might we be able to answer this question definitively.

On the occasion of the feast, celebrated in Maximinus' presence, the people expected, according to Eusebius, that some extraordinary spectacle be given, namely that a Christian be cast into the theater[84] to be devoured by the wild beasts. It had long been the practice that on the arrival of the emperor new and foreign presentations should be given, such as recitations, remarkable shows of acrobatics, singing and music, display of exotic beasts from India, Ethiopia, and other places, performances with wild beasts, and gladiatorial shows.[85]

---

[81] Reifenberg 1950; Roller 1982a. In a survey and in a sounding of a limited scale excavated by Negev, few architectural fragments were found. See Negev 1966b: 144. The estimated size of the arena is: 62 x 95 m. Recently large scale excavations took place at the site on behalf of IAA. These are yet unpublished.

[82] The exact date of Maximinus' birthday is not known from any other source. It could have been c. Nov. 20, the *dies imperii*, rather than exactly on this date. See Kazhdan and Talbot 1991: 1322, although it cannot be excluded that Eusebius had misunderstood when saying that Maximinus' birthday, rather than a *dies imperii*, was the reason for the feast. In any case, the presence of the Caesar augmented the scale and splendor of the celebration, as is clear from Eusebius' narrative.

[83] Similarly Polycarp was threatened by a Pagan and Jewish mob to be cast to a lion in the stadium of Smyrna, escaping this fate only because the kynegesaic show was already concluded—*HE* 4.15.16 and 25, ed. Oulton and Lawlor 1973: 346–47 and 350–51. He was martyred c. 155. The stadium of Smyrna disappeared. It is conjectured to have been located in its western part. See Akurgal 1978: 122; Golvin 1988: 263.

[84] Sic. But the arena of his martyrdom was actually the stadium. See also n. 78 above.

[85] *MP* Gr. 6.1–2, ed. Bardy 1967: 138; Syr. 21, ed. Cureton 1861: 19. According to the Gr. (6.3, ed. Bardy 1967: 139) Agapius was already led to the beasts in the second year, together with Thecla, and to the stadium, with criminals, on more than three other occasions, but each time he was sent back to the prison, after various threats from the judge, being reserved for later combats. It is clear that the stadium was a regular place of execution for criminals.

Roman spectacles were generally comprised of hunting shows (*venationes*) in the morning, gladiatorial combats (*munera gladiatorum*) in the afternoon, and various other amusements, including the execution of criminals, in between. Hence their name—*meridiani*. The executions constituted a component separate from the hunting shows in the day-long program.[86]

Agapius was dragged round about in the midst of the stadium (*astdyn*), and a placard with his accusation—his being a Christian—was carried before him. A slave who had killed his master, who was also to be executed in a similar manner in the stadium, won clemency from the emperor, to the applause of the entire audience, but not the martyr. While being led round about in the stadium Agapius was asked to renounce his faith, but he replied boldly and loudly, standing in the center of the stadium, that he adhered firmly to his beliefs. Maximinus, enraged, gave orders for the wild beasts to be released. A fierce she-bear rushed upon him and tore him with her teeth. Still alive he was led back to prison for another day; then stones were tied about him, and he was thrown into the sea.[87] Silvanus, a veteran soldier, priest, and later bishop of the Church of Gaza, also underwent his first confession in the stadium of Caesarea, before being sent to the copper mines (8th year—310 CE).[88]

In the period under discussion Caesarea had four entertainment facilities: the theater, Herod's U-shaped "amphitheater" nearby on the seashore, the Roman circus on the eastern fringes of the city, and the oval amphitheater to its north. Which of these was the stadium mentioned in the Acts of Agapius and Silvanus? Without doubt, it was a landmark on the urban landscape, known to all. The theater and the circus might be excluded, since they are mentioned by Eusebius as the venues of other shows. The U-shaped amphitheater of Herod and the oval structure are left.

As mentioned, the oval amphitheater has not yet been properly explored. It is reasonable to assume that it was constructed in the second or third century.[89] On the other hand, Herod's "amphitheatre"

---

[86] Golvin and Landes 1990: 189–92.
[87] *MP* Gr. 6.1–7, ed. Bardy 1967: 138–40; Syr. 21–23, ed. Cureton 1861: 19–21. For a placard with the accusation being carried before the martyr in the arena, see *HE* 5.1.44, ed. Oulton and Lawlor 1973: 427, pertaining to Attalus in the amphitheater of Lyons.
[88] *MP* Syr. 51, ed. Cureton 1861: 47 (*astdyn*).
[89] Reifenberg 1950; 1951.

(*Ant.* 15.341; *War* 1.415) is quite well known, having been uncovered on the seashore during the 1992–98 excavations (mostly by the IAA expedition headed by Yosef Porath).[90] Attached to the palace of Herod, which became the *praetorium* of the Roman governors, it was a U-shaped structure, comprising an arena surrounded by seats on the east, south, and west. The estimated capacity was 10,000 spectators. A southern gate under the *sphendone* gave direct access from the *praetorium* to the arena. In its final phase, perhaps in the mid-third century, the arena was truncated, and the southern third of the structure was converted into a small amphitheater. On that occasion the *loggia* or *pulvinar*, occupied by the dignitaries, was removed from its original location facing the center of the arena, and placed in the new center of the *cavea*. The *sacellum*, the tiny shrine of this arena, was underneath. Frescoes on the podium wall, depicting hunting scenes, are attributed by Porath to this phase. Identifiable here are the deer, fox, wild boar, tiger, and a right leg of a hunter.[91] A subterranean system of tunnels was also installed in the reduced amphitheater.[92]

In that early period the term amphitheater as used by Josephus indicated a multifunctional arena surrounded by seats for spectacles. There are other instances in which Josephus confused the terms amphitheater and hippodrome. It had not yet assumed the definitive meaning it acquired in the later empire, as an arena intended just for Roman spectacles.[93] In the days of Pontius Pilate it was known as the "Great Stadium" of the city.[94] I maintain that from those early times it was a familiar landmark in the urban landscape, known by this name—the city stadium—to all inhabitants. These included Eusebius and his fellow Christians, the addressees of his long recension of *The Martyrs of Palestine*.

Since its inauguration, the performances staged therein, being a part of the emperor's cult, included gymnastic contests, horse and chariot

---

[90] Porath 1994; 1995a; 1998: 40–41; 1996b: 93–99; Patrich 2001b. See also Chapter Seven above.

[91] Porath 2000b. The suggested dark-skinned elephant is actually a boar with a typical twisted tail.

[92] The tunnel was never a part of a *spina*, as was suggested by Porath. See Patrich 2001b; 2003b.

[93] On the ambiguity in applying technical terms to spectacle structures that existed in the Late Hellenistic/Late Republican and Early Imperial periods, see Jeremias 1931; Humphrey 1996; and Porath1995a: 23–27.

[94] *War* 2.9, 3 (172); in *Ant.* 18.3, 1 (57), simply a stadium is mentioned. The context suggests that the event took place near the Roman *praetorium* at the site of Herod's palace, namely in the Herodian entertainment structure under discussion.

races, and Roman spectacles—namely *munera* and *venationes*. These
shows, celebrated every four years, were known as "Isactian Games,"
following their institution by Herod in 10 BCE. A Greek inscription
from Laodicea dated to 221 CE indicates that these games continued
to be celebrated in Caesarea at least until that time. These contests
presumably continued to be held in that same arena due to their association with the emperor's cult.[95]

A stadium is mentioned in many Greek epigrams from the eastern
provinces as the arena of gladiatorial combats. Robert recognized that
this was a result of the metric difficulty of inserting *amphitheatron*
in pentametric or hexametric verses, yet he noted that this fact alone
does not prove that the combats actually took place in a stadium.[96] On
the other hand, Golvin indicated the paucity of oval amphitheaters
in the eastern provinces,[97] where *munera* and *venationes* were staged
mainly in elongated stadiums[98] with one or two *sphendone* at the short
ends, or in mixed edifices.[99] These were former theaters converted into
amphitheaters by raising the stage and erecting a podium wall under
the *cavea* delineating the orchestra, or by the construction of a low
barrier wall with poles for a protective net around the orchestra. Stadiums were used in the East also as arenas for chariot races.[100]

Porath dated the truncation of the arena to the second century, and
related it to the construction of the eastern circus at that time.[101] But
my excavation indicated that the arena was still functioning at its full

---

[95] Patrich 2002d.

[96] Robert 1940: 21, 35.

[97] They are somewhat more numerous in the provinces of Syria and Palestine, yet
with comparison to the western part of the empire the numbers are very small. Oval
amphitheaters existed only at Pergamon and Cyzicus in Asia Minor. In Syria and
Palestine such structures were erected in Antioch, Caesarea, and Bostra, all provincial
capitals. The case of Eleutheropolis is exceptional. A small amphitheater was constructed in Dura Europos, an important Roman garrison. Those of Scythopolis and
Neapolis were truncated hippodromes. No remains of the amphitheater erected by
Herod Agrippa in Berytus (*Ant.* 19.7.5, [335–37]) were found. This might have been
a wooden structure, as was common at that early period in Rome. See Patrich 2002e.

[98] Humphrey 1988: 1153–65; Aupert 1994; Welch 1998a; 1998b. The reality of
hunting scenes staged in a stadium is also familiar in the rabbinic sources. See *M
Baba Qamma* 4, 4; cf. *M 'Abodah Zarah* 1, 7.

[99] These were "édifices mixtes," "théâtres transformés," according to Golvin 1988:
237–49, 317; Golvin and Landes 1990: 8–10, 204–6; Welch 1999.

[100] Humphrey 1986: 438ff; 1988.

[101] Porath 1995a: 23; *idem* 1996b: 99.

length in the early third century, when according to Porath the short-ened complex was already out of use.[102]

Moreover, there are good grounds to believe that the old stadium of Caesarea was the arena of the Acts of Agapius and Silvanus, since its *sacellum* was converted into a martyrs' chapel; this would have been possible only following the persecutions.[103] Three foundation stones for altar legs were found *in situ*, a common find in chapels and churches. At least some of the niches carved in the rock wall are apparently from this phase. In any event, the large niche in the middle room, the aedicule of the pagan *sacellum*, certainly functioned in this phase as an apsidal niche, and the elongated niches in the side room to the north seem to be *loculi* for the emplacement of martyrs' remains, as was the case in the Christian catacombs in Rome.[104]

There is no reason at all to assume that the oval amphitheater, con-structed solely for Roman spectacles, was also known locally as the city stadium, when an earlier structure in the city, Herod's "amphitheatre," still functioning simultaneously with it,[105] was already known by this name.

Thus we may conclude that Eusebius' stadium is the same structure mentioned by Josephus by that name. This was the arena of the Acts of Agapius, and the *pulvinar* exposed above the *sacellum* was the *loggia* where Caesar Maximinus and Governor Urbanus sat watching Aga-pius' martyrdom in the arena.

The stadium, together with the adjacent *praetorium* with its prison and law court, constitute the venue where many of the Acts of the Martyrs of Caesarea took place.[106]

---

[102] For a presentation of the archaeological data, see Patrich, *supra*, n. 92. Porath seems, therefore, to be mistaken in the chronology he gave in his preliminary reports. We'll have to wait for the final report to be able to evaluate his claim on the basis of the archaeological small finds and stratigraphy, which have not been presented so far.

[103] Also the *sacellum* in the amphitheater of Salonae was converted into a Christian chapel in the fourth century. See Dyggve 1933: 102–7.

[104] See, for example, Fiocchi-Nicolai *et al.* 1999; Rutgers 2000.

[105] If the Roman oval amphitheater was constructed already in the second century, as is assumed, Porath also would agree that at least during that century both structures had functioned simultaneously.

[106] Thanks are due to Prof. I.L. Levine of the Hebrew University of Jerusalem for his useful comments on the original article.

BIBLIOGRAPHY

PRIMARY SOURCES

Abu al-Fath al-Samiri al-Danafi, *Continuatio—The Continuatio of the Samaritan Chronicle of Abu al-Fath al-Samiri al-Danafi*, text translation with annotations by Milka Levy-Rubin, Princeton, N.J: Darwin Press 2002.

Anastasius Persae—Acta martyris Anastasii Persae, ed. H. Usener. Bonn 1894; B. Flusin, ed. *Saint Anastase le Perse et l'histoire de la Palestine au début du VIIe siècle*. 1: Textes; 2: Commentaire: les moines de Jérusalem et l'invasion perse. Paris: Éditions du Centre national de la recherche scientifique 1992.

Antoninus of Placentia, *Itinerarium*, ed. P. Geyer, in *Itineraria et alia geographica*, CCSL 175. Turnhout 1965:127–153.

Avot de Rabbi Nathan, edited Schechter. Vienna 1887.

Babylonian Talmud: Translated Into English with Notes, Glossary and Indices (35 vols.). 1935–1952, ed. I. Epstein. London.

al-Baladhuri, *Futuh al-buldan—The Origins of the Islamic State*, ed. K. Hitti. New York 1916.

Chronicon Paschale, ed. Migne, *PG* 92: 69–1028.

Cod. Just.

Doctrina Jacobi, ed. N. Bonwetsch, Berlin 1910.

Evagrius, *Historia Ecclesiasticae*, ed. J. Bidez and L. Parmentier. London 1898 (Amsterdam 1964).

Expositio totius mundi et gentium, ed. J. Rougé, Paris 1966.

Jerome, *In Hiezech*. Hieronymus, *Commentarium in Hiezecheilem libri XIV*, ed. F. Glorie. CCSL 75, Turnhout 1964.

——, *Epistulae*, ed. J. Labourt, *Letters*. Paris 1949–1955; ed. I. Hildberg, CSEL 56, Vienna 1918; PL 22: 825–1224.

Jerusalem Talmud, First Order: Zeraim, tr. H. W. Guggenheimer, Berlin and New York 2003.

John of Nikiu, *Chronicle—The Chronicle of John, Bishop of Nikiu*, trans. from Zotenberg's Ethiopic text by R.H. Charles. London and Oxford 1916.

Josephus, Flavius, *War*, tr. H.S.J. Thackeray, *LCL* 203. London 1927.

——, *Antiquities XV*. LCL 489. London 1963.

——, *Antiquities XVI*. LCL 410. London 1963.

——, *Antiquities XVIII*. LCL 433. London 1965.

Kyrillos von Scythopolis, ed. Ed. Schwartz, Leipzig 1949 [Texte und Untersuchungen Vol. 49 ii].

Lamentations Rabba, ed. S. Buber. Vilna 1897.

Malalas, *Chronographia*, ed. L. Dindorf, Bonn 1831; ed. I. Thurn, Berlin 2000.

Marc le Diacre, *Vita Porphyrii*, ed. H. Gregoire and M.A. Kugener, Paris 1930.

Midrash Mishle, ed. S. Buber. Vilna 1893; *A critical edition based on manuscripts and early editions with an introduction and annotated*. English translation of chapters One through Ten, edited by B.L. Visotzky. The Jewish Theological Seminary of America 1990.

Midrash Shoher Tov to Psalms, ed. S. Buber. Vilna 1891.

Mishnah, ed. H. Albeck and H. Yalon. Jerusalem and Tel Aviv 1952–1958 (Hebrew); Eng. tr. H. Danby, *The Mishnah*, Oxford 1933; *Mishnah. A New Translation*. J. Neusner, New Haven and London 1988.

Mishnah, Tractate Oholot, ed. A. Goldberg, Jerusalem 1955.

Philo, *Legatio ad Gaium*. Philo of Alexandria, *The Embassy to Gaius*, with an English translation by F.H. Colson and G.H. Whitaker. London: LCL, X: 2–187; edited with an introduction, translation and commentary by E. Mary Smallwood, 2nd ed., Leiden: E.J. Brill, 1970.

Pirkei Hekhalot Rabbati, ed. S.A. Wertheimer, *Batei Midrashot* I. Jerusalem 1950.

Pliny, *Historia Naturalis*. ed. H. Rackham. LCL, Oxford: W. Heinemann, 1949–1963.

Procopius, *Anecdota*. Procopius of Caesarea, *The Anecdota, or Secret history*, ed. H.B. Dewing, LCL, London: W. Heinemann 1954.

Procopius of Gaza, *Panagyr. Anast. PG* 87.

Prudentius, *Contra Symmachum*.

Synopse zur Hekhalot Literature, ed. P. Schäfer, Tübingen 1981.

Talmud Babli (= TB), Babylonian Talmud. Printed edition. Vilna 1880–1886.

Talmud of the Land of Israel, A Preliminary Translation and Explanation, Vol. 5: *Shebi'it*, tr. A. J. Avery-Peck, Chicago and London 1991.

——, *A Preliminary Translation and Explanation*, Vol. 9: *Hallah*, tr. J. Neusner. Chicago and London 1991.

——, *A Preliminary Translation and Explanation*, Vol. 3: *Demai*, tr. R.S. Sarason, Chicago and London 1993.

——, *A Preliminary Translation and Explanation*, Vol. 13: *Pesahim*, tr. B.M. Bokser and L.H. Shiffman, Chicago and London 1994.

Talmud Yerushalmi (= TY). *Printed edition*, Venice 1523–24, reprt. 1925; ed. Y. Sussman, Jerusalem 2001; English: *The Talmud of the Land of Israel: a preliminary translation and explanation*, tr. by Jacob Neusner. Chicago: University of Chicago Press, 1982–1994.

Theodoros Anagnostes, *Historia Ecclesiastica*. Theodore Lector, *Kirchengeschichte*, ed. G.C. Hansen. Berlin: Akademie Verlag, c. 1995. [GCS, Neue Folge, Bd. 3].

Theophanes, *Chronographia*, ed. D. Boor, Leipzig 1883.

Theophanes Confessor, *Chronicle,—The Chronicle of Theophanes Confessor. Byzantine and Near East history, A.D. 284–813*, trans. with introduction and commentary by C. Mango and R. Scott, with the assistance of G. Greatrex, Oxford: Clarendon Press, New York: Oxford University Press 1997.

Tosefeth Rishonim, ed. S. Lieberman, Vol. II. Jerusalem 1939.

Tosefta Kifshuta, Zeraim B: Shebiit, ed. S. Lieberman, New York 1956.

Tosefta, Eng. translated from the Hebrew. Sixth Division: Tohorot (Order of Purities), ed. J. Neusner, New York 1977.

——, Eng. translated from the Hebrew. Second Division: Mo'ed (The Order of Appointed Times), ed. J. Neusner, New York 1981.

Tosefta with Hasdei David commentary, VIII: Purities A (first pr. 1970). Commentary by R. Isaac Pardo (1718–1790). Jerusalem 1994.

Tosephta based on the Erfurt and Vienna codices with parallels and variants, ed. M.S. Zuckermandel 1881; New edition with *Supplement to the Tosephta* by S. Liebermann, Jerusalem 1970.

Tractate 'Mourning' (Semahot), ed. A. Heiger, New York 1931; *Tractate 'Mourning' (Semahot)* [regulations relating to death, burial, and mourning], transl. from the Hebrew, with introduction and notes by D. Zlotnick, New Haven and London 1966.

Vitruvius, *De Architectura*, ed. F. Granger, Cambridge MS: LCL 1970.

Yerushalmi Kifshuto, ed. S. Lieberman, 2nd ed. Vol. I.1. New York and Jerusalem 1995.

Zacharia Rhetor, Ps. *Historia Ecclesiastica, PG* 85: 1011–1114; Eng. tr. F.J. Hamilton and E.W. Brooks, *The Syriac chronicle known as that of Zachariah of Mytilene*. London: Methuen & Co. 1899.

STUDIES

Abbott, Frank F. and Johnson, Allan C. (1926), *Municipal Administration in the Roman Empire* (Princeton: Princeton University Press).

Abel, Félix-Marie (1923), 'La list géographique du papyrus 71 de Zénon', *RB* 32:409–15.

—— (1952), *Histoire de la Palestine depuis la conquête d'Alexandre jusqu' à l'invasion arabe, 2 Vols.* (Paris: J. Gabalda).

Abel, Félix-Marie and Barrois, Augustin Georges (1931), 'Fragment de Césarée la metropole', *RB* 40: 294–95.

'Ad, Uzi (2005), 'Water-mills with Pompeian-type millstones at Nahal Tanninim', *IEJ* 55: 156–71.

Akurgal, Ekrem (1978), *Ancient Civilizations and Ruins of Turkey* (Istanbul: Haset Kitabevi).

Albricci, Anna (1962), 'L'orchestra dipinta del teatro Erodiano di Caesarea Maritima', *Bollettino di Arte* 4: 289–304.

—— (1965), 'L'orchestra dipinta del teatro Erodiano di Caesarea Maritima', in A. Frova *et al.* (ed.), *Scavi di Caesarea Maritima* (Milan): 93–120.

Alchermes, Joseph (1994), 'Spolia in Roman Cities of the Late Empire: Legistlative Rationales and Architectural Reuse', *DOP* 48: 167–78.

Alföldi, Andreas (1937), *A Festival of Isis in Rome under the Christian Emperors of the Fourth Century* (Budapest: Institute of Numismatics and Archaeology of the Pázmány University).

Alföldi, Geza (1999), 'Pontius Pilatus und das *Tiberieum* von Caesarea Maritima', *SCI* 18: 85–108.

—— (2002), ' Nochmals: Pontius Pilatus und das *Tiberieum* von Caesarea Maritima', *SCI* 21: 133–48.

Alicu, Dorin and Paki, Adela (1995), *Town Planning and Population in Ulpia Triana Sarmizegetusa* (BAR Int. Ser. 605; Oxford).

Alon, Gedaliahu (1957), *Studies in the History of the Jewish People (Hebrew)* (I; Tel Aviv: Hakibbutz Hameuchad).

—— (1957), *Studies in the History of the Jewish People, 2 vols. (Hebrew)* (Tel Aviv: Hakibbutz Hameuchad).

—— (1971), *History of the Jews in Eretz Israel in the period of Mishnah and Talmud (Hebrew)* (II; Tel Aviv: Hakibbutz Hameuchad).

Amit, David, Seligman, John, and Zilberbod, Irena (2000), 'The Monastery of Theodoros and Kyriakos on the eastern Slope of Mount Scopus (Hebrew, with an English summery in pp. 11*–12*)', in Avraham Faust and Eyal Baruch (eds.), *NSJ* (6; Ramat Gan): 166–74.

Amit, David, Patrich, Joseph, and Hirschfeld, Yizhar (eds.) (2002), *The Aqueducts of Israel* (JRA Suppl. 46, Portsmouth, RI: Journal of Roman Archaeology).

Amit, Moshe (2002), *History of the Roman Empire (Hebrew).* (Jerusalem: Magnes Press).

Appelbaum, Shimon (1977a), 'The Burial Place of Rabbi Aqiva (Hebrew)', *The 7th World Congress of Jewish Studies, Jerusalem* (Jerusalem): 46.

—— (1977b), 'Judaea as a Roman Province: the Countryside as a Political and Economic Factor', *ANRW* (2, 8): 355–96.

Arav, Rami (1989), 'Some Notes on the Foundation of Straton's Tower', *PEQ* 121: 144–48.

Arnon, Yael (2004), 'Early Islamic Period Caesarea (640–1110 C.E.) (Hebrew)', *Qadmoniot* 37: 23–33.

Attwater, Donald (1965, reprt. 1974), *The Penguin Dictionary of Saints* (Ayllesbury: Penguin Books).

Aupert, Paul (1994), 'Evolution et avatars d'une forme architecturale', in Christian Landes *et al.* (eds.), *Catalogue de l'exposition: Le stade romain et ses spectacles* (Lattes, Cedex): 95–105.

Aviam, Mordechai (1999), 'Christian Galilee in the Byzantine Period', in Eric Meyers (ed.), *Galilee Through the Centuries, Confluence and Cultures* (Winona Lake, Indiana: Eisenbrauns): 281–300.

Avi-Yonah, Michael (1952), 'Mount Carmel and the God of Baalbek', *IEJ* 2: 118–24.

—— (1956), '"Caesarea", Notes and News', *IEJ* 6: 260–61.

—— (1957), 'Césarée. Chronique archeologique', *RB* 64: 243–46.

—— (1960), 'The Synagogue of Caesarea-Preliminary Report', *Louis Rabinowitz Bulletin for the Exploration of Ancient Synagogues* (II; Jerusalem): 44–48.

—— (1962), *Geographical History of the Land of Israel (Hebrew)* (Jerusalem: Bialik Institute).

—— (1964), 'Survey of Population Density, and Settlements Quantity in Ancient Eretz Israel (Hebrew)', *Essays and Studies in the Lore of the Holy Land* (Tel Aviv: M. Newman): 114–24.

—— (1970), 'The Caesarea Porphyry Statue', *IEJ* 20: 203–08.

—— (ed.), (1975), *Encyclopedia of Archaeological Excavations in the Holy Land* (Jerusalem: Israel Exploration Society).

—— (1976), *Gazetteer of Roman Palestine* (Qedem. Monographs of the Institute of Archaeology; Jerusalem: The Institute of Archaeology of the Hebrew University and Carta).

Avi-Yonah, Michael and Negev, Avraham (1963), 'Notes and News: Caesarea', *IEJ* 13: 146–48.

Avner, Tamar (1999), 'Early Byzantine Wall Paintings from Caesarea', in Kenneth G. Holum, Avner Raban, and Joseph Patrich (eds.), *Caesarea Papers 2 (JRA, Suppl. Ser.* 35; Portsmouth, RI: Journal of Roman Archaeology): 109–28.

Ayalon, Eithan (1991), 'Giant Jars from Yavneh Yam (Hebrew)', in Moshe Fisher (ed.), *Yavneh Yam and its Environment* (Jerusalem): 80–88.

—— (2000), 'Typology and chronology of water-wheel (saqiya) pottery pots from Israel', *IEJ* 50: 216–26.

—— (2005), *The assemblage of bone and ivory artifacts from Caesarea Maritima, Israel, 1st–13th centuries CE* (BAR Int. Ser., 457; Oxford).

Ayalon, Etan, Frankel, Rafael, and Kloner, Amos (eds.) (2009), *Oil and wine presses in Israel from the Hellenistic, Roman and Byzantine Periods* (Oxford: Archeopress).

Bagatti, Bellarmino (1971), *The Church from the Circumcision. History and Archaeology of the Judaeo-Christians* (Jerusalem: Franciscan Printing Press).

Ball, Warwick (2000), *Rome in the East* (London and New York: Routledge).

Ball, Warwick *et al.* (1986), 'The North Decumanus and the North Tetrapylon at Jerash', in F. Zayadine (ed.), *Jerash Archaeological Project 1981–1983* (I; Amman): 351–410.

Balty, Janine (1969), *Apamée de Syrie: Bilan des recherches archéologiques 1965–68.* (Fouilles d'Apamée de Syrie. Miscellanea 6; Bruxelles: Centre belge de recherches archéologiques à Apamée de Syrie).

Balty, J. Ch. (1969), 'L'édifice dit 'au triclinos', in J. Ch. Balty (ed.), *Apamée de Syrie* (Bruxelles): 105–16.

Balty, Jean Charles (ed.), (1984), *Apamée de Syrie (Bilan des recherches archéologiques 1973–1979, aspects de l'architecture domestique d'Apamée)* (Bruxelles: Centre belge de recherches archéologiques à Apamée de Syrie).

—— (1984), 'Notes sur l'habitat romain, byzantin et arabe d'Apamée: rapport de synthèse', in J. Balty (ed.), *Apamée de Syrie* (Bruxelles): 471–501.

Barański, Marek (1995), 'The Great Colonnade of Palmyra', *Aram Periodical* 7: 37–46.

Barag, Dan (1964), 'An Inscription from the High Aquaduct at Caesarea—Reconsidered', *IEJ* 14: 250–52, pl. 45.a–d.

—— (1996), 'The Legal and Administrative Status of the Port of Sebastos during the Early Roman Period', in Avner Raban and Kenneth G. Holum (eds.), *Caesarea Maritima. A Retrospective after Two Millennia* (Leiden, New York and Köln): 609–14.

Baras, Zvi (1982), 'The Persian Conquest and the End of Byzantine Rule (Hebrew)', in Zvi Baras *et al.* (eds.), *Eretz Israel from the Destruction of the Second Temple to the Muslim Conquest* (Jerusalem: Yad Yizhak ben Zvi): 300–49.

Barghouti, A. (1982), 'Urbanization of Palestine and Jordan in Hellenistic and Roman Times', *SHAJ* I: 209–18.

Bar-Nathan, Rachel and Mazor, Gabi (1992), 'City Center (South) and Tel Iztaba Area; Excavations of the Antiquities Authority Expedition', *ESI* 11: 43–44.

Barnes, Thimoty D. (1981), *Constantine and Eusebius* (Cambridge, MA: Harvard University Press).

Baslez, Marie-Francoise (1991), *Saint Paul* (Paris: Fayard).

Beaucamp, Joelle (2000), 'Le droit successoral relatif aux curiales: Procope et Justinien', in S. Puliatti and A. Sanguinetti (eds.), *Legislazione, cultura giuridica, prassi dell'Impero d'Oriente in eta giustinianea tra passato e futuro* (Modena): 379–95.

Becker, Jürgen (1995), *Paul, "l'apotre des Nations" (tr. from German)*, trans. J. Hoffmann (Paris).

Bejor, G. (1999), *Vie colonnate: Paesaggi urbani del mondo antico* (Rivista di archeologia. Supplementi 22; Roma).

Bengtson, Hermann (1979), *Die Flavier: Vespasian, Titus, Domitian: Geschichte eines römischen Kaiserhauses* (Munich: Beck).

Ben-Shalom, Israel (1994), *The House of Shammai and the Struggle of the Zealots against Rome (Hebrew).* (Jerusalem: Yad Izhak Ben-Zvi).

Ben-Zvi, Izhak (1961), 'A Lamp with a Samaritan Inscription', *IEJ* 11: 139–42.

Berchem, Denis-Van (1976), 'Le plan de Palmyre', *Palmyre, bilan et perspectives. Colloque de Strasbourg (18–20 Octobre 1973) [3e colloque du Centre de Recherche sur le Proche-Orient et la Grece Antiques]* (Strasbourg: A.E.C.R.): 165–73.

Berger, Albrecht (1982), *Das Bad in der byzantinischen Zeit* (Miscellanea Byzantina Monacensia 27; Munich: Institut für Byzantinistik und neugriechische Philologie der Universität).

Berlin, Andrea (1992), 'Hellenistic and Roman Pottery, Preliminary Report, 1990', in R.L. Vann (ed.), *Caesarea Papers 1: Straton's Tower, Herod's Harbor, and the Roman and Byzantine Caesarea* (JRA Suppl. Ser. 5; Ann Arbor MI): 112–12.

Blakely, Jeffrey A. (1984), 'A Stratigraphically Determined Date for the Inner Fortification Wall of Caesarea Maritima', in H.A. Thompson (ed.), *The Answers Lie Below: Essays in Honor of Laurence Edmund Toombs* (Lanham, MD): 3–38.

—— (1987), *The Joint Expedition to Caesarea Maritima Excavation Reports 4: The Pottery and Dating of Vault 1: Horreum, Mithraeum and Later Usage* (Lewiston, NY: The Edwin Mellen Press).

—— (1988), 'Ceramics and Commerce. Amphorae from Caesarea Maritima', *BASOR*, 271, 31–50.

—— (1989), 'The City Walls of Straton's Tower: A Stratigraphic Rejoinder', *BASOR* 273: 79–82.

—— (1992), 'Stratigraphy and the North Fortification Wall of Herod's Caesarea', in R.L. Vann (ed.), *Caesarea Papers 1: Straton's Tower, Herod's Harbour, and Roman and Byzantine Caesarea* (JRA Suppl. Series, 5; Ann Arbor): 26–41.

Blatt, Franz (ed.), (1958), *The Latin Josephus I* (Acta Jutlandica 30, I, Aarhus: Universitetsforlaget).

Boudignon, Cristopher (2004), 'Maxime le Confesseur était-il Constantinopolitain? In Philomathestatos', in B. Janssens and P.V.D.B. Roosen (eds.), *Studies in Greek*

Patristics and Byzantine Texts Presented to Jacques Noret for his Sixty-Fifth Birthday (Orientalia Leuvenensa Analecta 137; Leuven and Paris: Peeters.): 11–43.

Bowersock, G.W. (1995), *Martyrdom and Rome* (Cambridge; New York: Cambridge University Press).

Brandon, Christopher (1996), 'Cements, Concrete, and Settling Barges at Sebastos: Comparisons with Other Roman Harbor Examples and the Descriptions of Vitruvius', in Avner Raban and Kenneth G. Holum (eds.), *Caesarea Martima: A Retrospective after Two Millennia* (Leiden, New York, and Köln): 25–40.

Brettler, Marc Zvi and Poliakoff, M. (1990), 'Rabbi Simeon ben Lakish at the Gladiator's Banquet: Rabbinic Observations on the Roman Arena', *HTR* 83: 93–98.

Brockelmann, C. (1928, reprinted 1966), *Lexicon Syriacum* (Hale: Hildesheim, G. Olms).

Brodie, Israel and Rabinowitz, Jacob (eds.) (1956), *Studies in Jewish History. The Adolph Büchler memorial volume* (London, New York and Toronto: Oxford University Press).

Broshi, Magen (1980), 'The Population of Western Palestine in the Roman-Byzantine Period', *BASOR* 236: 1–10.

Bruneau, Philippe (1961), 'Isis Pélagia à Délos', *BCH* 85: 435–46.

—— (1963), 'Isis Pélagia à Délos', *BCH* 87: 301–8.

—— (1965), *Exploration Archéologique de Délos. Fasc. XXVI: Les Lampes* (Paris: E. de Brocard).

Budge, Ernest Alfred Wallis (1909), *Texts Relating to Saint Ména of Egypt and Canons of Nicea in a Nubian Dialect* (London: British Museum).

Bull, Robert J. (1973), 'Notes and News: Caesarea', *IEJ* 23: 260–62.

—— (1974a), 'A Mithraic Medallion from Caesarea', *IEJ* 24: 187–90.

—— (1974b), 'Notes and News: Caesarea', *IEJ* 24: 281–82.

—— (1975), 'Césarée Maritime', *RB* 82: 278–80.

—— (1978), 'The Mithraeum at Caesarea Maritima', *études Mithraiques, textes et mémoires* 4: 75–89.

—— (1981), 'The ninth season of excavations at Caesarea Maritima', *AJA* 85: 188.

—— (1982), 'Caesarea Maritima. The search for Herod's city', *BAR* 8: 24–40.

—— (1984), 'Caesarea Maritima 1980, 1982, 1984', *ESI* 3: 15–16.

Bull, Robert J. and Toombs, L.E. (1972), 'Notes and News: Caesarea', *IEJ* 22: 178–80.

Bull, Robert J. *et al.* (1985), *The Joint Expedition to Caesarea Maritima: Preliminary Reports in microfiche* (Madison, NJ: Drew University Institute for Archaeological Research).

—— (1990), 'The Joint Expedition to Caesarea Maritima: tenth season, 1982', *BASOR Suppl.* 27: 75–82.

Bull, Robert J. and Storvick, Olin (1993), 'The Gold Coin Hoard at Caesarea', *BA* 56: 116–20.

Bull, Robert J., Krentz, E., and Storvick, Olin J. (1986), 'The Joint Expedition to Caesarea Maritima. Ninth Season, 1980', *BASOR Suppl.* 24: 31–55.

Burkhard, Büttger (2002), *Die kaizerlichtlichen Lampen von Kerameikos. Kerameikos: Ergebnisse der Ausgrabungen, 16* (München: Hirmer Verlag).

Burnett, Andrew, Amandry, Michel, and Ripollès, Pere. P. (1992), *Roman Provincial Coinage. Vol. 1: From the Death of Caesar to the Death of Vitellius (44BC–AD69)* (London: British Museum Press: Paris: Bibliothéque Nationale).

Burrell, Barbara (1993), 'Two Inscribed Columns from Caesarea Maritima', *ZPE* 99: 287–95.

—— (1996), 'Palace to Praetorium: The Romanization of Caesarea', in Avner Raban and Kennet G. Holum (eds.), *Caesarea Maritima. A Retrospective after Two Millennia* (Leiden, New York and Köln): 228–47.

Burrell, Barbara and Gleason, Kathryn. L. (1995), 'The Promontory Palace at Caesarea, Israel. The 1993 and 1994 Seasons', *AJA* 99 (2): 306–7.

Burrell, Barbara, Gleason, Kathryn. L. and Netzer, Ehud (1993), 'Uncovering Herod's Seaside Palace', *BAR* 19: 50–57, 76.

Burton, G.P. (1975), 'Proconsuls, Assizes and the Administration of Justice under the Empire', *JRS* 65: 92–106.

Butler, Howard Crosby (1914), *Publications of Princeton University Archaeological Expedition to Syria, Div. II: Architecture. Section A: Southern Syria, Part 4: Bostra* (Leiden: E.J. Brill).

Caetani, L. (1911), *Annali dell'Islam* (4; Milano: U. Hoepli).

Callmer, C. (1954), 'Antike Bibliotheken', *Opuscula Archaeologica* III: 144–93.

Cameron, Alan (1976), *Circus Factions. Blues and Greens at Rome and Byzantium* (Oxford: Clarendon Press).

Cameron, Averil (1985), *Procopius and the Sixth Century* (London and Barkley).

Carriker, A. (2003), *The Library of Eusebius of Caesarea* (Leiden: Brill).

Castagnoli, Ferdinando (1971), *Orthogonal Town Planning in Antiquity* (Cambridge, MA: The Massachusetts Institute of Technology).

—— (1984), 'Influenze allessandrine nell'urbanistica della Roma Augustea', *Alessandria e il Mondo Ellenistico-Romano. Studi in Onore di Achile Adriani (Studi e Materiali. Inst. di Arch. Univ. di Palermo 6)* (Rome): 520–26.

Chastagnol, André (1978), *L'Album municipal de Timgad* (Bonn: Gabelt).

Clark, Elizabeth A. (1992), 'Eusebius on Women in the Early Church History', in H.W. Attridge and G. Hata (eds.), *Eusebius, Christianity and Judaism* (Detroit): 256–69.

Claude, Dietrich (1969), *Die byzantinische Stadt im 6. Jahrhundert* (München: Beck).

Coleman, K.M. (1990), 'Fatal Charades: Roman Executions Staged as Mythological Enactments', *JRS* 80: 44–73.

Conder, C.R. and Kitchener, H.H. (1882), *Survey of Western Palestine II: Samaria.* (London: Palestine Exploration Fund).

Conrad, Lawrence I. (1992), 'The Conquest of Arwâd: A Source-Critical Study in the Historiography of the Early Medieval Near East', in A. Cameron and L.I. Conrad (eds.), *The Byzantine and Early Islamic Near East, 1: Problems in the Literary Source Material (Studies in Late Antiquity and Early Islam)* (Princeton: Darwin Press): 317–401.

Cope, Carol (1999), 'Faunal Remains and Butchery Practices from Byzantine and Islamic Contexts (1993–94 seasons)', in Kenneth G. Holum, Avner Raban, and Joseph Patrich (eds.), *Caesarea Papers 2 (JRA, Suppl. Ser.* 35, II; Ann Arbor: Journal of Roman Archaeology): 405–17.

Cotton, Hannah M. and Geiger, Joseph (1996), 'The Economic Importance of Herod's Masada: the Evidence of the Jar Inscriptions', in Klaus Fittschen and Gideon Foerster (eds.), *Judaea and the Greco-Roman World in the Time of Herod in the Light of the Archaeological Evidence* (Göttingen): 163–70.

Cotton, Hannah M. and Eck, Werner (2001), 'Governors and their Personnel in Latin Inscriptions from Caesarea Maritima', *Proceedings of the Israel Academy of Sciences and Humanities*, 7 (7): 215–40.

—— (2002), 'A New Inscription from Caesarea Maritima and the Local Elite of Caesarea Maritima', in Leonard V. Rutgers (ed.), *What Has Athens to Do with Jerusalem: Essays in Honor of Gideon Foerster* (Leuven: Peeters): 375–91.

—— (2003), 'Eine Provinz Entsteht: Alte und neue lateinische Inschriften in Iudaea unter Vespasian', in Edward Dąbrowa (ed.), *The Roman Near East and Armenia (Electrum 7)* (Krakaw: Jagiellonian University Press): 30–35.

Cotton, Hannah M., Lernau, Omri, and Goren, Yuval (1996), 'Fish Sauces from Herodian Masada', *JRA* 9: 223–38.

Coulton, J.J. (1976), *The Architectural Development of the Greek Stoa* (Oxford: Clarendon Press).

Cross, Frank Leslie and Livingstone, Elizabeth A. (eds.) (1974), *The Oxford Dictionary of the Christian Church, 2nd edition* (London-New York-Toronto).

Crowfoot, John Winter *et al.* (1942), *The Buildings at Samaria* (London: Palestine Exploraton Fund).

Crown, Alan David (1989), 'The Byzantine and Moslem Period', in Alan David Crown (ed.), *The Samaritans* (Tübingen: J.C.B. Mohr (Paul Siebeck)): 55–81.

Dahari, Uzi (2000), *Monastic Settlements in South Sinai in the Byzantine Period. The Archaeological Remains* (Israel Antiquities Authority Reports, 9; Jerusalem: Israel Antiquities Authority).

Dan, Yaron (1981), 'Circus Factions (Blues and the Greens) in Byzantine Palestine', in I.L. Levine (ed.), *The Jerusalem Cathedra: Studies in the History, Archaeology, Geography and Ethnography of the Land of Israel* (1; Jerusalem and Toronto): 105–19.

—— (1984), *The City in Eretz Israel during the Late Roman and Byzantine Periods (Hebrew)* (Jerusalem: Yad Yizhak Ben Zvi).

Dauphin, Claudine (1999), 'From Apollo and Asclepius to Christ. Pilgrimage and Healing at the Temple and Episcopal Basilica of Dor', *LA* 49: 397–430; Pls. 1–4.

Davies, P.S. (1989), 'The Origin and Purpose of the Persecution of AD 303', *JTS* 40: 66–94.

Degrassi, Attilio (1926), 'Il papiro 1026 della Società italiana e I diplomi militari romani', *Aegyptus* 10: 242–54.

Delehaye, Hippolyte (1910), 'L'invention des reliques de saint Ménas à Constantinople', *AB* 29: 117–50.

—— (1923, Repr. 1962), *Les Saints Stylites* (Brussels: Société des Bollandistes; Paris: A. Picard).

Delplace, Christiane and Dentzer-Feydy, Jacqueline (2005), *L' Agora de Palmyre* (Pessac: Ausonius; Beyrouth: Institut français du Proche-Orient).

Di-Segni, Leah (1990), 'The Church of Mary Theotokos on Mount Gerizim: the Inscriptions', in G.C. Bottini, L. Di-Segni, and E. Alliata (eds.), *Christian Archaeology in the Holy Land. New Discoveries* (Jerusalem: Franciscan Printing Press): 343–50.

—— (1994), 'Eis Theos in Palestinian inscriptions', *SCI* 13: 94–115.

—— (1996), 'Metropolis and Provincia in Byzantine Palestine', in A. Raban and K.G. Holum (eds.), *Caesarea Maritima: A Retrospective after Two Millennia* (Leiden-New York-Köln): 575–92.

—— (1998), 'The Samaritans in Roman-Byzantine Palestine: Some Misapprehensions', in Haim Lapin (ed.), *Religious and Ethnic Communities in Later Roman Palestine* (Bethesda, MD: University Press of Maryland): 51–66.

—— (2000), 'The Inscriptions from the Chapel of St. Paul at Caesarea', *LA* 50: 383–400.

—— (2002a), 'Epigraphical and literary sources on Aqueducts', in David Amit, Joseph Patrich, and Yizhar Hirschfeld (eds.), *The Aqueducts of Israel* (*JRA, Suppl. Ser.* 46; Portsmouth, RI: Journal of Roman Archaeology): 37–67.

—— (2002b), 'Inscription on a *Eulogia* Stamp', *IMSA* 1: 33–38.

Di-Segni, L. and Frankel, R. (2000), 'A Greek Inscription from Kibbutz Shomrat', *IEJ* 50: 43–46.

Di-Segni, Leah, Patrich, Joseph, and Holum, Kenneth G. (2003), 'A Schedule of Fees for Official Services from Caesarea Maritima', *ZPE* 145: 273–300.

Djobadze, Wachtang (1986), *Archaeological Investigations in the Regions West of Antioch-on-the-Orontes.* (Stuttgart: F. Steiner Verlag Wiesbaden).

Donner, Fred M. (1981), *The Early Islamic Conquests* (Princeton: Princeton University Press).

Downey, Glanville (1937), 'The Architectural Significance of the Use of the Words *Stoa* and *Basilike* in Classical Literature', *AJA* 41: 194–211.

—— (1958), 'The Christians Schools of Palestine', *Harvard Library Bulletin* 12: 297–319.

—— (1975), 'Caesarea and the Christian Church', in Ch. T. Fritsch (ed.), *Studies in the History of Caesarea Maritima* (BASOR Suppl. 19; Missoula, MA): 23–42.

Drei, Yeshua (2003), 'The process of wine production in the elaborate Byzantine winepress (Hebrew)', *SJS* 12: 219–28.

Dresken-Weiland, Jutta (1991), *Relieferte Tischplatten aus Theodosianischer Zeit* (Roma, Citta del Vatticano: Pontificio Instituto di Archeologia Cristiana).

Dunand, Françoise (2000), *Isis: Mère des Dieux* (Paris: Editions Errance).

Duran, Robert (1992), *The Lives of Simeon Stylites* (Cistercian Studies Vol. 112; Kalamazoo, Mich.: Cistercian Publications).

Duval, Noel (1984), 'Les maisons d'Apamée et l'architecture 'palatiale' de l'antiquité tardive', in J. Ch. Balty (ed.), *Apamée de Syrie [Bilan des recherches archéologiques 1973–1979, aspects de l'architecture domestique d'Apamée]* (Bruxelles): 457–64.

Dyggve, Ejnar (1933), *Recherches à Salone* (II; Copenhague: J.H. Schultz).

Eck, Werner (1996), 'Zu Lateinischen Inschriften aus Caesarea in Iudaea/Palaestina', *ZPE* 113: 129–43.

—— (1998), 'Ein Prokuratorenpaar von Syria Palaestina in P. Berol. 21652', *ZPE* 123: 249–55.

—— (2000), 'Provincial Administration and Finance', in Alan K. Bowman, Peter Garnsey, and Dominic Rathbone (eds.), *The Cambridge Ancient History. 2d ed., vol. 11: High Empire, A.D. 70–192* (Cambridge: Cambridge University Press): 266–92.

—— (2002), 'Compte rendu', *Topoi* 10: 538–39.

—— (2007), *Rom und Judaea. Fünf Vorträge zur römischen Herrschaft in Palaestina*, (Tübingen: Mohr Siebeck).

—— (2009), 'The presence, role and significance of Latin in the epigraphy and culture of the Roman Near East', in Hannah M. Cotton, *et al.* (eds.), *From Hellenism to Islam* (Cambridge: Cambridge University Press): 1–42.

Eck, Werner and Cotton, Hannah M. (2009), 'Inscriptions from the Financial Procurator's Praetorium in Caesarea', in Leah Di-Segni, *et al.* (eds.), *Man Near a Roman Arch. Studies presented to Prof. Yoram Tsafrir* (Jerusalem: Israel Exploration Society): 98*–114*.

Edelstein, Gershon (1996), 'Binyamina (Hebrew)', *HA* 106: 174.

—— (1998), 'Binyamina', *ESI* 18: 114.

El'ad, A. (1982), 'The Coastal Cities of Palestine during the Early Middle Ages', *The Jerusalem Cathedra* 2: 446–67.

Elitzur, Yoel (2008), 'The Siloam Pool—'Solomon's Pool'—was a swimming pool', *PEQ* 140: 17–25.

Ellis, Simon (1985), 'The 'Palace of the Dux' at Apollonia, and Related Houses', in Graeme Barker *et al.* (eds.), *Cyrenaica in Antiquity* (BAR International Series 236): 15–25.

Erim, Kenan T. (1969), 'The ninth campaign of excavations at Aphrodisias in Caria', *Türk Arkeoloji Dergisi* 18/2: 87–110.

Etienne, Robert (1966), 'La naissance de l'amphithéâtre le mot et la chose', *Révue des études latines* 43: 213–20.

Evans, A. (1999), 'Procopius', in Peter Brown, Glen Bowersock, and Oleg Grabar (eds.), *Late Antiquity* (Cambridge Mass. and London): 654.

Everman, Diane (1992), 'Survey of the coastal area of Caesarea and of the aqueducts: preliminary report', in L. Vann (ed.), *Caesarea Papers 1 (JRA Suppl. Ser. 5)* (I; Ann Arbor, MI: Journal of Roman Archaeology): 184–93.

Fabre, Pierre Demargne (1965), 'La date de la rédaction du périple de Scylax', *Les études classiques* 33: 353–66.

Farmer, David Hugh (1987), *The Oxford Dictionary of Saints* (2 edn.; New York: Oxford University Press).

Fears, J. Rufus (1988), 'Ruler Worship', in M. Grant and R. Kitzinger (eds.), *Civilization of the ancient Mediterranean, Greece and Rome* (II; New York: Scribner's): 1009–25.

Fedalto, Giorgio (1988), *Hierarchia Ecclesiastica Orientalis* (Padova: Edizioni Messagero).

Feig, Nurith (1994), 'A Byzantine Bread Stamp from Tiberias', *LA* 44: 591–94.

Festugière, André Jean (1962), *Les moines d'Orient III.2, Les moines de Palestine (Cyril de Scythopolis, Vie de Saint Sabas)* (Paris: Les Editions du Cerf).

Finley, Moses I. and Pleket, H.W. (1976), *The Olympic Games: The first thousand years* (New York).

Finocchi, Silvana (1965), 'La cinta Erodiana', in A. Frova *et al.* (eds.), *Scavi di Caesarea Maritima* (Milano): 247–92; Figs. 85–90.

Fiocchi Nicolai, Vincenzo, Bisconti, Fabrizio, and Mazzoleni, Danilo (1999), *The Christian Catacombs of Rome* (Regensburg: Schnell and Steiner).

Fischer, M. (1990), *Das korinthische Kapitell im Alten Israel in der hellenistischen und römischen Periode* (Mainz).

Fisher, M.L., Magaritz, M., and Pearl, Z. (1992), 'Decoration and Marble Sources of Sarcophagi from Caesarea: a case study', in R.L. Vann (ed.), *Caesarea Papers 1 Straton's Tower, Herod's Harbor, and Roman and Byzantine Caesarea (JRA, Suppl. Ser.* 5; Ann Arbor, MI): 214–21.

Fittschen, K. and G., Foerster (eds.) (1996), *Judaea and the Greco-Roman World in the Time of Herod in the Light of Archaeological Evidence* (Göttingen).

Flinder, A. (1976), 'A Piscina at Caesarea—A Preliminary Survey', *IEJ* 26: 77–88.

—— (1985), 'The Piscinas at Caesarea and Lapithos', in A. Raban (ed.), *Harbour Archaeology. Proceedings of the First International Workshop on Ancient Mediterranean Harbours. Caesarea Maritima* (British Archaeological Reports, Inter. Ser. 257; Oxford): 173–8.

Flusin, B. (1992), *Saint Anastase le Perse et l'histoire de la Palestine au début du VIIe siécle, vol. 2: Commentaire* (Paris: éditions du Centre national de la recherche scientifique).

Flusser, David (1975), 'The Great Goddess of Samaria', *IEJ* 25: 13–20.

Foerster, G. (1975), 'The Early History of Caesarea', in Ch. T. Fritsch (ed.), *Studies in the History of Caesarea Maritima* (BASOR Suppl. 19; Missoula, MA): 9–21.

—— (1995), *Masada V: Art and Architecture* (Jerusalem).

Foss, C. and D. Winfield (1986), *Byzantine Fortifications—An Introduction* (Pretoria).

Fox, R.L. (1986), *Pagans and Christians* (Harmondsworth: Penguin).

Fradkin, Arlen and Lernau, Omri (2008), 'The fishing economy at Caesarea', in Kenneth G. Holum, Jeniffer A. Stabler, and Edward Reinhardt (eds.), *Caesarea Reports and Studies* (Oxford: BAR Int. Ser. 1784): 189–200.

Frankel, Z. (1967), *Introduction to the Yerushalmi (Hebrew)* (Jerusalem).

Frankel, Rafael (1999), *Wine and oil production in antiquity in Israel and other Mediterranean countries* (Sheffield: Sheffield Academic Press).

Fredkin, E. (Habas) (1980), 'The Regulations of Rabbi pertaining to the borders of Eretz Israel (Hebrew)', unpublished M.A. thesis (Tel Aviv University).

Frend, W.H.C. (1965), *Martyrdom and Persecution in the Early Church: A Study of a Conflict from the Maccabees to Donatus* (Oxford).

Fritsch, Ch. T. (1975), *Studies in the History of Caesarea Maritima* (BASOR Suppl. 19; Missoula, MA).

Fritsch, Ch. T. and Ben-Dor, I. (1961), 'The Link Expedition to Israel', *BA* 24: 50–56.

Frova, Antonio (1959), *Caesarea Maritima (Israele): Rapporto preliminare della prima campano della Missione Archeologica Italiana* (Milano).

—— (1961-1962), 'Gli Scavi della Missione Archeologica Italiana a Cesarea (Israele)', *Annuario della Scuala Archeologica di Atene*, 39–40, n.s.: 23–24, 649–57.

—— (1962), 'La statua di Artemide Efesia a Caesarea Maritima', *Bollettino d'Arte del Ministero della Pubblica Istruzione* 4: 305–13.

—— (1963), 'Italian Excavations in Israel: Caesarea', *CNI* 14: 3–4, 20–24, pls. 1–4.

—— (1975), 'Caesarea', in Michael Avi-Yonah (ed.), *EAEHL* (Jerusalem: Israel Exploration Society): 274–277.

Frova, Antonio *et al.* (1965), *Scavi di Caesarea Maritima* (Milano: Istituto lombardo).
Gadot, Yuval and Tepper, Yotam (2008) *Archaeological Survey of Israel. Map of Regavim (49)* [online text], Israel Antiquities Authority.
Gafni, Reuven (2006), 'To One Hundred and Twenty Birds (Hebrew)', *Ethmol*, XXVIII/4 (184): 10–12.
Galavaris, George (1970), *Bread and Liturgy. The Symbolism of Early Christian and Byzantine Bread Stamps* (Madison Milwaukee and London: University of Wisconsin Press).
Galili, Ehud, Rosen, Baruch, and Sharvit, Jacob (2010), 'Artifact Assemblages from two Roman Shipwrecks off the Carmel Coast', *'Atiqot*, 63: 61–110.
Galling, Kurt (1938), 'Die syrisch-palästinische Küste nach der Beschreibung bei Pseudo-Skylax', *ZDPV* 61: 66–96.
Gardiner, Edward Norman (1910), *Greek Athletic Sports and Festivals* (London: Macmillan and co.).
—— (2002), *Athletics of the ancient world 1930, repr.* (Mineola, New York: Dover Publications).
Garland, Robert (1988), 'Greek Spectacles and Festivals', in Michael Grant and Rachel Kitzinger (eds.), *Civilization of the ancient Mediterranean, Greece and Rome* (II; New York: Scribner's): 1143–52.
Garnsey, Peter (1968), 'The Criminal Jurisdiction of Governors', *JRS* 58: 51–59.
Gebhard, Elizabeth R. (1975), 'Protective devices in Roman theaters', in Djordje Mano-Zisi (ed.), *Studies in the antiquities of Stobi* (II; Belgrade: Tiho Najdovski): 43–63.
Geiger, Joseph (1994), 'Latin in Roman Palestine', *Cathedra* 74: 3–21 (Hebrew).
—— (1996), 'How Much Latin in Roman Palestine?', in Hannah Rosén (ed.), *Aspects of Latin: Papers from the Seventh International Colloquium on Latin Linguistics, Jerusalem, April 1993* (Innsbrucker Beiträge zur Sprachwissenschaft; Bd. 86; Innsbruck: Institut fur Sprachwissenschaft der Universität Innsbruck): 39–57.
—— (2001), '"Voices Reciting the Shma" in Greek': Jews, Gentiles and Greek Wisdom in Caesarea', *Cathedra* 99: 27–36 (Hebrew).
Gendelman, Peter (2007), 'From Strato's tower to Caesarea Maritima. Hellenistic and Early Roman Ceramic Assemblages.', Ph.D. Dissertation (University of Haifa).
Gersht, Rivka (1984), 'The Tyche of Caesarea Maritima', *PEQ* 116, 110–14.
—— (1996), 'Representation of Deities and the Cults of Caesarea', in Avner Raban and Kenneth G. Holum (eds.), *Caesarea Maritima. A Retrospective after Two Millennia* (Leiden, New York and Köln: Brill): 305–24.
—— (1996), 'Imported Marble Sarcophagi from Caesarea', *Assaph, Studies in Art History* 2: 13–26.
—— (1999), 'Roman Statuary used in Byzantine Caesarea', in Kenneth G. Holum, Arvne Raban, and Joseph Patrich (eds.), *Caesarea Papers 2*: 389–98.
Gerst, Rivka (1987), 'The Sculpture of Caesarea Maritima. Ph.D. dissertation (Hebrew)', (Tel Aviv University).
—— (1995), 'Seven New Sculptural Pieces from Caesarea', in J. Humphrey (ed.), *The Roman and Byzantine Near East [JRA, Suppl. Ser. 14]* (Ann Arbor, MI): 108–20.
Geva, Hillel (1993), 'Jerusalem. The Second Temple Period', in Ephraim Stern (ed.), *NEAEHL* (Jerusalem): 717–57.
Gignoux, Philippe (1984), 'L' organisation administrative sasanide: le cas du Marzaban', *JSAI* 4: 1–29.
Gil, Moshe (1983), *Eretz Israel in the Early Islamic Period (634–1099), 3 Vols. [Hebrew]* (Tel Aviv: Tel Aviv University and Ministry of Defense Publishing House).
—— (1992), *A History of Palestine, 634–1099, trans. from Hebrew by E. Broido* (New York: Cambridge University Press).
Gleason, Kathryn L. (1996), 'Ruler and Spectacle: The Promontory Palace", in Raban and Holum 1996,' in Avner Raban and Kenneth G. Holum (eds.), *Caesarea Maritima. A Retrospective after Two Millennia* (Leiden, New York and Köln: Brill): 208–27.

Gleason, Kathryn L. *et al.* (1998), 'The Promontory Palace at Caesarea Maritima: Preliminary Evidence for Herod's Praetorium', *JRA* 11: 23–52.

Goldfus, Haim (1997), 'Tombs and Burials in Churches and Monasteries of Byzantine Palestine (324–628 A.D.)', Ph.D. Dissertation (Princeton University, UMI Dissertation Services).

Golvin, Jean-Claude (1988), *L'amphithéâtre romain* (Paris: Diffusion de Boccard).

Golvin, Jean-Claude and Landes, Christian (1990), *Amphithéâtres et gladiateurs* (Paris: Presses du CNRS).

Gordon, Hirsch Loeb (1931), 'The Basilica and the Stoa in Early Rabbinical Literature', *The Art Bulletin* XIII: 352–75.

Govaars, Marylinda, Marie, Spiro, and L., White Michael (eds.) (2009), *The Joint Expedition to Caesarea Maritima Excavation Reports, Volume IX: Field O: The "Synagogue" Site*, eds. Robert J. Bull and Olin J. Storvick (ASOR).

Grant, Michael and Kitzinger, Rachel (1988), *Civilization of the Ancient Mediterranean, Greece and Rome* (II; New York: Scribner's).

Gregoire, Henri (1950), *Les persécutions dans l'empire Romain* (Brussels: Palais des Académies).

Griffiths, Gwyn J. (1978), 'Isis in the Metamorphoses of Apuleius', in Benjamin L. Hijmans and R.Th. van der Paart (eds.), *Aspects of Apuleius' Golden Ass* (Groningen: Bouma): 141–66.

Grimal, Pierre (1983), *Roman Cities*, trans. G.M. Woloch (Madison, WI.: The University of Wisconsin Press).

Grossmann, P. (1989), *Abu Mina I, Die Gruftkirche und die Gruft. [Deutsches Archaeologisches Institut, Abteilung Kairo, Archaeologische Veroeffentlichungen 44]* (Mainz am Rhein).

Guidoboni, Emanuela, Comastri, A., and Traina, G. (1994), *Catalogue of Ancient Earthquakes in the Mediterranean Area up to the 10th Century*, trans. B. Phillips (Rome: Istituto nazionale di geofisica).

Habas, Efrat (1996), 'The Hallachic Status of Caesarea as Reflected in the Talmudic Literature', in Avner Raban and Kenneth G. Holum (eds.), *Caesarea Martima: A Retrospective After Two Millennia* (Leiden, New York, and Köln: Brill): 454–68.

Haefeli, Leo (1923), *Caesarea am Meer: Topographie und Geschichte der Stadt nach Josephus un Apostelgeschichte* (Münster: Aschendorffschen).

Haensch, Rudolf (1997), *Capita provinciarum. Statthaltersitze und Provinzialverwaltung in der römischen Kaiserzeit* (Mainz am Rhein: P. von Zabern).

Hall, S.G. (1993), 'Women among the Early Martyrs', in Diana Wood (ed.), *Martyrs and Martyrologies: Papers Read at the 1992 Summer Meeting and the 1993 Winter Meeting of the Ecclesiastical History Society* (Oxford): 1–21.

Hamburger, Anit (1959), 'A Greco-Samaritan Amulet from Caesarea', *IEJ* 9: 43–45 and Pl. 4 A, B.

—— (1968), 'Gems from Caesarea Maritima', *'Atiqot (English Series)*: 8.

Hamburger, H. (1949), 'Caesarea Coin Finds and the History of the City (Hebrew)', *Bulletin of the Jewish Palestine Exploration Society* 15: 73–82.

—— (1955), 'Minute Coins from Caesarea', *'Atiqot* 1: 118–19, 27–31, pls. X–XI.

—— (1970), 'The Coin Issues of the Roman Administration from the Mint of Caesarea Maritima', *IEJ* 20: 81–91.

Harel, Menashe (1988), 'Caesarea: City of Water and Prosperity (Hebrew)', in Rechavam Zeevy (ed.), *ILP* (Tel Aviv: Eretz Israel Museum): 163–78.

Harris, Harold Arthur (1966), *Greek Athletes and Athletics* (Bloomington: Indiana University Press).

—— (1968), 'The starting gates for chariots at Olympia', *Greece and Rome* 15: 113–26.

—— (1972), *Sport in Greece and Rome* (Ithaca: Cornell University Press).

—— (1976), *Greek athletics and the Jews* (Cardiff: The University of Wales Press).

Hauben, H. (1987), 'Philocles, King of the Sidonians and General of the Ptolemies', in E. Lipinski (ed.), *Phoenicia and the East Mediterranean in the First Millennium B.C.* (Orientalia Lovaniensia Analecta 22; Leuven: Peeters): 413–42.

Hayes, C.E. (2002), *Gentile Impurities and Jewish Identities: Intermarriage and Conversion from the Bible to the Talmud* (Oxford and New York: Oxford University Press).

Hesberg, von H. (1996), 'The Significance of the Cities in the Kingdom of Herod', in K. Fittschen and G. Foerster (ed.), *Judaea and the Greco-Roman World in the Time of Herod in the Light of Archaeological Evidence* (Göttingen: Vandenhoeck and Ruprecht): 9–26.

Hildesheimer, N.H. (1965), 'Geography of Eretz Israel', in S. Klein (ed.), *Studies in the Geography of Eretz Israel (Hebrew)* (Jerusalem: Mossad Harav Kook): 1–115.

Hill, D.R. (1971), *The Termination of Hostilities in the Early Arab Conquests A.D. 634–656* (London: Luzac).

Hillard, Thomas W. (1992), 'A Mid-1st c. B.C. Date for the Walls of Straton's Tower?', in Robert L. Vann (ed.), *Caesarea Papers 1: Straton's Tower, Herod's Harbor, and the Roman and Byzantine Caesarea* (JRA Suppl. Ser. 5; Ann Arbor, MI: Journal of Roman Archaeology): 42–48.

Hirschfeld, Yizhar (1995), 'The Early Roman Bath and Fortress at Ramat Hanadiv near Caesarea', in J. Humphrey (ed.), *The Roman and Byzantine Near East (JRA, Suppl. Ser.* 14; Ann Arbor, MI: Journal of Roman Archaeology): 28–55.

—— (2000), *Ramat Hanadiv Excavations* (Jerusalem: Israel Exploration Society).

Hirschfeld, Yizhar and Birger-Calderon, Rivka (1991), 'Early Roman and Byzantine Estates near Caesarea', *IEJ* 41: 81–111.

Hitti, Philip Khuri (1916), *The Origins of the Islamic State* (New York: Columbia University).

Hoenle, Augusta and Henze, Anton (1981), *Römische Amphitheater und Stadien* (Zuerich: Atlantis).

Hohlfelder, Robert L. (ed.), (1983), *City, Town, and Countryside in the Early Byzantine Era* (East European Monographs, 120, Byzantine Series, 1, Boulder: Distributed by Columbia University Press).

Hohlfelder, Robert (1989), 'Underwater Survey and Excavation. Link Expedition', in Avner Raban *et al.* (eds.), *The Harbours of Caesarea Maritima, 1: The Site and the Excavations: Results of the Caesarea Ancient Harbour Excavation Project 1980–1985* (BAR INt. Ser. 491; Oxford): 65–71.

—— (1992), 'The first three decades of marine explorations', in R.L. Vann (ed.), *Caesarea Papers 1*: 291–94.

—— (1996), 'Caesarea's Master Harbor Builders: Lessons Learned, Lessons Applied?', in Avner Raban and Kenneth G. Holum (eds.), *Caesarea Martima: A Retrospective After Two Millennia* (Leiden: Brill): 77–101.

Holum, Kenneth G. (1983), 'Caesarea and the Samaritans', in Robert L. Hohlfelder (ed.), *City, Town, and Countryside in the Early Byzantine Era [East European Monographs, 120, Byzantine Series, 1]* (Boulder): 65–73.

—— (1986a), 'Andreas Philoktistes, A Proconsul of Byzantine Palestine', *IEJ* 36: 61–64.

—— (1986b), 'Flavius Stephanus, proconsul of Byzantine Palestine', *ZPE* 63: 231–39.

—— (1989), 'The End of Classical Urbanism at Caesarea Maritima, Israel', in R.I. Curtis (ed.), *Studia Pompeiana & Classica in Honor of Wilhelmina F. Jashemski* (2; New Rochelle, NY: Caratzas): 87–104.

—— (1992a), 'Archaeological Evidence for the Fall of Byzantine Caesarea', *BASOR* 286: 73–85.

—— (1992b), 'Hadrian and Caesarea: An Episode in the Romanization of Palestine', *AW* 23: 51–61.

—— (1993), 'Temple Platform', in Avner Raban, Knnethe G. Holum, and Jeffrey A. Blakely (eds.), *The Combined Caesarea Expeditions: Field Report of the 1992 Season* (Haifa: Center for Maritime Studies): 53–60.

—— (1995), 'Inscriptions from the Imperial Revenue Office of Byzantine Caesarea Palaestinae', in J. Humphrey (ed.), *The Roman and Byzantine Near East (JRA, Suppl. Ser. no. 14)* (Ann Arbor, MI: Journal of Roman Archaeology): 333–45.

—— (1996a), 'In the blinking of an eye: the Christianizing of Classical cities in the Levant', in Adele Berlin (ed.), *Religion and Politics in the Ancient Near East*, (Bethesda, MD: University Press of Maryland): 131–50.

—— (1996b), 'The Survival of the Bouleutic Class at Caesarea in Late Antiquity', in Avner Raban and Kenneth G. Holum (eds.), *Caesarea Martima: A Retrospective After Two Millennia* (Leiden, New York, and Köln): 626–27.

—— (1997), 'Caesarea', in Eric Meyers (ed.), *The Oxford Encyclopedia of Archaeology in the Near East* (1; New York and Oxford): 399–404.

—— (1998a), 'Caesarea Palaestinae: The Byzantine-Islamic Transition', *Twenty-Fourth Annual Byzantine Studies Conference Abstracts 5–8 November* (University of Kentucky): 42–43.

—— (1998b), 'Identity and the Late Antique City: The Case of Caesarea', in Haim Lapin (ed.), *Religious and Ethnic Communities in Later Roman Palestine* (Bethesda, MD: University Press of Maryland): 157–177.

—— (1999), 'The Temple Platform: progress on the excavations', in Kenneth G. Holum, Avner Raban, and Joseph Patrich (eds.), *Caesarea Papers 2 (JRA, Suppl. Ser. 35*, Ann Arbor: Journal of Roman Archaeology): 13–26.

—— (2004a), 'Building Power. The Politics of Architecture', *BAR* 30 (5): 36–45, 57.

—— (2004b), 'The Combined Caesarea Expeditions Excavations: The Warehouse Quarter alongside the Harbor and Temple Platform (Hebrew)', *Qadmoniot* 37: 102–12.

—— (2009), 'Et dispositione civitatis in multa eminens: Comprehending the Urban Plan of Fourth-Century Caesarea', in Leah Di-Segni, *et al.* (eds.), *Man Near a Roman Arch. Studies presented to Prof. Yoram Tsafrir* (Jerusalem: Israel Exploration Society): 169*–89*.

—— (forthcoming), 'Caesarea Palaestinae: A Paradigmatic Transition,' in: Holum, Kenneth G. and Lapin, Haim (eds.), *Shaping the Middle East: Jews, Christians, and Muslims in an Age of Transition* (Bethesda, MD: University Press of Maryland): 11–32.

Holum, Kenneth G. *et al.* (1988), *King Herod's Dream: Caesarea on the Sea* (New York and London: Norton).

—— (1992a), 'Preliminary Report on the 1989–1990 Seasons', in R.L. Vann (ed.), *Caesarea Papers 1: Straton's Tower, Herod's Harbor, and the Roman and Byzantine Caesarea* (JRA Suppl. Ser. 5; Ann Arbor, MI: Journal of Roman Archaeology): 100–09.

—— (1992b), 'Roman and Byzantine Caesarea', in Robert L. Vann (ed.), *Caesarea Papers 1* (Ann Arbor, MI: Journal of Roman Archaeology): 79–193.

Holum, Kenneth G. and Raban, Avner (1993), 'Caesarea', in Ephraim Stern (ed.), *The New Encyclopedia of Archaeological Excavations in the Holy Land* (Jerusalem): 270–72, 82–86.

—— (1996), 'Introduction: Caesarea and Recent Scholarship', in A. Raban and K.G. Holum (eds.), *Caesarea Maritima. A Retrospective after Two Millennia* (Leiden, New York and Köln): xxvii–xliv.

Holum, Kenneth G., Raban, Avner, and Patrich, Joseph (eds.) (1999), *Caesarea Papers 2: Herod's Temple, The Provincial Governor's Praetorium and Granaries, The Later Harbor, A Gold Coin Hoard, and Other Studies (JRA, Suppl. Ser. 35*, Portsmouth, Rhode Island).

Holum, Kenneth G., Stabler, Jeniffer A., and Reinhardt, Edward (eds.) (2008), *Caesarea Reports and Studies* (BAR Int. Ser. 1784, Oxford).

Holum, Kenneth G. and Lapin, Haim (eds.) (forthcoming), *Shaping the Middle East: Jews, Christians, and Muslims in an Age of Transition* (Bethesda, MD: University Press of Maryland).

Homo, Leon P. (1949), *Vespasien, l'empereur du bon sens (69–79 ap. J.C.)* (Paris: A. Michel).

Horton, Fred L. (1996), 'A Sixth-Century Bath in Caesarea's Suburbs and the Transformation of Bathing Culture in Late Antiquity', in A. Raban and K.G. Holum (eds.), *Caesarea Retrospective* (Leiden, New York, Köln: Brill): 177–89.

Howard-Johnston, James (2000), 'The Education and Expertise of Procopius', *Antiquité Tardive* 8: 19–30.

Humphrey, John (1974), 'Prolegomena to the Study of the Hippodrome at Caesarea Maritima', *BASOR* 213: 2–45.

—— (1975), 'A Summary of the 1974 Excavations in the Caesarea Hippodrome', *BASOR* 218: 1–24.

—— (1986), *Roman Circuses: Arenas for Chariot Racing* (London: Batsford).

Humphrey, John H. (1988), 'Roman Games', in Michael Grant and Rachel Kitzinger (eds.), *Civilization of the Ancient Mediterranean, Greece and Rome* (II; New York: Scribner's): 1153–65.

Humphrey, J.H. (1996), 'Amphitheatrical' Hippo-Stadia', in Avner Raban and Kenneth G. Holum (eds.), *Caesarea Maritima. A Retrospective after Two Millennia* (Leiden, New York and Köln: Brill): 121–29.

Isaac, Benjamin (1980–81), 'Roman Colonies in Judaea: The Foundation of Aelia Capitolona', *Talanta* 12–13: 31–53.

—— (1984), 'Judaea after A.D. 70', *JJS* 35: 44–50.

—— (2009), 'Latin in cities of the Roman Near East', in Hannah M. Cotton, *et al.* (eds.), *From Hellenism to Islam* (Cambridge: Cambridge University Press): 43–72.

Israeli, Yael (2008), 'Chapter 7. The Glass Vessels', in Joseph Patrich (ed.), *Archaeological Excavations at Caesarea Maritima Areas CC, KK and NN. Final Report. Volume I: The Objects* (Jerusalem: Israel Exploration Society): 367–418.

Israeli, Yael and Mevorah, David (2000), *Cradle of Christianity* (Jerusalem: The Israel Museum).

Japp, Sarah (2000), *Die Baupolitik Herodes' des Großen: Die Bedeutung der Architektur für die Herrschaftslegitimation eines römischen Klientelkönigs* (Internationale Archéologie 64; Rahden Westfalen: Leidorf).

Jastrow, Marcus (1985), *A Dictionary of the Targumim, the Talmud Babli and Yerushalmi, and the Midrashic Literature* (New York: Judaica Treasury).

Jeremias, Joachim (1931), 'Der Taraxippos im Hippodrom von Caesarea Palaestinae', *ZDPV* 54: 279–89, pls. XII–XIII.

Johnson, Barbara L. (2008), 'Chapter 2. The Pottery', in Joseph Patrich (ed.), *Archaeological Excavations at Caesarea Maritima Areas CC, KK and NN. Final Report. Volume I: The Objects.* (Jerusalem: Israel Exploration Society): 13–206.

Jones, Arnold H.M. (1940), *The Greek City: From Alexander to Justinian* (Oxford: Clarendon Press).

—— (1964, repr. 1973), *The Later Roman Empire 284–602. Vol. 1* (Oxford: Basil Blackwell).

—— (1968), *The Later Roman Empire (AD 284–602)* (Oxford: Basil Blackwell).

—— (1971), *The Cities of the Eastern Roman Provinces. 2d ed.* (Oxford: Clarendon Press).

Kadman, Leo (1957), *The Coins of Caesarea Maritima (Corpus Nummorum Palaestinensium 2)* (Tel Aviv and Jerusalem Schocken).

Kaegi, Walter E. Jr. (1978), 'Some Seventh-Century Sources on Caesarea', *IEJ* 28: 177–81.

Kahn, Lisa (1996), 'King Herod's Temple of Roma and Augustus at Caesarea Maritima', in A. Raban and K.G. Holum (ed.), *Caesarea Maritima. A Retrospective after Two Millennia* (Leiden, New York and Köln): 130–45.

Kasher, Aryeh (1978), 'The Isopoliteia Question in Caesarea Maritima', *JQR* 68: 16–27.

Kaufmann, Carl Maria (1910a), *Zur Ikonographie der Menas-Ampullen* (Cairo).

—— (1910b), *Die Menasstadt und das Nationalheiligtum der altchristlichen Aegypter in der westalexandrinischen Wueste I, Ausgrabungen der Frankfurter expedition am Karm Abu Mina 1905–1907* (Leipzig).

Kazhdan, Alexander and Čevchenko, Nancy P. (1991), 'Menas', in Alexander Kazhdan and Alice-Mary Talbot (eds.), *The Oxford Dictionary of Byzantium II* (New York and Oxford: Oxford University Press): 1339.

Kazhdan, Alexander and Talbot, Alice-Mary (eds.) (1991), *The Oxford Dictionary of Byzantium* (New York and Oxford: Oxford University Press).

Keenan, J.K. (1973), 'The names Flavius and Aurelius as status designation', *ZPE* 11: 33–63.

—— (1974), 'The Names Flavius and Aurelius as Status Designations in Later Roman Egypt', *ZPE* 13: 283–304.

Keenan, J.K. (1983), 'An afterthought on the names Flavius and Aurelius', *ZPE* 53: 245–50.

Kempinski, Aharon and Reich, Roni (eds.) (1992), *The Architecture of Ancient Israel: from the Prehistoric to the Persian Periods; in memory of Immanuel (Munya) Donayevsky* (Jerusalem: Israel Exploration Society).

Kennedy, Hugh (1985a), 'From Polis to Medina: Urban Change in Late Antique and Early Islamic Syria', *Past and Present* 106: 3–27.

—— (1985b), 'The Last Century of Byzantine Syria: A Reinterpretation', *Byzantinische Forschungen* 10: 141–83.

Kindler, Arie (1968), 'Coins of the Roman Administration in the Roman Province Judaea in the Time of Caesar Domitian (Hebrew)', *Annual of HaAretz Museum* 10: 5–11.

Kiss, Zsolt (1989), *Les ampoules de Saint Menas decouvertes à Kom el-Dikka (1961–1981)* (Warsaw: Editions scientifiques de Pologne).

—— (1990), 'Evolution stylistique des ampoules de St. Menas', in Wlodzimierz Godlewski (ed.), *Coptic Studies. Acts of the Third International Congress of Coptic Studies, Warsaw 20–25 August 1984* (Warsaw: Editions Scientifiques de Pologne): 195–202.

Klawans, Johnathan (1995), 'Notions of Gentile Impurity in Ancient Judaism', *AJSR* 20 (2): 285–312.

—— (2000), *Impurity and Sin in Ancient Judaism* (Oxford and New York: Oxford University Press).

Klein, Shmuel (1965), 'The Borders of the Land in the *Mishnah* of the Tannaim', in S. Klein (ed.), *Studies in the Geography of Eretz Israel (Hebrew)* (Jerusalem: Mossad Harav Kook): 117–76.

Kofsky, Arieh (2006), 'Pamphilus and the Christian Library of Caesarea', *Cathedra* 122: 53–64 (Hebrew).

Kokkinos, Nikos (1998), *The Herodian Dynasty: Origin, Role in Society, and Eclipse* (Sheffield: Sheffield Academic Press).

Kornemann, Ernst (1900), 'Coloniae', *RE* (7, 1; Stuttgart): 511–88.

Kraeling, Carl Hermann (ed.) (1938), *Gerasa—City of the Decapolis* (New Haven: American Schools of Oriental Research).

Kraus, Samuel (1898), *Griechische und lateinische Lehnwörter im Talmud, Midrasch und Targum, II* (Berlin: S. Calvary).

—— (1902), 'Zur Topographie von Caesarea', *JQR (old series)* 14: 745–51.

—— (1925), '*Aseret Harugei Malkhut* (Hebrew)', *HaShiloah* 44b: 112–14. Republished in A. Oppenheimer (ed.), The Bar Kokhba Revolt, Jerusalem 1980: 258–260.

Krenz, E. (1992), 'Caesarea and Early Christianity', in R.L. Vann (ed.), *Caesarea Papers 1: Straton's Tower, Herod's Harbor, and the Roman and Byzantine Caesarea* (JRA Suppl. Ser. 5; Ann Arbor, MI: Journal of Roman Archaeology): 261–67.

Kümmel, W.G. (1975), *Introduction to the New Testament (Eng. tr. H.C. Kee)* (London: SCM Press).

Kushnir-Stein, Alla (1995), 'The Predecessor of Caesarea: On the Identification of Demetrias in South Phoenicia', in John Humphrey (ed.), *The Roman and Byzantine Near East: Some Recent Archaeological Research* (JRA Suppl. 14; Ann Arbor, MI: Journal of Roman Archaeology): 9–14.

—— (2007), 'Two Local Weights from the Colony of Caesarea Maritima', *INR* 2: 137–41.

Kushnir-Stein, Alla and Holland, Lionel (2008), 'New inscribed lead weights from Caesarea', in Kenneth G. Holum, Jeniffer A. Stabler, and Edward Reinhardt (eds.), *Caesarea Reports and Studies* (BAR Int. Ser. 1784; Oxford): 209–11.

Lafontaine-Dosogne, J. and Orgels, B. (1967), *Itinéraires archéologiques dans la région d'Antioch. Recherches sur le monastère et sur l'iconographie de S. Syméon Stylite le jeune* (Brussels: Byzantion).

Lambert, C. and Pedemonte, Demeglio P. (1994), 'Ampolle devozionali ed itinerari di pellegrinaggio tra IV e VII secolo', *Antiquité Tardive* 2: 205–31.

Lämmer, Manfred (1972), 'Eine Propaganda-Aktion des Königs Herodes in Olympia', *Perspektiven der Sportwissenschaft, Jahrbuch der deutschen Sporthochschule Köln* 1.

—— (1973), 'Griechische Wettkämpfe in Jerusalem und ihre politischen Hintergründe', *Perspektiven der Sportwissenschaft, Jahrbuch der deutschen Sporthochschule Köln* 2: 182–227.

—— (1974), 'Die Kaiserspiele von Caesarea im Dienste der Politik des Königs Herodes', *Kölner Beiträge zur Sportwissenschaft* 3: 95–164.

—— (1981), 'The Attitude of King Agrippa I towards Greek Contests and Roman Games', in U. Zimri (ed.), *Physical Education and Sports in the Jewish History and Culture* (Netanya): 7–17.

Lampinen, Peter (1999a), 'A Further Note on the Coins of 'Demetrias which is on the sea'', in Kenneth G. Holum, Avner Raban, and Joseph Patrich (eds.), *Caesarea Papers 2* (JRA Suppl. 35; Ann Arbor, MI: Journal of Roman Archaeology): 358–59.

—— (1999b), 'The gold hoard of 4th-c. solidi found in 1993', in K.G. Holum, A. Raban, and J. Patrich (eds.), *Caesarea Papers 2* (Ann Arbor, MI): 368–88.

Lancaster, Lynne (1995), 'Concrete Vaulted Construction: Developments in Rome from Nero to Trajan', Ph.D. dissertation (Oxford University).

Laniado, Avshalom (2002), *Recherches sur les notables municipaux dans l'empire protobyzantine* (Travaux et memoires du centre de recherche d'histoire et civilisation de Byzance. College de France. Monographies 13; Paris).

Lapp, Nancy L. (2000), 'Some Byzantine Pilgrim Flasks in the Pittsburgh Theological Seminary Bible Land Museum', in Lawrence E. Stager and Joseph A. Greene (ed.), *The Archaeology of Jordan and Beyond. Essays in Honor of James A. Sauer* (Winona Lake, Indiana: Eisenbrauns): 277–89.

Lassus, Jean (1932), 'Images de stylites', *Bulletine d' études Orientales* 2: 67–82.

—— (1947), *Sanctuaires Chrétiennes de la Syrie* (Paris: Geuthner).

—— (1972), *Antioch on the Orontes V: Les portiques d'Antioche* (Princeton: Princeton University Press).

Lauffrey, J. (1958), 'L'urbanism antique en proche orient', in Carsten Hoeg (ed.), *Urbanism and Town Planning: The Classical Pattern of Modern Western Civilization* (Acta Congressus Madvigiani, 4; Copenhagen: Ejnar Munksgaard): 7–26.

Lavan, Luke (1999), 'Late antique governor's palaces: a gazetteer', *Antiquité Tardive* 7: 135–67.

—— (2001), 'The praetoria of civil governors in late antiquity', in Luke Lavan (ed.), *Recent research in Late-Antique urbanism* (JRA Suppl. Ser. 42; Portsmouth, RI): 39–56.

Lawlor, Hugh Jackson (1912, reprt. Amsterdam 1973), 'The Earlier Forms of *The Ecclesiastical History*', in H.J. Lawlor (ed.), *Eusebiana. Essays on The Ecclesiastical History of Eusebius Pamphili, ca. 264–349 A.D., Bishop of Caesarea* (Oxford): 279–83.

—— (1973), 'The Chronology of Eusebius' 'Martyrs of Palestine', in Hugh Jackson Lawlor (ed.), *Eusebiana. Essays on The Ecclesiastical History of Eusebius Pamphili, ca. 264–349 A.D., Bishop of Caesarea* (Oxford 1912, reprt. Amsterdam: Philo Press): 179–80.

Le-Guen, Brigitte (2001), *Les associations de technites dionysiaques à l'époque hellénistique, I: Corpus documentaire; II: Synthése (études d'archéologie Classique, XI–XII)* (Paris: De Boccard).

Lehmann, Clayton M. (1994), 'The Combined Caesarea Expeditions: The Excavation of Caesarea's Byzantine City Wall, 1989', *AASOR* 52: 121–31.

—— (1999), 'The governor's palace and warehouse complex, west flank (areas KK 7–9, CV, 1993–1995 excavations)', in Kenneth G. Holum, Avner Raban, and Joseph Patrich (eds.), *CP II* (35; Porthsmouth, RI: Journal of Roman Archaeology): 136–149.

Lehmann, Clayton M. and Holum, Kenneth G. (2000), *The Greek and Latin Inscriptions of Caesarea Maritima* (The Joint Expedition to Caesarea Maritima, Excavation Reports, 5; Boston, MA: The American Schools of Oriental Research).

Lenzen, Cherie Joyce (1983), 'The Byzantine/Islamic Occupation at Caesarea Maritima as Evidenced through the Pottery', Ph.D. dissertation (Drew University).

Le-Strange, Guy (1965), *Palestine Under the Moslems* (Beirut).

Levick, Barbara M. (1999), *Vespasian* (London: Routledge).

Levine, Israel Lee (1973), 'A propos de la foundation de la Tour de Straton', *RB* 80: 75–81.

—— (1974a), 'The Hasmonean Conquest of Straton's Tower', *IEJ* 24: 62–69.

—— (1974b), 'The Jewish-Greek Conflict in First Century Caesarea', *JJS* 25: 381–97.

—— (1975a), *Caesarea Under Roman Rule* (Leiden: Brill).

—— (1975b), *Roman Caesarea: An Archaeological-Topographical Study* (Qedem 2; Jerusalem: The Institute of Archaeology, TheHebrew University of Jerusalem).

—— (1975c), 'R. Abbahu of Caesarea', in Jacob Neusner (ed.), *Christianity, Judaism, and Other Greco-Roman Cults: Studies for Morton Smith at Sixty* (Leiden: Brill): 56–76.

—— (1978), 'R. Simeon B. Yohai and the purification of Tiberias: history and tradition', *HUCA* 49: 143–85.

—— (1992), 'The Jewish Community at Caesarea in Late Antiquity', in Robert Lindly Vann (ed.), *Caesarea Papers 1: Straton's Tower, Herod's Harbour, and Roman and Byzantine Caesarea (JRA Suppl. Series 5)* (Ann Arbor, MI: Journal of Roman Archaeology): 268–73.

—— (1996), 'Synagogue Officials: The Evidence from Caesarea and Its Implications for Palestine and the Diaspora', in Avner Raban and Kenneth G. Holum (eds.), *Caesarea Maritima. A Retrospective after Two Millennia* (Leiden – New York – Köln: Brill): 392–400.

—— (ed.), (1981), *Ancient Synagogues Revealed* (Jerusalem: Israel Exploration Society).

Levine, Israel Lee and Netzer, Ehud (1986), *Excavations at Caesarea Maritima 1975, 1976, 1979—Final Report* (Qedem 21; Jerusalem: The Institute of Archaeology, The Hebrew University of Jerusalem).

Levy-Rubin, Milka (2006), 'The Influence of the Muslim Conquest on the Settlement Pattern of Palestine during the Early Islamic Period (Hebrew)', *Cathedra* 121: 53–78.

Lichtenberger, Achim (1999), *Die Baupolitik Herodes des Großen* (Wiesbaden: Harrassowitz Verlag).

Lieberman, Saul (1939–44), 'The Martyrs of Caesarea', *Annuaire de l'Institute de Philologie et d'Hisoire Orientales et Slaves* 7: 400–06.

—— (1944), 'Roman Legal Institutions in Early Rabbinics and the Acta Martyrum', *JQR* 35: 1–57.

—— (1963), 'How Much Greek in Jewish Palestine?', in A. Altmann (ed.), *Biblical and other Studies* (Cambridge, Mass: Harvard University Press): 123–41 (reprinted in idem, Texts and Studies, New York 1976: 216–234).

Lieberman, Shaul (1931), 'Tiqunei Yerushalmi (Emendations to the Jerusalem Talmud) (Hebrew)', *Tarbiz* 2: 106–14.

—— (1991), *Studies in Palestinian Talmudic Literature* (ed. David Rosenthal; Jerusalem).

Liebeschuetz, Wolfgang (1991), 'The Circus Factions', *Saggi di Storia Antica 13 [Convegno per Santo Mazzarino, Roma 9–11 maggio 1991]* (Bretschneider): 163–85.

—— (1992), 'The End of the Ancient City', in J. Rich (ed.), *The City in Late Antiquity* (London and New York: Routledge): 1–49.

Lifshitz, Baruch J. (1957), 'Une inscription byzantine de Césarée en Israel', *REG* 70: 118–32.

—— (1961), 'Inscriptions grecques de Césarée en Palestine', *RB* 68: 115–26, Pls. I.a–d, II.a–c.

—— (1962), 'Inscriptions latines de Césarée en Palestine', *Latomus* 21: 149–50, pls. IV.1–2, V.3–6.

—— (1963a), 'Inscriptions grecques de Césarée en Palestine', *RB* 70: 256–57.

—— (1963b), 'Inscriptions latines de Césarée en Palestine', *Latomus* 22: 783–84, pls. LXIII–LXIV.1–3.

—— (1964), 'La nécropole juive de Césarée', *RB* 71: 384–87.

—— (1965), 'Inscriptions grecques de Césarée en Palestine', *RB* 72: 98–107, pl. VII, a–c.

—— (1966), 'Inscriptions grecques de Césarée en Palestine', *RB* 73: 248–57, pl. XI. a–d.

—— (1967a), 'Donateurs et fondateurs dans les synagogues juives', *Cahiers de la Revue Biblique* 7: 50–54, nos. 64–68.

—— (1967b), 'Inscriptions grecques de Césarée en Palestine', *RB* 74: 50–59, Pl. IV, a–g.

—— (1977), 'Césarée de Palestine, son histoire et ses institutions', in H.I. Temporini (ed.), *ANRW* (II.8; Berlin: W. de Gruyter): 490–518.

Lightfoot, J.B. (1877–1887), 'Eusebius', in William Smith and Henry Wace (eds.), *Dictionary of Christian Biography, Vol. II* (London: J. Murray).

Lipkunsky, Doron (1998), 'Or 'Aqiva (East) (Hebrew)', *HA* 108: 53–54.

—— (2000), 'Or 'Aqiva (East)', *ESI* 20: 37.

Little, J. (1985), 'Urban Change at Ptolemais', in G. Barker *et al.* (eds.), *Cyrenaica in Antiquity* (BAR Int. Ser. 236; Oxford: British Archaeological Reports): 43–47.

MacDonald, William L. (1986), *The Architecture of the Roman Empire II: An Urban Appraisal* (New Haven: Yale University Press).

Magen, Yitzhak (1993), 'Shechem', in E. Stern (ed.), *New Encyclopaedia of Archaeological Excavations in the Holy Land* (4; Jerusalem: Israel Exploration Society): 1357–58.

—— (2008), *Judea and Samaria: Researches and Discoveries* (JSP 6; Jerusalem).

Magness, Jodi (2001), 'The Cults of Isis and Kore at Samaria-Sebaste in the Hellenistic and Roman Periods', *HTR* 94: 157–77.

—— (2003), *The Archaeology of the Early Islamic Settlement in Palestine* (Winona Lake, IN: Eisenbrans).

Magoulias, H.J. (1967), 'Lives of Byzantine Saints as Sources of Data for the History of Magic in the Sixth and Seventh Centuries A.D. Sorcery, Relics and Icons', *Byzantion* 37: 228–69.

Maier, P.L. (1969), 'The Episode of the Golden Shields at Jerusalem', *HTR* 62: 109–21.

Malkin, Irad (1987), *Religion and Colonization in Ancient Greece* (Leiden: Brill).

Mann, Jacob (1939), 'Some Midrashic Genizah Fragments', *HUCA* 14: 303–17.

Maoz, Zvi Uri (1985), 'On the Hasmonean and Herodian Town-Plan of Jerusalem (Hebrew)', *EI* 18: 46–57.

—— (1998), 'The Sanctuary of Pan at Panias (Hebrew)', *Qadmoniot* 115: 18–25.

Maraval, Pierre (1985), *Lieux saints et pélerinages d'Orient* (Paris: Les Editions du Cerf).

Margalioth, Mordechai (1976), *Encyclopedia for the Talmud Sages and the Geonim (Hebrew)* (II; Tel Aviv: Yavneh Publishing House).

Maricq, Andre (1951), 'Une influence alexandrine sur l'art augustéen. Le Lageion et le Circus Maximus', *RA* 37: 26–45.

Marsden, Peter (1980), *Roman London* (London: Thames and Hudson).

Martindale, John Robert (1992), *The Prosopography of the Later Roman Empire, 3: 527–641* (Cambridge: Cambridge University Press).

Matheson, Susan B. (1994), 'The Goddess Tyché', in Jerome Jordan Pollitt *et al.* (eds.), *An Obsession with Fortune: Tyche in Greek and Roman Art* (Yale: Yale University Art Gallery Bulletin): 19–33.

Matz, David (1991), *Greek and Roman Sport. A Dictionary of Athletes and Events from the eighth century B.C. to the third century A.D.* (Jefferson, NC and London: McFarland).

Mayerson, P. (1986), 'Choricius of Gaza on the Water Supply System of Caesarea', *IEJ* 36: 269–72.

Mazor, Gabi and Bar-Nathan, Rachel (1998), 'Beth Shean', *ESI* 17: 7–36.

McGuckin, John Anthony (1992), 'Caesarea Maritima as Origen Knew it', in Robert J. Daly (ed.), *Qrigeniana Quinta: Papers of the 5th International Origen Conference* (Leuven: University Press): 3–25.

McKenzie, J. (1990), *The Architecture of Petra* (Oxford: Oxford University Press).

—— (2003), 'Glimpsing Alexandria from Archaeological Evidence', *JRA* 16: 35–63.

Meiggs, R. (1973), *Roman Ostia* (2 edn.; Oxford: Clarendon Press).

Meinardus, Otto Friedrich August (1961), *Monks and Monasteries of the Egyptian Deserts* (Cairo: American University in Cairo Press).

Mendels, Doron (1999), *The Media Revolution of Early Christianity. An Essay on Eusebius's Ecclesiastical History* (Grand Rapids, MI: William B. Eerdmans).

Mércérian, J. (1952), 'Le monastère de saint Syméon le stylite du Mont Admirable', *Actes du VIe congrès international des études byzantines, Paris 1948* (II; Paris): 299–302.

Merkelbach, Reinhold (1963), *Isisfeste in griechisch-römischer Zeit: Daten und Riten. Beiträge zur klassischen Philologie, 5* (Meisenheim am Glan: A. Hain).

Millar, Fergus (1984), 'Condemnation to hard labour in the Roman empire, from the Julio-Claudians to Constantine', *Papers of the British School in Rome* 52: 124–47.

—— (1990), 'The Roman Coloniae of the Near East', in Heikki Solin and Mika Kajava (eds.), *Roman Eastern Policy and Other Studies in Roman History [Proceedings of a Colloquium at Tvärminne, 2–3 October 1987]* (Helsinki: Finnish Society of Sciences and Letters): 7–58.

Miller, Stephen G. (1980), 'Turns and lanes in the ancient stadium', *AJA* 84: 159–66.

Miranda, E. (1989), 'Osservazioni sul culto di Euploia', *Miscellanea Grecae Romana* 14: 123–44.

Mor, Menachem (2003), *From Samaria to Shekhem: The Samaritan Congragation in Ancient Times (Hebrew)* (Jerusalem: Zalman Shazar Center).

Moretti, Luigi (1953), *Iscrizioni agonistiche greche* (Roma: A. Signorelli).

Moulton, Warren J. (1919–20), 'Gleaning in Archaeology and Epigraphy: A Caesarean Inscription', *AASOR* 1: 86–90.

Müller, Carol (ed.), (1855), *Geographi Graeci Minores* (1; Paris: A.F. Didot).

Müller, E.B. (1938), 'The Hippodrome', in Carl Hermann Kraeling (ed.), *Gerasa—City of the Decapolis* (New Haven: American Schools of Oriental Research): 85–100.

Mühlenbrock, J. (2003), *Tetrapylon: Zür Geschichte des viertorigen Bogenmonumentes in der römischen Architektur* (Paderborn: Scriptorium).

Musurillo, Herbert Anthony (1972), *The Acts of the Christian Martyrs* (Oxford: Clarendon Press).

Nagorsky, Alla (2003), 'Or 'Aqiva (A-3265), (Hebrew)', *HA-ESI* 115: 33*–34*, 41–42.

Nasrallah, J. (1972), 'Couvents de la Syrie du nord portant le nom de Siméon', *Syria* 49: 127–57.

Nau, François (1903), 'Le texte grec des récits utiles à l'âme d'Anastase (le Sinaite)', *Oriens Christianus* 3: 56–90.

Neeman, Yehuda (1997), 'The Expansion of the Samaritans after the Bar Kokhba Revolt (Hebrew)', *Sinai* 120: 139–49.

Neeman, Yehudah, Sender, Shlomo, and Oren, Eldad (2000), *The Archaeological Survey of Israel. Map of Mikhmoret (52), Map of Hadera (53)* (Jerusalem: Israel Antiquities Authority).

Negev, Avraham (1961), 'Notes and News: Caesarea', *IEJ* 11: 81–83.

—— (1963a), 'The Palimpsest of Caesarea Maritima', *ILN* 6483 (Nov. 2): 728–31.

—— (1963b), 'Where Vespasian Was Proclaimed Emperor, Caesarea Maritima on the Coast of Israel', *ILN* 6482: 684–86.

—— (1964), 'The High Level Aqueduct at Caesarea', *IEJ* 14: 237–49, Pl. 17C.

—— (1966a), 'Caesarea (Hebrew)', *Mada* 10.6: 343–44.

—— (1966b), 'Caesarea (Hebrew)', *Mada* 11.3: 142–44.

—— (1967), *Caesarea* (Tel Aviv: E. Lewin-Epstein).

—— (1971), 'Inscription hébraiques, grecques et latines de Césarée Maritime', *RB* 78: 247–63, Pl. I–IX.

—— (1972), 'A New Inscription from the High Level Aqueduct at Caesarea', *IEJ* 22: 52–53.

—— (1975), 'Caesarea', in Michael Avi-Yonah (ed.), *EAEHL* (Jerusalem: Israel Exploration Society): 270–85.

—— (1993), 'Caesarea. Excavations in the 1950s and 1960s', in Ephraim Stern (ed.), *NEAEHL* (Jerusalem: Israel Exploration Society): 272–78.

Nelis-Clément, Jocelyne and Roddaz, Jean-Michel (eds.) (2008), *Le cirque romain et son image* (Bordeaux: Ausonius) [Proceedings from an international colloquium held in Bordeaux, Oct. 19–21, 2006; Ausonius Editions—Mémoires 20].

Nesbitt, J.W. (1999), 'Byzantine Lead Seals from the Vicinity of the Governor's Palace and Warehouses (CC and KK)', in Kenneth G. Holum, Avner Raban, and Joseph Patrich (eds.), *Caesarea Papers 2 (JRA, Suppl. Ser. 35)* (Portsmouth, RI: Journal of Roman Archaeology).

Netzer, Eehud (1985), 'The swimming pools of the Hasmonean period at Jericho (Hebrew)', *EI* 18: 344–52.

—— (1986), 'The swimming pools of the Hasmonean period at Jericho', *Leichtweiss Institut für Wasserbau der Technischen Universität Brownschweig, Mitteilungen* 89: 1–12.

—— (1987), 'The Augusteum at Samaria-Sebaste—A New Outlook (Hebrew).', *EI* 19: 97–105.

—— (1991), *Masada III. The Yigael Yadin Excavations 1963–1965. Final Reports: The Buildings, Stratigraphy and Architecture* (Jerusalem: Israel Exploration Society).

—— (1996), 'The Promontory Palace', in Avner Raban and Kenneth G. Holum (eds.), *Caesarea Maritima. A Retrospective after Two Millennia* (Leiden, New York and Köln): 193–207.

—— (1999a), *Die Paläste der Hasmonäer und Herodes des Großen* (Mainz: Philipp von Zabern).

—— (1999b), *The Palaces of the Hasmoneans and Herod the Great (Hebrew)* (Jerusalem: Yad Yizhak ben Zvi).

—— (2006), *The Architecture of Herod the Great Builder* (Tübingen: Mohr Siebeck).

Neubauer, A. (1868), *La Géographie du Talmud* (Paris).

Nielsen, Inge (1990), *Thermae et Balnea: The Architectural and Cultural History of Roman Public Baths* (Aarhus: Aarhus University Press).

Niese, B. (ed.), (1887), *Flavi Josephi Opera* (1).

Nir, David (1959), 'Artificial Outlets of the Mount Carmel Valley Through the Coastal "Kurkar" Ridge', *IEJ* 9: 46–54.

Noth, Albrecht (1994), *The Early Arabic Historical Tradition: a Source-Critical Study, in collaboration with L.I. Conrad, trans. M. Bonner* (Princeton N.J.: Darwin Press).

Ogg, George (1968), *The Chronology of the Life of Paul* (London: Epworth Press).

Oikonomides, N. (1986), 'Silk Trade and Production in Byzantium from the Sixth to the Ninth Century: The Seals of Kommerkiarioi', *DOP* 40: 33–53.

Olami, Jacob and Ringel, Joseph (1975), 'New Inscriptions of the Tenth Legion Fretensis from the High Level Aqueduct of Caesarea', *IEJ* 25: 148–50.

Olami, Ya'aqov, Sender, Shlomo, and Oren, El'ad (2005), *Archaeological Survey of Israel. Map of Binyamina (48)* (Jerusalem).

Oleson, John Peter (1984), 'A Roman Water Mill on the Crocodilon River near Caesarea', *ZDPV* 100: 137–52.

—— (1985), 'Area P: Piscina', in Avner Raban (ed.), *Harbour Archaeology. Proceedings of the First International Workshop on Ancient Mediterranean Harbours. Caesarea Maritima* (BAR Inter. Ser. 491; Oxford: British Archaeological Reports): 160–67.

—— (2000), 'Ancient sounding-weights: a contribution to the history of Mediterranean navigation', *JRA* 13: 293–310.

Oleson, John Peter and Branton, Graham (1992), 'The Technology of King Herod's harbour', in Robert L. Vann (ed.), *Caesarea Papers 1* (Ann Arbor, MI: Journal of Roman Archaeology): 49–67.

Oleson, John Peter *et al.* (1994), *The Harbours of Caesarea Maritima, 2: the finds and the Ship* (BAR Int. Ser. 594; Oxford: Archeopress).

Olivová, V. (1989), 'Chariot racing in the ancient world', *Nikephoros* 2: 65–88.

Oppenheimer, Aharon (ed.), (1980), *The Bar Kokhba Revolt (Hebrew)* (Jerusalem: Zalman Shazar Center).

Ostrasz, Antony A. (1989), 'The Hippodrome of Gerasa: A Report on Excavation and Research, 1982–1987', *Syria* 66: 51–77.

—— (1991), 'The Excavation and restoration of the hippodrome at Jerash. A synopsis', *ADAJ* 35: 237–50.

Otto, Walter (1913), *Herodes: Beiträge zur Geschichte des letzten jüdischen Könighauses* (Stuttgart: J.B. Metzler).

Owens, Edward J. (1991), *The City in the Greek and Roman World* (London and New York: Routledge).

Palm, B. (1999), 'Die Officia der Statthalter in der Spätantike: Forschungstand und Perspektiven', *Antiquité Tardive* 7: 85–133.

Palmer, Andrew, Brock, Sebastian, and Hoyland, Robert (1993), *The Seventh Century in the West-Syrian Chronicles (Translated Texts for Historians, vol. 15)* (Liverpool: Liverpool University Press).

Parker, Alton J. (1992), *Ancient Shipwrecks of the Mediterranean and the Roman Provinces.* (BAR Int. Ser. 580; Oxford: Archeopress, Hadrian Books).

Pastor, Jack (1997), *Land and economy in ancient palestine* (London: Routledge).

Patrich, Joseph (1992), 'Hyrcania (Hebrew)', in Ephraim Stern (ed.), *NEAEHL* (Jerusalem: Israel Exploration Society): 447–50.

—— (1995a), 'The warehouses (horrea) of Caesarea in light of the new excavations', *Caesarea, A mercantile city by the sea (The Reuben and Edith Hecht Museum, University of Haifa, Catalogue 12)* (Haifa: Hecht Museum): 12–17 (Hebrew) 14* 18* (English).

—— (1995b), *Sabas, Leader of Palestinian Monasticism, A Comparative Study in Eastern Monasticism, Fourth to Seventh Centuries* (Dumbarton Oaks Studies 32; Washington, DC: Dumbarton Oaks).

—— (1996), 'Warehouses and Granaries in Caesarea Maritima', in Avner Raban and Kenneth G. Holum (eds.), *Caesrea Maritima. A Retrospective after two Millennia* (Leiden: Brill): 146–76.

—— (1997a), 'Caesarea Maritima, Israel', in Marc Mayers and Isabel Rodé (eds.), *Ciutats antigues de la Mediterrània* (Barcelona: Diputacio di Barcelona and Lunwerg Editores): 302–05.

—— (1997b), 'A Roman Byzantine Government Compound in Caesarea (Hebrew)', *Ariel*, XIX (122–123): 10–17.

—— (1997c), 'The Starting Gates (carceres) of the Herodian Hippodrome at Caesarea', *ASOR News* 47.2: A 43–44.

—— (1998a), 'The Caesarea Excavations Project—March 1992–June 1994, Combined Caesarea Excavations (A)', *ESI* 17: 50–57.

—— (1998b), 'Urban Ruralization in Provincia Palaestina: The Demise of the Byzantine Praetorium at Caesarea', *Twenty Fourth Annual Byzantine Studies Conference (Abstracts)* (University of Kentucky): 41.

—— (1999), 'Caesarea Maritima: the Provincial Capital of Judaea Palaestina and its Praetoria', *1999 Roman Archaeology Conference (Abstracts)* (University of Durham): 26.

—— (2000a), 'A Government Compound in Roman-Byzantine Caesarea (English section)', in R. Margolin (ed.), *Proceedings of the Twelfth World Congress of Jewish Studies, Division B, History of the Jewish People* (Jerusalem: The World Union for Jewish Studies): 35*–44*.

—— (2000b), 'A Chapel of St. Paul at Caesarea Maritima?', *LA* 50: 363–82, pls. 27–30.

—— (2001a), 'Urban Space in Caesarea Maritima, Israel', in Thomas S. Burns and John W. Eadie (eds.), *Urban Centers and Rural Contexts in Late Antiquity* (East Lansing, MI: Michigan State University Press): 77–110.

—— (2001b), 'The *Carceres* of the Herodian Hippodrome/Stadium at Caesarea Maritima and connections with the Circus Maximus', *JRA* 14: 269–83.

—— (2001c), 'Césarée: Une chapelle dédiée à saint Paul?', *Le Monde de la Bible* 136: 57.

—— (2002a), 'On the Forgotten Circus of Aelia Capitolina (Hebrew)', *Cathedra* 102: 29–50.

—— (2002b), 'On the Lost Circus of Aelia Capitolina', *SCI* XXI: 173–88.

—— (2002c), 'Four Christian Objects from Caesarea Maritima', *IMSA* 1: 21–32.

—— (2002d), 'Herod's Hippodrome/Stadium at Caesarea and the Games Conducted Therein', in L.V. Rutgers (ed.), *What has Athens to Do with Jerusalem. Essays in Honor of Gideon Foerster* (Leuven: P. Peeters): 29–68.

—— (2002e), 'Herod's Theater in Jerusalem—a new proposal', *IEJ* 52: 231–39.

—— (2002f), 'The Martyrs of Caesarea: the urban context', *LA* 52: 321–46.

—— (2002g), 'Caesarea: The Palace of the Roman Procurator and the Byzantine Governor; Warehouses Complex and the Starting Gates of the Herodian Stadium (Hebrew)', *Qadmoniot* 35 (124): 66–86.

—— (2003a), 'Herod's Hippodrome/Stadium at Caesarea in the Context of Greek and Roman Contests and Spectacles (Hebrew)', in E. Reiner and Y. Ben Arie (ed.), *VeZoth-LeYehudah [Yehudah Ben Porath Festschrift]* (Jerusalem: Yad Yizhak Ben Zvi): 119–66.

—— (2003b), 'More on the Hippodrome-Stadium of Caesarea Maritima: a response to the comments of Y. Porath', *JRA* 16: 456–59.

—— (2003c), 'On Circus Carceres and a third farfetched hypothesis. Comments on Y. Porat's article in Qadmoniot 125 'Theatre, Racing and Athletic Installations in Caesarea (Hebrew)', *Qadmoniot* 36 (126): 119–20.

—— (2004), 'Tyche Feast in Caesarea and the Foundation Myth of Straton Tower (Hebrew)', *Etmol*, 28 (168): 6–9.

—— (2005), 'Herodian Caesarea—the urban framework (Hebrew).' in Menachem Mor *et al.* (eds.), *For Uriel: Studies in the History of Israel in Antiquity Presented to Professor Uriel Rappaport* (Jerusalem: Zalman Shazar Center): 497–538.

—— (2006a), 'Caesarea in Transition from the Byzantine to the Muslim Regime: The Archaeological Evidence from the Southwestern Zone (Areas CC, KK, NN), and the Literary Sources (Hebrew)', *Cathedra* 122: 143–72.

—— (2006b), 'The Wall Street, the Eastern Stoa, the Location of the Tetrapylon, and the Halachic Status of Caesarea (interpreting *Tosefta Oholot* XVII:13) (Hebrew)', *Cathedra* 122: 7–30.

—— (2007), 'Herodian Caesarea: The Urban Space', in Nikos Kokkinos (ed.), *The World of the Herods. Volume 1 of the International Conference The World of the Herods and the Nabataeans held at the British Museum 17–19 April 2001* (Oriens et Occidens 14; Stuttgart: Franz Steiner Verlag): 93–130.

—— (2008), 'Caesarea', in Ephraim Stern *et al.* (eds.), *NEAEHL* (5, Supplementary Volume; Jerusalem: Israel Exploration Society): 1673–80.

—— (ed.), (2008), *Archaeological Excavations at Caesarea Maritima Areas CC, KK and NN. Final Report. Volume I: The Objects* (Jerusalem: Israel Exploration Society).

—— (2009a), 'The Wall Street, the Eastern Stoa, the Location of the *Tetrapylon*, and the Halachic Status of Caesarea (interpreting *Tosefta Ahilot*, 18:13)', in Leah Di-Segni, *et al.* (eds.), *Man Near a Roman Arch. Studies presented to Prof. Yoram Tsafrir* (Jerusalem: Israel Exploration Society): 142*–68*.

—— (2009b), 'On the proclamation of Caesarea as a Roman Colony (Hebrew)', in Joseph Geiger, Hannah M. Cotton, and Guy D. Stiebel (eds.), *Israel's Land. Papers Presented to Israel Shatzman on his Jubilee* (Jerusalem: The Open University of Israel and Israel Exploration Society): 135–56.

—— (2009c), 'Herodian Entertainment Structures', in: D.M. Jacobson and N. Kokkinos (eds.), *Herod and Augustus.* [Papers Presented at the IJS Conference, 21st–23rd June 2005] (Leiden – Boston: Brill): 181–213, 455–467.

—— (2010), 'The *Praetoria* at Caesarea Maritima', in T. Capelle *et al.* (eds.), *Imperium—Varus und seine Zeit. Internationales Kolloquium des LWL-Römermuseums am 28. und 29. April 2008 in Münster.* (Veröffentlichungen der Altertumskommission für Westfalen, Vol. 18; Münster: Aschendorff-Verlag): 175–186.

—— (forthcoming-a), 'Caesarea in Transition: The Archaeological Evidence from the Southwest Zone (Areas CC, KK, NN)', in Kenneth G. Holum and Haim Lapin (eds.), *Shaping the Middle East: Jews, Christians, and Muslims in an Age of Transition* (Bethesda, MD: University Press of Maryland): 33-64.

—— (forthcoming-b), 'Roman *Hippo-Stadia*: The Hippodrome" of Gerasa reconsidered in light of the Herodian *Hippo-Stadium* of Caesarea Maritima, *Aram peridical.*

Patrich, Joseph *et al.* (1999), 'The warehouse complex and governor's palace (areas KK, CC, and NN, May 1993 December 1995)', in Kenneth G. Holum, Avner Raban, and Joseph Patrich (eds.), *Caesarea Papers 2 (JRA, Suppl. Ser. 35*; Portsmouth, Rhode Island: Journal of Roman Archaeology): 70–108.

Patrich, Joseph and Abu Shaneb, Mayada (2008), 'Chapter 4. The Clay Objects', in Joseph Patrich (ed.), *Archaeological Excavations at Caesarea Maritima Areas CC, KK and NN. Final Report. Volume I: The Objects* (Jerusalem: Israel Exploration Society): 301–32.

Patrich, Joseph and Amit, David (2002), 'The Aqueducts of Israel: an Introduction', in D. Amit, J. Patrich, and Y. Hirschfeld (eds.), *The Aqueducts of Israel* (JRA Suppl. Series 46; Portsmouth RI: Journal for Roman Archaeology): 9–20.

Patrich, Joseph and Pinkas, Shari (2008), 'Lamps and Flask Molds', in Joseph Patrich (ed.), *Archaeological Excavations at Caesarea Maritima Areas CC, KK and NN. Final Report. Volume I: The Objects* (Jerusalem: Israel Exploration Society): 296–300.

Patrich, Joseph and Rafael, Kate (2008), 'Chapter 8. The Jewelry', in Joseph Patrich (ed.), *Archaeological Excavations at Caesarea Maritima Areas CC, KK and NN. Final Report. Volume I: The Objects* (Jerusalem: Israel Exploration Society): 419–31.

Patrich, Joseph and Shadmi, Tamar (2008), 'Chapter 6. The Stone Vessels', in Joseph Patrich (ed.), *Archaeological Excavations at Caesarea Maritima Areas CC, KK and*

NN. Final Report. Volume I: The Objects (Jerusalem: Israel Exploration Society): 345–65.

Peilstöcker, Martin (1999), 'Or 'Aqiva (North), (Hebrew)', *HA-ESI* 110: 35*, 44–45.

Peleg, Michal and Reich, Ronny (1992), 'Excavations of a Segment of the Byzantine City Wall of Caesarea Maritima', *'Atiqot (English series):* 21: 137–70.

Peleg, Yehuda (1986), 'The Water Supply system of Caesarea', *Mitteilungen des Leicht-weiss-Institut für Wasserbau der Technischen Universität Braunschweig,* 89: 1–15.

Peña, Ignacio, Castellana, Pascal J., and Fernandez, Romuald (1975), *Les Stylites Syriens* (Jerusalem: Franciscan Printing Press).

Pflaum, Hans Georg (1950), *Les procurateurs équestres sous le haut-empire romain* (Paris: A. Maisonneuve).

Picard, Charles (1962), 'Lampes d'Isis Pelagia et Euploia à Délos et ailleurs', *RA* 228–30.

Piccirillo, Michelle (1992), *The Mosaics of Jordan* (Amman: American Center of Oriental Research).

Porath, Yosef (1990), 'Pipelines of the Caesarea water supply system (Hebrew; English Summary).' *'Atiqot* 10: 100–10.

—— (1994), 'Herod's amphitheatre at Caesarea: Preliminary Notice)', *'Atiqot* 25: 11*–19*.

—— (1995a), 'Herod's 'Amphitheatre' at Caesarea: A Multipurpose Entertainment Building', in J.H. Humphrey (ed.), *The Roman and Byzantine Near East: Some Recent Archaeological Research* (JRA Suppl.Series 14; Ann Arbor, MI: Journal of Roman Archaeology): 15–27, 269–72 (color pls.).

—— (1995b), 'Caesarea. Expedition of the Antiquities Authority', *ESI* 17: 39–49.

—— (1996a), 'The Evolution of the Urban Plan of Caesarea's Southwest Zone: New Evidence from the Current Excavations', in Avner Raban and Kenneth G. Holum (eds.), *Caesarea Maritima. A Retrospective after Two Millennia* (Leiden, New York and Köln): 105–20.

—— (1996b), 'Herod's "Amphitheatre" at Caesarea (Hebrew)', *Qadmoniot* 29 (112): 93–99.

—— (1998), 'The Caesarea Excavation Project—March 1992–June 1994: Expedition of the Antiquities Authority', *ESI* 17: 39–49.

—— (2000a), 'Caesarea—1994–1999', *HA* 112: 38–46, 34*–40*.

—— (2000b), 'The Wall Paintings on the Podium of Herod's Amphitheatron, Caesarea (Hebrew)', *Michmanin* 14: 42–48; English summary on pp. 17*–18*, colour pl. 7.

—— (2001), 'Caesarea (English and Hebrew)', *HA* 112: 38–46; 34*–40*.

—— (2002), 'The Water-Supply to Caesarea: A Re-assessment', in David Amit, Joseph Patrich, and Yizhar Hirschfeld (eds.), *The Aqueducts of Israel* (JRA Supp. Series 46; Portsmouth RI: Journal of Roman Archaeology): 104–29.

—— (2003), 'Theatre, Racing and Athletic Installations in Caesarea (Hebrew)', *Qadmoniot* XXXVI (125): 25–42.

—— (2006), 'Mansions on the Outskirts of Byzantine Caesarea (Hebrew)', *Cathedra* 122: 117–42.

—— (2008), 'Caesarea', in Ephraim Stern *et al.* (eds.), *NEAEHL* (5, Supplementary Volume; Jerusalem: Israel Exploration Society): 1656–65.

Porath, Yosef, Patrich, Joseph, and Raban, Avner (1998), 'The Caesarea Excavation Project—March 1992–June 1994', *ESI* 17: 39–77.

Potter, David Stone (1993), 'Martyrdom as Spectacle', in Ruth Scodel (ed.), *Theater and Society in the Classical World* (Ann Arbor, MI: University of Michigan Press): 55–88.

Pringle, Denis (1990), *The Churches of the Crusader Kingdom of Jerusalem. A Corpus. I* (Cambridge: Cambridge University Press).

Qidiocean, Nicola, Ayalon, Eitan, and Yosef, A. (1990), 'Two Winepresses from the Talmudic Period near Tell Qasila (Hebrew)', *ILP,* V–VI [23–24]: 23–36.

Quasten, Johannes (1950), *Patrology. Vol. 1: The Beginnings of Patristic Literature* (Utrecht and Antwerp: Spectrum).
—— (1990), *Patrology III* (Westminster, MD: Christian Classics, Inc.).
Raban, Avner (1987), 'The City Wall of Straton's Tower: Some New Archaeological Data', *BASOR* 268: 71–88.
—— (1992a), 'In Search of Strato's Tower', in Robert L. Vann (ed.), *Caesarea Papers 1: Straton's Tower, Herod's Harbor, and the Roman and Byzantine Caesarea* (JRA Suppl. Ser. 5; Ann Arbor, MI: Journal of Roman Archaeology): 7–22.
—— (1992b), 'Καισάρεια ἡ πρὸς Σεβαστῷ λιμένι: Two Harbours for Two Entities?' in Robert L. Vann (ed.), *Caesarea Papers 1: Straton's Tower, Herod's Harbor, and the Roman and Byzantine Caesarea* (JRA Suppl. Ser. 5; Ann Arbor, MI: Journal of Roman Archaeology): 68–74.
—— (1992c), 'Sebastos, the Herodian Harbor of Caesarea: How it was Built and Operated', *CMS News* 19: no page nos.
—— (1993), 'Maritime Caesarea', in Ephraim Stern (ed.), *The New Encyclopedia of Archaeological Excavations in the Holy Land* (Jerusalem: Israel Exploration Society): 286–91.
—— (1996), 'The Inner Harbor Basin of Caesarea: Archaeological Evidence for its Gradual Demise', in A. Raban, and K.G. Holum (ed.), *Caesarea Maritima. A Retrospective after Two Millennia* (Leiden, New York and Köln: Brill): 628–68.
—— (1998a), 'Caesarea Maritima—Land and Sea Excavations', *CMS News* 24–25: 32–.
—— (1998b), 'The Caesarea Excavation Project—March 1992–June 1994: Combined Caesarea Excavations (B)', *ESI* 17: 58–77.
—— (1999), 'The Lead Ingots from the Wreck Site (Area K8)', in Kenneth G. Holum, Avner Raban, and Joseph Patrich (eds.), *Caesarea Papers 2 (JRA, Suppl. Ser. 35)*: 179–88.
—— (2004), 'The History of Caesarea's Harbors (Hebrew)', *Qadmoniot* 37: 2–22.
—— (2009), *The Harbour of Sebastos (Caesarea Maritima) in its Roman Mediterranean Context. Edited by M. Artzy, B. Goodman and Z. Gal* (BAR Int. Ser. 1930; Oxford Hadrian Books).
Raban, Avner and Stieglitz, Rafael (1988), 'Caesarea, Ancient Harbor, 1987', *IEJ* 38: 276–78.
Raban, Avner et al. (1989), *The Harbours of Caesarea Maritima, 1: The Site and the Excavations: Results of the Caesarea Ancient Harbour Excavation Project 1980–1985* (BAR Int. Ser. 491; Oxford: Archeopress, Hadrian Books).
—— (1999), 'Land Excavations in the Inner Harbour (1993–94)', in Kenneth G. Holum, Avner Raban, and Joseph Patrich (eds.), *Caesarea Papers 2 (JRA, Suppl. Ser. no. 35)* (Portsmouth, RI: Journal of Roman Archaeology): 198–224.
Raban, Avner and Holum, Kenneth G. (eds.) (1996), *Caesarea Martima: A Retrospective After Two Millennia* (Leiden, New York, and Köln: Brill).
—— (1999), 'The Combined Caesarea Expeditions 1999 Field Season', *CMS News* 26: 9–12.
Raban, Avner, Holum, Kenneth G., and Blakely, Jeffery A. (1993), *The Combined Caesarea Expeditions Field Report of the 1992 Season* (Haifa).
Rackham, Richard Belward (1901, reprt. Ann Arbor, MI 1964), *The Acts of the Apostles* (Grand Rapids, Michigan: Baker Book House).
Rafael, Kate (2008), 'Chapter 9: The Metal Objects', in Joseph Patrich (ed.), *Archaeological Excavations at Caesarea Maritima Areas CC, KK and NN. Final Report. Volume I: The Objects* (Jerusalem: Israel Exploration Society): 433–69.
Rankov, Boris (1999), 'The Governor's Men: The Officium Consularis in Provincial Administration', in Adrian Goldsworthy and Ian Haynes (eds.), *The Roman Army as a Community (JRA Suppl. Ser. 34)* (Portsmouth, RI: Journal of Roman Archaeology): 15–34.

Ratner, Dov-Bear (1967), *Ahavat Tsion LeMoed Qatan (Hebrew)* (Jerusalem).

Rea, John (1977), 'Two Legates and a Procurator of Syria Palaestina', *ZPE* 26: 217–22.

Reich, Ronny (1985), 'On Some Byzantine Remains', *'Atiqot (Eng. Ser.)*, 17: 206–13.

Reifenberg, Adolf (1950), 'Archaeological Discoveries by Air Photographs in Israel', *Archaeology* 3: 40–46.

—— (1951), 'Caesarea: A Study in the Decline of a Town', *IEJ* 1: 20–32.

Reisner, George Andrew, Fisher, Clarence Stanley, and Lyon, David Gordon (1924), *Harvard Excavations at Samaria, 1908–1910* (Cambridge MA: Harvard University Press).

Reynolds, Joyce (1982), *Aphrodisias and Rome* (Journal of Roman Studies Monograph 1; London: Society for the Promotion of Roman Studies).

—— (1988), 'Cities', in David C. Braund (ed.), *The Administration of the Roman Empire 241BC–AD193* (Exeter: University of Exeter): 15–51.

Richardson, Peter (1996), *Herod. King of the Jews and Friend of the Romans* (Edinburgh: T & T Clark).

Rickman, Geoffrey (1971), *Roman Granaries and Store Buildings* (Cambridge: University Press).

Ringel, Joseph (1972–75), 'The Harbor Deity of Caesarea (Hebrew)', *Sfunim* 4: 19–23.

—— (1975), *Césarée de Palestine: étude Historique et Archéologique* (Paris: Editions Ophrys).

Robert, Louis (1940, reprint Amsterdam 1971: A.M. Hakkert), *Les gladiateurs dans l'Orient grec* (Paris: E. Champion).

—— (1960), 'Monuments de gladiateurs dans l'Orient grec', *Hellenica 11–12* (Paris) III: 112–50, Pl. vi–xiv; V: 77–99, Pl. v–xiv; VII: 26–51, Pl. xvi–xxii; VIII: 39–72, Pl. xi–xxii, xxiv–xxvii.

Robins, G.A. (1987), '"Fifty Copies of the Sacred Writings" (V.C. 4. 36): Entire Bible or Gospel Books?', *Studia Patristica* 19: 93–98.

Rochman, B. (1998), 'Imperial Slammer Identified', *BAR* 24 (1): 18.

Rodan, Shimona (1999), 'Marine Tyche-Fortuna: The Goddess of City, Luck and Chance in the Coastal Cities of Eretz-Israel', M.A. thesis (University of Haifa).

Rogers, Guy M. (1991), *The Sacred Identity of Ephesos: Foundation Myths of a Roman City* (London: Routledge).

Roll, Israel (1989), 'A Latin Imperial Inscription from the Time of Diocletian Found at Yotvata', *IEJ* 39: 239–60.

—— (1996), 'Roman Roads to Caesarea Maritima', in Avner Raban and Kenneth G. Holum (eds.), *Caesarea Maritima. A Retrospective After Two Millennia* (Leiden, New York, Köln: Brill): 549–58.

Roll, Israel and Ayalon, Eitan (1981), 'Two Large Winepresses in the Red Soil Regions of Israel', *PEQ* 113: 111–25.

—— (1989), *Apollonia and Southern Sharon. Model of a Coastal City and its Hinterland (Hebrew)* (Tel Aviv).

Roller, Duane W. (1980), 'Hellenistic Pottery from Caesarea Maritima: A Preliminary Study', *BASOR* 238: 35–42.

—— (1982a), 'The Northern Plain of Sharon in the Hellenistic Period', *BASOR* 247: 43–52.

—— (1982b), 'The Wilfred Laurier University Survey of Northeastern Caesarea Maritima', *Levant* 14: 92–96.

—— (1983), 'The Problem of the Location of Straton's Tower', *BASOR* 252: 61–66.

—— (1992), 'Straton's Tower: Some Additional Thoughts', in Robert L. Vann (ed.), *Caesarea Papers 1: Straton's Tower, Herod's Harbor, and the Roman and Byzantine Caesarea* (JRA Suppl. Ser. 5; Ann Arbor MI: Journal of Roman Archaeology): 23–25.

—— (1998), *The Building Program of Herod the Great* (Berkeley, Los Angeles and London: University of California Press).

Ronchey, Silvia (2000), 'Les procès-verbaux des Martyres Chrétiens dans les Acta Martyrum et leur fortune', *Mélanges de l'école française de Rome. Antiquité* 112: 723–52.

Rosenberg, Silvia (1996), 'The Wall Paintings in the Herodian Palace at Jericho', in K. and G. Foerster Fittschen (ed.), *Judaea and the Greco-Roman World in the Time of Herod in the Light of Archaeological Evidence* (Göttingen: Vandenhoeck and Ruprecht): 121–38.

Rosenthal, David (1993), ''Hql-dma'- 'Sde-Bokhin': On the Usage of the Apocrypha for the Establishment of the Right Version in the Rabbinic Literature (Hebrew)', *Mehqarei Talmud* 2: 490–516.

Rossiter, Jeremy J. (1989), 'Roman villas of the Greek east and the villa in Gregory of Nyssa Ep. 20', *JRA* 2: 101–10.

Rostovtzeff, Michael (1941, repr. 1998), *Social history of the Hellenistic world* (II; Oxford: Clarendon Press).

Roth-Gerson, Leah (1987), *The Greek Inscriptions from the Synagogues in Eretz-Israel* (Jerusalem: Yad Yizhak Ben Zvi).

Roueché, Charlotte (1993), *Performers and Partisans at Aphrodisias in the Roman and Late Roman Periods* (Journal of Roman studies monograph 6; London: Society for the Promotion of Roman Studies).

Runia, David T. (1996), 'Caesarea Maritima and the Survival of Hellenistic-Jewish Literature', in Avner Raban and Kenneth G. Holum (eds.), *Caesarea Maritima. A Retrospective after Two Millennia* (Leiden – New York – Köln: Brill): 476–95.

Russell, Kenneth W. (1985), 'The Earthquake Chronology of Palestine and Northwest Arabia from the 2nd through the Mid-8th Century A.D', *BASOR* 260: 37–59.

Rutgers, Leonard V. (2000), *Subterranean Rome. In Search of the Origins of Christianity in the Catacombs of the Eternal City* (Louvain: Peeters).

Safrai, Shmuel (1959), 'Beth She'arim in the Talmudic Literature (Hebrew)', *EI* 5 [Mazar Volume]: 206–12.

—— (1967), 'Mitzvat Shebi'it after the destruction of the Second Temple (Hebrew)', *Tarbiz*, 36: 43–60.

—— (1994), *In the Days of the Second Temple, the Mishnah and the Talmud: Studies in the History of the Jewish People (Hebrew)* (I; Jerusalem: The Magnes Press).

—— (1996), *In the Days of the Second Temple, the Mishnah and the Talmud: Studies in the History of the Jewish People (Hebrew)* (II; Jerusalem: The Magnes Press).

Safrai, Zeev (1980), *Boundaries and Rule in Eretz Israel in the Mishnah and Talmud Period (Hebrew)* (Tel Aviv: HaKibbutz HaMeuhad).

—— (1985), 'The permit of the borders of Caesarea from regulations related to the Land (Hebrew)', *Sinai*, 96: 217–28.

—— (1994), *The economy of Roman Palestine* (London and New York: Routledge).

Salzman, Michele R. (1991), *On Roman Time: The Codex-calendar of 354 and the Rhythms of Urban Life in Late Antiquity* (Berkeley: University of California Press).

Sandys, John Edwin (ed.), (1963), *A Companion to Latin Studies.* (3rd edn., New York and London: Hafner).

Saradi, Helen G. (2006), *The Byzantine City in the Sixth Century: Literary Images and Historical Reality [Monographs of Messenian Archaeological Studies]* (Athens).

Saradi-Mendelovici, Helen (1990), 'Christian Attitude toward Pagan Monuments in Late Antiquity and Their Legacy in Later Byzantine Centuries', *DOP* 44: 47–61.

Sartre, Maurice (1991), *L'Orient Romain: Provinces et sociétés provinciales en Méditerranée orientale d'Auguste aux Sévéres (31 avant J.-C.–235 après J.-C.* (Paris: Seuil).

—— (2001), *D'Alexandre à Zénobie: Histoire du Levant antique IVᵉ siècle av. J.-C.–IIIᵉ siècle ap. J.-C.* (Paris: Fayard).

Schalit, Abraham (1937), *Roman Rule in Eretz Israel (Hebrew)* (Jerusalem: Mosad Bialik).

—— (1964), *King Herod—Portrait of a Ruler (Hebrew)* (Jerusalem: Bialik Institute).

—— (1969), *König Herodes. Der Mann und sein Werk* (Berlin: De Gruyter).

Schemmel, F. (1925), 'Die Schule von Caesarea in Palästina', *Philologische Wochenschrift* 45: 1277–80.

Schick, Robert (1995), *The Christian Communities of Palestine from Byzantine to Islamic Rule. A Historical and Archaeological Study* (Princeton, N.J.: Darwin Press).

Schlumberger, Daniel (1935), 'Etudes sur Palmyre I: Le development urbain de Palmyre', *Berytus* 2: 149–62.

Schmid, Benno (1947), *Studien zu Griechischen Ktisissagen* (Freiburg in der Schwiez: Paulusdruckerei).

Schürer, Emil (1901), *Geschichte des jüdischen Volkes im Zeitalter Jesu Christi 4* (Leipzig: Hinrichs).

—— (1973–87), *The History of the Jewish People in the Age of Jesus Christ, 3 vols,* eds. Geza Vermes, Fergus Millar, and M. Black (Edinburgh: Clark).

Schwabe, Moshe (1950a), 'The Bourgos Inscription from Caesarea Palaestina (Hebrew)', *Tarbiz* 20: 273–83.

—— (1950b), 'The Synagogue of Caesarea and its Inscriptions (Hebrew)', in S. Lieberman (ed.), *Alexander Marx Jubilee Volume* (New York): 433–50, Pls. 1–4.

Schwabe, Moshe and Lifshitz, Baruch (1967), *Beth Shearim. Volume Two: The Greek Inscriptions (Hebrew)* (Jerusalem: Israel Exploration Society).

Schwartz, Daniel R. (1992), 'Caesarea and its 'Isactium': Epigraphy, Numismatics and Herodian Chronology', in D.R. Schwartz (ed.), *Studies of the Jewish Background of Christianity* (Tübingen): 167–81.

Scullard, Howard Hayes (1979), *Roman Britain* (London: Tames and Hudson).

Segal, Arthur (1995), *Theatres in Roman Palestine and Provincia Arabia* (Leiden: Brill).

—— (1997), *From Function to Monument: Urban landscapes of Roman Palestine, Syria and Provincial Arabia* (Oxford: Oxbow Books).

Seibert, Jakob (1970), 'Philokles, Sohn des Apollodoros, König der Sidonier', *Historia* 19: 337–51.

Seigne, Jacques (1992), 'Jérash romaine et byzantine: développment urbain d'une ville provinciale orientale', *SHAJ* IV: 331–41.

Seyrig, Henri (1972), 'La Tyché de Césarée de Palestine', *Syria* 49: 112–15.

Shalom, Israel Ben (1994), *The House of Shamai and the Struggle of the Zealots against Rome (Hebrew)* (Jerusalem: Yad Yizhak Ben Zvi).

Sharon, Moshe (1986), 'The Cities of the Holy Land Under Islamic Rule (Hebrew)', *Cathedra* 40: 83–120.

—— (2002), 'The Decisive Battles in the Conquest of Syria (Hebrew)', *Cathedra* 104: 31–84.

Shaw, Brent D. (1993), 'The Passion of Perpetua', *Past and Present* 139: 3–45.

—— (1996), 'Body/Power/Identity: Passions of the Martyrs', *Journal of Early Christian Studies* 4/3: 269–312.

Sherwin-White, Adrian N. (1970a), 'Citizenship, Roman', *The Oxford Classical Dictionary. 2d ed.* (Oxford: Clarendon Press): 243–44.

—— (1970b), 'Colonization, Roman', *The Oxford Classical Dictionary. 2d ed.* (Oxford: Clarendon Press): 266.

—— (1973), *The Roman Citizenship. 2d ed.* (Oxford: Clarendon Press).

Simon, R.P. and E. Smith (1971), 'Chronique Archéologique: Césarée', *RB* 78: 591–92, Pl. XXIX.

Sion, Danny (1998), 'A Roman House of Winepresses in Akhziv (Hebrew)', *'Atiqot* 34: 85–99.

Smallwood, Mary E. (1976), *The Jews under Roman Rule from Pompey to Diocletian* (Studies in Judaism in Late Antiquity 20; Leiden: Brill).

Sodini, Jean-Pierre (1989), 'Remarques sur l'iconographie de Syméon l'Alépine, le premier stylite', *Monuments Piot,* 70: 29–53.

— (1995), 'Habitat de l'antiquité tardive 1', *Topoi* 5: 151–218.
— (1997), 'Habitat de l'antiquité tardive 2', *Topoi* 7: 435–577.
Sperber, Daniel (1977), 'Greek and Latin Words in Rabbinic Literature (Hebrew)', *BIA*, 14–15: 9–60.
— (1984), *A Dictionary of Greek and Latin Legal Terms in Rabbinic Literature* (Ramat Gan).
— (1986), *Nautica Talmudica* (Jerusalem).
Spiro, Marie (1992), 'Some Byzantine mosaics from Caesarea', in Robert L. Vann (ed.), *Caesarea Papers 1 (JRA, Suppl. Ser.* 5; Ann Arbor: Journal of Roman Archaeology): 245–60.
Stabler, Jeniffer, Holum, Kennet G., *et al.* (2008), 'The Warehouse Quarter (Area LL) and the Temple Platform (Area TP): 1996–2000 and 2002 Seasons', in Kenneth G. Holum, Jeniffer A. Stabler, and Edward Reinhardt (eds.), *Caesarea Reports and Studies* (British Archaeological Reports, International Series, no. xx; Oxford: BAR Int. Ser. 1784): 1–40.
Stambaugh, John E. (1989), *The Ancient Roman City* (Baltimore: The Johns Hopkins University Press).
Stanley, Farlen H. (1999), 'The South Flank of the Temple Platform (Area Z2, 1993–95 Excavations)', in K.G. Holum, A. Raban and J. Patrich (ed.), *Caesarea Papers 2* (JRA Suppl. 35; Ann Arbor MI: Journal of Roman Archaeology): 35–39.
Stark, K.B. (1852), *Gaza und die philistäische Küste* (Jena: F. Mauke).
Ste-Croix, G.E.M. de (1954), 'Aspects of the "Great Persecution"', *HTR*, 47: 75–109.
Stein, Alla (1990), 'Studies in Greek and Latin Inscriptions on the Palestinian Coinage under the Principate', PhD diss. (Tel Aviv University).
Stern, Ephraim (1978), *Excavations at Tel Mevorakh (1973–1976). Part. 1: From the Iron Age to the Roman Period* (Qedem, Monographs of the Institute of Archaeology, Hebrew University, 9; Jerusalem).
— (ed.), (1993), *The New Encyclopedia of Archaeological Excavations in the Holy Land* (Jerusalem: Israel Exploration Society).
— (2000), *Dor, The Ruler of the Sea* (Jerusalem: Israel Exploration Society).
Stern, Henri (1953), *Le calendrier de 354* (Paris: Imprimerie nationale).
Stieglitz, Rafael R. (1993), 'Straton's Tower: The Name, the History, and the Archaeological Evidence', in J. Aviram (ed.), *Biblical Archaeology Today, 1990. Proceedings of the Second International Congress on Biblical Archaeology* (Jerusalem: Israel Exploration Society): 546–51.
— (1996), 'Stratonos Pyrgos—Migdal Sar—Sebastos: History and Archaeology', in Avner Raban and Kenneth G. Holum (eds.), *Caesarea Maritima. A Retrospective after Two Millennia* (Leiden, New York and Köln: Brill): 593–608.
— (1998), 'A Late Byzantine reservoir and piscina at Tel Tanninim', *IEJ* 48: 54–65.
— (1999), 'Straton's Tower and Demetrias Again: One Town or Two?', in Kenneth G. Holum, Avner Raban, and Joseph Patrich (eds.), *Caesarea Papers 2* (JRA Suppl. 35; Ann Arbor, MI: Journal of Roman Archaeology): 359–60.
Stillwell, Richard (1952), *Corinth, II: the theatre* (Princeton).
Stratos, Andreas Nikolaou (1968), *Byzantium in the Seventh Century*, trans. Marc Ogilvie-Grant and H.T. Hionides (Amsterdam: A.M. Hakkert).
Strong, Donald Emrys (1966), *Greek and Roman Gold and Silver Plate* (London: Methuen).
Sussman, Varda (2008), 'Chapter 3. The Oil Lamps', in Joseph Patrich (ed.), *Archaeological Excavations at Caesarea Maritima Areas CC, KK and NN, Final Report. Volume I: The Objects* (Jerusalem: Israel Exploration Society): 207–92.
Sussman, Yaacov (1974), 'The Halakhic inscription from Beth Shean Valley (Hebrew)', *Tarbiz* 43: 88–160.
— (1975), 'The Halakhic inscription from Beth Shean Valley (Hebrew)', *Tarbiz* 44: 193–95.

—— (1976), 'Baraita deThumei Eretz Israel (Hebrew)', *Tarbitz* 45: 213–57.

Swaddling, Judith (1980), *The Olympic games* (London: The British Museum Press).

Taft, Robert F. (1996), 'Byzantine Communion Spoons. A Review of the Evidence', *DOP* 50: 209–38.

Tchalenko, Georges (1953), *Villages antiques de la Syrie du nord* (1; Paris: Geuthner).

Thomas, D. and R., Buyce (1992), 'The Origin of the Mound in Area KK: A Geoarchaeological Interpretation, unpublished paper prepared for the Annual Meeting of the American Schools of Oriental Research, Nov. 21–24', (San Francisco, CA).

—— (1993), 'Geoarchaeological Survey', in Avner Raban, Kenneth G. Holum, and Jeffrey A. Blakely (eds.), *The Combined Caesarea Expeditions Field Report of the 1992 Season. 2 Parts* (University of Haifa: The Recanati Center for Maritime Studies; Haifa: Center for Maritime Studies, University of Haifa), Part I: 74–75; Part II: 105, Fig. 44.

Tomlinson, Richard (1992), *From Mycenaea to Constantinople: The Evolution of the Ancient City* (London and New York: Routledge).

Toombs, Lawrence E. (1978), 'The Stratigraphy of Caesarea Maritima', in R.P.S. Moorey and Peter J. Parr (eds.), *Archaeology in the Levant: Essays for Kathleen Kenyon* (Warminster: Aris & Phillips): 223–32.

Toueg, Ronny (1998), 'History of the Inner Harbour in Caesarea', *CMS News* 24/25: 16–18.

Tsafrir, Yoram (1998), 'The Fate of Pagan Cult-Places in Palestine: The Archaeological Evidence with Emphasis on Bet Shean', in Haim Lapin (ed.), *Religious and Ethnic Communities in Later Roman Palestine* (Bethesda, MD: University Press of Maryland): 197–218.

Tsafrir, Yoram and Foerster, Gideon (1989), 'From Scythopolis to Baysan—Changing Concepts of Urbanism', in R. Geoffrey, D. King, and Averil Cameron (eds.), *The Byzantine and Early Islamic Near East II: Land Use and Settlement Patterns* (Studies in Late Antiquity and Early Islam; Princeton: Darwin Press): 95–116.

—— (1994), 'The excavations of the Hebrew University of Jerusalem expedition in Beth Shean, 1980–1994', *Qadmoniot* 27 (107–108): 113–15.

—— (1997), 'Urbanism at Scythopolis-Bet Shean in the Fourth to Seventh Centuries', *DOP* 51: 65–146.

Tsafrir, Yoram, Di-Segni, Leah, and Green, Judith (1994), *Tabula Imperii Romani. Iudaea-Palaestina. Maps and Gazetteer* (Jerusalem: Israel Academy of Sciences and Humanities).

Tsatskin, A. (1994), 'Application of soil micromorphology and geochemistry techniques for examining of anthropic and constructional materials in Caesarea. Interim Report.'.

Vann, Robert L. (1983), 'Byzantine Street Construction at Caesarea Maritima', in Robert L. Hohlfelder (ed.), *City, Town, and Countryside in the Early Byzantine Era* (East European Monographs 120, Byzantine Series 1; Boulder: Distributed by Columbia University Press): 161–74.

—— (1983), 'Herod's Harbor Construction Recovered Underwater', *BAR* 9 (3): 10–14.

—— (1991), 'The Drusion: a candidate for Herod's lighthouse at Caesarea Maritima', *IJNA* 20: 123–39.

—— (1992), 'Early Travelers and the First Archaeologists', in Robert L. Vann (ed.), *Caesarea Papers 1: Straton's Tower, Herod's Harbor, and the Roman and Byzantine Caesarea* (JRA Suppl. Ser. 5; Ann Arbor MI: Journal of Roman Archaeology): 275–90.

—— (ed.), (1992), *Caesarea Papers 1: Straton's Tower, Herod's Harbour, and Roman and Byzantine Caesarea* (JRA Suppl. Series, 5; Ann Arbor).

Ven, P. van den (1970), *La vie ancienne de S. Syméon Stylite le Jeune (521–592). Part 2* ([Subsidia Hagiographica 32]; Brussels: Société des Bollandistes).

Vermeule, Cornelius Clarkson (1959), *The Goddess Roma in the Art of the Roman Empire* (Cambridge, MA: Boston, Museum of Fine Arts).

Veyne, Paul (1999), 'Païens et chrétiens devant la gladiature', *Mélanges de l'école fran-çaise de Rome. Antiquité* 111: 883–917.

Vikan, Gary (1991a), '"Guided by Land and Sea.' Pilgrim Art and Pilgrim Travel in Early Byzantium', *Tesserae. Festschrift für Josef Engemann, Jahrbuch für Antike und Christentum, Erganzungsband* (Erganzungsband, 19; Münster: Aschendorff): 74–92.

—— (1991b), 'Menas Flasks', *The Oxford Dictionary of Byzantium* (II; New York and Oxford: Oxford University Press): 1340.

—— (1997), 'Don't Leave Home without Them. Pilgrim Eulogiai Ensure a Safe Trip', *BAR* 23 (4): 56–59.

Ville, Georges (1981), *La gladiature en occident des origines à la mort de Domitien* (Rome: Ecole francaise de Rome).

Vogel, Lise (1969), 'Circus race scenes in the Early Roman Empire', *Art Bulletin* 51: 155–61.

Ward-Perkins, John B. (1955), 'Early Roman Towns in Italy', *TPR* 26: 126–54.

—— (1974), *Cities of Ancient Greece and Italy: Planning in Classical Antiquity* (New York: George Braziller).

Weingarten, Susan (2000), 'Jerome's World: The Evidence of Saints' Lives', Ph.D. Dissertation (Tel Aviv University).

Weiss, Zeev (1995), 'Roman leisure culture and its influence upon the Jewish population in the Land of Israel [Hebrew]', *Qadmoniot* 28 (109): 2–19.

—— (1996), 'The Jews and the Games in Roman Caesarea', in Avner Raban and Kenneth G. Holum (eds.), *Caesarea Maritima. A Retrospective after Two Millennia* (Leiden, New York, Köln: Brill): 443–53.

—— (1999), 'Adopting a novelty: the Jews and the Roman games in Palestine', in John H. Humphrey (ed.), *The Roman and Byzantine Near East, II: Some recent archaeological research* (Portsmouth, RI: Journal of Roman Archaeology).

Weiss, Zeev and Netzer, Ehud (1994), *Sepphoris (Hebrew).* (Jerusalem: Israel Exploration Society).

Welch, Katherine (1998), 'The Stadium at Aphrodisias', *AJA* 102: 547–69.

—— (1998), 'Greek stadia and Roman spectacles: Aphrodisias, Athens, and the tomb of Herodes Atticus', *JRA* 11: 117–27.

—— (1999), 'Negotiating Roman Spectacle Architecture in the Greek world: Athens and Corinth', in Bettina Bergmann and Christine Kondoleon (eds.), *The Art of Ancient Spectacles* (Studies in the history of art, National Gallery of Art; Washington, D.C.: National Gallery of Art): 125–45.

Wenning, Robert (1986), 'Die Stadtgöttin von Caesarea Maritima', *Boreas* 9: 113–29.

Wharton, Annabel Jane (1995), *Refiguring the Post-Classical City: Dura Europos, Jerash, Jerusalem and Ravenna* (Cambridge: Cambridge University Press).

White, K.D. (1970), *Roman Farming* (London: Thames and Hudson).

—— (1975), *Farm Equipment of the Roman World* (Cambridge: Cambridge University Press).

—— (1984), *Greek and Roman Technology* (London: Thames and Hudson).

Wiemken, Robert C. and Holum, Kenneth G. (1981), 'The Joint Expedition to Caesarea Maritima: Eighth Season, 1979', *BASOR* 244: 29, 40–41.

Will, Ernest (1983), 'La coupe de Césarée de Palestine au Musée du Louvre', *Monuments et mémoires*, 65: 1–24.

—— (1987), 'La Tour de Straton: mythes et réalités', *Syria* 64: 245–51.

—— (1997), 'Antioche sur l'Oronte, Métropole de l'Asie', *Syria* 74: 99–113.

Wilson, Roger John Antony (1983), *Piazza Armerina* (London, Toronto, Sidney, New York: Granada).

Wissowa, Georg (1903), *Römische Bauernkalender: Apophoreton der Graeca Halensis* (Berlin).

Witt, Reginald Eldred (1966), 'Isis-Hellas', *PCPS n.s.*, 192: 48–69.

Yegul, Fikret (1992), *Bath and Bathing in Classical Antiquity* (New York: MIT Press).

Yevin, Shmuel (1955), 'Excavations at Caesarea Maritima', *Archaeology* 8: 122–29.

—— (1957), 'Césarée, Chronique archéologique', *RB* 64: 259–60.

Yizhaki, Arieh (ed.), (1979), *Israel Guide. An Encyclopedia for the Study of the Land, VI: the Sharon, southern Coastal Plain, and the northern Negev (Hebrew)* (Jerusalem: Keter Publishing House).

Young, D.C. (1988), 'Athletics', in Michael Grant and Rachel Kitzinger (eds.), *Civilization of the Ancient Mediterranean, Greece and Rome* (II; New York: Scribner's): 1131–42.

Yule, Brian and *et al.* (1999), 'Evaluation of the Inner Harbour', in Kenneth G. Holum, Avner Raban, and Joseph Patrich (eds.), *Caesarea Papers 2* (JRA Suppl. 35; Ann Arbor, MI: Journal of Roman Archaeology): 261–357.

Zacos, G. and Veglery, A. (1972), *Byzantine Lead Seals, 1:1* (Basel: J.J. Augustin, Glückstadt).

Zanker, Paul (1990), *The Power of Images in the Age of Augustus, A. Shapiro (Eng. transl.)* (Ann Arbor: The University of Michigan Press).

Zori, I.S. (1926), *Rabbi Yose son of Hanina of Qisrin (Hebrew)* (Jerusalem).

INDEX OF ANCIENT AUTHORS AND LITERARY SOURCES

INDEX OF PERSONAL NAMES

INDEX OF PLACES AND PEOPLE

GENERAL INDEX

accountant. See *noumerarios*
Actian Games   28 n. 96, 88–89, 89 n.
  67, 179 n. 8, 184, 196
administration   213, 225
  Byzantine imperial   130, 134, 188
  civil   137 n. 107
  imperial   134, 188
  language of   94
  provincial   60, 74, 76 n. 23, 79, 94,
  96, 107
  Persian   130, 146, 148
  Roman   72, 74
  seal of civil   137 n. 107
aediles   75
Agathé (the Good). See Isis
Agathe, name of C. Tyche   22, 84
agora   7, 8
agoranomos   136
agricultural products, permitted in
  sabbatical year   66, 66 n. 90
album ordinis   75
amphitheater   6, 7, 8, 31, 43, 44, 68,
  91, 100, 107, 112, 177, 272, 194–199,
  277–280
  subterranean tunnel system in   199,
  297
  See also hippodrome/stadium
amphitheatrum, denoting hippodrome
  or stadium   195, 195 n. 46
amphorae   112, 121–122, 122 n. 32,
  126, 226
  burials in   10, 42, 42 n. 5
ampullae   235, 249, 252–57, 258
amulet, showing corn ears   134
Ansar, the first supporters of
  Muhammed at Medina   163
antals   126
Aphrodite   87 n. 63, 102
  temple of   105 n. 69
Apollo   11, 22 n. 68, 102, 184 n. 23
  depicted on Louvre cup   80, 80 n. 39
Apollo/Asclepius, temple of   13
apsidal buildings   26 n. 88, 138, 151,
  214–216, 218, 242
aqueducts   36–37, 44, 93–94, 109, 117,
  119, 134, 145, 162 n. 64
Aramaic speakers   71
Artemis, Ephesian   102

Asclepius   11, 22, 80 n. 39, 102
  alliance with Straton depicted on
  Louvre cup   80
assizes   37, 208, 209, 216, 240, 242, 265,
  267
Astarte   8, 11
Athena   102
athletics (*gymnika*)   180–84, 200, 202,
  279

baking   119
balaneum, urban   109
bathhouses and bathing   26–28, 37, 44,
  106, 109, 110, 111 n. 106, 112, 117,
  127, 138, 138 n. 110, 154, 207, 209,
  216, 242, 270
bears   199, 271, 278
beasts, wild   31, 80 n. 39, 179, 181, 191,
  194, 202
  Christian martyrs prey for   32 n.
  111, 83, 178 n. 5, 194 n. 43, 260–61,
  264 n. 21, 267–68, 271, 274, 276,
  277, 277 n. 85, 278
  corpses prey to   264 n. 21, 269
  execution of criminals by   194, 276
  n. 77
  Jewish captives fighting with   34, 90,
  192
beds, produced in C.   119
beneficiarii (soldiers with administrative
  jobs)   210, 267
bone and ivory industry   118, 132
bone objects   120
boxing   182
bread stamp   251–52 n. 9
  eucharistic   235, 251
  eulogia   248–252
  St. Paul *eulogia*   235, 243, 249–51, 258
bread   118
  white   233
brinefish   119. *See also* muria
building materials   13–14, 17
  looting of   25, 150, 153, 164
  white stone (*leukês petras*)   6, 7, 13
  opus signium   14
  pozzolana   14, 25 n. 86, 99, 206 n. 4
  See also kurkar; marble
building techniques   21 n. 64, 201 n. 70

ILLUSTRATIONS

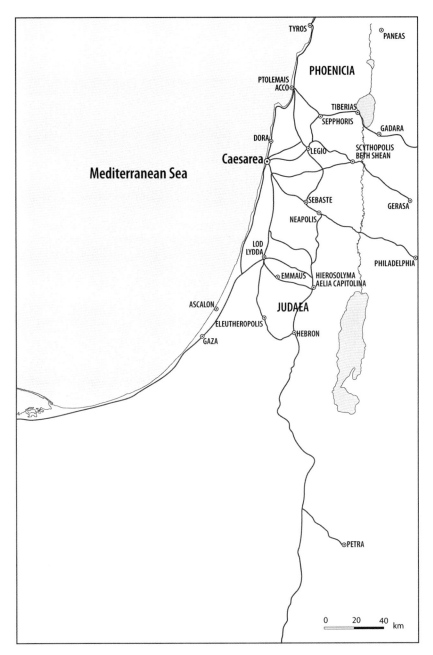

Fig. 1   Caesarea—Roads map (Soffer Mapping)

Fig. 2   Caesarea—aerial photograph, 10/04/1918 (Survey Of Israel—MAPI)

Fig. 3 Caesarea—aerial photograph, 12/12/1944 (Survey Of Israel—MAPI)

Fig. 4   Caesarea—aerial photograph, 21/11/2000 (Raqia-Ofek Aerial Photography)

Fig. 5   Areas CC, KK and NN as a pasture field in the early 1960's (courtesy A. Negev)

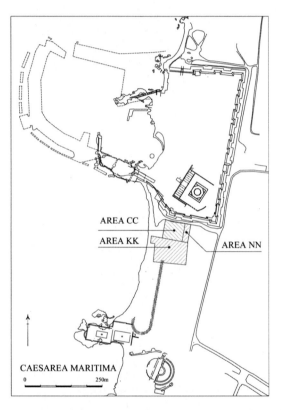

Fig. 6   Location map of the Excavated Areas CC, KK and NN (A. Iamim)

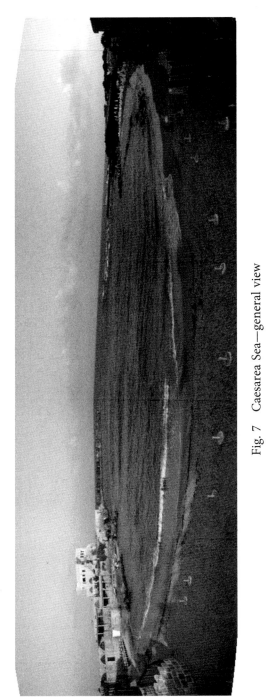

Fig. 7   Caesarea Sea—general view

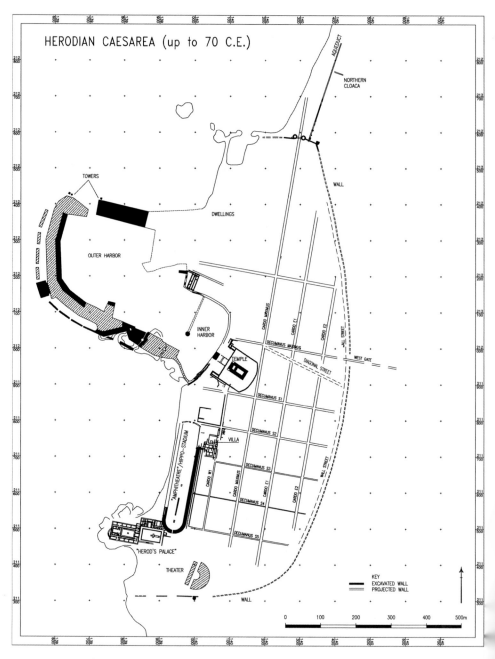

Fig. 8   Map of Herodian Caesarea (note new features: the diagonal street, suggested by
Ant. 15.349, and the peripheral "wall street", suggested by the Rabbinic sources, *m Oholot*
18:9 and *t Oholot* 18:13) (A. Iamim)

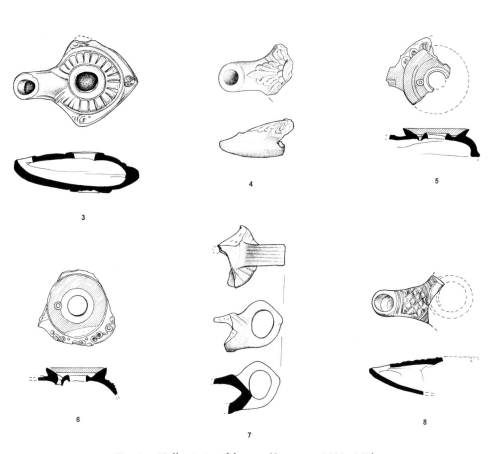

Fig. 9   Hellenistic oil lamps (Sussman 2008, 263)

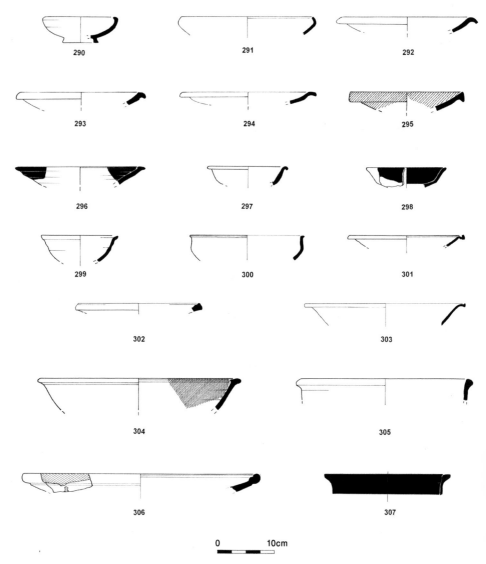

Fig. 10 Hellenistic bowls (Johnson 2008, nos. 290–305—various open bowls;
nos. 306–307—"West Slop" bowls)

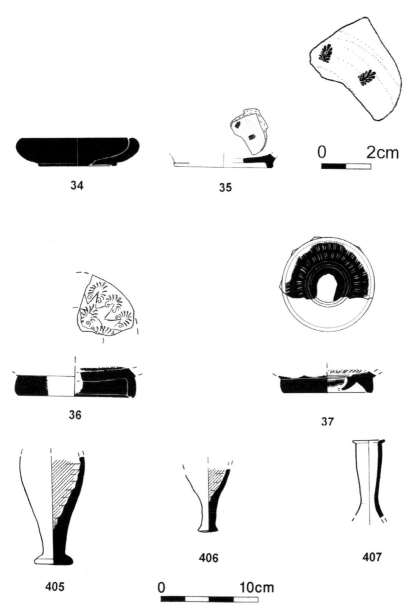

Fig. 11 Hellenistic pottery (Johnson 2008, nos. 34–37—Gray bowls;
nos. 405–407—Unguentaria)

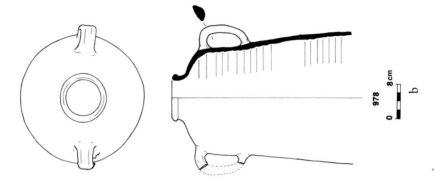

Fig. 12a–b   Jar burials in Area KK (Photo: Z. Friedman)

I) Libation in front of Tyche

II) Consultation in an oracle

III) Landing at a hostile shore

IV) Hand-shaking treaty between Straton and Asclepius

Fig. 13   The Louvre Caesarea Cup scenes, portraying a rite in front of the local
Tyche and the foundation myth of Straton Tower (Drawing: Sh. Patrich)

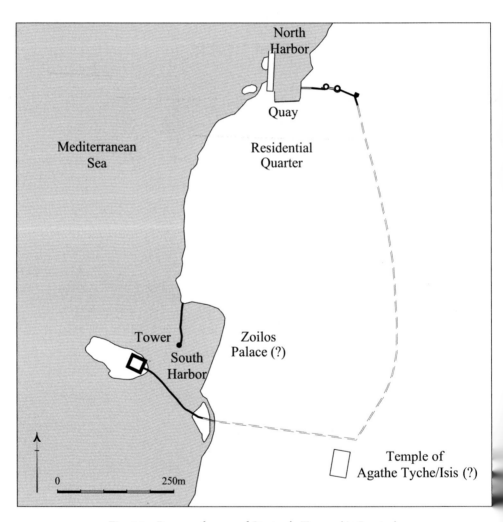

Fig. 14   Proposed map of Straton's Tower (A. Iamim)

a

b

Fig. 15a–b Herodian northern wall. a. Tower; b. Wall

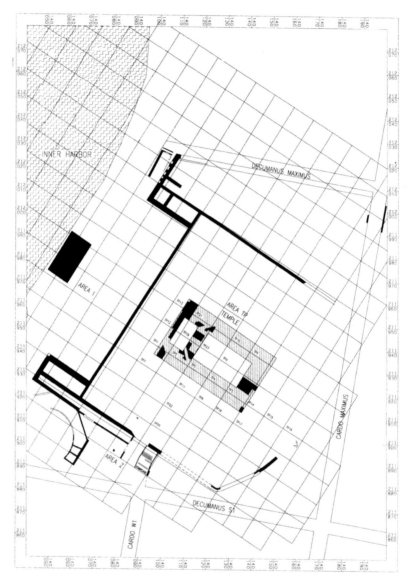

Fig. 16   The sacred *temenos* of Augustus and Roma (Holum 1999, 16, Fig. 4)

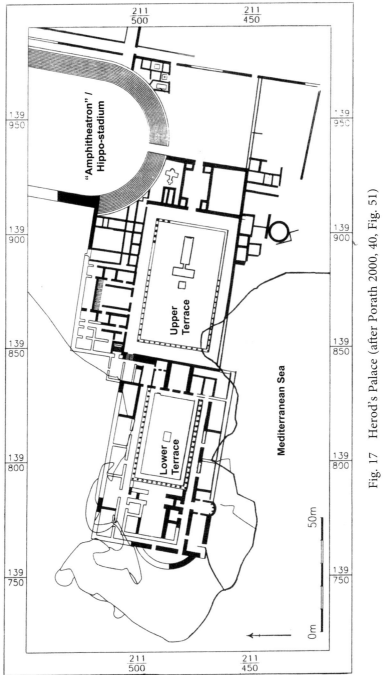

Fig. 17   Herod's Palace (after Porath 2000, 40, Fig. 51)

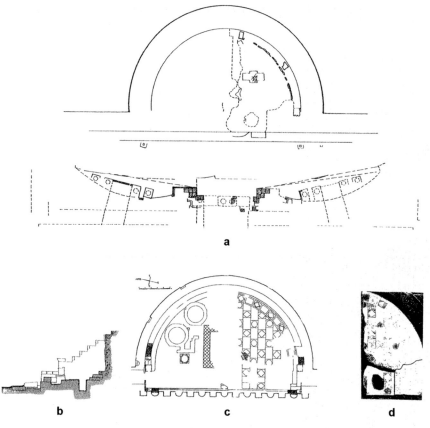

Fig. 18a–d The Herodian Theatre

a) Orchestra, *proscaenium* and *scaenefrons; proscaenium* line represents the
primitive Herodian phase (Frova *et al.* 1965, 129, Fig. 146);
b) Herodian pavement, *euripus*, stairs and seats under Roman *cavea* (Frova
et al. 1965, 86, Fig. 64);
c) Orchestra floor and *proscaenium*. The right side depicts the scheme of the
Herodian orchestra plaster floor (Frova *et al.* 1965, Fig. 72);
d) Herodian orchestra plaster floor (Frova *et al.* 1965, Pl. II, Fig. 93)

Fig. 19   The Herodian hippo-stadium, general view from south (A. Izdarechet)

Fig. 20   Head of emperor Hadrian, marble, found in debris in Area KK
(J.J. Gottlieb)

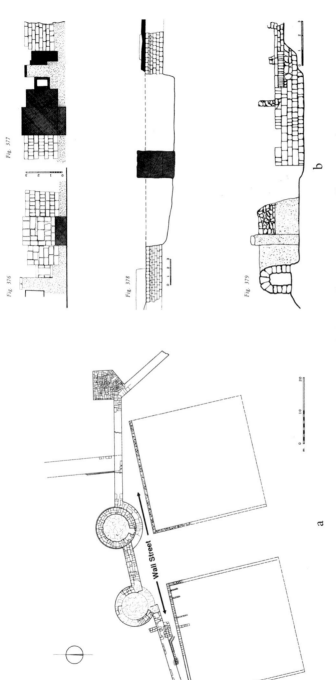

Fig. 21a–b   Remains of a wall street on the north (Finocchi 1965: 258–59, Ills. 285–90).

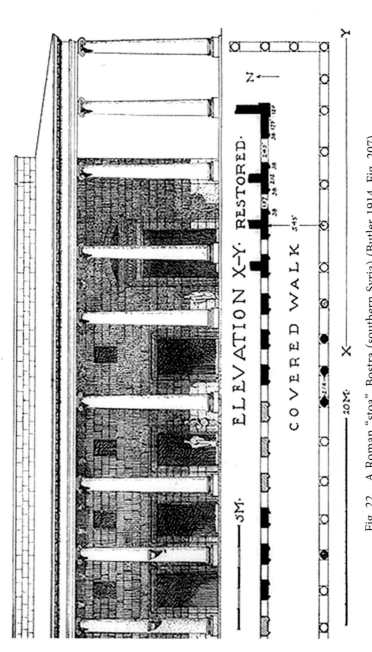

ELEVATION X-Y. RESTORED.

COVERED WALK

Fig. 22 A Roman "stoa", Bostra (southern Syria) (Butler 1914, Fig. 207)

Fig. 23   Gerasa, the northern *tetrapylon* of a *quadrifrons* type (Ball *et al.*
1986: 378, Fig. 14)

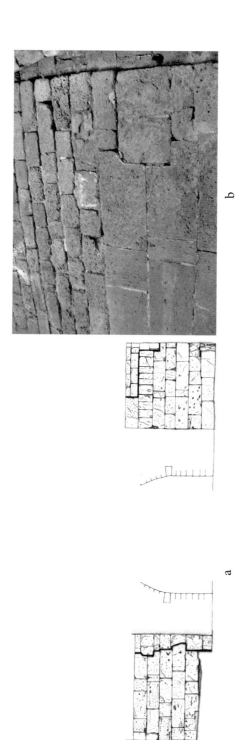

b

a

Fig. 24a–b Remains of a *terapylon* in the inner face of the eastern Crusaders' city gate (a. drawing: I. Levitt; b. photo: author)

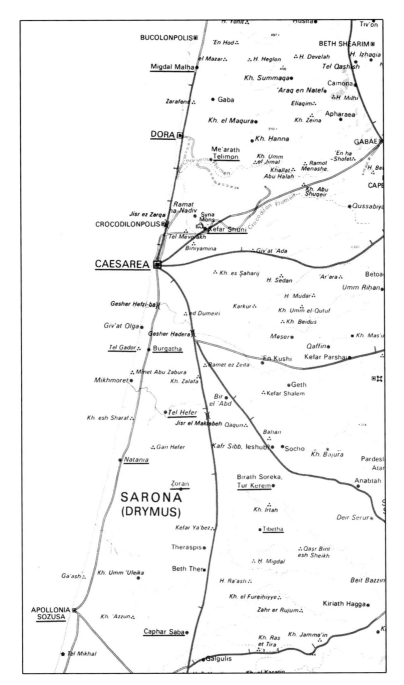

Fig. 25   Sites (underlined) in the permitted zone within the Land of Gentiles
around Caesarea in the Talmudic period (*TIR*)

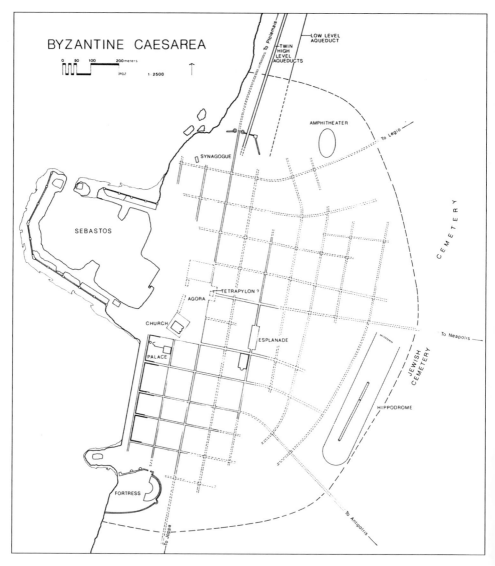

Fig. 26　Byzantine Caesarea (Holum *et al.* 1988: 163)

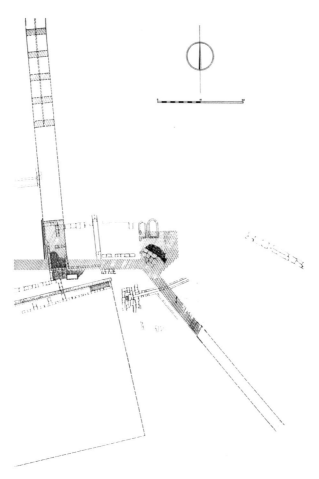

Fig. 27   Late-Roman remains exposed by the Italian Mission near the north-eastern tower of the Herodian city wall (Frova *et al.* 1965: Fig. 375)

IMP CAES VESPASIANVS AVG·PONT MAX
TRIB POT VIII IMP XIX P P COS VIII CENSOR ET
T CAES VESP AVG F PONT IMP XIIII TRIB POT VI COS VI
CENSOR

Fig. 28   Dedication inscription of the *praetorium* of the Roman procurator. Latin, 77/78 CE (Eck 2007, 219)

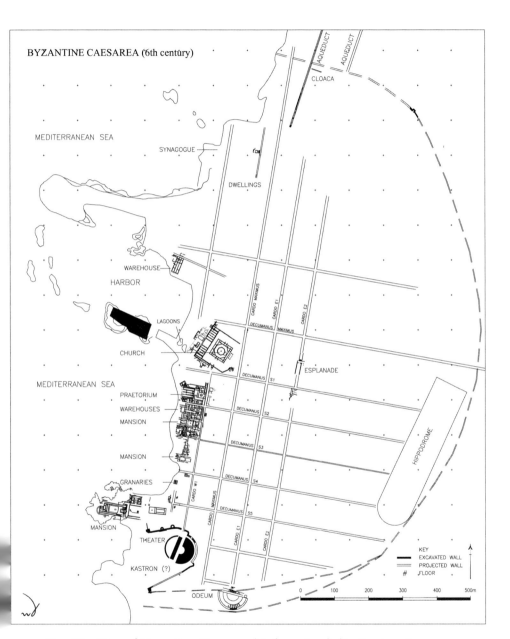

Fig. 29   Map of Byzantine Caesarea (sixth century) (A. Iamim, Caesarea
Graphics Archive)

Fig. 30 Corinthian marble capital decorated with crosses found near the
intersection of Cardo W1 and Decumanus S2

Fig. 31 Fresco depicting Christ and the twelve apostles, Area CC, Vault 9 (B. Haimov)

b

a

Fig. 32a–b   Remains of section of Cardo W1 between CC and NN. a. looking north; b. Looking south

Fig. 33   Decumanus S2, looking west (M. Piccirillo)

Fig. 34   Sacellum of Kore converted to martyrs chapel

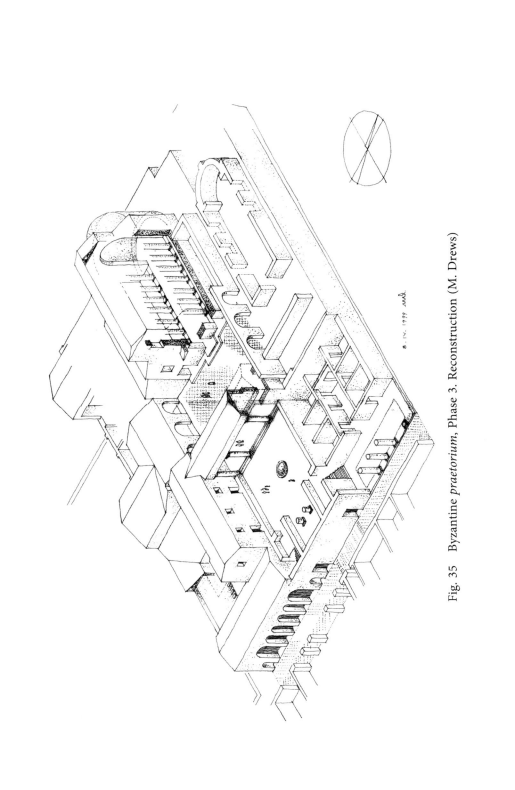

Fig. 35   Byzantine *praetorium*, Phase 3. Reconstruction (M. Drews)

Fig. 36   Caesarea SW zone, Looking south (Aric Baltineschter Aerial Photography)

Fig. 37   Herod's theater, the Roman imperial phase, looking west, 25/11/2000
(Raqia-Ofek aerial photography)

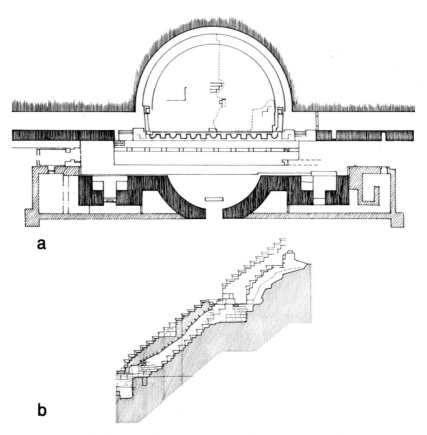

a

b

Fig. 38   Herod's theater, the Roman imperial phase: a. *Scaenefrons, pulpitum* and *orchestra*; b. Section across the *cavea* (Frova 1965, Figs. 23, 147)

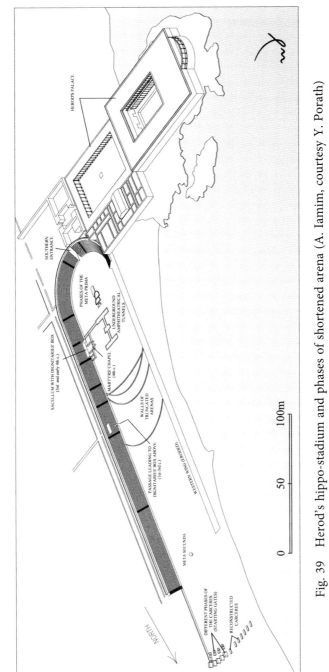

HEROD'S PALACE

SOUTHERN
ENTRANCE

PHASES OF THE
META PRIMA

UNDERGROUND
AMPHITHEATRICAL
TUNNELS

MARTYRS' CHAPEL
(4th c.)

SACELLUM WITH DIGNITARIES' BOX
(3rd and early 4th c.)

WALLS OF
TRUNCATED
ARENAS

PASSAGE LEADING TO
DIGNITARIES' BOX ABOVE
(1st-3rd c.)

WESTERN WING (IGNORED)

META SECUNDA

NORTH

DIFFERENT PHASES OF
THE CARCERES
(STARTING GATES)

RECONSTRUCTED
CARCERES

0   50   100m

Fig. 39   Herod's hippo-stadium and phases of shortened arena (A. Iamim, courtesy Y. Porath)

Fig. 40   Herod's hippo-stadium, general view from SW

Fig. 41   The Roman Circus near the SE Byzantine wall, looking north (A. Izdarechet)

Fig. 42   The warehouses complex in Area KK, general view, looking west (J.J. Gottlieb)

Fig. 43   Courtyard of Warehouse I, looking north

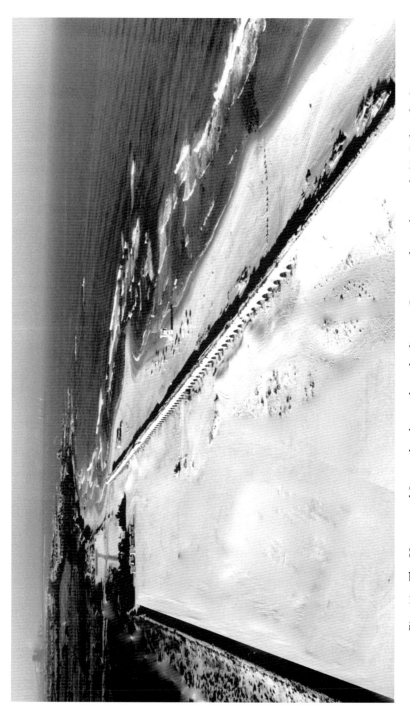

Fig. 44   The Upper- and Lower-level aqueducts leading to Caesarea from the north (A. Izdarechet)

Fig. 45 Nahal Tanninim dam and lake

Fig. 46   Public latrine at the intersection W1-S2, looking west

Fig. 47   *Nymphaeum* at the NW corner of the Temple Platform

Fig. 48   Hoard of 99 *solidi* hidden under floor in a dwelling in the northern zone of
Caesarea, Area G (A. Levine, courtesy JECM)

Fig. 49   Assemblage of pottery vessels, local and imported retrieved in the excavations at Areas CC, KK and NN (J.J. Gottlieb)

Fig. 50 Assemblage of pottery vessels, local and imported retrieved in the excavations at Areas CC, KK and NN
(J.J. Gottlieb)

a

b

Fig. 51   Roman bowls (J.J. Gottlieb)

a

0   10cm

b

Fig. 52a–b   Corinthian Relief Bowl depicting a chasing scene (Photo:
J.J. Gottlieb; drawing—Johnson 2008, no. 39)

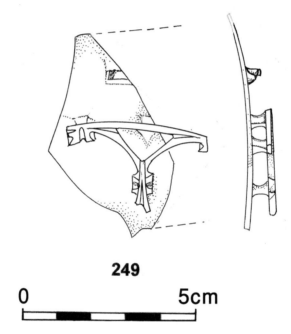

249

0   5cm

Fig. 53   A fragment of a "Cage Cup" (Israeli 2008, no. 249)

Fig. 54   Local amphorae (orange baggy-shaped and "Gaza" types) (G. Laron)

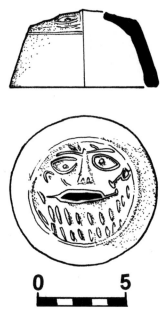

Fig. 55   A lid of a "safe box" (Patrich and Abu Shaneb 2008, no. 209)

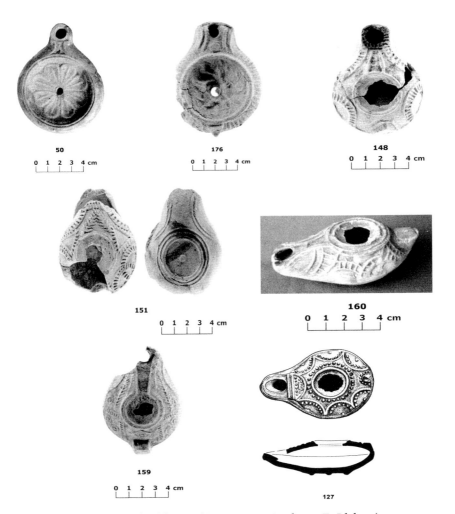

50

0 1 2 3 4 cm

176

0 1 2 3 4 cm

148

0 1 2 3 4 cm

151

0 1 2 3 4 cm

160

0 1 2 3 4 cm

159

0 1 2 3 4 cm

127

Fig. 56   Local oil lamps (Sussman 2008; photo: E. Idelson)

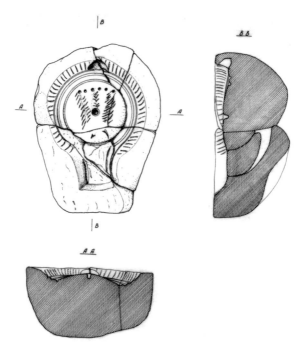

Fig. 57 A mold for an oil lamp type B10 (Patrich and Pinkas 2008)

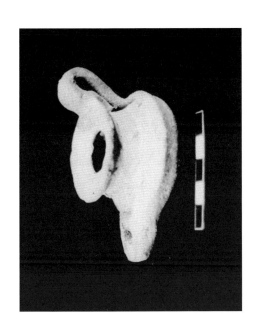

214

0 1 2 3 4 cm

Fig. 58   High and Low Boot-Shaped lamps (Photo: J.J. Gottlieb)

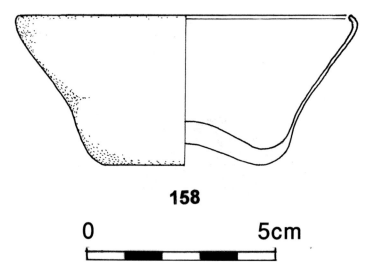

158

0   5cm

Fig. 59   Local small glass bowl (Israeli 2008, no. 158)

Fig. 60   A lead seal with the monograms of Georgios *kommerkiarios* on both sides (Nesbitt 1999: 130, no. 5)

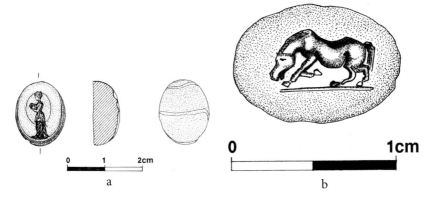

Fig. 61a–b   Gem stones (Patrich and Rafael 2008, nos. 22 and 80)

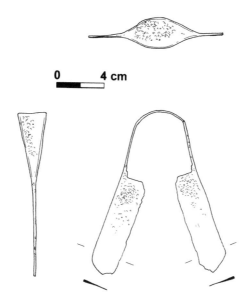

Fig. 62   Silver shears (Rafael 2008, no. 229)

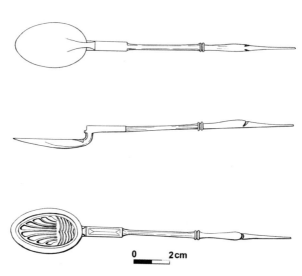

Fig. 63   Silver spoon (Rafael 2008, no. 250)

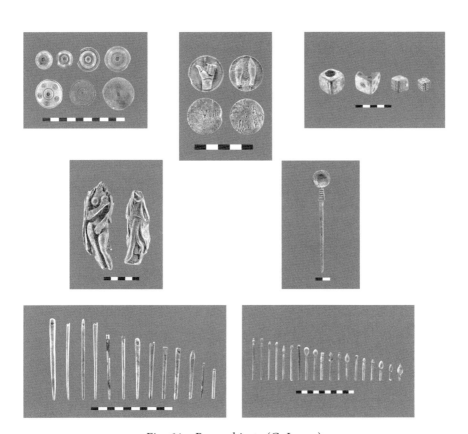

Fig. 64   Bone objects (G. Laron)

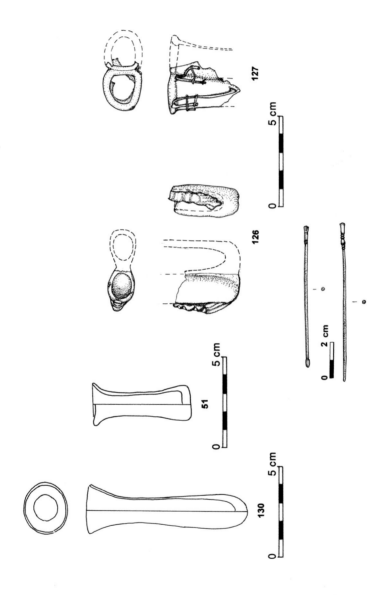

Fig. 65 Kohl bottles and sticks (Israeli 2008, nos. 51, 126, 127 and 130; Rafael 2008, nos. 197 and 203)

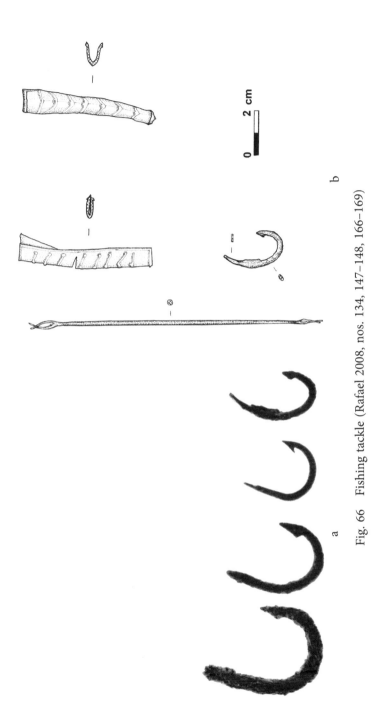

Fig. 66   Fishing tackle (Rafael 2008, nos. 134, 147–148, 166–169)

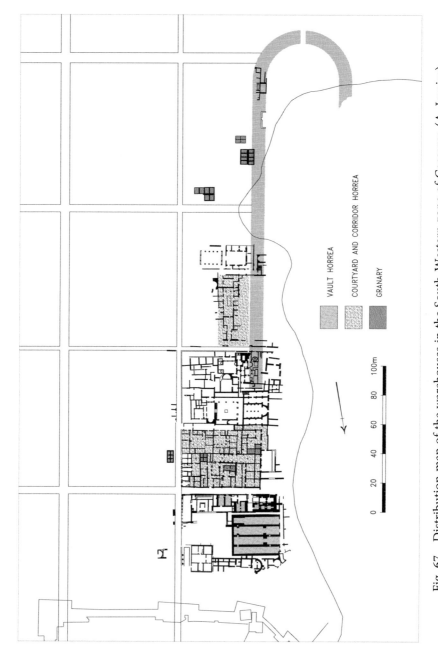

VAULT HORREA

COURTYARD AND CORRIDOR HORREA

GRANARY

0   20   40   60   80   100m

Fig. 67   Distribution map of the warehouses in the South-Western zone of Caesarea (A. Iamim)

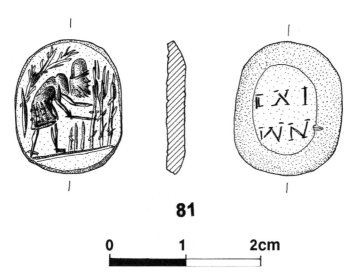

81

0   1   2cm

Fig. 68   Lumbago amulet (Patrich and Rafael, no. 81)

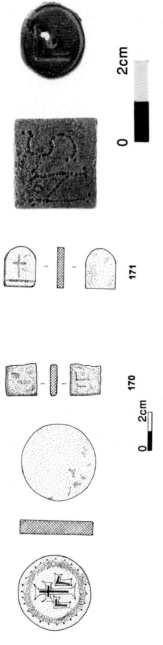

Fig. 69   Metal weights (Rafael 2008, nos. 170, 171, 174, 179, 182)

Fig. 70   Lead bullae (G. Laron)

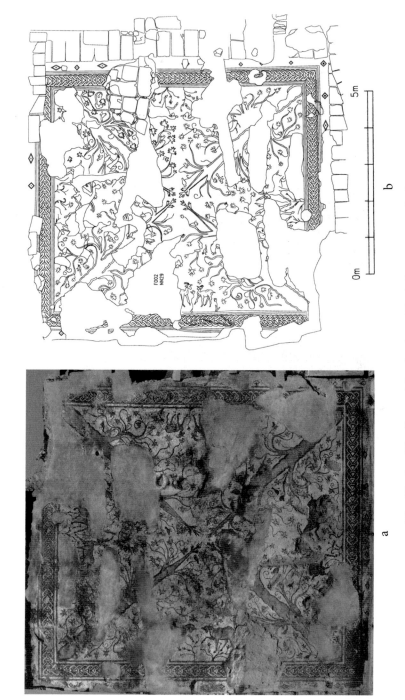

Fig. 71a–b   The Ibexes Mosaic, Area NN (Photo N. Davidov)

Fig. 72   Dionysius inscription (J.J. Gottlieb)

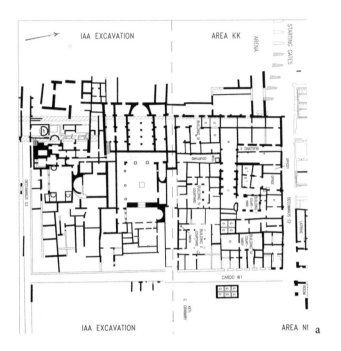

IAA EXCAVATION

AREA KK

ARENA

STARTING GATES

BUILDING II

BUILDING III

COURTYARD

OFFICE

DECUMANUS S2

OFFICE

BUILDING IV
COURTYARD

BUILDING V
COURTYARD

BUILDING VI
COURT.

BUILDING VII
COURT.

LATRINE

DECUMANUS S3

KEY:
G GRANARY

CARDO W1

ROOM

IAA EXCAVATION

AREA NI

a

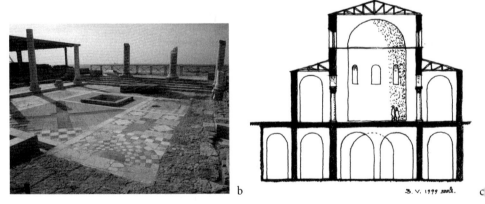

b

3. V. 1999

c

Fig. 73a–c Urban villa in the south-western zone of the city. a) plan; b) central courtyard; c) section N–S across the audience hall and its substructure, looking W (Plan: A. Iamim; photo: author; section: M. Drews)

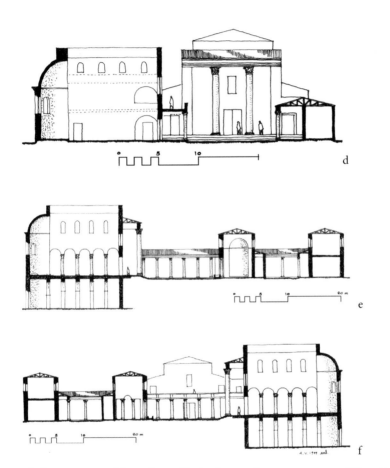

Fig. 73d–f   Sections of the urban villa in the south-western zone of the city.
d) N–S section, looking W, e) E–W section, looking N; f) E–W section,
looking S (M. Drews)

Fig. 74   A complex of warehouses. General view (A. Izdarechet)

Fig. 75   Villa corridor leading to the lower terrace and hence to the seashore

Fig. 76   The suburban villa with the Birds Mosaic, general view

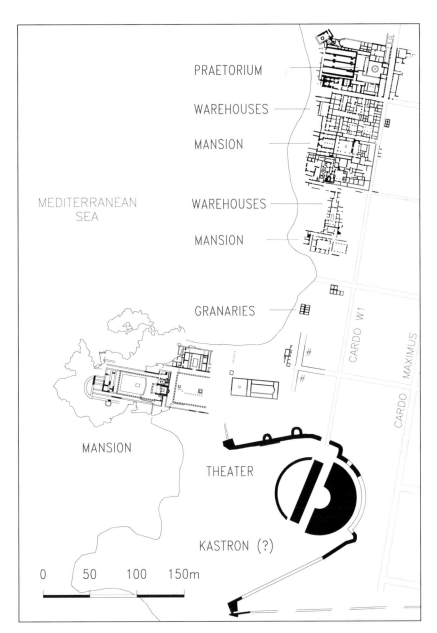

PRAETORIUM

WAREHOUSES

MANSION

MEDITERRANEAN
SEA

WAREHOUSES

MANSION

GRANARIES

CARDO W1

CARDO MAXIMUS

MANSION

THEATER

KASTRON (?)

0   50   100   150m

Fig. 77   Map of Southwest Zone (A. Iamim)

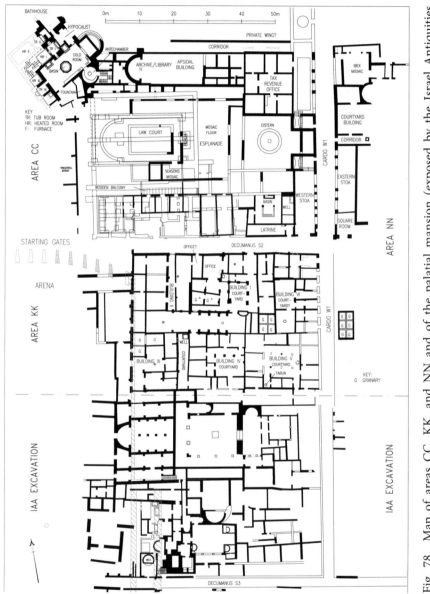

Fig. 78 Map of areas CC, KK, and NN and of the palatial mansion (exposed by the Israel Antiquities Authority) (A. Iamim)

Fig. 79   The latrine at the Cardo W1, Decumanus S2 intersection, looking east. Note the reduced dimensions of the later phase

Fig. 80a–c   a–b. The channel in vault 12, looking west; c. The channel in vault 6, looking west (J.J. Gottlieb)

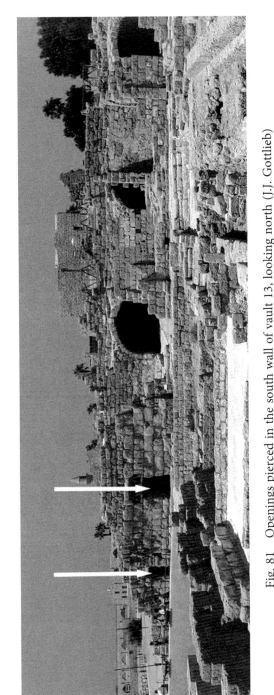

Fig. 81   Openings pierced in the south wall of vault 13, looking north (J.J. Gottlieb)

Fig. 82   Tavern couches on the north side of vault 13, looking northwest
(J.J. Gottlieb)

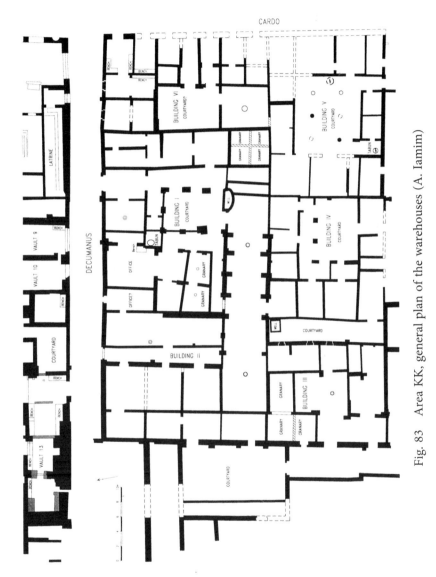

Fig. 83   Area KK, general plan of the warehouses (A. Iamim)

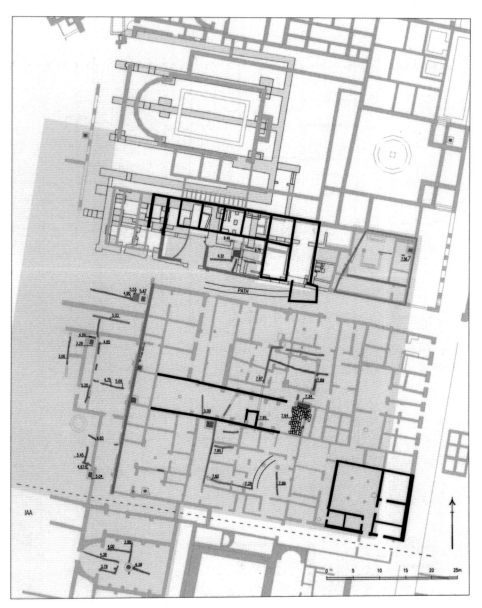

Fig. 84   General plan of the seventh-century irrigated garden plots above the Byzantine
structures in areas CC and KK (A. Iamim)

Fig. 85   Area KK, the *dolia*-hall of Building I, looking east. Note the bright sand layer (stratum II) above the dark garden soil (stratum IIIA) in the section to the east (Z. Friedman)

Fig. 86   Area KK, well and irrigation channel in the northwest corner of the area, looking south
(Z. Friedman)

Fig. 87   Area KK, irrigation channel on the south side of the area,
looking west (J.J. Gottlieb)

Fig. 88   Area CC, marble column incorporated into the wall of a terraced
garden in the southeast of the area, displaying a Christian cross incised when
the column had already fallen and lay in a horizontal position (J.J. Gottlieb,
B. Haimov)

Fig. 89   Area CC, segment of a marble Ionic capital built into the terrace wall of the garden plot established above the public latrine in the southeast of the area (J.J. Gottlieb)

Fig. 90 Lead seal with a monogram of Sergios (son of) John, the *patrikios* (Y. Dukhovni; Nesbitt 1999, no. 17)

Fig. 91 Area KK, burial layer (stratum I) above layer of fine sand (stratum II) and layer of garden soil (stratum IIIA) with an irrigation channel, in the southwestern corner of the area (J.J. Gottlieb)

Fig. 92   A small gate (wicket) in the northern Byzantine city-wall

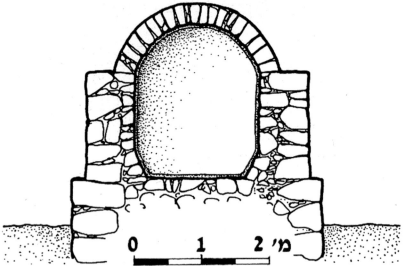

Fig. 93 The low-level aqueduct of Caesarea north of the city, photograph and section. The covered channel was high enough to permit a person to pass through it (Photo: A. Levine, Drawing: E. Cohen)

Fig. 94   Caesarea, the Herodian hippo-stadium, aerial view, 11/02/2000 (Raqia-Ofek Aerial Photography)

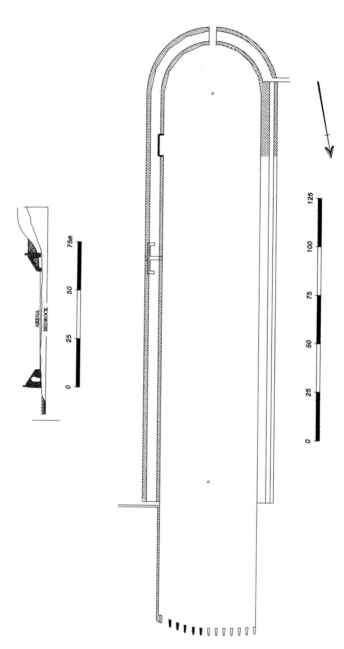

Fig. 95   Caesarea, the Herodian hipp-stadium (after Y. Porath 1995a, 18, Fig. 5; A. Iamim)

Fig. 96   Podium wall and seats on either side of the arched
passage leading up to the dignitaries *pulvinar*

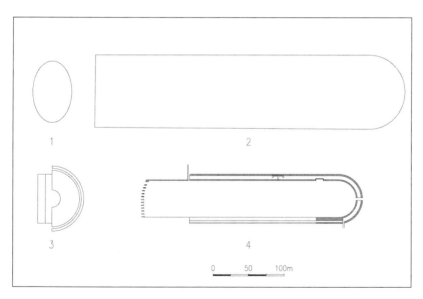

Fig. 97   Sports and entertainment structures in Caesarea: 1. Amphitheater;
2. Circus; 3. Theater; 4. Herod's Hippo-Stadium (A. Iamim)

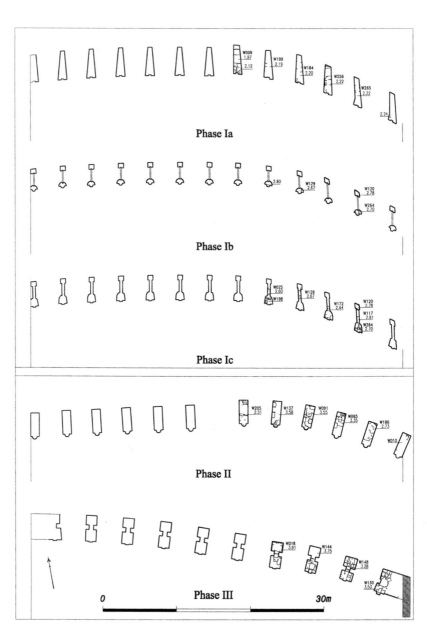

Fig. 98   Caesarea, the phases of the *carceres* (I. Levitt and A. Iamim)

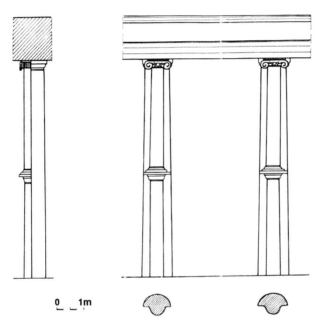

0 ‗ 1m

Fig. 99   Caesarea, reconstruction of the façade of the *carceres* dating to Phase
Ib (I. Levitt)

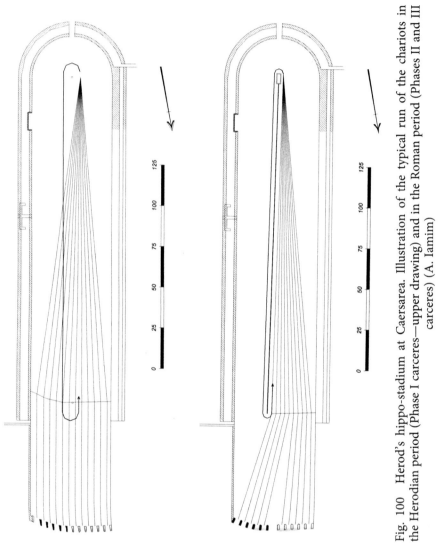

Fig. 100 Herod's hippo-stadium at Caersarea. Illustration of the typical run of the chariots in the Herodian period (Phase I carceres—upper drawing) and in the Roman period (Phases II and III carceres) (A. Iamim)

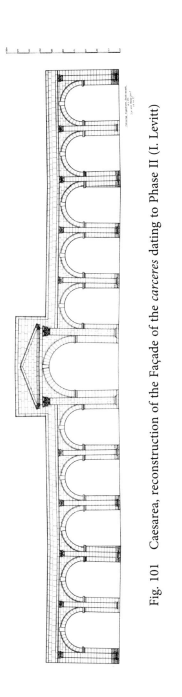

Fig. 101　Caesarea, reconstruction of the Façade of the *carceres* dating to Phase II (I. Levitt)

Fig. 102   Holes for fastening a protection net on top of the podium wall

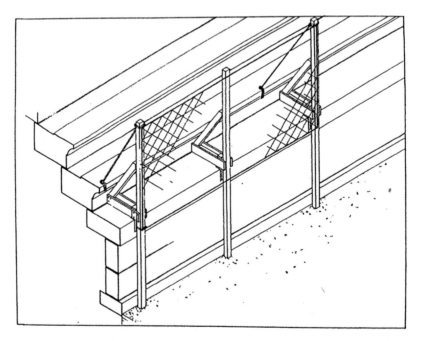

Fig. 103   Suggested reconstruction of a protective net attached to the podium
wall of Herod's hippo-stadium (D. Abu Hatzeira)

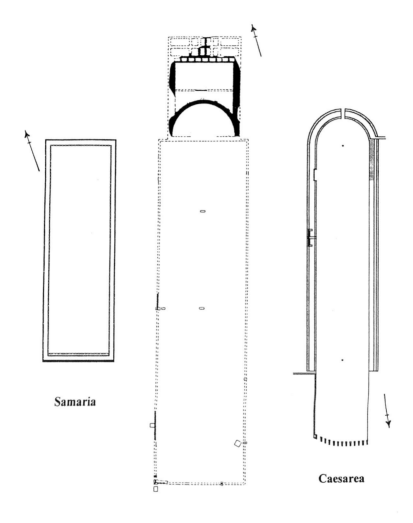

Samaria

Jericho

Caesarea

0   50

Fig. 104   Herodian stadiums: Samaria, Jericho, and Caesarea
(M. Abu Shaneb)

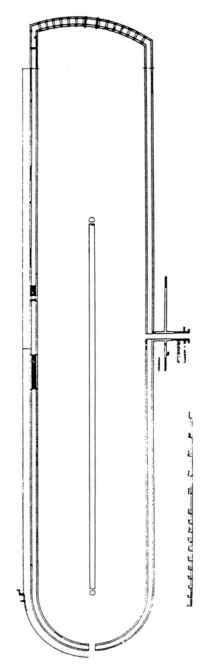

Fig. 105   The circus at Bovillea (Humphrey 1986, 563, Fig. 268)

Fig. 106   Herod's *praetorium*, general aerial view of the upper and lower
terraces, 21/11/1997 (Raqia-Ofek Aerial Photography)

Fig. 107   Herod's palace, aerial view of the upper terrace 11/02/2000 (Raqia-Ofek Aerial Photography)

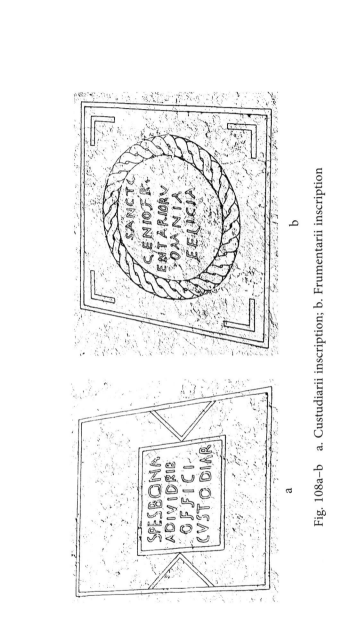

Fig. 108a–b   a. Custudiarii inscription; b. Frumentarii inscription

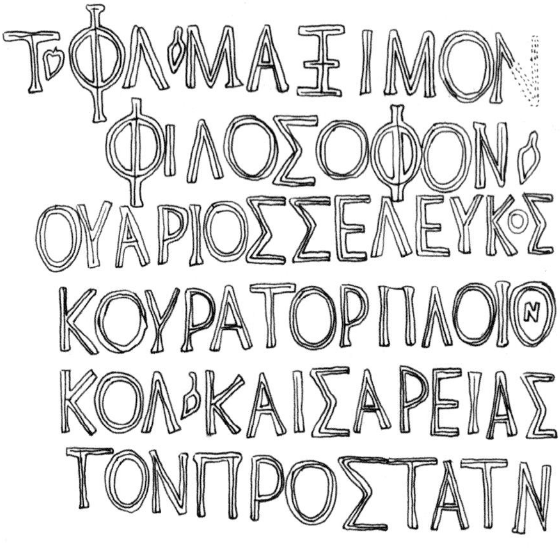

Fig. 109   Varios Seleukos inscription

Fig. 110 Byzantine *Praetorium*, aerial view from SE (A. Izdarechet)

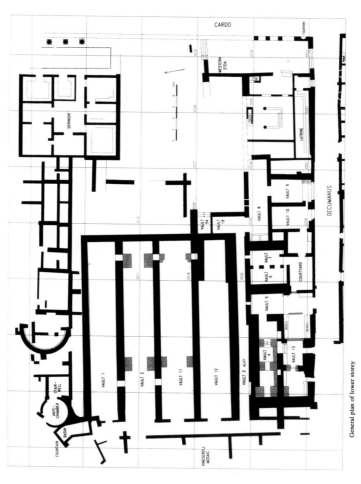

General plan of lower storey

Fig. 111 *Praetorium* of the Roman procurator. Plan of the lower floor, comprising of vaults on the west and on the south (A. Iamim)

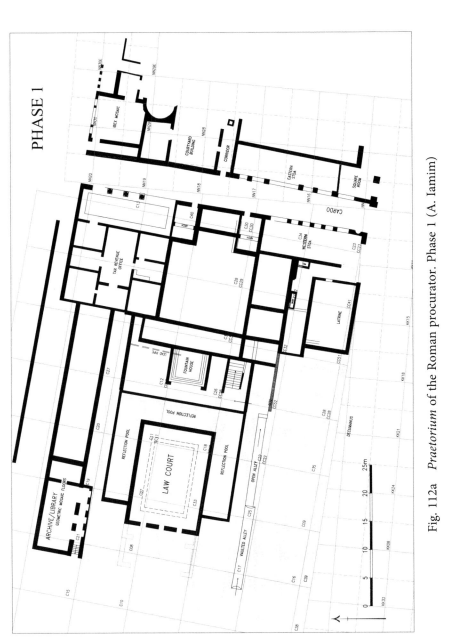

Fig. 112a   *Praetorium* of the Roman procurator. Phase 1 (A. Iamim)

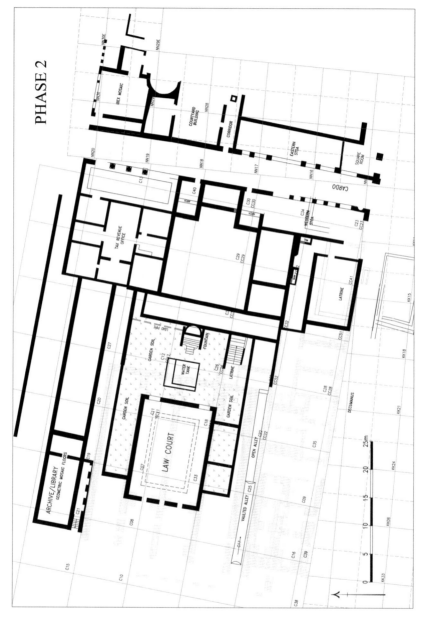

Fig. 112b *Praetorium* of the Roman procurator. Phase 2 (A. Iamim)

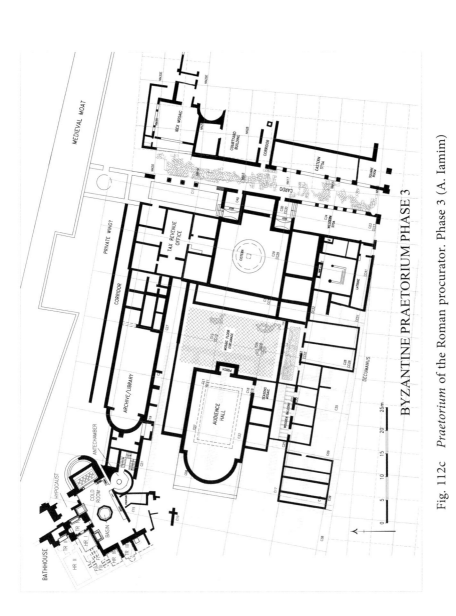

Fig. 112c   *Praetorium* of the Roman procurator. Phase 3 (A. Iamim)

Fig. 113 General view of the "Revenue Office", looking east

Fig. 114   The *Skrinion* inscription

89. Photo: Salvatore Mancini, JECM

a

88. Photo: Salvatore Mancini, JECM

b

Fig. 115a–b   Mosaic inscriptions in the "Revenue Office", citing Rom 13: 3 (Lehmann and Holum 2000, nos. 88, 89)

Fig. 115c   The "Revenue Office". General view of the NE room with medallion inscription in the center and benches around the walls

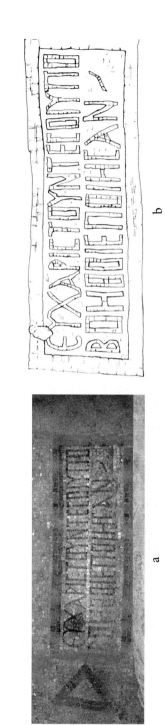

b

a

Fig. 116a–b   *Hypoboethoi* inscription. (a. photo: author; b. drawing: I. Levit)

Fig. 117   The SW *stoa*, looking north

Fig. 118 The audience hall of the *Praetorium*, remains of two floor levels

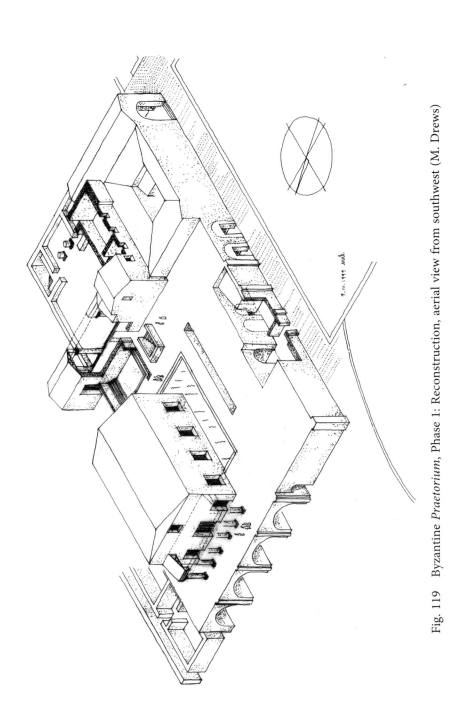

Fig. 119   Byzantine *Praetorium*, Phase 1: Reconstruction, aerial view from southwest (M. Drews)

Fig. 120   Fountain on the rear of the audience hall, looking east (J.J. Gottlieb)

Fig. 121   Latrine in Vault 54 (J.J. Gottlieb)

Fig. 122   Staircase leading to the upper floor (J.J. Gottlieb)

Fig. 123   Andreas the proconsul (*antypatos*) inscription (Lehmann and
Holum 2000, no. 39)

Fig. 124   Colorful mosaic floor in the rectangular hall (archive/library?),
that preceded the apsidal hall (J.J. Gottlieb)

Fig. 125   *Armarium* niche in the s wall of the rectangular hall
(library/archive?) (J.J. Gottlieb)

Fig. 126 Fountain hall of the bathhouse

Fig. 127 Antipatros the procurator (*epitropos*) inscription (W. Eck)

Fig. 128   The inscription of Valerius Valerianus, procurator (W. Eck)

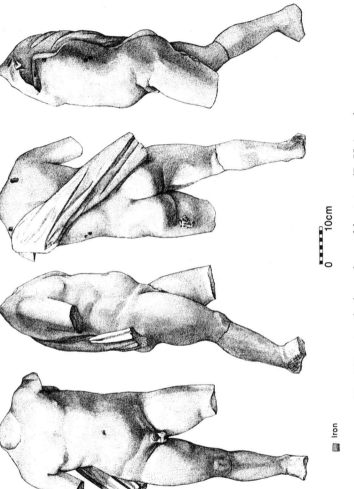

Iron

0   10cm

Fig. 129   A naked youth, marble statue (B. Haimov)

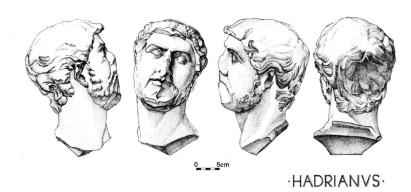

·HADRIANVS·

Fig. 130   Marble head of emperor Hadrian (B. Haimov; see also Fig. 20)

Fig. 131a   Vault 1 (the *Mithraeum*), looking east (J.J. Gottlieb)

Fig. 131b   Marble medallion portraying Mithras slaying a bull found by the
JECM in Vault 1 (the *Mithraeum*)

Fig. 132   Pottery sherds found in the thickness of the western vaults

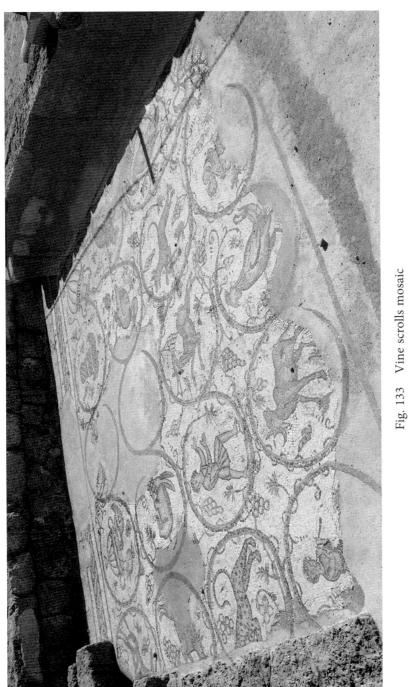

Fig. 133   Vine scrolls mosaic

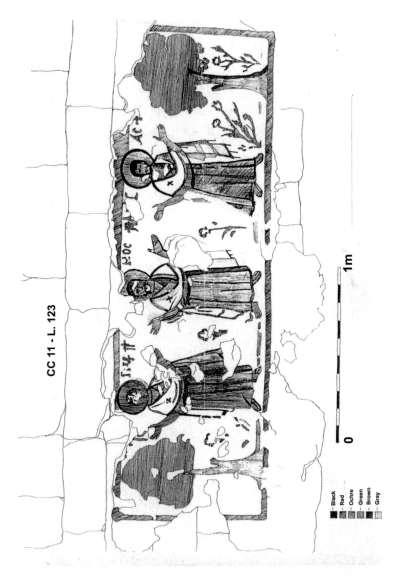

Fig. 134   Fresco depicting three saints on the S wall of Vault 11 (B. Haimov)

Fig. 135   The "*sportula* inscription" (G. Laron)

Fig. 136   Eusebius *noumerarius* inscription (N. Davidov)

Fig. 137   The "*Mithraeum Horrea*", vault 11, looking east (J.J. Gottlieb)

Fig. 138 The Inner Harbor *Horrea*, general view looking east

Fig. 139 The Inner Harbor *Horrea*, vault 3, general view looking east

Fig. 140   The courtyard of Building I in Area KK, looking north (J.J. Gottlieb)

Fig. 141   The "*dolia* hall" of building I, Area KK, general view
looking west (J.J. Gottlieb)

Fig. 142   Building I, Area KK, "*dolia* room" near the antechamber,
looking south

Fig. 143   Underground granaries in building I, Area KK (J.J. Gottlieb)

Fig. 144   The office of the courtyard *horreum*, building I, looking south
(J.J. Gottlieb)

Fig. 145   Building II in Area KK, corridor *horreum*, general view looking
south (J.J. Gottlieb)

Fig. 146   Corridor *horreum* in IAA Area I, south of the bath house of the palatial mansion, general view looking north

Fig. 147   Corridor *horreum* in IAA Area I, general view looking south

Fig. 148   Building III in Area KK, composite *horreum*, general view looking east (J.J. Gottlieb)

Fig. 149   Dolium (upper part), IAA excavations (Courtesy of Y. Porath)

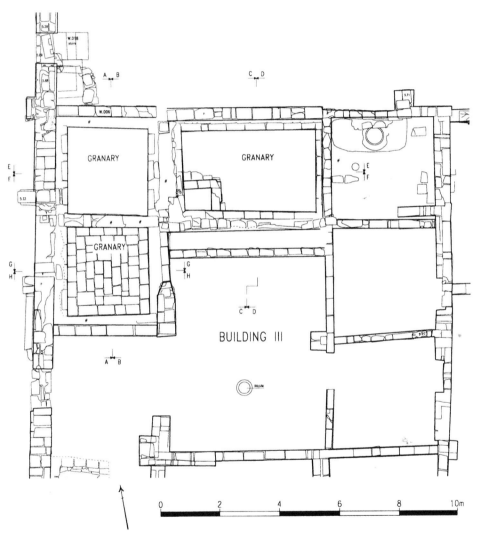

Fig. 150   Granaries 8 and 9 in building III, Area KK, plan (I. and N. Levit)

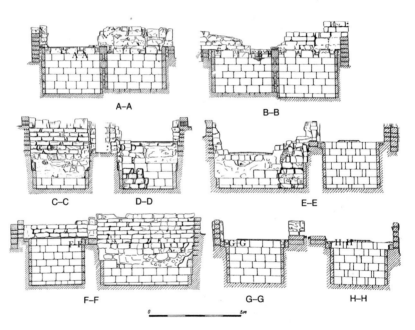

Fig. 151   Granaries 8 and 9 in building III, Area KK, elevations A-H
(cf. Fig. 150) (I. and N. Levit)

Ilja and Nadja Levit H.05.95.

Fig. 152   Granaries 8 and 9 in building III, Area KK, reconstruction (I. and N. Levit)

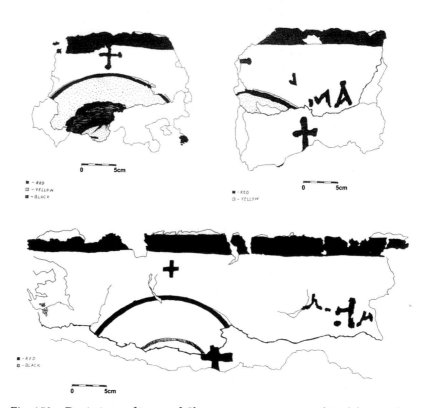

Fig. 153   Depictions of icons of Christian saints uncovered in debris in the antechamber of building I, Area KK (B. Haimov)

Fig. 154 Depiction of a *crux gemmata* found in debris in the *dolia* hall of building I, Area KK, fresco remains (J.J. Gottlieb)

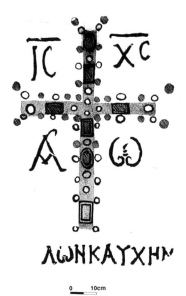

Fig. 155 *Crux gemmata* found in building I, Area KK, reconstruction (B. Haimov)

Fig. 156 Eucharistic bread stamp found in the north portico of the
courtyard of building I, Area KK

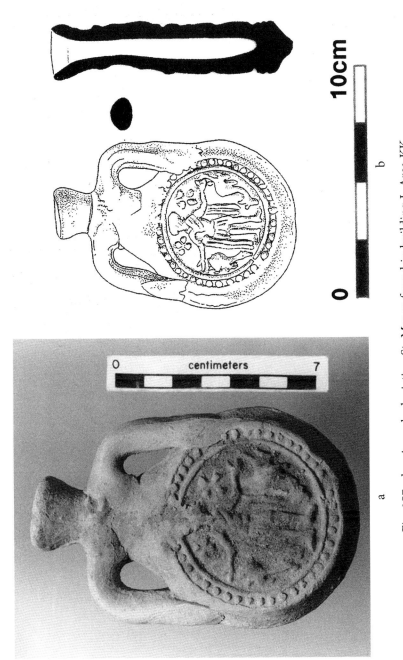

10cm

b

0

a

Fig. 157a–b   Ampule depicting St. Menas found in building I, Area KK

Fig. 158   Clay ampule depicting a stylite saint, found in building III,
Area KK (J.J. Gottlieb)

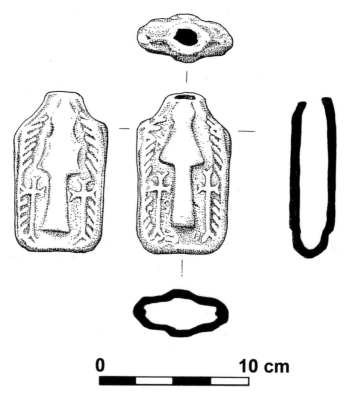

0   10 cm

Fig. 159   Clay ampule depicting a stylite saint from building III,
Area KK (Y. Dukhovnik)

Fig. 160   Fragment of a marble screen plate depicting a cross surrounded in a wreath, found in building VI, Area KK (Z. Friedman)

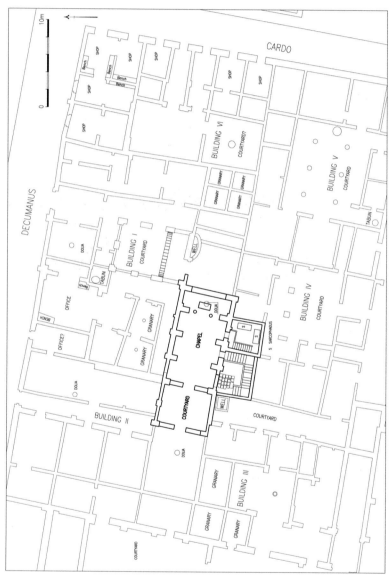

Fig. 161   Plan of suggested chapel in area KK within the complex of the warehouses (A. Iamim)

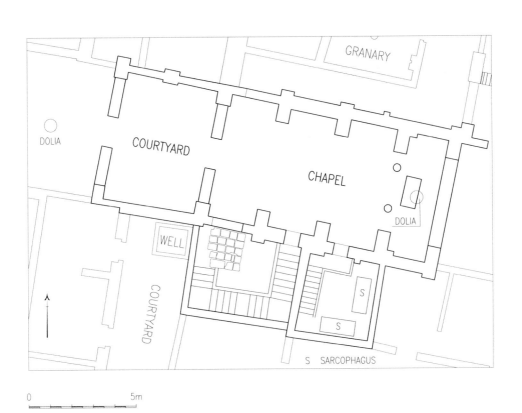

GRANARY

DOLIA

COURTYARD

CHAPEL

DOLIA

WELL

COURTYARD

S

S

S SARCOPHAGUS

0   5m

Fig. 162a   St. Paul Chapel. Plan (A. Iamim)

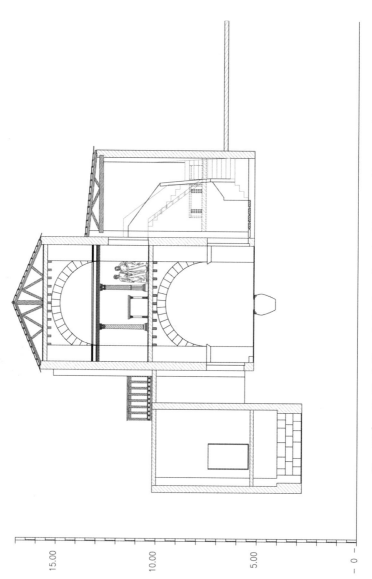

Fig. 162b St. Paul Chapel. N–S section, looking east (A. Iamim)

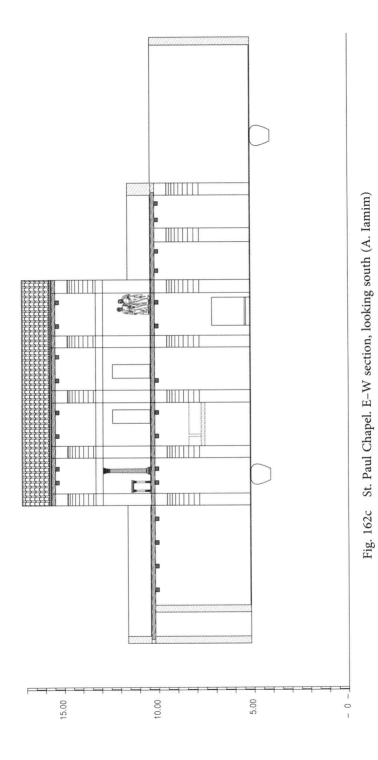

Fig. 162c   St. Paul Chapel. E–W section, looking south (A. Iamim)

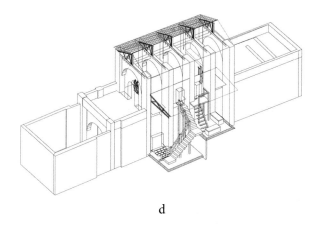

d

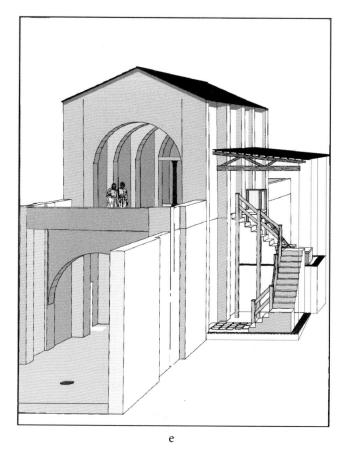

e

Fig. 162d–e   St. Paul Chapel. Suggested reconstructions, from southwest, including the staircase room and the burial chamber (A. Iamim)

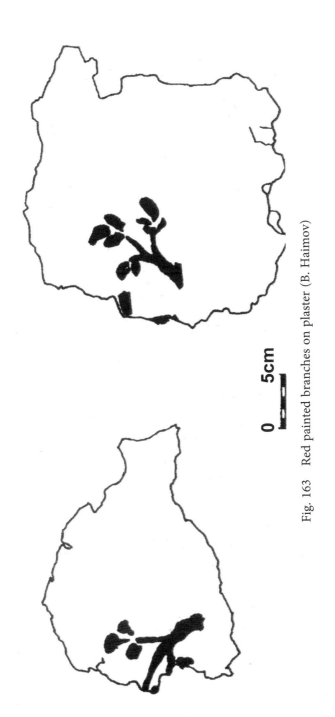

Fig. 163   Red painted branches on plaster (B. Haimov)

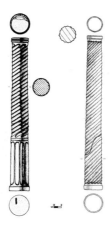

Fig. 164   *Ciborium* (*baldachino*) columns (B. Haimov)

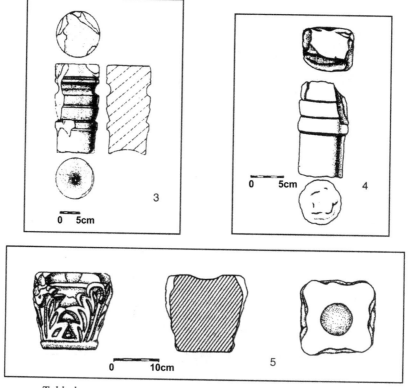

Table legs.

Fig. 165   Table legs (B. Haimov)

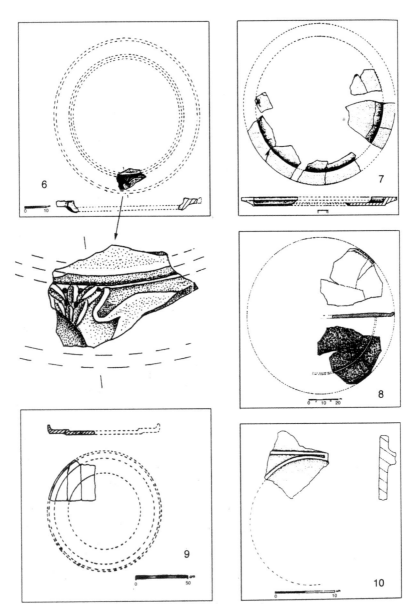

Fig. 166   Table plates (B. Haimov)

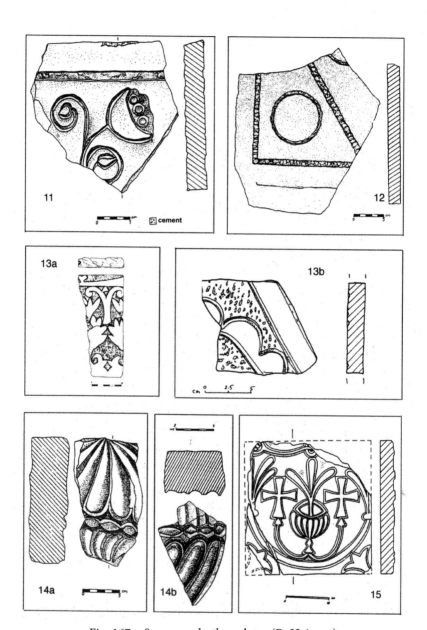

Fig. 167   Screen and other plates (B. Haimov)

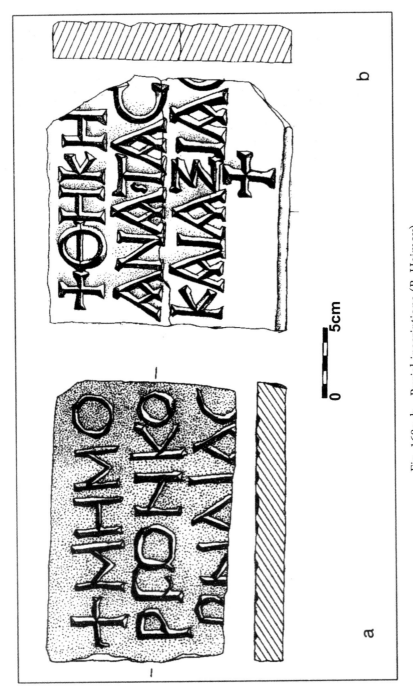

Fig. 168a–b   Burial inscriptions (B. Haimov)

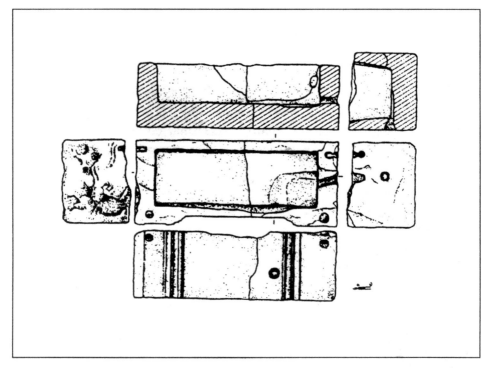

Fig. 169   Sarcophagus KK16 L.171 B0012 (B. Haimov)

Fig. 170   Fallen sarcophagus at the entrance of Vault 7 (J.J. Gottlieb)

Fig. 171   Stylite ampule from Beirut, obverse and reverse (after Lassus 1932)

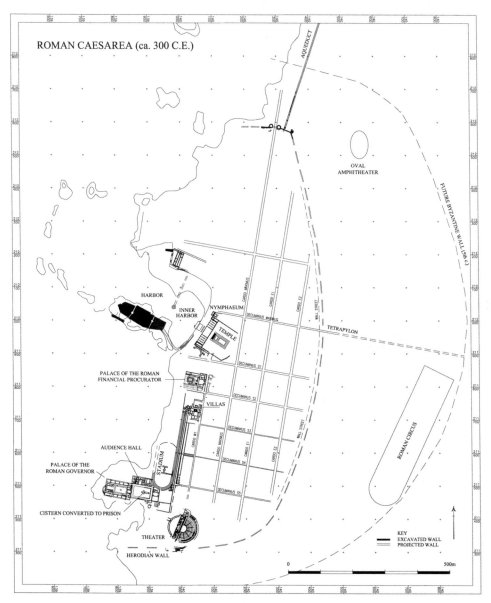

Fig. 172   Map of Caesarea in ca. 300 CE (A. Iamim)